A TEACHING METHOD
FOR BRAIN-INJURED AND
HYPERACTIVE CHILDREN

A Teaching Method
for Brain-injured and
Hyperactive Children
A Demonstration-pilot Study

WILLIAM M. CRUICKSHANK

FRANCES A. BENTZEN

FREDERICK H. RATZEBURG

MIRIAN T. TANNHAUSER

GREENWOOD PRESS, PUBLISHERS
WESTPORT, CONNECTICUT

Library of Congress Cataloging in Publication Data

Main entry under title:

A Teaching method for brain-injured and hyperactive chil-
    dren.

    Reprint. Originally published: Syracuse, N.Y. :
Syracuse University Press, 1961. (Special education
and rehabilitation monograph series ; 6)
    Includes bibliographies.
    1. Handicapped children--Education--Case studies.
2. Handicapped children--Case studies. I. Cruickshank,
William M. II. Series: Special education and rehabili-
tation monograph series ; 6.
[LC4019.T43 1981]   371.91'6   81-6255
ISBN 0-313-23071-4 (lib. bdg.)   AACR2

SYRACUSE UNIVERSITY

SPECIAL EDUCATION AND REHABILITATION

MONOGRAPH SERIES 6

WILLIAM M. CRUICKSHANK, *Editor*

First published in 1961. This is a reprint of the eighth
printing 1972.

Reprinted with the permission of Syracuse University
Press.

Reprinted in 1981 by Greenwood Press
A division of Congressional Information Service, Inc.
88 Post Road West, Westport, Connecticut 06881

Printed in the United States of America

10 9 8 7 6 5 4 3 2 1

The research reported herein was performed pursuant to Contract SAE-6415, United States Office of Education, Department of Health, Education and Welfare, and with funds granted from the Eugene and Agnes Meyer Foundation, Washington, D.C.

✦

The printing and publication of this monograph was greatly assisted through a grant from the

BENJAMIN ROSENTHAL FOUNDATION
City of New York

Preface

IN INTRODUCING the reader to this monograph, it should be said that the authors have provided an extensive amount of data dealing with an educational program for hyperactive and brain-injured children. Many decisions had to be made regarding the nature of the data to be included in the report. Since the study was in the form of a demonstration and pilot project, it was decided to include as much data as possible in the hope that the future would permit others to extend the demonstration-pilot study phase into a more fully controlled experiment in the knowledge of what had already been done. However, even within this broad goal, decisions had to be reached regarding the inclusion or omission of much data.

It was finally decided to include most if not all of the data which in any way related to education *per se*. In the authors' files there are the complete tracings of the electroencephalograms. Only a summary of these results are included, since this data does not immediately have a bearing on educational program or teaching materials. Similarly, only one group of case studies has been reproduced in the Appendix. All the data is available, however, for each of the 39 children studied. Much highly interesting psychological data dealing with the Draw-a-Person test and with the Bender-Gestalt test has had to be omitted from this report due to space limitations.

The reader may be concerned that too much detail has been included in spite of the deletions of data which have been mentioned. The authors have attempted to extract from the data every possible fact which might have a bearing on the education of the children under consideration. Few conclusions are reached, because of the limited duration of the intensive phase of the study. Numerous implications are drawn, since it is felt that implications are more appropriate to a pilot study than are decisive conclusions. The results of individual tests are therefore included in consideration of the test itself. The data which was finally used in the monograph has been included, first, because of its direct or indirect application to educational program, second, because of its ability to further illuminate a psychological understanding of hyperactive children, and finally because it corroborates or initially develops medical concepts regarding these children.

The authors are fully cognizant of the limitations of a demonstration-pilot study. They are cognizant of the large number of variables which remain uncontrolled when research is being done in a service-oriented agency such as the public schools. They are, indeed, aware of the limitations of this research, as the reader will also become during the course of his careful examination of the monograph. The authors, however, are also of the belief that the data contain many things of importance to educators who are seriously attempting to meet the needs of a group of children, each member of which presents extraordinarily complex demands on the school.

In approaching the problem of education of hyperactive and brain-injured children, the authors are aware of the inadequate state of knowledge of neurological processes. The inaccessibility of the physical system basic to behavior leaves many vacuums in understanding. This lack of knowledge about the physical basis of children's behavior may mean that the total orientation of this research will ultimately be found incorrect. In the absence of more exact information than that presently available in the literature, the study, however, has gone forward to the limits discussed in this monograph.

The reader will also immediately become aware of the bias of the authors. While there is, of course, a distinct orientation of this research to one point of view, the authors are fully aware that there may also be other approaches to the education of hyperactive and brain-injured children that in the future may be fully as important as the present one which is being examined. The present research has been conceived, neither as eclectic nor inclusive of all possible educational approaches, but as a careful examination of one method of education about which there has already been much written and much professional discussion. Within this frame of reference and within the limitations which have been pointed out, the authors invite the reader to consider carefully the chapters which follow in the hope that such an examination will produce a more refined experimental approach in the near future. The goal of the authors is the better understanding of a group of exceptional children about whom little is now known and the subsequent development of a method of teaching and a system of education adequate to meet the complex needs of these children.

Acknowledgments

THE COMPLETION of this demonstration-pilot study was not the work of a single individual, nor of the senior author of this monograph. It was the product of a large group of people representing the three co-operating agencies directly responsible for the study, and, in addition, representatives of the Montgomery County Health Department, Rockville, Maryland. In a large sense the demonstration-pilot study was an excellent example of professional teamwork and co-operation at its best.

Remarkable co-operation was received from the Montgomery County Health Department. Appreciation is extended to Dr. William J. Peeples, Director, whose personal support of the project made possible the splendid assistance of many of his colleagues. To Dr. Harold Mitchell, Director of the School Health Services, particular thanks are due, for throughout the entire project he gave unlimited time and effort to its success. Much of the co-operation received from health agencies, individual private physicians, and his departmental colleagues was due to Dr. Mitchell's splendid assistance.

Without question, the four people to whom greatest credit is due are the four teachers who devoted almost all of their time for nearly two years to the requirements of the teaching responsibility. The authors have never had the privilege of working with a more devoted staff of teachers. They invested their own time, far beyond any reasonable expectation, to learn their tasks and to meet the eccentric demands which were often placed upon them. They were ingenious, inventive, original, patient, and most intelligent in the pursuit of their responsibilities. Thanks which cannot appropriately be rewarded or phrased must go to Mrs. Sally R. Luke, Mrs. Mary J. McClurkin, Mrs. Wretha Petersen, and Mrs. Gertrude Knott. Miss Charlotte Larson, Visiting Lecturer at Syracuse University and a member of the faculty of the Joliet (Illinois) Public Schools, played an important role in teacher preparation which is more fully noted in Chapter V.

Mrs. Dorothy Meiklejohn and Mrs. Kathleen Pricer served as teacher-assistants during the demonstration. Their support and understanding of the teachers and their patient concern for the individual children in the classes went far to insure success to the pilot study.

Appreciation is further extended to the members of the Montgomery County Board of Education who originally approved the request to have the pilot study undertaken in the school system. Interpretation of the request to the Board members and support of the project as it continued was the responsibility of Dr. Forbes Norris, Superintendent of Schools, and of his successor, Dr. E. Taylor Whittier. The individual within the Board of Education who was most responsible for the smooth operation of the project was Mr. Maxwell E. Burdette, Director of Educational Services, to whom the project was generally assigned. His interest in the program and his readiness to serve the project staff as a trouble shooter and as an administrative guide was most appreciated by all who worked with him.

The project could not have been accomplished without the remarkable support of the members of the Diagnostic Team. These people were required to invest much more time than they had originally expected to give, but throughout the initial eight months of the project they gave generously of their time to the examination of the children and to staff meetings in evaluating the results of their examinations. Over the entire two-year period each continued to contribute valuable time as he was called upon to perform additional services. Members of the Diagnostic Team included:

Milton G. Glatt, M.D., Pediatrician, Assistant Chief, Handicapped Children's Clinic, Bureau of Maternal and Child Health, District of Columbia Department of Health, *Pediatrics.*

Christine W. Kehne, M.D., Director, Psychiatric Youth Services, Montgomery County Board of Health, Rockville, Maryland, *Psychiatry.*

Miriam Pauls Hardy, Ph.D., Associate Professor of Otolaryngology, Johns Hopkins Medical Institutions, *Audiology and Speech Pathology.*

Frederick H. Ratzeburg, Ph.D., Research Assistant Professor of Special Education, School of Education, Syracuse University, *Clinical Psychology.*

Bushnell Smith, M.D., Instructor in Neurology, Georgetown University Hospital, Washington, D.C., *Neurology.*

Mirian T. Tannhauser, M.A., Supervisor of Special Education, Montgomery County Board of Education, Rockville, Maryland, *Education.*

During the initial phase of the diagnostic work, Harry V. Bice, Ph.D.,

Clinical Psychologist, Constructive Health Bureau, Division of Maternal and Child Health, New Jersey State Department of Health, Trenton, New Jersey, also served as a consultant on the Diagnostic Team. Robert Cohn, M.D., of the United States Naval Hospital, Bethesda, Maryland, rendered an invaluable service to the study in connection with the administration and interpretation of electroencephalograms to each member of the subject population. Paul Lewis, O.D., provided much assistance in the appraisal of the visual characteristics of the children.

The teachers guide, Chapter V of this report, was prepared by three of the research teachers, Mrs. Luke, Mrs. McClurkin, and Mrs. Petersen, under the chairmanship of Mrs. Miriam Ulrich, speech therapist of the Montgomery County Board of Education. This group was assisted during the preparation of the guide by Miss Ruth Cheves, teacher of brain-injured children, Bibb County Board of Public Instruction, Macon, Georgia, and Mrs. Dorothy Zipperman, Montgomery Board of Education. During the teaching phase of the project, Mrs. Ulrich served as speech therapist to selected children of the two experimental classes. Appreciation of the authors for the excellent work of this group is gratefully given.

Appreciation is also extended to the principals of the three elementary schools in Montgomery County in which classes were organized: Mr. John Kneisley of the Bethesda Elementary School, Mr. Albert Gibson of the West Rockville Elementary School, and Mrs. Suzanne F. Waters of the Broad Acres Elementary School.

Mention must be made of the co-operative attitude and assistance of the parents of the forty children finally selected for the project. As the reader will note, each child, prior to his selection for the project, was submitted to extensive and time-consuming physical, psychiatric, and psychological examinations. To each of these examinations the children were accompanied by their parents. The parents often interrupted their family schedules to meet the restricted schedules of the examining personnel. They gave permission to obtain hospital birth records and information from family physicians. They responded to endless questions frankly and fully. They co-operated wholeheartedly and in a true spirit of experimentation with no guarantee that their children would be assisted, but with a hope that some light would be shed on the educational problems of children like their own.

During the study Mr. Sheffield Nasser, now Co-ordinator of Special Education, Sarasota County Board of Public Instruction, Florida, served as Research Assistant. The authors thank him for the excellent assistance he continually rendered to the study staff. Other Syracuse University Special Education staff members who participated in the study from time to time included Dr. Kathryn A. Blake, Dr. Donald Y. Miller, Dr. Leon Charney, Dr. E. Donald Blodgett, Dr. James R. Lent. To these also thanks are extended.

Mr. Paul Hutko, a graduate student in psychology at the University of Connecticut, assisted in psychological and statistical work with the study staff during several intervals in 1958 and 1959. His careful and excellent assistance was appreciated by all who were associated with him.

Appreciation for their excellent work must also be extended to Mrs. Evelyn Besansky, Educational and Medical Records Co-ordinator for the study, and to Mrs. Gertrude Weiss, Secretary, both of whom served the professional staff members most ably. Mrs. Claire Hirsch and Miss Irene Wolfe, as medical and statistical secretaries, performed their respective tasks with unusual ability and devotion to staff needs. Mr. Lionel Sharp of the Department of English in the College of Liberal Arts, Syracuse University, rendered an invaluable assistance in the editing of the manuscript.

The senior author of this monograph wishes especially to note the services of three of his close associates and co-authors. Mrs. Mirian T. Tannhauser, who served as liaison between the study staff and the Montgomery County Board of Education, has given continuous counsel and leadership to the staff. Her wise opinions and thorough understanding of the educational problem under consideration was of inestimable value. Mrs. Frances A. Bentzen served as Resident Co-ordinator for the study. She gave of herself to an almost superhuman degree and steered the study for two years in a remarkable fashion. Her tact and understanding in large sense contributed to effective team diagnosis and teaching. Dr. Frederick H. Ratzeburg functioned continuously as Resident Clinical Psychologist. The effect of his careful work and his detailed measures and analysis of growth is reflected throughout this report. To these three individuals much credit for the study and for the final report is gratefully given.

Appreciation is extended to the Dean and the Faculty of the Montgomery County Junior College who provided extensive office space and excellent work space with no charge for more than two years. Finally, the officials of the Syracuse University Research Institute made available facilities without which the study could not have been adequately completed.

The authors of this book are briefly described as follows. William M.

Cruickshank, Ph.D., is Professor of Education and Psychology, and Director of Education for Exceptional Children, School of Education, Syracuse University. He was Project Director of the demonstration-pilot study.

Mrs. Frances A. Bentzen was Resident Research Co-ordinator of the demonstration-pilot study throughout its entire period. She is currently serving as a Teaching Specialist in the Montgomery County Public Schools, Rockville, Maryland.

Dr. Frederick H. Ratzeburg was Resident Clinical Psychologist during the entire period of the demonstration-pilot study and Research Assistant Professor of Special Education, Syracuse University. He is currently Professor of Psychology, State University of New York College of Education at Oswego.

Mrs. Mirian T. Tannhauser was liaison between the study staff and the Montgomery County Board of Education where she served and continues to serve as Supervisor of Special Education.

W.M.C.

Contents

II. THE ORGANIZATIONAL AND PLANNING PERIOD, 35

III. THE DIAGNOSTIC PERIOD, 51

IV. MATCHING CRITERIA, GROUPING PROCEDURES, AND TEACHER SELECTION, 111

VI. PSYCHOLOGICAL, EDUCATIONAL, AND
PSYCHIATRIC EVALUATIONS, 255

VII. IMPLICATIONS OF THE DEMONSTRATION-
PILOT STUDY, 419

A TEACHING METHOD
FOR BRAIN-INJURED AND
HYPERACTIVE CHILDREN

. . . the conflict between fragmentation and incoherence on the one hand, and stability and poise on the other. . . .

GILBERT HIGHET in
The Powers of Poetry

CHAPTER I

The Educational Problem and Design

THE EDUCATION of children who are diagnosed as hyperactive in their behavior, with or without the diagnosis of brain injury, has been the source of serious concern and discussion among educators for more than two decades. This phase of special education stemmed initially from the important research of Heinz Werner and Alfred A. Strauss (1) [1] which was concerned primarily with the psychopathological characteristics of these children; its development was furthered by the resulting volume on educational methodology later authored by Strauss and his colleague, Laura A. Lehtinen (2). There is little question as to the importance of this contribution; in addition to being of value in its own right, the work of these authors has stimulated numerous other studies of the psycho-educational problems of brain-injured children. These, in turn, have gone far to break down the artificial barriers of the traditional medical classifications because they have served to reveal common psychological characteristics among some children diagnosed as cerebral palsy, epilepsy, and aphasia, as well as among those exhibiting exogenous mental retardation without motor disability, and, indeed, among hyperactive, emotionally disturbed children who have no apparent specific or generalized neurological disturbance.

The research of Werner and Strauss has been subject to some legitimate criticism in spite of the importance of the work. Essentially this criticism has revolved around two factors: the lack of statistical controls and the lack of rigorous control in the medical diagnosis. The most important of these criticisms is that of Sarason (3), who treats the research fairly and objectively in the light of its importance while recognizing the limitations which have been mentioned above. One notes

[1] References appear at the end of each chapter.

1

with interest, however, that recent research, which provided those controls that were absent in the original research, has in large measure supported the earlier findings of Strauss and Werner.

Masland, Sarason, and Gladwin (4) in this connection, state:

> The work of Strauss is perhaps the best example we have of the fruitfulness of an approach which is based on the integration of concepts in developmental neurology, diagnostic criteria of brain injury, and detailed program planning. Elsewhere one of us has criticized the logic and validity of some of the diagnostic criteria employed by Strauss. Although Goldenberg felt that these criticisms were somewhat severe, it should be noted that they lead to a conclusion identical to his own. . . . Although the validity of some of the diagnoses of minimal brain injury based on Strauss' criteria can be questioned, it should not be overlooked that Strauss' conceptions have given rise to ingenious educational procedures and an environmental structuring which undoubtedly have had positive therapeutic effects. It is likely that there are cases where one would feel that a diagnosis of minimal brain injury by Strauss' criteria was unwarranted but where the child's response to the program planned for him, while it cannot "prove" the correctness of the diagnosis, certainly cannot be used as evidence against it (4, pp. 366–367).

Dolphin (5), for example, in a pilot study utilizing two groups of matched pairs of 30 children each, one a cerebral palsy child the other physically normal, found psychopathological characteristics in the cerebral palsy children which were similar to those in the exogenous mentally retarded children observed by Strauss and Werner. Dolphin controlled her data statistically, but was at that time (1948) unaware of the psychological variability which might exist in subclassifications of children with cerebral palsy. Hence, the medical classification of the 30 children in her cerebral palsy group varied. Further, it was observed that some of the physically normal children demonstrated characteristics similar to those of the cerebral palsy group of children, although this did not affect the statistical significance between groups. However, nothing was done at that time to ascertain the importance of those characteristics in the normal population which, when they occurred in the cerebral palsy population, were termed psychopathological.

Shaw (6) later submitted a group of idiopathic epileptic children and a control group of endogenous mentally retarded children to many of the same tests which Werner, Strauss, and Dolphin had used; he found less significance statistically between the two groups than had previously been anticipated. Statistical controls and medical classification were maintained by Shaw. His results pointed up the fact that within the large group of children with central nervous system impairments there were apparently some children (his idiopathic epileptic population, for example) who functioned psychologically as normal children.

The findings of Dolphin and Shaw prompted a further study of the psychological characteristics of children with cerebral palsy. This study by Cruickshank, Bice, and Wallen (7) utilized large, homogenous populations of athetoid and spastic cerebral palsy children and a control group of physically normal children. In an effort to offset Sarason's earlier criticisms of Werner and Strauss, care was taken to control for medical diagnosis, chronological age, mental age, intelligence quotient, and presence or absence of speech; furthermore, a sufficiently large group of subjects was obtained so that sound statistical generalizations could be made. In general the study demonstrated statistically significant differences between athetoid and spastic groups of children, and between the athetoid and spastic groups and the control group of normal children. However, it was observed that children in all three groups showed some characteristics of psychopathology, in some degree related to chronological age, earlier reported by Werner and Strauss and their associates. While the spastic population deviated in the greatest extreme from the responses of the normal children, some normal children also showed deviations in figure-background relationship.

The essential conclusion reached from this series of research projects is that, while generalizations can be made about the psychological characteristics of children with central nervous system disorders, significant variability obtains within any particular group of such children. It has been stated, and it is certainly true, that this group of children represents the epitome of the concept of individual differences. Within the group are those children who demonstrate in an extreme fashion all the characteristics of psychopathology. There are some who show certain characteristics in large degree while other factors are less obvious. Finally, there are other children with known central nervous system impairment who appear to demonstrate none of the classical characteristics of psychological impairment. The need for individual diagnosis and appraisal is immediately apparent whenever educational placement or planning for a given child is seriously considered.

THE PSYCHOLOGICAL CHARACTERISTICS

What are the psychological characteristics to which reference has been made above? They have been described so fully in the literature elsewhere (7, 8) that space will be devoted here only in the degree that reader orientation to this monograph can be obtained. Several psychological characteristics have been described in the literature pertaining

to brain-injured children. These have usually included the factors of:
1. distractibility,
2. motor disinhibition,
3. dissociation,
4. disturbance of figure-background relationship,
5. perseveration,
6. absence of a well-developed self-concept and body-image concept.
Difficulties with angulation, closure, compression, rotation, and other factors related specifically to children's productions on the Bender-Gestalt test have been reported by various writers. It is felt, however, that these latter factors are closely related to, and indeed are undoubtedly an integral part of, certain broader characteristics mentioned earlier. As a matter of fact, whereas six major characteristics of psychopathology have been listed, it appears that probably three of these are in large measure variations of the characteristic of distractibility, and that perseveration may be the second major characteristic of brain-injured children. The matter of self-concept and body-image must be considered as a separate factor.

Distractibility

It is felt that distractibility is the chief characteristic of children with central nervous system disorders. While there is, of course, marked variability among the children, this trait is almost universally reported by investigators. Werner and Strauss (9) refer to this phenomenon as forced responsiveness to extraneous stimuli. Goldstein (10) calls it hyperactivity. Homberger (11) sees certain of his patients as being "stimulus bound," i.e., unable to refrain from reacting to environmental stimuli which are at the moment essentially unnecessary to adjustment. Kahn and Cohn (12) describe some of their patients as possessed of a "drive" to respond to unessential stimuli. In general, these investigators are observing the same thing, i.e., an inability of the patient to control his attention to stimuli which are immediately significant to his adjustment, the inability of the patient to adapt negatively to unessential stimuli, and an apparent hyper-awareness of visual, auditory, and tactual stimuli within the perceptive field of the observer. The attention span of these children is thus exceedingly short. Attention is interfered with in certain children by the most minute and insignificant extraneous factors. The behavior observed by educators is not to be interpreted as willed misbehavior, but may, when adequate diagnosis is at hand, be understood as an undetermined, but evident, lack of that cortical control which permits prolonged attention to the task and negative adaptation to the unessential.

Distractibility as it is being described here has frequently been reported in the literature of controlled experimentation. Werner and Strauss report this characteristic as predominate in their populations of exogenous mentally retarded children who lack pronounced motor disability. Dolphin observed it in her population of cerebral palsy children. Shaw reported it in some degree with idiopathic epileptic children. Qualtere (13), Trippe (14), Norris (15), and Neely (16), make various references to this factor in their studies of four other groups of cerebral palsy children. Cruickshank, Bice, and Wallen (7) make frequent references to distractibility as a factor in poor test performance of their two large groups of athetoid and spastic cerebral palsy children. Goldenberg (17), Morris Bender (18), and others likewise refer to distractibility as a major characteristic of psychopathology in their populations of both children and adults who have some form of central nervous disorder.

Motor Disinhibition

Motor disinhibition is defined as the failure of the child to refrain from response to any stimuli which produces a motor activity. This is definitely an aspect of distractibility which was described in previous paragraphs. Any object which can be pushed, pulled, twisted, folded, or bent may elicit a motor response from the child. Holes into which fingers can be poked, cracks in a desk top which can be traced with a pencil or a finger, doors on hinges, inkwell covers in old-fashioned desks, or locker handles in school corridors: all provide for the motor-disinhibited child a stimulus which may require a response. Here again, however, individual differences are manifest. Some children will be observed to be distractible in terms of auditory, visual, or tactual cues, but will not manifest motor disinhibition. The converse may also be true. There is, however, little doubt that the latter factor of motor disinhibition is related to the larger characteristic of distractibility.

Dissociation

Dissociation is herein defined as the inability of the child to conceptualize a totality, i.e., the inability to see things as a whole, as a unity, or as a Gestalt. The child tends to respond to a stimulus in terms of parts or segments, and has marked difficulty in bringing two or more parts together into a relationship to complete a whole.

It is hypothesized that this characteristic is also closely related to distractibility and hyperactivity. Many researchers have demonstrated the difficulty which different populations of brain-injured children have in completing simple abstract geometrical designs on a marble board, for example. An analysis of the marble board itself may indicate the reason for the dissociative tendencies of the children. The marble board originally used by Werner and Strauss (19), and later used by Goldenberg (see in 20), Cruickshank and Dolphin (21 and 24), Shaw (22), and many others is approximately 14 inches square. It is painted gray and contains 10 rows of 10 holes each. On the surface of 100 holes is constructed a design made of black marbles which the child is to copy on a second board of his own. Hence, in front of the child during the task are two boards, 200 holes, possibly 40 marbles on the stimulus board, and a box full of 40 or more marbles given the child to use on his own board. It is easy to see that within the task itself are several hundred extraneous stimuli to which a distractible child, and perhaps one characterized by motor disinhibition, may respond. If such be the case, it is quite likely that a trait which can be characterized as dissociation will be demonstrated because of the inability of the child to refrain from reacting to the extraneous stimuli within the test situation itself. However, dissociation as an entity, whether associated with distractibility, or with a separate clinical factor, has been demonstrated by numerous investigators working with different clinical groups and in several sensory modalities to be an important factor in the adjustment and learning of the children herein under consideration.

Figure-Background Disturbance

The close relationship between distractibility and the figure-background phenomenon has been clearly demonstrated by Cruickshank, Bice, and Wallen (7) in their study of psychopathology in children with cerebral palsy. The figure-background disturbance is characterized by the tendency of some children to confuse the figures and the background; others tend to reverse background and figure; and still others are unable to see any difference whatsoever between figures and background. This has been demonstrated in the visual modality on tachistoscopic tests administered by Werner (23), Dolphin and Cruickshank (24), and others. It has been shown in tactual sensation by Werner (23), Dolphin (25), Cruickshank, Bice, and Wallen (7). It can be observed through such tests as the Tactual-Motor Tests of Werner, the Syracuse Visual Figure-Background Test, and possibly even the Marble Board Tests earlier mentioned. Werner has suggested that there are clinical differences in figure-ground pathology between exogenous and endogenous mentally handicapped boys' performances on the Rorschach test (26), while many clinical psychologists interpret white-space responses on the Rorschach as, among other things, clinical evidence of possible organicity.

It is again suggested that the figure-background pathology may be related to the phenomenon of distractibility and forced responsiveness to extraneous stimuli. In all of the test situations mentioned above, particularly in the Rorschach, the tachistoscopic tests, and the tactual-motor tests, the background has contained a marked amount of stimuli. Cruickshank, Bice, and Wallen (7) observed significant differences in the ability of their groups to differentiate figures from background when the patients were blindfolded and asked to conceptualize tactually one of the Bender-Gestalt figures which had been embossed on a large board and embedded in a background of thumbtacks. The large number of thumbtacks in the background constituted extraneous stimuli to which the distractible child was forced to respond and to which he was unable to adapt negatively in favor of the tactually more prominent embossed figure. Similarly, it could be argued that the Rorschach cards contain much more stimulating features in the edges pertinent to the white spaces, and that thus the child who is hyperactive visually may be attracted to these areas for his responses. Certainly this is true in the case of the two-dimensional tachistoscopic tests used by Werner and by Dolphin, and in the three-dimensional modification of their tests as it appears in the Syracuse Visual Figure-Background Test developed by Cruickshank, Bice, and Wallen (7).

It thus appears that motor disinhibition, dissociation, and figure-background pathology may be closely related to hyperactivity. This latter factor has been herein so conceived. Such a conclusion may be of little importance in itself, but it has basic import in considering the total problem of a learning situation for these children.

Perseveration

Perseveration seems to be a more independent psychological factor than the four already discussed, yet it often characterizes children with central nervous system involvement. Perseveration is the inability to shift with ease from one psychological activity to another. More precisely, it is the apparent inertia of the organism which retards a shift from one stimulus situation to another, and it results in a prolonged after-effect of a given stimulus to which the individual has made an adjustment. There is an overlap in time between a shift from an old situation to a new situation. As is the case with many other characteristics which have been mentioned, perseveration is not restricted solely to children with central nervous system disorders. While it may be observed frequently in such patients, it is also a characteristic of psychopathology in many other clinical groups. It is difficult to understand how perseveration could be related to hyperactivity and distractibility, although Werner and Strauss on one occasion intimated that this might be possible.

Perseveration appears to be an independent psychological variable whose presence may impede learning in as significant a way as can distractibility in all of its various forms. Teaching experience indicates, however, that perseveration seems to be much more difficult to control than the other factors.

Self-concept and Body-image Concept

Bender and Silver (27), among others, have pointed out that brain-injured children often are characterized by inadequately developed concepts of the body image. Such impairment has also been found to be responsible for the development of inadequate self-concepts in brain-injured children. The lack of development of body-image concepts or the immature development of such concepts is not in and of itself a separate psychopathological characteristic. Rather, it is the effect of the psychological factors which have been mentioned in earlier paragraphs. It is hypothesized, however, that until a child has developed a relatively good concept of the body image, his own self-concept will be significantly impaired, and learning of all types will be significantly retarded. The development of a realistic body-image concept necessitates co-ordinated physical growth and sound emotional development, i.e., a generally secure person. If any of these facets of healthy growth are retarded for any reason, the individual's body image may be impaired, and learning and adjustment will be retarded as a result.

Cruickshank (28) has suggested that the self-concepts of cerebral palsy children were frequently disturbed and that their drawings of the body image were significantly mutilated. It is herein suggested that children who are characterized by hyperactivity, dissociation, and other forms of psychopathology observed in hyperactive and brain-injured children, have not yet had the opportunity to develop appropriate self-concepts nor have they been able to come to a good understanding of their own body images. Until such time when this can be accomplished within relatively normal limits, many types of learning will continue to be impaired. The evidences of insecurity which many of these children present to the careful observer are indicative of their unawareness of other human beings and their lack of well-formulated self-concepts. Hyperactive children are frequently observed to hug and caress their teacher, to run their hands over the teacher's face or arms, to pinch, push, or otherwise physically handle the adult or other children. Their visual perception of themselves and of others is so impaired that they appear to need constant tactual reminders that others are around them. The development of wholesome self-concepts in these children should be a major goal of educators and psychologists who work with them.

THE POPULATION: A FRAME OF REFERENCE

Achievement of an adequate definition of the population herein being considered is indeed difficult for many reasons, but primarily because of the lack of unanimity among the members of the medical, psychiatric, and psychological professions as to the cause and nature of the disability involved. It is difficult because of the inaccessibility of the brain and upper brain stem wherein disturbance is suspected. And also it is difficult because of the lack of detailed understanding as to the nature and function of the brain itself, either in terms of its separate lobes, or in terms of their interrelationship and their function as a totality.

The authors of this study and the members of the Diagnostic Team struggled for many hours to obtain a meeting of minds regarding definitions. They were hindered by the stereotypes of the several professions and by the literature which employs such terms as *brain injury, brain damage,* and *brain disorder.* The traditional medical classifications of cerebral palsy, aphasia, epilepsy, and others, and the literature pertaining to each, carry further implications for definitions and contain somewhat differing definitions.

The children about whom this monograph is concerned are those who are defined as hyperactive, with or without diagnosis of brain damage. Specific brain injury is difficult to delineate in every instance. While neurological examination and pediatric history in over half the cases supported the fact that brain injury was undoubtedly present, the Diagnostic Team members were frequently reluctant to agree that a brain injury or other form of central nervous system disorder did actually exist. The diagnostic and clinical data accumulated on the individual children, however, fell into a pattern or "clustering" which made it possible to describe the children in terms of behavioral and learning disorders. A group decision to include a child in the study was made on this basis.

Thus, children who demonstrated hyperactivity, dissociative tendencies, perseveration, figure-background reversals, and angulation problems in combination or as separate psychological characteristics; children who indicated traditional organic characteristics in pattern and scatter analysis on intelligence tests; and children who demonstrated these characteristics in appropriate ways in pediatric examinations, in neurological, audiological, and psychiatric examinations, as well as in the psychological examinations, were included in the group. Hyperactivity, in traditional terms, often applies to those children who are characterized by emotional disturbances and gross manifestations of behavior disorders. While some children in the population of the current study were characterized by these factors, hyperactivity is herein defined to include much more subtle deviations in behavior, and is more specifically considered to be related to matters of short attention span, visual and auditory distractibility, and disturbances in perception leading to dissociative tendencies. A careful examination of the Diagnostic Team's case studies which are included in the Appendix will impress the reader with the universality of these characteristics in this population of children. All of these characteristics have been observed in individuals with definitely diagnosed brain pathology. The case histories will indicate that many of the children presented marked evidence of hyperactivity in some form. In other instances, while psychopathology is evident, specific evidence of brain pathology is neurologically absent. However, as it will be noted later, certain children who did not demonstrate any evidence of brain injury were intentionally included in this population; yet they were hyperactive within the limits of the definition. Their behavior was indistinguishable from the behavior of children in whom the presence of brain injury was more clearly evident.

All of the children were having difficulties in school. Several of the children were undoubtedly candidates for exclusion from the public schools because of their inability to adjust to the typical school situation. In many instances the results of subsequent examinations which they underwent indicated that there were subtle psychological reasons for their deviant behavior which would not have been otherwise understood. This dramatically points up an important new direction for public schools in their attempt to meet the needs of children. It is not enough that school personnel believe in the concept of individual differences. Profession of a belief necessitates its implementation, and implementation with this particular segment of the school population —which is apparently much larger than had been anticipated—requires a full complement of clinical personnel capable of evaluating subtle psychological and behavioral changes which may have their etiology in central nervous system disorders. Frequently these children present no observable deviations other than emotional maladjustment. This is usually coupled with a failure to respond to good teaching situations. Ordinarily there will be no motor disability such as one finds with cerebral palsy children. There is often no mental retardation; or, if it is present, it may be a factor that is produced in the psychological examination situation by the same elements which limit or entirely restrict school achievement. There may be no speech involvement such as in aphasia, although there may be a noticeable lag of speech and language development. The most characteristic impression of these children is that they reveal a serious lag in development.

However, when they are subjected to understanding clinical appraisal by the psychologist, the neurologist, the pediatrician, and other members of an adequate diagnostic team, sufficient reason for their developmental lag will become immediately apparent. When appropriate information of a clinical nature is available, the schools are then in a position to implement a program appropriate to the peculiarities demonstrated by the child. It is the thesis of this monograph that it is possible through thoughtful educational planning to devise within the framework of public education, methods of identifying and compensating for the learning disabilities which are currently causing many school failures. This cannot be done, however, without a complete understanding of the subtle nuances of behavior which characterize these children. Examples of the fullness required to obtain the necessary understanding are to be found in the Appendix; but even in the case studies included therein, the thoughtful reader will perceive serious omissions of clinical data. More information is desirable; less is intolerable for adequate implementation of the concept of meeting children's needs.

Increasing numbers of educators are becoming more alert to the importance of minor deviations in child adjustment which are viewed as symptomatic of disorders in the integrative system affecting growth and maturation. The resulting unevenness in the child's development quickly brings him into conflict with the organizational pattern of the school system. Children characterized by a developmental lag do not really fit into the neat scheme of annual promotion, standardized grading, and other typical practices. The failure of these children to adapt to the standards of a child society, their failure to reach integrative standards typical of their chronological age and mental ability, and their failure to achieve and to learn on the level of their intelligence, all point to the need for different educational programs. These must not be conceived in terms of remediation or reduction of standards, nor in terms of repetition and drill, nor even in terms of greater emphasis on manual skills. Failure of these children to achieve in the regular grades cannot be viewed by the teacher as a failure on her part. An individual educational plan must be designed for the child in the light of the particular psychopathology demonstrated by him and in terms of new teaching which is geared to the unusual and unique characteristics which he illustrates. If psychopathology is organically based in a central nervous system disorder, the factors etiological to maladjustment cannot be removed. The educational program must work with the psychopathological characteristic and exploit it to advance the growth of the child. Until this can be achieved, the schools cannot legitimately say that they are meeting the needs of these children.

THE PROCESS OF LEARNING: A THEORETICAL VIEWPOINT

In order to appreciate the problem which the young hyperactive child faces, one must put oneself momentarily in his place. Learning and adjustment are essentially problems of perceiving and conditioning. It has been demonstrated many times that children with central nervous system disorders often evidence pathology of perception. Problems have been demonstrated in visual perception and in the subsequent interpretation of visual impressions into motor activities. Copying a design of marbles is not basically different from following a teacher's request to copy a word or problem from the blackboard. Werner and Bowers (29) and, much later, Norris (15) and Hunt and Patterson (30) have indicated that in various groups of persons auditory perception also may be impaired. An impairment in audio-motor performance may effect the child's abilities to write spelling words dictated by the teacher, to respond to pure tones in the audiological examination, to sing accurately tones which he has heard played for him on the piano, or to perform in accordance with his age and ability on other tasks which require motor interpretation of auditory stimuli. The applied research of the psychological laboratory does have much meaning to the educator, since tactual-motor deficiencies demonstrated by these children in the daily activities of the classroom are corollaries to laboratory experimentation.

Learning is conditioning; it takes place most advantageously under conditions of success. Children with perceptive disorders have predominately had failure experiences in the school situation. Guthrie speaks of ". . . the modification of behavior following . . . experience" as being the basis of positive growth and development (31, p. 22). Positive growth and development, however, is premised on the ability of the child to perceive things in the same way, or in generally the same way, as do other individuals in the same culture. Many children with a central nervous system disorder who also show evidence of psychopathology will not perceive life situations in the way that normal children do. Thus, their response to a given stimulus or situation will not be the same as that of the normally perceiving child. Conditioning will take place under such situations, but it will be learning which is counter to the standards which society expects in a child of that age. Teachers, parents, and neighbors interpret his learning as misbehavior. As one observes these children in a typical classroom situation, one is impressed by the few times during the course of a given day when the teacher can genuinely compliment the brain-injured or hyperactive child for a job well done. The child rarely has a genuine success experience.

Conditioning implies that a "combination of stimuli which has accompanied a movement will on its recurrence tend to be followed by the movement" (32, p. 26). Most learning in children is positive in terms of school achievement and social growth because the response inherent in a given stimulus has been appropriately perceived and has been accompanied by praise and a feeling of accomplishment on the part of the child. Learning and growth in the hyperactive child will be disorganized and disintegrated because distractibility prevents the perception of responses deemed socially appropriate to given stimuli. Both the stimuli perceived and the responses made are the result of change, as well as of unplanned trial-and-error behavior. Because the odds are small that the child will produce the socially correct response to a given stimulus or series of stimuli by chance, the possibility that his behavior will produce positive social rewards is exceedingly small. Inappropriate responses, however, bring some rewards even though they may be negative. Since the environmental situation does not change and since the organic condition producing perceptual pathology does not change or changes only slowly if at all, the trial-and-error behavior continues, and the child soon comes to learn that his rewards are going to be in the nature of failure which is often punitive. Since the stimuli present when the initial response occurred are also the cues for future responses, a vicious circle is almost immediately established for the deviant child. As age increases and emotional disintegration continues, his maladjustment becomes more and more apparent to those with whom he lives.

THE EDUCATIONAL PROGRAM

In consideration of the characteristics of psychopathology which have been delineated and in terms of factors essential in conditioning, an educational program has been devised. The essentials of this program were described by Strauss and Lehtinen and were employed by them around 1940 at the Wayne County Training School in Northville, Michigan, and subsequently at the Cove School in Racine, Wisconsin. The present writers have modified the procedures of Strauss and Lehtinen to some degree and have attempted to establish an initially controlled pilot study and demonstration to evaluate the practical effectiveness of the procedures which have been described.

In terms of educational efficiency, the psychopathology inherent in the child cannot be removed. This is true due to the fact that the psychological problems are inherent in damaged tissue somewhere in the vital areas of the central nervous system, or due to the fact that they are functional manifestations of a complex emotional problem which in itself is physical, and which only can be modified at too slow a rate to insure satisfactory educational and social growth. The educational program planned for normal children is in large measure completely unsatisfactory for the group of children herein under discussion. If the disability cannot be removed, and if the educational environment is unsatisfactory, there remains only the solution of creating another educational environment which takes into consideration the child's psychopathology and which *teaches directly to the disability*.

It is hypothesized that four elements comprise the essentials in a good teaching environment for brain-injured children with hyperactivity and for hyperactive children whose disturbance may result solely from emotional maladjustment. These four elements are:
1. reduced environmental stimuli,
2. reduced space,
3. a structured school program and life plan,
4. an increase in the stimulus value of the teaching materials which are constructed to cope with the specific characteristics of the psychopathology under consideration.

In addition to the above mentioned factors, an adequately prepared teacher should be in charge of the classroom, a teacher who has sufficient and appropriate teaching materials with which to carry out the designated program. The importance of this and other factors, such as understanding administrators, cannot be stressed too much and will be discussed at some length in chapters which follow. The four essential features mentioned above will be considered now.

Reduced Environmental Stimuli

The children herein under consideration are frequently characterized by marked and abnormal distractibility: they are unable to refrain from reacting to unessential stimuli, and they are unable to adapt negatively to environmental stimuli which are unnecessary to the specific adjustive task at hand. The reader is asked to imagine the best possible classroom which could be set up for a typical class of second-grade children. It would be filled with all types of motivational materials, i.e., stimuli which for the normal child are important factors in learning. A science corner, a transportation corner, a library corner, live pets, seasonal decorations on windows, bulletin boards full of appropriate features, pictures, growing plants, and beautifully decorated walls characterize the modern classroom. Open shelves are filled with books and teaching materials. Blackboards contain written material often retained from one lesson to the next. Both children's and teacher's desks are filled with many educational materials. Into this richly stimulating room, amply equipped for normal children without perceptual problems, are sent between 20 and 40 children and their teacher. Each child is individually dressed in brightly colored clothes which constitute additional stimuli to the other children. Color and the physical activity of the children and the teacher as they move around the room involve continual visual stimuli. In addition, auditory stimuli in the nature of hall noises, intercommunication systems, pencil sharpeners, and shuffling of children complete a stimuli picture of the normal, but nevertheless excellent, second-grade class.

The normal child can learn in this rich and highly varied environment. He can respond appropriately to appropriate motivational stimuli at appropriate times. He can do this because he can adapt negatively to or ignore stimuli inappropriate to the specific learning at hand. Most teachers can appreciate the inability of the normal child to adapt negatively when at the end of a tiring school day he and some of his friends become management problems and begin to react to things in the classroom which are not related to the learning situation then being considered. He begins to behave not unlike the hyperactive child.

A stimulating environment appropriate for a normal child is completely inappropriate for the hyperactive or distractible child who, because of an apparent lack of control, is unable to adapt negatively or to refrain from reacting to the unessential stimuli in the classroom. The library corner, the movement of pets, the colors in the room, the auditory stimuli, all—it is hypothesized—constitute hurdles to satisfactory achievement and learning for this child. If what has been described is true, it then follows that a learning environment appropriate to the distractible child is one in which extraneous and unessential stimuli are reduced to a minimum.

It is suggested that one feature of an appropriate learning environment for distractible children is a classroom as devoid of stimuli as possible. The color of the walls, woodwork, and furniture should match the floor; windows should be made opaque; bulletin boards and pictures should be removed; intercommunication systems should be disconnected and pencil sharpeners removed; ceilings and walls near halls should be sound-treated so as to absorb external noises; all furniture should be removed except that which is absolutely essential to the teaching program; and the number of children in the group should be significantly reduced below normal registration for an elementary classroom. The concept of reduction of environmental stimuli must be seriously considered, and every possible unessential stimulus in the classroom must be removed or reduced in its visual, auditory, or tactual impressiveness. If the learning environment can be stripped of unessential stimuli, other things being equal, it is hypothesized that the hyperactive child has an increased opportunity to attend for necessary periods of time to those stimuli which are essential to his learning and achievement. He is thus placed in a position where socially positive conditioning is likely to take place.

Reduced Space

As space increases, the number of stimuli in that space also increases. The opposite is also assumed to be true, that as space decreases, the number of stimuli is reduced. Since hyperactive children with a limited attention span find it difficult, if not impossible, to refrain from reacting to stimuli, the space in which their learning activities take place should be reduced to the smallest practicable area—that required for the child's desk and chair. It is therefore suggested that cubicles approximately three feet square be constructed for each child. The walls of the cubicles should be painted the same color as other structures in the room; they should be solid to the floor and approximately seven feet high. Each cubicle will be open on the fourth side. Each child's desk will be facing away from the open side toward the back wall. The two side walls will be constructed so as to terminate about six to eight inches beyond the child's back when he is seated at this desk to obviate distraction which may otherwise come peripherally to the child from the adjoining cubicles. The desk will be permanently fixed to the cubicle walls to minimize motor disinhibition. No teaching materials will be kept in the child's desk. No pictures or other items will be attached to the walls of the child's cubicle. Until the child has learned through conditioning to attend, all of his learning experiences in school will take place in this remarkably stimulus-free space.

Under optimum conditions a room smaller than the typical standard classroom would probably be most appropriate for the hyperactive child, and, although adjoining storage space must be available for the teacher's use, all cupboards and closets should be enclosed.

Insofar as the learning environment is concerned, a nonstimulating space has been created in which the insertion of stimuli can be carefully controlled. Such controls should also include restriction of the number of visitors admitted to the classroom. In the largest sense, a self-contained classroom has been achieved. An environment sufficiently devoid of unessential stimuli has been developed so that the hyperactive child can, for one of the first times in his educational experience, attend to the essential stimulus for a sufficiently long period of time without interruption and achieve a success experience, i.e., effect a socially positive conditioning.

A Structured School Program and Life Plan

It is the thesis of this monograph that many hyperactive children (with or without diagnosed brain damage) have been unable to attend to appropriate stimuli for a sufficiently long period of time to comprehend their meaning and to have a genuine success experience in terms of socially approved activities. Their lives have been filled with failure experiences, which are based on trial-and-error reactions, and confused responses to unessential stimuli in the immediate environment. This behavior is frequently misunderstood by parents, teachers, and others to the degree that the child is perceived as a behavior and management problem. Certainly, deviant behavior is apparent in terms of classroom and home standards. The behavior is not willed, however, but is the purposeless response to random stimuli. The child experiences failure and discipline which add further to the frustration which he may sense.

It is hypothesized that, if the learning environment can be simplified and highly structured, the hyperactive child will have greater opportunity for success experience, i.e., for positive conditioning. Hence, it is proposed that initially the educational program of the school day be completely teacher-directed with little or no opportunity for choice on the part of the child. Such a decision implies that the teacher will be fully capable of meeting the child's needs within such a restricted environment and that the teacher will have available the complete data regarding achievement levels and ability of the child in terms of all activities which may be planned by the teacher for the child.

Specifically, what is meant by a structured program? For example, upon coming into the classroom the child will hang his hat and coat on a given hook—not on any hook of his choice, but on the same hook every day. He will place his lunch box, if he brings one, on a specific shelf each day. He will then go to his cubicle, take his seat, and from that point on follow the teacher's instructions concerning learning tasks, use of toilet, luncheon activities, and all other experiences until the close of the school day. The day's program will be so completely simplified and so devoid of choice (or conflict) situations that the possibility of failure experience will be almost completely minimized. The learning tasks will be within the learning capacity and within the limits of frustration and attention span of the child. This will mean that a careful study of the child's attention span will have to be made. If it is determined that he has an attention span of four minutes, then all teaching tasks should be restricted to four minutes.

This procedure will be followed until such time as the teacher observes that the child is functioning with success in most of his activities, i.e., hanging up his coat, sitting at his desk, raising his hand, complying with the rules of the classroom, maintaining appropriate habits at lunch, achieving in abstract learning and other elements essential to approved social participation and intelligent conformity. At this juncture the teacher may begin to present the child with opportunities for making choices. "Do you wish to eat your lunch today in your cubicle, as you have been doing, or would you care to eat lunch with John and me at a table near the window?" "You may hang your coat and hat on any of these unused hooks today. Which do you choose?" If the teacher senses tension in the child during these simple choice situations, she should continue the structured program for a while longer.

Mention was previously made that class size will have to be restricted in this type of teaching. The optimum class size has never been scientifically determined; undoubtedly it depends in large measure on the degree of hyperactivity of the children to be included. It is proposed, however, that the procedures in initially organizing the class be carefully structured, whatever the size. To bring 8 or 10 hyperactive children into the classroom on the same day is to court disaster, for each of the children will bring his own pattern of misdirected behavior and background of failure into the school. The total situation is too complex for the majority of these hyperactive children. It also violates the concept of structure now under consideration. The presence of other children and a teacher in the classroom presents too many choice situations for a given child in the initial days of the school experience.

It is also proposed that during the weeks prior to the beginning of the school year the teacher should visit the children in their individual homes and become acquainted with them, make a careful study of the diagnostic data, and, possibly in conference with the Supervisor of Special Education or with appropriate psychological personnel, come to a decision as to which *single* child she desires to have come to school on the first day. The teacher will then work with this child until the latter is well adjusted to the schoolroom, to herself, and to the routine which has been established. It may take several days before the teacher decides that a second child should join the group and before she decides which child will be selected. This procedure is to be followed until the entire class roster has been assimilated into the group. In this fashion the teacher is able to observe that at no time is the adjustment of the group being impaired by reason of the situation becoming too complex. In the event the teacher finds that she has moved too rapidly in the admission of children to the group, temporary exclusion of one or more children may be required to reduce the complexity and to continue to insure success experiences for those children who remain in the classroom. Assuming that this procedure starts in early September with the opening of the school year, it may be the latter part of October or early November before the group is intact and operating together. Public relations with the families of those children not yet admitted is, of course, the responsibility of the school administration. Experience has demonstrated, however, that this does not constitute a major hurdle to the success of the program.

The major consideration in terms of structure is to keep all activities, including the total social organization of the classroom, within the limits of tolerance or within the level of success of the children, both as individuals and as a group. This consideration alone is not sufficient; but in combination with reduction in stimuli and space, and in terms of the remaining consideration for the teaching materials, a situation will be created that may specifically meet the peculiar psycho-pathological needs of the children concerned and that may make acceptable learning and adjustment more nearly possible.

Increased Stimulus Value of the Teaching Materials

It is hypothesized that if hyperactive children are distracted to stimuli, then their attention can be drawn to stimuli which are purposely organized and specifically placed within their visual field. It follows that if stimulating teaching materials are used the child is more likely to direct his attention to them than to usual teaching materials. The goal is to provide a learning situation so stimulating that the child's attention will be drawn to the task for a sufficient period of time to permit a positive conditioning to be effected. Hence, in preparing reading materials the teacher will utilize different colors in each word or in the numbers comprising a problem to be solved. The word, "dog," for example, can be increased threefold in stimulus value if different sizes, shapes, and colors are used in the three letters comprising the word. Pre-academic skills will be developed through the use of intensely colored blocks, form boards, peg boards, and similar materials. The teaching material must be of appropriate difficulty to the child's achievement level, but it must also be intensified in terms of its visual or tactual value. Once an appropriate reaction to a specific learning task has been completely achieved, it is possible to begin a transference to less stimulating materials and ultimately to bring the child to typical texts, workbooks, or teacher-made instructional materials. It is important to note that it may be necessary to present only single, highly stimulating items to the child one at a time. This may mean a single word on a card, a single sentence on a paper, a single arithmetic problem on a page. The desk top will be free of all other stimuli except those necessary to the specific task at hand. All unnecessary materials will be removed from the desk and placed in enclosed cupboards or out of sight.

Mention was made above of the problem of adjusting in space. Frequently, hyperactive children will be helped to attend to the specific area of the desk on which, for example, an arithmetic problem is placed, if the space of the desk top is restricted. The visual field can be restricted by placing a brilliant piece of construction paper or blotter paper under the book, paper, or form board, or by adding colors to the work itself. The brilliant color not only assists in restricting the visual field, but also simultaneously helps the child to direct his attention to the task at hand.

When provided in concert, the four elements which have been discussed above offset the impact of hyperactivity in the hyperactive child. Even though the causes of hyperactivity cannot be removed, it is possible through success experiences and conditioning for the child to learn positively. In keeping with the standards of society, and through successful learning and social adjustment, he can also learn to tolerate more effectively the highly stimulating environments of so-called typical classrooms, playgrounds, or home environments.

The factors which have been discussed, however, are not the sole answers to all of the problems of psychopathology which may be observed in individual brain-injured or hyperactive emotionally disturbed children. These factors are basic, but at the same time consideration must be given to the development of teaching materials and environmental modifications involving such other factors as dissociation, figure-ground disturbance, and motor disinhibition. If it is true that these latter factors are aspects of distractibility, then what has been outlined is also appropriate for them. Other modifications can be made, however, which will permit the teacher to teach more directly to these disabilities. These modifications will be discussed more fully in Chapter V, wherein the specific teaching techniques will be outlined. Similarly, for the second major psychological disorder, perseveration, considerations can be made which will also immeasurably assist the child and lessen the impact of this on learning and adjustment.

BACKGROUND AND SETTING FOR THE RESEARCH STUDY

The purpose of this section is to outline the factual, concrete aspects of both the setting and the research design. Certain administrative and theoretical problems will be mentioned where pertinent, because they were associated with a pilot study in a public school system, and because in addition to education they involved the psychological, medical, and social sciences.

Were it the purpose of this monograph to report the results of an experiment in physics or chemistry, the general acceptance of an already established body of proven facts and theory would obviate the need to report in detail professional viewpoints, specific information concerning the environmental setting in which the experiment was conducted, and conflicting interpretations of the results of the experiment. In the psychological, medical, and social sciences relating to the present problem, however, no such proven body of facts and theories has been established. Diethelm, in commenting on this fact, cogently observes that ". . . nowhere is bias more marked than in the behavioral sciences.

The personal psychodynamics of the individual will influence him, theories will affect his way of looking at the facts, his selection of special data, and his differentiation of the essential from the nonessential. . . . None of us are able to avoid bias, but by keeping this possibility in mind we will succeed in being constructively self-critical and avoid the danger of building fortifying systems" (33, pp. 149–50).

In connection with these remarks, it is appropriate to comment briefly upon the implications of various research methods. If one thinks of research design in terms of levels of rigorousness and control of variables, then among the simplest forms of inquiry are the survey and the pilot study. The survey is a method by which pertinent information and data are identified and collected about a general problem area, and the pilot study is a method of exploring an aspect of the problem area under relatively controlled conditions. It is not unusual, for example, for pilot studies to develop out of research problems which are identified, defined, or delineated as a result of a survey.

These two exploratory research methods appear to be particularly well suited to interdisciplinary research in the problem area of emotional disorders and learning difficulties among children—an area about which there is so little known and around which there are so many conflicting theories. This statement is not meant to imply that the more rigorous methods of research do not produce basic information about human behavior, but only that these methods are perhaps more productive, more easily manipulated, and better controlled when conducted within the framework of one particular discipline.

For example, it was appropriate that a pilot study such as this one— which presumed to explore the usefulness to children without brain injury of a specific type of instructional program devised for children with brain injury—would, as a matter of course, seek to provide a means by which the existence of brain injury could be identified. Thus, although it was not the purpose of the diagnostic staff members to determine what brain injury is, to isolate the various causes, or to resolve the complicated neurological and medical problems of differential diagnosis associated with the concept of brain injury, it was their business to decide as a medical staff when and if gross brain injury existed. Discovery of the answers to the other problems may well be within the province of carefully controlled, long-range experimental problems in basic research initiated by those disciplines directly concerned with the structure and physiology of the central nervous system.

These general remarks would be incomplete without some comment which recognizes the importance of the setting in which this research was conducted. One needs only to call attention to the vast number of variables which exist in a public school classroom setting to realize the difficulties one would encounter in attempting to conduct a classic experiment in basic research. The following paragraphs describe in considerable detail the background from which the current pilot study developed and the setting in which it was conducted. The purpose of including this information is to illustrate a basic fact of considerable importance: that is, that the setting in which educational research is conducted is most appropriate when the problem, procedures, aims, and goals are compatible with the philosophy and needs of the public school program.

In Montgomery County, Maryland, the public school administrative personnel had been keenly aware for some time of the need to explore the basic causes of the learning difficulties of children who were not responding satisfactorily to existing methods of classroom management, instructional programs, or classroom assignments. Some of these children had been excluded from the school system and others were eligible for exclusion. Under Maryland state law, children whose educational needs are not met by existing school services are eligible for state aid when they are transferred to private schools and treatment centers having programs more appropriate to the children's needs (34). It was of immediate importance that the educational needs of these children be met in some way.

A second factor in the setting was the experimental nature of the Board of Education's philosophy. For a period of approximately five years prior to the initiation of the pilot project, the Supervisor of Special Education and her teaching staff had explored a wide variety of classroom environments, teaching methods, instructional devices, and principles of classroom grouping with particular references to the educational, emotional, and social needs of children known to have disorders of the central nervous system. She had also employed the same exploratory procedures with emotionally disturbed children whose learning difficulties were customarily associated with an aggressive, acting-out, hyperactive behavior response pattern.

Classroom grouping and instructional techniques for the children with central nervous system disorders had been worked out to the satisfaction of the children, parents, and the Supervisor of Special Education. Such was not the case with the children without brain injury, who may be descriptively referred to as hyperactive, underachieving, and emotionally disturbed.

Toward the close of the fifth year of informal classroom experimentation, it became evident that the learning disabilities and behavioral response patterns of the hyperactive, emotionally disturbed children were strikingly similar to those of the children with central nervous system involvement. That is, the latter group of children behaved *as if* they were brain-injured, even though the available diagnostic and clinical data had ruled out the existence of demonstrable organic pathology.

As a result of these observations, and after very careful planning for the individual child in order to eliminate possible dangers to his self-esteem, the Supervisor and her administrative staff arranged for a number of hyperactive, emotionally disturbed children to be class-based with groups of brain-injured children in a structured classroom situation. For the first time in their school experience they appeared able to adjust satisfactorily to the group situation, and for the first time they showed academic gains.

As a result of the controls imposed by the structured classroom routines, group teaching approach, and specialized techniques of instruction, it was possible for the children to develop an ability to conform to the classroom situation. Academic progress was slow but consistent, varying from a gain of one to three grade levels in achievement in less than one academic year. The classroom units developed social cohesiveness, and peer-group identification was noticeable among several subunits within the total group structure. It was felt that these results justified and substantiated the continued use of classroom procedures and grouping policies designed to meet the children's educational needs, rather than their unresolved emotional needs.

The next step evolved out of the recognition that a diagnostic study should be undertaken of all the possible causes which might contribute to, or result in, the learning disabilities and behavior response patterns of the acting-out, aggressive child who is emotionally disturbed but not brain-injured. The educational philosophy and instructional programming had advanced to the point where classes for emotionally disturbed children were no longer appropriate; instead, emotionally disturbed children were grouped in terms of "classes" or types of educational handicaps.

It was then possible to identify two basic requirements in the County Special Education Program:

1. the need for more adequate and intensive medical, psychiatric, and psychological diagnostic data, and better reporting of the educational backgrounds and social histories of children in question;

2. the need for public school systems to initiate pilot studies in educational research projects within their own framework.

Once these needs were recognized, it followed that a research project would require adequate and intensive medical, neurological, psychiatric, and psychological diagnostic data, as well as more refined methods of reporting the educational backgrounds and developmental histories of the children in question. Furthermore, it was felt that, until more adequate diagnostic information became available, any further attempts to explore the causal factors in conjunction with or separate from the clinical base of disorders in the learning processes of these children should be postponed. This exploration could best be conducted within a planned, controlled, interdisciplinary pilot study. The research facilities and administrative direction of the Office of Research in Special Education and Rehabilitation of the Syracuse University Research Institute were made available to this favorable public school setting. The resulting experimental design, which was directed toward the development of a specialized teaching method for hyperactive, emotionally disturbed, and brain-injured children, was formulated and submitted to the United States Office of Education. The project was approved and a grant for a two-year pilot project and demonstration was awarded to Syracuse University.

Thus, the Co-operative Research Project in Specialized Teaching Methodology was jointly sponsored and financed by the Montgomery County Board of Education and Syracuse University, the major funds coming from the United States Office of Education. Just prior to the termination of the project an additional grant from the Eugene and Agnes Meyer Foundation made it possible to extend the program for an additional six months in order to prepare this monograph and to provide follow-up testing for the children participating in the project.

THE RESEARCH DESIGN: A DEMONSTRATION-PILOT STUDY

The Problem

A pilot study was developed to investigate the value and effect of a nonstimulating classroom environment, specially prepared teaching materials, and highly structured teaching methods upon the learning problems and school adjustment of hyperactive, emotionally disturbed children with and without clinically diagnosed brain injury.

Specific Aims

There were two chief aims in the minds of the investigators:
1. in terms of their appropriateness to the instructional and social

needs of hyperactive, emotionally disturbed children with or without evidence of brain injury, to investigate and evaluate the usefulness of teaching methods developed in an experimental setting for brain-injured children;

2. to carry out the pilot study within the framework of the administrative policies and procedures of a public school system.

Methods of Procedure

THE LOCATION

The proposed study was conducted within the public school system of Montgomery County, Maryland, and was housed in four classrooms in three elementary schools: two classes are referred to as experimental and two as control. The two experimental groups were housed in one school which was chosen on the basis of available space, feasibility of making structural changes in the classrooms, location, and staff attitudes toward educational research. The two control classes were housed separately in two other elementary school buildings. All standard instructional equipment, classroom space, and facilities normally available were provided without cost to the four research classes.

THE STAFF

The administrative, clinical and medical, and secretarial staff members were selected on the basis of anticipated needs in the diagnostic, administrative, teaching, evaluating, and reporting processes. They co-operated in compiling complete information on medical case histories, learning pathology, behavior disorders, teaching methods, and the adaptation of materials. They assisted in writing up the research findings. The selection of staff members and consultants was made on the basis of their professional competency, interest in the pilot study, experience with children of the type to be studied, and previous contributions in their respective fields. One of the most important considerations in the current project was the selection of teacher personnel for the four classrooms. Four teachers and two teacher-assistants were selected. Each teacher received training at an approved teacher education center. Each had been noted as a competent, successful teacher and had had no less than two years teaching experience. All had demonstrated success in handling groups of children and in relating to individual children within the group. The teachers were creative and willing to utilize new teaching materials in an experimental setting. Each teacher had an appreciation of the research design and the learning theory within which this particular study was being conducted. Teacher-assistants had the same personality characteristics but somewhat less teaching experience. The teacher-assistants for the experimental classes had recently been oriented to the research problem. These individuals had responsibility for the groups only in the case of the major teacher's illness or absence. Their responsibilities included assistance in the preparation of teaching materials, observation, record-keeping, operation of audio-visual equipment, and provision of teacher relief. All four teachers and the teacher-assistants received special instruction in the experimentally designed specialized teaching method.

THE SELECTION OF THE CHILDREN

Forty children were selected whose emotional difficulties were characterized by hyperactive, aggressive behavior and who were educationally retarded. They were between the chronological ages of 6–11 and 10–11 years. They had mental ages not less than 4–8 years and intelligence quotients not less than 50. They were referred to research personnel through the Montgomery County Public School Department of Special Education.

A diagnostic work-up for each child included complete pediatric, neurological, electroencephalograph recording, psychiatric, psychological, educational, speech, and hearing evaluations. Developmental and environmental data were collected, and case histories were prepared. On the basis of these data the candidates were separated into two diagnostic groups:

1. those children with clinically diagnosed neurological and medical evidence of brain injury;

2. those children whose case histories demonstrated psychological behavior and learning disabilities typical of those observed among brain-injured children, but whose diagnostic studies revealed no conclusive evidence of specific birth injury, neurological signs or evidence of accident, disease, or injury which might account for the observed behavior and learning disorders.

GROUP ORGANIZATION

After the diagnostic classification of the 40 subjects into two groups, they were placed in four matched groups of 10 each. Five in each group of 10 had a diagnostic classification of brain injury, and the other 5 had a diagnostic classification of emotional disturbance. The four groups were matched further in terms of chronological age, mental age, instructional levels, degree of hyperactivity and perseveration, and previous experience in special classes. Two of the four groups were designated as experimental, two as control.

THE CLASSROOMS

Four classrooms of maximum efficiency were chosen on the basis of their location and the adequacy of such facilities as lights, space, toilets, sinks, and storage closets.

As previously indicated, the two groups designated as experimental were located in one school. The two control groups were located in two additional schools. Environmental alterations in the two experimental classrooms were largely made according to the recommendations of Strauss and Lehtinen. Further modifications made by the senior author of this monograph included the use of uniformly colored walls, individual cubicle work units from which all extraneous stimuli had been removed for each member of the class, closed closets for clothing and supplies, and opaque windows. Other alterations not specified, were compatible with the design for a stimulus-free classroom environment.

The two control classrooms were subject to no environmental alteration of any kind other than temporary adjustments normally made by the teacher in special education classes during the academic year.

Methods and Materials

The teaching methods and instructional materials used in the two experimental classrooms were evolved as part of the research project. They were designed to enlist the use of the auditory, kinesthetic, and tactile sensory processes in the learning experiences. The instructional time and activity was rigidly scheduled. No deviation from the experimental programming took place during the academic phase of the project unless the educational welfare of a child was subject to question.

The teaching methods and materials used in the two control groups included any of the traditional instructional methods and any aspect of the experimental programming which appealed to the interest of the teacher. Such matters as scheduling and planning of activities were left to the discretion of the teacher.

Recording and Evaluating

Anecdotal records were kept by all four teachers and the assistant-teachers. Tape recordings of activities and classroom discussions were made as frequently as good teaching practice would allow. Observation by the administrative staff was scheduled on a regular basis, and the results were recorded for later study. Teaching techniques received constant critical evaluation as to their usefulness to individuals and the group as a whole. Psychiatric, psychological, and educational evaluations were conducted at the beginning and end of the first academic year. Classroom observation by the psychiatrist and psychologist was scheduled at regular intervals. Other members of the diagnostic staff were available for consultant purposes, but they were not requested to participate in classroom observation.

Psychological examinations included:

1. the Marble Board Tests devised by Strauss and Werner,

2. the Tactual-Motor Test devised by Strauss and Werner and modified by Cruickshank, Bice, and Wallen,

3. the Syracuse Visual Figure-Background Test by Cruickshank, Bice, and Wallen,

4. the Bender Gestalt Test adapted by Cruickshank, Bice, and Wallen as a tactual test,

5. the Draw-a-Person Test adapted for children from Machover,

6. the Rorschach Test,

7. the Vineland Scale of Society Maturity.

Intelligence and mental age levels were determined by standard instruments including:

1. the Terman-Merrill Revision of the Stanford-Binet Intelligence Test, Forms L or M,

2. the Wechsler Intelligence Scale for Children.

Educational achievement was assessed on appropriate forms of Stanford Achievement Test—1953. Other appropriate psychological tests were used as needed.

Parent Conferences

Since the specific aim of the pilot project was to evaluate the usefulness of a specialized teaching method within the public school system, the research staff did not provide any form of individual or group psychotherapy or counseling for the parents. When parents indicated their interest in such assistance, they were referred to appropriate services.

Parent meetings were scheduled periodically when there appeared to be sufficient factual information concerning the progress of the children, or when the results of the study warranted such meetings. Teacher-parent conferences were scheduled at the discretion of the individual research teachers in collaboration with their principal and in line with the policy of the school. All parents were kept informed of the project's progress, and their co-operation was enlisted prior to the release of any and all information which involved medical or clinical data about their children.

Interpretation of Purposes

During the course of the pilot project the research personnel attempted to determine whether or not a nonstimulating, rigidly controlled teaching approach, combined with specialized teaching techniques, could effect a more adequate school adjustment and academic achievement with hyperactive, aggressive, emotionally disturbed children with or without brain injury. The project was both important and timely. It was important because it proposed to evolve an educational program for such children whose behavior response patterns and learning disabilities constitute one of the most acute and clearly delineated general problem areas in the fields of education and mental health. It was timely because current research reports in the fields of neurology, psychiatry, physiology, biochemistry, and psychology dealing with various aspects of deviations in development and growth were providing more encouraging leads to the nature and results of dysfunction in the learning process and behavior disorders.

Psychological and educational observations conducted in experimental or clinical situations had earlier indicated that hyperactive, aggressive, emotionally disturbed, brain-injured children did make adequate school adjustment and academic progress in a highly structured environment which included the use of special teaching methods and materials. This type of methodology had not been adequately tested and evaluated in a public school program for either hyperactive brain-injured children or hyperactive children without brain injury. It was, therefore, significant to determine the extent to which such a program, devised for brain-injured children, would meet the instructional and emotional needs of children with similar behavior patterns who showed no demonstrable neurological evidence of brain injury.

It has been generally assumed that emotional difficulties retard or limit the learning process. This project attempted to explore the concomitant possibility that some emotional problems are a symptom of dysfunction of the learning process, and that appropriate instructional programs could alleviate or remediate the emotional difficulties as well as the learning disabilities without the necessity for recourse to individual or group psychotherapy.

If measurement by objective tests and statistical analysis of the diagnostic and clinical data proved that the specific instructional program and teaching methods developed in this project were useful, then they could be made available immediately to educators throughout the nation who are able to provide adequate diagnostic studies necessary to identify the type of learning problems in their underachieving, emotionally disturbed school population.

Significant By-products

The diagnostic and clinical data were analyzed to determine evidence of social and academic growth or the lack of it. Significant questions for further investigation are:

1. What additional criteria in selecting, matching and grouping emotionally disturbed children for instructional purposes should be utilized in addition to the traditional criteria based on achievement levels, chronological age, intelligence, and behavioral response patterns?

2. What factors are significant in selecting teachers for children who have learning problems and emotional disorders?

3. Can administrative policies and procedures, combined with intensive diagnostic studies and therapeutically sound teaching programs, provide adequate resources within the framework of the public schools for handling acutely disturbed, hyperactive, underachieving children in a classroom situation?

4. What functional and organic components are combined in the life history of children which produce that type of behavior response pattern commonly referred to as hyperactive?

5. To what extent can psychological test responses and their interpretations be used diagnostically in determining the existence of central nervous system dysfunction?

6. Should neurological reports indicating the existence of damage to the brain and central nervous system be evaluated with respect to their implications for educational programming; and, if so, what are the responsibilities of educators and neurologists?

7. Considerable research in the field of electroencephalography (EEG) indicates a high correlation between EEG electrical patterns, certain types of behavior response patterns, and variations in the learning process. What are the educational implications of these findings?

8. Current information concerning the role and function of the reticular formation as an integrative center of the central nervous system indicates that the impact of stress or trauma may result in disturbance of the integrative processes basic to the development of lan-

guage formulation and communication. What educational implications are there in these data for the planning of instructional programs for children lacking integration in all levels of adaptive behavior? [2]

9. Current developments in the fields of physiological psychology and optometry indicate that disturbance in body image, self-concept, visual-perceptual processes, and lack of co-ordination in fine and gross motor function are associated with experiential deprivation or injury of one or more of the motor sensory processes. What are the educational implications for the development of new curricula for children with these problems?

10. The experience of mastery has long been established as a necessary component for the development of physical and emotional growth and maturation. If a child's learning and behavior disorders are characterized by a consistent pattern of inappropriately immature responses to external and internal stimuli, is it possible to provide experience in an instructional program which translates the needs of an immature organism into an appropriate educational frame of reference, thus eliminating the possibility of academic failure and consequently activating or preserving the immature or damaged nervous system which controls or guides his adaptive behavior?

These questions, and those contained in the original design, are discussed in the chapters which follow. Rational solutions to these questions have important implications for special education.

The remainder of this monograph is a report of the demonstration-pilot study conceived to explore several of the hypotheses stated in this chapter. Since the original study was a demonstration, and since the number of variables presented to the investigators was initially very large, this report will be somewhat more informal than that which is appropriate to a rigorous experimental design. In the hope that future investigators will be able to test more adequately the effectiveness of the authors' opinions, and in order to give some direction to school administrators who may be considering the establishment of an educational program based upon this monograph, the authors will discuss extensively their numerous problems. The findings of this pilot study are not all positive. Nevertheless, considerable information herein contained may serve to challenge serious and thoughtful educators as they seek ways to meet the needs of many children who appear unable to profit from otherwise rich school programs.

---

[2] While this problem remains important to the authors, the nature of the diagnostic and post-test data did not lend itself to discussion of this question. It remains for further research to implement present data.

REFERENCES

1. The work of WERNER and STRAUSS appeared in numerous journals during the period 1940–50. For complete bibliography see, STRAUSS, A. A., and LEHTINEN, L. E. *Psychopathology and Education of the Brain Injured Child.* New York: Grune and Stratton, 1947.
2. STRAUSS and LEHTINEN, *op. cit.*
3. SARASON, S. B. *Psychological Problems in Mental Deficiency.* Third Edition. New York: Harper & Brothers, 1959.
4. MASLAND, R. L., SARASON, S. B., and GLADWIN, T. *Mental Subnormality.* New York: Basic Books, 1958.
5. DOLPHIN, J. E. "A Study of Certain Aspects of the Psychopathology of Children with Cerebral Palsy." Unpublished doctoral dissertation, Syracuse University, 1950.
6. SHAW, M. C. "A Study of Some Aspects of Perception and Conceptual Thinking in Idiopathic Epileptic Children." Unpublished doctoral dissertation, Syracuse University, 1955.
7. CRUICKSHANK, W. M., BICE, H. V., and WALLEN, N. E. *Perception and Cerebral Palsy.* Syracuse: Syracuse University Press, 1957.
8. CRUICKSHANK, W. M., and BICE, H. V. "Personality Characteristics," Chapter IV in *Cerebral Palsy: Its Individual and Community Problems* Syracuse: Syracuse University Press, 1955.
9. STRAUSS, A. A. and WERNER, H. "Disorders of Conceptual Thinking in the Brain-Injured Child," *Journal of Nervous and Mental Diseases,* XCVI (1942), 153–72.
10. GOLDSTEIN, K. *The Organism.* New York: American Book Co., 1939.
11. HOMBURGER, A. *Vorlesungen uber Psychopathologie des Kindersalters.* Berlin: Julius Springer, 1926.
12. KAHN, E., and COHN, L. H. "Organic Driveness, a Brain-Stem Syndrome and an Experience," *New England Journal of Medicine,* CCX (April, 1934), 748.
13. QUALTERE, T. J. "An Investigation of the Relation Between Visual Figure-Background Disturbance and Performance on Raven's Progressive Matrics Test in Cerebral Palsy Children." Unpublished doctoral dissertation, Syracuse University, 1957.
14. TRIPPE, M. J. "A Study of the Relationship Between Visual Perceptual Ability and Selected Personality Variables on a Group of Cerebral Palsy Children." Unpublished doctoral dissertation, Syracuse University, 1957.
15. NORRIS, H. "An Exploratory Study of the Relation of Certain Theoretical Constructs to a Behavioral Syndrome in Brain Pathology." Unpublished doctoral dissertation, Syracuse University, 1958.
16. NEELY, J. "A Study of the Relation of Figure-Background Differences and School Behavior in Cerebral Palsied Children." Unpublished doctoral dissertation, Syracuse University, 1958.

17. GOLDENBERG, S. "Some Aspects of Diagnosis of Cerebral Damage in Children." *Dissertation Abstract,* XIII (1953), 1259.

18. BENDER, M. *Disorders in Perception.* Springfield, Ill.: Charles C. Thomas, 1952.

19. WERNER, H., and STRAUSS, A. A. "Types of Visuo-Motor Activity in Their Relation to Low and High Performance Ages," *Proceedings American Association on Mental Deficiency,* XLIV (1939), 163–69.

20. STRAUSS, A. A. and KEPHART, N. C. *Psychopathology and Education of the Brain-Injured Child,* Vol. 2. New York: Grune and Stratton, 1955.

21. DOLPHIN, J. E. and CRUICKSHANK, W. M. "Visuo-Motor Perception in Children with Cerebral Palsy," *Quarterly Journal of Child Behavior,* III (1951), 198–209.

22. SHAW, M. C., and CRUICKSHANK, W. M. "The Use of the Marble Board Test to Measure Psychopathology in Epileptics," *American Journal of Mental Deficiency,* LX (1956), 813–17.

23. WERNER, H., and STRAUSS, A. A. "Pathology of Figure-Background Relation in the Child," *Journal of Abnormal and Social Psychology,* XXXVI (1941), 236–48.

24. DOLPHIN, J. E., and CRUICKSHANK, W. M. "The Figure-Background Relationship in Children with Cerebral Palsy," *Journal of Clinical Psychology,* VII (1951), 228–31.

25. DOLPHIN, J. E. and CRUICKSHANK, W. M. "Tactual Motor Perception of Children with Cerebral Palsy," *Journal of Personality,* XX (1952), 466–71.

26. WERNER, H. "Perceptual Behavior of Brain-Injured, Mentally Defective Children: An Experimental Study by Means of the Rorschach Technique," *Genetic Psychology Monographs,* XXXI (1945), 51–110.

27. BENDER, L., and SILVER, A. "Body Image Problems of the Brain Damaged Child," *Journal of Social Issues,* IV (1948), 84–89.

28. CRUICKSHANK, W. M. (ed.). "Psychological Considerations with Crippled Children," Chapter VI in *Psychology of Exceptional Children and Youth.* Englewood, N.J.: Prentice Hall, Inc., 1955.

29. WERNER, H., and BOWERS, M. "Auditory-Motor Organization in Two Clinical Types of Mentally Deficient Children," *Journal of Genetic Psychology,* LIX (1941), 85–99.

30. HUNT, B., and PATTERSON, R. M. "Performance of Brain-Injured and Familiar Mental Deficient Children on Visual and Auditory Sequences," *American Journal of Mental Deficiency,* LXIII (1958), 72–80.

31. GUTHRIE, E. R. *The Psychology of Learning.* New York: Harper & Brothers, 1935.

32. SPENCE, K. W. *Behavior Theory and Conditioning.* New Haven: Yale University Press, 1956.

33. DIETHELM, O. "Presidential Address: The Psychopathologic Foundation of Psychiatry," Chapter X in *Psychopathology of Communication.* Edited by HOCH, P. H., and ZUBIN, J. New York: Grune and Stratton, 1958.

34. *Annotated Code of Maryland,* Part B. Article 77, paragraph 234.

CHAPTER II

The Organizational and Planning Period

As HAS BEEN stated previously, the current demonstration-pilot study was a co operative undertaking among three major agencies; one provided the funds, and the remaining two provided the professional implementation. The approximate cost of the two-year investigation was $200,000. The term "approximate" is used advisedly, since numerous costs could not be computed specifically. These are particularly reflected in several administrative costs of Syracuse University and the Montgomery County Board of Education which were in excess of direct overhead costs paid by the United States Office of Education. A small grant from the Eugene and Agnes Meyer Foundation to continue the study for six additional months is not included in the above figure.

THE UNIVERSITY

Through its Research Institute and Office of Research in Special Education and Rehabilitation, Syracuse University provided professional leadership and direction to the study. The contract covering the expenditure of government funds was made between the United States Office of Education and Syracuse University. Thus, all administrative details covering the expenditure of the government and foundation grants were assumed by the university. Professional personnel at Syracuse University provided continuous leadership for the study, approved and participated in the selection of the diagnostic staff, appointed the resident staff, and co-operated in the selection of the research teachers. With the establishment of a Syracuse University office within the school district, close and continuous supervision could be effected. The Project Director attended nearly all of the staff conferences of the Diagnostic Team and in other ways participated in the active phase of the study on an average of three full working days per month after the diagnostic phase had been completed. This was adequate to maintain close contact with the study, to confer with the teachers, to learn to know the children and to be known by them, to observe in the classrooms, to participate in parent meetings, and to confer with public school administrators when it was necessary. The availability to the Project Director of a competent research assistant enabled the Project Director to make much more effective use of his time when he was in the school district.

The authors have often been asked why a university and a school system separated from each other by so many miles would undertake such a study. Over the years the Project Director and the local Supervisor of Special Education had observed their mutual interest in the etiology, psychological characteristics, and educational problems of hyperactive children with or without diagnosed brain injury. On the one hand, psychological research had been undertaken and completed; on the other, exploratory educational planning had been attempted with these children. When the opportunity presented itself for an initial investigation, the mutual interests of those who were administratively responsible for the program made it logical and important that a joint project be undertaken. In this climate of mutual interest and respect, distance was no barrier to successful professional enterprise.

Table of Organization

The administrative organization established for the completion of the study is noted in Figure 1. In large measure the relationships between Syracuse University and the school district were completely cooperative. No one person was employed by both agencies with any administrative responsibility. The Supervisor of Special Education had a relationship with the research staff which technically was stronger than that of any other person, but these relationships were never defined specifically and simply evolved over the months as questions and problems arose. The Resident Co-ordinator, as is indicated below, secured all of her administrative authority through offices and other persons already possessed of such authority. In no instance did she administer the project in the sense that she directed it. Co-operation is always time-consuming. In the end, however, if carried through in the proper spirit, it should lead to stronger understandings and greater *esprit de corps*. This proved to be the case in the present situation.

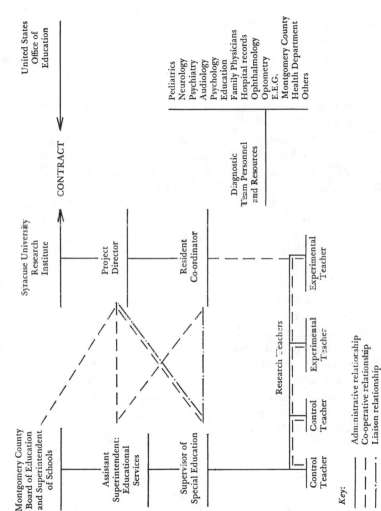

TABLE OF ORGANIZATION FOR THE STUDY

Fig. 1. Administrative Plan for the Pilot Study.

The Public School District

The Montgomery County Board of Education's contribution included the salaries of the four project teachers and two teacher-assistants, instructional supplies and equipment normally available to the teaching staff of elementary public schools, office space, equipment and supplies for the administrative staff, and the reconditioning of the two experimental classrooms to provide a stimulus-free environment.

The Assistant Superintendent in charge of the Department of Educational Services of the Montgomery County Board of Education was delegated the responsibility for making those policy decisions resulting from the pilot study which fell within the jurisdiction of the Board of Education. He authorized and supervised the introduction of the research staff's ancillary personnel into the classroom situations. It was through the Assistant Superintendent that the Resident Co-ordinator channeled all requests for project needs other than those provided by the research project funds. It was from him that guidance and assistance was sought in resolving problems which required deviations from the accepted Montgomery County School Board educational policies and procedures.

Since this was a project involving the Department of Special Education, the Supervisor of that department was delegated large administrative responsibilities. Selection of the teachers for the research classes was her responsibility. All referrals of children for examination were made after initial screening in the Supervisor's office. Diagnostic Team members were appointed on the basis of her experience and many whose interests in the project were known to her were initially recommended by her for consideration. In dozens of indirect and intangible ways she made significant contributions to the study.

Related Personnel

School psychologists, remedial reading teachers, special education and regular elementary teachers, school principals and guidance counselors from the school district, all participated, formally or informally, in the initial referral of subjects for evaluation. Persons outside of the Montgomery County Board of Education also were vital in the development and implementation of the project. The Administrator of School Health Services of the Montgomery County Board of Health was professionally associated with the study. He participated in the diagnostic case conferences and acted as Health Department liaison in providing the diagnostic staff with examination rooms, nursing personnel, and the past medical histories of the children scheduled for examination.

The Resident Co-ordinator

The Resident Co-ordinator was responsible for co-ordinating and integrating the project for the public school, for supervising the full-time residential office staff, for scheduling staff meetings and working out agendas, and for channeling questions of policy and personnel to the appropriate administrative head. In addition to these duties the Resident Co-ordinator participated with the administrative assistant in the selection, matching, and grouping of the project children. She conducted parent interviews, acted as liaison with the Health Department personnel in providing the diagnostic staff with clinic facilities, nursing personnel, and secretarial services. In general, she was responsible for the continuous development of the project in all its phases.

THE DIAGNOSTIC STAFF

". . . The problem of multidisciplinary research is basically the problem of small group organization in which two or three, rarely more than four, technically distinct disciplines are represented. This requires clear and precise communication, as well as a definition of compatible goals. . . ." (1, p. 467). The four disciplines represented in the present study are education, medicine (including pediatrics, neurology, psychiatry), psychology, and audiology and speech pathology.

Two major factors facilitated the development of a smoothly operating group organization. First, each member of the diagnostic staff was professionally acquainted with the type of child typical of the subject population of the research project; and second, all members were sympathetic to the research goals and had had previous experience in diagnostic investigations of the clinical, medical, and psychological factors operating in underachievement and behavior disorders.

The speech pathologist and audiologist, for example, as a result of her professional affiliation with Johns Hopkins University Hospital's Department of Otolaryngology and Environmental Medicine and the Diagnostic Speech Clinic of the Montgomery County Health Department, was professionally acquainted with a number of the children and parents who participated in the project. In addition to her familiarity with some of the subject population, she had for a number of years been deeply concerned with the diagnostic and treatment problem resulting from the presence of speech and language formulation difficulties when no demonstrable evidence of end-organ hearing loss or central nervous system damage existed.

The staff neurologist, in addition to having had long-term professional association with some of the children from whom the project selections were made, had also been instrumental in organizing a clinic to provide for multidisciplinary study of diagnostic and treatment problems associated with retarded mental development and damage to the central nervous system. It should also be mentioned that the neurologist had assisted in the original planning of the research design. Thus, the project design, aims, methods, and goals all reflected the neurologist's research interest in the possible neurological basis of specific types of learning problems and behavior disorders.

The project pediatrician was, at the time of his appointment as a member of the diagnostic staff, the pediatrician at the District of Columbia Department of Public Welfare, Children's Center, Laurel, Maryland. In this work the staff pediatrician had become keenly aware of the role that underachievement and unsatisfactory school experience played in delinquency and emotional disorders. Thus, the long-range goal of the project, i.e., the development of specialized teaching methods and instructional programs geared to the learning difficulties and emotional problems of underachieving, hyperactive children, coincided with an area of his specialized pediatric interest.

The psychiatrist had worked closely with public school teachers and administrative personnel, particularly in the Montgomery County Department of Special Education. As a result of establishing herself in a participant-observer role in the classroom situation, the psychiatrist had acquired a clear and practical understanding of the group-teaching problems associated with classroom management and instruction of children with behavior disorders and learning problems.

Thus, the main criterion of selection which determined the appointment of the individual members of the diagnostic staff were: first, a high degree of professional competence and maturity; second, professional and personal interest in the research problem and an awareness of the need and importance of developing teaching programs for underachieving children with associated emotional disorders; and, third, professional experience with the school population from which the research subjects were chosen.

To the above staff were added the services of a full-time research clinical psychologist whose professional background and orientation in the problems of differential diagnosis in children with central nervous system involvement added much to the over-all competency of the Diagnostic Team. The experience of the clinical psychologist included institutional work with mentally retarded children and professional responsibilities in a child guidance center. For an extended period of time he functioned as a clinical psychologist under the supervision of the Project Director in an out-patient diagnostic and evaluation center for the psychological study of physically and mentally handicapped children. Thus, his experience was extensive in relation to children and intensive with relation to the project immediately at hand.

It will be noted that the clinical psychologist was employed in the study on a full-time basis whereas all other diagnostic staff members were employed on a part-time basis. There were numerous, obvious reasons for this. The primary basis for the decision was encompassed in the nature of the services to be performed by the psychologist. His work included the pre- and post-examination of all the children wherein he utilized a very extensive and time-consuming battery of psychological instruments. This work could not have been concluded on a part-time basis. As a matter of fact, much additional part time psychological assistance was provided to this member of the professional team. In addition, the clinical psychologist was responsible for scheduled observations of the children throughout the school year and for the interpretation of psychological test data on each of the children to the teachers. Much time was spent by this individual in teacher conference. Finally, statistical treatment of his data and preparation of written reports concluded his professional obligations.

Two other individuals also participated in the actual function of the Diagnostic Team during staff conference periods. The Supervisor of Special Education in the Montgomery County Public Schools served as a liaison between the school system and the research staff. Her interest in the education of these children has been previously recorded. She thus brought to the Diagnostic Team conference table not only an excellent understanding of the educational characteristics of the children being discussed, but also a complete understanding of each child's school behavior history and a broad background of interdisciplinary information regarding the nature of the children under discussion.

The Project Director also participated in the Diagnostic Team conferences. His background as a psychologist and educator, and his previous psychological research with the learning problems of the children being considered—in conjunction with the insights of the Supervisor of Special Education—made it possible to integrate the numerous specialists' reports and to obtain group decision regarding the admissibility of a given child to the project.

From time to time as various specialized problems arose, other individuals representing the disciplines of psychology, medicine, and education participated in the staff conferences.

At this point the thoughtful reader will be alert to the fact that there were some omissions from the Diagnostic Team. The authors are quick to point out these omissions for they were immediately apparent to them and to the others participating in the study. The sole reason for any and all of the omissions was the problem of finance. While funds were available for the study, they were not sufficient to provide as complete a diagnostic picture as had originally been hoped. It must be pointed out that this was not due to initial inadequate planning, but rather to a reduction in the size of the grant originally requested.

The most serious omission was that of a social caseworker. Were the study to be reinstigated at a future time, a full-time medical social caseworker would be considered by these authors as a member of the Team. In the present study this function was not completely filled at any time, although the pediatrician, the psychologist, and the coordinator each and together provided much background data which would normally be provided by the caseworker. The other important functions of medical social casework, however, were simply not fulfilled, and the study suffered to this degree.

It may appear that nursing personnel were not represented. They were not included as permanent members of the Team. Nursing services were available to diagnostic personnel during the period of the examinations when they were necessary.

Complete ophthalmological and optometric services were missing. Both disciplines were represented in the community by highly specialized personnel. Because of the limitation of funds, however, such services were utilized only for those children who presented visual symptoms in other clinical situations. The authors recognize the importance of complete visual information, particularly in this type of an educational study. However, it was impossible to provide routinely for this in what was originally considered to be the priority list for minimal professional services. To compensate for this general lack of information, all other diagnostic personnel were sensitive to the visual status of the patients who were being examined and liberal use of referral was made.

THE ROLE OF THE RESIDENT CO-ORDINATOR

The success of the organizational and planning periods depends to a great extent on the competencies of the Resident Co-ordinator and on the continuing successful operation of the staff conference.

The definition of roles and the delineation of responsibilities in educational research programs and projects for atypical children may create problems in school administration, policies, and procedures. Class size, specialized teaching methods, adapted curriculum, and instructional materials frequently result in policy problems between special and regular teachers, their principals and supervisors. Unusual or bizarre behavior on the part of disturbed children frequently precipitate feelings of anxiety and uncertainty in teachers, parents, and principals.

Research projects carried out within the framework of departments of special education further complicate the existing professional and interpersonal situations by introducing criteria and controlled variables which frequently appear to run counter to traditionally accepted methods of providing for the educational welfare of the children assigned to research classes.

Therefore, it is particularly important for a co-ordinator of an educational research project to possess:

1. the professional training and work experience which have prepared him or her to handle complicated, anxiety-laden, interpersonal situations with warmth, objectivity, and professional maturity;

2. a working knowledge of the traditional elementary public school administrative and personnel policies, curriculum manuals, instructional methods, and status problems associated with the teaching profession;

3. an awareness of the impact of educational research upon research teachers' morale, and, furthermore, the preparation to handle these anxieties with reality-based techniques;

4. a thorough and complete understanding of the particular research design as well as its aims and goals, and the ability to translate the procedures, aims, methods, and goals into an instructional frame of reference.

For example, when a research project is introduced into a public school setting, the first response of the teaching and administrative staff is one of enthusiastic support. However, once the planning and organizational phase is completed and the class or project is integrated into the school setting, the initial enthusiasm is likely to wane for the following reasons.

1. The principal and teachers are apt to feel that their authority and status are threatened by the presence of specialists associated with the research project.

2. The regular teachers may become resentful of the small groups of children who are utilized for research purposes and of the research teachers who receive so much special attention while the regular teachers and their groups of 30 or 40 children receive no additional help or guidance.

3. The project teachers find their instructional day interrupted by observers, testing procedures, extra conferences, and additional work over and beyond that which is normally required of all teachers.

A co-ordinator who does not anticipate and plans for these potential conflict situations will quite justifiably be blamed if things go wrong. In such situations additional tensions develop and "those specialists" or "that project" become hooks on which very serious and time-consuming parent-teacher, teacher-principal, teacher-teacher, and teacher-research staff interpersonal and professional problems are hung. An individual who, previous to co-ordinating a research project, has become an accepted and valued member of a regular and special teaching staff is in an excellent position to become an effective member of the administrative staff of an educational research project.

The person best equipped to evaluate school and medical records for an educational research project involving classroom practices is one who is able to understand the meaning of school reports and recording language. It is important to be able to translate these understandings and clues to various types of medical and psychiatric conditions into specific reasons for the child's learning difficulty, and finally, he must be able to assess those difficulties in terms of their applicability to the specific research design in question.

In those cases where the research design is interdisciplinary, a co-ordinator with some background or experience in psychiatry, medicine, education, counseling, and, if possible, previous work in educational research can be put to excellent use in assisting in the selection of the diagnostic staff for the project.

In addition to assisting in the selection of the staff, the Resident Co-ordinator arranges individual conference appointments for each member of the proposed staff with the Project Director, School Health Administrator, and Board of Education liaison. This initial conference is important in order that professional approaches to and interests in interdiscipline diagnostic problems and the research project goals can be explored. During such conferences, it is helpful to identify areas of special interest in each discipline which may be related to the research design in a mutually profitable way, thus establishing areas of professional compatibility.

After the staff is employed, the arrangement of staff conferences becomes an important function of the Resident Co-ordinator. Conferences including the Project Director, representatives from participating agencies, Board of Education administrative personnel, secretarial and clerical help, and the diagnostic staff should be arranged so that each member of the conference is provided with an agenda which permits organizational problems to be handled through an objective exploration of the factual material related to the problems at hand. It is the structure of operation rather than the problem itself which is emphasized.

Areas of interdisciplinary controversy frequently caused by differing viewpoints on problems of differential diagnosis, status and role problems of the individuals participating in the study, matters of scheduling and referrals, procedural methods, and problems associated with the question of medical ethics—all may be handled by the Resident Co-ordinator through the administrative technique of the written agenda and the staff conference. Time for the satisfactory rationalization and solution of these controversies and problems must be arranged. In preparing the agenda and arranging the staff conference, it is essential that the Resident Co-ordinator be free of any personal investment or bias in favor of any one of the particular disciplines represented and that he or she be familiar with each discipline's traditionally accepted method of organizing and interpreting diagnostic data. Helpful, but not essential, is the Co-ordinator's understanding of the major problems and conflict areas within a discipline and among the various disciplines involved.

If possible, it is wise to schedule the order of business so that the first two items planned for discussion are noncontroversial, thus providing the staff with a solidly realistic feeling of achievement *before* group discussion of anxiety-laden problems arise. The use of the agenda is an excellent technique for setting limits and controlling the overflow of anxiety which frequently manifests itself in staff conferences in the form of rambling digressions. Without the aid of the agenda, there is little chance of handling this overflow of anxiety in an impersonal manner.

If it is possible to arrange the staff conferences so that the Resident

Co-ordinator does not act as chairman or as an authority figure in any capacity, it is wise to do so. In the current study the chairman was almost always the Project Director. This arrangement diminishes the status role of the Resident Co-ordinator; making it possible to maintain a free-flowing interpersonal communication with each of the staff members.

It is important that the subjects for discussion on the agenda remain specific, concrete, and concerned with exploration of various techniques of handling a given situation, so that the selection of a particular technique for dealing with a problem results from concerted group action and not from the impression that one person's way appears to be better than another person's way.

The roles of the Resident Co-ordinator were that of the assistant, the planner and writer of agendas, and the originator of arrangements for such matters as scheduling the time and place of staff conferences. The Co-ordinator's careful, methodical, and well-planned staffings served as the means by which problems and needs were channeled to the Project Director, to other administrative personnel, or to other appropriate authority figures.

Staff discussions of problems of differential diagnosis were recorded fully and accurately. The records were held for the time when diagnostic emphasis might tend to fluctuate, and for the stage when the problem of matching and grouping the children would have to be resolved.

There is perhaps no more critical period during an educational research project than the one during which the project and its personnel are new to the school system, the parents, family physician, and the related agencies with which the project necessarily and appropriately becomes involved. If the services of a Co-ordinator are utilized, it is necessary that the individual selected have sufficient personal maturity and professional insight to understand that, no matter how competently this initial period is handled, there will be periods of interpersonal and interdepartmental conflict. The initiation of educational research projects which provide additional classroom space for children with learning needs may precipitate competition and rivalry among various departments of the school system, the health department, and related agencies. It is imperative that an individual acting as a research project Co-ordinator realize that this rivalry is not associated with a role *per se,* but that it is due to the existence of large numbers of school-age children whose emotional, social, and educational problems may not be provided for under current conditions. Understanding and acceptance of this problem help Co-ordinators to keep in mind the fact that no matter how personalized a situation may seem to be, it develops in fact because a research project represents a new source of help and possible school placement for troubled children. The methods, means, and available facilities for resolving the problems of children with emotional disturbances and learning difficulties are so meager in the face of established needs that those who are employed in an attempt to resolve the problems and provide facilities may experience failure—not because they do not know what is needed, but because the professionally trained help, classroom space, and teachers needed to solve the problems are not available within the provisions of a single research project or within the public school system.

It is important for the person appointed Resident Co-ordinator to realize that during the first three to five weeks of the academic year, teachers regularly experience one of the most anxiety-producing periods associated with, or perhaps even a part of, the teaching profession. Among teachers, this period is referred to as "holding my group," and the close of the period is indicated by the teacher's informal announcement that she "has her group now."

For example, in discussing the stresses and strains of this period, one teacher said flatly, "No one can teach a collection of individuals who haven't even learned to work with each other, let alone work with the teacher. The hardest job in the world is to teach the children how to work together. Once that's done, half your teaching worries are over. . . . Anybody can do a good teaching job once they 'hold their group.' "

The Resident Co-ordinator, while recognizing that teacher anxiety is normal to this particular phase of the instructional year, must exercise the firmest kind of self-discipline in order to avoid over-identification with teaching personnel during this period. His or her job is to be available, on a round-the-clock basis if possible, in order to provide missing supplies, instructional equipment, teacher breaks, and whatever classroom additions are needed, such as desks, chairs, and tables. The Co-ordinator does not under any circumstances attempt to explore the anxiety in the interest of providing supportive therapy, even though the teacher may make a verbal request for this type of assistance.

Co-ordinators who fail to observe this cardinal rule of good professional ethics will find, first, that, even though the teacher may feel temporary relief from anxiety, she is justified in feeling extremely hostile because, as a teacher, she has demonstrated that she is uncertain in her own mind as to whether she can consider herself equal to the task of "holding her group" during the rest of the year. Second, the children are keenly aware of any situation where there is any indication that "my teacher can't handle us and had to ask for help." Once this suspicion has been justified, it may take as long as six months for the teacher to "hold her group."

Some teachers frequently feel during this initial period that certain children were improperly assigned to their group. The Co-ordinator who acts on the assumption that this is an indirect request to have the child transferred substantiates the teacher's false suspicions of her own professional inadequacies. These fears are usually completely inappropriate and unrealistic in terms of the teacher's total teaching strength.

For example, if the teacher feels that one child is much too tall (or too old, or too young, or too disturbed) for her group, will be excessively unhappy as a result of his placement, and should be transferred to another group where he can establish better relationships, the Co-ordinator (if the child is taller than the other children, for example) makes certain that the desks which have been provided for the teacher include one of the correct height for this child, and works out with the teacher the best seating arrangements in terms of seating proximity to the next tallest children. He does not explore the teacher's unexpressed concern as to the child's possible reasons for being unhappy, or the teacher's personal reasons for thinking that he is unhappy. He does *handle* the situation on a reality-based level of assistance. The Co-ordinator gets things done, no matter how much time it takes, or how many people have to be seen. Once this initial period is over for the teacher, for the children, and for the Co-ordinator, the Co-ordinator absents himself from the classroom situation in order that the teacher may be free to get on with her teaching program.

If the Resident Co-ordinator has established the fact that he is useful and helpful during this anxiety period, the teacher can then be expected to request the use of the Co-ordinator's services when she needs them, and not when the Co-ordinator thinks the teacher needs them. When this particular *status quo* has been reached, both can turn their attention to other and more pressing matters.

These philosophical considerations were basic to this study. In conclusion, a good Co-ordinator is one who helps to define the role and function of individual members of the staff in relation to every other individual and to the research project's philosophy and goals. Success in filling this role can best be measured when the staff with whom the Co-ordinator is associated is unable to define the Co-ordinator's role or function, but knows that the program just would not work if he were not available.

THE STAFF CONFERENCE

It was initially felt that all children should be individually presented at a staff conference by the several disciplines represented in the Diagnostic Team. The original purpose was to develop as quickly as possible a unanimity of feeling regarding the problem being considered. It was also felt that as soon as staff members felt that there was a "meeting of the minds" among themselves, the diagnostic phase would proceed at a more rapid rate and with greater assurance.

The Diagnostic Team members spent many full days together in these discussions. For each child finally selected as a member of the study groups the pediatric, psychological, neurological, audiological, psychiatric, and educational data was extensively presented and thoroughly discussed. Seven children, not ultimately included in the groups, were screened out at this point. It was in the staff conferences that numerous digressions occurred, stimulated by professional differences, lack of understanding of one another's vocabulary, and differing personal orientations to the problem. It was here that the role of the Resident Co-ordinator played a crucial part. For while the Co-ordinator did not chair the staff conferences, she was present to hear discussions, to observe confusions objectively, and to make notes on those points which should be considered individually with a member outside of the group environment. This individual contact by the Co-ordinator made possible a high degree of group participation and function when the Diagnostic Team operated together. In general, the staff conferences were characterized by a marked degree of unanimity of point of view and always by a healthy feeling of mutual co-operation.

Since so much of the result of any special education experimentation depends on the adequacy of physical data regarding the subjects, it goes without saying that the selection of the diagnostic personnel is among the most important elements of any design. This is oftentimes not thoroughly understood by educational administrators or those related to fund-granting agencies. The inclusion of these noneducational representatives in an educational experiment is not looked upon as essential or appropriate. The contrary is, however, true and is apparent to the thoughtful scientist. No educational experimentation in the field of special education can be undertaken without the support of medical disciplines and psychological disciplines in at least the diagnostic and subject-finding phase of the study. The results of too many educational experiments must be looked upon with distrust because the reader is unable to ascertain the nature of the problem of the children included in the study and because the principal investigator was professionally unprepared to make these decisions himself. Thus, in the present educational experiment, a major proportion of the research funds was spent in medical and psychological diagnosis and in an attempt to describe sufficiently each of the children ultimately studied, so as to provide the reader with as complete a picture as possible of the subject population. The findings of educational experimentation are relatively worthless if the reader does not have a good understanding of the population to which the findings apply. In the present pilot study nearly ten months were spent in selecting the Diagnostic Team members, orienting them to the problem, scheduling and completing examinations, and holding staff conferences. The nature of the activities specific to this period will be discussed in Chapter III of this monograph.

REFERENCE

1. RIOCH, D. McK. "Multidisciplinary Methods in Psychiatric Research," *American Journal of Orthopsychiatry*, XXVIII (July, 1958), 467–482.

The Diagnostic Period

IN THIS chapter the authors desire first to provide a frame of reference in the form of a descriptive composite out of which the research problem was developed and on the basis of which the children were selected for the project. Second, to report the methods and techniques utilized in the prediagnostic screening, selection, and referral of the project candidates to the staff. Third, to reproduce in detail the individual diagnostic and clinical reports of the examinations of one child as they were recorded by the examining physicians for the staff conferences. Finally, to present diagnostic data collected from hospital obstetrical records and to discuss this together with the implications drawn from electroencephalographic studies made of each child during the diagnostic period.

A COMPOSITE AS A FRAME OF REFERENCE

A family and child composite represents a departure from established methods of reporting clinical data which customarily outline the behavior pattern to be used as a guide in designing the research problem and in the prediagnostic selection of the group of children who are to participate in the project. The composite not only accomplishes these purposes, but also provides a frame of reference for the remaining portions of this chapter. This particular frame of reference is one in which children are, at first glance, seen as problem children; but, as the results of the examination are accumulated, the children gradually emerge and are viewed as a group of individuals whose specific learning disorders and behavior patterns pinpoint unresolved problem areas in all the disciplines which are concerned with processes of birth, growth, development, maturation, and learning.

Keeping in mind that no such child or family as that described in the composite exists in reality, some aspects of the composite behavior response pattern which are familiar to parents will be seen as an entirely different behavior pattern to teachers, and *vice versa*. Psychiatrists, neurologists, and pediatricians will recognize herein some of their most difficult, distracting, and likable patients. Thus it is entirely possible that if such a child did exist, he might, under various circumstances, be classified as brain-injured, or as one who demonstrates evidence of organicity or minimal brain injury. He might be viewed as emotionally disturbed; as having a home problem; as a psychopathological personality; as having a weak ego or lack of ego integration; as lacking inner controls and requiring a rigid, controlled, and highly structured environment; or as needing an environment which is warmly permissive. He could be regarded as needing immediate long-term residential treatment, or as not being amenable to psychiatric treatment. In some situations such a child might be classified as being a "real boy" whose discipline problems are ones which he will outgrow.

The child is usually a boy. His parents are white, as were their mothers and fathers before them. They may believe in the Catholic, Protestant, or Jewish religion, but do not necessarily attend the church of their faith. The father, a rather quiet man in his late thirties or forties, may be a truck driver, nuclear physicist, manager of a chain store, biochemist, or theoretical mathematician, but no matter what his profession, he performs his chosen occupation with outstanding efficiency, dependability, and intelligence. During the week he works long hours, frequently leaving the house before his son is up and returning after he is asleep.

On weekends, if he is not working, he tries very hard to spend some of his time with his son and to find things to do together; but when he succeeds in initiating some joint enterprise, his son for no apparent reason wrecks the afternoon by carelessly thrusting the hammer into the power saw while it is going at high speed, kicking over a bucket of freshly mixed paint, or sticking his finger into a light socket and then exploding into yelling fury when he is jerked to safety. The father, unable to comprehend the violence of the explosion or to control his son's behavior, more often than not retreats to the bastions of his work, remarking to his wife as he does so that she is too easy on the child, that he needs more discipline.

His wife is an attractive, outgoing, intelligent woman who, up to the time of her son's birth, thoroughly enjoyed her job as a secretary, nurse, teacher, economist, or mother of the two previous children. Before children were born to her, she was active in civic affairs and frequently participated in various types of adult study groups. She enjoys a good fight, although she has learned for the most part to control her aggressive drives in the interest of maintaining harmony in the family and neighborhood.

At this point, her relationships with her son are at an all-time low because he demands constant attention and rebels fiercely when he gets it. He refuses to share his toys with his little sister and knocks her down when she asks to play with his truck collection. He fights with the neighbors' children, except those much younger than himself with whom he spends more time than a boy of his age should. Although he is constantly hungry, especially for sweets, during the family dinner hour—to which he is customarily a half hour late—he fiddles with his food until, under threat of maternal violence, he gulps it down, frequently eating with his hands instead of the silverware which he throws to the floor upon being reprimanded for bad manners. Although he is an alert, attractive lad, he is failing in school and may have been retained a year, or even excluded from school, because he refused to settle down and get to work.

At their wits' ends, the parents finally take their boy to his pediatrician who more often than not finds him physically healthy, somewhat hyperactive, of normal or superior intelligence and, most comforting of all, a child who will probably "outgrow" his current behavior problems. It is to be noted, however, that during this conference and the many others which follow with teachers, principals, school psychologists, counselors, and therapists, the parents' conversation is apt to have a curiously detached quality, almost as though they were helping the professional to understand the problems of a close friend's child for whom they feel a great deal of warmth and a very deep personal concern but no real responsibility.

The boy established his reputation as a classroom discipline problem between the ages of 6 and 9. He may have had a trial period in a nursery school or a kindergarten group around 5 years of age, but after a very hectic week or so, he was probably sent home as being too immature and not ready for group experience.

In the third grade, if he has not already been excluded from school, he is frequently disruptively aggressive. He talks out of turn, forgetting or neglecting to raise his hand. He appears unable to sit still and is constantly wiggling, fidgeting, twisting, and jouncing up and down in his seat. He runs in the halls, no matter who is watching, nor how often he is reprimanded. His shoelaces, zippers, and buttons, once undone, remain untied, unzipped, and unbuttoned, until standards of decency and orderliness are finally re-established by weary adults. His pockets bulge with miniature trucks, cars, and playing cards with which he plays all day, frequently humming, making odd noises, or talking to himself as he does so.

He is physically attractive, well-built, and appears to have good motor co-ordination. Even though he is frequently awkward and clumsy on the playground and in the classroom, it is assumed that he does not take time to look where he is going.

In the classroom during work periods, he is unable or refuses to follow directions. If pictures, for example, are to be pasted at the top of the page, he pastes his at the bottom and frequently on the wrong side of the paper. If his teacher takes time to give him the directions again, he loses the thread of what she is saying before she has finished the first sentence. If he manages to complete any work at all, it is in-describably sloppy and carelessly executed. He agrees with everything the teacher says and on occasions treats her with great respect. The next minute he denies he took from her desk the pencil which is sticking out of his pocket. His books are torn and dirty.

He shrieks and crys like a frightened two-year-old if he cuts his finger. However, when the basketball lands on the roof of the school, he climbs the side of the building (with no visible means of support), retrieves the ball, which he refuses to throw to the waiting players, and shinnys down the drainpipe, kicking at someone's head as he jumps the last five feet to the ground.

No matter what he scores in terms of a functioning IQ (intelligence quotient), the school psychologist reports that the test results are charac-terized by an unusual spread. He fails, for example, in some tasks at a level four years below his chronological age. In general, his greatest strengths are on the performance level and greatest weaknesses in the area of verbal concepts. The examiner frequently concludes his report with a statement that he does not feel the final score is a valid estimate of the child's potential.

The boy may not be able to read at all, and he may test at the same readiness level for three consecutive years. Or he may read with great fluency two years above his chronological age, but be so lacking in comprehension that, if he is asked to repeat the story in his own words, he will be unable to think of a single thing to say that is relevant.

He is somewhat better at arithmetic; but his worksheets, which he twists about or turns at an odd angle as he works, are usually in shreds by the time he should have completed the assignment. His spelling and handwriting, if they are at all comprehensible, are atrociously inaccurate and carelessly executed. In his everyday speech, as well as in his reading, writing, spelling, and arithmetic papers, one notes reversals, substitutions, and omissions of words. He dislikes art class, refuses to participate in finger painting, and frequently loathes clay, which he throws at the other students. He likes fans, motors, small trucks, and the pets which he mistreats.

He rarely has friends, although he frequently has accomplices both at home and at school. In playground activities, he is something of a bully. He refuses to participate in organized group games, but then harries his classmates from the sidelines. He appears to be completely devoid of even a rudimentary sense of fair play or of the existence of rules. In general, he gets along better with adults than with children. Adults are often attracted by his graceful charm, but are apt to have the feeling that they are unable to reach him.

On occasions he explodes into temper tantrums or apparently unprovoked rage reactions of such violence that he may constitute a danger to himself or others. At times it appears that his only regret after such episodes is that he did not kill or demolish the offending object.

He loves ritual, marching, and making up elaborate rules. He would give his immortal soul to be a member of the school patrols, but even if he is able to read and understand the patrol pledge, he forgets it two days later, as he does the rules and regulations. He loses his patrol badge, coat, belt, and hat, and has a difficult time giving directions at the intersection because he apparently does not remember the difference between left and right.

And finally, in the neighborhood he may be, or he may only be suspected of being, a thief, a fire setter, or both. On the other hand, he may be the idol of the neighborhood mothers and his teachers, because in both deportment and dress he is always the perfect gentleman. But no matter how he appears to others, after the long day's frustrations and failure to get along with others, at night he wants closeness and warmth more than almost anything else in the world, even when he twists his body sharply out of the very arms which would give him what he needs and wants most.

Whether this boy is brain-damaged, emotionally disturbed, or both, it was the assumption of the educators who developed the research design that the available educational methods by which he was expected to learn how to learn and how to behave at home and at school, were inappropriate to the ways in which his particular mind, ears, eyes, and body operated in a learning situation.

PREDIAGNOSTIC SCREENING PROCEDURES
AND TECHNIQUES

The lack of uniformity and standardization of special education programs and services makes it impossible for recommendations and suggestions regarding any one particular method or methods of screening and selecting children for purposes of educational research projects. It may be helpful to the reader, therefore, at this point to report the specific procedures followed in the present project in screening and selecting the children for later referral to the diagnostic staff.

Underachieving children with learning problems and emotional disorders are frequently known to many agencies and may have long histories of educational, medical, psychiatric, and community problems, as illustrated in the preceding composite. Background histories on children with these difficulties are rarely accumulated in one place. Therefore, it was most fortunate that the personnel (the Resident Coordinator and the Supervisor of Special Education) responsible for prediagnostic screening and referral were familiar with the services, personnel, policies, and procedures of the Board of Education Department of Special Services, Pupil Personnel Department, Department of Psychological Services, Health Department, local nonschool mental health clinics and facilities, as well as the clinic and treatment centers in the area which had established working relationships with the public school system. As a result, the staff knew where to go to locate pertinent information for review and evaluation of the background history of the children's difficulties. It was also extremely useful to know, in each particular case, through whom to channel requests for the review of confidential information in each department or agency.

With this backlog of experience and information, it became possible to operate smoothly through interagency channels of authority and to resolve problems of referral procedures and policy matters with a minimum amount of time and friction. Awareness on the part of project personnel responsible for the selection of children of specific areas of intradepartmental and interagency conflict was frequently found to be helpful in maintaining good public relations.

It was important that the right of free access to confidential records had been previously established. It should be pointed out that this can be expected only if the person selected for the coordinating role has had an opportunity to work closely with the administrative personnel who are responsible for confidential records and that the relationship is characterized by professional integrity, good sense, and discretion.

In this first step in the screening process, the task was to look for children who met the specific research criteria in regard to chronological age and intelligence. Individual children whose scores did not meet the criteria received consideration only when the administrative and diagnostic staff were provided with documentary evidence that the existing testing measurements and diagnostic skills did not provide accurate measurements of the individual potential. Evidence or clues indicating the existence of a hyperactive behavior pattern, academic underachievement, and brain injury were carefully noted. The names and folders of children excluded from consideration as a result of this gross record screening were returned immediately to whatever referral source had made the name and record available. Great care was taken in returning these records to specify exactly why the case did not meet the needs of the project; and, when possible, the opportunity was used to explain, in as much detail as was appropriate, the nature of the project, its aims and goals, and any aspects which could be expected to provide assistance to the department or agency in question.

Once the gross record screening was completed, a detailed examination of the teacher and principal reports and anecdotal records was begun in which information pinpointing the individual behavior response pattern and outlining the learning problems of each child was carefully noted. Following this, the school psychological reports were examined for comments which offered clues as to the nature of the learning and emotional difficulties of individual children.

Examination of the application for special education or special services, when available, frequently provided information on previous schools attended, as well as teacher reports of academic weaknesses and strengths. Information regarding past medical and psychiatric histories was also regularly included in these records.

The subject population of the four research classes was selected for prediagnostic screening from a total of 460 referrals from the above indicated sources. It included children already enrolled in the Department of Special Education classes who were not felt to be achieving at their maximum potential; children who had been accepted for Special Education classes, but whose class assignment was pending due to lack of classroom space or teachers; and children who had been referred for Special Education case study and placement by school principals, health department officials, pupil personnel workers, school psychologists, parents, private physicians, or therapists.

Selection of the Sample

Prediagnostic screening of the referral population of 460 children eliminated all but 67 of the total number referred. These 67 children showed a range in chronological age of 6–10 through 9–9, in mental age from 4–8 through 8–10, and an IQ range from 51 through 107.

The research-design criteria specified that the total subject population was to have clinically demonstrable evidence of forced responsiveness to stimuli, short attention span, visuo-motor or other perceptual difficulties, hyperactivity, disturbance in figure-background relationships, impulsivity, perseveration, with or without evidence of language and speech formulation difficulties. In the prediagnostic screening, the selection of the 67 children in terms of the criteria of specific learning disabilities was guided by clues obtained from the anecdotal records of teachers, and the reports of school psychologists. Examples of such clues include the following kind of comments:

". . . fails to pay attention." ". . . refuses to follow directions." ". . . stubborn." ". . . lazy." ". . . resents authority." ". . . refuses to cooperate." ". . . is a nonreader but does well in arithmetic." ". . . dislikes art and ceramics but is very good with his hands." ". . . talks constantly without regard for others." ". . . is a mirror reader." ". . . has many reversals." ". . . is above average in intelligence but lacks motivation." ". . . is a word-caller." ". . . reads two years above his age-grade level but lacks comprehension." ". . . insists on a great deal of personal attention." ". . . is a discipline problem and refuses to participate in group activities." ". . . is a good speller but unable to write his spelling words correctly." ". . . clumsy." ". . . awkward." ". . . deliberately trips other children." ". . . dresses sloppily." ". . . seems to have a hearing problem." ". . . seems to need glasses." ". . . has disorganized work habits which he refuses to correct." ". . . needs limits." ". . . is a playground problem in organized games."

These particular comments were evaluated in terms of the existence of specific learning problems. It was assumed, for example, that the failure to pay attention, refusal to follow directions, refusal to cooperate, resentfulness of authority figures, ability to read above grade level without adequate comprehension, or an apparent hearing loss when health and medical records ruled out end-organ damage to the ear, might well indicate the existence of learning problems associated with difficulties in language formulation, auditory comprehension, or both.

Mirror reading, ability to spell verbally and inability to write words, clumsiness, awkwardness, apparent visual problems (when health records and eye examinations ruled out eye defects), disorganized work habits, and classification as a nonreader were evaluated, for example, as possible manifestations of visual-perceptual and visuo-motor problems. Children reported as discipline problems in the classroom, those in need of limits, or those who constituted playground problems during organized games, and who also were characterized by one or more of the above difficulties, were evaluated as probably evidencing hyperactive or perseverative behavior response patterns, or both, to overstimulating and loosely structured group activities.

The research design specified that, although all the final selectees were to have common learning and behavioral response patterns, half of the total complement of 40 were to demonstrate conclusive medical and neurological evidence of injury to the central nervous system. The remaining half, while sharing the behavior and learning problems, were to have medical and neurological histories which ruled out gross evidence of central nervous system damage.

During the prediagnostic screening period, selection guides and clues indicating damage to the central nervous system were frequently located in school medical histories, health department records, the reports of family physicians, parent conference reports concerning their child's adjustment and learning problems, and specific notations of convulsive disorders, birth injury, accidents, or diseases. Indications of organicity reported by the psychologist or noted by psychotherapists were considered clinical evidence only if this information was associated with a compatible medical and neurological history. In the absence of such medical and neurological data, the child was tentatively classified as not brain-injured and referred as such to the diagnostic staff.

Parent Contact

Once the evaluation of the available data was completed, parent conferences were scheduled in order to explain the nature of the research project, the specific reasons why the child had been selected as a possible candidate for the program, and in order to receive parent permission for the child to participate if he were found later to be admissible.

In connection with these parent conferences, it is important to bear in mind that this particular project was designed in order to explore the learning problems of a particular group of children and to develop an appropriate instructional program. The particular individual behavior response patterns, therefore, were regarded simply as evidence of the child's learning difficulties in attempting to adjust to a classroom situation and instructional program which had not in the past provided him with the skills and techniques which might have made it possible for him to achieve academic mastery in the tool subjects. It was, for example, assumed that a hyperactive, aggressive, acting-out behavior pattern was a result of, or associated with, a child's learning difficulties and not necessarily a psychopathological symptom of deep-seated emotional problems amenable only to some form of psychotherapy. A teaching, not treatment, program was contemplated in the study.

This viewpoint was clearly stated during the parent conference, and the relation of the child's particular learning difficulties to project goals was outlined as clearly as available information permitted. Problems of transportation and scheduling dates for the diagnostic examinations were worked out, and reasons for requests for parent releases for purposes of collecting additional medical information from the family physicians were clearly explained. Discussion of school, neighborhood, and home problems which might develop as a result of project participation was thoroughly explored. As a result of the care taken at this point, only one parent, and she only on the advice of her pediatrician, withdrew her child's name from possible project participation.

It is the impression of the research staff that the parents co-operated just as fully as their understanding and acceptance of their child's problem in relation to the research project design permitted, and that this was a direct result of a clear-cut presentation which neither minimized nor evaded discussion of their child's school problems. Furthermore, although the project goals were related whenever possible to the instructional difficulties of the child, at no time was it stated or implied that there was any certainty that the child would gain from the specialized teaching method; rather that it was the staff's feeling that the placement would be well worth trying.

The Family Physician

Accompanying the medical release forms provided by the parents was a letter prepared by the staff pediatrician which explained the long-range instructional goals of the project to the family physician and indicated the nature of the diagnostic examinations scheduled for the patient. The letter included a request for any information which the physician felt might be helpful in the study. The family physician was subsequently provided with copies of the unrevised reports of the examining physicians in order that parents might turn to him for an explanation of the results of the diagnostic examinations.

Although direct participation and personal interest by the family physicians in providing medical data to the research staff varied a great deal, only one physician failed to provide the diagnostic staff with information which might have been helpful in evaluating the child.

Scheduling of Referrals to the Diagnostic Staff

After careful study of all the available medical and educational data, conferences with the parents, and clearance from the family physicians, 46 of the 67 possible candidates were selected as constituting the group for intensive diagnostic study. The remaining children were held in reserve until the diagnostic studies were completed on the 46 selectees, when it would be apparent that the screening had been careful enough so that it was possible to provide the project with the 40 children necessary for the classes from the first 46 referrals.

A face sheet and flow chart of the diagnostic examinations were devised which provided a summary of the past medical and clinical history (when available), and a brief statement reporting the results of previous psychological tests. In those cases where the child was known to the School Health Service of the Department of Health, this chart was clipped to the chart for the examining physicians who reviewed the material prior to their own examinations.

Insofar as possible, the examinations were scheduled in the following order: psychological testing, pediatric examination, neurological examination, speech and hearing testing, electroencephalogram, and psychiatric evaluation. Each specialist dictated the results of his examination the same day, or as soon thereafter as possible, and the transcription was made immediately. Thus, it was possible for each staff member, with the exception of the psychologist, to have the report of the previous physicians available at the time of the examination.

Staff Conference

Once the examinations were completed, the children were evaluated by the combined diagnostic and administrative staff as to their suitability in terms of the project design and degree of organic involvement. A preliminary evaluation was made of the possible usefulness of the proposed specialized methodology in terms of specific learning problems and behavior disorders.

Forty of the 46 children were selected: 37 boys and 3 girls. Two of the 46 children moved from Montgomery County, and an additional 4 children were excluded for the following reasons. One child demonstrated no evidence of the existence of the type of learning problems which were characteristic of the other children, and, although he was severely disturbed, it was the consensus that his adjustment was primarily schizophrenic rather than the hyperactive, aggressive, acting-out pattern of the other children. One child, whose reported IQ was in error, was found by the research psychologist to be so retarded that the placement in an academic group would have been unrealistic. One child, whose previous school records and related data gave every indication of meeting the prediagnostic selection criteria, had made so much progress in his special class placement the preceding year that he no longer needed the special class placement and was transferred to a regular class. One child, who met all the selection criteria and qualified in every other way, was rejected by the staff because not only would he have been the youngest child in the entire group, but he had had no previous public school experience. His placement at that time was in a residential treatment center, and it was the consensus of the staff that the combination of these reality factors argued against transfer to a full-time academic program in the public schools.

INDIVIDUAL DIAGNOSTIC EXAMINATIONS

This section of this chapter consists of the individual examination reports of the pediatrician, neurologist, audiologist, psychiatrist, and psychologist. The reports here and in the Appendix have been arranged by discipline, since it was felt that this method of presenting the medical and clinical data provided an over-all view of the diagnostic patterning of the total group from the standpoint of each discipline. In each case, the reports are preceded by an outline of the examination procedure and conclude with a general statement as to what was considered to be the most important aspects or implications of the study from the standpoint of each particular discipline.

This presentation of diagnostic and clinical data was agreed upon by the research staff after many other methods had been considered and rejected as unsatisfactory. What finally became apparent was that in attempting to revise the raw data in line with the traditional methods of reporting case history material, a number of the most important aspects of the research project were being left out.

These aspects included the following:

1. the research staff's own conflicting opinions and disagreements concerning the interpretation of the results of the diagnostic examinations;

2. the learning experience they shared in working through these conflicts in order to maintain the integrity of the research design;

3. the gradual revision of some of the examination procedures and methods of recording medical and clinical impressions as a result of the staff's growing awareness and agreement of the clinical uncertainties in establishing brain injury as a definitive diagnostic classification.

The decision to make the raw data available is indeed a tribute to the individual integrity, maturity, and professional objectivity of the members of the diagnostic staff. This is in contrast to the more popular practice of eliminating contradictory material and differences of opinion in favor of publishing smoothly edited case histories, thus creating an illusion of perfect accord and harmony.

It can be predicted with considerable accuracy that from whatever personal bias or professional viewpoint this material is studied and evaluated, substantiating evidence supporting that bias or viewpoint becomes available as a result of selected aspects of the raw data itself. This opportunity is deliberately offered the reader, in preference to reporting the research staff's own personal opinions and interpretations of what they thought was significant to the project problem and their own personal discipline.

As has been previously indicated, there has been no attempt to make it appear as though there was complete, or even general, agreement among the physicians as to the specific diagnostic classification considered appropriate to each of the individual children. What will become clear after even the most cursory reading of the reports from any one discipline is the similarity in the developmental patterns of these children. Whether they demonstrated clear-cut evidence of organic damage to the central nervous system, or symptoms of what has been frequently referred to as "minimal" brain injury, or behavior and learning problems similar to those of the brain-injured child but with no evidence of minimal or any other kind of central nervous system damage, their developmental histories were startlingly similar.

It appears particularly appropriate at this point to refer to the work of Masland, Sarason and Gladwin who, in reporting on other significant studies in this general problem area, make the following statement concerning the need for detailed case histories on children who demonstrate this particular kind of problem in differential diagnosis.

. . . The work of Strauss is perhaps the best example we have of the fruitfulness of an approach which is based on the integration of concepts in developmental neurology, diagnostic criteria of brain injury, and detailed program planning. . . . Unfortunately, we do not have the kind of detailed case reports which would allow one to gauge the frequency of this type of case. If we had such comprehensive case descriptions one could also get a better idea of the role of the 'therapeutic milieu' in producing behavioral changes regardless of the presence or absence of brain injury. For example, we obviously have been impressed with the educational techniques and over-all therapeutic approach designed by Strauss and Lehtinen. But one cannot avoid raising the following question: To what extent would children with no brain injury but with severely disabling learning difficulties and/or behavior problems benefit from the kinds of programs adapted to the presumably peculiar needs of brain injured children? (1, pp. 366–367.)

It is the belief of the research staff that this pilot study and demonstration provide at least a partial answer to this question, that it is a favorable one, and that the following detailed case report may help in the task of working toward the solution to some of the questions raised by Masland, Sarason, and Gladwin.

In the opening paragraph of this chapter it was stated that there would herein be recorded the unrevised individual diagnostic and clinical reports of the diagnosticians. Since these are oftentimes exceedingly lengthy and since the inclusion of all of them at this point would interrupt the reader, only one case study will be presented. Ten additional studies will be found in the Appendix. Information on the children continued to accrue over the months, and there thus appears in the data which follow some information which was not available at the staff conference when the child's admission was considered. The initial data can be ascertained, however, from the dates which are indicated after each psychological test. The data are presented below in the general order in which the child received the diagnostic examinations: psychology, pediatrics, neurology, speech and hearing, and psychiatric.[1]

THE POPULATION: A CASE STUDY, CHILD NO. C-1-6

Psychological Evaluation

  Stanford-Binet, Form L (Pre-test) (4–2–57).

  CA: 8–3; MA: 6–3; IQ: 76.

  The IQ is at the lower limits of the Slow Learning range. The Mental Age is 6–3 years, with a range of performance from a Basal Age of IV to a Ceiling of IX. These results are quite similar to those obtained a year previously by another psychologist when a Mental Age of 5–2 years was obtained, IQ 70.

---

[1] The Appendix does not contain the total balance of 39 case studies. Several parents withheld written permission to include the case data on their children. In deference to parent attitudes, the authors have not included these data. The additional material would not, however, change the characteristics of the group in any significant manner from that presented in the monograph. The case studies of one entire group have been included to provide the reader a complete understanding of the nature of the children in the total study.

In the present examination all items were passed at the Year IV. C-1-6 was unable to repeat four digits which is expected at Year IV-6. At Year V he was unable to fold a triangle after being shown how by the Examiner or to repeat simple sentences. At Year VI he was unable to copy a bead chain from memory, differentiate essential aspects of a situation from nonessential, and showed poorly developed number concepts. When asked to give the Examiner 3 blocks he did so, but could not do the same for 5 or 9 blocks. He could count by rote, but was unable to count concrete things correctly. He started to play with the blocks, making a tower, and it was somewhat difficult to get him away from this. At Year VII he was unable to see the absurdity in pictured situations, see similarities, repeat five digits, or copy a diamond. When asked to draw a diamond, he produced something resembling a rectangle, called it a boat, and proceeded to elaborate this concept. At the Year VIII level he passed only one item, which involved comprehension of a concrete situation. All items were failed at the Year IX.

Stanford Binet, Form M (Post-test) (5–22–58).

CA: 9–5; MA: 7–0; IQ: 74.

Intelligence is at the borderline between the Slow Learning and Retarded range. The range of performance is from a Basal Age at Year VI to a Ceiling at Year IX.

At the Year VII two items were passed. He was able to give the number of fingers, and could see the absurdity in pictorially presented materials. He could not reverse three digits, however, and memory for sentences was extremely poor. He could not count the number of times a block was tapped.

Four items were passed at the Year VIII level. Comprehension of verbally described situations and problems was good, and he could see the similarity between two things. He could name the days of the week in order, and give the day that preceded certain specified days. He could not resolve verbal absurdities, and opposite analogies were too difficult.

All items were failed at the Year IX.

Ammons Full-Range Picture Vocabulary Test (12-2-57).

CA: 9–0; MA: 8–0.

The mental age obtained on this test was 1.5 years above that obtained on the Stanford-Binet. The following words, which the average child of 9-0 is expected to pass, were failed: customer, sale, meal, broadcast, safe, protection, and cleanliness.

Goodenough Intelligence Test.

Pre-test (11–25–57), CA: 8–11; MA: 6–3.

Post-test (5–21–58), CA: 9–5; MA: 6–9.

Both drawings were crudely drawn, with odd, peanut-shaped bodies, stick legs, and elongated necks. Both drawings were concerned with a figure doing some activity. The first was, "A man sawing some two-by-fours." The second was, "A man writing." In the second figure the arms were in two dimensions, and fingers were drawn. The facial detail was more complete. Although the over-all impression is better, the actual scorable details result in only a six-month difference in mental ages between the two tests.

Block Design and Coding from WISC (4–2–57).

Block Design: raw score, 1; scaled score, 3; test age equivalent, 4–10.

Coding: raw score, 4; scaled score, 2; test age equivalent, 4–10.

On the Block Design Test, Design A was passed on the second attempt. From that point on the colors seemed to be confusing. Inappropriate colors were used, and he could not construct the figures.

On the Coding Test, Form B, 21 symbols were attempted, but 17 were errors.

Both of the above tests were well below the level one would expect on the basis of the over-all mental age of this child.

Bender-Gestalt Test. The pre-test drawings (4–2–57) were very poorly conceived and executed. There were 23 errors in all, with 4 drawings categorized as immature, 5 dissociations, 1 closure, 4 incorrect elements, 1 unrecognizable, 3 distorted angles, 4 rotations, and 1 compression. There was little change in the post-test (5–21–58) where 23 errors were made. One was categorized as concrete, 3 perseverations, 4 dissociations, 1 closure, 5 incorrect elements, 3 distorted angles, 1 rotation, 3 enlargements, and 1 disproportion.

Syracuse Visual Figure-Background Test. In the pre-test (11–19–57) there were 9 correct responses to the figure, no background responses, and 1 perseveration. In the post-test (5–21–58) performance was much poorer, with 6 correct responses to the figure, 3 background responses, and 2 perseverations.

Tactual-Motor Test (11–19–57). This child was unable to draw a single figure. The addition of a thumbtack background seemed to make little difference. He seemed quite certain that he knew what was behind the screen, but each drawing was incorrect. When feeling the diamond his face suddenly lighted up, and he said: "I *know* what that is! It's a box."

Marble Board Test (10–3–57). On the Marble Board 1, the child looked at the board, then said: "I've got the shape of it. You put one in the middle, and one in the middle, and. . . ." He then proceeded to completely fill in every square with a marble. His drawing was constructed in the same manner, showing rows of filled-in spaces. When presented with Marble Board 2, he said: "What is it? It's a Z!" He then proceeded to make a backwards Z. His drawing, however, was of three sides of a square.

Vineland Social Maturity Scale.

Pre-test (*11–19–57*): total score, 74; age equivalent, 9–0; social quotient, 101.

Post-test (*5–11–58*): total score, 75; age equivalent, 9–4; social quotient, 103.

There are few changes between the pre- and post-test interviews. C-1-6 can now make telephone calls, does small remunerative work, and does routine household tasks, things that he could not do at the beginning of the year. In general, however, his rate of social development has remained quite constant.

Summary. Intelligence is at the borderline between the slow-learning and retarded range. The rate of intellectual development is quite consistent over the course of the last three years, as may be seen in the similar test results obtained at yearly intervals. The main intellectual weaknesses on the Stanford-Binet are to be found in those areas requiring sustained attention, ability to reproduce designs, abstract abilities (seeing similarities and differences), and ability to differentiate essential from nonessential elements. Relative strengths are to be found in areas requiring comprehension of concrete situations and vocabulary. On tests requiring visual-perceptual ability, such as the two subtests from the WISC, the Bender-Gestalt, and Syracuse Visual Figure-Background Test, performance was quite poor. Both subtests from the WISC were at a level considerably below the mental age on the Stanford-Binet. No improvement was noted on the Bender-Gestalt reproductions, and the performance was actually poorer in the post-test period on the Syracuse Visual Figure-Background Test, where there were more perseverative responses, fewer correct responses to the figures, and more background responses. The rate of social development, as shown on the Vineland Scale of Social Maturity, was approximately the same, with relatively few changes occurring over the course of the year.

Pediatric History

Problem. The history was obtained from both parents who were seen together. The problem was stated to consist of three parts:

1. Physically, he seems more awkward than other boys of his own age. He is somewhat lacking in co-ordination.

2. One leg is shorter than the other and this discovery apparently was made last year when he was examined after having complained of foot pain. Measurements were taken at this time and the difference was noted. In addition, one arm is and has always been large in circumference and there is mottling of the skin on the arm, leg, and buttocks. Reference was made to his awkwardness by stating that he skips on only one foot at a time and goes down a flight of steps only one step at a time, lacking the automatic movements which would be required for such an act.

3. Brain damage: the diagnosis of brain damage apparently came about as a result of a neurological examination.

It should be stated here that the parents have been to innumerable physicians and clinics, inasmuch as the father is in the service and has been referred, depending on his assignment, to various specialized clinics. As a result, they have reports which they carry with them and have a pretty good working knowledge of the type of problems which their son presents. The mother, who is pregnant, was more outgoing and seemed to be less serious than was her husband. He seemed to be very stable and serious and tried to pinpoint all of his answers as best he could.

It was stated that the mottling of the skin was first noted at about 3.5 years of age. Physicians were consulted for this and the difference in the arm circumference was discovered then. At this time he was not yet talking, but the parents were not concerned about it. In 1953, while in nursery school (when he was 4 years of age) he still did not talk. Speech had not been stimulated, as had been anticipated, by enrolling him in nursery school. In 1954, EEG's (electroencephalograms) were done and were said to have been normal. Speech therapy was begun and the term "aphasia" was used for the first time. The speech therapy apparently had some initial success. In 1955, when the family came to this area, C-1-6 began to see a speech therapist and has continued to work with her under the supervision of an audiologist. The boy was given a neurological examination in the spring of 1956 at which time the term "brain damage" was used for the first time in explaining the etiology of his condition.

Present status. His schooling in general is said to be coming along nicely although slowly. He is talking more satisfactorily now. He is beginning to read and beginning to do arithmetic. He apparently is being worked with a great deal at home and his writing is definitely improving. He has never had any difficulty making his wants known.

Marriage. They have been married for fourteen years. It has been a compatible, fairly happy, normal married life. It is a second marriage for the mother. The responsibility for the home and the raising of the children is a mutually shared responsibility. They are both of the same religion.

Siblings. A sister, 12½ years of age. She is aware of her brother's situation and tries to treat him as normally as possible. A brother, age 2. C-1-6 is said to be very fond of the sister and is said to be very affectionate by nature. Because of the younger brother's age and the frequency with which he gets into C-1-6's things and into his hair, in general, they are usually separated; but once in a while when such interference does occur, C-1-6 will explode.

Maternal history during pregnancy and delivery. The mother is pregnant now for the fourth time. She was 31 years of age when she delivered C-1-6. She received prenatal care after the third month of her pregnancy. He was a desired baby. He was born fourteen days overdue according to her calculation. Apparently the pregnancy was not remarkable. There were no unusual emotional or physical strains, no medications and no X-rays. There was a very short labor period and it is extremely interesting to note that apparently the baby was *held back*. He is said to have had a large head. He weighed 7 pounds, 8 ounces. He was seen during the first twenty-four hours. He was breast fed for only the first few days until a viral infection of the mother seemed to make it advisable to stop nursing him. He thrived on a formula, sucked well; there were no GI symptoms in early infancy. He slept well and quite a bit of the time. There was no history of head-banging or rocking or thumb-sucking. Solids were started at 3 or 4 weeks of age. He was said to be a hungry baby and thrived.

Past medical history. DPT and smallpox vaccinations received during first year of life, and subsequently the three Salk immunizations. Mumps at 3 years of age, chickenpox at 4 years of age, measles at the age of 6. Except for occasional colds and other febrile illnesses, the remainder of the medical history is not remarkable.

Developmental history. He started counting last year. He is said to be right-handed. He was toilet-trained quite late and progress was slow. He did not achieve bladder control until 4 or 4½ years of age and bowel control at approximately 5 years of age. His attention span is very short and he is beginning to make positive progress in school. He prefers boys of his own age or younger. There is no difficulty sleeping, he can sit through TV, he goes to regular Sunday School. He loves to swim and is fearless of water. He plays baseball, and rides a two-wheeler bicycle alone. He likes to play cowboy and use guns. He has his own record player; likes to be read to and to read. He likes to play games with other people. The mother works with him at home under supervision in order to improve his speech. He used a spoon and a fork well and at the moment is learning how to use a knife. He can dress himself, but does have difficulty with his shoelaces. When punished he blows up quickly and violently, but only for a short time. He is discouraged from fighting, or at least was discouraged from fighting and now, apparently, does not know how to fight back. When questioned about how he handles hostility, the mother said he is more likely to be "the St. Bernard type." He is said to be a lot less uninhibited in making new friends. He does not handle frustration well. When thwarted he will explode and cry out.

Past medical history notation. A neurological examination in 1956 revealed a high probability of a vascular anomaly of the left cerebral hemisphere. It was felt to be of the large vessel type rather than capillary in nature. The localization was considered to be probably in the superior temporal parietal region.

The child walks with a minimal right hemiparetic gait. He is clumsy bilaterally. There are no cerebellar signs. Tonus is slightly increased on the right side.

Physical Examination

Blood pressure 105/70.

General appearance. C-1-6 has puffy eyes, and is a big boy for his age. He is chubby, friendly, and sympathetic looking. In the examining room he kept saying "What's this? What's this?" for everything he picked up. He speaks deliberately and will say words that he has been taught, even though they do not apparently make much sense. When asked about three wishes he replied that it was a secret and he couldn't tell. When the four o'clock siren was heard it disturbed him markedly. He said that it was his little brother (who was with his mother in the waiting room) who was frightened by the siren. Although he undressed without too much difficulty, later, in getting dressed, he was unable to tie his shoelaces. He kept asking the examiner to tie them and to do other things as well. It may be that the subject expects not to be able to do them by himself. His posture and gait were grossly normal.

Skin and mucous membranes. C-1-6 has vascular anomalies of the left hand and arm and the right thigh and right leg. The left arm is bigger than the right and the right leg and foot are smaller than the left. *Lymph nodes.* Not remarkable. *Head.* Position and shape not remarkable. *Face.* There were no facial tics apparent. *Ears.* The external ear was normal. There were no discharges or mastoid tenderness. Hearing was grossly normal and otoscopic examination was negative. *Eyes.* Extra-ocular movements were normal. There was no ptosis of the lids or strabismus. Pupils were round and regular and reacted to light. Vision was grossly normal. Fundi were negative. *Nose and sinuses.* Not remarkable. *Mouth and throat.* Not remarkable. The teeth were in good condition, numbering 12 on top and 12 on bottom. The tonsils were still present. The palate was of normal contour. The pharynx was negative. *Neck.* There was no nucha rigidity or any masses palpable. The thyroid was not enlarged. The trachea was in the mid-line. There was no evidence of venous engorgement. *Chest.* The shape of the chest was somewhat concave, symmetrical with normal respirations. The lungs were clear to palpation, percussion and auscultation. The heart was clinically not enlarged. The point of maximum impulse was in the sixth interspace in the mid-clavicular line on the left. No murmurs were audible. Femoral and radial pulses were normal. *Abdomen.* Abdomen was somewhat protuberant. There were no masses palpable. The liver, spleen and kidneys were not enlarged. *Gentalia.* Normal male external genitalia. *Extremities.* Right extremity measured 32 inches and the left extremity 31 inches in length.

Neurological Examination

   Cranial nerves. First cranial nerve: not tested. Second cranial nerve: the fundi are normal. There are no abnormalities of the vessels present. The discs are well outlined. The fovea are normal. Third, fourth, and sixth cranial nerves: the extraocular movements are intact. No nystagmus is present. Fifth cranial nerve: the boy was able to chew without difficulty. There is no sign of sensory loss on either side. Seventh cranial nerve: muscles of facial expression are all normal. Eighth cranial nerve: air conduction is greater than bone conduction. The tuning fork is heard without difficulty. There is no lateralization. Ninth and tenth cranial nerves: the uvula was in the mid-line. The vocal cords were not seen. The boy was able to swallow without difficulty. Eleventh cranial nerve: the boy is able to shrug his shoulders without difficulty. Twelfth cranial nerve: the tongue protrudes in the mid-line. There is no sign of atrophy or fasciculations.

   Sensory. Pinprick, vibratory, position, touch, stereognosis were all well performed. He has good two-point discrimination and pinprick localization. He is able to identify his body parts without any great difficulty, although he seemed to hesitate a little when it came to which was his right and which was his left. However, once he had that established in his mind he went right ahead and identified one side against the other without difficulty. This boy does not have any signs of apraxia. He understood the majority of the commands that were issued to him and carried them out with alacrity. When asked to identify parts of the examiner's clothing, he was able to identify all of them and usually gave a correct response. When it came to identifying things with stereognosis, he misnamed thimble. When corrected he went back and gave the correct name for it. He appears to be able to do things very well insofar as the parietal lobe is concerned. *Reflexes.* Reflexes were brisk throughout. No pathological reflexes were present. *Motor.* The boy seems to have moderately good strength. *Cerebellar.* The boy was able to do finger-to-nose and heel-to-shin tests without any difficulty. Diadochokinesis was well performed. He could walk without staggering. *Station and gait.* Romberg was negative. He could walk on his heels and on his toes without any difficulty. *Movements.* No extrapyramidal movements were noted. He had no choreiform movements at any time.

Electroencephalogram

Attitude and condition of patient: alert, co-operative. Fundamental frequency: Slow waves: around 4.5 to 5 per second dominate the record, at times more in the bi-occipital derivations. Fast waves: except of muscle origin, are not prominent. Amplitude characteristics: high voltage (150 microvolts); regular modulation. Hyperventilation: generates generalized 2 to 3.5 per second waves; persists long after the cessation of deep breathing. Impression: generalized abnormal EEG.

Speech and Hearing Evaluation

Language and speech development. C-1-6 had been diagnosed as a child with expressive aphasia. Parents had never questioned the child's ability to hear or to understand the language. In retrospect they feel that he never vocalized freely as an infant and did not experiment with vocal play. He developed an elaborate gesture language. At age 5 he had no speech. He was taken to the speech clinic where the therapist began training with picture cards. The child had the ability to mimic the word, but there was no spontaneous recall or carry-over. He associated the syllables with the cards rather than the idea of verbal communication. As a result of training he began to add a great many words and also began phrasing, but language sequence was his greatest problem.

General behavior observations. The child came willingly to the test situation. He was friendly, co-operative, and displayed a great deal of social maturity.

Oral examination. Oral examination is unimpressive. There is good length and lift to the velum and also good control of the articulators.

Articulation. C-1-6 has some articulation errors but they are minimal. The most persistent and consistent errors are an *f* substitution for *th,* and *sh* substitution for *ch, br* for *dr,* and *pr* for *cr* and *tr. L* blends are also unstable. There is some vowel prolongation.

Voice. Voice is of good quality. There are many changes in rate and pitch. There tends to be a sing-song quality and a different rate pattern. There are times when his utterance is almost compulsive. This occurs when he gets excited, at which time his speech tends to get labored and articulation is slurred. It is as if he does not have control of the rate of speech.

Propositional speech. C-1-6 has shown much progress in his ability to express himself freely. He now talks in complete sentences, using complex sentences as well as extensive vocabulary. He is now using words such as *pause* and *recognize*. His speech is characterized by the marked changes in rate and pitch which are described above. There is a great deal of perseveration which takes the form of repeating the same sentence or phrase several times. For example, when asked to do something, he commented, "Never can do that, never can do that, never can do that, never can." This happens many times during a conversation. There were occasional lapses into incorrect grammatical usage, such as the wrong pronoun or the wrong verb tense. He can repeat long sentences accurately. His auditory memory is improving steadily. He reads with reluctance and is somewhat defensive about his reading.

Hearing. A pure-tone audiogram was done. C-1-6's hearing is well within normal range. However, it may be significant that he had some difficulty in localizing which earphone he was hearing from. He was able to repeat spondee words and a standard list of PBK words with ease and accuracy.

Psychiatric Examination

C-1-6 made a real effort for the entire hour to be understood, but at times he lapsed into unintelligible syllables. He had a short attention span, but it was sufficiently long to tell a ten-minute story about cowboys and Indians. In telling this story and in playing with the puppets, the child destroyed the Indians and a witch, roles that were taken by the examiner. His puppet play consisted of expressing interest in puppets; he was himself and the examiner was the witch. The witch was hanged.

The subject was interested in BoBo the Clown. However, his punches were very mild, as though he were too afraid to hit out. His co-ordination was fair for this activity.

He spent most of the hour shooting several guns. For this activity his stance was very realistic and he threw himself into the shooting. He appeared confused when asked his three wishes. When pressed he changed the subject. No answer was received. He said he liked to draw, and quickly drew a boy hitting BoBo the Clown with obvious pleasure and relish. When asked to sign his name, he said, "I can't," but followed the remark with a creditable signature.

Psychiatric re-evaluation. C-1-6 was his usual friendly self who put on a serious face "to act like a grownup and behave myself." In the playroom, he turned at once to the guns and could have continued with this activity for the full hour. When asked if all the shooting meant that he was unhappy he replied, "They are too busy." After several pauses and changes of the subject, he replied that he went to Sunday School with his father.

Conversation with mother: the mother feels that the child's progress can be summed up by the phrase "more confidence." She went on to say that he was no longer afraid of dogs. Previously, he had a great fear of them. His mother felt that the increase in his ability to communicate had much to do with this change in his attitude.

Although the child still asks questions he knows the answers to, the parents feel that C-1-6 has made many strides toward independent behavior in other directions. The mother was at a loss to remember any incident which would lead him to be more than ordinarily irritated at one or more members of the family.

The mother was relaxed, concerned, intelligent, and impressed with the child's progress.

PRENATAL, NATAL, AND POSTNATAL DATA

Part of the diagnostic evaluation included an effort to try to discover what developmental factors might have been involved in producing the clinical picture in each child included in this study. Thus, an attempt was made to study the prenatal, natal, and postnatal data that were available. A study was undertaken [2] to examine the available clinical data by verbatim copying of data from hospital obstetrical charts and new-born charts of each of the mothers and the child in the study. Those data which are missing from Tables 1 through 6 indicate either that home deliveries occurred, or else that no record at all was available to the research personnel. As the reader can see from Tables 1 through 6 inclusive, there are more blank spaces than reported data. Many times even the same hospital was inconsistent in the manner in which the information was recorded. Obviously this kind of retrospective study has many defects. What is needed is a prospective kind of recording of information which could later be carefully studied and correlated. In this way, possible factors which are influential in the production of congenital abnormalities could be isolated and viewed in terms of their relative importance. In the absence in the present study of such a forward-looking plan on the part of hospital administrators and physicians, the data insofar as they may have value in pointing up a problem are presented here for consideration.

The data included in Table 1 are all essentially negative. This table indicates the respective ages of father and mother at the time of the birth of the subject and presents data regarding previous pregnancy history of the mother. Data were available for 28 of the 40 children. The average

[2] Following clearance from parents and family physicians, these entire data were collected by Milton Glatt, M.D., pediatrician on the study staff during its duration. All data were copied from hospital records personally by Dr. Glatt. They are his notations which appear in Tables 1 through 6, inclusive, in this chapter.

TABLE 1

Prenatal Data Regarding the Mothers and Fathers of the Experimental and Control Subjects (N = 28)

Subject	Age (in years)		Total Number of Previous Pregnancies	Number of Previous Abortions (and time)	Number of Previous Stillbirths	Number of Premature Births	Number of Neonatal Deaths
	Mother	Father					
C-2-2	29	33	2	2 (Before the 5th month.)	0̄	0̄	0̄
E-1-1	33	36	1	0̄	0̄	0̄	0̄
E-1-8	31		0̄ Had difficulty in becoming pregnant. Appendix and ovarian cyst removed.	0̄	0̄	0̄	0̄
E-1-4	28	28	0̄	0̄	0̄	0̄	0̄
C-1-6	31	29	b				
C-2-3	30	30	0̄	0̄	0̄	0̄	0̄
E-2-10	25	28	0̄	0̄	0̄	0̄	0̄
E-1-3	31	34	2				
C-1-9	29	31	2	0̄	0̄	0̄	0̄
E-2-6	32	29	1	0̄	0̄	0̄	0̄

TABLE 1, *continued*

Subject	Age (in years) Mother	Age (in years) Father	Total Number of Previous Pregnancies	Number of Previous Abortions (and time)	Number of Previous Stillbirths	Number of Premature Births	Number of Neonatal Deaths
C-2-1	27	34	0	0	0	0	0
C-2-4	25	28	3	0	0	0	0
C-1-2	26	30			0		0
E-2-7	22	25	1	0	0	0	0
E-2-2	29	33	1	0	0	0	0
C-2-6	18	25	0	2 abortions at 6 weeks of gestation. Between 1st and 2nd, then 2nd and 3rd child.	0	0	0
E-2-1	20	20	0	0	0	0	0
C-2-8	27	31	1	0	0	0	0
E-2-8	32	32	2	0	0	0	0
C-1-4	25	30	1	0	0	0	0
C-1-5	26		2	0	0	0	0
C-1-7	37	42	0	0	0	0	0

TABLE 1, *continued*

Subject	Age (in years) Mother	Age (in years) Father	Total Number of Previous Pregnancies	Number of Previous Abortions (and time)	Number of Previous Stillbirths	Number of Premature Births	Number of Neonatal Deaths
C-1-1	32	33	0̄	0̄	0̄	0̄	0̄
E-2-3	26	26	1	0̄	0̄	0̄	0̄
E-1-5	23	29	0̄	0̄	0̄	0̄	0̄
E-1-9	25	27	2	0̄	0̄	1	0̄
E-1-6	26	32	2	1 First trimester	0̄	0̄	0̄
E-1-2	34	36	3	0̄	1 Impacted shoulders.	1	0̄
Total			27	5 (for 3 mothers)	1 (for 1 mother)	2 (for 2 mothers)	
Range	18–37	20–42	0–3				
Unknown	6	2	2				
Average	27.8	30.4	–1				

a 0̄ = Recorded as negative.
b Blank spaces indicate no hospital record notation.

76

age of the mother was 27.8 years (N = 28); of the fathers, 30.4 years (N = 26). For the group on whom data were available, there are recorded 27 previous pregnancies involving 15 mothers. The range is from 1 to 3 previous pregnancies. Five previous abortions are noted in the case of 3 mothers, 1 previous stillbirth in 1 mother. Two premature births are reported for 2 mothers. No neonatal deaths are reported in the mothers of this group. In themselves, none of these figures is noteworthy; and in combination a relatively normal picture is presented. The data regarding stillbirth, premature deliveries, and previous abortion are considerably more favorable for this group of mothers than for those reported by Hopkins, Bice, and Coulton (2) in their survey of birth records of New Jersey mothers of cerebral palsy children.

Table 2 presents gestation information of the mothers in the experimental and control groups (N = 28). Data obtained are essentially negative. The average length of gestation in weeks reported for 27 mothers was 39.3. Complications during the gestation period were reported for 19 mothers. Ten of the reports were negative. Complications which arose during pregnancy and reported were as follows: 1, threatened abortion; 3, spottings; 3, edemas; 1, pre-eclampsia one week prior to delivery; 2, "falls"; 1, depression; 1, mild anemia; 1, hyperosis; 1, twins; 1, leucorrhea; 1, scarlet fever.

Two mothers had X-rays during the gestation period and 1 mother received medication (1 additional mother, medication questionable).

The data included in Table 3 indicate labor and delivery information of the mothers in the experimental and control group (N — 28).

The average length of delivery was 12.8 hours (M = 23). Complications arising from labor are negative in all but 4 mothers. One mother had a ruptured membrane; 1 had a rupture of the membrane-transverse; 1 had a pelvic arrest; 1 fetus had a weak heartbeat. Of the 28 mothers, 20 had drugs administered to them during labor.

Twenty-four mothers had spontaneous labor, and 1 mother had labor induced.

Fourteen mothers had their BOW[3] ruptured spontaneously; 9 had their BOW artificially broken; 1 mother had a premature rupture.

The paranatal and the blood data contained in Table 4 are also negative when taken as a group.

Seven mothers were delivered by spontaneous control; 6 had outlet forceps used; 7 had low forceps used; 4 had a Caesarean section; 1, a Kieland rotation; 1, a Scanzoni rotation; 1, a single footling extraction; 1 delivery was reported as "normal." The percentage regarding Cae-

[3] Bag of water.

TABLE 2
*Gestation Data Regarding Mothers of Children in the Experimental
and Control Groups (N = 28)*

Subject	Length of Gestation (in weeks)		Complications of Gestation	X-rays during Gestation	Medication during Gestation
C-2-2	LMP ᵃ	7/17/48	Threatened abortion (spotted until 10/26).	ō	Stilbestrol
	EDC ᵇ	4/24/49 (3/24/49) 33 weeks	20 lbs. weight gain		
E-1-1	LMP	7/28/49	ō	ō	ō
	EDC	5/4/50 (5/2/50) 40 weeks	18½ lbs. weight gain		
E-1-8	LMP	5/21/47	ō	ō	ō
	EDC	2/28/48 (1/6/48) 32 weeks	19 lbs. weight gain		
E-1-4	LMP	9/2/49	ō	ō	ō
	EDC	6/9/50 (6/16/50) 41 weeks	20 lbs. weight gain		
C-1-6		(12/20/48)			
C-2-3	LMP	11/15/46	Ankle edema		
	EDC	8/22/47 (9/4/47) 42 weeks			
E-2-10	LMP	7/4/48	Nausea, vomiting. Edema, pre-eclampsia, one week prior to delivery.	ō	
	EDC	4/11/49 (3/30/49) 38 weeks			
E-1-3		39 weeks			
C-1-9	LMP	7/12/47	ō	ō	ō
	EDC	4/19/48 (4/26/48) 40 weeks			
E-2-6	LMP	1/18/49	ō	ō	ō
	EDC	10/25/49 40 weeks	20 lbs. weight gain		

Subject		Length of Gestation (in weeks)	Complications of Gestation	X-rays during Gestation	Medication during Gestation
C-2-1	LMP EDC	10/1/48 7/8/49 (6/25/49) 39 weeks	Ankle edema. 23 lbs. weight gain (Ovarian cyst removed in 1948)	ō	ō
C-2-4	LMP EDC	4/25/48 2/1/49 42 weeks (2/17/49)	Fell down steps in November '48, hip bruise, no spotting.	ō	ō
C-1-2	LMP EDC	12/15/47 9/22/48 (9/17/48) 39 weeks			
E-2-7	LMP EDC	10/24/49 8/1/50 (8/11/50) 41 weeks	ō	ō	ō
E-2-2	LMP EDC	8/19/48 5/26/49 (4/21/49) 35 weeks	ō Mother had rheumatic fever as child.	ō	ō
C-2-6	LMP EDC	9/7/49 6/14/50 (7/13/50) 44 weeks	Spotting in 2–3 months. Confined to bed for 2 weeks. No treatment, 7/14/50—fracture of right fibula following fall.	Yes, at term. Cephalo-pelvic dispro-portion.	ō
E-2-1	LMP EDC	5/27/48 3/4/49 (2/18/49) 38 weeks	Mild anemia 10.5 gm. hemoglobin	ō	ō
C-2-8		40 weeks	ō	ō	
E-2-8	LMP EDC	11/15/48 8/22/49 (8/13/49) 39 weeks	Nausea and weight gain "blues"	ō	ō
C-1-4	LMP	9/18/49			

Subject		Length of Gestation (in weeks)	Complications of Gestation	X-rays during Gestation	Medication during Gestation
	EDC	6/27/50 (7/12/50) 42 weeks			
C-1-5	LMP EDC	5/1/48 2/1/49 (2/13/49) 42 weeks	Hyperemesis		? for hyper-emesis
C-1-7	LMP EDC	4/24/49 5/1/50 40 weeks	? of endocrine treatment—not confirmed.		
C-1-1	LMP EDC	4/20/48 1/27/49 (2/8/49) 42 weeks	? of spotting not on chart from mother's history.	ō	ō
E-2-3	LMP EDC	10/20/49 7/20/50 (7/20/50) 40 weeks	ō	ō	ō
E-1-5	LMP EDC	6/25/48 4/2/49 (3/17/49) 38 weeks	Twins	Fifth month for diagnosis	ō
E-1-9	LMP EDC	1/28/48 11/4/48 (11/1/48) 40 weeks	ō		ō
E-1-6	LMP EDC	4/24/49 1/31/50 (1/3/50) 36 weeks	Leucorrhea (fun-gus infection)		ō
E-1-2	LMP EDC	2/13/48 11/20/48 (11/13/48) 39 weeks	Spotting first 2 months Scarlet fever in second month.	ō	ō
			Comments on 19 mothers	Two for 2 mothers	One plus, 1 in question

ᵃ Last menstrual period.
ᵇ Expected date of confinement.

TABLE 3

Labor and Delivery Data Regarding Mothers of Children in the Experimental and Control Groups (N = 28)

Subject	Length of Labor	Complications of Labor	Treatment During Labor (including analgesia)	Time Prior to Delivery	Labor S[a] or I[b]	BOW[c] Rupture S[a] or A[d]	Time Prior to Delivery
C-2-2	6 hrs. 10 min.	ō			S	S	20 hrs.
E-1-1	6 hrs. 44 min.	ō	Seconal (250 mgs.) Demerol (100 mgs.) Nembutal (I.V.) (250 mgs.)	2 hrs. 9 min. 30 min.	S	S	6 hrs. 44 min.
E-1-8	60 hrs.	ō	Seconal (250 mgs.) Demerol (100 mgs.)	1 hr. 43 min.	S	S	60 hrs.
E-1-4	12 hrs.	ō	Hykinone (4.8 mgs. I.M.) Seconal (100 mgs.) Demerol (100 mgs.) Nembutal (250 mgs. I.V.)	3 hrs. 5 min. 3 hrs. 10 min. 1 hr. 15 min.	S	S	20 min.
C-1-6	2 hrs. 35 min.	ō	Demerol Scopolamine		S		
C-2-3					S	S 4:15 P.M.	29 min.
E-2-10	2 hrs. 25 min.		Nembutal (250 mgs. I.V.)		S	S 10:15 P.M.	
E-1-3							

81

TABLE 3, *continued*

Subject	Length of Labor	Complications of Labor	Treatment During Labor (including analgesia)	Time Prior to Delivery	Labor S[a] or I[b]	BOW[c] Rupture S[a] or A[d]	Time Prior to Delivery
C-1-9	2 hrs. 30 min.	Premature rupture of membrane; transverse cephalo-pelvic disproportion, cervix long and closed.	Demerol (100 mgs.) Seconal (250 mgs.)		S	S	Premature.
E-2-6	4 hrs. 35 min.	ō	Seconal (300 mgs.) Demerol (100 mgs.) Seconal (250 mgs.)	2 hrs. 30 min. 2 hrs. 30 min. 1 hr.	S		
C-2-1	14 hrs. 5 min.		Morphine (10 mgs.) Seconal (300 mgs.) Demerol Seconal (100 mgs.) Demerol (50 mgs.) Demerol (50 mgs.) Nembutal (250 mgs.)	17 hrs. 55 min. 13 hrs. 5 min. 8 hrs. 30 min. 6 hrs. 10 min. 4 hrs. 30 min.	S	A	6 hrs. 15 min.
C-2-4	12 hrs. 55 min.	ō	Nembutal (100 mgs.) Demerol (100 mgs.) Demerol (100 mgs.) Luminal (250 mgs.)	7 hrs. 10 min. 2 hrs. 20 min. 1 hr. 40 min.	S	S	

TABLE 3, *continued*

Subject	Length of Labor	Complications of Labor	Treatment During Labor (including analgesia)	Treatment Time Prior to Delivery	Labor S[a] or I[b]	BOW[c] Rupture S[a] or A[d]	BOW[c] Rupture Time Prior to Delivery
C-1-2	8 hrs. 23 min.	ō			S	S	13 hrs. 23 min.
E-2-7	2 hrs. 30 min.	ō	Devaral (5.0 cc.) Pitocin (0.5 cc.)		I	A	2 hrs. 30 min.
E-2-2	5 hrs. 56 min.	ō			S	A	11 min.
C-2-6	—	—	—	—	—	A	At the time of delivery
E-2-1		ō	Nembutal (500 mgs.) Demerol (100 mgs.) Demerol (100 mgs.)	4 hrs. 48 min. 4 hrs. 48 min. 1 hr. 13 min.	S	A	48 min.
C-2-8	2 hrs. 47 min.	ō	ō		S	S	47 min.
E-2-8	5 hrs. 20 min.	ō	Morphine sulphate (8 mgs.)		S	A	
C-1-4	4 hrs. 34 min.	ō	Atropine paraldehyde		S	A	4 hrs. 34 min.
C-1-5	37 hrs. 54 min.		Morphine sulphate (15 mgs.) Seconal (200 mgs.) Seconal (200 mgs.)	1 hr. 29 min.	S	A	
C-1-7	17 hrs.	Premature rupture of membrane	Demerol (200 mgs.) Seconal (350 mgs.)			Premature rupture of membrane	

TABLE 3, *continued*

Subject	Length of Labor	Complications of Labor	Treatment During Labor (including analgesia)	Time Prior to Delivery	Labor S a or I b	BOW c Rupture S a or A d	BOW c Rupture Time Prior to Delivery
C-1-1	57 hrs. 30 min.	Pelvic arrest	Seconal (100 mgs.) Demerol (100 mgs.) Seconal (275 mgs.) I.V. .05 g/w e Morphine (15 mgs.) Hykinone (4.8 mgs.) Duracillin Morphine (15 mgs.) I.V. protein hydrolysate f	53 hrs. 33.5 hrs. 33.5 hrs. 21.25 hrs. 16 hrs. 16 hrs. 16 hrs. 7.5 hrs. 6.5 hrs.	S	A	4 hrs.
E-2-3	8 hrs.	ō	Demerol (100 mgs.) Nembutal (275 mgs.) Nembutal (275 mgs.)	3 hrs. 30 min.	S	S	26 min.
E-1-5	11 hrs. 25 min.	One fetal heart weak	Seconal (300 mgs.) Luminal (120 mgs.) Demerol (100 mgs.) Scopolamine		S	S	7 hrs.
E-1-9	1 hr. 30 min.	ō	I.V. Nembutal (200 mgs.)		S	S	15 min.
E-1-6	7 hrs. 50 min.	ō	ō		S	S	10 min.

TABLE 3, *continued*

Subject	Length of Labor	Complications of Labor	Treatment During Labor (including analgesia)	Time Prior to Delivery	Labor Sᵃ or Iᵇ	BOWᶜ Rupture Sᵃ or Aᵈ	Time Prior to Delivery
E-1-2	None	Caesarean section breech presentation, question. Cephalo-pelvic disproportion, large baby, previous history.	Nembutal (100 mgs.) Scopolamine		none	A	

ᵃ Spontaneous.
ᵇ Induced.
ᶜ Bag of waters (amniotic fluid).
ᵈ Artificial.
ᵉ I.V. intraveneous 5 per cent glucose in water.
ᶠ Enumeration of treatment completed in last box "neonatal complications."

TABLE 4

Paranatal and Blood Data Regarding Mothers of Children in the Experimental and Control Groups (N = 28)

Subject	First Stage	Second Stage	Presentation Position	Method of Delivery	Third Stage	Placenta and Abnormalities Thereof	Anesthesia Type	Duration	Blood Group and Rh Mother	Infant
C-2-2	4 P.M. 3/21 6 hrs.	10 P.M. 3/24 10 min.	LOA a	Outlet forceps	10:10 P.M.	Spontaneous complete	Gas			
E-1-1	2:30 A.M. 5/2 6 hrs. 20 min.	8:50 A.M. 24 min.	LOA	Outlet forceps	9:14 A.M.	Spontaneous complete	Gas			A (+)
E-1-8	11:45 A.M. 1/4 59 hrs. 35 min.	11:20 P.M. 1/6 22 min.	LOA	Outlet forceps	11:42 P.M.	Spontaneous complete	Gas			B (−)
E-1-4	11:20 P.M. 6/15 11 hrs. 50 min. 22 min.	11:10 A.M. 6/16	LOA	Outlet forceps	11:32 P.M.	Spontaneous complete	Gas			O (+)
C-1-6	4:30 A.M. 2 hrs.	6:30 A.M. 35 min.	ROA b	Spontaneous controlled	7:05 A.M.	Spontaneous and intact, 1 coil of cord about neck	Pudental block			(+)
C-2-3			ROT c	Kielland rotation	4:44 P.M.	Expressed intact	Gas, O₂ and ether			

Sub-ject	First Stage	Second Stage	Presen-tation Position	Method of Delivery	Third Stage	Placenta and Abnormalities Thereof	Anesthesia Type	Dura-tion	Blood Group and Rh Mother	In-fant
E-2-10	8:30 P.M. 3/30 1 hr. 50 min.	10:20 P.M. 30 min.	LOA	Low forceps	10:50 P.M.		Ethylene and O₂		(+)	
E-1-3				Repeat CS d (low cervical ovarian cyst dystocia)			Spinal and Pentothal			
C-1-9	9 A.M. 4/26 2 hrs. 25 min.	11:25 A.M.	Transverse (back up)	CS		Cord around baby's neck	Pentothal, ether, and O₂		(+)	(+)
E-2-6	4 A.M. 10/26 4 hrs. 32 min.	8:32 A.M. 3 min.	LOA	Spontaneous	8:35 A.M.	ō	Ethylene and O₂	34 min.	A (+)	
C-2-1	3 P.M. 6/25 14 hrs. 2 min.	5:02 A.M. 6/26 3 min.	LOP e Low mid-rotation	LOA Forceps	5:05 A.M.	Spontaneous and intact 2 loops about neck	Ether, ethylene, and O₂	1 hr.	B (+)	
C-2-4	12 M. 2/17 12 hrs. 55 min. 5 min.	12:55 P.M. 2/17	LOA	Spontaneous	1 P.M.	Intact	Ether and O₂	30 min.		

Subject	First Stage	Second Stage	Presentation Position	Method of Delivery	Third Stage	Placenta and Abnormalities Thereof	Anesthesia Type	Duration	Blood Group and Rh Mother	Infant
C-1-2	10 A.M. 9/17 8 hrs. 13 min.	6:23 P.M. 2 min.	LOA	Spontaneous	6:25 P.M.	Intact	Gas, ether, and O$_2$			
E-2-7			ROA	Spontaneous		Intact	Devanal 6.0 cc.			(+)
E-2-2	1 A.M. 4/21 5 hrs. 56 min.	6:56 A.M. 4 min.	OA	Spontaneous	7 A.M.	Intact	Ether and O$_2$			
C-2-6	—	—		CS cephalo-pelvic disproportion 1 month past due date		None	Gas-ether	45 min.		
E-2-1		18 min.	Vertex LOA	Outlet forceps	7 min.	None	Ethylene and O$_2$	30 min.		
C-2-8	5 A.M. 7/12 2 hrs. 47 min.	2 min.	Vertex LOA	Spontaneous delivery	5 min.	None	Ethylene and O$_2$			

TABLE 4, *continued*

Sub-ject	First Stage	Second Stage	Presen-tation Position	Method of Delivery	Third Stage	Placenta and Abnormalities Thereof	Anesthesia Type	Dura-tion	Blood Group and Rh Mother	Blood Group and Rh Infant
E-2-8	5 hrs. 20 min.		Vertex LOA		10 min.	None	Ethylene and O_2		A (+)	
C-1-4	11:30 A.M. 7/12	4 P.M. 7/12	Vertex ROA	Outlet forceps	3 min.	None	Ether and O_2			
C-1-5	10 A.M. 2/12	11:54 P.M. 2/13		Low forceps	12 P.M. 6 min.	None	Pentothal, ethylene, and O_2	25 min.	(+)	
C-1-7	15 hrs.	2 hrs.	Vertex ROA	Low forceps		None	Ethylene not well tolerated		O (+)	
C-1-1	6 A.M. 2/6 57 hrs.	3:30 P.M. 2/8 23 min.	LOP	Low mid-forceps with Scanzoni rotation		ō	Spinal	43 min.	A (+)	
E-2-3	8:50 P.M. 7/19 7 hrs. 45 min.	4:35 A.M. 7/20 11 min.	ROP f	Low outlet forceps	2 min.	ō	Gas		B (+)	
E-1-5	9:30 P.M. 3/16	8 A.M. 3/17	LOA (still birth) LSA g	Single footling extraction	5 min.	ō	Ethylene, ether, and O_2	30 min.		

TABLE 4, *continued*

Sub-ject	First Stage	Second Stage	Presentation Position	Method of Delivery	Third Stage	Placenta and Abnormalities Thereof	Anesthesia Type	Duration	Blood Group and Rh Mother	Infant
E-1-9	5 A.M. 11/1	6 A.M. 11/1	LOA	Outlet forceps	15 min.	ō	Ether and O₂	30 min.		(+)
E-1-6	12 A.M.	7:30 P.M.	LOP	Normal spontaneous delivery	3 min.	Multiple infarcts with hemorrhage into placental tissue	Caudal ethylene O₂			
E-1-2			RSPʰ	Low cervical CS		ō	Ether and O₂	1 hr.		

ᵃ LOA = occipital left anterior.
ᵇ ROA = occipital right anterior.
ᶜ ROT = occipital right temporal.
ᵈ CS = Caesarean section.

ᵉ LOP = occipital left posterior.
ᶠ ROP = occipital right posterior.
ᵍ LSA = sacrum left anterior.
ʰ RSP = sacrum right posterior.

90

sarian deliveries when compared to the group of mothers used in the Pasamanick, Rogers, and Lilienfield (3) study is considerably larger. Caution must be noted in that their study had a total N of 830 (white and nonwhites).

The condition of the placenta was reported in 26 mothers (N = 28). Two babies had the cord wrapped around their necks once; 1 had the cord wrapped around twice; and 1 placenta exhibited multiple infarcts with hemorrhage. The majority of mothers showed a spontaneous and intact placenta.

All mothers had gas or spinal blocks given to aid delivery.

Only one infant's blood group was reported and that was the same as the mother's.

The postnatal factors as related to the birth of the children (N = 28) are negative. Fifteen mothers were reported as having an episiotomy as part of the process of delivery; 3 mothers had a Caesarean section (one mother who was reported in Table 4 as having a Caesarean section, was not reported in this table as to the delivery procedure used); 1 mother was reported as having a first degree laceration as part of the operative procedure. Post-partum complications were negative except for moderate bleeding in 2 mothers; 1 mother was depressed; a 1 degree laceration reported for one mother (see Table 5).

Birth weight ranged from 3.2 pounds to 9.1 pounds. Four babies were under 5 pounds and may be considered premature. Infant length ranged from 16 inches to 23 inches.

Respiration data are generally negative. Respiration time was reported for 11 infants. The time ranged from immediately to five to six minutes. Four infants had respiration established after one minute.

Additional postnatal factors as reported in Table 6 show generally negative information. In the column Birth Injury, only one report was noted. This was a bruise caused by forceps on the right side of one infant's face. Only two anomalies were reported and both concerned the infant's testicles. One was quite small and one infant was reported as having a testicle that was undescended.

The Neonatal Complication column reveals the following: 6 infants were jaundiced; 1 had the possibility of a subdural hematoma; 1 had forcep injuries; 1 exhibited a bilateral talipes equina varus; 1 might have had an intracranial hemorrhage.

Seven mothers reported feeding their babies by the breast, 6 by formula, and 1 by both methods.

TABLE 5

Postnatal Factors Related to Birth of Children (N = 28)

Subject	Operative Procedures	Post-partum Complications	Infant Weight (pounds-ounces)	Length (inches)	Respiration Established S^a	A^b	Time	Resuscitation	Cry
C-2-2	Episiotomy	ō	5-3	19					
E-1-1	Episiotomy	ō	7	20.75					
E-1-8	Episiotomy		4-4	17	Yes-no, sluggish, did not breathe readily.	Yes		Yes, O$_2$	Weak
C-1-4			6-5	19.5					
C-1-6	Episiotomy	ō	7-75	22.5					Normal
C-2-3									
E-2-10			5-13	19	Yes				
E-1-3	Caesarean section, low cervical		8-10		Yes, dusky in color.				Vigorous
C-1-9	Caesarean section	ō	8-13	22	Yes				Spontaneous and good

TABLE 5, *continued*

Subject	Operative Procedures	Post-partum Complications	Infant Weight (pounds-ounces)	Length (inches)	Respiration Established S	A	Time	Resuscitation	Cry
E-2-6	Episiotomy	Moderate bleeding, given 500 cc. of whole blood	8-3	23		Yes	2 min.	Suction and O_2 4-5 min.	
C-2-1	Episiotomy	ō	6-3.5	19		Yes	2 min.	Suction and O_2 4 min.	
C-2-4			6-7	19.5	Yes			Suction and O_2	
C-1-2		First degree laceration	7-11.5	21					
E-2-7		ō	5-6	20		Yes	5-6 min.	Suction, artificial respiration O_2 Coramine	Weak and "obstinate"
E-2-2	Episiotomy	ō	4-10	16	Yes				
C-2-6	Caesarean section	ō	8-5	20.5	Yes		Immediately	Subsequent to spontaneous cry, good color, breathing less active than normal—stimulation and suction—normal breathing and good color	Good

93

TABLE 5, *continued*

Subject	Operative Procedures	Post-partum Complica- tions	Infant Weight (pounds- ounces)	Length (inches)	Respiration Established S[a]	A[b]	Time	Resuscitation	Cry
E-2-1	Episiotomy	ō	7–1	20.5	Yes			ō	Good
C-2-8	First degree laceration	ō	9	22				Resuscitated and suctioned	Good
E-2-8	Episiotomy	"Blues"	7–9.75	21				Routine	
C-1-4			6–2	19					
C-1-5	Episiotomy	ō	6–10	20		Yes	2 min.		Good
C-1-7	Episiotomy	Moderate blood loss; foul-smelling amniotic fluid	7–12			Yes	20 sec.	Yes, O₂	O.K.
C-1-1	Episiotomy and Scan- zoni rotation	ō	6–11	20.5					
E-2-3			8–2	23	Yes		20 min.	Aspirateur and given O₂	

TABLE 5, *continued*

Subject	Operative Procedures	Post-partum Complications	Infant Weight (pounds-ounces)	Length (inches)	Respiration Established S[a]	A[b]	Time	Resuscitation	Cry
E-1-5	Episiotomy		4-12				3 min.	Positive pressured, O₂ and suctional	Weak
C-1-9	Episiotomy		6-14	20	Yes		at birth	O₂	Lusty
E-1-6	Episiotomy		3-2		Yes		1 min.	Continuous O₂ and suction	Yes
E-1-2	Episiotomy		8-13	21			1 min.	ō	Lusty

[a] Respiration established spontaneously.
[b] Respiration established artificially.

95

TABLE 6

Additional Postnatal Factors in the Children ($N = 28$)

Subject	Condition at Birth	Caput	Molding	Anomalies	Birth Injury	Feeding	Neonatal Complications
C-2-2						Breast	Sluggish—jaundiced 3/26/49
E-1-1						Formula	ō
E-1-8						Formula	Prematurity; irregular respiration with apnea; moderately cyanotic diagnosis: atelectasis 1/10/48—seems jaundiced; no definite area of atelectasis fontanelle full; subdural hematoma may be considered; diagnosis: "central" respiratory impairment; 1/11/48—O_2 no longer necessary
C-1-4						Formula	6/18—seems to be cyanotic—improved with O_2—given penicillin; diagnosis: interstitial atelectasis; 6/19—penicillin; 6/20—O_2 discontinued; jaundice—penicillin; 6/21—out of O_2—penicillin
C-1-6	Good		Cephalo-hematoma, left occiput	Left testicle quite small			

Subject	Condition at Birth	Caput	Molding	Anomalies	Birth Injury	Feeding	Neonatal Complications
C-2-3							
E-2-10							Admitted to hospital 3/22/49—37th week of gestation—pre-eclampsia, mild (edema and hypertension 142/100)—salt free diet 3/22: Nembutal 100 mgs. 4 P.M., Demerol 100 mgs. 6:30 P.M., Nembutal 100 mgs. 9:30 P.M.; 3/23: Nembutal 100 mgs. 7:30 A.M., Nembutal 100 mgs. 7 P.M., Nembutal 100 mgs. 8 P.M.; 3/24: Nembutal 100 mgs. 10 A.M., Nembutal 100 mgs. 7 P.M., Nembutal 100 mgs. 9 P.M.
E-1-3							
C-1-9	Cyanotic						
E-2-6	Dusky color						General condition good
C-2-1	Dusky						Breast Formula Draining parietal, forceps injuries

97

Subject	Condition at Birth	Caput	Molding	Anomalies	Birth Injury	Feeding	Neonatal Complications
C-2-4	"Baby jittery," skin dry and peeling			Right testicle undescended		Breast	Normal spontaneous delivery of male infant; amniotic fluid deeply colored with meconium; infant of poor color, very dirty
C-1-2	Good						
E-2-7	"Fair"						Baby failed to breathe spontaneously, born with cord around neck, was not tight; no cyanosis, heart good, no voluntary, spontaneous breathing; suctioned; Coramine—O_2. After rather vigorous resuscitation, began to breathe 5–6 minutes later. X-ray of chest, right lung atelectasis.
E-2-2	Good	ō	ō	ō	ō		Bilateral talipes equinovarus; placed in incubator and O_2—received hypodermoclysis; regained birth weight —8th day
C-2-6	Good	ō		ō	ō	Formula	Jaundiced 4th day; discharged on 22nd of July

TABLE 6, *continued*

Subject	Condition at Birth	Caput	Molding	Anomalies	Birth Injury	Feeding	Neonatal Complications
E-2-1	Good					Breast	Circumcision
C-2-8	Good					Formula	
E-2-8	Good					Breast	
C-1-4	Satisfactory						
C-1-5	Dusky color, muscle tone O.K.					Breast	Slightly jaundiced on 3rd day
C-1-7	O.K. amnionitis					Breast	
C-1-1							Slightly jaundiced and dehydrated 3rd day given clysis 75 cc 2-5 per cent G.W. 4th and 5th days; Hgh-18 mgs.; RBC-5.86; WBC-8.6; circumcised 8th day. Continuation of "Treatment during labor" Duracillin, Pitocin 0.03cc 4 hrs.; Pitocin 0.06cc 3.5 hrs.; Nembutal 4cc CU 2 hrs.; Pitocin 0.06cc 20 min.

99

TABLE 6, *continued*

Subject	Condition at Birth	Caput	Molding	Anomalies	Birth Injury	Feeding	Neonatal Complications
E-2-3					Bruise of forceps— marks on right side of face		ō
E-1-5						Formula	Placed in incubator with O_2; weak cry: color good except for hands and feet which were cyanotic and edamatous 3/21—extremely jittery —shrill cry (? intracranial hemorrhage) given phenobarbital; discontinued 3/28—discharged 3/29
C-1-9	Good	Slight	Slight	ō	ō		
E-1-6	Fair	ō	ō	ō	ō		Continuous O_2—cyanotic, out of O_2 1/8/50; discharged 1/26/50; 23 days old weight = 4 lbs. 7.5 oz.
E-1-2	Good	ō	ō	ō	ō	Breast	

ELECTROENCEPHALOGRAPHIC STUDY

In clinical medicine and in clinical psychology, after a syndrome has been described, clinicians frequently seek to find a laboratory procedure which in itself is not too complicated and which, therefore, can be used as a confirmation of the clinical diagnosis. Whatever term is used as a label for children with behavior and learning disabilities (organic brain damage, hyperactive, physiologic maturational lag, and so forth), the implication seems to be that the difficulty must be in the central nervous system. Teachers, psychologists, and physicians, after describing a clinical picture, therefore frequently turn to the neurologist for his evaluation and hopefully look to the electroencephalograph for further help.

All of the 40 subjects were administered at least one EEG during the diagnostic period. Although 22 of the 40 EEG recordings showed abnormal electrical activity, what was considered to be of greater significance insofar as this particular study was concerned was the fact that an extraordinarily high percentage of the recordings demonstrated a persistent occipital slow wave.[4] There was provided to the authors by Dr. Robert Cohn, self-administered and interpreted electroencephalograms and neurological examinations of the research project selectees (in addition to those performed by the staff neurological diagnostician). His interpretation of the significance of this particular finding in these 40 children, plus a control group of 130 children, is summarized below:

In EEG recordings from children it has become common practice to accept non-paroxysmal occipital slow activity as a normal phenomenon. A randomly selected normal control series of 130 children ranging in age from 6 to 12 years (selected from the same public school population as the children of the pilot study), showed 22 subjects (17 per cent) with slow waves in each occipital derivation, sometimes synchronous, but more often of greater prominence on one side. This slow activity consisted of variable length sequences of 180 to 250 millisecond waves. In a series of 47 individuals (including all of the above mentioned 40 children), ranging in age from 6 to 11 years, who showed clinical disturbances in reading, writing, and adaptive behavior, bioccipital slow waves were observed in 29 cases (62 per cent). Sometimes this occipital slow output was coterminous with indisputable paroxysmal discharges. From this data it is concluded that occipital slow activity cannot

---

[4] In terms of this particular finding, it is important to note that Dr. Robert Cohn of the United States Naval Hospital, Bethesda, Maryland, although not a member of the diagnostic staff of the research project, co-operated with the staff insofar as the project met his research interests in determining the possible relationship of the bioccipital slow waves behavior and learning difficulties.

categorically be considered as a benign phenomenon in children. By means of a frequency correlation of age versus occipital slow activity, and from clinical neurological data, there is good evidence that persistent occipital slow waves are representative of retarded physiological maturation processes of the brain.[5]

As a part of the diagnostic phase, then, group findings were obtained with respect to the EEG which have important implications in understanding the children of the pilot study. As a result of the EEG findings, the authors and their associates were further convinced that children's progress must be adjusted to individual growth patterns, if behavior problems and educational retardation were not to be even more pronounced than that already described in the case summaries. While the EEG did not demonstrate abnormal brain wave patterns in each child, nevertheless a statistically significant difference (p = .001) obtains between the control group of Cohn and the subjects of the present pilot study for the occipital slow waves, which warrants further investigation of this problem by others in the future.

NEUROLOGICAL FINDINGS

Following the pediatrician's examinations, the staff neurologist saw the children.[6] The results of the neurological examinations are summarized for the total group.

Jackson (4) speaks of the positive and negative aspects of the neurological system. Nowhere is this better exemplified than in the immature brain. The loss of function with resulting weakness of the limb is the negative, while the hyper-reflexia is the positive. This can be further applied to the loss, or absence, of cortical function (negative) and the generalized hyperactivity of the brain stem (5). The maturation of the brain results in cortical control upon this reflex mechanism. This may be clearly seen with the change in postural reflexes with age or in disease and, should be kept in mind in considering the children of this study.

The following neurological examination was done on each of the subjects. For convenience, it was arbitrarily divided into four parts: I. cranial nerves; II. sensory; III. motor; IV. association.

---

[5] Abstract from a paper titled "On the Significance of Bioccipital Slow Wave Activity in the Electroencephalograms of Children" presented by Dr. Robert Cohn at the American Electroencephalographic Society Annual Meeting, June, 1958.

[6] Neurological examinations were performed by Bushnell Smith, M.D., staff neurologist and, at the time of the study, Instructor in Neurology, Georgetown University Hospital, Washington, D.C. The data included in this section were summarized by Dr. Smith.

I. Cranial Nerves

With the exception of smell (cranial nerve I) and taste (cranial nerve VII for the anterior two thirds of the tongue), all cranial nerves were tested. Visual acuity was reported elsewhere. Auditory and speech evaluation is reported in detail by the audiologist elsewhere in this chapter.

II. Sensory

Peripheral: the modalities of touch, vibration, pain, and passive movement were tested. Temperature was omitted.

Central: identification of objects by feel (stereognosis), pinprick localization, two-point discrimination, and double simultaneous stimulation of face, hands, and feet were noted whenever possible.

III. Motor

Muscle power and bulk, as well as tone, were evaluated. Co-ordination was studied by hand-patting, rapid alternating hand movements (diadokokenesis), finger-to-nose, finger-to-finger-to-nose, and heel-to-shin tests. Deep tendon reflexes tested were biceps, triceps, patellar, and achilles. Abnormal reflexes were noted when present (Babinski and Hoffman). Tests for clonus were also done. Tremors, choreiform, athetotic and other abnormal movements were recorded whenever they occurred. Abnormal posturing was looked for with the subject standing, eyes closed, feet together and arms extended horizontally before him. Specific tests for dominance employed a piece of paper, with a small hole centrally placed, to determine which eye was used for sighting, observation as to which hand was used for writing and performing other manual tasks, and which foot was used to kick a ball. Dominance was reported as the side doing the act (i.e., left hand, left eye, left foot equals left-sided dominance).

IV. Association

Orientation as to time and place, and right-left orientation. Identification of body parts. A general evaluation of how well the subject understood the examiner. Writing, reading, drawing, numbers and calculation were evaluated roughly. Attention span and hyperactivity were noted. Speech defects were noted.

The neurological examination was primarily concerned with the demonstration of defect in function of the central nervous system, specific or generalized, attributable to structural abnormality or neurological deficit.

In four cases (E-1-5, E-2-2, E-2-4, E-2-6) weakness in one hand, leg or a hemiparesis, coupled with appropriate reflex changes and abnormal movements such as structural abnormality could be visualized with ease. Often cranial nerves were involved also in these cases. In 15 cases (C-1-1, C-1-4, C-1-8, C-1-9, C-1-10, E-1-1, E-1-2, E-1-8, C-2-4, C-2-8, C-2-9, C-2-10, E-2-5, E-2-9, and E-2-10) the neurological deficit affected the motor system. Here inco-ordination, impairment of fine movements and clumsiness, either unilateral or bilateral, were found. Either right-left disorientation or perseveration or both occurred in 10 of these cases. The central nervous system was immature as seen by the right-left disorientation in 15 cases (normally done at age 6). The high incidence of unresolved double simultaneous stimulation also speaks for immaturity of function. No localization can be attributed to this (7). This immaturity of motor function, as well as impairment of memory and concentration, is stated to be a reflection of insult to the nervous system irrespective of its location by Kugelmass (8). Francis and Rarick (9) have demonstrated that motor abilities of retarded children fall significantly below standards for normal children. Two cases (C-2-6 and E-2-7) stand out for extreme hyperactivity and short attention span coupled with other findings. These are conveniently diagnosed as brain-injured children (10). Nine cases (C-1-2, C-1-3, E-1-9, C-2-1, C-2-3, C-2-5, E-2-1, E-2-3, and E-2-8) had no neurological abnormality of the cranial nerves, the sensory of motor examinations. All but three (C-2-1, C-2-3, and E-2-1) had speech defects in addition to other central difficulties.

The evidence for neurologic deficit is not so clear cut, yet the combination of signs and symptoms are compatible with such a deficit. In the opinion of the neurologist only those cases with a clearly demonstrable specific defect without concomitant defects in other portions of the central nervous system can be attributable to psychological factors only. Strephosymbolia is an example of this. According to Kanner (11) it is distinguished from primary reading disorders due to neurologic deficit and reading disorders seen with demonstrable brain damage.

In the following pages, the neurological examination for each child is set forth. Only the abnormal findings are recorded unless the test could not be done, in which case it is so stated. Under IV. *Association*, additional tests done on some subjects are recorded.

SUBJECT C-1-1. *Cranial nerves.* Normal. *Sensory.* Normal. Double simultaneous stimulation was not done. *Motor.* Co-ordination and fine movements slightly impaired. Dominance: right-sided. *Association*. Writing: poor. Attention span: short. Hyperactivity: none noted.[7]

SUBJECT C-1-2. *Cranial nerves*. Normal. *Sensory*. Normal. *Motor*. Normal. Dominance: left-sided. *Association*. Reading: poor. Attention span: normal. Hyperactivity: none noted. Speech defect: slight.

SUBJECT C-1-3. *Craniel nerves*. Normal. *Sensory*. Normal. *Motor*. Normal. Dominance: right-sided. *Association*. Reading: poor. Attention span: short. Hyperactivity: moderate. Speech defect: yes.

SUBJECT C-1-4. *Cranial nerves*. Normal. *Sensory*. Subject unable to resolve double simultaneous stimulation. *Motor*. Bilateral anterior tibial weakness. Incoordination both hands. *Association*. Right-left disorientation. Writing: fair. Numbers: good. Calculation: poor. Drawing: fair. Comprehension: fair. Perseveration: present. Attention span: normal. Hyperactivity: none noted.

SUBJECT C-1-5. No neurological examination.

SUBJECT C-1-6. *Cranial nerves*. Normal. *Sensory*. Normal. *Motor*. Normal. Right-handed. *Association*. Right-left disorientation. Writing: poor. Comprehension: adequate. Attention span: normal. Hyperactivity: present. Perseveration: present. Speech defect: yes

SUBJECT C-1-7. *Cranial nerves*. Normal. *Sensory*. Vibration could not be adequately evaluated. Subject unable to resolve double simultaneous stimulation. *Motor*. Normal. Dominance: right-sided. *Association*. Disoriented for time. Right-left disorientation. Writing: poor. Drawing: unable to reproduce a diamond. Comprehension: poor to fair. Attention span: short. Hyperactivity: present. Speech defect: yes.

SUBJECT C-1-8. *Cranial nerves*. Normal. *Sensory*. Subject unable to resolve double simultaneous stimulation. *Motor*. Slight bilateral incoordination. Dominance: right-sided. *Association*. Disoriented for time. Right-left orientation normal. Reading: unable to read. Numbers: fair. Calculation: poor. Drawing: unable to reproduce a diamond. Comprehension: good. Attention span: fair. Hyperactivity: none noted. Speech defect: yes.

SUBJECT C-1-9. *Cranial nerves*. Normal. *Sensory*. Normal. Subject unable to resolve double simultaneous stimulation. *Motor*. Slight difficulty with fine

---

[7] Hyperactivity as used by Dr. Smith in these neurological examinations is defined somewhat differently than that as used by other authors and diagnosticians in this study. He has considered hyperactivity as ". . . motor agitation accompanied by nervousness, restlessness, and fidgetiness . . ." (Kugelmass, Newton I., *Management of Mental Deficiency*, New York: Grune and Stratton, 1954, p. 277). If the patient responded to the examiner and appeared interested in the examination procedures he was not classified as hyperactive. When the child persisted in running about, would not respond to the examiner, and the examination could be carried out only with the use of restraint, he was classified as hyperactive. Obviously, the one hour period of examination time in an individual situation with an adult can not be compared to the stimulus value of many hours in a classroom group. It is in this light that there are numerous subjects reported as having no hyperactivity in the neurological examination.

movements of the hands. *Association.* Reading: unable to read. Drawing: unable to reproduce a diamond. Comprehension: fair. Attention span: short. Hyperactivity: present.

SUBJECT C-1-10. *Cranial nerves.* Normal. Eighth cranial nerve could not be evaluated. *Sensory.* Normal. *Motor.* Impairment of fine movements. *Association.* Comprehension: fair. Attention span: short. Hyperactivity: none noted. Perseveration: present. Speech defect: yes.

SUBJECT E-1-1. *Cranial nerves.* Normal. *Sensory.* Two-point discrimination and double simultaneous stimulation could not be evaluated adequately. *Motor.* Unable to hop on right foot. Co-ordination: poor bilaterally. Left-eyed, right-handed, both feet used equally. *Association.* Right-left disorientation. Writing: unable to write. Reading: poor. Drawing: diamond poorly drawn. Comprehension: fair. Attention span: moderate. Hyperactivity: moderate.

SUBJECT E-1-2. *Cranial nerves.* Normal. *Sensory.* Partial resolution of double simultaneous stimulation. *Motor.* Impairment of fine movements. Right-handed. *Association.* Right-left disorientation. Reading: unable to read. Numbers: good. Calculation: poor. Drawing: unable to reproduce a diamond. Attention span: normal. Hyperactivity: none noted.

SUBJECT E-1-3. *Cranial nerves.* Normal. *Sensory.* Unable to resolve double simultaneous stimulation. *Motor.* Normal. Dominance: not tested. *Association.* Right-left disorientation. Numbers: fair. Comprehension: fair. Attention span: moderate. Hyperactivity: none noted. Speech defect: yes.

SUBJECT E-1-4. No neurological examination.

SUBJECT E-1-5. *Cranial nerves.* Nystagmus on left lateral and upward gaze. *Sensory.* Sterognosis was not valid. Two-point discrimination and double simultaneous stimulation could not be evaluated adequately. *Motor.* Right hemiparesis. Right hyper-reflexia. Right Babinski present. Marked limitation in fine movements and gross inco-ordination. Right-handed. Dominance: right-sided. *Association.* Disoriented for time and place. Right-left disorientation. Comprehension: poor. Drawing: unable to reproduce a diamond. Attention span: short. Hyperactivity: present.

SUBJECT E-1-6. *Cranial nerves.* Nystagmus on gaze to either side. Strabismus. *Sensory.* Two-point discrimination and double simultaneous stimulation could not be evaluated adequately. *Motor.* Normal. Left-eyed, right-handed and right-footed. *Association.* Disoriented for time. Writing: poor. Drawing: unable to reproduce a diamond. Comprehension: poor. Attention span: moderate. Hyperactivity: none noted.

SUBJECT E-1-7. *Cranial nerves.* Normal. *Sensory.* Unable to resolve double simultaneous stimulation. *Motor.* Normal. Right-handed. *Association.* Drawing: unable to reproduce a diamond. Comprehension: good. Attention span: normal. Hyperactivity: none noted. Speech defect: yes.

SUBJECT E-1-8. *Cranial nerves.* Horizontal nystagmus on lateral gaze to either side. *Sensory.* Normal. *Motor.* Impairment of fine movements and co-ordination in the hands. Right-handed. *Association.* Right-left disorientation.

Comprehension fair. Attention span: short. Hyperactivity: moderate. Speech defect: yes.

SUBJECT E-1-9. *Cranial nerves.* Normal. *Sensory.* Normal. *Motor.* Un sustained ankle clonus bilaterally. Right-handed. *Association.* Writing: fair. Drawing: unable to reproduce a diamond. Comprehension: fair. Attention span: moderate. Hyperactivity: slight. Speech defect: yes.

SUBJECT E-1-10. *Cranial nerves.* Normal. *Sensory.* Two point discrimination and double simultaneous stimulation could not be evaluated adequately. *Motor.* Normal. Dominance: right-sided (uses left hand for writing). *Association.* Right-left disorientation. Writing: reversal of letters. Reading: unable to read. Comprehension: poor. Attention span: short. Hyperactivity: none noted.

SUBJECT C-2-1. *Cranial nerves.* Normal. *Sensory.* Normal. *Motor.* Normal. *Association.* Numbers: fair. Calculations: poor. Comprehension: slow. Attention span: good. Hyperactivity: moderate.

SUBJECT C-2-2. *Cranial nerves.* Normal. *Sensory.* Unable to resolve double simultaneous stimulation. *Motor.* Normal. Dominance: right-sided. *Association.* Reading: poor. Comprehension: fair to poor. Attention span: moderate. Hyperactivity: none noted. Speech defect: yes

SUBJECT C-2-3. *Cranial nerves.* Normal. *Sensory.* Normal. *Motor.* Normal. Dominance: right-sided. *Association.* Writing: poor. Comprehension: slow. Attention span: short. Hyperactivity: none noted.

SUBJECT C-2-4. *Cranial nerves.* Normal. *Sensory.* Normal. *Motor.* Impairment of fine movements of right hand. Left-eyed, right-handed. *Association.* Right-left disorientation. Writing: reversal of letters. Reading: poor. Comprehension: fair. Attention span: moderate. Hyperactivity: none noted.

SUBJECT C-2-5. *Cranial nerves.* Normal. *Sensory.* Normal. *Motor.* Normal. Dominance: left-sided. *Association.* Disoriented for time. Right-left disorientation. Reading: poor. Comprehension: fair. Attention span: moderate. Hyperactivity: none noted. Speech defect: slight.

SUBJECT C-2-6. *Cranial nerves.* Visual fields could not be done. Ninth and tenth cranial nerves could not be adequately tested. *Sensory.* Passive movement and central sensory could not be adequately evaluated. *Motor.* Normal. Dominance: right-sided. *Association.* Writing: words crowded to one side of page. Drawing: unable to reproduce a diamond. Comprehension: poor. Attention span: short. Hyperactivity: extreme. Speech defect: yes.

SUBJECT C-2-7. *Cranial nerves.* Horizontal nystagmus on lateral gaze to either side. Vertical nystagmus on upward gaze. *Sensory.* Unable to resolve double simultaneous stimulation. *Motor.* Normal. Dominance: right-sided. *Association.* Writing: reversal of letters. Drawing: unable to reproduce a diamond. Comprehension: poor. Attention span: normal. Hyperactivity: none noted.

SUBJECT C-2-8. *Cranial nerves.* Normal. *Sensory.* Normal. *Motor.* Impairment of fine movements bilaterally. *Association.* Comprehension: slow. Attention span: moderate. Hyperactivity: none noted. Speech defect: yes.

SUBJECT C-2-9. *Cranial nerves.* Horizontal nystagmus on lateral gaze to either side. Eighth cranial nerve not adequately evaluated. *Sensory.* Normal. *Motor.* Poor co-ordination and impairment of fine movements of the hands. Fine tremor right hand. Left-eyed and right-handed. *Association.* Right-left disorientation. Writing: poor. Numbers: fair. Calculation: poor. Drawing: unable to reproduce a diamond. Comprehension: poor. Attention span: short. Hyperactivity: moderate. Perseveration: present. Speech defect: yes.

SUBJECT C-2-10. *Cranial nerves.* Normal. *Sensory.* Unable to resolve double simultaneous stimulation. *Motor.* Impairment of co-ordination and fine movements of hands. Clumsiness of feet. *Association.* Right-left disorientation. Reading: unable to read. Numbers: fair. Calculation: poor. Drawing: unable to reproduce a diamond. Comprehension: fair. Attention span: moderate. Hyperactivity present.

SUBJECT E-2-1. *Cranial nerves.* Normal. *Sensory.* Normal. *Motor.* Normal. Left-eyed, right-handed and right-footed. *Association.* Reading: poor. Drawing: unable to reproduce a diamond. Comprehension: good. Attention span: normal. Hyperactivity: none noted.

SUBJECT E-2-2. *Cranial nerves.* Normal (gag reflex not tested). *Sensory.* Normal. *Motor.* Motor power in lower extremities limited because of talipes varus of the feet. Weakness in right arm. Poor co-ordination in right hand. Heel-to-shin tests not performed because of weakness. Spooning of the right hand with choreiform movements noted when arms are extended. Right-eyed. Subject tends to use the right hand, but has to use the left because of poor function of the right. Dominance in feet was not tested. *Association.* Writing: poor. Reading: poor. Comprehension: good. Attention span: normal. Hyperactivity: none noted.

SUBJECT E-2-3. *Cranial nerves.* Normal. *Sensory.* Normal. *Motor.* Normal. Left-eyed, right-handed and footed. *Association.* Reading: unable to read. Writing: name only. Drawing: unable to reproduce a diamond. Comprehension: slow. Sequence: unable to do three things in sequence when asked. Attention span: fair. Hyperactivity: none noted. Speech defect: yes.

SUBJECT E-2-4. *Cranial nerves.* Normal. *Sensory.* Normal. *Motor.* Weakness right hand and foot. Spooning of right hand. Fine movements and co-ordination impaired in right hand. Left-eyed, left-handed. *Association.* Right-left disorientation. Writing: name only. Reading: poor. Drawing: inversion of house. Comprehension: fair. Attention span: good. Hyperactivity: none noted. (Note: Left side of head and face larger than right; no asymmetry of extremities noted.)

SUBJECT E-2-5. *Cranial nerves.* Normal. *Sensory.* Unable to resolve double simultaneous stimulation. *Motor.* Co-ordination slightly impaired left hand and leg. Left-eyed, right-handed and right-footed. *Association.* Writing: poor. Reading: unable to read. Drawing: unable to reproduce a diamond. Comprehension: good. Attention span: fair. Hyperactivity: none noted. Speech defect: yes.

SUBJECT E-2-6. *Cranial nerves.* Visual fields not done because of poor cooperation. Divergent strabismus. *Sensory.* Unable to resolve double simultaneous stimulation. *Motor.* Weakness: dorsiflexion, right foot. Left-eyed, right-handed. *Association.* Comprehension: fair. Attention span: short. Hyperactivity: none noted.

SUBJECT E-2-7. *Cranial nerves.* Visual fields could not be tested. Eighth, ninth and tenth cranial nerves could not be adequately evaluated. *Sensory.* Pinprick and touch: normal throughout. Vibration and the higher modalities of sensation could not be assessed adequately. *Motor.* Reflexes could not be evaluated. Muscle power and tone: normal throughout. Left-handed. *Association.* Orientation: could not be evaluated. Writing: name only. Reading: unable to read. Comprehension: poor. Attention span: short. Hyperactivity: extreme. Speech defect: yes.

SUBJECT E-2-8. *Cranial nerves.* Normal. *Sensory.* Stereognosis was invalid. Passive movement: subject unable to comprehend directions. Unable to resolve double simultaneous stimulation. *Motor.* Normal. Dominance: right-sided. *Association.* Drawing: unable to reproduce a diamond. Comprehension: poor. Attention span: moderate. Hyperactivity: none noted.

SUBJECT E-2-9. *Cranial nerves.* Divergent squint. *Sensory.* Two point discrimination and double simultaneous stimulation could not be evaluated. *Motor.* Impairment of co-ordination and fine movements of the left hand. (Note: When excited, the subject raised both arms and shaking movements of the arms and hands were noted without impairment of consciousness. When asked to do so the subject voluntarily stopped the movements.) Dominance: right-sided. *Association.* Right-left disorientation. Drawing: unable to reproduce a diamond. Comprehension: poor. Attention span: short. Hyperactivity: none noted. Speech defect: yes.

SUBJECT E-2-10. *Cranial nerves.* Transient nystagmus on left lateral gaze. *Sensory.* Unable to resolve double simultaneous stimulation. *Motor.* Fine movements impaired in the right hand. (Note: When excited, the subject rapidly clenches and opens his hands with the thumbs flexed across the palms.) Dominance: left-sided. *Association.* Right-left disorientation. Writing: poor. Reading: poor. Comprehension: adequate. Attention span: good. Hyperactivity: slight. Speech defect: yes.

STUDY GROUP ORGANIZED

As a result of the procedures which have been delineated above, 40 children were selected. The diagnostic team temporarily concluded its work, waiting the outcome of matching the children into four relatively equated groups on the basis of factors which have been shown above. However, once the diagnostic phase of the project had been completed and the second phase of the project had been initiated, the appointments of the diagnostic staff members (with the exception of the pediatrician, psychiatrist, and psychologist) were officially terminated. The pediatrician and psychiatrist were retained on a continuation basis for the duration of the project. The pediatrician acted as the school physician to the children participating in the research classes and the psychiatrist acted on a consultant basis to the research teachers and provided a psychiatric re-evaluation of the children's progress prior to the termination of the project. The research clinical psychologist's duties for the duration of the study have been delineated previously.

REFERENCES

1. MASLAND, R. L., SARASON, S. B., and GLADWIN, T. *Mental Subnormality.* New York: Basic Books, 1958.
2. HOPKINS, T. W., BICE, H. V., and COTTON, K. C. *Evaluation and Education of the Cerebral Palsied Child; New Jersey Study.* Washington: International Council for Exceptional Child, 1954.
3. PASAMANICK, B., ROGERS, M. E., and LILIENFIELD, A. M. "Pregnancy Experience and the Development of Behavior Disorders in Children," *American Journal of Psychiatry,* CXII (February, 1956), 613–18.
4. JACKSON, J. H. *Selected Writings.* Two volumes. Edited by TAYLOR, J. New York: Basic Books, 1931.
5. MYERSON, S. Discussion of Kahn and Cohen, "A Brain Stem Syndrome and an Experience," *New England Journal of Medicine,* CCX (1934), 748.
6. TEICHER, W. H. "Preliminary Survey of Motility in Children," *Journal of Nervous and Mental Diseases,* XCIV (1941), 277.
7. BENDER, M. *Disorders in Perception.* Springfield, Ill.: Charles C. Thomas, 1952.
8. KUGELMASS, N. *Management of Mental Deficiency in Children.* New York: Grune and Stratton, 1954.
9. FRANCIS, R. J., and RARICK, L. L. "Motor Characteristics of the Mentally Retarded," *Journal of Mental Deficiency,* LXIII (1954), 792.
10. KALISKI, L. "The Brain Injured Child—Learning by Living in a Structured Setting," *Journal of Mental Deficiency,* LXIII (1959), 688.
11. KANNER, L. *Child Psychiatry.* Springfield, Ill.: Charles C. Thomas, 1957.

CHAPTER IV

Matching Criteria, Grouping Procedures, and Teacher Selection

THE ACADEMIC phase of the project involved the investigation of the reliability, effectiveness, and instructional usefulness of a specialized teaching method which included a stimulus-free classroom environment, a highly structured teaching program, and specially designed teaching equipment and materials. This phase was divided into four separate but overlapping steps. First, the 40 research project selectees were separated into four groups, two experimental and two control. Second, the four research teachers and the teacher-assistants were selected and trained in the preparation and use of the instructional materials and in the programming of the specialized teaching method; also the two experimental classrooms were reconditioned. Third, the specialized teaching method was used experimentally in classroom situations during the academic year 1957–58. Fourth, the total group was retested by the clinical psychologist and re-evaluated by the psychiatrist in order to assess the effect of the diagnostic grouping, specialized teaching method, and classroom environment on the learning problems and behavior response patterns of the children. This chapter covers the first two steps.

The two primary purposes of this chapter are to define the composition of the four groups of children, and to explain the basis for the selection of the four teachers. Some of the most thought-provoking problems raised by the study occur in connection with the results of the grouping criteria which were utilized in matching the four classes and in connection with the educational implications of matching the teachers to their groups. The nature and significance of these problems are explored in Chapter VII.

A discussion of the specific nature of the methods and instructional programming is not within the province of this chapter. However, the reconditioning of classrooms to provide a nonstimulating environment is described insofar as it distinguished the experimental from the control groups and insofar as it directly related to classroom management in the experimental groups.

MATCHING CRITERIA

Before the designation of the two experimental groups, all four groups were matched in terms of the following criteria and instructional factors: chronological age (CA), mental age (MA), intelligence quotient (IQ), Stanford-Binet mental age range, instructional or achievement levels in previous school experience, perseveration, hyperactivity, ratio of students with no previous experience in special education classes, and diagnostic evidence of specific damage to the central nervous system. Tables 7 and 8 indicate the extent of the matching on the first four of the above factors.

The specific matching criteria are noted in Table 7. No statistically significant differences exist in any of the items in the table. The groups ranged in average chronological age, from 7–11 years to 8–2 years;

TABLE 7
Matching Criteria for the Four Groups

Group	Average CA	Average MA	Average IQ	Stanford-Binet MA Range
Experimental I	8– 0	6–2	78.0	5.4
Experimental II	7–11	6–6	81.0	5.1
Control I	8– 2	6–9	80.2	5.3
Control II	8– 2	6–8	82.2	5.3

TABLE 8
Range in Matching Criteria for the Four Groups

Group	CA (Inclusive)		MA (Inclusive)		IQ (Inclusive)		Stanford-Binet MA Range (Inclusive years)
Experimental I	6–10	9–2	4–8	7–10	51	102	5 through 7
Experimental II	6– 9	9–9	5–2	8–10	62	107	2 through 7
Control I	6–10	9–5	5–0	8– 4	61	102	3 through 8
Control II	6–11	9–7	5–5	8–10	68	107	2 through 7

and in average mental age, from 6–2 years to 6–9 years. Intelligence quotients in the four groups ranged from an average of 78 through 82.2, with an average mental age range on the Terman-Merrill Revision of the Stanford-Binet Scale of from 5.1 years to 5.4 years.

The range for the individual groups on the four matching criteria is noted in Table 8. Some comment needs to be made regarding the intelligence quotient range. The range in Experimental Group I, for example, is from 51 through 102. This disparity violates the principle of grouping by intelligence as it is ordinarily conceived in the field of special education. A decision to permit this unusual range was made: first, because small groups of children were involved: second, because the nature of the work was highly individualized; and third, because the reliability of the initial intelligence quotients was questioned by the staff psychologist and others. The question concerning reliability arose because factors which resulted in poor achievement in school learning tasks could also operate to depress the intelligence quotient scores. While the range was great and would not be normally recommended, it did not act as a deterrent to satisfactory function of the classes.

GROUPING PROCEDURES

Tables 9, 10, 11, and 12 illustrate the readiness characteristics of the children in each of the four groups (as measured by the Metropolitan Readiness Test in November, 1957) after the matching had been completed. Care had been taken to ascertain that no more than three instructional groups were assigned to each teacher, i.e., pre-academic, primary, or elementary. The grouping was necessarily based arbitrarily on the traditional criteria of CA, MA, IQ, and achievement level.

The other factors considered in grouping the children were:

1. *Perseveration.* Although perseveration was a learning difficulty characteristic of the total group, no more than 4 children were assigned to any group whose perseverative tendencies, as informally evaluated from teachers' records, constituted the primary instructional problem to the teacher.

2. *Hyperactivity.* In matching the children to balance the four groups an attempt was made to place in each group approximately 5 children whose hyperactive response pattern appeared, at least superficially, to be a response to environmental stimuli and unstructured group situations. This type of hyperactive behavior is in contrast to that which has a persistent driven quality and which appears to be more internalized and less subject to environmental and group modification.

TABLE 9

Metropolitan Readiness Test, November, 1957, Group Experimental I (E-1)

Subject	Word Meaning	Sentences	Information	Matching	Total 1–4	Numbers	Copying	Total 1–6	Reading	Readiness Number	Readiness Total	Percentile Rank
E-1-4	18	12	13	15	58	15	5	78	B[b]	C[c]	C	68
E-1-3	17	11	11	18	57	17	10	84	B	B	B	84
E-1-1	16	9	12	11	48	15	2	65	C	C	C	37
E-1-9	17	10	11	15	53	19	6	78	C	B	C	68
E-1-7	16	13	11	0	40	11	4	55	D[d]	C	D	19
E-1-5	18	12	13	12	55	14	7	76	B	C	C	63
E-1-8	19	14	13	17	63	20	8	91	A[a]	B	A	96
E-1-10	13	5	12	11	41	8	1	50	D	D	D	13
E-1-2	18	14	14	16	62	24	5	91	A	A	A	96
E-1-6	16	6	9	9	40	10	3	53	D	C	D	17

Summary of Group Instructional Levels

	Number of Children
1. First half of kindergarten	4
2. First half of first grade	3
3. Second half of first grade	3

[a] A = Superior
[b] B = High Normal
[c] C = Average
[d] D = Low Average

114

TABLE 10

Metropolitan Readiness Test, November, 1957, Group Experimental II (E-2)

Sub-ject	Word Meaning	Sen-tences	Infor-mation	Match-ing	Total 1–4	Num-bers	Copy-ing	Total 1–6	Reading	Readiness Number	Total	Percentile Rank
E-2-5	18	8	13	14	53	14	4	71	C [c]	C	C	51
E-2-3	15	8	9	14	46	20	4	70	D [d]	B [b]	C	48
E-2-9	18	11	12	15	56	20	4	80	B	B	B	73
E-2-7	14	8	11	10	43	15	1	59	D	C	D	25
E-2-4	18	11	14	18	61	23	10	94	A [a]	A	A	99
E-2-2	18	13	14	18	63	24	7	94	A	A	A	99
E-2-1	19	13	13	16	61	23	8	92	A	A	A	97
E-2-6	15	7	11	11	44	16	6	66	D	B	C	39
E-2-8	19	5	11	9	44	7	1	52	D	D	D	15
E-2-10	17	14	14	16	61	17	4	82	A	B	B	79

[a] A = Superior
[b] B = High Normal
[c] C = Average
[d] D = Low Average

Summary of Group Instructional Levels

	Number of Children
1. Second half of kindergarten	4
2. First half of first grade	3
3. Second half of first grade	3

TABLE 11

Metropolitan Readiness Test, November, 1957, Group Control I (C-1)

Subject	Word Meaning	Sentences	Information	Matching	Total 1-4	Numbers	Copying	Total 1-6	Reading	Readiness Number	Total	Percentile Rank
C-1-5	16	12	14	16	58	19	10	87	B [b]	B	B	90
C-1-4	14	7	12	13	46	6	3	55	D [d]	D	D	19
C-1-3	18	12	13	18	61	24	10	95	A [a]	A	A	99
C-1-8	18	13	14	13	58	18	6	82	B	B	B	79
C-1-6	18	11	13	15	57	13	1	71	B	C [c]	C	51
C-1-7	17	7	12	12	48	12	4	64	C	C	D	35
C-1-1	18	13	14	16	61	24	9	94	A	A	A	99
C-1-10	16	9	10	11	46	7	1	54	D	D	D	18
C-1-9	14	8	12	13	47	20	8	75	C	B	C	61
C-1-2	18	13	14	18	63	23	10	96	A	A	A	99

[a] A = Superior
[b] B = High Normal
[c] C = Average
[d] D = Low Normal

Summary of Group Instructional Levels

	Number of Children
1. First half of first grade	3
2. First half of second grade	5
3. Second half of third grade	2

TABLE 12
Metropolitan Readiness Test, November, 1957, Group Control II (C-2)

Subject	Word Meaning	Sentences	Information	Matching	Total 1–4	Numbers	Copying	Total 1–6	Reading	Readiness Number	Readiness Total	Percentile Rank
C-2-7	18	9	14	13	54	15	6	75	C[c]	C	C	61
C-2-1	18	13	14	18	63	24	10	97	A[a]	A	A	99
C-2-10	17	10	12	15	54	21	8	83	C	A	B[b]	81
C-2-5	17	9	13	16	55	14	6	75	C	C	C	61
C-2-6	17	10	12	10	49	11	6	66	C	C	C	39
C-2-2	18	14	14	18	64	23	9	96	A	A	A	99
C-2-9	16	11	13	8	48	10	2	50	C	C	D[d]	27
C-2-4	19	13	13	18	63	20	10	93	A	B	A	98
C-2-3	18	12	14	16	60	20	6	86	B	B	B	88
C-2-8	17	10	9	10	46	15	4	65	D	C	C	37

[a] A = Superior
[b] B = High Normal
[c] C = Average
[d] D = Low Average

Summary of Group Instructional Levels

	Number of Children
1. First half of kindergarten	3
2. First half of first grade	3
3. First half of second grade	4

3. *Previous Special Education Class Placement.* The administrative staff responsible for grouping the children had long felt that children with specific learning problems and behavior disorders made their greatest progress after their initial adjustment in a special education class than in any year thereafter. Therefore, 5 children who had had no previous special education experience were assigned to each group.

4. *Diagnostic Evidence of Injury to the Central Nervous System.* Matching the groups with reference to this particular criterion of the research design was medically and neurologically complicated. Moreover, the entire group, regardless of the clinical picture, demonstrated varying degrees of the learning and behavior characteristics customarily associated with injury to the central nervous system. The research design required that at least 20 of the 40 children demonstrate not only clinical evidence of these types of learning problems, but that the problems appear in association with medical and neurological evidence of central nervous system damage without gross motor involvement.

However, it was still possible to use gross evidence of organic pathology as one of the guides to class assignment. For example, no more than 5 children for whom the complete diagnostic evaluation demonstrated gross evidence of damage to the central nervous system were assigned to any group. One of these children demonstrated no abnormality in the EEG tracing, while 2 of the children with no other medical or neurological evidence of central nervous system damage did demonstrate grossly abnormal EEG's.

TRANSPORTATION

Once the task of matching the children was completed, the proposed class lists were submitted to the special education transportation secretary who reorganized the entire schedule in an effort to meet the transportation needs of the project children and at the same time maintain the proposed class lists intact. Consequently, it was necessary to reassign only 4 children, of which 2 were shifted by simply reversing the school assignment of matched pairs. The end result was that not only were the four groups matched in terms of the research design criteria, but each child (with the exception of 2) matched one other child in each of the other three groups.

THE TEACHING SITUATIONS

Once the task of matching the four groups was completed, two groups of 10 children each were designated as experimental, and 2 were designated as control.

The difference between the experimental and control groups consisted of: first, strict adherence to the prescribed use of the specialized teaching method and, second, the use of the nonstimulating classroom environment in the experimental groups. The latter will be described here.

The two experimental groups were housed in one elementary school in order to facilitate the renovation of the two classrooms and provide for maximum instructional assistance from the teacher-assistant. The two control groups were assigned to two separate schools where classroom space was available and where the school administrators were receptive to the research program. No modifications were initiated in these two classrooms other than those which are customarily employed by special education teachers, such as the temporary use of screens to separate highly distractible children.

In line with the recommendations of Cruickshank and Dolphin, Strauss, and Lehtinen, the two experimental rooms were painted a uniform color closely matching the honey-colored woodwork. Individual work cubicles with built-in desk tops were constructed to meet the height and weight requirements of the individual children in each group (Figures 2a, 2c, 3a, 3c). Open coat closets and supply cabinets were provided with sliding doors (Figures 2d, 3d). Windows were made opaque with a plastic medium (Figures 2b, 3b). Individual two-shelf lockers equipped with snap-lock doors were built for each child (Figures 2b, 3b). These lockers fit snugly below the window ledges and between the heating units, thus, not only providing the children with adequate storage space for their daily work, but also eliminating a number of distracting spatial interruptions.

Aside from any other contribution which these lockers made toward establishing a uniformly nonstimulating learning environment, their use became one of the main organizing experiences of the children. Each locker's measurements, 30 by 14 by 17 inches, allowed space for two shelves. On the top shelf the teacher placed the instructional material for each of the daily assignments in the order in which the tasks were to be completed.

Every assignment during the day was checked by the teacher and only when the task was correctly completed was the child allowed to file his work on the bottom shelf. This practice introduced into the classroom learning situation a rigid order of sequential procedures for both the child and teacher which, by its very nature, developed organized work habits and increased the child's personal sense of responsibility for order and cleanliness.

Fig. 2. Photographs of interior of Experimental Classroom 1. Figures 2a, 2b, 2c, and 2d were taken about five months after the program started. Furniture in the center of the room has been added since the program started. Small group work illustrated in Figures 2e and 2f indicates progress which some children have made in tolerating larger space and increasing stimuli. The latter were taken five months after initiation of program.

Fig. 3. Illustrating interior arrangement of Experimental Classroom 2. Photographs taken about five months after initiation of program illustrate seating adaptations made for children in various stages of tolerance of stimuli. Figures 3e and 3f illustrate a group reading experience with children seated and working in situations most comfortable to them psychologically.

In addition, the systematization required of the teacher in checking each piece of work as it was finished meant that each child repeatedly experienced success in a series of given tasks before he moved on to the next step in the learning process.

Initially, all individual work assignments were completed in the cubicles. Later in the year, arrangements for group work were made possible by providing a set of three trapazoidal tables for each of the experimental classrooms (Figures 2a, 3a). When arranged in a half circle, the three tables provided sufficient work space for all 10 children, and enabled the teacher, who was seated at the center of the half circle, to hold her group and provide individual guidance without moving about the room. The flexibility with which the tables could be arranged also made it possible to provide the same type of working arrangements for one or two separate activities or sub-groups. When not in use, the tables were easily moved to the side of the room and concealed by a screen, thus freeing the entire classroom space of non-essential furniture.

The usual paintings, drawings, maps and charts, handwriting guides, school calendars, flowers, aquariums, murals and class projects—and all other types of traditional motivating equipment considered appropriate in a regular classroom—were displayed only during a specific work period or project assignment and then removed. Once the object or objects had served their immediate instructional purpose, they were returned to the storage and supply cabinets. As the year progressed and the children's hyperactivity and distractibility decreased, it became possible for the teacher to increase the number of instructional guides which were left out in the classroom. In one group, for example, the classroom calendar and handwriting chart were the first items to become a permanent part of the classroom environment (Figure 3b).

(It is interesting to report that while the nonstimulating atmosphere was obviously beneficial as a means of assisting highly distractible children to control their responses to the classroom environment and each other, its effect upon adult observers, whose sole occupation was to sit quietly in the room, was to reduce their mental alertness to a soporific calm. After approximately twenty minutes of observation, visitors to the experimental classrooms were frequently found strolling up and down the hall in a dignified effort to contain their need to stretch and yawn.)

Although a detailed statistical analysis of the pre- and post-test differences between the experimental and control groups is provided in a later chapter, it is indeed unfortunate that there is apparently no method by which the significance of such environmental adjustments can be isolated and objectively measured in terms of their contribution to the children's development of organized work habits and a sense of personal responsibility about instructional materials and equipment, nor can the assistance provided a teacher in fulfilling her instructional responsibilities to the children's particular rate of learning and acquisition of skills be objectively measured. However, one cannot help but conclude that many nonmeasurable benefits were derived from the modified classroom environment, particularly during the first few months of the academic year. Many of these advantages were reflected in the amelioration of time-consuming details associated with good classroom management and housekeeping. As has already been indicated, the development of organized individual and group work habits and the organization of instructional materials were all facilitated through the use of lockers, cubicles, and a nonstimulating classroom environment.

Perhaps one of the most important uses of the cubicles for a number of the more seriously emotionally disturbed children was a retreat, a shelter, in which they were better able to deal with their fears and anxieties concerning the external world. One teacher made the following observation about a child with prepsychotic tendencies:

> If X hadn't had his cubicle at the beginning of the year, I just don't think he could have made the grade. You know, it reminded me of the way tired two-year-olds climb in their crib when they find the world too much for them. Of course, by the end of the year, he used the cubicle as his office like some of the others did at the beginning of the year.

In general, the main differences between the control and experimental groups may be summarized as follows:

The classrooms of the two control groups had no structural changes (Figures 4 and 5). They were typical elementary classrooms. One of the rooms had closed cabinets (Figure 5c), as did the experimental classrooms. It had previously been a kindergarten room and the cabinets had been used for storing the children's rest mats. The control group teacher used the cabinets in the same way that the cabinets were used by the experimental group teachers. The second control teacher, who had no cabinets, used designated spaces on a wide window ledge for the prepared and finished work of each child (Figure 4b). The control classrooms had no cubicles and were not repainted. Shades were

Fig. 4. Figures 4a to 4f inclusive illustrate classroom seating and instructional arrangements for Control Class 1.

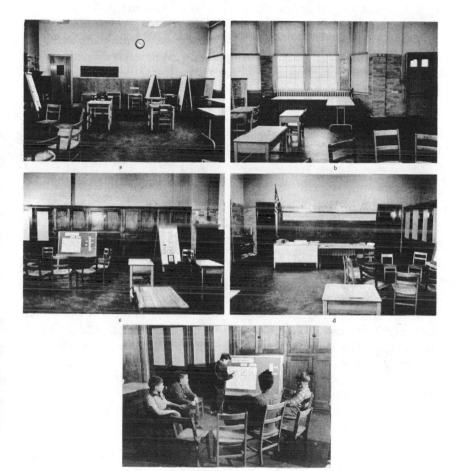

Fig. 5. Figures 5a to 5e inclusive illustrate seating and instructional arrangements for Control Class 2.

lowered when it was necessary to eliminate outside distractions. Chart racks were used for screening purposes, and desks were arranged in such a way as to provide minimum distraction for each child (Figure 5a). Displays and illustrative materials were minimized. Very insecure children sat near the teacher's desk (Figure 4c).

The two experimental group teachers agreed to maintain strict adherence to the specialized techniques and instructional goals. They further agreed to implement any changes in procedures that the Project Director recommended and to use any additional materials or techniques which might be devised during the research period.

The two control teachers were free to vary their programming in any way they felt might be helpful to the children in their groups, as long as they did not deviate too far from the established educational policies and standards of the Department of Special Education. Without direction from the Project Director, they were to devise appropriate techniques and materials.

TEACHER SELECTION

All four research teachers were unanimously recommended by their previous supervisors and administrators as being the best possible choices for teaching children with the particular combination of learning problems and behavior response pattern which characterized the research selectees. All had received past training at a college of education and had been adjudged successful in their previous teaching assignments. Each was creative and experimental in her approach to the use of instructional materials. Two of the four teachers had had no previous experience as special education teachers, while the remaining two had been instructing special classes for approximately three years. One teacher with regular class experience and one with special class experience were assigned to each of the control and experimental situations.

The particular method used in the initial selection of the teachers, although somewhat unusual, was a most effective one. The Supervisor of Special Education held a conference with members of the Montgomery County Elementary School Supervisors, and representatives of the Pupil Personnel Department, and the Psychological Services. During this meeting, the Supervisor described to the group the behavior disorders and instructional problems of a typical research-project child as though he were a member of a regular third-grade class.

The kind of teacher the research staff was looking for was described as follows:

First and foremost, the teacher must be professionally competent in the use of the skills and tools of the teaching profession. Second, she should have had several years experience in teaching and possess the skills essential to the management of an average size elementary class of around 30 children. She should be rated by her supervisors and principals as consistently superior in her ability to provide group instruction and to maintain a learning environment which the children enjoy. She should have demonstrated exceptional ability in meeting the individual and group instructional needs of children in kindergarten, first, second, or third grades. She must have a thorough knowledge and understanding of the developmental sequence in the growth of children and understand and respect the social, emotional, and educational needs associated with the maturational processes at each developmental level.

She should be professionally interested in, curious about, and intrigued by the unresolved instructional problems of the times; and her attitude toward new and unfamiliar teaching concepts, instructional methods and techniques should be characterized by elasticity, creativity, and professional objectivity. She should be more an eclectic than a devotee of curriculum guides and methods, and she should be able to determine quickly what particular techniques and procedures to use at a specific time with a given child with a particular problem. Since the members of the group she was to be teaching would be easily distracted, have a short attention span, and lack impulse control, her sense of timing and skill at transition devices must be developed to such a degree that the instructional day would be experienced by the children as a smooth-flowing, many-faceted continuum of learning.

She must be a good group teacher. That is, she would need to be able to use the group structure as one of her instructional techniques for communicating the skills which, in the end, would make it possible for the children to learn how to learn when they were independent of the group situation. She would be expected to mobilize all her talent, experience, drive, and professional ability in an almost final attempt to provide previously unsuccessful, disorganized, underachieving children with those skills which would lead to successful experiences and a sense of well-being in positive, well-organized classroom activities and achievement.

The supervisors, pupil personnel workers, and psychologists were asked to recommend teachers who could meet these requirements. Four teachers were selected from the names which were submitted. Each of the four teachers was independently recommended by three or more persons. The project administrators were satisfied that the four teachers recommended were matched in terms of teaching strength and professional maturity.

The teacher-assistants assigned to the two experimental groups shared the same general background and personality characteristics of the project teachers but lacked formal academic training in an accredited school of education.

Once the teachers and teacher-assistants were selected, they were given a six-week training period in the specialized teaching methodology.[1] This course included theory, methods, and supervised practice teaching. The work included the preparation of materials and specific instructional aids appropriate to the learning problems of the project children. A demonstration class was maintained, and each of the teachers and the teacher-assistants were supervised in actual work with children.

In concluding this chapter, the authors would like nothing better than to be able to define and itemize the specific factors by which teachers for classes comparable to the project groups can be selected and assigned with satisfaction guaranteed to both the teachers and the children. Unfortunately, the project staff is in no better position to set up such criteria than anyone else who has struggled with this problem. What has been attempted in this chapter is the sharing of the few clues and guides which were found to be useful in this particular project and which made a significant contribution in the selection of four master teachers. Use of the criteria for teacher selection which were itemized in this chapter, resulted in the remarkably wise selection of the four research teachers who participated in this pilot study. The criteria used would remain unchanged were these authors to re-establish a second study of the same nature.

---

[1] The teacher preparation program was under the supervision of Miss Charlotte Larson, teacher of brain-injured children, Joliet Public Schools, Illinois, who was appointed as a visiting lecturer at Syracuse University during the program. Only the research teachers and the teacher-assistants were admitted as members of the program.

CHAPTER V

The Teaching Method

IN CHAPTER I and in Chapter IV some attention was given to the nature of the nonstimulating classroom environment. The present chapter will describe the teaching methods [1] and many of the materials used with the four groups. General information about the children, like that provided to the teachers, is also presented in the paragraphs which follow and serves as an introduction to and rationale for the teaching materials. Since some of this information has already been mentioned in the preceding chapters, this chapter should be read from the point of view of the teachers' needs. What do they need to know and how should it be presented? It is in answer to these latter questions that the pages which follow present informally and graphically the concepts, techniques, and materials which could prove helpful in seeking to meet the needs of some or all of the children.

The material contained in this chapter is included in the monograph for two reasons. First, its contents essentially comprise the instructions given to the research teachers during the intensive training period; therefore, the reader can view the results as consequences of the method

[1] Miss Charlotte E. Larson of the Joliet Public Schools was responsible for the teacher preparation in the Demonstration-pilot Study. Both Miss Larson and the present authors recognize their debt to Dr. Alfred A. Strauss and Miss Laura Lehtinen of the Cove Schools for many of the ideas contained in this chapter. Miss Larson has graciously suggested that the study teachers incorporate many of her ideas into their teaching, and this has been liberally done. The authors recognize the important contribution of Miss Larson and also recognize the original source of all of the educational techniques which were attempted. Since the present authors feel no more ownership to the concepts which are herein presented than did Dr. Strauss or Miss Lehtinen or, indeed, Miss Larson, other educators are urged to utilize the concepts presented herein as freely as they desire when they can be used for the good of children.

utilized. Second, since this monograph is a report of a demonstration-pilot study, it is assumed that in the future a more refined investigation may be undertaken either by the present authors or by others. A relatively complete description of the teaching method [2] and the instructions provided to the teachers are, therefore, necessary to the total report for purposes of later corroborative research.[3]

WHY DO THEY "MISBEHAVE"?

The diagnostic staff could not develop all of the answers regarding the children, because not all of the answers were known. However, in both the group of brain-injured children and in the group without apparent brain injury certain factors stood out clearly. The diagnostic data showed that many children were characterized by developmental delays in sitting, crawling, standing, walking, toilet-training, speech and language development, motor co-ordination, weaning, and feeding. Eye-hand co-ordination often appeared inadequate. Visual difficulties (not connected with eye pathology) were frequently observed in many activities: lack of fusion while following a moving target with the eyes, periodic divergent strabismus (crossed eyes) under "stress," and related visual-perceptual activities.

As teachers work with these children, they come to talk about "developmental gaps," because the children can do some things well, others poorly. One of the striking characteristics is the wide range of performance demonstrated by psychological examinations. This range in mental age would indicate to a teacher that the formal IQ score alone would hardly be a valid index or measurement of the child's learning potential. In a later section of this chapter it will be shown how the teachers tested each child informally to find out where to begin and how to determine the child's learning disability so that he could be brought to the point where he could feel success.

[2] The reader is referred also to *The Montessori Method,* by Maria Montessori, London: William Heinemann Publisher, 1930, for excellent additional suggestions for teaching method. While the Montessori method was not originally developed for hyperactive or brain-injured children, much of the method appears to be appropriate for this work, and many of the teaching suggestions contained in the present chapter are modifications of those of Montessori.

[3] For the pages in this chapter which follow, the authors are indebted to a committee of six educators who were employed during the summer of 1958. The group included three of the research teachers: Mrs. Sally Luke, Mrs. Mary McClurkin, and Mrs. Wretha Peterson. These were joined by Mrs. Dorothy Zippermann of the Montgomery County Public Schools, and Miss Ruth Cheves of the Bibb County Board of Public Instruction, Macon, Georgia. The committee was under the chairmanship of Mrs. Miriam Ulrich of the Montgomery County Board of Education, Rockville, Maryland.

If a child has a healthy body, but one that will not do what he wants it to—if he has eyes that see, but that do not see things the way other eyes see them—if he has ears that hear, but that have not learned to hear the way other ears do—he can not tell anyone what his difficulty is: it just seems to him that he is always wrong. No one can see that he is not like everyone else, so he is expected to act like everyone else. These are the things that happen to such children. This is the kind of behavior in a learning situation which the teacher will have to understand if she is to help the child. These are the symptoms of developmental lags in the child's experience which develop into "specific learning disabilities."

LEARNING CHARACTERISTICS

Hyperactivity-distractibility and Disinhibition

The children of this study are apparently abnormally responsive to the stimuli of the environment. They are inclined to over-react to everything around them. When placed in a situation where the visual and auditory stimuli are constant and widespread, they try to react to everything at once and move from one place to another. The individual child in the group cannot fix his attention on any one thing. One is reminded of a toddler who moves from one object to another, picks it up, drops it, and moves on to the next stimulus. This is appropriate behavior at 21 months; it is not appropriate to 5, 6, or 7 years. Control, then, must be learned. The child must have a place to anchor. As with the young child, all bric-a-brac is removed to a safe place so that the environment is simplified. This enables him to concentrate on the problem at hand.

Another type of hyperactive child appears in this special class. He is the one who sits quietly at his desk, apparently absorbed in work, but at the end of the period his lesson has not been completed. He is judged to be lazy or a daydreamer. This child is attracted by pictures and page numbers in his book, by flaws and marks on the paper, or by any features of the material which are for most children irrelevant. His seeming inattentiveness is the expression of an abnormally attentive condition. If he is to get his work done, he must have nothing to distract him from the job at hand.

Dissociation

Children are often unable to synthesize separate elements into integrated and meaningful wholes (Gestalts). Figures involving interlocking squares or triangles are reproduced as separate and unrelated (see Figure 7).

Perseveration

Children with brain injury are among the ones in whom the characteristic of perseveration, as a learning and behavior characteristic, is usually most prominent. Perseveration makes it necessary to do a different kind of teaching from that which is ordinarily used. If one uses drill or repetition in setting a learning pattern, perseveration is intensified. No matter what new material is introduced, the child may be unable to shift. In reading, a child may repeat a phrase several times before he is able to continue. In writing, a word incorrectly spelled will be erased and may be written again with the same error. In arithmetic, dots or blocks are counted several times. If a page of arithmetic problems starts with a row of problems in addition, the child may ignore subtraction signs and perform addition in every problem on the page. In the use of standardized tests, such as the Metropolitan Reading Readiness Test, the examiner must be alert to the possibility of perseveration. If the correct answer in a given task happens to be the third one, the child is likely to mark the third answer all the way down the page.

The teacher is normally inclined to insist that a paper be correct before the pupil leaves it; but if the child is inclined to perseveration, she will need to have him do something else before he can come back to his errors and correct them. There is probably no characteristic more exasperating than perseveration to the teacher who does not know what she is dealing with. One must learn to sense it in all types of behavior and working situations and to develop techniques for dealing with it.

Catastrophic Reaction

Catastrophic reaction is another characteristic that has been attributed to the brain-injured person. The child will be working happily, and then suddenly may burst into explosive crying, or may get up and turn his desk over. This may occur because he is confronted with a new task, with a slightly more difficult problem, or it may occur as a result of success. Catastrophic reactions need to be differentiated from temper tantrums. The outward manifestations are the same but the causes and the management are different. For example: One of the children in the study had a catastrophic reaction to his first reading success. This was handled by placing a calm and sympathetic hand on his arm until the storm passed. The next time the same set of circumstances arose, rather than bursting into crying, the child said, "Put your hand on my arm."

Instability of Performance

Instability of performance is characteristic of most children of which those in this study are typical. The new teacher has often been frustrated by the discovery that a skill that appears to be mastered on one day will be approached as if for the first time on the next. Some days a child will seem alert and bright and capable of many things; on other days he will be sluggish, inept, and extremely distractible. So-called "forgetting" is usually the result of lack of understanding. Learning accompanied by insight and understanding is retained; automatization is soon lost. Weather, minor cuts or bruises, and so on, cause irritability toward the environment. On such occasions a teacher gains best results by assigning a minimum requirement and avoiding introduction of any new skills.

THE CHILD AND THE TEACHER

As a group, these children need a special kind of handling that comes with the understanding of their problems. Class games designed to motivate and interest the normal or the familial mentally retarded children are overstimulating for this group. Scolding or deprivation, reasoning, subtle approaches by precept or example are equally ineffectual since the cause of the reactions and the irritating situations remains. Repeated experiences of failure and the unrelenting demands of school and home have compounded the children's problems. Their first need is a simple, quiet environment where they can relax, and a structure of activities so designed that they know what is expected of them and what they can expect to have happen to them. In this setting they can find out who they are and what they can do.

In this controlled environment the teacher becomes the focal point. It is important that she dress with thought to the effect her appearance will have on the children. Whereas many teachers wear eye-catchers such as jewelry and flowers for the children to notice, this teacher will find that her problems multiply if she wears something that calls attention to itself. Similarly, any speech mannerisms or unusual voice quality will lead the child to listen to how she talks rather than to what she says.

CASE STUDIES

If there is one principle which stands out more than any other in the teacher's experiences with these classes, it is the paramount importance of the injunction, "Know your child." To know the child: where he is handicapped, where he is strong, how he feels about himself and about the world as he is able to conceive it, and, most of all, how all these factors figure in his behavior, to know these things is to hold the key to helping him.

In one class, for example, are three children who present the same symptom: a habit of making loud, meaningless noises. But in no case is the reason for this behavior the same, nor is the cure. Consider the children: Jane, one of the few girls, is a mite of a 7-year-old, piquant and apparently alert, who charmed the little boys. But she has no interest in charming anyone; and is not alert in the usual sense of the word. Confused and terrified by the disastrous experiences which have attended her constant failures, not only in school but in all group experiences, she is convinced that the world is against her; she is alert only to danger. Offers of kindness and friendliness arouse her contempt and suspicion. Severity arouses her fear; but, a born fighter, she will go down fighting. Her noises warn the world that she is ready to pay it back in kind, and she often does so with real physical violence. A combination of unperturbed acceptance—no overt friendliness—and detached firmness ("no work, no playtime") encourage her to remain in her cubicle work unit doing puzzles, her only accomplishment. Between her spells of loud, raucous singing or shouting, she listens to the background of fun and developing friendships in the room. In the end it is her strengths that draw her forth. She longs for a friend and, characteristically, she seeks one with her usual do-or-die determination. The chosen one must tell her categorically in the presence of all that she will be her friend. She must tell her not once, but many times. If the writing paper looks too hard, or before she can try to answer the teacher's question, there is a pause while Jane draws herself together rigidly and asks this other child in her tight, clipped little voice, "Are you my friend, Betty?" Betty is no noisemaker. As a matter of fact, she can scarcely talk. Most of her sentences come out, "Me do this," "Me say that," and what she further does or says is meaningless. But one day Jane lets her love of music draw her to the group around the record player only to find her fears return and force her to sit with eyes darting like a frightened cat's, looking as if she were not sure whether to run or to hit someone. This time Betty's understanding of her friend's need destroys her own fear as she leans forward and says in words that anyone could understand, "I'm your friend, Jane." And Jane looks tensely at her, asks for and gets another reassurance, then relaxes and settles back in her chair, a real little girl again.

Joe's noises do not begin at first. His enormous, disorganized eyes look oddly in two different directions, and his exaggeratedly stiff, awkward movements suggest that he has good reason to feel uneasy in a world with which neither his eyes nor his body can entirely cope. Indeed, he takes no chances. An only child, unaccustomed to other children and accustomed to few adults, he sits quietly at his desk, keeping himself as inconspicuous as possible and doing, as nearly as possible, no work. Loss of playtime is no punishment to him. He is afraid of the large, strange playground that seems good only for activities which he detests, such as running, jumping, climbing, or playing with a ball. He chills quickly and hates to be out in cold weather. He cries so hard when required to go outdoors that for most of the winter he is allowed to stay inside by himself. But he, too, finds a friend, or rather lets the friend find him and accepts the friendship. Later he seems so much stronger that one day the teacher insists that he come outside. She has to pull him by main force, with Joe crying and pleading at the top of his voice, while the children watch open-mouthed at her cruelty. Suddenly she looks down to discover that his eyes are crinkling with merriment and that this time he is playing a game with her.

After this, Joe began to make noises. At first he used only a vexed "tsl tsl" to which he soon added a little stamp of the foot. Next came a piercing "No! No!" at the top of his voice—and finally a large, full-bodied scream. Between these outbursts, he learned, if not to run and play, at least to carry a chair outside and to carry it back. Later he could be persuaded to play tag with the teacher, and eventually to go outside with his friend. He had a success experience with writing and began to do his work. He electrified the class by telling someone to shut up. ("Joe said 'shut up,'" came delightedly from all sides.) Joe's noises were a boast of strength, and he was so much stronger by the time he made them that they could be dealt with summarily.

The noises Chuck makes go by the name of conversation. An eager, friendly, little boy, his normal, alert curiosity about the world around him is exaggerated by a distractibility which draws his attention to every detail. The perseveration of which he is equally a victim keeps him harping on the subject long after everyone else has ceased to care. "Are we going out to play today?" "What are those notices about?" "When can I show the toy I brought?" A dozen times in a morning he asks the same question. When the group begins a new activity, he talks incessantly, trying to inform himself of every move which he is about to make, expressing his pleasure or displeasure.

Chuck is not afraid in the sense that Joe and Jane are afraid. His cute, little-boy appearance and friendly ways have done much to cushion the difficulties of not doing well in school; and his parents have devised many ways to give him extra support at home. He finds three or four willing best-friends in the weeks when Joe and Jane are making contact with one, and finally he settles down to one real chum and several cronies.

He does have some uneasiness about his inadequacies with numbers, peg boards, parquetry block designs, and his probable inadequacies in new situations. These fears are by no means always justified, but his distractibility and vocal perseveration are especially pronounced in moments of tension. His therapy is found to involve the protective devices which are standard for this type of group. The room must be free of the physical stimuli that provide fuel for ever more questions. He must have a place to work in solitude. Alone, he can be quiet and often industrious. The cardinal injunction to *go slowly* in work and to let the child give the cue has a special importance with Chuck. He is one of those children whose performance fluctuates mysteriously (even his vision and neurological pattern fluctuate, giving totally different results in the same tests administered at different times). For this reason, a pattern of work with which he is entirely comfortable for many weeks, may for no apparent reason, suddenly cause him to be irresponsible and apathetic as he unhappily protests that everything he knew before is "too hard"—and yet he is talking a mile a minute.

Here are three children with common symptoms; but each has his own distinct pattern of causes which is not quite like that in any other child. The teacher must begin with the basic reasonableness of the child's reaction to the world as he sees it and proceed from there to rehabilitation.

PROBLEMS OF INSTRUCTION

Bender says, "Children with severe reading disabilities show lags in neurological patterning . . . they are awkward in motor control. . . . Motor tone is more variable . . . general behavior is disorganized and impulsive; motor perceptual patterns or capacity to develop gestalten remains primitive and full of motion and fluidity; personalities are immature, impulse driven and dependent. . . . They also suffer from anxiety and feeling of inadequacy . . ." (1, p. 158). These, then, are problem areas of instruction in the research classes.

Motor Control

When observing a class in this study, one is struck by the great number of scarcely noticeable physical disabilities. Almost without exception, this is a group of apparently physically "normal" children, generally attractive and personable. However, scrutiny is likely to reveal one boy who stands or sits with every muscle stiff, his arms held rigidly at his sides; two others who have a habit of rising to their toes or walking on their toes; still others who wave their hands and forearms in the air in moments of excitement, much as a baby or toddler does. Some move in a slow, clumsy shamble, and cannot follow directions for simple movements such as crossing arms over chest, hopping, or extending arms or feet in a given direction. The introduction of a simple exercise period is a really startling experience for the teacher. Arms, legs, and heads go in every direction but the one specified; and the sheepish, embarrassed faces of the children show that they have no more idea than the teacher where a given motion is going.

On jungle gym and climbing bars, the group as a whole is far behind the usual level of performance for its age. Even the most ordinary motions are unpredictable and are liable to cause mishaps. A child moves eagerly to the cupboard and bumps into the teacher's desk; or a child tries to pass a pile of papers and drops half of them; waste paper dropped toward the basket misses it and hits the floor. The sound of scattering pegs and falling chairs is a daily occurrence in the early weeks, and spills at lunch-time are common. Frequently someone stumbles and nearly falls, even in walking across a room.

While working with these children, one comes to the realization that these mishaps are not accidents in the sense of being isolated, unrelated occurrences. The succession of small mishaps and inadequacies is the result, in part, of the fact that even in situations requiring the use of the large muscles the child does not notice the things around him. He can *see* the teacher's desk when it comes to his attention. But he does not *notice* it as part of the total Gestalt of the room. When he is thinking of the cupboard he notices the cupboard and only the cupboard. When he stacks dishes at lunch and puts a saucer on top of a cup or a large plate on a small dish, he can *see* the dishes, but he does not *notice* more than the one which catches his attention. Nor does he observe the difference in *form* of a cup and a saucer which make the safer way of stacking so obvious.

Here, as always, the difference is a matter of degree. To be sure, any group of young children has its share of spills and mishaps. But when, day in and day out, eyes do not notice the bulk of a desk or the shape of a cup, it becomes clear that they must have even greater difficulty with the shape and arrangement of letters and numbers.

In general, the stumbling, tumbling, bumping, spilling, dropping that goes on reminds one of a group of much younger children— sometimes kindergarteners, sometimes even those in nursery school. For the sake of emphasis, the foregoing discussion deals with failures in large-muscle activity. There are, however, many similar disturbances in the area of speech. A child cannot protrude his tongue to say "th"; or cannot move his tongue from side to side or up and down as directed; or he cannot purse his lips.

Here, again, the over-all impression is one of almost bizarre immaturity. It is not unusual for a child in this group to speak of himself habitually in the third person. Speech sounds are inaccurate or babyish, even where speech organs are physically perfect. The children make less use of complete sentences than groups of comparable age.

Even in play they may prefer activities which are popular in first grade, kindergarten, or even nursery school. Toy cars and trains are in great demand. Play with blocks attracts restless children who have been interested in nothing else.

As the medical histories show, many of the children did not do, or did not do until very late, many of the things which are part of the usual developmental activities of infants and toddlers. Some walked without ever having crawled; some talked late, but were physically too active to play with blocks or with fitting, piling, or counting toys. Others were inactive physically and had little experience in running, skipping, hopping, and climbing. Discovering the reasons why they did not do these things is a matter for the theorist. The fact that they did not do them and a knowledge of which ones were skipped are matters of great importance in bringing such children up-to-date in academic areas. If a child cannot follow a pencil with his eyes, but must turn his whole head as a baby does, he is at a disadvantage in reading. If he still needs to grasp objects in order to count them, he will not be able to count merely by pointing and certainly not with his eyes alone.

Eye-hand Co-ordination

One of the ways to evaluate a child's visual perception is to have him draw what he sees. Psychologists have been studying eye-hand co-ordination for a long time and have partially standardized the performance of the average child. On the following pages (Figures 6 and 7), are samples of the drawings made at the time of the initial testing for the study. These samples indicate both the nature and the scope of the eye-hand problem. Almost all the techniques in the chapter require eye-hand co-ordination. Drawing a square is required at the five-year level on the Binet. The other items are from the Bender-Gestalt Test for Visuo-Motor Ability. It will be noted that each child's performance falls into the "primitive" level. In struggling to find their places in a regular class these children had unsuccessfully tried to go through the conventional procedures for learning to write and to read. Little wonder they took refuge in "aggressive, acting-out behavior." Crossing a *t* would have been a major triumph for them.

Other tests that involve matching and sorting forms or copying block designs frequently show results that are just as bizarre as those noted in Figure 7. The teacher's use of these tests will be discussed in a later section of this chapter.

Foreground-background Disturbances

These children often have difficulty perceiving foreground-background relationships. Normally, in spite of talking or other sounds, one child has no trouble talking to another. To some of these children, however, the distraction is so great that it may cause a catastrophic reaction. Any noise on the playground may make it impossible for them to attend to what is going on in the classroom. They may not see a word on a page because their attention is attracted to pictures and numbers, or the background may be lost to something in the foreground. For example, a child was asked the color of a church in a picture. His perception of a tiny blue window brought the answer, "blue," but the church was actually yellow. As one studies the techniques for teaching, it will be observed that much emphasis is placed on using picture material in which foreground and background cannot be confused.

Language and Speech

There is probably no area more important to education than language and speech, yet it is the least understood. The largest portion of intelligence tests deals with the ability to understand language and express it. If a child has an obvious speech defect, he gets sufficient sympathy for his problem and allowances are made. Only when expressive speech is defective is the teacher aware that there may be a language problem.

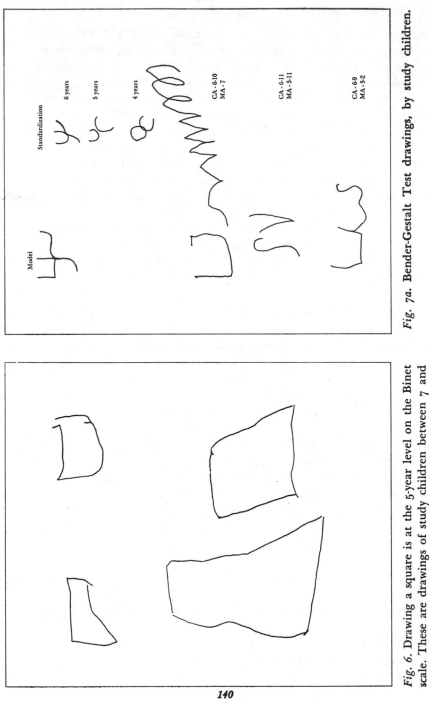

Fig. 7a. Bender-Gestalt Test drawings, by study children.

Fig. 6. Drawing a square is at the 5-year level on the Binet scale. These are drawings of study children between 7 and 10 years.

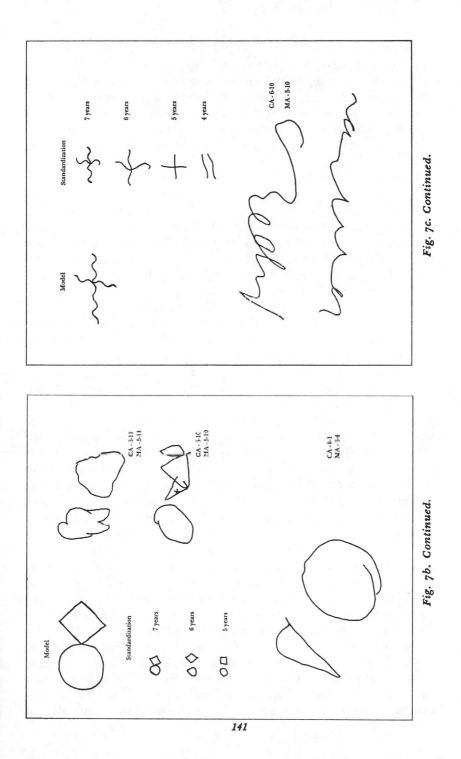

Fig. 7c. Continued.

Fig. 7b. Continued.

Speech is divided into two areas, language and speech. Language is the ability to comprehend and use symbols (words, pictures, numbers, letters) as the accepted means of communication in society. Their use is based on the desire to communicate and convey wants, feelings, and thoughts. Speech, on the other hand, is merely the uttering of the articulate sound, the mechanism or tool, serving the higher function of language.

Language can be divided into three categories: inner, receptive, and expressive. Inner language is the symbol system used for thinking, memory, imagination, reason, and so on. At the lowest level it is a simple association between the word and concrete experiences, such as associating the word "mama" with feeding and generalized feelings of well-being. Receptive language is the symbol system used to understand the ideas of others. Expressive language is the symbol system used to communicate ideas to others.

Inner language must develop first. The average infant must be exposed to spoken language for about 8 months before he begins to comprehend the speech of others. Some associations must be made between experience and the word before the words themselves become intelligible. When such associations have been accomplished to a certain extent, inner language has been sufficiently well established so that receptive language can begin. (In the average child this begins at approximately 8 months.) During the next 4 or 5 months inner and receptive language develop at the same time to the level which makes expressive language possible. This means that at about 12 to 13 months the child speaks his first word. It seems that no child talks until he first has acquired inner and receptive language. Looking ahead, it can be assumed that no child learns to read normally unless he first acquires oral language. It seems essential that he first be able to understand spoken language before he can learn to read normally.

It has already been noted that speech and language constitute one of the delayed areas in these children. Even if they are without speech, it is possible to test the inner language of children by observing their use of materials, their ability to see likenesses and differences, their ability to arrange a group of pictures into a sequence that tells a story. They can express this inner language by manipulation of materials if they have the necessary eye-hand co-ordination. Receptive language can be tested by giving directions and observing the child's ability to carry them out. If one says, "Give me the pencil," and the child hands one a ball, it is likely that he does not understand what is said to him and that he is responding to the extended hand since he understands only that the examiner wants something. Or if a child is asked a question about what shoes are made of and he says, "My daddy went to work this morning," one may suspect that he has some defect in receptive language. It is altogether possible for a child to have learned to talk by imitation without being able to make sense out of what is said to him. This is closely akin to the "word-caller" in reading. The question arises, "If some of these children are unable to understand what is said to them, could this be why they do not 'mind' when given a direction?"

This is a major area of concern in instruction. Just as awareness of form is rooted in visual perception, so are speech and language largely rooted in auditory perception. Auditory perception leads one to select out of the total mass of auditory stimuli certain groups of sounds, each of which has a unique quality. Thus one learns to recognize the song of a bird, the sound of the wind in the trees, the ringing of the telephone or front door bell. Still other combinations of sounds come to have significance because they form the sounds of speech. These clusters become the symbols of language as words, phrases, and sentences.

In order to perceive Gestalts or patterns of speech, one must call upon auditory memory to hold these sound units in mind. If auditory memory is poor, the individual finds it difficult to recognize the speech sounds individually and almost impossible to remember the longer series of sounds which make up the word, phrase, and sentence. As the infant develops he learns to distinguish between sounds; he learns to repeat them, combine them, and give them meaning. Through this developmental process he eventually learns to make fine distinctions between *pat* and *pot; God* and *dog;* among *pin, pen,* and *pan.*

Looking at auditory perception this way, it is possible to see how a child can achieve a perfect audiogram in a pure-tone audiometer test and still be able to understand speech. There are no complex patterns of sound in the test for him to analyze; there is no background noise to attract his attention. The child has ears that hear, but he has not learned to attach association to the sounds of speech he hears.

This, then, is the heart of the language problem with nonachieving children. As it was found necessary to discover the level of ability in visual perception and help develop the missing steps, so is it necessary to fill in the gaps in auditory training before one can expect to get the sound discrimination necessary for phonetic training in reading. So one must build receptive language and expressive language to the point where one normally expects language to be when a youngster is handed his first book.

PROCEDURES

Determine the Child's Needs

When a child has been referred because of behavior or learning disability or both, it is essential that every bit of available information be gathered about him. There are four areas in which information is needed.

1. The *family history* should be gathered by a social worker or pupil-personnel worker who is trained in dealing with the home. The teacher will want to have her interview with the parents, but usually parents are reluctant to give intimate data to the person who will work with the child. The teacher's chances of working with the parents for the good of the child will be better if she does not get too involved with them at this level. The family is an important source of information, and it may be necessary to inform the social worker of the type of developmental information that is desired for understanding the child's problems.

2. The *medical history* should include information about prenatal, birth, and postnatal factors. This may include psychiatric evaluation also. The Health Department is the proper agency to work with in this area. The school nurse is an invaluable resource when she knows the kind of help and information that is desired. She can call the family physician or ask the school physician to get the information. Doctors are reluctant to give confidential history to school personnel; but when authorized by the parents to release information, they will give it to the School Health Physician who is then in position to interpret the findings. The School Health authorities should be thoroughly familiar with the program for these children so that they will be in a position to work with the school.

3. The *psychological testing* should be done before the child is considered for special handling and teaching. When the psychologist knows the type of information desired and why it is desired, he is most helpful in discussing developmental deviations and the needs of the child. The teacher will be infinitely more helpful to the child if she can learn to communicate her needs to the psychologist. If she convinces him that she is more interested in mental age and deviations from the norm rather than IQ, if she asks him what the test data mean in relation to this particular child or group of children—then both the psychologist and the teacher have learned to help the child.

4. The *school records* are to be studied for any crumb of informa-

tion. Many times previous teachers will add samples of the child's work to explain the latter's frustrations. These should be studied carefully for reversals, spatial relationships, kinds of errors, number of erasures, perseveration, and "unfinishedness." The results of reading readiness tests and other group tests are frequently found in the cumulative records. One should be more concerned with the way in which the final score was achieved rather than with the score itself. Is there a wide range of ability shown? Is there a discrepancy in the language and nonlanguage areas? Was the child retained? Many times the tests show little more than the child's name. This is information nevertheless: the child was not able to take a test. No matter how much or how little information is gathered, the teacher's final decision as to the needs of the child will come as a result of her own observations and testing. This will be discussed in a later section.

Meet the Child's Needs

If the information gathered on the child indicates that he has the characteristics of children either with brain or central nervous system injury, or with developmental deviations—and if it is decided that he is in need of the kind of program suggested here—then it is recommended that he have a quiet, uncluttered spot in which to grow. Because of his hyperactivity, his forced response to the stimuli in his environment, and his confusion of foreground and background, it is best to select a room that is free of extraneous sights and sounds. The preparation of the room will be discussed in the section on classroom management.

Here, then, is the child with all his deviations, his accumulation of failures, and his need for living with himself and his world. Out of all this information, the teacher must determine what he is like *now*. To do this she must consider what is normal for all children at all levels. The child comes to her as an 8-year-old, for example. What things can he do that a normal 8-year-old can do? Which of his activities are like those of a 6-year-old? What are his potentialities and limitations? The proper developmental pattern for *this* child must be worked out. This is a therapeutic process because of his deviations. He must go on as an 8-year-old, but he must have therapy where he deviates. The farther the developmental and therapeutic levels are from each other, the greater become his frustrations. One must take note of his mental age and deviations. He is getting special help because his deviations are so great. Consider the areas in which he is below his mental age; likewise, consider the areas in which he is above his mental age.

A program of instruction must be planned to help overcome the basic and specific dysfunctions which seem to underlie the problems of poor school performance. The program must include work that will develop finer muscular control, eye-hand co-ordination, form perception, and perception of figure-background relationships; it must help in establishing left-right progression and integration of behavioral responses. This is a therapeutic program and as such cannot be justified if the child is allowed to keep on doing only the things he is able to do. One must *lead him through the things he cannot do—step by step up the developmental ladder.* Six factors will help the teacher to start her program.

1. Begin with work where the child is able to succeed.

2. Be sure the child understands what is expected of him. Do more demonstrating than talking. Make directions concise and meaningful.

3. Be consistent. Plan a program with requirements that can be met. The child will find himself, because the teacher has defined his limits clearly and reasonably.

4. Use the child's strengths to correct his weaknesses and to supply the crutches he needs. He will discard them when they are no longer needed.

5. Observe carefully. The child will show when he is ready for the next step, or when he needs to go back.

6. Remember that progress comes slowly. When the child has confidence in himself, he will move ahead. He will learn just as much and just as fast as he can, if the teacher takes her cue from him.

THE TEACHER'S TASK

It has been said that the task in Special Education is to minimize the deviations of each child and bring him to the highest possible level. This kind of teaching offers a tremendous challenge. A word of warning: tension transfers from teacher to children very quickly, and these children have had too much tension all of their lives. This chapter attempts to identify those factors that have made it possible for the teacher to carry out her activities with minimum stress. The teacher must be poised, calm, and objective in the classroom. The discussion that follows is interspersed with the warning to "progress slowly." This means a relaxed pace. The children must not feel hurried.

The teacher should not carry her problems to the teachers' lounge. It is essential to discuss the children constructively. She should share in the whole school program wherever possible and take a fair share of school duties, remembering that she is "special" only in that she has the opportunity to do exciting work. She should share her experiences with other teachers, but not bore them with every detail. They will ask for information as they become interested.

Further, there is the matter of professional ethics. The teacher in Special Education will have more confidential information at her disposal than most teachers have. It should be guarded as a precious possession and should be shared only for the betterment of the child; confidential material will be discussed only with the professional personnel engaged in working with the child's problems.

Much of what the teacher has been trained to do in normal educational situations is reversed with these children. For example, whereas in reading the usual method is to start with the whole word (the Gestalt), in this type of teaching it has been found necessary to begin with the part and build to the whole. The child must be taught to see every part of a word. Because of his inability to grasp the Gestalt, he may fix on only one part of the word. For example, if he has learned the word *family* because of the *y*, it is possible that every word he sees that ends in *y*, such as *Monday, pretty*, and so on, he will call *family*. The *gh* in *eight* may be his clue to this word so that when he sees *high, though, night,* he will call them *eight*.

Normally one does not teach a child to put his finger under each word as he is reading but it is frequently a great help to these children. It may be necessary to go so far as to make a frame for each word so that he cannot possibly see more than one word at a time.

Commercially prepared materials are sometimes very useful. Teachers tear such books apart, cut out the pictures, or use the printed matter without the pictures because these children cannot tolerate the amount of material put on the commercial book page. The list of suggested materials states: "These books are excellent for cutting up." Further, when old books are being discarded from the school stock, they should be treasured for "cutting up." Adaptation of prepared materials is most important.

One can recognize many of the techniques suggested here as "outmoded" according to modern educational theory. But they may be the ones that work with these children.

VARIETY IN TECHNIQUES

The wide variety of techniques found in this chapter is helpful for varying the approach to learning difficulties and for assisting in the development of learning skills. For example:

1. The following techniques have been found helpful in breaking

up patterns of rigidity and perseveration. Drill on such things as number combinations helps to develop meaningful automatization. If perseveration persists in spite of the use of varied drill techniques, it is well to substitute another activity for a time and then return to the subject later.

2. When dealing with a short attention span, it is helpful to give short assignments. For example: only the number of arithmetic problems that a child can handle is put on his paper; thus he is able to finish the entire assignment because it is within the range of his attention span.

3. Utilize all of the senses in the approach to learning. The child learns through using his whole body and self.

4. Motor disinhibition can be used to the child's advantage by providing materials of learning which involve muscular movement, such as the abacus and peg boards.

CLASSROOM MANAGEMENT

Preparation

CHOICE OF CLASSROOM

If there is an opportunity to choose a classroom for this special group of children with specific learning disabilities, there are several things to be taken into consideration.

It should be located away from the main work and play areas of the school. Hence, a room on an inner court would be best. Opaque windows are desirable; these can be made by painting over the lower part of the window. Venetian blinds are very distracting; window shades that blow about can ruin an otherwise peaceful environment. Opaque glass should be on the doors to the hall, also.

Color appears to be an important factor. The experimental classes of the study were held in rooms whose walls and fixtures were painted the color of the school furniture. One room happened to have a tile floor that was almost a perfect match. The room was so free of stimulation that observers had to struggle to stay awake. The only contrasting note was the chalkboard, and this made it possible to hold attention there when it was in use. The control rooms were regular schoolrooms: one was in an old building; the other was in a modern one.

Although class size may vary, a room should be large enough so that busy hands and feet cannot reach out to touch anyone; but it should be small enough to keep stimuli to a minimum. There should also be several work areas available. Because they need to feel that limits have been set, a room that is too large can be just as unsettling to these disturbed children as one that is too small. The teacher should avoid using an "all-purpose" room unless arrangements are made for partitioning it to appropriate size.

Other distractions are cut down if the room has an adjoining bath, sink, and drinking facilities.

Lighting and heating equipment should be of a high quality. Flickering lights or banging radiators are distracting.

ROOM EQUIPMENT

In spite of the blandness of such a neutral environment, the group situation itself may be disturbing for some children. Those children may be moved to the edge of the group by facing their work tables against a wall. Strauss and Lehtinen (2) explain that the reason for the separation is explained to the child in such a way that he understands that its purpose is constructive rather than punitive—that it is meant to help him "work better where other children won't disturb him." In dealing with a very hyperactive and disinhibited child these authors "have even resorted to the expedient of isolation behind a clinic screen."

The present study advocates going a step further and having a cubicle for each child. This procedure was followed in the experimental classes. All children could not tolerate the enclosure and worked better with the desk-to-the-wall arrangement, but this was the exception rather than the rule. Each child had his "office" where he went to do his work free of distraction. Each child seemed to know when he needed to withdraw from a group and do his work there. These cubicles were in no sense punitive. The child could "calm down and be happier when . . . alone."

The teachers of the control groups created blank walls with chart racks and other natural barriers for the children who seemed to need isolation. It would be an advantage to have folding screens in a classroom where cubicles were not available. The lighting must be adequate in the cubicle areas.

Cabinets. Enclosed cabinets and other storage space are particularly important for eliminating extraneous stimuli. The experimental rooms had cabinets built-in, so that each child had a place of his own to keep his work, a place where work could be placed out of sight. The rooms had ample shelf space in the closets and files. The importance of such equipment cannot be overstressed because only the work being used is in sight at any time.

The teachers of the control group did not have cabinets. One teacher put an extra chair beside each child's desk for his work; the other used a large table with a box for each child.

Furniture. It is important that all furniture be designed to fit the child. Tops may be put over the desks so that there will be a large working area. For group activities trapezoidal tables may be supplied. This makes an ideal working situation because the teacher can be within arm's reach of several children.

The formica top of such a table makes an excellent work surface for many activities. One can readily see from the examples (Figure 8) the

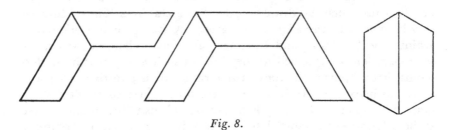

Fig. 8.

possibilities for arrangements which provide for a controlling position for the teacher and which provide enough separation for the children.

Blackboards. Black chalkboards with yellow or white chalk are preferred. Blackboards are kept free of daily schedules and old work. Only the work being attended to at the moment is placed on these boards.

Bulletin boards. Such bulletin boards as are regularly installed in rooms should not be used for displaying the children's work until late in the school year and then only for a specified time. They can be covered. In the experimental rooms, cubicles were built in front of the bulletin boards. Bulletin boards in the hall outside the room are most satisfactory for display of class work because they make it possible for everyone to share in the children's activities.

INSTRUCTIONAL EQUIPMENT

The teachers in the experimental classes were privileged to have the following items for their own use, and they considered them indispensable: record player, tape recorder, filmstrip projector with tachistoscope attachment, full-length mirror, typewriter with primary type.

The following items should be accessible in the school: records, piano, metronome, rhythm instruments, mats, autoharp, tone blocks, movie projector, opaque projector.

INSTRUCTIONAL MATERIALS

A suggested list of instructional materials is noted below. The use of these materials will be discussed in the appropriate context. The items listed here will be mentioned in the succeeding sections on method: colored one-inch cubes and quarter-inch cubes, large and small wooden beads, mosaic color blocks, parquetry blocks, large dice blocks, pegs and peg boards, puzzles, magnets and magnet boards, large pocket chart, seat pocket charts, flannel board, abacus (one for each child, specially constructed so that beads can be removed), ten's board, hundred's board, number rack, numerous teacher (or parent) prepared gadgets, picture stamps, workbooks to cut up for pictures, print set for words and pictures; "Magic Markers," individual jars of paste and brushes, specially prepared paper (See Fig. 41, p. 200), books and workbooks (these are discussed in detail in the section on reading).

TEACHER-ASSISTANT

Because of the children's hyperactivity and motor disinhibition, and because of the need for constant and close supervision, an assistant is highly desirable. The assistant needs a personality and an understanding similar to the teacher's. The assistant is a teacher at heart, but does not have the professional training and experience that make her eligible for the position.

The assistant is there to help the teacher achieve her goal—to carry the child to the highest possible social and achievement level. It is important that the teacher take the time to explain the reasons the children act the way they do and why she handles the program the way she does. Errors in judgment were made when an assistant felt the teacher was being too strict with children. When she had them alone for a "break," she thought it would be nice if they had some fun. If she had been briefed on the teacher's reason for handling the children as she did, she would not have lost her effectiveness with the group.

In this project the children recognized that the teacher was the authority figure. They also recognized that the assistant was one who was there to help them, and that they were to do for her exactly what they would do for the teacher. Consequently, it is important that the assistant be a co-operative person. The children are quick to sense any conflict and take advantage of it.

Usually the assistant spent a good part of her time preparing materials for class use. As she learned the class procedures, she was most helpful in working with individuals or taking a group for an activity so that the teacher could do individual work or have a brief rest period.

If the school budget does not allow for an assistant, it is possible to use willing parents to assist in preparing materials. They should work on the materials at home because the children should not be aware that they are in the building. At no time would it be considered wise to have a parent of one of the children as an assistant in the room; should she come to school to get her assignment or deliver materials, it should be at the end of the school day so that there is no opportunity for a break in the day's routine or the emotional tone of the school setting.

The "homeroom mother" can be of great assistance to the teacher by telephoning to explain any change of schedule, planning holiday parties, and so on.

School Begins for the Teacher

The class has been assigned, the room has been selected and equipped, the materials are in place, and the teacher reports to school to make her final preparations. The beginning of the school year with this class should be different from the same period in other classes. Most of these children have had a traumatic experience with school—at least with group experiences. Whatever their past experience has been and whatever their reaction to it has been, they have been told that they are going to a different kind of class. Consequently, arrival at school should be different from their past experience. Furthermore, the teacher has a different kind of job to do. She must find out for herself what the child's educational needs are, so that she can begin at the proper place for each child.

It is to be hoped that when the administration of the school system has agreed to set this type of class in operation, they have understood the problem and the program projected and they will permit flexibility in the scheduling of such a class. If one thing has stood out clearly in the research classes of this study, as well as in experimental classes held in other areas of the country, it is the method which has proved most satisfactory for getting the school year off to a good start: the method of bringing in one or two children at a time. In this way the teacher can study them, test them, and get them working at their level before the next ones come to school. This is a point that must be understood and agreed upon by the parents when a child is accepted for placement.

If the teacher has had a part in selecting the personnel of the class, she will be familiar with the children, will have studied all of the data, and will know which ones she wants to take first. Otherwise it will be necessary for her to study the data that have been gathered for her before she can make out a schedule. She will want to consider which children she can probably guide easily to a degree of independent work. For as she brings one child to the place where he can take his day's work and attend to it with a minimum of help, she will be ready for the next. When she has made out a schedule for the order in which she will take the children, she will call the parents. It is to be understood that appointments cannot be made far in advance because, until the teacher and child have begun to work together, she has no idea how long it will take. There have been classes in which this reception program went on for six weeks. The teacher must be convinced that what she is doing is for the best of all of the children because she will have to keep reassuring the parents of the latest arrivals that in this way their children are really going to profit the most.

School Begins for the Parent and Child

An appointment is made for the parents (preferably both of them) to bring the child in. The parents must understand that their presence is required; no exceptions can be permitted. The purposes of the conference are as follows:

1. to establish rapport with parents and child,
2. to relieve any misapprehension,
3. to observe the child's relationship with his parents,
4. to explain the school program, and to familiarize the child with the classroom environment,
5. to suggest attitudes to be established at home,
6. to get further information needed to complete the picture of child,
7. to answer parents' questions, and
8. to inform the parents regarding the nature and purpose of the conference.

THE PARENT CONFERENCE

Parents of hyperactive and brain-injured children have had many, many conferences regarding their children. They are often defensive and insecure. Guilt feelings are frequent. It is important that the teacher try to put the parents at ease and to let the parents feel that educators too are still seeking answers to many of the problems which the children present. It is important that during the initial contact between parents and teacher the former have an ample opportunity to discuss their feelings about the child to the teacher.

It is also important to make certain tests to establish the child's level of performance. By the time the parents conference has been completed the parents may be very comfortable because they knew all the time that their son could not do these things for which he was tested. There will be other parents who will explain that the child was just nervous, not used to the teacher, and consequently did not perform up to his ability. "He knows all of those things. He has played with those things all of his life. There really isn't anything wrong with Joe at all." The teacher may need to ask the parents why the child has been assigned to this group.

This is the point at which a careful explanation of the program must be given. The parents should be made to understand that school people do not yet have all of the answers. "This approach to learning problems has worked out very well with many children, and we think this will help your child. We will do everything in our power to meet his needs, but we never make any guarantees. Many people have spent many, many hours studying your child so that we may use the best possible professional skill to help him. We ask two things: one, that you have confidence in us, knowing that if this does not work out, we will be the first ones to say so; two, that you give us your full co-operation."

The parents' part in the program may be explained in the following terms:

1. to understand the child's needs and meet them;

2. to recognize his need for acceptance as he is and not pressure him for high scholastic attainment;

3. to become a good listener and observer in order to find out what the child is really like. "Do not ask him what he has done at school because he probably can't tell you. You will learn through observation and listening."

4. to call the school when there are questions about the school program or child's progress, asking that the teacher call at her convenience;

5. to help the child to become independent by not overprotecting him and permitting him to do as much for himself as he can;

6. to attend all conferences and meetings that the school feels are important.

At this point during the parent conference the parents are informed of the fact that the teacher desires to get acquainted with the child and to have him spend a sufficient period of time with her so that she may obtain an initial understanding of the child's strengths and weaknesses. An appointment for this meeting is made, and the child is brought to the teacher at the designated time.

This conference is child-centered because this is his school and is his schoolroom; he is to feel a part of it right from the start. Even though he has learned to react to situations with a shout of bravado, basically he is very uneasy about the situation. As soon as possible he should be told that this is "a get-acquainted time" and the testing and observation should begin.

One does not sit with pencil and paper to write down every word. The child, however, is used to school tests by this time, and he must know that the teacher needs to put things down on paper so that she can remember all about him. Notes taken during this period are important for later observation of progress. Questions of a personal nature are likely to make him very uncommunicative, so it is probably better to begin a task that is easy and fun for him.

Throughout the testing, watch for preferred hand, co-ordination (walking, writing, and so on), fatigue, distractibility, and perseveration. Also observe speech and understanding of directions.

If a child fails a task, the teacher must ask herself, "Why?"

Did he understand what was expected of him?

Were too many elements presented at once?

Was the material too distracting?

Did the activity lack structure, so that foreground could be confused with background?

Was the child's perception fragmented?

Did he lose sight of the whole by fixation on details?

Did he seem to understand but fail because of perseveration?

Sorting. Sorting colors: Put two small boxes and a number of blocks of different colors on the table in front of the child. Put a red block in one box and a blue one in the other. Ask him to "put all the blocks like this in this box and all the blocks like this in this box." If he is not able to do it, do not correct him (he is being tested, not taught); try another pair of colors. If he is unable to select two colors from many, try putting just the two colors of blocks before him.

Sorting forms: Use the same technique as for color but use differently shaped beads, parquetry blocks, or the form cards as in Figure 13 and have him sort according to form.

Eye-hand co-ordination. For copying forms make a set of test cards. Use 4 by 6 inch cards and put each of the following forms on a separate card with heavy black lines (Figure 9). They are arranged in order of

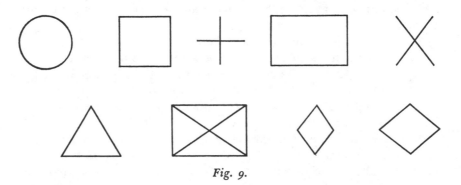

Fig. 9.

difficulty. The square is a test at the 5-year level, the diamond at the 7-year level.

Give the child a sheet of paper and a crayon or pencil and have him copy the forms as you present them one at a time. Observe how he gets his results.

Does he need help with vertical, horizontal, or oblique lines? Is he able to make corners, to make lines come together? Inability to perform in this area may indicate need for peg board and stencil work.

Puzzles. Give him a complete puzzle. Can he tell you what the picture is? Take out the pieces and ask him to work it. If this seems too complicated, try him out on one of the puzzles in Figures 14 and 15.

Peg board design. Set up a peg board with the design seen in Figure 21. Give him another peg board and pegs, and let him copy the design. Try to take note of the way this test is performed. Does he work in an organized way, or are the pegs put in at random? After he feels that he has completed his work, remove his board and ask him to "draw a picture" with the teacher's model present. Observe closely the sequence and direction in which the lines were drawn. The young normal child, or the familial type of mentally retarded, characteristically work in an orderly and continuous sequence of placement of the pegs along the outlines of the pattern. The brain-injured child or the child with visuo-motor disturbance works in a discontinuous and incoherent fashion. He may start or stop at any point in the pattern, placing the pegs in a sporadic and erratic fashion without regard for continuity or the squares of the pattern.

If he cannot handle this particular peg design, it indicates his need to work with peg boards. The next step is to find his work level in this area.

Parquetry designs. Have him do a parquetry design as described and illustrated in Figures 25, 26, and 27.

Coloring. Present a page torn from a coloring book and ask him to color it. Can he stay within the lines? Does he have any sense of form? If he is unable to stay within the lines, stencil work is advised.

Writing. "Can you write your name on these papers for me?" "Can you spell any words that you would like to write for me?" Watch the way he writes. If he can write, note the direction of the strokes. Does he reverse any of the letters? What is the spatial relationship between letters? Have him copy a word written by the teacher.

Language and vocabulary. "How old are you? Where do you live? Do you know your telephone number? What is your daddy's name? What does your daddy do? What is mother's name? Tell me about your pets," and so on. How does he express himself? How does he see his world? Can he tell you a story about something he has seen or done?

Reading. Have him sort letters as described in first steps in reading procedure. Can he see their form? Does he indicate that he knows their names?

Give him words to match to Dolch cards. Can he see the form of a word? This is a good point at which to run through a few Dolch basic vocabulary cards as a check on basic vocabulary.

Give him a story sequence in pictures to see if he can arrange them in the correct order and tell you the story.

Have him tell a story about a picture that you show him, or ask him to relate the story of "The Three Bears," and so on.

If there are indications that he can read or has at least had reading experience, give him appropriate material and question him to see if he understands what he has read.

Arithmetic. Have him count blocks. Observe whether or not he can touch a block for each number.

"How far can you count?" "You know lots of numbers. Give me 3 blocks, 4 red blocks," and so on. Does he have number concept?

Number content questions: "You are alone here today. Monday there will be 5 more boys. Do you know how many there will be then?" "Can you write a 5? An 8?" Have him do sorting with numbers.

These are the areas in which the teacher will seek information so she will know how to plan the first day's work. All of these suggestions will not be used for every child, and usually only a small part of the testing can be done the first time the teacher is with the child. The data will give a clue as to the degree of sophistication she is likely to meet. It is always safest to start testing at a low point because the purpose of this test is to find the level of the child's performance—to find those deviations that have caused the difficulty.

When the child has reached a stopping point, the teacher may give him something from the "free play" materials with which to entertain himself while she terminates this interview with the waiting parents.

Organizing the Work

When the child comes to school alone the first day, the teacher will begin by teaching him school routines. He will learn about the school, will be taken through the daily schedule, will learn where things are and what is expected of him. Testing will continue until the instructional level can be determined and his approximate developmental pattern worked out.

In the beginning most of the child's work will be on a perceptual level. The developmental stages for such activities are presented in the chapter on the instructional program. This will include work with peg boards, color cubes, parquetry blocks, stencils, and puzzles. Some tasks from each of these activities will be included in the daily planning. Such activity will be continued at progressively higher levels as long as there is need for it. When the time comes that no such activity is needed, the child should be ready to move on to a class for normal children or, as his ability indicates, to a special class for children with less severe learning difficulties.

For a child needing a beginning level of work, one day's activities might include the following: sorting color block forms (see p. 166), puzzle (Figure 14), stencil (Figure 18, Stencil a), peg board (Figure 20, Peg Board b), block design (Figure 23).

As the child learns to do more kinds of work, the teacher begins to plan a program that will include some work in each of the following areas: perceptual training, writing, arithmetic, reading.

Two kinds of plans are needed for this class: individual plans and group plans. Teachers have found that having a folder for each child simplifies the individual planning. It will be necessary for some time to plan by the day, though a day will come when plans can be made by the week.

Each child's work will be prepared in advance so that it is ready and waiting for him when he enters the room. He will know where to find it, for the teacher will make sure that he has a place of his own. He will know how to get his material, what to do when he has finished, and where to put it when it is completed.

MANAGING DAILY WORK

With many of these children it will be necessary to give out one piece of work at a time in the beginning. To some, the sight of "all that work" would discourage them, and they would not be able to begin the first piece. In order to reduce distractions the teacher must take the work to the child. His greatest need may be to learn to stay in one place until a task is completed.

It is important that the teacher see that the child succeeds with each task. If the child becomes frustrated, the teacher needs to stay close by and see him through. When such a situation arises she should ask herself:

1. Did anything happen before the child left home, or on the bus?
2. Has anything happened in the room?
3. Is he testing me?
4. Was the work too hard?

She may need to change to an activity that will divert him so that he does not perseverate in his behavior pattern.

KEEPING RECORDS OF DAILY WORK

Too much emphasis cannot be put upon the importance of anecdotal records. Whenever the child makes a response worth noting, if the situation permits, it should be written down immediately and *dated*. Noting the time may be important also; for example, if a child has an emotional outburst at the same time every day, it may be necessary to change his schedule. Observations may be put on the planning sheet or kept in a notebook with a page for each child (see Figure 10).

Records of this type are important for several reasons. First, it is a guide to the teacher and a morale booster; she can see where she has come from when she feels that no progress has been made. A later problem may have its answer in earlier records.

Progress reports are frequently requested by a supervisor, principal, or doctor. These records make it possible to write a meaningful report. In the parent conference, or in reporting to parents, such records make objective reports possible and believable.

The best record of any child is his own work. It has been found best to keep samples of these papers for the parents as an over-all view of

Mary Smith
Age: 7 years, 6 months
Perceptual:

9/9/57	Simple peg design—1 color—2 sides. No difficulty.
9/10/57	Color within black crayoned lines. Terribly upset. Insisted on scribbling alone. May need to drop this activity. Try stencils.
9/20/57	Block designs—6 blocks—2 colors. No difficulty.

Writing:

9/12/57	Tracing colored lines. Well executed.
9/30/57	Tracing half-rounds in black. Go back to color. How well does she see? May want to refer for visual evaluation.

Arithmetic:

9/16/57	Matching domino configurations. Gave too many. Try with 1 and 4.

Phonics:

9/20/57	No sense of sound discrimination. Work on auditory perception. Confer with speech therapist.

Motor:

9/18/57	Couldn't hop on either foot. Tried jumping. Appears afraid to leave floor.

Fig. 10. Example of anecdotal record.

the child's work. Sending work papers home seldom accomplishes any real purpose unless the parent can understand what is being accomplished and what they mean in terms of the child's development.

SETTING THE PATTERN FOR A DAY'S WORK

A carefully planned schedule for the day's activities must be made and adhered to. Consistency in the program helps the child to become organized. He is no longer anxious or fearful of what is to come next because he knows what is expected of him, how to do it, and when. When the routines of the day are set, the environment becomes a quiet background. The foreground is the task at hand. He learns exactly where to put his coat, hat, the material he uses, and his finished work. He learns what to do first, second, third.

The teacher must be consistent in her demands; what is expected one day is expected every day. The tasks given to the child are within his abilities, so he can be expected to succeed. Her instructions must be structured, brief, and clearly understood. She is firm but supportive. She supervises as closely as possible and checks every piece of work as it is finished. The child will learn to wait his turn at his seat until she can get to him. She has him correct his mistakes unless it appears that the task has been too difficult for him, in which case she gives help and makes a note that the next project must be within his range. Each task is finished correctly before he goes on to the next. He must learn the sense of accomplishment of a job well done.

Time limits may help the structuring and speed up activity. Arithmetic must be finished by morning recess; writing by lunch time, and so on.

Teaching the Class

Up to this point the individual has been emphasized. The teacher will take advantage of every situation to teach to the individual's needs, and one of his greatest needs is to be a member of a group. The most difficult problem the teacher has when she begins in this type of program is to meet the needs of the individuals and still maintain a class structure. "What is their common denominator? How can I make a class out of these emotionally disturbed, hyperactive, aggressive, acting-out children?"

One of the chief reasons for bringing the children in one or a few at a time has been to teach the rules of the class, build the group slowly, and keep the situation controlled as the teacher builds. The schedule for the day will be carefully planned to include some activities that will be interesting for all and within the range of every child's capabilities. In the beginning all activities will be very highly structured. There will be no question in anyone's mind about what is to be done. The teacher doesn't ask, "Would you like to do so and so today?" At this stage these children do not really know what they want to do; they need to be told. No question arises about succession of turns. A system should be developed for selecting leaders, for example. One successful method is to make a name card for each child with a number on it. The cards are rotated so that each child knows who is to be leader for the day.

Outdoor play periods need to be planned. The children should know before they go outside what they are going to do. It has been found helpful to perform an activity inside before going out. Limits must be known and understood.

"Are these children never to have any free play?" The goal is to develop controls from within, but first they must learn to follow controls from without. With decreased interference from disturbances comes an increased responsiveness to the learning situation. Control of behavior makes learning possible; knowledge gained makes possible more effective control of behavior. The measure of how far the group can go in free play or in games is the ease with which they can be brought under control again. If the excitement perseverates, they have gone too far. The controls must be rigid at first, just as the room must be free of all distractions.

Group Activity

Each of these children needs to strengthen his self image, his sense of personal worth. Until he is comfortable with himself, it is not likely that he can be successful in peer relationships. It is necessary to set up the room so that he is not distracted by the other children. As he grows in stature with himself, he will be able to move in with his peers. There are times in the day when almost everybody does the same thing at the same time. *Listening time* will draw in most of the group at the beginning. *Lunch time* will find most of them wanting to be a part of the group. The teacher will watch carefully for every clue that the outsider wants to move into the group. She will watch for signs of a friendship blossoming that can be encouraged as a move toward group activity. Two can be considered a group for instructional purposes. For some, a group activity lasting five minutes indicates real progress.

The use of the film strip projector has proven to be a most successful device for working with the class as a whole. In the darkness of the room, the projected story is important to the most withdrawn child. He can move toward the group without feeling that anyone is noticing him. The use of a darkened room also significantly further reduces environmental visual stimuli.

The tape recorder has likewise proven a good instrument for developing group activity. Teachers find that having the children sit on the floor in a group for such activity works well if each child sits on his own mat. In this way they have to keep a distance between them that discourages intermingling of busy hands and feet.

One of the best periods in the day for developing group feeling is the *lunch period*. "We eat together. We talk together. We work together (setting the table, stacking dishes, trays, sorting silver). We learn about health. We learn about manners." This program should be structured as carefully as the rest of the day. If an assistant takes over occasionally to give the teacher a rest, it will be with understanding of the purposefulness of the lunch activities.

Other activities that are conducive to group work are counting, language development, auditory training, telling time, work in art or music, motor training and trips.

The presence of a teacher-assistant makes it possible to do a more successful job. The assistant can take care of one individual while the teacher is working with a group. It has been found helpful to have an "acting-out" child taken from the room for a period of time until he can calm down.

The Special Class as Part of the School

When a principal accepts this type of special class for his school, he does it with the understanding that the children are in this group because they have not been able to conform to the usual school routines. It may be necessary for the teacher to further his understanding by explaining the nature and needs of these children. Since this class is therapeutic, one of the goals is to help the children overcome their difficulties so that they can gradually move back into a regular program. It is hoped that the school will welcome them to all activities when they are ready. The teacher should be free to develop a schedule that meets the needs of the children rather than the routines of the school. Such a group may not be ready for elaborate opening exercises with the salute to the flag, a patriotic song, and so on. They need to be readied for this activity. A school assembly may undo days of work and personal growth in the structured classroom. The cafeteria experience can be so stimulating that the children who walked in quietly are wildly excitable for the rest of the day. These children should be permitted to have their lunch in the classroom, using this as part of their educational program. It is often necessary for this group to have a different time for outdoor play or a protected area on the playground because of the distractions and noise. Principals are most sensitive to these needs and are helpful in arranging such variations in schedule.

Two exceptions to rigidly kept routines are fire drills and air raid drills. Tolerance for safety routines must be built up. Understanding the purpose and extra practice in knowing exactly what to do and where to go fit in with the children's structured program. With proper training, the deviation in routine has seemed to inspire them to adhere to this kind of active regimentation with pride, and they have given excellent performances. The teacher will need to expect behavior interruptions in the children after returning to the classroom following these emergency drills.

The teacher will want to enlist the aid of the principal in limiting interruptions of class activity. Visitors, including parents, should be strictly limited in the early months. Parents will be invited for observation when the teacher feels that the individuals in the group are ready. The usual visiting week in November is probably too soon for a new class. On the other hand, the teacher will want the children to learn to accept professional personnel—such as the principal, psychologist, supervisor, or speech therapist—who are part of the team working for the children. Children can learn to accept these people as part of the environment and continue with their activities if the teacher can also accept their presence without comment. In one class the teacher preferred to have the speech therapist come to the room for the children. When the therapist entered the room, she would walk to the child wanted and touch him on the shoulder. All but one child accepted this without notice—all but Jane who has been mentioned before. Jane did not go out for speech, but she resisted the departure of any other child. "You can't have John. I won't let you have him!" Jane, too, finally learned to accept this interruption as part of the routine. This was as important a part of Jane's learning as any other activity.

MATERIALS OF INSTRUCTION

The responses of children with perceptual problems can be directed or organized through the use of special instructional material and devices. The way these materials are constructed depends upon the particular problems each child possesses. One must not mistake the devices and materials for the method itself. Although the materials are used extensively, they are but one means of reaching the child. Unless the teacher thoroughly understands the child's problem and knows what she hopes to accomplish by using a teaching device, she will have little success. No matter how many ideas are presented here, the teacher must always be alert to the need for a new device that will reach a particular child. No school, no classroom, no instructional materials are of any value without the teacher. She is the core of the program.

Many of the materials for training eye-hand co-ordination will be seen to be similar to the educational toys designed for the preschool level. They include peg boards, puzzles, form boards, stencils, blocks, and so on. In the regular classroom these materials are usually on the leisure-time activities shelf; not so here. These are *materials of instruction* and should be given to the child for a definite reason. At no time is he to be allowed to "play" with them in the classroom. Children ready for school activities are assumed to have visuo-motor skills, perception of spatial relationships, sound discrimination, and language skills fairly well developed. Testing has shown, however, that many of these children are at a very low level perceptually. Hence, teaching must begin at a pre-academic level, i.e., learning to distinguish *form* and *sound*.

It has frequently been pointed out that no two children are on the same level of development. Therefore, all the steps suggested in this chapter may not be needed for all children. To be on the safe side, it is better to take nothing for granted, but to start all children at a low level. Materials interestingly created will attract even the most sophisticated 8- or 9-year-old, and with them he may have his first experience of success in a school setting.

Goals in the Preparation of Teaching Material

The teacher tries to provide motor activity which engages the child directly in his task and which fixes his attention on the process involved. She tries to create materials that are self-tutoring, so that the child is helped to become independent of the teacher. She designs materials that are free of unnecessary detail, that do not distract the child, and that enable him to focus his attention on the task at hand. For example, she uses only simple forms. The child is to think of color or form and is not to be distracted by cats, trees, or rabbits.

TEACHING THE CHILD TO CO-ORDINATE EYES AND HANDS

The teacher will probably find most of these children inadequate in visual discrimination. If they cannot distinguish forms such as squares, triangles, and circles, it will be almost impossible for them to do formal work in reading, writing, and arithmetic. The teacher must, therefore, find very elementary tasks for the children to do, tasks which will develop their ability to perceive shapes and forms in a more definite way—tasks which help them to see the whole of a picture instead of only a part of it and which are so simple that they can be performed successfully.

Sorting Color and Form

COLOR [4]

"It has been found that color perception and responsiveness to color remain intact in spite of the severest disturbance of perceptual and general integration. . ." (3, p. 137). Thus the teacher can rely heavily upon color as a means of reaching these children.

For example, cut 2-inch squares of colored construction paper, using only the 6 primary and secondary colors, and mount them on cardboard (see Figure 11). Have the child sort them according to color.

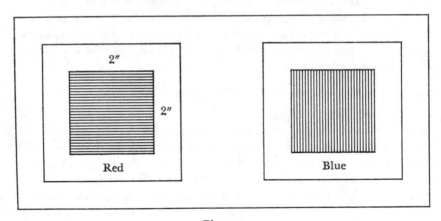

Fig. 11.

Make colored dominoes (without spots), using 2-inch squares cut from construction paper (again only the 6 primary and secondary colors), and mount them on cardboard strips 2 by 4 inches (see Figure 12; these cards are identical to the cards of Set B, described in the section on Arithmetic). The child is shown how to match color to color, as in dominoes.

BLOCK FORMS

Use large nursery beads. Give the child 2 or 3 red square beads and 2 or 3 blue round beads, for example. Have him sort them according

---

[4] The use of colors as illustrated in this section should not be construed to mean that the color will always be used in the same position and direction. Variation of position, color, and direction is important from day to day.

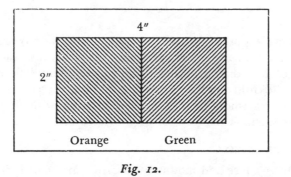

Fig. 12.

to color. To enlarge on this activity, add additional shapes in different colors, and perhaps use parquetry blocks as well. At a later stage, mix the colors within the shapes: red, blue, and yellow squares, for example. And finally, plan other similar sorting activities according to shape.

PAPER FORMS

Cut squares, circles, and triangles (see Figure 13) from colored construction paper, and mount them on cardboard. Have all the square blue, all circles red, and so on, then mix them together. The child is then asked to sort them according to shape; the color becomes only a clue.

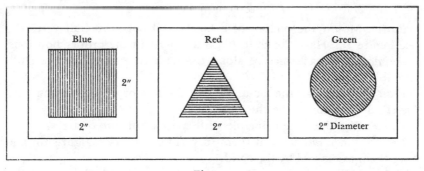

Fig. 13.

Have each shape cut in *different* colors. Mix them, and have the child sort them according to shape; now the color offers no clue.

Finally, have all shapes cut in the same color, and ask the child to sort them according to shape. Do not use more shapes than he can handle.

Puzzles

Teacher-made puzzles (geared to reduce dissociation) are more successful than commercial puzzles at this point because they have the simplicity of line that is needed. The puzzles should be cut in such a way that the child sees the entire picture immediately. He should see the picture as a whole first. (Clean-cut pictures without background may also be used.)

TEACHER-MADE PUZZLES

Faces. Draw a face and mount it on cardboard. Cut it into 2 pieces across, each the same size; into 3 pieces; into several pieces (see Figure 14). Have the child assemble the pieces in each case.

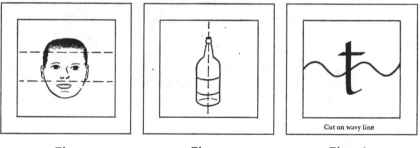

Fig. 14.   *Fig. 15.*   *Fig. 16.*

Bottle. Mount the picture of a bottle and cut it in half vertically (see Figure 15). Have the child place the parts in the proper positions.

Animals. Cut each picture along the neck line and have the child assemble the pieces.

Man with hat. Cut the pictures along the line of the crown and have the child "put the hat on the man."

Circles. Use the same principle with a circle cut into quarters.

Letters and numbers. Cut them in various ways (see Figure 16) and have them assembled by the child.

Colored-pattern squares. Draw several squares with designs similar to those in Figure 17; mount them on cardboard, cut them into quarters, and have the child assemble them.

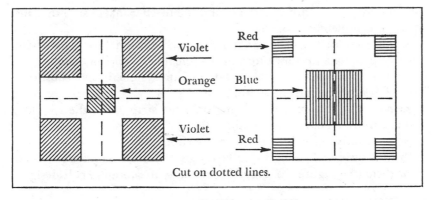

Fig. 17.

COMMERCIAL PUZZLES

Commercial puzzles, from the simplest to the more complex, are useful. Always keep in mind the need for a plain background and the child's need for seeing the whole picture.

Stencils

The first stencils should be made of strips of heavy cardboard or corrugated board, and should not be too small (see Figure 18, a to e).

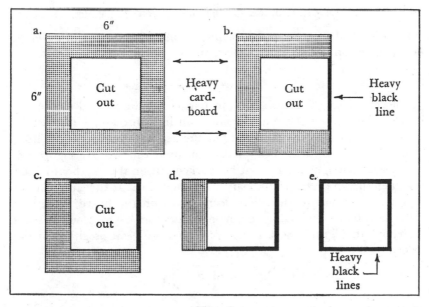

Fig. 18.

The child colors within the frame, and the teacher makes sure that the square is completely colored.

Remove a side strip, making a stencil shaped like a hollow square with one side missing and substitute a heavy line for the missing strip.

Remove the top strip, making an L-shaped stencil, and substitute heavy lines for the missing strips.

Remove the bottom strip, leaving only the strip along the left side, and again draw heavy lines to finish the square.

Now use only heavy lines to guide the child.

Draw a variety of forms, using heavy guide lines, and have the child color them (see Figure 19). Progress gradually to more difficult designs.

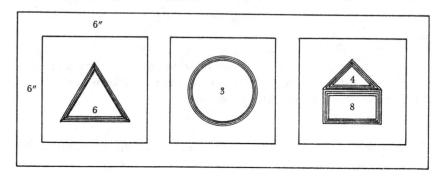

Fig. 19. 3 = Red. 4 = Orange. 6 = Green. 8 = Violet.

Let the child first trace, then color, commercial stencils of animals, birds, and so on. Work from the very simplest to the more difficult.

Peg Boards

Colored designs are made first on paper and then taped to the peg board. The holes must not only be punched through, but must be large enough so that the child can put the peg into the opening. These, too, progress from the very simplest to the more difficult (see Figure 20).

Peg board designs should first be worked out on the peg board itself and then drawn on the chalkboard with solid lines. If the child cannot reproduce the design which has been drawn on the board, have him draw it on paper first. Observe how he draws the design. Does he see it correctly? In Figure 20g, for example, does he see it as either of the below?

An ✕ , or a ⋈ ?

Watch for clues in perceptual problems.

The design the child is to copy is set up on a peg board. Designs similar to those in Figure 20 which the child then reproduces on another peg board may be used.

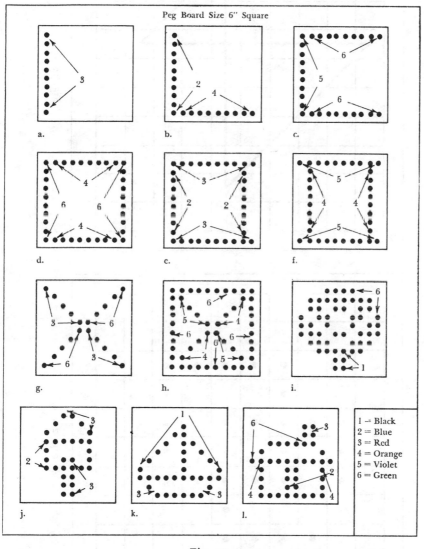

Fig. 20.

The child looks at a design made with dots on paper and works it out on his peg board. Start at his level and work into the more difficult patterns (see Figure 21).

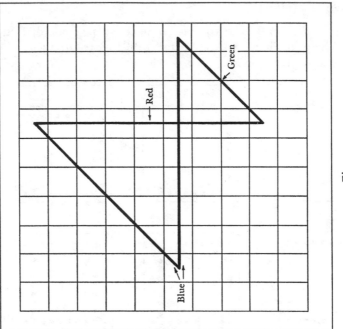

Fig. 22.

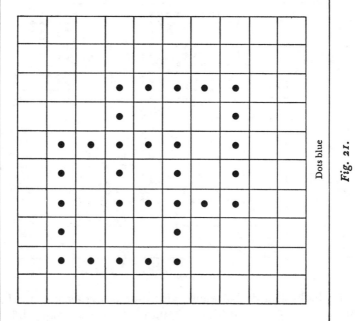

Dots blue

Fig. 21.

The child looks at the design drawn with lines on paper (see Figure 22) and works it out on his peg board. Progress from the child's level to the more difficult (see Figures 27–29).

Block Designs

Use colored 1-inch-cube counting blocks. Make designs using colored inch squares of paper mounted on cardboard. The children use the block cubes flat on their desks to make the designs. If a child places the blocks on top of a pattern, praise him; then ask him if he can make the design on his desk (see Figures 23 to 26).

Use colored 1-inch-cube blocks with various colors on the same block, some sides in solid color, some sides divided into 2 triangles of different colors. The teacher can make designs for these blocks (see Figures 27 to 29), or she may use the designs furnished with the blocks if they are simple enough and large enough for the child.

Parquetry blocks may be used as above. The teacher will make the designs using colored paper blocks mounted on cardboard.

Use colored 1-inch-cube counting blocks in building upright designs from patterns drawn on cardboard by the teacher, the drawings to be first in color, then in black and white (see Figures 30 and 31).

Sorting and Matching

PICTURES

Put like pictures in the same group. Use only as many groups of pictures as the child can handle, working toward more groups of pictures. Use desk pocket chart or small box for sorting and matching. Tell the child, "Put the pictures like this in that row (or box)." Start with pictures that are identical, then with pictures that are similar, and so on.

Source of pictures: "Match Me" picture cards, reading readiness workbooks, and so on.

LETTERS AND NUMBERS

Put like letters or numbers into the same groups, using the number of groups the child can handle (see Figure 32).

1. A's green, B's red, C's orange, and so on.
2. Mixed colors for each letter or number.
3. Make all letters black.

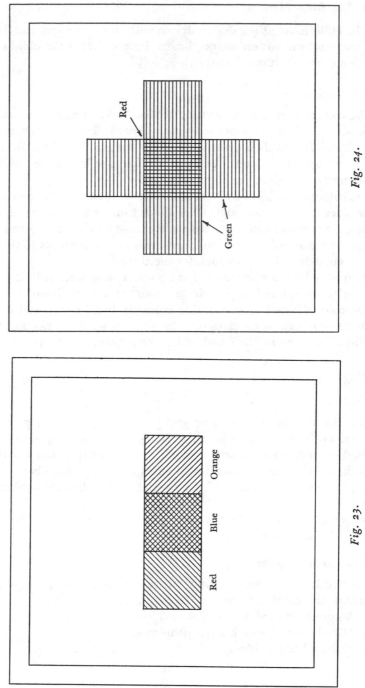

Fig. 24.

Red

Green

Fig. 23.

Red   Blue   Orange

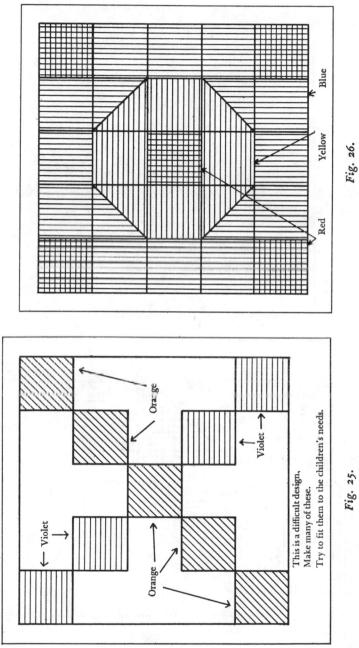

Blue

Yellow

Red

Fig. 26.

Orange

Violet

Violet

Orange

This is a difficult design,
Make many of these.
Try to fit them to the children's needs.

Fig. 25.

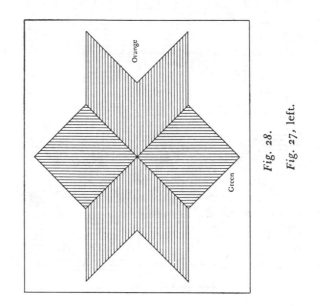

Orange

Green

Fig. 28.

Fig. 27, left.

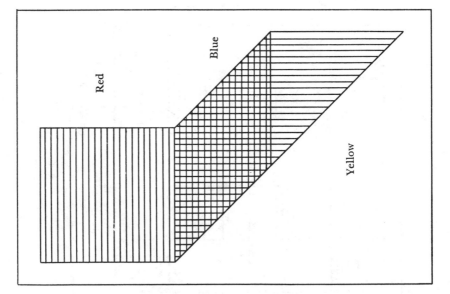

Red

Blue

Yellow

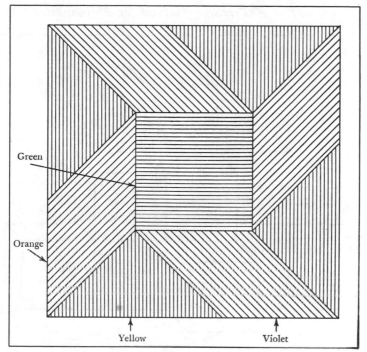

Green

Orange

Yellow   Violet

Fig. 29.

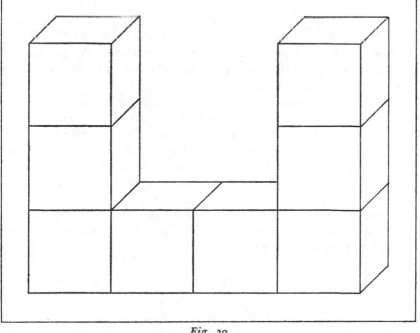

Fig. 30.

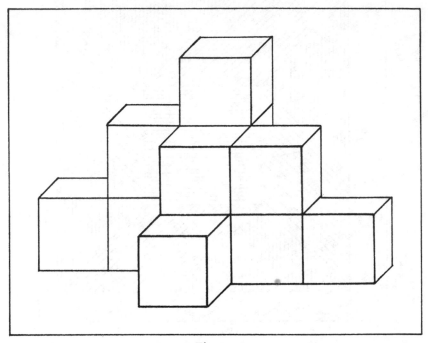

Fig. 31.

Afterimage and Recall

Show the child a card made in color, such as seen in Figures 33a and 33b. Cover the card. Have him reproduce the design on his own blank card. The order of difficulty might be as follows:

The following game is another way to help develop recall:

Show the child 3 objects. Have him identify them, then turn his back. Remove 1 object. Now have him look again, and tell what object is missing. Many objects may be added as the child can handle them.

Expose a picture out of a catalog or magazine which contains a number of familiar objects. Cover it and have the child tell as many things as he remembers seeing.

Have a child look at one of his classmates; then have him turn his back. Now have him tell you the color of shirt the classmate is wearing, the color of his trousers, and so on.

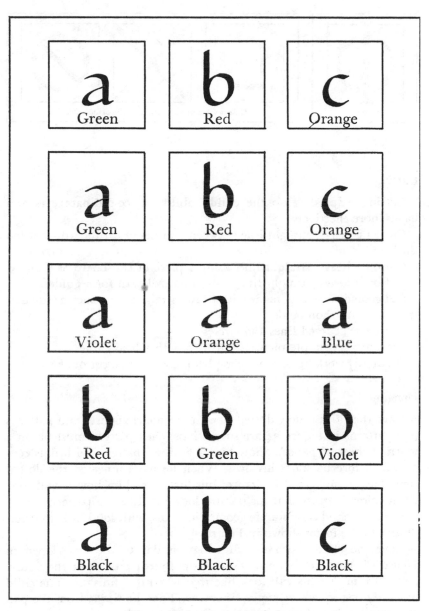

Fig. 32. Make several in each set.

179

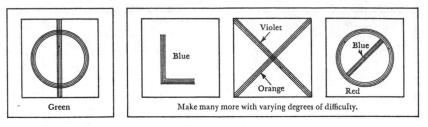

Fig. 33a.   Fig. 33b.

Cutting

Cutting helps develop the child's ability to co-ordinate eyes and hands more effectively.

Cut on a heavy, straight line between 2 pieces of cardboard—not too thick.

Cut on a heavy, straight line, using 1 piece of cardboard as a guide.

Cut on a heavy, straight line, using no cardboard for a guide.

Cut geometric figures made with heavy, straight lines, such as squares, triangles, and rhomboids.

Cut heavy, curved lines and circles.

Cut out very simple pictures outlined with a heavy line.

Gradually work up to more complex pictures to be cut out.[5]

Drawing

Have the child follow dotted lines in geometric figures and patterns (the patterns in Figure 34 are suggestions; each pattern must be on a separate sheet of paper). Show him a finished pattern, with dots connected, before he starts his own. When he has connected the dotted lines, have him color the picture; but first show him how it will look when colored. Insist that his picture look just like the pattern.

Have the child copy simple geometric forms, with solid lines in color, similar to the forms shown in Figure 35.

Have the child reproduce drawings similar to the one shown in Figure 36. First call his attention to the fourth picture of the figure, and tell him that his will look like that when it is finished. The child uses only one square of paper, of course. Then he works from the pattern step by step, the teacher directing the procedure.

---

[5] The pictures may be mounted on cardboard by the child. This helps him establish the foreground-background concept.

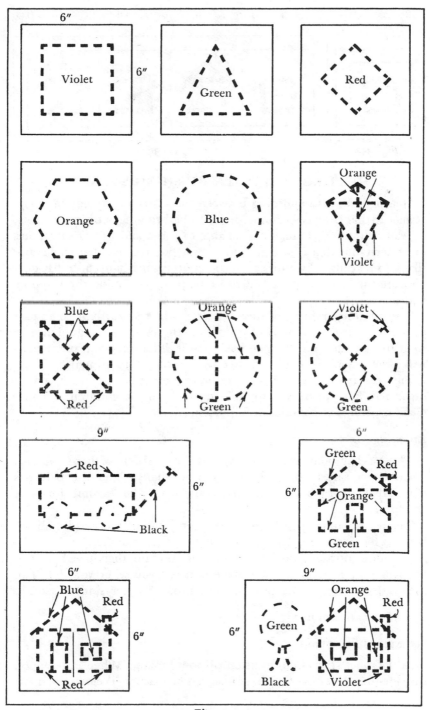

Fig. 34.

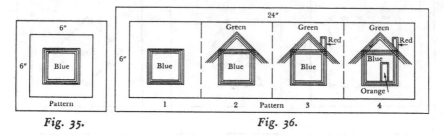

Fig. 35.   Fig. 36.

HEARING AND DISTINGUISHING SOUNDS

Hearing and distinguishing between sounds is a frequent problem. It may be that the child cannot identify a bell ringing, a train whistling, or water running. He may not be able to listen and follow directions, or understand what is said to him. It was pointed out that this is not likely to be caused by a defect in the auditory mechanism, but it does indicate that the child needs definite help in developing the listening abilities.

The auditory training of these children will necessarily become part of the daily program. It is obvious that the child needs guidance in what to listen for, and how to listen for it. The following suggestions will prove useful, but the teacher will think of additional activities as the need arises. Always bear in mind that every activity must be well organized, both to be meaningful and to keep the children in hand. Good control is of paramount importance.

Listening Games

The teacher bounces a ball. The children listen without looking. Then when called on, a child tells how many times the ball was bounced. Two or 3 bounces (perhaps only 1) may be the limit for these children.

The teacher taps a pencil on a desk (2 or 3 times). The children listen without looking and individually give the proper number.

Provide a cup and spoon. Show them to the child, then have him turn his back. Stir in the cup, then have him tell you what you did. Tap the cup, and repeat the process; and provide other similar sounds.

Training with Sounds

DISTINGUISHING SOUNDS

In the room. The children listen without looking. When called upon they identify the sound they have heard. The teacher (1) closes the door;

(2) knocks on the door; (3) rings a bell; (4) blows a whistle; (5) sharpens a pencil; (6) turns on the water, and so on.

On a walk outdoors. Have the children let you know when they hear (1) a bird singing; (2) a dog barking; (3) an automobile motor running; (4) water rippling in a stream.

CONTRASTING SOUNDS

Loud or soft. (1) The teacher walks noisily, then tiptoes; (2) calls attention to a noisy situation and a quiet one (for example, a noisy game on the playground and the rest period).

Fast or slow. (1) The teacher walks rapidly, then slowly; (2) has a child walk fast, then slowly.

High and low. (1) Teacher talks in a high voice, then very low; (2) listen for sound of a whistle and a horn; (3) demonstrate high and low on piano, if possible.

FOLLOWING DIRECTIONS

Give simple directions, such as (1) come here; (2) shut the door; (3) look up; (4) look down, and so on.

Increase the complexity of the directions as the child can handle them. The next step might include two directions, the teacher saying, "I am going to give you two things to do. Listen carefully. One, go sit in your seat; and two, put your head on your desk."

HEARING THROUGH POETRY

Read poetry to the children for sheer enjoyment. As an aid to good listening, the children may pick out the rhyming words.

Read favorites, frequently. Stop and let the children fill in the last words in rhyme.

LISTENING SKILLS THROUGH STORIES

Read a story to the children. Before starting, tell them that they will be asked some questions about the story when it is finished.

MUSIC TO DEVELOP THE ABILITY TO HEAR AND DISTINGUISH SOUNDS

Music is perhaps the first medicine that come to mind when one thinks of developing more discernment in hearing and distinguishing sounds. However, *great care must be exercised in using music or the children will become overstimulated.* If any part of the music program does cause the children to become excited, discontinue its use until you feel the group can handle it. Learning self-control is of prime importance. Music should not be used in the early days of class organizations, but only after the teacher has carefully evaluated the tolerance of the children to these stumuli.

Steps in using music. In the beginning quiet music might be played during the rest period when everyone is already in his place. The teacher will need to evaluate the effectiveness of this music, for it may prove to be a stimulus which some children are unable to accept.

Have the children learn *My Country 'Tis of Thee*. Be sure of the pronounciation of the words. Establish meaning insofar as possible. Listen for rhyming words.

Later the children may gather in a group to listen to a musical story such as *Mary Had a Little Lamb*. Ask the children to find out why the lamb loved Mary so.

Teach *loud* and *soft* through music. A record player could be used here. Play first a loud selection, such as a march. Then play a soft selection, such as a lullaby. Use short selections. You may need to use many variations of the above. Songs can be used to teach *loud* and *soft*. A good song is "Clocks and Watches," from *Music in Our Town*, Silver Burdette.

Use songs in which familiar sounds are imitated, such as transportation songs (*The Train Is Coming Down the Track*), animal imitations (*Old MacDonald Had a Farm*), and others. Do not use these if they are too stimulating, but by midterm the children may be able to handle them. If they can, this type of song adds interest and variety, as well as helping the children to hear with more meaning.

Use songs to establish *high* and *low*. *The Pussy Willow Song* is a good example. Use only hands to show going up and down until the children are stable enough to use their bodies. This may not be for several months. And change "Scat" on the end of the song to "Meow" to hold down excitement.

Rhythms may be used to develop a feeling for *fast* and *slow*. The children may listen to marching music and running music. Later they may beat time to each selection with their two forefingers. Still later they may clap. Show them how to clap *noiselessly*, otherwise, discontinue clapping. And much, much, later they *may* be able to move about the room on tiptoe. Keep body activity down until the group can be controlled in this situation. Introduce it very slowly. The other rhythms (skipping, galloping, and so on) can be presented in much the same way. However, these may not be introduced at all during the first year.

Music has great potential for teaching more than sound discrimination. It can provide individual therapy if handled skillfully. It can promote relaxation, and it provides an ever broadening field of recreation for the child as he grows in his feeling for it. On the other hand, music can be a detriment to learning in some children, if they are not ready for it. Music, of necessity, must be a *group* activity. Some children are not ready for group experiment. Even if a child is not a part of a music activity group, the child cannot avoid the sound stimuli produced by others and tension may result. It is with this reason in mind that the utilization of all music must be approached cautiously.

TOUCH AND SMELL

Developing the Sense of Touch

The sense of touch is frequently underdeveloped in these children. If it is, this is a serious handicap because developmentally the tactual percept precedes the visual percept.

How does the teacher determine if the child does need help in this area? Does he know the feel of soft and hard, smooth and rough, smooth and sticky; of cotton, fur, velvet, leather, wood, metal? If not, then the teacher looks for ways to help him. Following are some suggestions:

Give him a hard block and a wad of cotton (familiar objects). He feels and sees the difference at the same time he says "hard," "soft." It may be necessary to introduce one at a time.

Make up games and riddles with objects. Put objects in view. The child picks up all the hard objects, soft objects, rough objects, smooth objects, and so on.

The child closes his eyes and feels something, then gives the correct description of it as, "It is hard."

The teacher says, "I am thinking of something hard. It is in this room. What is it?"

The child who guesses correctly becomes the leader. See to it that everyone gets a turn.

"Let's name 3 (or 2, or 1)" hard things, soft things, sticky things, furry things, and so on.

Blocks and objects may be identified through touch. Put 2 or 3 differently shaped blocks on a desk. Let the child feel them, look at them, identify them. Now put them inside the desk. The child feels them without looking at them.

1. He names the shapes.
2. He draws the shapes.

Use objects the same way—request drawing only if they are not too difficult for him.

Paste different shapes made of felt on cardboard.

1. The child feels and names one with his eyes open.
2. The child feels and names the same one with his eyes closed.
3. Omit step "1" as soon as possible. Increase the number of objects slowly.

Use flannel board and follow the same procedure as in pasting felt shapes on cardboard.

Make use of raised figures, numbers and letters. First, cut 3 by 3-inch cards. On each card make a number or a letter with glue. Sprinkle with sand and let it dry. Let a child feel a letter or a number without looking at it. Can he tell what it is? If not, let him look at it. Then tell its name.

Next, use a stencil of an animal, or food, or an object. Shellac inside the stencil. Sprinkle with sand and poster paint. When it dries have the child feel it, look at it, if necessary, and name it. Have him name it without looking as soon as possible.

Developing the Sense of Smell

Learn to identify familiar foods such as bananas, apples, chocolate, peanut butter, and so on.

Circumstances can dictate when recognition of odor should be developed.

If there is a cafeteria in the building, let the child guess what is cooking.

It is a matter of safety to be able to identify the odor of gas, smoke, gasoline, and so on. The family can be asked to help in this situation.

Awareness of the odor of flowers, weather, and so on, all serve to heighten perception.

MOTOR TRAINING

Discovering Child's Need for Motor Training

The characteristics of the children under consideration here have been outlined in earlier sections of this monograph. They include the following: little apparent physical malformation, but considerable lack of physical control; emotional involvement as a result of repeated failures to achieve, and striking patterns of misbehavior; and wide gaps in developmental patterns. The gaps may result in infantile behavior in a 7-year-old; in the inability to hop, climb, or run; or in difficulty with "normal" activities such as moving the eyes without moving the head, or pointing in a given direction.

How can the teacher know where these gaps occur? Obviously she cannot study completely each child's developmental pattern. But she can gain insights into a particular child's problems by observing from three points of view.

She will watch closely the physical behavior of each child. She will be alert in standard situations in the classroom, notice which child is likely to bump into desks, drop papers, or move with less than normal gracefulness. She will discover the type of situation the child finds difficult and how often this occurs. One of her richest sources of information will be the free play period, both indoors and on the playground; for this is the time when the child is most himself. What he does, how well or how poorly he does it, and with whom—these facts will tell her a great deal about how old he really is.

She will get clues from his parents. She can gather information about how far he has progressed in caring for himself. She can learn revealing facts about the progress he has made in dressing or bathing himself and in the care he takes of his possessions. She can find out about his play habits and what he does "for fun" at home.

She will look for answers to specific questions. Can he tie his shoes? Can he catch, throw, and kick a ball? Can he open a door by turning the doorknob (one of the children in these groups could not)? Can he climb, hop, skip, jump, and run easily? Can he sort objects? Continuing observation in these areas will supply the teacher with additional valuable clues to gaps in the child's development.

Perhaps no aspect of the job more strongly gives one the feeling of exploring unchartered territory. It may be observed with great frequency that, in general, the children most lacking in elementary physical skills are also the children most handicapped in reading, writing, and arithmetic. As physical skills improve, children relax and seem more competent in academic areas as well.

It is impossible to say to what extent this improvement is due to motor training rather than to other aspects of the learning process. Large blocks of time may be devoted to physical activities (larger than is usual for these age groups: 7 to 9 years), but this seems to bring forth less fatigue and supports more sustained interest in purely academic periods.

Considerable variation in this activity may be expected from one class to another; half an hour daily, in addition to playtime and other physical activities, is the most usual amount. Since the skills required in academic subjects demand intense effort from the children, it follows that frequent changes of activity are helpful. Short periods of time devoted to the activities described below can thus be made to serve a double purpose. The degree of interest and enthusiasm which children usually show for these activities seem to indicate that they are enjoyed not only as breaks in the routine, but also because they introduce skills which the children are eager to learn. In making up a list of large and small muscle activities to meet the needs of a particular child or group, a most useful resource book is one by Prudden (4).

It may also be possible to ask the help of the physical education instructor in working out some parts of the program. A word of warning is in order here. Since the regular physical education program will be planned in terms of chronological ages, the instructor in that program must know the mental and physical age level represented by the special group or child. Probably the teacher can do this best by indicating the motor skills she hopes to develop. She will want games that require only the number and kinds of actions that she feels sure her group can carry out without confusion and excitement—actions that call for only the number and complexity of instructions the children can readily understand.

It is of paramount importance to note that the program of physical activity will not begin until after all the children have made a successful adjustment to the structured daily program and have begun to evidence a degree of success in school achievement. The program will begin very slowly under highly structured conditions.

Planning a Program for Large Muscle Activity

The teacher's first care in planning for large muscle training is to introduce situations which provide for movement without excitement. *Excitement arises when the children do not know exactly what to do.* It is important to organize each activity so that:

1. each child knows from brief, simple directions where he is to be at each moment, how to get there, what to do, and how to get back;

2. neither the skill needed in the activity nor the amount of waiting for his turn be beyond his capacity;

3. the amount of stimulation from noise, movement, laughter, and so on, is kept within the endurance of the less stable members of the group;

4. provision for skill variations is made where possible.

The activities listed here are arranged roughly in order of the extent to which they meet these requirements.

OUTDOORS

Pre-Kick-ball. Players form a line and take turns kicking to the pitcher. This is probably plenty to start with. When the group is able, add the step of running to a base, then two, then three. How many days it will take to move into Kick-ball depends a good deal on how soon there are enough catchers to do the necessary minimum of fielding.

Catch-ball and Roll-ball. Same as above but the players catch the kick-ball and throw it back to the pitcher. In Roll-ball they roll it.

Track meet. Children run around the black top, or playground as many times as seems to fit each child. All can run together, but this is not a race. Competition means only trouble for most of the children, and it is important—particularly at first—to eliminate it in every way possible. Hopping, skipping, jumping, running with arms outspread, and so on, can vary the activity.

Jungle gym or bars. The children play tag in and around the jungle gym. This keeps the game within a limited area so that more people are tagged, and it encourages climbing.

Call-ball. Each player has a number. The one in the middle calls a number, throws the ball in the air, and the child who has the number tries to catch it.

London Bridge, Duck, Goose, Red Rover, Ring Around a-Rosie. These and other familiar games involve valuable practice in co-ordination for this group.

1 2 3. Players in a circle are numbered one to three. The teacher (until a child can do it) calls "All the one's run" (or two's or three's). All with the number called must try to run around the circle and back to place before another child who is "it" can catch them.

Relays. These can be arranged more easily outdoors. Walking, hopping, skipping can replace running. *Farmer and Crows* may be possible late in the year. First children in line are farmers, who "plant seed" (four counters) about 10 feet in front of the lines. Next ones are crows who eat them up, i.e., pick them up and return them *one at a time* to the third children who replant them, and so on until the first children are back in front. Make sure in playing a second round that places are moved to give each child a turn at each activity.

INDOORS

Following directions. Children sit at own desks and take turns carrying out some action command: hop, skip, jump, place arms, legs, torso, and so on, in various positions. This is a good way for the teacher to find out what skills she needs to teach.

Calisthenics. Records are helpful in this. Exercises should include as wide a range of muscles as possible, not forgetting hands. Later lessons can concentrate on areas where particular work is needed. To reduce both stimulation and frustration, slow rhythms should come first. The children will tire very quickly, especially at first. Rest on mats should probably follow. Mats are also useful in keeping each child in his own place. More advanced people can do further exercises while others rest and watch.

Marching, clapping, walking, skipping, running. These activities are accompanied with motions of arms: elephant walk, duck walk, and so on, preferably to music.

Balancing. Have children walk on line or 2 by 4-inch board. (A lumber yard will make wooden supports or slots to hold the board up on its narrow edge for that step.)

Eraser-bowling. Children sit in 2 rows to form an alley down which players take turns rolling kick-ball to knock down 3 or 4 up-ended erasers. Teacher, or child if possible, keeps tally on board. Best score out of 2 tries gives better chance of success and reduces frustration. The distance of the roll should vary according to the skill of each player.

Chair-ball. Same formation as above. Roll the ball under 1, later 2 chairs from whatever distance is appropriate to the skill of the player. Keep score as above. Two tries as above.

Erasers-in-basket. Same formation as above. Toss erasers in empty wastebasket from most feasible distance. Keep score. This game may be only for 2 or 3 more physically skilled, while the rest of the group play something else.

Building. The children use desks, chairs, tables, and so on, to build tunnels for crawling, trains, rocket ships, and so on. This activity comes later in the year, about in time for long periods of indoor weather. By this time the children have developed their own leaders and can use this as independently creative play with much opportunity for conversation and invention.

Care of room. Erasing and washing boards. Washing lunch tables or sink. (Running water is a great distraction to many of the children. Any activity which involves it needs careful control.) Picking up papers and crayons, putting chairs onto tables and down again.

Small Muscle Activity

Most of these are self-explanatory:
1. folding,
2. cutting,
3. dealing and holding cards,
4. block building (both large and small blocks),
5. picking up things (pegs, paper, beads),
6. squeezing sponge ball,

7. finger and wrist activity,
8. lacing and tying,
9. winding a spool,
10. weaving,
11. tapping,
12. blow down and pick up (fold little pieces of paper, have child blow them down, then pick them up),
13. speech muscles,[6]
14. eye exercises [6] (following target with eyes without moving head, in horizontal, vertical, and oblique planes),
15. foot exercises [6] (marching),
16. eating (chewing, using tools, sorting, stacking, carrying plates, trays).

WRITING

Writing as Therapy

Writing is one of the most crucial learning activities. The difficulties in motor co-ordination which are such a basic part of the child's problem are more evident (though not necessarily present to a greater degree) here than in any other academic subject. The developmental kinesthetic approach to learning is here available as an indispensable aid to reading; the senses of touch and motion are used to help fix in the child's mind the look and sound of letters. The physical activity of writing channels his restless energy and gives him the rare experience of using that energy in a way which calls forth praise. It is perhaps for this reason that the child most often begins to take great pleasure in writing. Certainly this is an activity that often provides the experience of success which he needs to overcome his initial feelings of fear and failure; and in the process his bizarre or frustrated behavior is lessened. Indeed, a restless, unruly child often becomes a model of industrious virtue when he is presented with a specific and suitably simple writing assignment.

Writing is also an invaluable tool in helping the child to see letters and words as wholes (Gestalts) instead of as the disconnected parts in which they usually appear to him.

In reproducing the sound and shape of a letter, the child concentrates every part of his physical system: eyes, large and small muscles, and (in the present therapy) vocal cords, and ears. This helps him in two ways, first because senses and muscles are in use he is free from the

[6] Give motions to imitate as in "Follow Directions" or "Simon Says."

many distractions which usually pull at him from all directions; and second, because several senses unite to bring the impression to his brain, he achieves a clearer and more satisfactory result than he could obtain by the use of any one sense alone.

Principles

CURSIVE WRITING

In view of these considerations, it may be stated that only cursive writing should be taught because the child uses a continuous flowing motion which carries him on by its own momentum. Cursive writing helps his disorganized, unco-ordinated movements to fall into a coherent pattern. Letters flow into each other, and this fact reduces sensitivity to the external distractions of the non-continuous motions and the disconnected letters of manuscript. Further, words are written as connected wholes; consequently improper connections are not the problem as they often are in manuscript. For example,

Th ebo yꞇd nu pt hehill

The connections between letters in cursive writing also help to emphasize left-to-right progression. Cursive letters, moreover, are not subject to reversals (compare b and d printed with *b* and *d* cursive); and, finally, if the child is taught the new skill of cursive writing, there is no need for the teacher to correct the errors that may have developed in his wrongly formed manuscript.

If a child has already been taught manuscript, he must be led to feel that this is also a worthwhile accomplishment. This is important, for he has few achievements to take pride in. He should not be given many opportunities to use manuscript, however; he should learn that cursive is another higher step which he is now ready to understand. Manuscript may be avoided by using print sets, printed letter cards, a typewriter, and so on. A possible exception to the avoidance of manuscript might occur with the child on the second- or third-grade level who needs to do longer assignments, or who works with spelling lists which go beyond the cursive letters he has learned so far.

COLOR AND SOUND

Two of the most dependable aids in teaching writing are color and sound. Just as color is one of the first things an infant notices, and just as color holds a powerful attraction for the young child, so it catches and holds the attention of the immature and hyperactive child also. Being a stronger stimuli than others in the environment, it frees him a little from external distractions. Heavy colored lines help him to see actual shapes and directions and to locate lines or strokes which have been confusing him. (See below for details on the use of color.)

The other important aid is sound. The child softly says the sound—not the name—of each letter as he writes it. When he can put two or three letters together, he learns at the same time how to sound them and how to blend them into a word. At the beginning he will write only phonetic words.

Writing Readiness

Every child will probably not be ready to begin with the first steps in writing—namely, learning to form the letters. It is extremely rare to find every child at the same level of co-ordination and behavior. This fact supports the cardinal principle that the teacher cannot work the same way with every child. She watches each child, observes what he uses to help himself (color, shape, touch, and so on), as well as what he avoids, and plans her work accordingly.

A major prerequisite to the small muscle work of writing is gross muscle development. Extreme lack of skill here may be the signal for delaying all formal writing activities. Deficiency in this area is so prevalent that it should never be overlooked as a factor in writing difficulty. The section on motor training discusses the methods whereby the teacher can detect and evaluate lack of motor skill, and discusses measures that have proved helpful in treating the deficiency.

It is probable that some children will have to begin with certain preliminary activities; others may be able to proceed directly to the formation of letters. The clues are given by the children themselves; in general, the level of co-ordination and the type of behavior provide those clues and indicate the point at which each child must begin.

Insofar as co-ordination is concerned, the child may not be able to copy simple lines:

— ⌐ / ⌐ U

Perhaps he cannot make curved lines (his *m* may contain jagged peaks); or he cannot keep reasonably well within guide lines; or he cannot cut, or cannot follow directions for simple physical activities (see the section on motor training).

He may lose, tear, or mark the paper; he may yawn, wriggle, play, make silly noises, or annoy other children. Obviously, misbehavior can stem from many causes. *In general, however, a child finds such pleasure in doing a task that is within his power well, that marked and continuous need for discipline should always be a signal for re-examining the amount and difficulty of the work he is being asked to do.* From time to time the teacher may need to ask herself questions such as the following:

If the child is not working well, is the work too hard? Is it so easy that it offers no challenge? Is it too familiar, and does it need to be presented in a new guise? Does the child feel humiliated because he thinks the material is babyish (even thought it may be difficult for him to do)?

Sometimes understanding the purpose of the task is enough to spur the child on. At other times, ways must be found to make the work look more "grown-up."

If symptoms in either of these categories (co-ordination and behavior) raise doubt as to the child's readiness for conventional writing, the teacher should draw on the following list of activities, experimenting to find the one suited to the child's needs. They may be used in addition to longer or shorter writing assignments, or as substitutes, depending upon the child.

Techniques

LARGE MUSCLE WORK

Many children gain from practice in drawing inside and outside of large and small cardboard stencils which are thumbtacked to a board or an easel (5). Shapes similar to the type of line which is causing trouble should be chosen; the stencils may be constructed as shown below (Figure 37). Both the inside and the outside patterns should be drawn

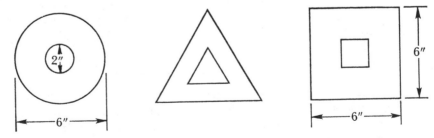

Fig. 37.

by the child. The inside pattern should be done first so that he has something to push against. The outside pattern will prove to be more difficult, for the crayon or large pencil will tend to wander away from the pattern. Forms such as those shown here will give the child his directional lines.

A variant of this approach is one in which the child traces very large letters, figures, or shapes. The chalkboard may be used, or a large paper may be placed on the child's desk; the latter is less likely to distract the rest of the class. The ideal method is to project the items to be traced with the slide attachment of a filmstrip projector. Letters or pictures (pumpkins, hearts, circles, cats, and so on) which call for the type of line being developed at the time may be projected onto an easel. A sheaf of large papers may be thumbtacked to the easel, and the children may trace in turn. The teacher may find it necessary to guide the child's hand at first.

SMALL MUSCLE WORK

Strips of modeling clay or *Play-Doh* (the latter is preferred because of its greater malleability) may be used by the child to copy models of letters. The activity of shaping or modeling contributes to the development of the small muscles and co-ordination. Further, the child both sees and feels the letter he is working on and comes to understand its shape more clearly.

Cutting and pasting. These will be treated in other subject areas but should be included in generous amounts for children with writing problems.

Coloring. This is a particularly important activity. Since background-foreground disturbance is a major problem, the usual commercial coloring book is not often satisfactory. Coloring books whose pictures are simple enough, whose outlines are sharp enough, can be found. But to use the common type of coloring book, with small pictures and decorations intertwined, and with many objects on a page, is simply to compound the child's already existing confusion.

Before they are ready for even the clearest, simplest coloring book, many children will need a period of work with such subjects as apples, pumpkins, and so on, culled from reading readiness books or drawn by the teacher.

Stencils. Sometimes coloring is so difficult and frustrating for the child that it is necessary to introduce stencils.

Tracing. Many children profit by a long period of tracing, either in addition to or before independent writing. A number of page-size cards of white tagboard are needed. The cards first in the series should contain short vertical lines. The next cards should contain simple abstract lines as shown below.

These ought to include many of the strokes which will be needed in writing (see ₁Figures 38 and 39). Following these should come cards with large numbers and cursive letters. Lines, letters, and numbers on the early cards should be 1½ inches high with 4 lines to a page. Letters on the later cards should fit the writing paper used at this stage (see

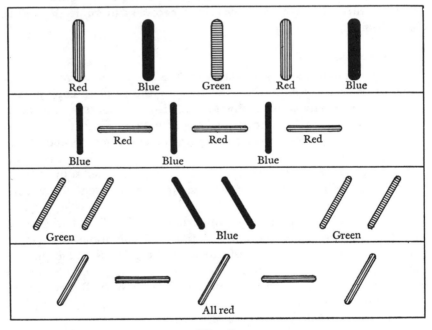

Fig. 38.

Figure 40). All lines, letters, and figures should be in color (felt pens may be used). The card is covered with onion skin or tracing paper held in place with paper clips or masking tape, and the child traces in crayons, whose colors match colors on the card. It may be necessary to make cards showing one line at a time. The child should have only the amount of work that he can successfully complete.

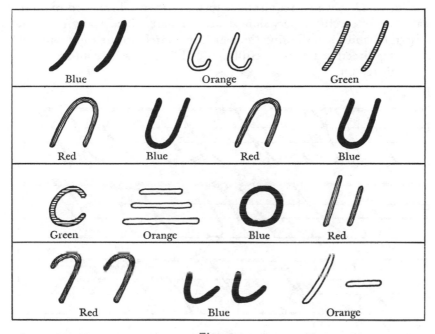

Fig. 39.

From there he can go on to tracing, in crayon or pencil, letters and words on dittoed sheets, or on papers made to suit his individual needs. (The teacher may write letters and words on a ditto stencil, not more than two or three different letters per sheet—a line of *m's,* a line of *i's,* a line of *mi,* each line repeated—and keep a supply for the child to trace over directly on the ditto copy.) As he moves into independent writing, some papers will include both tracing and space for his own writing.

Steps in Formal Writing

Since motor development is immature, the first letters to be taught are those requiring motions which develop earliest in the young child —those moving away from the body. (A list of letters in the usual order of teaching appears in Figure 40, but exceptions may be made for an individual child if his performance reveals a reason for doing so.) Although the letter *n* might appear to be the next choice (after *m*), it should be delayed until other letters have intervened because children confuse the number of humps. The pointed letters, *i, u, w, t* and *s* are at approximately the next level of ease. Most difficult as a rule are *a, o, d, c* and *g*, which require first forward, then a backward motion. Particularly careful supervision is needed here, since many children form the habit of continuing the pencil in a circle to the right without reversing direction unless carefully guided. They easily confuse *a* and *s* for this reason.

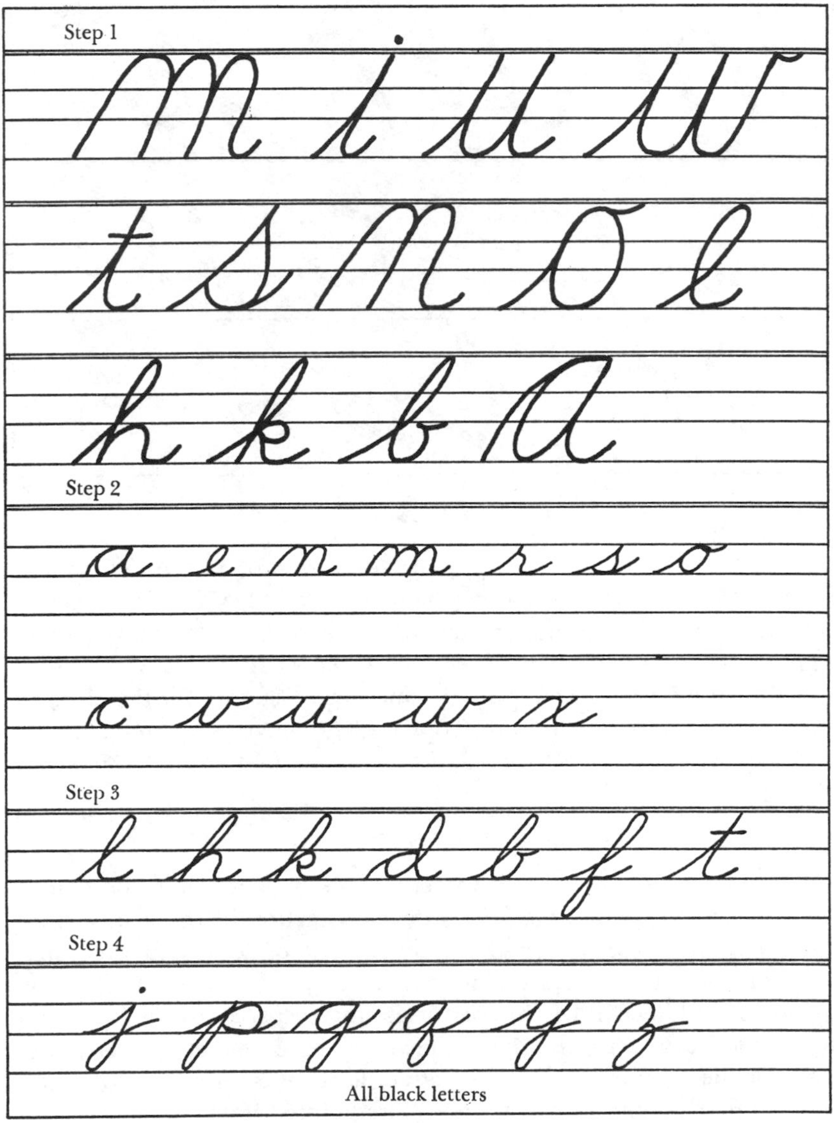

Fig. 40.

PAPER AND LETTER SIZE

It must always be borne in mind that the child's main problem is immature development. The teacher should begin with large letters which are easy for the child's eyes to perceive and for his muscles to make. In formal writing, large letters will be at least three spaces high.

Special lined paper should be used (see Figure 40). At first, the top and bottom lines are drawn in contrasting colors (using crayons or felt pens) until the child is able to stay easily within the lines. The lines in Figure 37 are usually not strong enough to guide the beginner. When he can make a few large letters successfully, he may try letters two spaces high. These two spaces should again be outlined in color if necessary. If he goes above or below the lines, or does not touch them; or if his letters are not as well formed as he can make them; or if he begins to resist writing, this is evidence that he needs the colored line. He will probably be ready for one-space letters by the time he is writing the letters with tails (see Figure 40, steps 3 and 4). If he is not, his paper should be specially ruled with spaces of the width he can handle (see Figure 41).

The teacher can experiment with the size of letters. Children vary considerably in the size of the writing with which they feel most comfortable; they are often able to select wisely if consulted. The paper should be lined in color as long as necessary. In later stages only the line to which attention must be drawn should be colored. The use and location of the lines will vary with the problem: for example, the space enclosed to guide one-space letters, the bottom lines to show how far the tails come down, the bottom line of the middle space to stress that letters stay on the line. Colored lines should be omitted as soon as the child can do without them. The teacher must always beware of setting up rigid patterns that will be hard to break.

WRITING TOOLS

The choice of writing tools often has a great deal to do with the child's comfort and degree of success. Here, too, he can often help in choosing the best instrument for his particular level. In general, the more immature and ill-co-ordinated the child, the larger and more colorful the writing tool he will need: large crayons, smaller crayons, colored felt pens, "Magic Markers," [7] large thick pencils, conventional pencils. Sometimes an older child's preference for a thin pencil comes

[7] "Magic Marker" is a commercial product, useful because the child can grasp it easily and because it adds zest to the writing process.

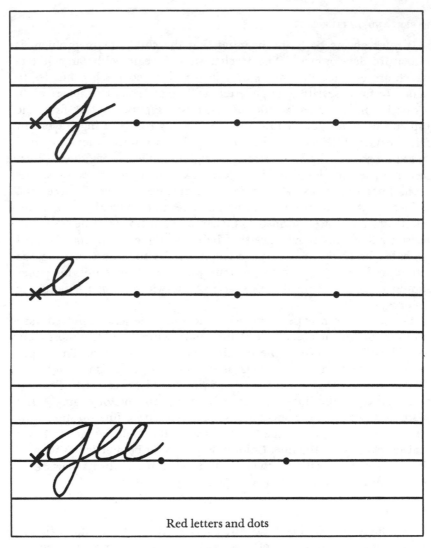

Red letters and dots

Fig. 41.

not because he is able to handle it but because use of a first-grade pencil intensifies his feeling of humiliation about his poor writing. In such a case, wrapping the pencil in modeling clay may give him the thicker, nonslippery surface he needs. For children whose posture is poor, the use of a 12-inch or 18-inch "novelty" pencil, sold in many variety stores, sometimes helps to keep the pencil pointed over the shoulder.

BEGINNING TO WRITE

The child should be seated facing away from all possible distractions; nothing should be within reach or sight but his paper, outlined in color, and his crayon or pencil. At the beginning of the top line, the teacher draws an *m* three spaces high. She says, "This letter says *mmm*," and she gives him one or two examples (milk, mother, his own or a familiar name). Then she says, "Now let me hear you say *mmm*." Next she takes his hand and has him make several *m's* with his index finger, then with his pencil until she can feel that he is beginning to sense the form. The teacher points out that he must start on the line for this and every letter. She has him sound each *m* as he makes it. Finally she may let him try one or two alone. If his effort is something like an *m*, he may get enough help from specific reminders and crutches to go on with independent writing.

COMMON PROBLEMS

If letters are too short or uneven in height, it may be enough to have the child repeat them until they touch the top and bottom lines. The teacher should not accept anything that does not meet standards. If a child cannot succeed here, the activity should be postponed. If the *m* has the wrong number of humps, the teacher should write each hump in a different color; the child should then do the same. This device may also help if the child tends to write too hastily—which happens often (see Figure 42). If he makes too many letters on a line for proper form and spacing (perseveration), the teacher should draw a line where each letter should go (*m* __ __ __ __ __). If this is not sufficient, she may block off each space with a vertical line, colored if necessary (*m* | *m* | *m* | |), or with masking tape.

If his co-ordination is such that the paper slides and wrinkles under his hand, he may need a *writing block*. This can be a piece of board thick enough to take thumbtacks and large enough to take his paper. The child can soon learn to prepare the board himself. He may get and replace the board, and tack and untack the paper. These are among the activities the teacher may devise to give him intervals of physical activity without getting him out of the mood for work. If a board is not available, a clipboard or a piece of heavy cardboard may be used (experiment to find the most comfortable size for a given child). The teacher or the child can attach the paper, using masking tape at the corners.

If the child cannot remember to start on the line, the teacher may

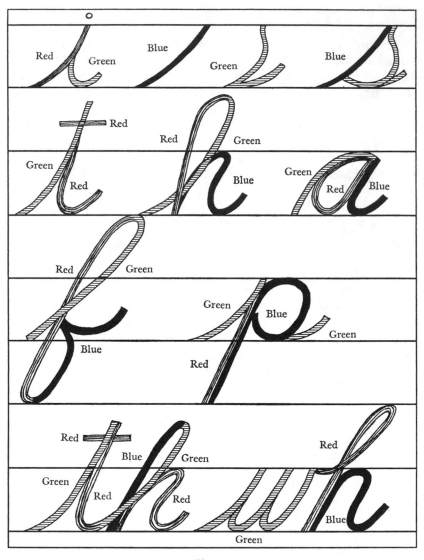

Fig. 42.

draw a colored dot or small star to indicate the beginning of each letter (Figure 41).

The teacher, working with each child, watches not so much what he does but *how he does it*. New techniques for solving the problem that stump the child will occur to each teacher.

COMBINING LETTERS INTO WORDS

As soon as he can write *m* and *i*, the child is ready to write and read phonetic syllables. The short sound of the vowels should be taught, and combinations such as *mi, mu, wi, wit, it, sit* and so on should be made. As succeeding letters are introduced, *all combinations must be sounded.* This method may be continued through the alphabet. It is of great importance that writing be closely correlated with reading.

Just as the humps of the *m* must sometimes be highlighted in different colors, many of the other letters will also call for special guides. Most faithful and reliable of all helpers to the immature child is color. If he makes his *t's* like tents, the teacher may make the upstroke in red, the down in green; she may give different colors to the dips of the *w;* she may color the arm of the *b* to help him distinguish it from the *l;* she may make the upstroke of the *a* one color, the swingback and around another. Wherever he has trouble, color may solve the immediate problem.

Another helpful approach, which relies on the early childhood interest in the sense of touch, is the use of the clay pan. A large flat pan is filled (by the child if possible) with modeling clay or "Play-Doh," and he writes the troublesome letter with a stylus prepared by sharpening a dowel, stick (or an awl, or metal skewer from the kitchen). The resistance of the clay helps to fix the feel of the stroke in his mind.

Sometimes when the effort to combine more than one stroke into a letter is too much for a child, he can learn to do half the letter independently beginning by tracing the first part, then finishing on his own, as shown below.

If numbers are among his strong points, a dot-to-dot puzzle may help: for example,

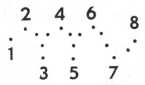

The teacher must bear in mind that the children find it hard to change any habit once it is formed; it is therefore important to have them try to write newly learned letters and words correctly and independently as soon as possible. This is better done in small doses. "My, that is a nice *m!* Let's see if you can make one without looking at mine." Such comments do much good.

Personality Factors

All of the foregoing are valuable teaching techniques, but the teacher will succeed or fail in using them to the degree that she appreciates the special factors involved in the children's learning.

First of all, it is hard to overstress the importance of going slowly. This applies to the following:

LENGTH OF LESSON

Many children can do only one or two lines of writing in a day; very few can do a whole page. As always, the child and all his reactions must be watched to determine the size of assignment he should have.

INTRODUCTION OF NEW MATERIAL

Ample time must be allowed for new learnings to settle in and become familiar. Enough days must go by before the teacher can be sure the child is really at home with the letters and words he has learned before he is presented with others. In this respect his judgment is not too sure a guide. He may be ready for another step, or he may only be eager to succeed or to please the teacher. She must judge his strength and protect him from more of the failures which have accompanied all his efforts.

USE OF THE GROUP AS A TOOL

One of the most effective tools in reducing and relaxing this fear of failure is the group. A child can be so shy and tense alone that his mind scarcely seems to function at all. Yet the same child, watching or listening to another child falter, comes through time and again with answers and insights that were previously out of his reach. When his turn to perform comes, he too may falter; but by that time other children are having their turn at success, and the total amount of learning increases tremendously.

The teacher will use groups very sparingly in the early weeks; but writing, with its need for physical activity, is one of the safest areas in which to begin. This can be done at the board, with children taking turns writing and sounding letters and words; 4 to 6 children, if necessary, may be writing at a large table while the teacher supervises each in turn. She will do a better job with 4 than with 6; she must continually make a choice, particularly during the first year, in the process of trying to be in as many places as possible. The important point is that no child should ever be left to do his writing unsupervised until the teacher has made sure he has learned to make correctly the letters he is using: habits once formed are so hard for him to break that the unlearning will be worse for the child than the learning.

PEER RELATIONSHIPS

The handicaps under which these children labor have been discussed elsewhere. Those handicaps have prevented the development of normal, comfortable relationships with other children and with adults. Shyness, overaggressiveness, and a conviction that "nobody likes me" are so common that much real learning power does not become effective until the children can begin to feel happy with the people around them. One of the most productive situations for this type of growth is the writing group. With physical activity channeled into writing, the children begin to get acquainted through talking, through listening, and through simply being together. Since the ostensible purpose is not conversation, shy people can lie low and get their bearings while enjoying being with a group. Aggressive people learn to use speech instead of teasing and horseplay. Particularly at first, the teacher controls the talk to help keep down excitement and distraction, and she is as alert to teach good ways of getting along together as she is to teach good writing.

A variation of this approach is the practice of letting the children work together when friendships begin to develop. Often a job which seems like drudgery alone becomes fun when two work together. Often, too, a child who cannot feel at ease either with the teacher or in a group learns avidly from a friend—who in turn benefits for the first time from the experience of having something to give.

NEED FOR REST INTERVAL

There are many times in the teaching of writing—as in every other area—when a particular step seems impossible for a child to master. It has been presented in every imaginable way, from every angle, and through every possible sensory approach. The child feels—and the teacher must almost agree with him—that this is something he will never learn. This is the time for the *rest interval*. The letter, word, or the activity must be dropped entirely. Let the child put it out of his mind, and the teacher likewise. It must remain out of mind for two weeks, a month, even months, until the child has had enough success in other areas to face up to it again. As always, the teacher takes her cue from the child. He may "ask" to take it up again, either by coming to watch the teacher working with someone else or by trying it on his own. When the task is taken up again after a sufficiently long interval, the teacher will frequently find that the child seems to have learned it almost magically in the meantime; he will have no further trouble. Sometimes he has actually matured in the interval to a point at which he is now ready for the task. Sometimes perseveration has blocked him, driving him helplessly to do over and over the very action he wants to avoid. Because perseveration may be operating, the teacher can do much to avoid the need for long rests by immediately changing any activity in which the child repeats the same mistake several times. Whatever he does he is learning _something_. If he cannot be taught that he _can_ do it, he should not be taught that he _can't!_

ARITHMETIC

The number concept is rooted in the child's perception of objects in space. Numbers help the child to organize his environment, and they help him to view the world in quantitative fashion. For example, he finds that 8 blocks take up more space than 3 blocks, that one thing is twice as large as another, that time and distance are divided into measurable units. All of these experiences involve ways of viewing the world; _form perception_ is basic to them. Until the child is able to perceive form, he cannot go on with arithmetic.

No matter how old the hyperactive child is, he should be started at the beginning, both to get a new approach to numbers and to be sure he has a workable number concept. With the normal child, one can count milk bottles, rabbits in a picture, and so on. The child in this study, however, becomes more interested in the objects than in the number, but nothing must be allowed to distract him from the actual process of counting. A child may be able to say that $4 + 4 = 8$, but can he look at dots in configurations and arrive at the right answer? Does he know that a similar mental process is at work? One cannot know; for this reason, one must begin at the beginning.

Because of hyperactivity, distractibility, and perseveration, the number experiences which normal children have in abundance lose their significance for a child in this group. Arithmetic must involve numbers and numbers alone, and activities should not be included which may cause the child to become lost in them.

For much of the time, the teacher must prepare and provide the materials that the child uses. This is necessary for many reasons.

1. The child will need many manipulative materials to help overcome motor disinhibition and perseveration.

2. The worksheets must call for only the amount of work he is able to do successfully.

3. Each new factor must be repeated over a longer period of time, and it must be varied in as many ways as possible.

4. The page of a commercial workbook is so crowded and full that the child cannot tolerate it.

5. The purposeful use of color on each teacher-prepared paper will help the child attend to the task before him.

6. He must be given a carefully calculated starting point and ending point to help him establish himself in space.

The following material need not necessarily be presented to the child in the order given here. It is, however, set down in developmental sequence. Testing will show the teacher where the gaps are. If she remembers that progress comes slowly, and if she learns to take her cue from the child, she will be able to determine when he is ready to go on to another step.

Materials

The most important of the manipulative materials needed in the beginning stages are sets of cards variously shaped and variously colored. Each type of card will be seen to have a particular purpose. The teacher may find it convenient to make these materials well in advance of class use; or she may find an interested parent who is willing to take over their preparation. In the discussion of techniques which follow these directions, the cards will be referred to by the names given them here.

SET A. COLOR-PATTERN SORTING CARDS

Cut about 30 cards 2½ inches square from tagboard. Draw a circle or spot in blue on each of 5 cards, 2 spots in yellow on the next 5, 3 in orange on the next 5, and so on through 6 spots. The spots are to be arranged in domino patterns (see Figure 43). (Since many of these have to be prepared, stencils could be made. The stencils could be used by the children to good advantage.)

SET B. TWO-COLOR MATCHING CARDS

Cut 36 strips of cardboard (heavy weight or corrugated) about 2 by 4 inches. Then cut 72 squares of construction paper 2 by 2 inches, using only the 6 primary and secondary colors. Paste one of the colored squares on each half of each cardboard strip, taking care to vary the color

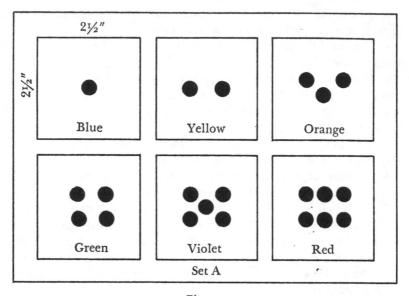

Fig. 43.

combinations as widely as possible, and bind the edges with tape (see Figure 44).

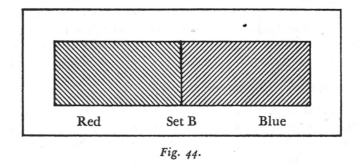

Fig. 44.

SET C. VARICOLORED DOMINO CARDS

Cut about 30 strips of tagboard 2 by 4 inches, and draw a black line down the middle of each strip to mark the strip into 2 squares. In each square draw from 1 to 6 spots in the standard domino patterns. However, all the 1's are to be drawn in one color (blue, for example), the 2's in another, and so on through the 6's (see Figure 45).

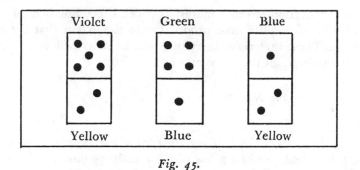

Fig. 45.

SET D. SOLID COLOR DOMINO CARDS

Prepare about 30 or more domino cards, as in Set C, and divide them into 6 decks of 5 or more cards each. Again draw the standard domino combinations; now, however, each *deck* is to be in a different color: one deck with all blue spots, another deck with all yellow, and so on (see Figure 46).

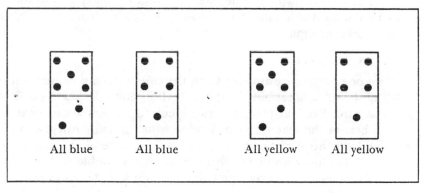

Fig. 46.

SET E. BLACK AND WHITE DOMINO CARDS

Prepare about 30 or more domino cards, as in Set C, and draw the standard domino patterns in black.

(Note: the domino spots in Sets A, C, D, and E can be stamped by using the eraser end of a new pencil and a variety of colored stamp pads. The gummed, gloss-paper forms listed under "Materials to Order" will save much time.)

The preparation of other materials (worksheets, number cards, and so on) will not require mass production to the extent that the sets of cards do. Those materials, therefore, will be described in connection with the techniques they accompany.

Getting Ready for Numbers

MATCHING PATTERNS

Using the cards of Set A, place one card of each configuration on the child's desk, and give him a few of the remaining ones. He is to match his cards with the 6 "models," using color as a guide. If he cannot handle many cards at once, reduce the number of models from 6 to 3.

MATCHING COLORS

Using the cards of Set B, let the child match color to color on his desk in the manner of a domino game. Give him a starting point, and see that he matches color to color with no gaps. Check to be sure that he does not go back and add any remaining cards at random. He should stop when he can go no further. The essential point of this step is to introduce him to the domino shape and to the principle of domino matching —using color as a guide.

MATCHING END-TO-END

Place one domino card of Set C on the child's desk, give him a few cards of the set, and let him find a card whose end matches the end of the first card. Let him place the two identical configurations next to each other, in the manner of a domino game; he will still use color as a guide at this step, but he may also gain a sense of the configuration itself. Let him continue in this way. If he has trouble at this point, it may be necessary to cover one half of the card, or even to return to Set A for a time.

MATCHING WITHOUT COLOR GUIDE

Using Set D, begin another domino sequence similar to that introduced with Set C. The essential point at this step is gradually to free the child from dependence on color, and to fix his attention on the configuration or form itself. Here again, if the child is not successful, he should return to working with one of the earlier sets of cards. To the extent that he is successful, the variously colored decks in Set D may be used interchangeably or all together.

INDEPENDENT MATCHING

Set E may be used in the same manner. At this point the child's recognition of forms is (or should be) so well established that he does not have to rely on color at all.

Introducing Numbers

NUMBER SYMBOLS

Prepare several cards 2 by 2 inches containing only the number symbols from 1 to 6. Place 2 of the symbol cards (for example, 1 and 5) on his desk, give him several other 1's and 5's, and have him match the latter with the models. Each day, add to the symbols until he can distinguish clearly and easily among all 6 of the numbers. At this stage, the names of the numbers are not introduced; the goal here is only to be able to distinguish one symbol from another.

NUMBER NAMES

Now the dot configurations and symbols may be brought together. Use the symbol cards and a deck of the cards from Set A. Point to the first card of the "A" set and say, "This is *one*"; then point to the first symbol card and say, "Here is another way to say *one*." Work backward and forward between dot and symbol, and add other dots and symbols as the child's comprehension allows.

MATCHING NUMBERS AND SYMBOLS

Use a few cards from Set A and the number-symbol cards from 1 to 6. Let the child match the symbols and configurations (spots). It may be possible also to use the cards from Set E (black and white domino cards) and continue the matching technique. (The use of Set E rather than Set A will tend to remove any possible color cue for the child; the color cue, essential at the early levels, must eventually be done away with.)

REFERENCE CHART

When the child is sufficiently skilled at recognizing symbols and matching with configurations, he may be given a chart made as in Figure 47. The chart should be kept at his desk for constant reference. (The blank third column is for the words—number names—themselves, which will be added at a later stage.)

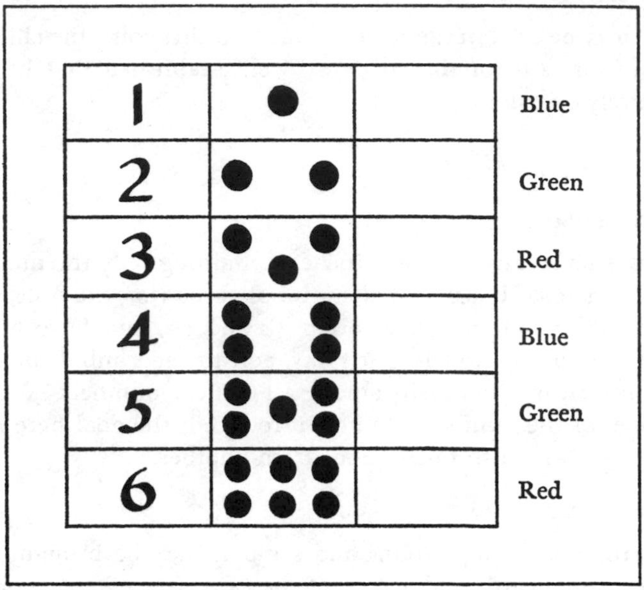

1	●		Blue
2	● ●		Green
3	● ● ●		Red
4	● ● ● ●		Blue
5	● ● ● ● ●		Green
6	● ● ● ● ● ●		Red

Fig. 47.

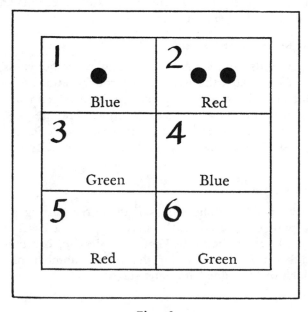

Fig. 48.

WORKSHEETS

The teacher may now introduce worksheets (see Figures 48 and 49) for the child to complete. The child may draw in the spots, or he may paste in 1-inch squares or circles of colored paper supplied by the teacher. These papers may be presented in a number of ways to help him with his attention span and distractibility.

1. Vary the colors of the numbers until you think he can select whatever color he wishes, then write the symbol in black.

2. Use different colored stamp pads and the eraser of a new pencil so that he can stamp the number pattern.

3. Let him make his own number patterns with his crayons. (It may be helpful to fold the paper and expose only one example at a time.)

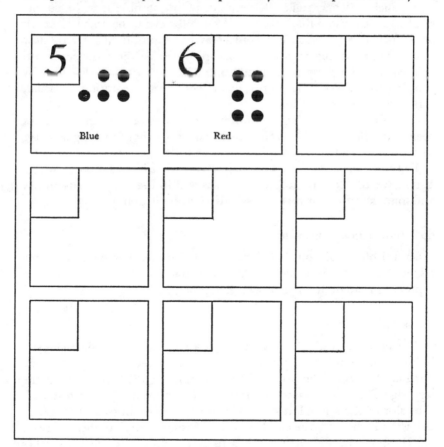

Fig. 49.

Counting and Tallying

As configurations and names are recognized, the child should start counting orally. This is a complicated process. He will know the names of the numbers (up to "six," at least); at this point every effort must be made to bring the names into relationship with the quantities represented by them. The child may be able to "count" more or less correctly and still have no number concept—no meaning for the words. Some children need many different devices to help them to learn sequence and to keep their place in that sequence. The child may point to 3 objects but meanwhile count up to 7; he may skip numbers or repeat them; and the devices are necessary to correct these faults.

In general, it may suffice if the child points to objects as he counts them. But it is more than likely that he will have to be asked to touch or, even better, to grasp each object as he counts it, if only to slow him down. Grasping each object will prove to be the most successful method, for the grasping reflex is one of the earliest to develop; by grasping the object as he counts, he arrives at an integration of visual, verbal, and motor functions.

From this point of view, the following devices and techniques have been found helpful. The teacher must remember that touching is better than pointing, and that grasping is better still.

The child must be *helped* to understand what he is supposed to do. It is above all necessary to keep his tasks within the range of his ability and to make sure that he understands what he is doing.

COUNTING BLOCKS OR BEADS

Several blocks are put before the child. The teacher says, "Give me 1 block"; then, "Give me 2 blocks," and so on. The average limit of perception as a single impression is a group of 4 blocks.

LARGE PEG BOARD

The number symbols are written on a strip of tagboard, each symbol in a different color, and the symbols are spaced as far apart as the horizontal rows on the peg board allow; this strip is then taped at the left edge of the board (see Figure 50). The child, using pegs to match the color of the symbol, inserts the proper number in each row. When this work is checked, the child is asked, "Show me the number that says 3." He shows it, and then is asked to give it to the teacher. He takes the pegs out one at a time, counting each one as he removes it.

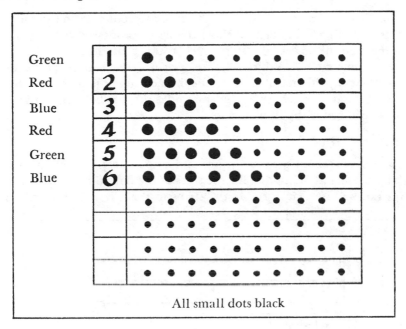

Green	1			
Red	2			
Blue	3			
Red	4			
Green	5			
Blue	6			

All small dots black

Fig. 50.

COLORED CUBES

A series of dowel rods of different lengths, mounted on a board, and a number of drilled, colored cubes or spools are needed (see Figure 51). The child puts as many on each dowel as it will hold, counting each cube (or spool) as he places it on the rod. At this point, the questions,

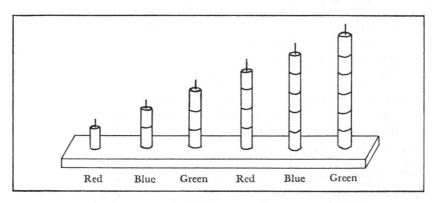

Red   Blue   Green   Red   Blue   Green

Fig. 51.

"Which is more" and "Which is less" can be introduced; and parallel to this, counting 1 through 6. Have the child count the cubes as he puts them on the dowels. Questions such as this could be asked: "Show me 4." "Show me 6." "Which is more, 4 or 6?" The teacher points to the 4 as she says it, and likewise to the 6. Each time she must wait for the child to give his answer. When she thinks this has been established, she may proceed with, "Which is less?"

BEAD BOX

Make a box about 9 by 12 inches and 1 inch deep; mount in it a set of 5 cardboard divisions. (Slit the sides of the box so that cardboard strips can be inserted, or staple the strips to the sides.) The numbers

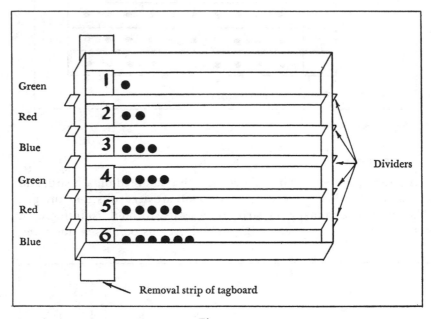

Fig. 52.

that the child is learning are placed in varying arrangements on strips which are slipped in turn under the division strips (see Figure 52). The child puts the corresponding number of beads into each section. Check in the same way as mentioned above.

OTHER DEVICES

A piece of construction paper is marked off with black crayon lines across the paper. A number the child is learning is placed at the left of each row. The child puts a corresponding number of objects (blocks, magnets, and so on) in the spaces beside each number (see Figure 53).

This work may be varied by pasting, stamping; and last, after much success, he may draw as many as he needs.

Desk charts may be used; put number symbols at left. Then the child places the correct number of cut-outs of colored paper or pictures by the number symbol.

6	Red
4	Green
1	Violet
3	Orange
5	Red
2	Blue
6	Green

Fig. 53.

A flannel board may also be used; number symbols and circles are cut out, and flannel or rough paper is glued to their backs so they will stick to the flannel board.

THE ABACUS

The abacus has been found to be the basic tool the child uses in understanding numbers. A concrete concept of numbers is taught with the use of the abacus. The child can readily see the differences in spatial relationships. Each row is a different color to help the child locate the number row. It is very important that each child have an abacus of his own so that when he is ready to use it, it is at his side.

Have the abacus strung 1 to 6 or simpler if necessary (see Figure 54).

As the child counts the beads, he pushes them over. For 1, he pushes over the row with one bead on it; for 2, the row with two beads on it, and so on.

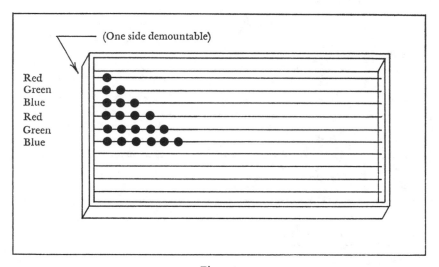

Fig. 54.

Another advantage of the abacus, for example, is that the child learns to see the threeness of a number. Ask the child to make each row say "3." He begins the row "3" on the left, then makes all the other rows match it by pushing the extra beads to the right on each of the following rows. Then he may do the same for the other numbers.

When the teacher feels that the child has a good understanding of numbers 1 to 6, she is ready to teach him groupings. She asks the child to push over "4." Then she shows him all the ways he can make 4, such as pushing 1 and then pushing over 3 (in the same row), and so on.

A standard abacus with all but one row removed can be introduced at this point (see Figure 55). Here the child is helped to see numbers in a linear position. Ask the child to push over 2 beads, 3 beads, and so on. It is hoped that by this time the child will see 4 has 2 and 2 and will push over the beads in groups. Use of this abacus will thus be another means of helping the child to learn groupings. All of the work with the abacus should be done orally.

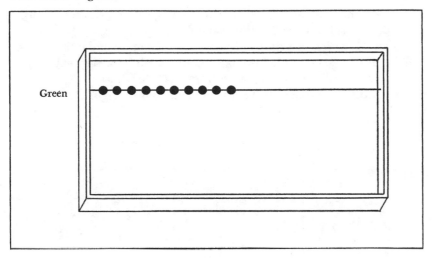

Fig. 55.

Groupings

A device can be prepared from corrugated cardboard as follows (see Figure 56). (The Stern Blocks for Structural Arithmetic, Houghton Mifflin, are ideal if money is available.)

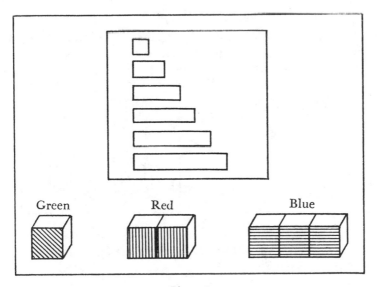

Fig. 56.

Glue together colored half-inch cubes to make the desired grouping. Make several sets, each a different color.

Individual flannel boards may be used by children who need to work with larger pieces. Cut large number symbols with flannel glued to the backs of each. Cut 2-inch squares from colored construction paper with a backing of flannel. The suggestions shown in Figure 57 may be helpful.

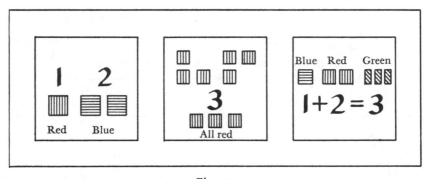

Fig. 57.

A magnet board may be used in much the same manner as the flannel board. Here the child *hears* how many he puts on the board.

Analysis of Configurations

Give the child several 1-inch blocks of the same color. Place 3 blocks in this pattern (see Figure 58a). Then ask the child to add as many as

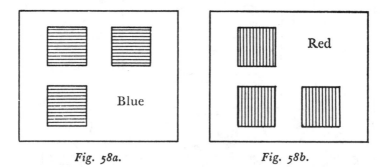

Fig. 58a.   *Fig. 58b.*

he needs to make it say 4. Then change the configuration as seen in Figure 58b, and repeat.

On a piece of paper write the configuration. Ask the child to complete it to make 4, and so on.

Later the configuration may be completed in a linear arrangement —6— □ □ □ _____. In this problem the child is asked to add enough squares to make it say 6.

The following suggestions may be helpful:

1. The child may be given plain blocks and work orally.
2. He may work with pasting and stamping papers.
3. He may draw the squares himself with crayons.

Add Sign

The most concrete presentation is to call the add sign "and." First use beads or blocks and show the child that "2 blocks *and* 1 block are 3 blocks."

Papers such as shown in Figure 59 may be prepared. In writing the number combinations, use a different color for each number; the plus (add) sign should be in black. The child first pastes or stamps the num-

Red $2 + 1$ Green	● ● ● Red Green	3
Blue $3 + 2$ Red		
Green $1 + 2$ Violet		
Red $2 + 2$ Blue		
Blue $1 + 3$ Green		
Green $3 + 3$ Red		
Red $1 + 1$ Violet		

Fig. 59.

ber of colored circles to make the combination. Then he writes the answer in the box at the right of the line. It is important that the child should be shown how to get his answer by counting (using the num-

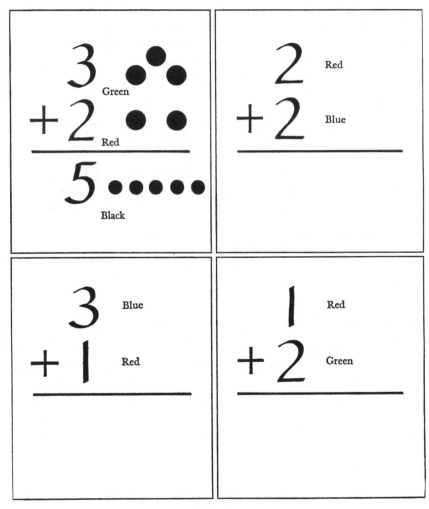

Fig. 60.

ber 2 as his starting point); he places his finger on the second circle and says "two," on the third circle and says "three," and so on.

Likewise in another form (see Figure 60). The number 3 and the number pattern are made in the same color; similarly other numbers and number patterns must agree. The child is asked to fill in the right number of dots (as in the illustration) and write the answer.

Still another version may take the form seen in Figure 61. The

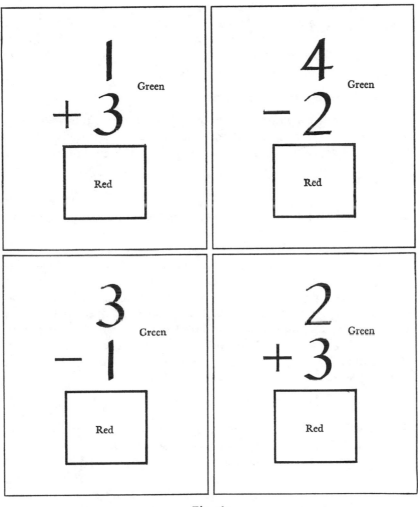

Fig. 61.

numbers are written in one color, and the boxes in another. The add sign is in black.

Later papers may be made with pen or pencil (that is, without color), and may contain several examples on each paper.

Numbers 7 to 10

Add to the large abacus rows 7, 8, 9, 10, each in a different color. Work with these numbers in the same way as you did in teaching 1 to 6. Make use of color and *work slowly*.

Begin by making individual papers with the numbers in different colors. Use colored squares, colored circles, the stamp pads, and the large peg board. Another device similar to Figure 56, but made for the rows 7 to 10, may be made here.

Working Toward the Abstract

Many worksheets may be made now. (The teacher will have to decide whether or not the child can tolerate written instructions.) The examples may be written on lined paper, as seen in Figure 62.

Teaching Subtraction

This may be done as soon as the teacher feels that the process for adding is *well* established. This does not mean that all addition facts are taught before subtraction is introduced.

Using the one string abacus, have the child push (to the right) 5 beads. Ask him to take away 2. Then ask him to tell you how many are left. Do this many times with different combinations. Then write an example on a piece of paper. Show the child how to begin with the number written on top. Have him push over on his abacus that number. Then show him the number under the top number and the minus sign (see example below) and say, "This tells us to take away this number."

Example:

$$\begin{array}{r} 5 \\ -2 \\ \hline 3 \end{array}$$

Show him how to take from the number he has pushed over. Show him that what is left is his answer and that he is to write it on his paper. Go through several examples with him until you feel that he can do it alone.

It might be to the child's advantage if the minus sign is made in a color to help the child remember that this is a new process.

You may find that some child or children need to "see" the process of subtraction in a more concrete way. Use the flannel board here so that you are able to actually "take away" from the board and let the child see how many are left. The Stern arithmetic materials are also excellent for this.

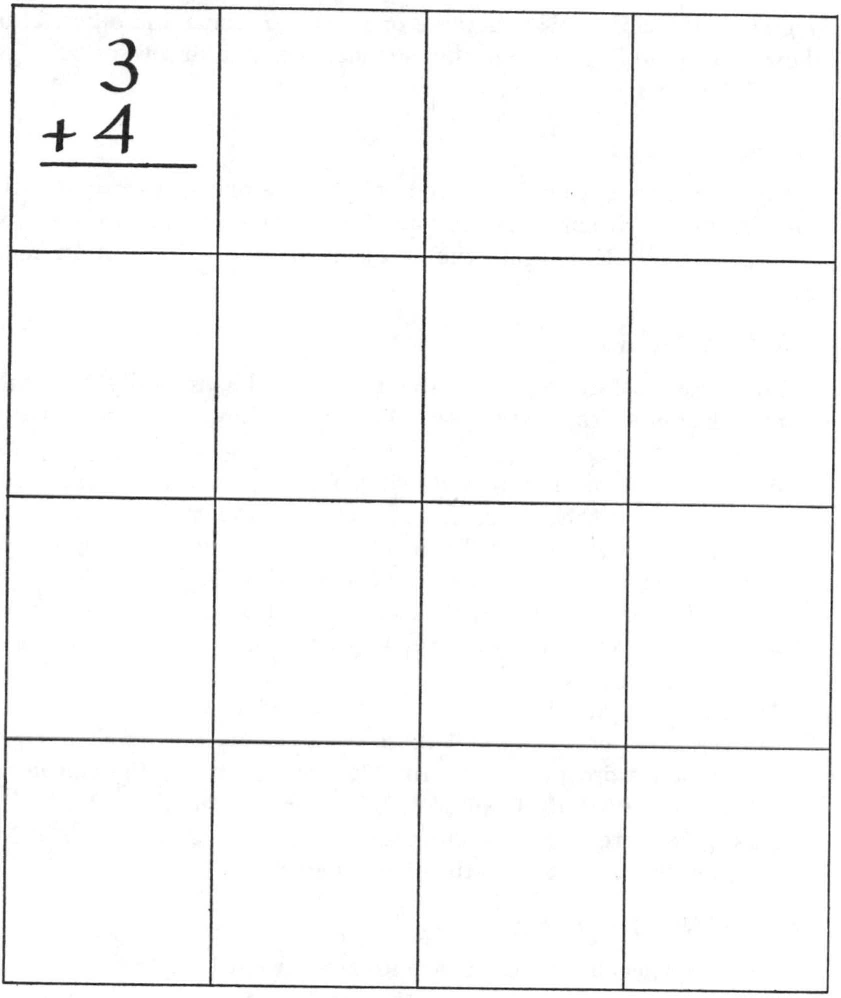

$$3$$
$$+4$$

Fig. 62.

Take your cue from the child; when you feel that he is secure in this process, make papers for him that have mixed examples, such as:

$$\begin{array}{cccc} 3 & 4 & 2 & 6 \\ +1 & -2 & +4 & -3 \end{array}$$

Make the process signs in different colors to avoid perseveration.

Write individual problems on cards 2 by 3 inches. Give several cards to the child and have him copy them on "blocked off" paper (see Figure

61). Show the child how you write one number under the other; also show that the add sign goes to the left side, and that his answer belongs *directly under* the example.

Column Addition

Sums up to 10 may be introduced. Worksheets may be prepared with the directions written across the top. Use the combinations in as many ways as possible. Here again the add sign may be written in another color.

Simple Problems

Introduce this section by giving simple problems orally in small groups. Example: there are 2 boys here and 3 boys there; how many boys are there altogether?

Write problems such as the following: 1 boy and 2 boys are _____ boys; 4 cats and 3 cats are _____ cats. The numerals *must* be written in color at first, so that the child may select the essentials of the problem. Later the color cue may be dispensed with.

Many children can do arithmetic calculation far in advance of their reading. Do not introduce reading problems unless the child can read.

At this point add the number names (words) to the chart shown as Figure 47; and perhaps extend the chart by using the numbers (symbols, dots, and words) from 7 to 10. Then write simple problems using number words instead of symbols. Example: two girls and four girls are six girls. Here again, the number words must be written in color at first. Let the child refer to the chart at all times.

Writing Numbers 1 to 50

Prepare papers lined off in 1-inch squares, 10 across and 5 down. Write the numbers from 1 to 10 across the top row, and the number 20 below the 10. Then have the child write in the missing numbers (11 to 19).

Continue by writing in the number 30 and having the child complete the row (21 to 29).

Continue in this manner to 50. Always have a chart available for the child's use if he needs it.

Adding to 10

The child is now ready to use the abacus strung with 2 rows, each row in a different color. He should be very familiar with 10 by this time. First give the examples orally: have the child push over 5, then ask him to push over 7 (sometimes he will immediately say that he can't). Show him then how to use the 5 that are left in the first row and to use 2 from the second row. Then show him his answer as one 10 and two 1's. Next, write the example on paper and write the answer, saying as you write, "one 10 and two 1's make 12." Show him that the 10's column is written under the add sign and that the 1's are written under the 1's column. Stay with this step until *you are sure* that the child can go further on his own.

A "tens pocket chart" may be prepared to help the child see the 1's and 10's better (see Figure 63). Here the child can readily see one bundle of 10's in the tens pocket, and he can count the 1's in the ones pocket.

Telling Time

Prepare a large clock face, with movable hands, of cardboard or paper plates (long hand red, and the short hand black as color cues). Make large pictures of clocks on paper, and give one to the child. Have the child use the cardboard clock to set the hands at a specified hour. Then let him copy on his paper clock, with the use of a red and black crayon, the position of the hands. Do this many times, helping the child to see that the hour hand is short and the minute hand is long. Stay with the hour time until the child feels secure in telling the time (hour) from another clock.

Then go to half past the hour. Use the cardboard clock with the movable hands as long as the child feels it necessary.

Subtracting 10 to 19

Using the two-stringed abacus, write an example on paper:

$$\begin{array}{r} 15 \\ -8 \\ \hline \end{array}$$

Have the child push over 1 ten and 5 ones (15). From this number ask him to take away 8. He should know what makes 8. Using the 5, he adds 3 from the top row; he pushes these away, leaving 7 (when 3 are left your answer is 7). Go through several problems such as this before you leave the child to work alone.

When you feel that the child is secure in this process, make papers for him with examples.

Adding by 10's

The child is now ready for a 10-string abacus (100 beads) with each row in a different color.

Begin by asking the child to push over 1 ten, 2 tens, have him say 20, each to 100. Keep this on an oral basis for a time.

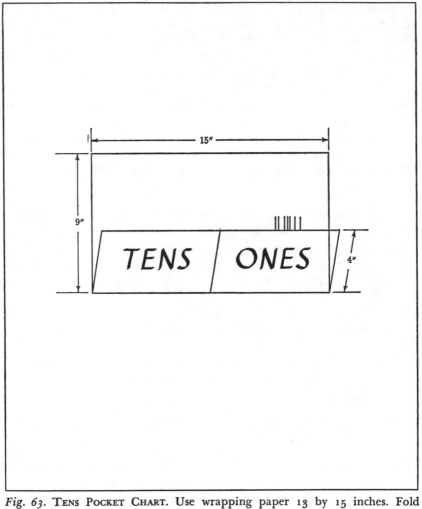

Fig. 63. TENS POCKET CHART. Use wrapping paper 13 by 15 inches. Fold back 4 inches, making the pocket chart 9 by 15 inches. Staple the edges, and staple between the "Tens" and "Ones" pockets. The words on the face of the pocket should be written in color—a different color for each word. Colored counting sticks may be used singly and in bunches of ten.

At the same time let him use this process in rote, writing to 100 as a guide.

When you feel that he is ready, show him how to find the answer to the example: 11
                     $+12$

by first pushing over 1 ten and 1 one (11). There are 9 beads left on the second row. Use those 9 beads and 1 bead from the third row to make the second ten. Then push over 2 more to complete the 12. The child writes his answer 23 (the tens under the tens column and the ones under the ones column).

If this is too difficult, show the child how to add the ones column, then the tens column. Much of this will probably be done without the use of the abacus. However, do *not* take the abacus away from the child; let him discard it when he feels that he no longer needs it. This he will do of his own accord when he feels secure.

For two column addition here again show the child how to begin adding the ones column, then the tens column. At first have all the tens column with answers less than ten. Stress over and over that you begin adding the ones column first. Be sure you, as the teacher, call the tens column by its correct name at all times.

Learning About Money

This can best be done by using real money. Have the child close his eyes and see if coins of different size sound differently when dropped on the floor or desk top. Have him close his eyes and see if he can arrange them by size—dime, penny, nickel.

Identify the names of coins, using real money: pennies, nickels, dimes. Ask the child, "Give me 2 pennies," and similar questions. Show the child that a nickel is worth as much as 5 pennies, or that you can buy as much with 5 pennies as with a nickel. Go slowly. This is a difficult concept for some.

Later say, "Give me 6 cents," and "1 penny and a nickel." The child needs to know what things he can buy for this amount of money. This is very important.

Many papers can be made at this point introducing the cent mark in another color from the examples. Stress the position of the "¢" mark in relation to the answer.

Counting by 5's

Here is a good place to begin counting by 5's—using nickels. Also, another 10-string abacus could be set up with a different color for each 5 on each row. After oral work the child can begin to write by 5's. If he needs the abacus to guide him, let him use it. This is a good place to make a "hundreds board," made as the "fiftys board" in the section, "Writing Numbers 1 to 50," above. Make each multiple of 5 in red. The child counts by 5's; but he must understand that each number on the clock face represents a group of 5 minutes (when the minute hand passes over them) as well as an hour.

Now he is ready to learn how to tell time with the quarter hour.

Measurements

At this point the child should be ready to learn about a ruler, and that 12 inches make a foot. The teacher may also be able to introduce liquid measurements in an elementary fashion: pints, quarts, and gallons.

Carrying in Addition

Occasionally a child will find this process easy, especially if he has a good mental picture of the 10-string abacus and of 10. Other children find it very difficult merely because it is something new.

Write down an example: 36
                          +47

Remind the child to begin adding the ones column first. Using the 10-string abacus, the child pushes over 6. There are 4 beads left. He uses the 4 and adds as many as he needs from the next line to make 7. He sees 1 ten and 3 ones. Show him how to write the 3 ones under the ones column. Show him then that 1 ten is still left on the abacus (top row) and that he may write a small 1 above the 3 in the tens column. Then he adds the tens column, and he has his answer. Go over several examples in this manner.

For some time let the child have only 1 ten to carry. Go very slowly. The important thing to remember is that the process must become stabilized to the extent that it becomes part of his thinking. Check each paper each day. Be sure that every example is correct before the child leaves the work.

Borrowing in Subtraction

Use the 10-string abacus. Write an example: 43
                                              −16

Show on the abacus that you cannot take a large number from a smaller number. Show him 3 and that you cannot take away 6. With your pencil show him how to borrow a ten from the tens column, thus changing the 4 to a 3 and making the 3 into a 13.

Arrange the combinations so that your first examples do not have the sum of 11 since this is confusing to the child (one ten and one 1 = 11).

Add and Check

By the time the child is ready to learn to check his own examples, this is an easy and comfortable process.

Write down an example: 243
$$+232$$

Have the child add to find the sum. By this time he will perhaps proudly tell you that he does not need an abacus. Call attention to the number next to the add sign. Tell him to copy this number down under his answer, reminding him to copy number under number. Tell him to subtract to get his answer. Then show him that it is the same number as the one at the top of his example. (Some children will make this discovery for themselves.) Use only simple combinations at first, and defer carrying and borrowing until much later.

Subtract and Check

This process is essentially the same as that described in the previous section, except that to check subtraction the child adds. Mix the problems so that the child will be able to transfer from one process to the other without difficulty.

Counting by 2's

Use the "hundreds board," made in the section, "Counting by 5's," above, but now write the odd numbers in blue and the even numbers in red. Have the child read the red numbers until he gets the feel of counting by 2's. The names *odd* and *even* are introduced here. Then give him a squared paper and let him fill in the numbers for himself. Start off with one line only, and then add more lines as soon as he is ready for them. He may discover for himself the possibility of skipping spaces and writing only the red numbers in their proper places. Another possibility is for the teacher to write in the blue (odd) numbers and then to let the child fill in the missing (red) numbers.

Dollar Sign and Decimal Point

Work papers may be made by writing the examples in blue and the decimal point and dollar sign in red. Show the child how to make the dollar sign and where it is put. Do the same for the decimal point.

After the child has learned to make the dollar sign, call out money numbers for him to write.

Later, work papers may be made on which he reads the number words and writes the amount of money indicated.

Written Problems

Written problems must be very simple at first. It is very important to use only vocabulary with which the child is familiar. This type of work is very difficult for him. Use the number symbols in the problems at first; later the number words may be used. Make the problems so simple at first that the child immediately knows what process to use. *Gradually* increase their level of difficulty. The child should be able to begin to organize and use what he has been taught.

Multiplication

Multiplication has a great psychological influence upon the child. There is a "grown-up-ness" about it. Further, it is a dramatic moment when he discovers that multiplication is a quick way to do addition. The multiplication sign itself with its oblique lines mean mastery over the difficulties of eye-hand co-ordination. By the time he has reached this stage, it is hoped that he no longer needs the abacus; let him use it, however, until he is ready to discard it.

USE OF ABACUS

Begin teaching very simple examples orally to show the child how to do it. Take for example:

$$\begin{array}{r} 2 \\ \times 3 \\ \hline \end{array}$$

Have the child push over 3 groups of two; then 2 groups of three. Let him discover that a 2 × 3 and 3 × 2 are the same. Do several examples such as this before you write one on paper for the child to work. Stay with him until he feels secure. Tell him to call you immediately if he needs help.

THE MULTIPLICATION BOARD

Some children understand multiplication better if the multiplication board is used before the abacus. The multiplication board is made by using 2 pieces of heavy cardboard, 6 by 21 inches (see Figure 64). Cut six 2-inch windows in each piece as shown. The 2 large pieces are pasted together with strips of the cardboard between the windows and at each end so that the strips of tagboard can be moved. Now make 6 tagboard strips 2 by 18 inches. Mark off into 2-inch squares and make the dominoes as illustrated. Thread the board with the strips. The problems: 3 × 2 means to show 3 windows, each containing 2 dots.

Division

USE OF ABACUS

This is usually an easy process for most of the children. Begin by asking the child to push over a given number, e.g., "8." Then say to him, "How many 4's do you have?" He then groups the 8 into 2 fours. After several oral problems show him how to write a division example.

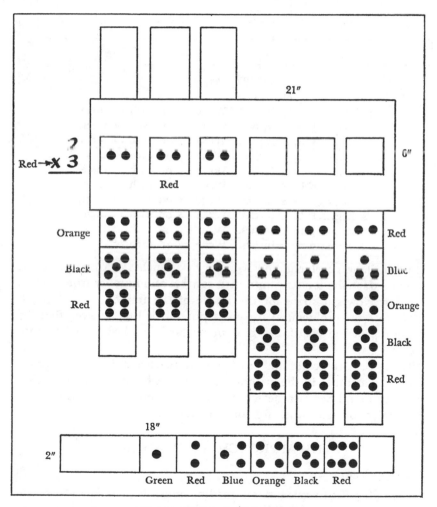

Fig. 64. Multiplication board.

THE DIVISION BOARD

This useful device is made as follows: Cut a piece of heavy cardboard 6 by 22 inches (see Figure 65). Frame the board by pasting a strip

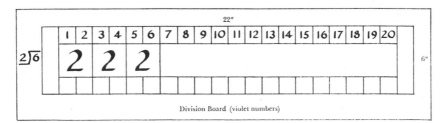

Fig. 65.

20 strips 1 by 2 inches. Write *1* on each of these.
10 strips 3 by 2 inches. Write *2* on each of these.
 7 strips 3 by 2 inches. Write *3* on each of these.
 5 strips 4 by 2 inches. Write *4* on each of these.
 4 strips 5 by 2 inches. Write *5* on each of these.
 3 strips 6 by 2 inches. Write *6* on each of these.
 2 strips 7 by 2 inches. Write *7* on each of these.
 2 strips 8 by 2 inches. Write *8* on each of these.
 2 strips 9 by 2 inches. Write *9* on each of these.
 2 strips 10 by 2 inches. Write *10* on each of these.

1 by 6 inches on each end and a strip 1 by 20 inches across the top and bottom. Mark the top strip into inch squares and number from 1 to 20 in color. Now cut strips for the inside of the frame.

To work the problem: 2$\overline{)\,6}$, put a pin on the line between 6 and 7 at the top of the board. See how many cards marked 2 will fit into that space.

By the time the child and teacher have reached this stage in arithmetic, the methods in the arithmetic texts will be usable. The teacher will have found her own devices for teaching concepts and can follow the regular course of study for further progress.

THE APPROACH TO READING

Reading Readiness

The following discussion on reading must be considered as one approach to reading for children with specific learning disabilities. It cannot stand alone as a treatise on reading and should not be approached unless the full content of this monograph has been read and understood. Reading is presented last because everything else is, by and large, preparation for reading. Kirk (7) lists the following factors in development as necessary for reading readiness:

1. a mental age of 6 or more,[8]
2. adequate language development required for reading,
3. memory for sentences and ideas,
4. visual memory and visual discrimination,
5. auditory memory and discrimination,
6. correct enunciation and pronunciation,
7. motor ability,
8. visual maturity,
9. motivation.

Any authority on reading would list these factors and would add the matter of social adjustment and the ability to cope with the day-to-day class situation.

The Problem

When a child has difficulty in reading, the first task is to try to discover the reason. If, for example, he cannot distinguish a square from a triangle, he will not be able to tell *A* from *H*. If a picture of a swing and a picture of a table look the same to him, he cannot see the difference between *M* and *W*. If he cannot stack plates, saucers and cups, or does not know what size piece of paper will best fit on his desk, he needs help in organizing spatial relationships, for in reading he may confuse said–and, the–then, you–yes, on–no. If he cannot direct his attention to specific sounds or cannot differentiate between high and low, loud and soft, he needs help in sound discrimination. If he cannot follow a simple direction, such as "put the book on the table," cannot ask or answer a simple question, is unable to speak understandably, he needs help in speech and language development.

He may have difficulty seeing the whole picture. One teacher asked a child to identify the picture of a farm. The child's response was "cat." A very small cat was sitting on the ground by the barn. This is the type of child who will identify a word by one part of it. He will learn *family*, for example, and then call any word ending in *y family*.

It is essential to fill the gaps within each successive stage of development, if the child is to learn to read. The techniques presented in this study are for the purpose of "filling the gaps" so that the child is ready

[8] At the 1958 meeting of American Association for Mental Deficiency, Hegge recommended a mental age of 8 for beginning reading with retarded children.

for the reading process. The more he can do and learn by seeing, feeling, hearing, and saying simultaneously, the greater his success in learning will be.

Many of the children in the study had had numerous failure experiences with reading; the presentation of a book for them to read would set off behavior reactions of aggression or withdrawal. Regardless of what grade they had come from or whether they were beginners, the same test procedures were used to find a point of beginning. As has been pointed out, the developmental lag or deviation had made function uneven. It is the goal in these procedures to get back to the basic tools necessary for reading and to build from there to the reading level. In the section on the instructional program these steps have been worked through very carefully. In looking toward the reading process, it may be well to ask questions that will aid in finding the right beginning point.

VISUAL DISCRIMINATION

1. Can the child sort colors into groups?
2. Does he know the names of colors?
3. Can he sort forms? Can he put all of the squares in one group and all of the round forms in another? Can he do this even though the forms are of different sizes and colors?
4. Can he do this with more than two forms? Can he draw any or all of the forms from the teacher's example?
5. Does he know the names of the forms?
6. Does he associate any meaning with any of the forms? E.g., "This is round like a ball," or "Round-Ball."
7. Can he reproduce a pattern from a model such as a red square, a blue square, and a green square in a vertical row? Can he do this horizontally?
8. Can he sort letters as described earlier?
9. Can he match pictures?
10. Can he match words to words?
11. Can he match pictures with letter, sound and word?
12. Can he speak clearly and understandably?
13. Can he imitate sounds?
14. Can he repeat a sentence after you?
15. Can he pick out the beginning or ending sounds?

LANGUAGE DEVELOPMENT

1. Can he answer questions?
2. Does he seem to understand what is said to him?

3. Does he have an adequate basic vocabulary (the Dolch cards are suggested as a starting point)?

4. Can he keep to a subject or does he wander to irrelevant topics?

5. Is his language satisfactory for his age level?

Left-to-right Progression

One sign of the developmental lag with children is the lack of established handedness. They are inclined to be ambidextrous. This may account in part for the clumsiness described in earlier sections. Studies by Gesell, McCarthy, Karlin, and others have shown that there is a simultaneous development of higher mental functions, cerebral dominance, handedness, and language skills.

In his study, Karlin found that the more strongly handedness was developed, the higher was the language ability. He found a positive correlation between the degree of brain development and the development of language and handedness.

Certainly in the area of reading and writing, the left-to-rightness is of utmost importance and requires specific training. This training needs to be started early and continued in every activity until well established. The purposes of training are:

1. to help determine and establish handedness,
2. to learn direction,
3. to gain a better self image,
4. to match forms and words in correct sequence,
5. to help establish spatial relationships.

TECHNIQUES

Begin with the left hand, since it is left-to-right that must be established. Place the child's left hand on paper and have him trace around it with a black crayon (even if it is necessary to guide his hand). Tell him this is his left hand. Write the word "left" on the paper copy, as well as on the back of his hand with chalk. Follow the same procedure with his right hand. See if he can cut out the hand forms and match them to his hands. *The goal is to see the form, and to match the form.* If he needs help in cutting or tracing, help him. He will say "left" and "right" with the teacher, repeat after her, and then do it by himself. Next have him trace his left hand on the blackboard with chalk, and later the right hand. Label the tracings "left" or "right."

While he is tracing, one can get a clue as to which hand does the best tracing. This may show which hand he should use in writing. Talk about and take turns demonstrating left ear and right ear, side, and foot, and so on. (*Be sure to face the same way as the child in these initial stages*.) Help him to know the left and right sides in tracing and writing; point out the fact that he starts at the left and goes to the right. A color cue is very helpful. Mark left with green and the stopping point with red. This is also a guide for him to follow and an aid in stopping.

Show pictures of left hand and right hand. Let him match them with his own.[9] Ask him to show you his left hand, his right hand—help him if he has forgotten. Devise games that are simple and not exciting; the goal is to learn left and right, not to play an exciting game.

Activities in motor training should be planned with establishing of dominance in mind. Sing "Looby Lou" and teach the proper motions, if this is not too exciting. Apply left and right to his immediate environment whenever possible. Setting the table is a good activity for learning left and right. The fork is on the left side; ask him to "put the fork on the left side." Teach him that, "The spoon is on the right side." Combine seeing, feeling, and doing, whenever possible.

Try as soon as possible to establish a definite purpose for one hand, "We salute the flag with our right hand." "We always shake hands with our right hand."

Keep making him conscious of left and right: ("The orange line is on the left side,") or testing ("On which side do you see the orange line?").

Visuo-motor Training

The activities introduced here have their beginning in the perceptual training as outlined earlier. The steps that follow lead from those activities *toward* reading. Good form and color discrimination will have been developed before this part of the program is followed.

USING FORMS AND SHAPES

Use paper geometric forms. The teacher puts a green square and, at its right, a red circle on the child's desk which has nothing else on it. Have him watch you do this. Now give him duplicate forms. Ask him to make the same design *under* the one already made. Be sure he knows the word "under." Guidance may be needed so that he will put the square on the left side and the circle on the right. Start working now for left to right progression.

Again use the squares and circles as above, but use all forms of the same color.

This time the teacher uses two green squares and one red circle

---

[9] Excellent picture of hands may be found in *Look and Say*, Teacher's Edition, World Book Company.

to make a horizontal pattern of a square, a circle and a square. The child is given duplicate forms and asked to duplicate the teacher's design under hers. Now use the same procedure but vary the shapes and colors, keeping two alike and one different. An added step is to tell which one is different.

Do the same exercise using a desk chart.

Give the child a similar exercise on ditto paper. Let him mark through the form that is different in each line. Then have him cut out the forms in the bottom line and paste them in the proper sequence in the spaces provided.

Go through the same steps as in the above paragraphs, but have the child now make the pattern to the right of the one he is copying.

Similar work may be found in reading readiness workbooks. Tear out such pages, cut them in strips if necessary. When the child is ready, increase the number of forms needed to make the designs, also the number of designs to be copied at one time.

MATCHING PICTURES

Match pictures which are exactly alike. Start with a few pictures. Increase the number and the difficulty as the child can handle them. The Dolch *Match-Me Picture* cards are excellent. If the teacher feels that at this time the child needs more help in this type of work, she may cut out clear pictures and mount them on tagboard for the child to match. Additional sets of picture cards should be made if necessary.

MATCHING LETTERS

This step is for matching, not learning, letter sounds or names. Begin with letters that are very different in forms, such as *o* and *t*. For example: On the first day take 2 *t*'s and 2 *o*'s. Put one *o* in one box and a *t* in the other. Give child the other *o* "Put this in the box that has one just like it." Then give the *t* and follow the same procedure. If he can do this, give him several of each and let him sort them himself. The desk pocket charts are good for this type of sorting.

Gradually work toward differences in letters which have more similar forms. The following pairs of letters are quite dissimilar:

m – t	q – r	h – j
c – b	s – t	k – p
d – e	w – o	l – n
f – g	y – z	a – i

However, the letters listed below are difficult to differentiate and so would be matched last:

h – k	i – j	e – c	m – w
r – h	b – p	h – n	m – n
n – u	t – f	o – e	b – d
i – l	a – s	o – c	x – w

(Suggested materials: Beckly Cardy letters, letters from printing set or primary typewriter, plastic letters, letters cut from workbooks or advertisements, dittoed letters in blocks, dittoes in two rows for matching.)

MATCHING WORDS

Follow the same procedure as in "Matching Letters" above, using words. Begin with words of very different configuration, for example: ball – me; go – run; little – come. Make them more similar as skill develops. Use words with capitals.

BUILDING WORDS

Give the child a desk chart with 3 or 4 word cards that are familiar to him. In a small box have only the letters needed to make these words. Guide the child to build words. Here the teacher stresses the left-to-right process. Caution: Do not allow the child to put the letters in the chart in any way other than the proper order.

Phonetic Training

At the same time that the teacher is working with visual training, she gives definite instruction in auditory perception. It is customary with normal children to begin ear training or phonics after a basic sight vocabulary is established; but for many of these children phonetic training is often the means of acquiring the first words of a reading vocabulary. It is necessary to have the all-sensory approach in order for them to organize the processes needed for reading. The children must be helped to realize that the symbols on the page represent speech sounds. They will learn the whole words if they understand how they are put together. The approach presented here has proven successful with the children in this study.

Ear Training

Techniques for listening suggested earlier are as basic to work on phonics as the eye-hand coordination exercises are for the visual approach to reading. In addition to listening, the children must learn to imitate sounds.

Imitate the sound of a fire engine. Some children will have their own variety of fire engine. A prolonged *oo–oo–oo* going up and down makes a fine fire engine. Make it start far away, come close, and go away again.

The sound of an airplane can be an *m–m–m*.

A tea kettle, a leaky tire, a radiator, or a snake can be *s–s–s–s*.

A mad cat says *f–f–f*.

A goose says *th–th–th* (voiceless).

Sounds need not have animals or objects connected with them. "Let me see if you can make this sound: 'ee,' 'ah,' 'k,' 'o,' " and so on. The purpose of this is to hear a sound and imitate it. Unless a child can give it back correctly, the hearing-speaking mechanism is not working correctly. If at all possible, correct the speech sound before putting it into the phonetic drill. Practice on the incorrect sound will only make its correction more difficult at a later date.

Correction of Defective Sounds

It is to be remembered that many articulation disorders are due to poor auditory perception. The child thinks he is saying the sound the right way. Test him to see if he can hear the error when you say the word the way he does. See if he can imitate the correct sound when you make it alone. For example, if the child says "tee" for "see," try him on games that would make him say s–s–s. Play "right and wrong." "I am going to say some words. You be the teacher and tell me when I make a mistake." Show pictures of objects beginning with *s*. Say several the right way. Then make a mistake on a very familiar one as "taw" for "saw." "Is this a taw?" If he can hear the difference in someone else and can say the sound by itself, then the suggested procedures for phonetic training will be very helpful in correcting his speech.

Beginning Sounds

Show pictures of two objects whose names begin with *m* (preferably words that end with a distinctly different sound) such as *milk* and *mop*. Say them as you point to them, strongly emphasizing the beginning sound. Have the child repeat them. Show several more pictures that begin with the same sound. Be sure he understands about "beginning." In words such as *moon* and *man* there is the possibility of confusing the *m* and *n*; it is best to leave them until the *m* is well established.

Find the pictures that begin with the *m* sound from a set that the teacher gives to the child.

Find pictures with this same *m* sound from magazines or old workbooks. Let the child cut out the pictures (outlined in black crayon, if necessary). Mount on paper. Each child might keep a book with his pictures.

By now the child probably can *write* the letter *m,* saying the sound as he does so. Have him write it under each picture.

Give him three clear-cut pictures, one of which shows an object whose name does not begin with the *m* sound and which has a distinctly different beginning sound: meat, cat, mouse. Ask the child to name each picture and to give the teacher the pictures of objects whose names begin with *m.*

Give the child several pictures, some of which show objects whose names begin with the *m* sound, to work with by himself. Have him sort these, putting all *m* words in one group, all others in another group.

AUDITORY AND VISUAL RECOGNITION COMBINED

Present the printed form of *m.* "You have learned to write *m.* Now I am going to show you how *m* looks in books and newspapers and magazines." Present different sizes, cut from a magazine, a printed card, from the print set. Let him stamp several *m*'s with the print set, type some on the typewriter, select some from a box of mixed letters. Let him go back to his pictures under which he has written *m,* and stamp or paste a letter there. "Now you know two ways to make *m.* You can write it and you can print it." "This letter has a sound and a name. Its name is 'em.' " (At this point the teacher should be sure that the child is always presented with cursive or printed form—not manuscript.)

Put several pictures in the pocket chart, using one or two that do not begin with *m.* Have him put the letter beside the pictures that begin with *m.*

THE "WINDOW CHART"

See example and directions on the following page (Figure 66). Put pictures in pockets. The child uses a print set to stamp the appropriate letter in window or to place a printed letter in the window. As he learns to write, he can write the sounds. Give him just the letters he needs to complete the activity.

Use the same general procedure in introducing each beginning consonant sound. Continue with each sound until the child seems ready to learn a new one. Go slowly, but do not risk boring him. If one sound seems too difficult, drop it for the time and try another one. The second

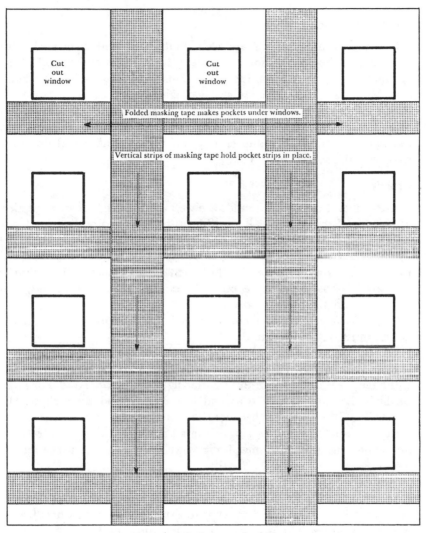

Fig. 66. Window Pocket Chart.

sound and letter should be different in both sound and configuration. *T* is a good choice for a second sound because it satisfies both requirements and is easy to write. With the exception of *m* and *n*, the voiceless consonants should be taken first; *g, d, b,* are best taught directly with short *u* as in *duck, bus, gun.* In presenting the diagraphs *th, sh* and *ch,* the use of color will help the recognition that two letters represent one sound.

Final Consonants

If the beginning sounds are well established and associated with letter forms, the final consonants usually come easily and quickly. The techniques used for beginning consonants can be used for the finals also. Whether final consonants are taught before or after vowels is dependent upon the child's need. Many of these children are inclined to omit final consonants. Therefore, it is important that they learn to pronounce the final sound clearly; the visual symbol will do much to correct the speech pattern.

Vowels

After several consonant sounds are well established, the introduction of one vowel sound makes it possible to begin building words. If one is following the procedure suggested in the section on writing, the short *i* would be the best one to use. This is limiting because of the few picture words with three sounds that include the short *i*. The short-*a* in "family" has many more possibilities: *cat, rat, hat, bat, fat,* and many other similar words exist.

Two pitfalls that may come with the usual approach to teaching vowels must be kept in mind:

Whereas most systems of teaching phonics treat the short vowels first, it is well to remember that a child who is weak in auditory perception will have great difficulty in differentiating them. Short *i* and *e* are particularly difficult. Many words end in *n* or *ng*, and these should be avoided until sound is set because the vowel blends into the nasal consonant (example: *pin, pen, ring*). The sounds *a* (as in *hat*) and *o* (as in *hot*) cause difficulty for some. Long vowels are easier to make and to hear.

Many of these children will find it very confusing to associate a sound with a specific object such as the *a* in *apple*. As in arithmetic, where one worked on the number concept to get twoness or threeness free of bunnies and cars, here it is important that the sound and its relationship to a symbol be established free of the distraction of pigs and apples.

As the child has learned to sound consonants when he sees the symbol, so he can learn the vowel sound. "This is the letter A and it says *a*." When this idea is set—"Now we can put some letters together." Use a different color for each letter.

1. Put down *m* and have him say it.
2. Put *a* after *m* and have him say m–m–a–a–.
3. Now add *t*. Point to each letter and say *m–a–t*.

4. Have the child do it with you.

5. When he seems sure of the sounds, have him do it alone.

6. Emphasize the fact that "We start at the left and go to the right."

Building Word Families

Dolch *Picture-Word* Cards are useful. Put the picture-word card in large chart rack. Build and sound the word for him as you place single letters in correct order beside picture-word card. Color for letters will help. Then let the child do it. When he is sure he knows how to do it, give him a similar exercise at his own desk, using a small desk chart. Put letters he will need in an envelope. When his work is checked, he is to sound the letters of a word as he moves his finger from left to right. Other cards can be made. Paste the picture(s) and print the word(s) on a small card. Have available to the child a set of individual letters (Figure 67) with which he can make the word(s) which the teacher has placed on the card.

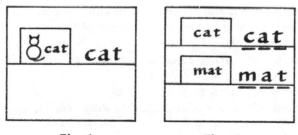

Fig. 67.   Fig. 68.

When he can do the first exercise successfully, replace the picture word card with just the word printed on plain paper clipped to seat chart (Figure 68).

Use Dolch cards *Teaching Short Vowels*, or make a set of flash cards of the word family needed. It helps to put the vowel in red, for example, $C - t$.

Adapt window cards to vowel sound.

Make a vowel sound booklet combining pictures and words.

Stay with one vowel sound until the child knows it well and can substitute many beginning and ending sounds, recognizing and saying each new word. In this word-building procedure there is a close correlation between spelling and reading. He can soon learn to spell words in word families. At this stage he learns to spell only those words that are spelled just the way they sound. In the beginning, spelling is oral; but when he can call the letter names in sequence without looking at the word, he is getting excellent work in visual and auditory memory and recall.

For reinforcement and variety in practice on phonics, the following filmstrips will be found valuable: *Beginning Consonant Sounds—A, Beginning Consonant Sounds—B, Hearing Vowels Sounds—A, Hearing Vowels Sounds—B, Hearing Rhymes,* all from the series *The New Spelling Goals* (Webster Publishing Company).

Sight Words

Sight words are taught when needed. But the child's first attempt at seeing words in a sentence should be with as many words from "word families" as possible. The first sentence may contain just one word he can recognize as the teacher says the rest of the words, e.g., "The *cat* is black." Teacher may say: "Find the word here you know. Put your finger under it. When it is time to say that word—you say it." Teacher reads, "the," child says, "cat," teacher says, "is black." She points to each word as she says it and encourages the child to point to each word but only to say the word he knows. The accomplishment the child feels here may be his next cue that he *can* do something. A smile or "Isn't this fun?" from the teacher gives support and encouragement.

First sight words might be *color* words (blue, orange, etc.), number words, and words needed to follow simple directions, such as *color, draw,* and *come.* Color words and number words can be matched with objects.

Language Development

Though there can be a time set aside for language development in the class, this is an ongoing process that is working every minute of the day. Directions are given clearly and carefully. Understanding of every object and every activity is kept in mind at all times. There are the "gaps" to fill, and one must never take anything for granted; the teacher must be sure that each child understands what is expected of him and how to do it. This is training in language reception. It was noted in the psychological tests that many children failed on the subject of what things are made of, what things are used for. The inability to answer questions is a major problem with children who have difficulty in communication.

Games can be played in learning how to communicate and receive communication from others.

Make an action game for prepositions. Have children put an object *in, on, under, beside, below, above, behind,* the box. The teacher gives the direction first. When the children are skilled in following the directions, let them give the directions to each other. When the group can tolerate such activity, ask them to stand *on* a chair, lie *under* the desk, sit *on* the mat, hide *behind* the desk.

Make an action game for adverbs. Walk *quickly, slowly, sadly, quietly, noisily, happily,* and so on.

Make an action game for adjectives. Have a child bring the *blue, red, big, little, striped, smooth, hard, soft, fuzzy* ball and so on. Have him pretend he is *big, brave, little, happy, unhappy, kind, old, young,* and so on.

Make an action game for verbs. *Walk, run, hop, work, play,* and so on.

Make a game for sentence structure. Give each child an object which he can hide in his hand or behind him. "What do you have?" He answers with a complete sentence: "I have a car." Let a child ask the question, for it is important that he know how to ask as well as how to answer; each child must get used to hearing different people ask questions. Use a shoe box with a peep hole cut in one end. Put an object in the box. "What do you see"? Answer: "I see a doll." Look through a paper tube or use the slide or film strip projector and have each child tell what he sees. Question the child: "What can a boy do"? A girl, a mother, a father, a dog, a truck, a tractor. "A boy can run." "A father can drive a car." Ask a child to cut some paper and keep cutting. "What is Billy doing"? "Billy is cutting." Work up many situations and use pictures for "What is _____ doing"? Hide objects around the room. Have one child hunt at a time. "What did you find"? I found _____."

Some children will need much work in this area. The sentences can get longer and more complicated. By the teacher's use of the question-answer technique, the child will learn correct word order, clear speech and words that will appear in reading. Memory span is increased.

All games will be planned with an instructional purpose. "I Spy" is excellent. Card games such as "Go Fish" should have consistent questions or answers. "May I have your fives"? Assign each child a question that is within his ability to say, and hold him to it.

Reading Stories

Since the building of concepts is an important factor with these children, true-life stories are important for them. Attention span is a factor to take into consideration in selection of story material. Following is a list of stories that have been proven satisfactory: *Stories to Begin on* by Rhoda Bacmeister (E. P. Dutton and Company); *Come to the City, Come to the Farm,* and *Come to the Zoo* by Ruth M. Tensen (Bailey and Lee); *The Cat in the Hat* by Dr. Seuss (Random House); *Littlest House* by Elizabeth Coatsworth (Macmillan); *True Book of Holidays* by John Wallace Purcell (Children's Press); "I Know a Story," *Supplementary Primer* (Row Peterson); "On the Way to Storyland," *The First Reader* (Laidlaw Brothers); *The Toy Train* (A Golden Book, Simon and Schuster).

Stories on film strips have been found to be especially useful with distractible children. The darkened room with one focal point of light will frequently hold the attention of a group when other devices fail. The following film strips are recommended: *The Billy Goats Gruff, The Ugly Duckling, Cinderella, The Gingerbread Boy, Winter in Country and Town, Spring in Country and Town, Summer in Country and Town* (all titles, Curriculum Filmstrip Series).

The children learn to "tell" stories by arranging pictures in sequence. Many of the stories in readiness books can be cut out and pasted on separate cards. The child learns to say what comes first, what comes next, and so on. Later he may be encouraged to cut and paste a familiar story so that he can use for "Share and Tell."

CHART STORIES

After the child has acquired some skill with words, chart stories can be introduced. The purposes of chart stories are:

1. to show that there are symbols that represent verbal language,

2. to increase understanding of correct sequence of words in a left to right direction,

3. to record a unit of spoken thought,

4. to provide participation in a group activity,

5. to provide an opportunity to recognize familiar words in context.

Chart stories may begin with one sentence: "The ball is blue and red," or "The cat is on the mat."

Making or finding a representational picture to color, cut, and paste is valuable to help expand the memory for the sentence. More sentences can be added as they seem appropriate to interest and attention span.

The First Book

When the child knows all of the words from the book he is to get, when he has established the process of and reason for left to right progression, when he has a clear association between picture and object and understands the meaning of the words used, when he has a reasonably fluent speaking vocabulary, when he shows an interest in books and pretends to read or picks out words he does know—then he is ready for a book.

Here it is important that one know the child. The commercial book may be too distracting for some children. The book may need to be cut up so that he gets one short story at a time. It may be necessary to eliminate pictures. Some children will be able to use the book as it is intended to be used, following the teacher's manual. Let the child use his finger or a marker if he needs it. Accompanying workbooks should be used though they may need to be cut up.

Remedial Techniques

There are among these children those who appear to read well and rapidly. They are "word callers" who have no idea what they have read. Others may perseverate and say the same word or phrase over and over again, unable to proceed. These children will need "crutches" to help them slow down. Such devices as pointing to each word, marking between the words, making each word a different color, or using a frame to slide from word to word or phrase to phrase can be very helpful. Exercises in following directions will make the child slow down and pay attention to the words he is reading.

The young child's early reading is naturally oral. The brain-injured child is permitted to study his reading lesson by actually speaking the words he is reading, or by articulating them subvocally. Silent reading is not emphasized until the child's oral reading is fluent and until his rate of reading begins to approach the rate of his speech. We have found that too early inhibition of peripheral movements of articulation distracts the child from arriving at the sense of the material he has read. Also, the experience of hearing one's own voice speaking the words contributes toward strengthening the necessary auditory-visual relationships.

ART

Purpose of Art in the Special Class

Although art is usually thought of as free expression, in this program for children with learning disabilities it will be considered as one more way to practice skills and develop understandings. The goals are: to develop visual perception, to develop motor control, to aid in the teaching of writing, reading, and arithmetic, to establish spatial relationships, and to help the child in his socialization with the group.

Planning the Art Lesson

The art lesson must be as carefully structured as other activities. The teacher must know what she wants to accomplish, how she will motivate the lesson, and how to relate this activity to the children's needs and abilities. The room should be arranged so that the teacher can be close to all of the children at once. (This is a situation in which the trapezoidal tables can be used effectively.) All materials should be arranged in advance according to a systematic plan for distribution. A completed sample of what is to be done is before the children so that they can see the Gestalt before them at all times. A step-by-step procedure should be followed; plans for cleaning up and putting away should be a part of the lesson. Gradually the children can be trained to get ready, work, and clean up with fewer controls.

Materials to be Avoided

Finger paint, wet clay, and chalk have been found to create distracting situations. "Play-Doh" is a satisfactory substitute for clay.

Skills

CUTTING

Cutting is an important skill because it develops motor control and visuo-motor performance.

PASTING

The use of individual jars of paste for each child is more effective than giving out a small portion at a time. Pasting is a skill that should be taught step by step. Show the children how to open the jar, where to put the lid, how to dip the paste brush into the paste, how much paste to get on the brush, how to put paste on the paper, where to place the brush, how to turn the paper over, and so on.

PAINTING

Have paint mixed for the children and poured into containers that do not tip easily. Start with simple projects such as filling in a stencil. When the stencil is removed they can brush paint away from the stencil and make such things as sun rays. (See Figure 70a.)

Suggested Art Projects

USE OF STENCILS AND PATTERNS

Use forms such as the square, circle, and diamond for interesting effects (Figure 69).

Circles:

Squares:

Triangles:

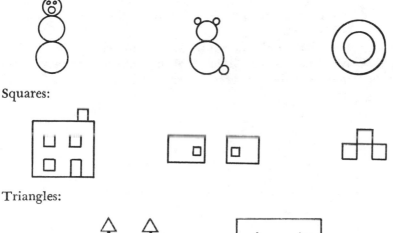

Fig. 69.

Color is used for filling in the forms. Start with one and work up to a combination, using first primary and then secondary colors.

Place mats can be made for use at the lunch period or in decorations for a party (Figure 70b and 70c).

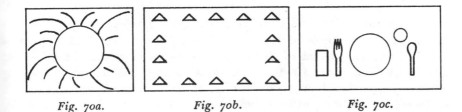

Fig. 70a.   Fig. 70b.   Fig. 70c.

STENCILS USED FOR SOCIAL STUDIES

For the holidays there are pumpkins, turkeys, bells, stars, hearts, and so on. The creation of the ornaments can be a fine group project and can be worked at Christmas. Sketch an outline of a tree on the bulletin board in the hall. The children can put their ornaments on it with paste or thumbtacks.

Stencils of farm animals, houses, fruits, vegetables, jungle animals, and so on, can be used advantageously. Representations of transportation and communication units lend themselves well to the use of stencils.

Stencils should have unbroken lines so that the child can see the Gestalt. Many commercial stencils are broken into sections and are not desirable for use with these children (Figure 71).

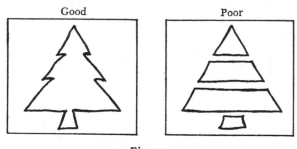

Fig. 71.

MURALS

From the objects created by simple cutting and pasting rather complicated murals can be made. In a unit on "Travel to Nearby Places," a background of brown paper can be put on the bulletin board. Cut and paste the blue sky, white clouds, cars, busses, boats, telephone poles, people walking, and so on.

SCIENCE

Nature study offers endless ways of integrating the classroom program. The same type of bulletin board display as was described above for Christmas can be used in the fall to show change of color and falling leaves. Use a simple leaf pattern (no veins), have children color (after observing trees outdoors), cut, and paste or thumbtack.

In the spring bring in sprays of forsythia and pussy willow. Have the children observe that on the forsythia the flowers are opposite each other, on the pussy willow they alternate. This leads into further study of growing plants, trees, and so on.

In studying animals have children observe animals in different positions. Then draw (stencil or free hand). In motor training, children can try to imitate, walk, and so on.

CRAYON TECHNIQUE

An interesting technique is to use the broad side of the crayon. It helps add depth to the work. Use crayons about 1 inch long (Figure 72).

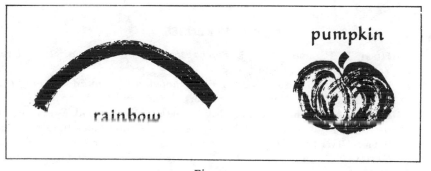

Fig. 72.

COLOR MIXING

After the children have learned the primary and secondary colors and have used them in crayons and paint, color mixing becomes very interesting. Work first with the crayons and then the paints.

NUMBERED PICTURES

Numbered pictures for coloring must be very simple at the start. The teacher can make these very easily by using coloring books (Figure 73).

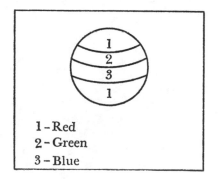

Fig. 73.

Handicraft

Simple handicraft can be done with these groups after their motor and perceptual abilities are developed. Simple woodworking, weaving, and so on, can be done. The block design technique used for training can be carried over by the use of floor tiles. These make beautiful hot pads. Odds and ends of tile can be found in the supply companies or can be bought as art supplies.

REFERENCES

1. HOCH, P. H., and ZUBIN, J. *Psychopathology of Communication.* New York: Grune and Stratton, 1958.
2. STRAUSS, A. A., and LEHTINEN, L. E. *Psychopathology and Education of the Brain-Injured Child.* Vol. 1. New York: Grune and Stratton, 1947.
3. STRAUSS, A. A., and KEPHART, N. C. *Psychopathology and Education of the Brain-Injured Child.* Vol. 2. New York: Grune and Stratton, 1955.
4. PRUDEN, B. *Is Your Child Really Fit?* New York: Harper & Brothers, 1956.
5. GETMAN, G. N., and KEPHART, N. C. *Plastic Templets.* Loveland, Colorado: Child Care Co., 1956.
6. KIRK, S. A. *Teaching Reading to Slow-Learning Children.* Boston: Houghton Mifflin Co., 1940.

CHAPTER VI

Psychological, Educational, and Psychiatric Evaluations

IN THE PRECEDING chapters of this monograph, problems of diagnosis, teacher selection, room treatment, teaching method, and other matters pertinent to the demonstration-pilot study have been discussed. It remains now to consider in detail the reactions of the children themselves to the educational program. It should be kept in mind that the children were under the described instructional program *for a maximum of ten months*. Not all children received this amount of school experience, since many began their school attendance later than others. Vacations and illness also shortened the school experience in varying amounts.

The children were carefully evaluated psychologicaly and psychiatrically at the beginning of the school year and at its close. This chapter includes a brief description of each of the psychological tests used, as well as the administration and the scoring techniques. Included also is a second psychological post-evaluation which was completed twelve months after the close of the formal demonstration year. Finally, the psychiatric evaluations made at the beginning and at the end of the demonstration year are discussed.

PSYCHOLOGICAL INSTRUMENTATION

The test battery consisted of thirteen tests designed to investigate intelligence, social development, perceptual ability, readiness, and academic achievement. The pre-test period consisted of two phases: the period of the screening battery which was administered before the children were grouped; and the period of the remaining tests completed after the children were assigned to the research classes.

In the diagnostic phase the children were seen either at the school in which they were enrolled, or else they were brought to the psychologist's office by a parent.

The screening battery consisted of:

1. Terman-Merrill Revision of the Stanford-Binet; Test, Form L;
2. Goodenough Intelligence Test;
3. Block Design and Coding subtests from the Wechsler Intelligence Scale for Children;
4. Bender-Gestalt.

After the diagnostic period was completed and the children were class based, the remainder of the pre-test program was completed.

This involved the use of:

1. Vineland Scale of Social Maturity;
2. Ammons Full-Range Picture Vocabulary Test;
3. Marble Board Test;
4. Tactual Motor Test;
5. Syracuse Visual Figure-Background Test;
6. Rorschach;
7. Metropolitan Readiness Test;
8. Stanford Achievement Test.

The choice of tests used in this study was guided by several considerations. The first problem was to determine the possible presence of organicity. To this end, tests were chosen which have been used extensively with brain-injured children, especially cerebral palsy children, such as the Tactual-Motor Test, Marble Board Test, and the Syracuse Visual Figure-Background Test, the last being a tachistoscopic test originally used by Strauss and Werner (59) and others (47) but greatly modified at Syracuse University. Two items chosen from the Wechsler Intelligence Scale for Children, the Block Design and Coding, have at times revealed the presence of organicity.

The second factor determining the choice of tests was the time available for testing. It was necessary to obtain a maximum of information in the shortest possible time. Each child was seen once during the diagnostic phase of the testing; the time ranged from forty-five minutes to an hour and a half. Since many of the children were hyperactive and emotionally disturbed, it was felt that this represented an absolute maximum of time for one testing session. Time was also an important consideration once the classes were grouped and once the academic experience for the children had started. The children were in the classroom only from 9:30 A.M. until 2:00 P.M. They were primarily in school for an academic experience, not for the purpose of serving as continuous subjects for psychological evaluation. Therefore, the testing program necessarily had to be fitted into the school program. This was worked out with each teacher; she selected the child who would be least disturbed by leaving the room with the examiner at a particular time.

Considering both the expended time and the amount of information gained, four tests used in the pre-testing period were discarded in the final, post-test period. They were the two items from the Wechsler Intelligence Scale for Children (Block Design and Coding), the Tactual-Motor Test, and the Marble Board Test. It was felt that these tests contributed little additional information and merely duplicated the information obtained from other instruments.

The total post-test battery consisted of:

1. Stanford-Binet, Form M;
2. Goodenough Intelligence Test;
3. Vineland Scale of Social Maturity;
4. Bender-Gestalt;
5. Syracuse Visual Figure-Background Test;
6. Stanford Achievement Test;
7. Rorschach.

The post-test phase was composed of three separate testing sessions with each child:

1. the Stanford-Binet, Form M, was administered during one session;
2. the Goodenough Intelligence Test, Bender-Gestalt, and Rorschach were given during the second session;
3. the Syracuse Visual Figure-Background Test was administered during the third session.

Because of the special conditions required for the last test—i.e., darkened room and special equipment—a separate session was required. The Vineland Scale of Social Maturity involved a separate interview with the parents. The psychologist administered the Stanford Achievement Test during the pre-test phase, but the teachers assumed the responsibility for the post-test administration because of the pressure of time.

Although both pre- and post-test Rorschachs were administered, the results have not been included in the present report for reasons to be discussed elsewhere. (See p. 431.)

In the presentation that follows, a brief background for each test will be given, the administration and scoring will be described, and statistical results will be presented.

Stanford-Binet Scale

The choice of a psychological instrument for the evaluation of intelligence was quickly narrowed down to the two most commonly used tests for this purpose: the Stanford-Binet and the Wechsler Intelligence Scale for Children.[1]

During the planning stages of this project, the main interest was in detection of central nervous system dysfunction rather than emotional dysfunction. It was generally agreed among the diagnostic staff that the determination of an intellectual level of functioning was in itself of little diagnostic value when considering brain injury *per se*. As Goldenberg has pointed out:

> Although there is a real problem in the choice of the most effective measures of intelligence for use with organic groups, this is more or less extraneous to the problem of detection of organicity (33, pp. 145–146).

Many authors (17, 19, 20, 22, 42, 44) have reported that brain-injured children have intellectual ability well within the range of the normal. Among many others, Benton and Collins (17) have pointed out that brain-injured children show a *selective* impairment of intellectual functioning. Hence, the use of general tests of intelligence as diagnostic tool in the detection of brain injury has centered first upon attempts to detect patterns of performance indicative of brain injury, and second upon attempts to identify particular test items which might be of value for discriminating the effects of such impairment of intellectual functioning.

One reason for choosing the Stanford-Binet rather than the WISC is that there are relatively few studies (9, 62) which report the use of the WISC with brain-injured children. There are several such studies which mention the use of the Stanford-Binet. Hopkins, Bice and Colton (40), and Cruickshank and Bice (23) have presented evidence showing the difficulty for cerebral palsy children of certain items of the Binet. Failure was generally observed to occur on items requiring judgment, discrimination, memory, visuo-motor abilities, and locomotion. The largest percentages of passes occurred on language development items.

Another factor which made the choice of the Binet desirable was that many of the children had previously had the Binet administered to them either by a school psychologist or in a clinic contact. Thus, comparison of results was possible.

[1] Referred to hereinafter as the WISC.

Since the Binet was not primarily constructed for the purpose of evaluating organicity, most of the information derived from such use is arrived at by inference and empirical observations. Hoakley and Frazeur (39) compared matched groups of exogenous and endogenous retarded children on the Binet Scale. The only statistically significant differences found between the groups occurred on items requiring perceptual or visuo-motor performance, such as the drawing of a diamond. It should be noted that Sarason (49) has called into question the diagnostic significance of this finding because none of the 15 pairs of children taking that item made equal scores.

Sarason (49) found that 9 subjects in a group of 18 mentally defective children were completely unable to reproduce the diamond item on the Binet and that their performance was very poor on other items requiring the reproduction of form relationships.

Frazeur and Hoakley (31) compared groups of exogenous and endogenous boys (matched for CA and Binet IQ) for differences in performance on the Arthur Point Scale. The only significant differences found were on the Porteus Mazes, which distinguished the performance of the two groups at the .05 level of confidence.

Feifel (29) found that brain-injured children and adults as well as many psychotic patients, show a lower level of conceptualization in Stanford-Binet vocabulary definitions than do matched control subjects. Bijou and Werner (18), however, found that when exogenous and endogenous children were matched on MA and IQ, and when comparison was made on the Binet vocabulary test, the definitions of the brain-injured were superior.

Although the use of the Binet as an instrument *diagnostic* of brain injury is open to some question, there are, nevertheless, research findings to indicate that:

1. brain-injured children do perform differently on at least some of the items, especially those requiring perceptual or visuo-motor performance;

2. there seems to be an order of item difficulty, at least for cerebral palsy children who are known to be brain-injured.

RESULTS

Table 13 shows the means, standard deviations, and *t*-test for the pre– and post-test Stanford-Binet Intelligence Test IQ's. It can be seen that there are no statistically significant differences between the pre-test and post-test means, either for the group as a whole or for the four indi-

TABLE 13

Mean IQ, Standard Deviations, t-Tests, and Probabilities of Chance Differences in Means for the Pre- and Post-test Stanford-Binets

| Class | N | Pre-test | | Post-test | | |
		$\overline{X}$	σ	$\overline{X}$	σ	t
C-1	10	80.20	11.58	80.00	14.16	.11
C-2	10	82.10	13.48	83.80	13.43	.62
E-1	10	78.00	14.13	75.30	13.00	1.36
E-2	9	81.33	14.89	82.00	14.61	.33
Total	39	80.39	13.63	80.23	14.16	.14

vidual groups.[2] This is, of course, what is to be expected from the process of careful screening and matching. As a further check on the comparability of the groups, an analysis of variance was made on the

TABLE 14

Mean IQ, Standard Deviations, t-Tests, and Probabilities of Chance Differences in Means for the Control and Experimental Groups on the Stanford-Binet Intelligence Test

Group	N	$\overline{X}$	σ	t
Combined Control Groups, Pre-test	20	81.15	12.60	
				.35
Combined Experimental Groups, Pre-test	19	79.58	14.59	
Combined Control Groups, Post-test	20	81.90	13.93	
				.74
Combined Experimental Groups, Post-test	19	78.47	14.19	
Comparison of Control Group, Pre-test, and Control Group, Post-test	20	.75	7.51	.44 [a]
Comparison of Experimental Group, Pre-test, and Experimental Group, Post-test	19	.58	4.56	.05 [a]

[a] All *t*-tests in this chapter were computed on basis of paired observations. The mean and standard deviation are based on the differences between pairs of observations, according to the formula given in Allen L. Edwards, *Experimental Design in Psychological Research* (New York: Rinehart and Company, Inc., 1950), p. 150.

[2] The accepted statistical significance level in this report is .05 level. In the discussion which follows, only figures at this level are considered significant. The .10 level is reported as "approaching significance."

pre-test IQ scores, post-test scores, and the differences between the pre–
and post-test scores. No significant F values were obtained.

Table 14 shows the comparison of Stanford-Binet IQ scores for the
control and experimental groups. This analysis was made as a further
check on the possibility of differential growth in the experimental
groups as compared to the control groups. As can be seen from the table,
no statistically significant differences were observed.

There seemed to be a narrowing of the age range on the Stanford-
Binets of the year. It was felt that there might be a "consolidation"
of ability; and that, as a result of the year's experience, performance
at the lower levels of the scale had been brought more nearly into line
with the child's potential ability. Table 15 shows the means, standard

TABLE 15

*Means, Standard Deviations, and Probabilities of Chance Differences in
the Means for the Age Range for the Pre- and Post-test
Stanford-Binets*

| Class | N | Pre-test | | Post-test | | t |
		$\overline{X}$	σ	$\overline{X}$	σ	
C-1	10	5.30	1.49	5.10	1.58	.41
C-2	10	5.30	1.27	4.30	1.74	1.72
E-1	10	5.40	.92	4.80	.75	1.59
E-2	9	5.11	1.45	4.66	1.15	1.28
Total	39	5.28	1.30	4.72	1.40	2.39 †

† $p < .05$

deviation, and *t*-tests of significance between means for the age range
on the pre– and post-test Stanford-Binets. There were no significant
differences by class; but the age range of the total group was significantly less ($p. < .05$) at the end of the school year. To check on whether
or not there were systematic changes in age range, comparison was
made between the experimental and control groups, the results are
shown in Table 16. No significant differences were found.

Although there are some differences between the order of difficulty of
test items used in the present study and the order of difficulty reported
by Cruickshank and Bice (23), the same general types of difficulty may
be seen, i.e., the most difficult items require visuo-motor ability (drawing a diamond, copying a bead chain), followed by items involving
memory, judgment, and discrimination.

The most difficult single item was the drawing of a diamond. Only

TABLE 16

*Means, Standard Deviations, t-Tests, and Probalities of Chance
Differences in Means for the Control and Experimental
Groups on the Stanford-Binet Age Range*

Group	N	$\overline{X}$	σ	t
Combined Control Groups, Pre-test	20	5.30	1.38	
				.09
Combined Experimental Groups, Pre-test	19	5.26	1.21	
Combined Control Groups, Post-test	20	4.70	1.71	
				.09
Combined Experimental Groups, Post-test	19	4.74	.96	
Comparison of Control Group. Pre-test, and Control Group, Post-test	20	.60	1.74	1.50
Comparison of Experimental Group, Pre-test, and Experimental Group, Post-test	19	.53	1.09	.65

7 out of the 39 children were able to draw a diamond which met the Binet scoring criteria. The mean age of these 7 children was 8–7, and the mean IQ was 93.71. The mean age for all the children was 8–3, and the mean IQ was 80.39. Of the 7 children who were able to draw a diamond, one had been diagnosed as having definite neurological involvement. It is also of interest to note that of these 7 children, 4 had abnormal electroencephalograms.

The children did not show significant changes in IQ over the course of the year. The total group showed a significant narrowing of the age range when comparison was made of the pre-test (Form L) and post-test (Form M) results, but there were no differences between the children in stimulus-free classrooms and those in regular classrooms.

Goodenough Intelligence Test

The Goodenough test is widely used with children. Bender (13) has stressed its importance in evaluating post-encephalitic and brain-injured children. She emphasized one important diagnostic clue: the discrepancy between the Goodenough MA and the Binet MA, i.e., she considers a Goodenough mental age two years lower than the Binet MA as being highly suggestive of organicity.

Benton and Collins (17) believe that the Goodenough contributes to the diagnosis and detection of brain injury in about 50 per cent of the cases, but they have not offered controlled observations or data to support this contention.

While the influence of brain pathology may be sufficient in many cases to lead to poor performance on this test, other authors, notably Machover (44), have shown that poor performance may be found in conditions of psychosis, neurosis, or other emotionally based conflict states. Goldberg (32) found that while normals tend to produce the best drawings, and organics the poorest, there is a great deal of overlap in the performance of various psychiatric groups.

Goodenough and Harris (35) have reviewed the studies dealing with reliability, scorer agreement, and test-retest reliability; and they have shown that these aspects of the test meet the usual requirements up for good clinical tests.

Goldenberg concluded his review of the literature as follows:

The Goodenough test has not yet been established as having a sufficient validity as a discriminator of brain injury in children to justify its general clinical use for this purpose (33, p. 159).

The Goodenough test was included in the present battery as an additional source of information regarding the intellectual and perceptual functioning of these children, not as a test for discriminating the presence or absence of brain injury. Its inclusion could be justified as a rapport-gaining device, if nothing else. All of the children, with one exception, seemed to enjoy "drawing a man" and looked upon this activity as a game.

ADMINISTRATION AND SCORING

The pre-test drawings were included as part of the diagnostic battery. Administration and scoring were based on Goodenough's directions (35).

The child was seated at a desk on which there were several sheets of paper (8½ by 11 inches), a pencil, and an eraser. He was told: "I would like you to draw a picture of a whole man for me. Take your time, and make it the best picture of a man that you can possibly draw." Any questions from the child about his drawing were referred back to his judgment. Any spontaneous remarks made by the child were recorded.

The drawing was scored by the examiner as soon as possible. In the present study, two judges independently scored all of the pre-test Goodenough tests; then the IQ's were correlated. The Pearson product moment correlation coefficient was .91. The two judges went through all the scorings and, through discussion, arrived at a decision in the few instances where there was a discrepancy. In no case was there difficulty in resolving a scoring problem.

RESULTS

Table 17 shows the means, standard deviations, and *t*-tests of the significance of differences between means for the Goodenough IQ's. IQ's rather than MA's were used because interest was focused on the

TABLE 17

Mean IQs, Standard Deviations, and Probabilities of Chance Differences in Means for the Pre- and Post-test Goodenough Intelligence Tests

Class	N	Pre-test $\overline{\mathrm{X}}$	Pre-test σ	Post-test $\overline{\mathrm{X}}$	Post-test σ	t
C-1	10	79.50	20.48	85.30	9.92	1.27
C-2	10	73.20	13.92	75.50	11.80	.50
E-1	10	72.10	11.00	76.50	16.13	1.22
E-2	9	85.57	12.51	75.00	10.21	2.95 ‡
Total	39	77.39	15.84	78.15	13.02	.10

‡ p < .02

rate of development. As can be seen from the table, three of the four classes made small, nonsignificant gains in IQ over the course of the year. The one exception (Class E-2) made significantly lower average Goodenough IQ's at the end of the year (p. < .02).

Table 18 shows comparison of the combined control groups with

TABLE 18

Means, Standard Deviations, t-Tests, and Probabilities of Chance Differences in Means for the Control and Experimental Groups on the Goodenough Intelligence Test IQ Scores

Group	N	$\overline{\mathrm{X}}$	σ	t
Combined Control Groups, Pre-test	20	76.35	17.79	
				.41
Combined Experimental Groups, Pre-test	19	78.47	13.53	
Combined Control Groups, Post-test	20	80.40	11.95	
				1.09
Combined Experimental Groups, Post-test	19	75.79	13.67	
Comparison of Control Groups, Pre-test, and Control Groups, Post-test	20	4.05	14.65	1.21
Comparison of Experimental Groups, Pre-test, and Experimental Groups, Post-test	19	2.37	13.43	.75

the combined experimental groups. There were no significant differences in comparing the control with experimental groups, or in comparing the pre- with the post-test control groups, or in comparing the pre- with the post-test experimental groups.

The above data show no differences between the experimental classes and control classes. It is of interest to note, however, that in the pre-testing only one child drew a man who was "doing something." None gave spontaneous secondary elaborations or descriptions. In the post-testing, however, 15 children (38 per cent) either drew a man "doing something" or gave a number of secondary elaborations, i.e., "A janitor," "I drew a cowboy, with a gun," "He's wearing a striped shirt," "He's sitting down at a table, on a mat," and so on. Of these latter 15 children, 9 were in the stimulus-free classrooms and 6 were in the control classrooms.

Ammons Full-Range Picture Vocabulary Test

The decision to include the Ammons Full-Range Picture Vocabulary Test [3] in the pre-test psychological battery was made because no reading, writing, or speech is required of the testee. This was especially desirable in view of the severe speech difficulties of some of the children. In the FRPV, the child is required to point, and no spoken language is necessary.

The norms for the FRPV—which were established on a population carefully controlled for age, sex, grade placement in school, and occupation of father—have been reported in a series of articles by Ammons and others (2, 3, 4, 5, 6).

Reliability is uniformly high, ranging for various groups from .86 to .99. In general, validity has also been shown to be quite good. Pearson product moment correlation coefficients have been reported as follows: .76 with Stanford-Binet for 60 male mental defectives (53), .82 with Wechsler Intelligence Scale for Children for 90 children who were reading cases (54), .78 with Leiter International Performance Scale for 50 cerebral palsied (41), .85 with full Binet for 120 preschool children (3), and .88 with Binet Vocabulary for 71 rural children (5).

The FRPV was not included in the post-test battery for two reasons. First, the test did not contribute enough additional data. Its high correlation with the Stanford-Binet, Form L, in the present study was .83, which shows that the test measures essentially the same thing as the Stanford-Binet and, also, that it can be used advantageously as a quick estimate of general intellectual functioning. Second, the time limita-

[3] Referred to hereinafter as the FRPV.

tion made it necessary to administer the entire test battery to all of the children in approximately one month; consequently, an attempt was made to obtain a maximum of meaningful information in the shortest possible time.

ADMINISTRATION AND SCORING

The FRPV consists of 16 cards; on each card there are four cartoon-like line drawings. The examiner's answer sheet lists the words to be used with each card. The child is asked to point to the drawing which best represents a particular word. Each response is checked right or wrong. Adult percentiles and mental ages from 2 years through 16 are available.

RESULTS

Table 19 shows the means and standard deviations for the mental ages on the FRPV. Comparison of the two combined control groups with the two combined experimental groups does not show a significant difference between the means.

TABLE 19

Mean Mental Ages and Standard Deviations for the Ammons Full-Range Picture Vocabulary Test: Form A

Group	N	$\overline{\text{X}}$	σ
C-1	9	102.56	21.99
C-2	10	90.00	16.76
E-1	7	91.57	19.62
E-2	9 [a]	100.00	27.71
Total	35	96.11	22.55

[a] One child terminated due to necessity for 24-hour treatment.

The above results show that at the beginning of the present project, the FRPV mental ages of the children in stimulus-free environments were quite similar to those of the children in control classrooms. These results are consistent with the findings on the Stanford-Binet and Goodenough Intelligence Test which showed that the four classes were quite comparable in their intellectual functioning.

Block Design and Coding from WISC

Block design problems have been included in a number of tests of general ability (56) as well as in tests designed to evaluate impairment of the abstract attitude (34). The value of this type of test in diagnostic work with children is based largely on uncontrolled clinical observations, and from studies where the tests have been used with mentally defective children.

The Block Design and Coding subtests from the WISC were included because it was felt that they might provide additional information about the children's learning problems.

RESULTS

Table 20 gives the test age means and standard deviations for the WISC subtest Block Design. Comparison of the means of the combined

TABLE 20

Mean Test Ages and Standard Deviations for the Wechsler Intelligence Scale for Children Subtest: Block Design

Group	N	X̄	σ
C-1	10	73.60	12.32
C-2	10	79.20	23.94
E-1	10	62.80	9.77
E-2	9	76.67	12.65
Total	39	72.97	17.41

experimental and combined control groups resulted in a *t*-test of 1.03 which does not reach the level of significance accepted for this study.

Table 21 gives the test age means and standard deviations for the WISC subtest Coding. A *t*-test of the significance of the differences be-

TABLE 21

Mean Test Ages and Standard Deviations for the Wechsler Intelligence Scale for Children Subtest: Coding

Group	N	X̄	σ
C-1	10	80.00	20.71
C-2	10	74.80	19.90
E-1	10	68.80	12.27
E-2	9	79.33	15.39
Total	39	75.64	18.19

tween the means of the combined experimental and combined control groups was not significant ($t = .08$).

The above results reflect the careful matching of the children at the beginning of the academic year. The control and experimental groups were equal in the types of ability called for in the Block Design and Coding subtests.

Metropolitan Readiness Test

The Metropolitan Readiness Test, Form R, was administered by the staff psychologist to all 39 of the children at the beginning of the academic year. The test is devised to measure the traits and achievements that contribute to readiness for first grade instruction. It is designed to be administered at the end of the kindergarten year or at the beginning of the first grade. The test was administered to all of the children because many were unable, in spite of their age, to do many of the things required for its satisfactory completion.

The Metropolitan Readiness Test is composed of six subtests: word meaning, sentences, information, matching, number, and copying. The first four subtests (word meaning, sentences, information, and matching) are grouped together to give a reading readiness estimate, test 5 (number) is considered the number readiness test; the total of the results on all six subtests gives a total readiness estimate. Descriptions of the six subtests follow:

SUBTEST 1. WORD MEANING

Understanding and comprehension, rather than language usage, are involved in this subtest. The child's task is to select the one picture out of four that illustrates the word the examiner uses.

SUBTEST 2. SENTENCES

Comprehension of phrases and sentences is required. Successful performance on this test requires more sustained attention.

SUBTEST 3. INFORMATION

This subtest is related to vocabulary. The child is required to select the one picture out of four that best suits the examiner's description.

SUBTEST 4. MATCHING

This is a test of visual perception involving the recognition of similarities. Each item contains four different pictures of animals, figures, objects, words or letters. In the center of the row, there is a framed picture which is just like one of the other four. The child is to circle the picture that looks just like the one with a frame around it.

SUBTEST 5. NUMBERS

This involves ordinal numbers, recognition of fractional parts, recognition of forms, time, and number vocabulary.

SUBTEST 6. COPYING

This test involves visual perception and motor control. Geometric forms and letters are the stimulus figures. Much the same type of activity is called for in this subtest as that required in the Bender-Gestalt.

In the manual of directions distributed with the test booklets, note is made that groups larger than 15 are not recommended and that smaller groups are even more desirable. Because of the distractibility of the children, each examination was administered individually. In no instance was there a departure from the directions made. The tests were carefully timed, and no help other than that explicitly stated in the directions, was given. The individual tests were given in as non-stimulating a room as the schools could provide. An attempt was consistently made to obtain the most accurate estimate of readiness ability.

RESULTS

Table 22 gives the means and standard deviations for each of the subtests of the Metropolitan Readiness Test. Table 23 gives a comparison of the combined control and combined experimental groups. There were no statistically significant differences between the groups on any of the subtests.

These results of the Metropolitan Readiness Test show that all of the four classes were very evenly matched.

Tactual-Motor Test

This test was originally devised by Werner and Strauss (59) to determine perceptual ability in the tactual sense modality. While blindfolded, a subject must feel a board which has a raised design on it and then indicate his perception of the design by drawing it on paper provided for that purpose. Several variations have been used. In the present study, it was decided not to blindfold the children because of the fear this might cause. Instead, a screen was used through which the child extended his two hands. In no case did a child experience observable anxiety about this procedure. Several children became curious and wanted to look behind the screen but were easily discouraged from doing so.

TABLE 22

Means and Standard Deviations for the Metropolitan
Readiness Tests, (N = 39)

Test	Group									
	C-1		C-2		E-1		E-2		Total	
	X̄	σ	X̄	σ	X̄	σ	X̄	σ	X̄	σ
Word Meaning	16.70	1.55	17.50	.81	16.80	.20	17.00	1.76	17.00	1.63
Sentences	10.50	2.38	11.10	1.70	10.60	2.97	10.00	2.94	10.56	2.57
Information	12.80	1.25	12.80	1.47	11.90	1.38	12.11	1.66	12.41	1.50
Matching	14.50	2.34	14.20	3.54	12.40	4.98	14.11	3.18	13.80	3.74
Numbers	16.60	6.39	17.30	4.69	15.30	4.65	18.33	5.03	16.85	5.36
Copying	6.20	2.52	6.70	2.45	5.10	2.62	5.00	2.87	5.77	2.98
Percentile Rank	65.00	31.19	69.00	26.39	56.10	30.56	63.79	30.99	63.46	30.23

TABLE 23

Means, Standard Deviations, t-Tests, and Probabilities of Chance
Differences in Means for the Combined Control and
Experimental Groups on the Metropolitan
Readiness Test: Pre-test $(N = 39)$

| | Combined Groups | | | | |
| | Control | | Experimental | | |
Sub-test	X̄	σ	X̄	σ	t
Word Meaning	17.10	1.30	16.89	1.92	.39
Sentences	10.80	2.09	10.32	2.94	.57
Information	12.80	1.36	12.00	1.52	1.69
Matching	14.35	3.00	13.94	3.06	.41
Numbers	16.95	5.62	16.74	5.07	.12
Copying	6.45	3.04	5.05	2.74	1.47
Percentile Rank	67.00	28.96	59.74	31.08	.74

Werner and Strauss used this test initially to determine the negative effects of background on the perception of form perceived through touch rather than through sight. They found that when simple figures were presented as solid forms, both brain-injured and retarded children who were not classified as brain-injured were able to reproduce them without difficulty. When the designs were constructed of rubber thumbtacks over a thumbtack background, however, the children without brain injury showed definitely superior performance. Dolphin (28) and Shaw (50) obtained similar results with cerebral palsy and idiopathic epileptic groups.

For a detailed discussion of this test and its administration, see Cruickshank, Bice and Wallen (24). In the present study a triangle and Figures 4 and 6 of the Bender-Gestalt Test were used. The three designs were first presented without a background; and then were presented as raised figures against a background of thumbtacks.

ADMINISTRATION AND SCORING

Three designs were chosen from those used by Cruickshank, Bice and Wallen. Each design was made of rubber-headed tacks; each appeared on two boards, one with a plain background and the other with a thumbtack background. The figures were presented to the child in the following order:

1. Triangle, plain;
2. Bender Figure 4, plain;

3. Bender Figure 6, plain;
4. Triangle, Background (reversed);
5. Bender Figure 4, Background (reversed);
6. Bender Figure 6, Background (reversed).

The child was seated at a table upon which was clamped a screen; he could feel the forms behind the screen but could not see them. The examiner then said: "I'm going to place some boards behind the screen. Now you can't see them, but you can feel them. On the top of each board is some kind of a design or pattern. I want you to feel the board until you can draw for me what you feel, just the way it would look. When you are ready to draw, tell me. Do you understand?" The child was encouraged to feel the design for a minimum of thirty seconds and a maximum of two minutes. If the child asked questions about how he should draw what he felt, he was told, "Just draw what you felt the best way you can."

Scoring consisted of placing each drawing into one of the five following categories:

1. correct figure;
2. incorrect figure;
3. correct figure with background also drawn;
4. incorrect figure with background also drawn;
5. background only.

Cruickshank, Bice and Wallen (24) have developed a much more refined procedure for evaulating tactual-motor performance, but, in view of the extreme difficulty with this test experienced by most of the children, the system described above seemed more appropriate. As will be seen in the discussion of results, very few of the children were able to identify the figures with any accuracy.

RESULTS

The Tactual-Motor Test proved to be too difficult. Only 17 out of 36 who attempted the test managed to identify the triangle with plain background (Table 24), and 2 drew pictures with a background. Not one child could correctly identify or draw Figures 4 (Table 25) and 6 (Table 26) with the plain background from the Bender-Gestalt. The confusing effect of the thumbtack background may be inferred from the smaller number of children who could identify and draw the triangle when such a distracting background was introduced. Only 10 of the 33 who attempted the test could correctly identify the triangle on a thumbtack background, and 7 children drew figures with a background (Table 27). No child was able to identify Figure 4 (Table 28)

TABLE 24
Tactual-Motor Test: Triangle, Plain

Variable	Class				
	C-1	C-2	E-1	E-2	Total
Correct figure	4	5	5	3	17
Incorrect figure	5	3	4	5	17
Correct figure with background	0	0	0	0	0
Incorrect figure with background	0	0	0	1	1
Background only	1	0	0	0	1
Total	10	8	9	9	36

TABLE 25
Tactual-Motor Test: Bender Form 4, Plain

Variable	Class				
	C-1	C-2	E-1	E-2	Total
Correct figure	0	0	0	0	0
Incorrect figure	9	7	8	9	33
Correct figure with background	0	0	0	0	0
Incorrect figure with background	0	1	0	0	1
Background only	1	0	0	0	1
Total	10	8	8	9	35

TABLE 26
Tactual-Motor Test: Bender Form 6, Plain

Variable	Class				
	C-1	C-2	E-1	E-2	Total
Correct figure	0	0	0	0	0
Incorrect figure	6	6	9	9	30
Correct figure with background	0	0	0	0	0
Incorrect figure with background	0	1	0	0	1
Background only	0	1	0	0	1
Total	6	8	9	9	32

TABLE 27
Tactual-Motor Test: Triangle, Background (Reversed)

	Class				
Variable	C-1	C-2	E-1	E-2	Total
Correct figure	2	4	3	1	10
Incorrect figure	3	1	4	6	14
Correct figure with background	1	1	0	0	2
Incorrect figure with background	1	1	0	1	3
Background only	2	1	1	0	4
Total	9	8	8	8	33

TABLE 28
Tactual-Motor Test: Bender Form 4, Background (Reversed)

	Class				
Variable	C-1	C-2	E-1	E-2	Total
Correct figure	0	0	0	0	0
Incorrect figure	7	6	7	7	27
Correct figure with background	0	0	0	0	0
Incorrect figure with background	1	1	0	1	3
Background only	0	1	0	0	1
Total	8	8	7	8	31

TABLE 29
Tactual-Motor Test: Bender Form 6, Background (Reversed)

	Class				
Variable	C-1	C-2	E-1	E-2	Total
Correct figure	0	0	0	1	1
Incorrect figure	4	7	6	7	24
Correct figure with background	0	0	0	0	0
Incorrect figure with background	0	0	0	0	1
Background only	0	1	0	0	1
Total	4	8	6	8	26

with a thumbtack background from the Bender-Gestalt, and only one child was able to do so with Figure 6 (Table 29).

The drawings made by the children bore little relationship to the stimulus figures. Squares, circles, and wild scribbling were the usual productions.

Marble Board Test

The Marble Board Test was originally developed by Werner and Strauss (59). It was devised to assess visuo-motor ability. Strauss and Kephart (55) have emphasized its diagnostic value in detecting the effects of brain injury. For a more detailed description, see Goldenberg (33), and Cruickshank, Bice and Wallen (24).

ADMINISTRATION AND SCORING

The subject must reproduce designs made of marbles on a specially constructed board. The examiner makes a design in such a way that the child cannot see the actual process of construction; and then, with the examiner's design in full sight, the child attempts to reproduce it on his board. Careful note is made of how the child constructs the designs, and of any changes or shifts in the marbles. The examiner's design is then removed from sight, and the child is given a standard-size sheet of paper and is asked to draw the design. His marble board construction, of course, is left in full view while he is drawing.

Only two designs were used in this study: two overlapping squares, and two overlapping triangles.

The scoring scheme is Goldenberg's; for complete scoring directions, this reference should be consulted. A brief description of the scoring categories is given here, but it is by no means to be considered as a substitute for Goldenberg's complete directions.

A. Accuracy:
    1. Perfectly accurate: score 5
    2. Generally accurate: score 3
    3. Little or no accuracy: score 1
B. Method:
    1. Continuous: this involves a consecutive placement of marbles in a single direction of movement.
    2. Segmental: two or more series of consecutive placements of adjacent marbles occur along one or more sides of a subform.
    3. Incoherent: a reproduction was scored as incoherent if it did not qualify as continuous or segmental.
C. Organization:
    1. Articulate: each subform must be completed, and overlapping subforms must overlap.
    2. Global: the outline of the total configuration is followed, and other remaining parts of the pattern are fitted into this frame.

3. Aggregate: successive closed units of the pattern are completed but not according to the two basic subforms; overlapping subforms must overlap.

4. Linear: lines or portions of lines within the configuration are followed, and the production is composed of lines or closed units not corresponding to the stimulus pattern.

The drawings of the marble board designs were examined for evidences of response to the background.

RESULTS

Tables 30 and 31 show a comparison of the accuracy score of the two combined control groups with the accuracy score of the two combined

TABLE 30

Means, Standard Deviations, and t-Tests of the Significance of Differences Between Means for the Combined Control and Combined Experimental Groups on the Marble Board No. 1: Accuracy Score

Class	N	$\overline{X}$	σ	t
C-1	9	1.89	1.37	
C-2	10	2.60	1.95	
				1.51
E-1	10	1.20	.60	
E-2	9	1.89	1.37	
Total	38	1.89	1.50	

TABLE 31

Means, Standard Deviations, and t-Test of the Significance of Differences between Means for the Combined Control and Combined Experimental Groups on the Marble Board No. 2: Accuracy Score

Class	N	$\overline{X}$	σ	t
C-1	9	2.33	1.89	
C-2	10	1.80	1.32	
				.75
E-1	10	1.20	.60	
E-2	8	2.25	1.71	
Total	37	1.86	1.50	

experimental groups. There were no significant differences between the means of the combined groups.

Tables 32 and 33 give the method or organization for the two designs.

TABLE 32

Method of Organization on the Marble Board No. 1

Class	N	Articulate	Global	Aggregate	Linear
C-1	9	3	1	0	5
C-2	10	2	2	1	5
E-1	10	1	1	0	8
E-2	9	2	1	1	5
Total	38	8	5	2	23

TABLE 33

Method of Organization on the Marble Board No. 2

Class	N	Articulate	Global	Aggregate	Linear
C-1	9	3	1	0	5
C-2	10	2	3	1	4
E-1	10	2	1	1	6
E-2	8	2	1	0	5
Total	37	9	6	2	20

The results are quite consistent for the two designs. The least number of reproductions are categorized as aggregate, followed by global, articulate, and linear. The small numbers, and absence of post-test information, make any sort of meaningful statistical description impractical, so the information is being included merely for comparative purposes.

TABLE 34

Method of Approach on the Marble Board No. 1

Class	N	Continuous	Segmental	Incoherent
C-1	9	4	1	4
C-2	10	3	1	6
E-1	10	2	1	7
E-2	9	2	2	5
Total	38	11	5	22

Tables 34 and 35 indicate that the method of approach on the two designs is quite consistent. The order of frequency, from greatest to least, is incoherent, continuous, and segmental. On Design 1, 22 children (57 per cent) produced incoherent reproductions; and on Design 2, 21 children (56 per cent) produced incoherent reproductions.

TABLE 35
Method of Approach on the Marble Board No. 2

Class	N	Continuous	Segmental	Incoherent
C-1	9	4	1	4
C-2	10	1	3	6
E-1	10	2	2	6
E-2	8	2	1	5
Total	37	9	7	21

Evidence of responses to the backgrounds rather than to the figures indicates that the classes are quite similar. For Figure 1, the background responses are as follows: C-1 had 2; C-2, 1; E-1, 0; and E-2, 3. For Figure 2, the background responses were as follows: C-1, 0; C-2, 1; E-1, 0; and E-2, 3.

Analysis of the Marble Board results yields no information that would indicate anything other than comparability between the experimental and control groups at the beginning of the academic year. Similar performance is observed in method of approach, method of organization, accuracy score, and background responses.

Bender-Gestalt

The Bender-Gestalt Test (14) was administered routinely. Several considerations made the inclusion of this instrument desirable. (1) The test is easy, helps establish rapport; all of the children, without exception, enjoyed "drawing the pictures." (2) The test has been used extensively in the psychological investigation of celebral pathology. (3) One of the most important learning problems manifested by these children occurs in visuo-motor activity.

Difficulty in reproducing visually perceived forms has often been considered a characteristic of brain-injured children. This type of task has been included in tests of general intelligence (21, 56), as well as in various specialized tests. Bender (10, 11), Bakwin (7), and others (43, 61) have emphasized the importance of such tasks in various types of organic conditions.

A number of tests have been used which involve the reproduction of visually perceived forms, including that of Benton (16), Graham and Kendall (36), Healy, Bronner, *et al.* (38), and Bender (14).

The diagnostic value for identifying brain-injured patients has been mainly established with regard to adult groups (15, 16), but recently some work has been reported on children. Baroff (8) administered the

Bender-Gestalt Test to 84 twin individuals who were institutionalized because they were mentally defective. Seventy-six of his subjects seemed to meet the requirements for classification as endogenous. Although the number of children in his sample definitely diagnosed as brain-injured (N = 8) was too small for generalization, he noted that their performance tended to be much poorer than that of children not similarly diagnosed.

Shaw and Cruickshank (51, 52) compared the Bender-Gestalt Test performance of a group of 25 institutionalized, idiopathic epileptic children who were matched with a group of 25 institutionalized, non-convulsive children on the basis of age, sex, and intelligence. The Pascal and Suttell scoring system was used. Comparison of the total scores for the two groups by means of the *t*-test revealed no significant difference. When comparison was made on the basis of the configuration score, however, there was a difference significant at the .02 level of confidence. In other words, the results indicate that there is a real difference between the epileptic and control subjects in the placement, size and order of the design on the paper. The authors point out that background cannot be considered the disturbing factor in this study, because the original background is only a blank piece of paper. The authors conclude:

> From the present results, we might infer that it is not the confusing background which results in misperception, but an inability to organize thought processes in what might be considered an orderly fashion (51, p. 193).

Goldberg (32) administered the WISC and the Bender-Gestalt Test to three groups of 15 white male children who were schizophrenic, retarded and "normal," and who ranged in age from 11 to 16 years. The results showed a significant difference between the performance of the normal and both the schizophrenic and retarded groups. The difference between the schizophrenic and the retarded children approached but did not attain significance. Goldberg concluded that the Bender-Gestalt Test score (as measured by the Pascal and Suttell scoring system) was primarily a function of intelligence, but that emotional factors also seemed to have an effect upon the score.

Aaronson (1) compared the performance on the Porteus Mazes and Bender-Gestalt recall of a sample of epileptic subjects with a high incidence of feeblemindedness. The moderate correlation of .46 between these two variables shrunk to .21 when age was held constant. Aaronson concluded that there is no practical relationship between recall of Bender figures and intelligence.

Hanvik (37) concluded that rotations usually occurred in the records of only the most disturbed children, and that very often among children producing rotations there was evidence pointing toward the probability of brain damage. He is even more emphatic in saying that rotation is a more malignant sign in children than it is in adults, and that rotation is a visual-motor aberration almost pathognomic in brain-damaged children.

Bice and Cruickshank (23) compared the performance of cerebral palsy children on the Bender-Gestalt. They concluded that there is a relationship between the major medical classifications in cerebral palsy and certain scoring categories devised by them. The scoring system used in the present study is the one which was developed by these authors.

ADMINISTRATION

The method of administration closely followed that described by Bender (14) and others (48). The child is seated at a table, and is given a pencil with an eraser and a sheet of 8½ by 11-inch paper. On the table there is a pile of paper the same size. The directions are as follows: "I have some simple designs here which I want you to draw for me on this paper. Each design is on one of these cards which I will show you one at a time. You have as long as you want to draw these designs for me. Try to make your drawings look as much like the card I show you as you possibly can." This last statement, to make the drawings look as much like the cards as possible, was made quite emphatically because the children frequently looked upon this as an opportunity to draw. The child's questions were referred back to his own judgment. For example, if the child asked, "Should I count the dots?" the response was, "Just try to make your drawing look as much like the card as possible."

The order of presentation was in the numerical order of the cards. An attempt was made to discourage the child from turning the paper, but if he persisted, this was noted as part of the testing information.

SCORING

A number of scoring schemes which have been advanced for the Bender-Gestalt (14, 23, 48) were considered before the scoring scheme devised by Cruickshank and Bice (23) was chosen. Even the most disorganized drawings can be classified in their system. What was lost in fineness of scoring was more than compensated for in meaningful categorization of responses. A brief description of the categories will be given here, and the reader interested in scoring procedures and problems may consult Cruickshank and Bice (23).

Drawings were categorized according to the types of errors and distortions. While many descriptive categories have been proposed by various authors, some distortions occurred with such infrequency that they were not included in the following list. A description of the scoring categories follows:

Immature. The Stanford-Binet mental age of the child was taken into consideration in scoring for this category, and Bender's (14) summary chart was used as the basis for determining the maturational level of a drawing. The child's drawing had to be at least two years below his Binet mental age for inclusion here. To avoid overlapping of categories, a drawing that was considered in this category was not included in any other. Detachment and separation, for example, may represent either immaturity or form dissociation, depending upon the mental age of the child. Similarly, Figure 5 [4] drawn with solid lines may represent either immaturity or incorrect elements.

Concrete. The only responses assigned to this category were those in which the child named the design, i.e., while drawing Figure 6, a child said: "This is a piece of string." Compulsive counting was not included here because the nature of the visual-perceptual training procedures used with these children, such as peg boards, blocks, and other materials, have taught many of them to count in an attempt to reproduce designs. Of course, note was routinely made of such counting and was included in the qualitative evaluation of the test results. One boy, when starting to draw Figure A, lost sight of the goal set for him and elaborated his drawing into a boy. This was scored as Concrete, even though a second, more firm request to draw the design resulted in a figure A that was quite acceptable. After finishing Figure A, a girl proceeded to embellish the drawing, saying, "This is a kite." This was scored not only as Concrete, but also for Form Dissociation and Distorted Angles.

Perseveration. Perseveration, as used in this category, is the continuation of an activity after it is no longer appropriate. On the Bender-Gestalt, this usually shows up on Figures 1 and 2. The stimulus for Figure 1 consists of 12 dots. If the number of dots in the drawing was more than 14, the drawing was scored for Perseveration. The stimulus for Figure 2 consists of 11 columns of circles. If the child drew more

[4] All references in this section to figure numbers relate to the numbering of figures in the Bender-Gestalt Visual-Motor Test.

than 13, the figure was scored for this category. The stimulus for Figure 3 is made of 16 dots, so if a child drew more than this number the figure was scored for Perseveration. If Figure 3 were made of loops, it might or might not indicate Perseveration, depending on the mental age of the child.

Erratic Approach. This category was used when there was no clear pattern in the drawing; it usually occurred in those figures made of dots or loops. Some children scattered dots across the page, thereby demonstrating little ability to hold to the basic pattern.

Form Dissociation. This category included detachment, displacement, and incompleteness. *Detachment* referred to a complete separation of the figure. A minimum gap of 3 millimeters was needed for inclusion here. The most frequent figure in which the elements were detached was Figure A, followed by 4 and 7. *Displacement* refers to a distortion of the basic configuration so that parts that should touch are actually in contact but at the wrong point. *Incompleteness* refers to a drawing in which an important element is missing. The stimulus for Figure 1 consists of 12 dots, so if it was drawn with less than 10 dots it was considered incomplete. The stimulus for Figure 2 consists of 11 columns, so if it was drawn with less than 9 columns, it was included here. If Figure 3 was drawn with less than 16 dots, it was considered to be incomplete.

Closure. For inclusion of a drawing in this category, there must be an addition of parts, resulting in a closing of the pattern. Figures 4 and 5 are the only open designs in the series. Thus, the addition of a line to make an enclosed rectangle of Figure 4, or the addition of dots to make a circle in Figure 5 would require the inclusion of the figure in this category. Errors in this category were infrequent.

Incorrect Element. A drawing made of inappropriate parts would be included here: for example, Figure 6 drawn with loops or dots. Figure 5 made of solid lines may either represent this category or immaturity, depending upon the mental age. Similarly, loops in Figure 3, dots in Figure 2, or lines in Figure 3 would qualify a figure for this category.

Unrecognizable. A drawing so poorly executed that it must be numbered at the time it is drawn for future identification would represent this type of error. This occurred most often in designs made of dots, although the line drawings were also frequently distorted beyond recognition.

Distorted Angles. This included any marked inadequacy in the construction of angles. The most easily recognized is an inversion of the angle so that it points toward the center of the figure rather than outward. Other angle distortions may occur by arbitrarily adding of an extra angle, by abruptly changing the direction of a line so that it results in a well-defined extra angle, or by using curves instead of angles.

Rotation. A 45 degree, or more, rotation was required for inclusion in this category. A knowledge of the position of the paper in relation to the child was necessary in evaluating this error.

Compression. A marked reduction in size was the error under consideration here. Reduction of at least 50 per cent was the criterion.

Enlargement. Enlargement of at least 50 per cent was necessary for inclusion here.

Disproportion. The internal elements of a figure had to be markedly out of balance to be considered an example of Disproportion. A variation of 50 per cent or more in a major element was the criterion.

A number of the above categories contained so few responses that individual analysis was not possible. These categories included Concrete, Erratic Approach, Closure, Unrecognizable, Compression, Enlargement, and Disproportion. These results are in essential agreement with Cruickshank and Bice (23). Psychologically, a number of these categories seem to "fit" together, so they were added together to form combined categories. For example, Immature, Concrete, Perseveration, and Erratic Approach were combined into *Inadequate Method.* Form Dissociation, Closure, Incorrect Element, Unrecognizable, Distorted Angles, and Rotation were grouped together and called *Distortion of Configuration.* Compression, Enlargement and Disproportion were combined under *Size.* All errors were added to produce the *Total* score.

Further analysis was based on the number of rotations; the scoring system devised by Pascal and Suttell (48) was followed. Further analysis was necessary because of the importance assigned to the presence of rotations by various writers. Pascal and Suttell have devised a weighted score for various types of rotations, and their approach is as follows:

Figure 1. Rotation is scored for this design if the figure is reproduced vertically rather than horizontally, or if the reproduction is rotated from the horizontal 45 degrees or more. *Score 8.*

Figure 2. Scored as Figure 1. *Score 8.*

Figure 3. When the design is rotated 45, 90, or 180 degrees. *Score 8.*

Figure 4 a. Curve rotation. For perfect reproduction, one line should bisect the curve and the adjacent angle of the square. The line bisecting the curve should form an angle of 135 degrees with the adjacent side of the square. When this angle is reduced to 90 degrees or less, the deviation is scored. *Score 3.*

Figure 4 b. Design rotation. This is scored when the base of the square is rotated 45 degrees or more from the horizontal, or when the curve is attached to the square more than one-third of the distance along that side of the square. *Score 8.*

Figure 5 a. Rotation of extension. This is scored when the extension begins at or below the approximate mid-dot of the right side, or when the direction of the extension is reversed to the left rather than to the right, or when the extension begins to the left of center. *Score 3.*

Figure 5 b. Design rotation. This is scored when the design is rotated 45 degrees or more from the horizontal. *Score 8.*

Figure 6 a. This is scored when the vertical line is rotated to the left, more than 10 degrees from perpendicular. *Score 8.*

Figure 6 b. This is scored when the horizontal line is rotated 45 degrees or more. *Score 8.*

Figure 7 a. This is scored when the lateral hexagon is rotated so that the 30 degree angle of the stimulus design is increased to 90 degrees or decreased to 0 degrees. *Score 8.*

Figure 7 b. This is scored when the entire reproduction is rotated. *Score 8.*

Figure 8. This is scored when the base of the design is rotated 45 degrees or more from the horizontal. *Score 8.*

Immature. Table 36 shows the means, standard deviations, and *t*-tests of the significance of the differences between pre-test and post-test means for the Bender-Gestalt category, Immature. When the means of the pre-test results are compared with the means of the post-test results by classes, two classes (one control and one experimental) produced significantly fewer Immature drawings ($p < .02$); the other two classes approached significance ($p < .10$) but did not reach the level used in

TABLE 36
Mean Errors, Standard Deviations, and t-Test of the Significance of Differences between Means for the Bender-Gestalt Category: Immature

Class	N	Pre-test		Post-test		t
		$\overline{X}$	σ	$\overline{X}$	σ	
C-1	10	1.36	1.49	.20	.60	2.18 *
C-2	10	1.50	1.36	.20	.40	2.90 ‡
E-1	10	2.90	1.92	1.20	.87	2.94 ‡
E-2	9	2.22	1.75	1.11	1.59	2.01 *
Total	39	1.97	1.76	.67	1.07	5.17 #

* $p < .10$
‡ $p < .02$
\# $p < .001$

this study. When the pre-test and post-test means for the total group were compared, however, the difference was highly significant (p < .001).

When the two combined control groups' pre-test results were compared with the two combined experimental groups' pre-test results, the means were significantly different at the .05 level (See Table 37). In

TABLE 37

Mean Errors, Standard Deviations, t-Tests, and Probabilities of Chance Differences in Means for the Control and Experimental Groups on the Bender-Gestalt Category: Immature

Group	N	$\overline{X}$	σ	t
Combined Control Groups, Pre-test	20	1.40	1.43	
				2.16 †
Combined Experimental Groups, Pre-test	19	2.58	1.87	
Combined Control Groups, Post-test	20	.20	.51	
				3.05 §
Combined Experimental Groups, Post-test	19	1.16	1.27	
Comparison of Control Groups, Pre-test, and Control Group, Post-test	20	1.20	1.44	3.65 §
Comparison of Experimental Group, Pre-test, and Experimental Group, Post-test	19	1.42	1.66	3.62 §

† p < .05
§ p < .01

other words, at the beginning of the project, the experimental groups produced significantly more drawings that were at least two years below their Binet mental ages than did the control groups. This same relationship held true at the conclusion of the project, the two combined control groups produced significantly fewer Immature responses than did the two combined experimental groups. Both the experimental and control groups made significant growth (p < .01) over the course of the year, as may be seen in comparing pre- and post-test categories.

The above results show that at the beginning of the academic year, the combined control groups were significantly superior to the combined experimental groups with regard to the number of Bender-Gestalt reproductions which were scored as Immature; this superiority was maintained at the conclusion of the year. When comparison is made between the pre- and post-tests results, however, it can be seen that both the experimental and control groups produced significantly fewer Immature responses at the end of the year.

Perseveration. Table 38 shows the means, standard deviations, and *t*-tests of the significance of differences between means for the Bender category, Perseveration. When considered individually by classes, or when considered as a total group, there are no significant changes in

TABLE 38

Mean Errors, Standard Deviations, t-Tests, and Probabilities of Chance Differences in Means for the Bender-Gestalt Category: Perseveration

Class	N	Pre-test $\overline{X}$	σ	Post-test $\overline{X}$	σ	t
C-1	10	1.50	1.02	1.80	.87	.38
C-2	10	1.80	.98	1.30	1.10	.83
E-1	10	1.30	1.27	1.50	.81	.36
E-2	9	1.67	1.41	1.56	1.07	.23
Total	39	1.56	1.19	1.54	.98	.08

the number of perseverative responses between the pre-test and post-test phases of the project.

Table 39 shows a comparison of the combined control and combined experimental groups. Again there are no differences between the total control and total experimental groups on a test—retest basis, or between the pre-test and post-test scores for the control groups or the experimental groups.

TABLE 39

Mean Errors, Standard Deviations, t-Tests, and Probabilities of Chance Differences in Means for the Control and Experimental Groups on the Bender-Gestalt Category: Perseveration

Group	N	$\overline{X}$	σ	t
Combined Control Groups, Pre-test	20	1.65	1.01	
				.46
Combined Experimental Groups, Pre-test	19	1.47	1.35	
Combined Control Groups, Post-test	20	1.55	1.02	
				.06
Combined Experimental Groups, Post-test	19	1.53	.94	
Comparison of Control Group, Pre-test, and Control Group, Post-test	20	.15	1.70	.39
Comparison of Experimental Group, Pre-test, and Experimental Group, Post-test	19	.05	1.47	.02

The above results show no differences in the number of perseverations made between the pre-test and post-test phases on the Bender-Gestalt.

Form Dissociation. Table 40 shows the means, standard deviations, and *t*-tests of the significance of differences between pre-test and post-test for the Bender-Gestalt category, Form Dissociation. The post-test

TABLE 40

Mean Errors, Standard Deviations, t-Tests, and Probabilities of Chance Differences in Means for the Bender-Gestalt Category:
Form Dissociation

Class	N	Pre-test		Post-test		t
		$\overline{X}$	σ	$\overline{X}$	σ	
C-1	10	2.90	1.81	2.20	1.54	.15
C 2	10	2.80	1.25	1.90	1.30	2.21 *
E-1	10	4.50	2.29	2.50	1.50	2.34 †
E-2	9	3.22	2.09	1.22	.92	2.13 *
Total	39	3.36	2.02	1.97	1.42	4.34 §

* p < .10
† p < .05
§ p < .01

scores indicate that only one experimental class produced significantly fewer responses in this category. However, a comparison of the pre-test and post-test means of the total group indicates that significantly fewer form dissociations (p < .01) were produced in the post-test results.

Table 41 shows a comparison of the combined control and combined experimental groups. Neither on the pre-test nor on the post-test scores were there significant differences between the means of the two combined control group means and the two combined experimental groups. However, both the combined control and combined experimental groups produced significantly fewer responses in this category in their post-test scores.

The above results show that all of the children produced significantly fewer Form Dissociation errors but that there were no differences between the experimental and control groups.

Incorrect Element. Table 42 shows the means, standard deviations, and *t*-tests of the significance of the differences between means for the Bender-Gestalt category, Incorrect Element. When considered individually by classes, three of the four classes produced about the same number, or fewer, errors in the post-testing as they did in the pre-

TABLE 41

*Mean Errors, Standard Deviations, t-Tests, and Probabilities of Chance
Differences in Means for the Control and Experimental Groups
on the Bender-Gestalt Category:* Form Dissociation

Group	N	$\overline{X}$	σ	t
Combined Control Groups, Pre-test	20	2.85	1.43	
				1.67
Combined Experimental Groups, Pre-test	19	3.89	2.29	
Combined Control Groups, Post-test	20	2.05	1.43	
				.34
Combined Experimental Groups, Post-test	19	1.89	1.41	
Comparison of Control Group, Pre-test, and Control Group, Post-test	20	.80	1.33	2.63 ‡
Comparison of Experimental Group, Pre-test, and Experimental Group, Post-test	19	2.00	2.32	3.66 §

‡ p < .02
§ p < .01

TABLE 42

*Mean Errors, Standard Deviations, t-Tests, and Probabilities of Chance
Differences in Means for the Bender-Gestalt Category:*
Incorrect Element

Class	N	Pre-test		Post-test		t
		$\overline{X}$	σ	$\overline{X}$	σ	
C-1	10	2.10	1.51	3.40	1.02	2.22 *
C-2	10	2.20	.75	2.20	1.16	0.00
E-1	10	2.40	1.02	2.00	1.26	.69
E-2	9	1.89	1.52	1.78	1.03	.23
Total	39	2.15	1.25	2.36	1.29	.83

* p < .10

testing. The fourth class (a control class) produced more errors in the
post-testing, but this only approached a significance (p < .10) which
did not reach the level of confidence established for this study. A comparison between the means for the pre-test and post-test scores did not
indicate a significant difference for the total group.

Table 43 shows a comparison of the total control and total experimental groups. At the beginning of the academic year, the groups were

TABLE 43

Mean Errors, Standard Deviations, t-Tests, and Probabilities of Chance Differences in Means for the Control and Experimental Groups on the Bender-Gestalt Category: Incorrect Element

Group	N	$\overline{X}$	σ	t
Combined Control Groups, Pre-test	20	2.15	1.19	
				.36
Combined Experimental Groups, Pre-test	19	2.00	1.31	
Combined Control Groups, Post-test	20	2.80	1.25	
				2.29 †
Combined Experimental Groups, Post-test	19	1.89	1.17	
Comparison of Control Group, Pre-test, and Control Group, Post-test	20	.65	1.37	2.06 *
Comparison of Experimental Group, Pre-test, and Experimental Group, Post-test	19	.26	1.55	.72

* $p < .10$
† $p < .05$

quite comparable. When the post-test scores are compared, however, the experimental group showed significantly fewer Incorrect Element errors than did the control group.

Therefore the above data show that the children in the experimental classes made signficantly greater gains than did the children in the control classrooms. The children in the control classroom actually made *more* Bender-Gestalt reproductions containing Incorrect Elements at the end of the academic year than they did at the beginning. Thus, while the children in stimulus-free environments were improving in performance, the performance of the children in control classes was actually becoming worse.

Distorted Angles. In Table 44 are given the means, standard deviations, and *t*-tests of the significance of the differences between the means for the Bender category, Distorted Angles. There are no significant differences between means either for the classes considered individually, or for the group as a whole, in the pre-test and post-test phases of this study.

Table 45 shows a comparison of the total control and total Experimental groups; there are no significant differences between the control and experimental groups.

The above data show that there were no differences between the experimental and control groups in Distorted Angles errors.

TABLE 44

Mean Errors, Standard Deviations, t-Tests, and Probabilities of Chance Differences in Means for the Bender-Gestalt Category:
Distorted Angles

Class	N	Pre-test X	σ	Post-test X	σ	t
C-1	10	2.80	.60	2.90	.70	.55
C-2	10	2.80	.40	2.50	.50	1.27
E-1	10	3.00	.52	2.90	.53	.06
E-2	9	2.67	1.05	2.78	.79	.42
Total	39	2.82	.64	2.77	.66	.05

TABLE 45

Mean Errors, Standard Deviations, t-Tests, and Probabilities of Chance Differences in Means for the Control and Experimental Groups on the Bender-Gestalt Category: Distorted Angles

Group	N	X	σ	t
Combined Control Groups, Pre-test	20	2.80	.51	
				.19
Combined Experimental Groups, Pre-test	19	2.84	.74	
Combined Control Groups, Post-test	20	2.70	.64	
				.65
Combined Experimental Groups, Post-test	19	2.84	.67	
Comparison of Control Group, Pre-test, and Control Group, Post-test	20	.10	.62	.70
Comparison of Experimental Group, Pre-test, and Experimental Group, Post-test	19	0.00	.65	0.00

TABLE 46

Mean Errors, Standard Deviations, t-Tests, and Probabilities of Chance Differences in Means for the Bender-Gestalt Category: Rotations

Class	N	Pre-test X	σ	Post-test X	σ	t
C-1	10	1.20	1.66	.70	.64	.84
C-2	10	.90	1.03	.90	.94	.67
E-1	10	1.10	1.22	1.00	1.27	.16
E-2	9	1.33	1.25	.67	.47	1.63
Total	39	1.13	1.32	.82	.90	1.17

Rotations. Table 46 shows the means, standard deviations, and *t*-tests of the significance of differences between means for the category, Rotations. There are no significant differences between the number of rotations produced in the pre-test and post-test phases where the means are considered individually by classes, or when the means for the total groups are compared.

Table 47 shows a comparison of the combined experimental and combined control groups; there are no statistically significant differences between pre-test and post-test performance.

TABLE 47

Mean Errors, Standard Deviations, t-Tests, and Probabilities of Chance Differences in Means for the Control and Experimental Groups on the Bender-Gestalt Category: Rotations

Group	N	$\overline{X}$	σ	t
Combined Control Groups, Pre-test	20	1.05	1.74	
				.32
Combined Experimental Groups, Pre-test	19	1.21	1.24	
Combined Control Groups, Post-test	20	.80	.81	
				.14
Combined Experimental Groups, Post-test	19	.84	.99	
Comparison of Control Group, Pre-test, and Control Group, Post-test	20	.25	1.61	.68
Comparison of Experimental Group, Pre-test, and Experimental Group, Post-test	19	.37	1.63	.96

The above results show no changes in the pre-test and post-test means for the category, Rotations. The use of the scoring criterion of 45-degree rotations may be too gross an approach to evaluating rotations.

The Pascal and Suttell scoring system takes into account partial rotations as well as rotations of the complete design. Their system also uses weighted scores for various types of rotations. An analysis of rotation based on their scoring system follows.

Table 48 shows the means, standard deviations, and *t*-tests of the significance of differences between means for the number of rotations scored according to the Pascal and Suttell scoring system. Only one class (an experimental class) approached significance (p < .10) when its score was compared to the pre- and post-test rotation score. When the 39 children are considered as a total group, there is no difference between the pre- and post-testing.

Table 49 shows a comparison of the combined control and combined experimental groups. At the beginning of the academic year, the mean

TABLE 48

Mean Errors, Standard Deviations, t-Tests, and Probabilities of Chance Differences in Means for the Number of Rotations, Scored According to the Pascal and Stuttell Scoring System

Class	N	Pre-test $\overline{X}$	σ	Post-test $\overline{X}$	σ	t
C-1	10	13.40	9.76	13.30	11.41	.02
C-2	10	14.70	13.40	13.60	9.55	.21
E-1	10	18.20	10.87	13.90	8.51	.94
E-2	9	15.89	13.51	7.78	7.89	2.08 *
Total	39	15.54	12.09	12.26	9.78	1.36

* p < .10

TABLE 49

Mean Errors, Standard Deviations, t-Tests, and Probabilities of Chance Differences in Means for the Combined Control and Combined Experimental Groups on the Number Rotations, Scored According to the Pascal and Stuttell Scoring System

Group	N	$\overline{X}$	σ	t
Combined Control Groups, Pre-test	20	14.05	11.74	
				.78
Combined Experimental Groups, Pre-test	19	17.11	12.25	
Combined Control Groups, Post-test	20	13.45	11.00	
				.77
Combined Experimental Groups, Post-test	19	10.52	8.77	
Comparison of Control Groups, Pre-test, and Control Groups, Post-test	20	.60	16.43	.16
Comparison of Experimental Groups, Pre-test, and Experimental Groups, Post-test	19	6.105	11.15	2.33 †

† p < .05

of the combined control groups for the rotation score (14.05) was less than the mean for the combined experimental groups (17.11); but this difference was not statistically significant. At the end of the academic year, this situation had been reversed: the mean of the combined control groups' rotation score (13.45) was slightly more than the mean of the combined experimental groups' (10.52); again this difference was not statistically significant. When the combined control groups' means for the pre- and post-tests are compared, the *t*-test is .16, which is not significant. A comparison of the pre-test and post-test means of the combined experimental groups, however, results in a *t*-test of 2.33, which is significant at the .05 level of confidence.

The Pascal and Suttell scoring system indicates that the children in the experimental classrooms produced significantly fewer rotations at the end of the academic year than they did at the beginning. The children in the control classroom did not make similar progress.

Inadequate Method. Table 50 shows the means, standard deviations, and *t*-tests of the significance of differences between pre-test and post-

TABLE 50

Mean Errors, Standard Deviations, t-Tests, and Probabilities of Chance Differences in Means for the Bender-Gestalt Category:
Inadequate Method

Class	N	Pre-test		Post-test		
		$\overline{X}$	σ	$\overline{X}$	σ	t
C-1	10	2.80	1.78	2.70	2.37	.12
C-2	10	3.40	1.80	2.10	1.22	1.71
E-1	10	4.20	2.60	3.30	1.49	.90
E-2	9	4.11	2.33	3.22	2.44	3.02 ‡
Total	39	3.62	2.20	2.82	1.99	2.66 †

† $p < .05$
‡ $p < .02$

test means for the Bender-Gestalt category, Inadequate Method. This category is a sum of our other categories, i.e., Immature, Concrete, Perseveration, and Erratic Approach. As can be seen from Table 50, the only class that showed significantly fewer errors in this category in the post-test phase is one of the experimental classes, E-2. This difference is significant at the .02 level of confidence. When the means of all four groups are compared on a pre-test and post-test basis, the difference between means is significant at the .05 level of confidence, showing that the total group produced fewer Inadequate Method errors in the post-test phase.

Table 51 shows a comparison of the combined control and experimental groups. The combined control groups did not make significant gains in their post-test results, but the combined experimental groups did, at the .05 level of confidence.

The above results show that the children, when considered as a total group, made significantly ($p < .05$) fewer drawings in the post-test

TABLE 51

Mean Errors, Standard Deviations, t-Tests, and Probabilities of Chance Differences in Means for the Control and Experimental Groups on the Bender-Gestalt Category: Inadequate Method

Group	N	$\overline{X}$	σ	t
Combined Control Groups, Pre-test	20	3.10	1.81	
				1.51
Combined Experimental Groups, Pre-test	19	4.16	2.43	
Combined Control Groups, Post-test	20	2.40	1.91	
				.35
Combined Experimental Groups, Post-test	19	2.42	1.57	
Comparison of Control Group, Pre-test, and Control Group, Post-test	20	.70	2.51	1.22
Comparison of Experimental Group, Pre-test, and Experimental Group, Post-test	19	1.74	2.92	2.53 †

† p < .05

phase that could be considered under the category of Inadequate Method. The children in the experimental classes made fewer errors (p < .05) in the post-testing, but the children in the control classes did not.

Distortion of Configuration. Table 52 shows the means, standard deviations, and *t*-tests of the significance of the differences between pre-test and post-test means for the Bender-Gestalt category, Distortion of Configuration. This category is a combination of six other categories:

TABLE 52

Mean Errors, Standard Deviations, t-Tests, and Probabilities of Chance Differences in Means for the Bender-Gestalt Category: Distortion of Configuration

Class	N	Pre-test $\overline{X}$	σ	Post-test $\overline{X}$	σ	t
C-1	10	10.60	4.29	9.70	3.47	.42
C-2	10	9.90	2.74	7.70	3.23	2.13 *
E-1	10	13.60	4.69	9.90	2.95	1.93 *
E 2	9	10.67	5.60	7.56	2.46	1.85 *
Total	39	11.21	4.65	8.74	3.25	3.42 §

* p < .10
§ p < .01

Dissociation, Closure, Incorrect Element, Unrecognizable, Distorted Angles, and Rotation. When the classes are considered individually, each of the four made fewer Distortion of Configuration errors in the post-test results; but when the means are compared on a pre-test and post-test basis, three of the class means approached significance but did not reach the level of confidence used in this study. When all of the children are considered as a total group, however, the difference in means is significant ($p < .01$), showing that there was a decrease in the number of errors in the post-test results.

Table 53 shows a comparison of the two combined control and the two combined experimental groups. Initial comparability of the groups may be seen in the lack of a difference between the control and experi-

TABLE 53

Mean Errors, Standard Deviations, t-Tests, and Probabilities of Chance Differences in Means for the Control and Experimental Groups on the Bender-Gestalt Category: Distortion of the Configuration

Group	N	$\overline{X}$	σ	t
Combined Control Groups, Pre-test	20	10.25	3.62	
				1.31
Combined Experimental Groups, Pre-test	19	12.21	5.35	
Combined Control Groups, Post-test	20	8.70	3.49	
				.08
Combined Experimental Groups, Post-test	19	8.79	2.96	
Comparison of Combined Control Groups, Pre-test, and Control Groups, Post-test	20	1.25	2.67	2.04 *
Comparison of Experimental Groups, Pre-test, and Experimental Groups, Post-test	19	3.47	5.29	2.97 §

* $p < .10$
§ $p < .01$

mental classes in the pre-test phase of the project. A comparison of the pre-test and post-test scores for the combined experimental groups shows a significant decrease ($p < .01$) in the number of errors. A similar comparison for the combined control groups approaches significance (.10) but does not reach the level of confidence used in this study.

The above data show that the children in the experimental classes made significantly fewer Distortion of Configuration errors; although the children in the control classes made fewer errors in the post-test phase, this did not reach the level of confidence set for this study.

Size. Table 54 shows the means, standard deviations, and *t*-tests of

TABLE 54

*Mean Errors, Standard Deviations, t-Tests, and Probabilities of Chance
Differences in Means for the Bender-Gestalt Category: Size*

Class	N	Pre-test X̄	σ	Post-test X̄	σ	t
C-1	10	2.70	1.27	3.50	2.58	1.18
C-2	10	2.90	1.92	2.70	2.45	.18
E-1	10	3.10	1.87	2.20	1.08	1.22
E-2	9	2.67	1.56	1.44	.96	1.91
Total	39	2.85	1.69	2.49	2.07	.86

the significance of differences between pre-test and post-test means for
the Bender-Gestalt category, Size. Three other categories were included
in this category: Compression, Enlargement, and Disproportion. No
class made significantly fewer errors.

TABLE 55

*Mean Errors, Standard Deviations, t-Tests, and Probabilities of Chance
Differences in Means for the Control and Experimental Groups
on the Bender-Gestalt Category: Size*

Group	N	X̄	σ	t
Combined Control Groups, Pre-test	20	2.80	1.63	
				.16
Combined Experimental Groups, Pre-test	19	2.89	1.74	
Combined Control Groups, Post-test	20	3.10	2.55	
				1.94
Combined Experimental Groups, Post-test	19	1.84	1.09	
Comparison of Control Group, Pre-test, and Control Group, Post-test	20	.30	2.85	.46
Comparison of Experimental Group, Pre-test, and Experimental Group, Post-test	19	1.05	2.04	2.19 †

† $p < .05$

Table 55 shows a comparison of the combined control and combined
experimental groups. There was not a significant reduction of errors
in the combined control groups when comparing the pre-test and
post-test results. A similar comparison for the two combined experimental groups, however, resulted in a statistically significant difference
$(p < .05)$.

When the pre-test and post-test results were considered individually by classes or as a total group, a significant reduction in errors is not indicated. When the analysis was made in terms of combining the two control classes and comparing them on a pre-test and post-test basis, no difference was observed. Comparison of the two combined experimental classes on a pre-test and post-test basis, however, showed a difference that was significant at the .05 level of confidence. In other words, the children in the experimental classes made significantly fewer errors of size (Compression, Enlargement, Disproportion) at the end of the academic year; but the control groups did not show a similar gain.

Total. Table 56 shows the means, standard deviations, and *t*-tests of the significance of differences between pre-test and post-test means for

TABLE 56

Mean Errors, Standard Deviations, t-Tests, and Probabilities of Chance Differences in Means for the Bender-Gestalt Category: Total

| Class | N | Pre-test | | Post-test | | |
		$\overline{X}$	σ	$\overline{X}$	σ	t
C-1	10	15.50	4.59	15.90	6.89	.22
C-2	10	16.20	4.31	12.50	5.20	2.29 †
E-1	10	20.90	7.98	15.40	4.80	1.97
E-2	9	17.44	7.99	12.22	4.18	2.91 ‡
Total	39	17.51	6.76	14.05	5.64	3.23 §

† p < .05
‡ p < .02
§ p < .01

the Bender-Gestalt category, Total. When the pre-test and post-test scores are considered individually by classes, only two classes showed significantly fewer errors: one was a control group and the other was an experimental group. When all four classes were combined, however, the total group made statistically significantly fewer errors (p < .01) in the post-test period.

Table 57 shows a comparison of the two combined control and two combined experimental classes. There were no significant differences between the means of the combined control and combined experimental groups on either pre-test or post-test scores. There was not a significant difference between the combined control groups' pre-test and post-test scores, but there was a difference (p < .01) between the means of the combined experimental groups' pre-test and post-test scores. In other words, the experimental groups showed greater improvement

TABLE 57

Mean Errors, Standard Deviations, t-Tests, and Probabilities of Chance Differences in Means for the Control and Experimental Groups on the Bender-Gestalt Category: Total

Group	N	X̄	σ	t
Combined Control Groups, Pre-test	20	15.85	4.46	
				1.60
Combined Experimental Groups, Pre-test	19	19.26	8.17	
Combined Control Groups, Post-test	20	14.20	6.34	
				.11
Combined Experimental Groups, Post-test	19	13.89	4.79	
Comparison of Control Group, Pre-test, and Control Group, Post-test	20	1.65	5.61	1.28
Comparison of Experimental Group, Pre-test, and Experimental Group, Post-test	19	5.37	7.02	3.24 §

§ p < .01

over the course of the year, as may be seen in the significantly fewer total number of errors made in the post-test phase.

The above data show that the total group improved markedly in their ability to reproduce the Bender-Gestalt figures, and that the children in the experimental classes showed significantly greater improvement in this ability than did the children in the control classes.

SUMMARY

So few errors occurred in a number of categories (Concrete, Erratic Approach, Closure, and Unrecognizable) that statistical analyses were not possible. A study of those categories that were amenable to statistical analyses, however, showed that the children who were in stimulus-free rooms made significant progress over the course of the year in 6 out of 10 categories, while the children placed in control classrooms did not make such progress. Since the children had been carefully matched for chronological age, mental age, and intelligence quotient, differences between the groups may be assumed to be reflections of the environmental differences and specialized teaching methods.

The categories in which the children in the nonstimulating rooms showed significant improvement were: Incorrect Elements (lines for dots, dots for loops, and so forth), Rotations, Distortion of the Configuration, Size (Enlargement, Compression, Disproportion), Inadequate Method (a combination of Immature, Concrete, Perseveration, and Erratic Approach), and the Total category.

No differences between the experimental and control groups were found for the categories: Immature, Concrete, Perseveration, and Erratic Approach. The number of errors classified as Concrete and Erratic Approach was so small that individual analyses were not undertaken. However, these four categories were combined to produce the category, Inadequate Method; and when this category is considered, the children in the stimulus-free rooms were seen to make significant progress over the course of the year, while the children in the control classes did not. Similarly, there were too few errors classified as Closure and Unrecognizable. For Form Dissociation and Distorted Angles, there were no differences between the experimental and control groups. However, when Form Dissociation, Closure, Incorrect Element, Unrecognizable, Distorted Angles, and Rotations were combined to form the category, Distortion of the Configuration, the scores for the children in the experimental classes showed significantly fewer errors than the scores for the children in control classes.

These results demonstrate the ameliorative effect both of a non-stimulating environment and of a specialized teaching methodology on the visuo-motor performance of children having specific learning disabilities.

Syracuse Visual Figure-Background Test

The Syracuse Visual Figure-Background Test [5] is a variation of a tachistoscopic test which was used originally by Werner and Strauss (59), Dolphin (28), and Myklebust (47). For a more detailed description of its administration, construction, scoring, and theory see Cruickshank, Bice and Wallen (24).

The SVFB consists of 16 pictures arranged in four series which are projected on a screen for times varying from .50 to .04 second. The pictures are of common objects embedded in a structured background. The first picture in each series is presented without the distracting influence of background.

Various writers have emphasized the significance of impairment of the figure-background relationship in brain injury. The rationale for the SVFB is based on the Gestalt conceptions developed by Vernon (57), Goldstein (34), and others.

PROCEDURE

The screen was placed 82 inches from the projector, and the child was seated so that his head was about a foot in front of the projector. The room was darkened as much as possible. The child was given the

[5] Referred to hereinafter as the SVFB Test.

following instructions: "Watch the screen. I'm going to show you some pictures for just a short time and then ask you tell me what you saw. Watch very carefully." Then the demonstration slides were shown, the first two for an indefinite time greater than .5 second, and the third at .05 second. When each slide was shown, every attempt was made to direct the attention of the child toward the stimulus materials. After each picture was flashed on the screen, the examiner said only: "Tell me what you saw." The child's responses were taken down verbatim on the record sheet. The same procedure was followed for series B at .2 second, series C at .1 second, and series D at .04. If the child responded with "Don't know," it was permissible to say, "What do you think it was"?

SCORING

The scoring procedure is the same as that used by Cruickshank, Bice and Wallen (24). Each response was categorized into one of eight categories. The categories are as follows:

1. *Correct Figure.* Identification in terms of either the original figure or of a figure which, in the judgment of the examiner is equally well represented by the slide. Plural identification of the correct figure is not included in this category.

2. *Slightly Incorrect Figure.* Identification in terms of any figure which, in the judgment of the examiner, closely approximates the intended figure but not closely enough to be "1." This category includes plural identification of correct figures where the plurality, in the judgment of the examiner is not due to the background.

3. *Correct Figure with Background.* Identification of the figure as defined in 1, plus any general reference to background such as lines, circles, design, pattern, and so forth; also any interpretation of background such as eggs, pillows, lips, screen, rug, tablecloth, wallpaper.

4. Same as "3" but with figure as defined in "2," i.e. slightly incorrect figure with background.

5. *Incorrect Figure.* Any response to the figure but one which is so poorly represented by the projected figure that it prohibits classification under "2."

6. *Incorrect Figure with Background.* Same as "3" but with figure defined as in "5."

7. *"Don't know."* All "don't knows," plus any other comment which does not commit the subject to a response.

8. *Background Only.* Any response which, in the judgment of the examiner, relates to the background exclusively.

Reliability data for the above categories have been reported elsewhere (24). The split-half reliability for "number correct" was .89; and for "number background," .92.

The performance of the children was also examined for evidences of perseveration. Many children gave the same response to several of the tachistoscopic presentations; or, when the pictures were projected more rapidly, they would repeat the responses which had been correct when the pictures had been presented at a slower rate. The number of repetitions was totaled and considered as evidence of perseveration.

RESULTS

Number Correct. Table 58 shows the means, standard deviations, and *t*-tests of the significance of the differences between means for the Num-

TABLE 58

Means, Standard Deviations, t-Tests, and Probabilities of Chance Differences in Means for the Syracuse Visual Figure-Background Test: Number Correct Score

Class	N	Pre-test		Post-test		t
		X̄	σ	X̄	σ	
C-1	10	5.70	3.10	7.40	3.32	2.83 ‡
C-2	10	5.10	2.17	7.60	2.29	8.59 #
E-1	10	2.20	1.66	5.00	3.07	3.75 §
E-2	9	3.78	3.52	7.22	2.62	5.65 §
Total	39	4.21	3.01	6.79	3.05	8.35 #

‡ p < .02
§ p < .01
# p < .001

ber Correct score on the SVFB. Each class saw significantly more correct slides in the post-test phase than they did in the pre-test phase. Considered as a whole, the group also made significant gains (p < .001).

Table 59 shows a comparison of the total control and total experimental groups. The control groups made significantly more correct responses at the beginning of the project than did the experimental groups (p < .05). At the end of the academic year, however, this difference had decreased to the point where it was no longer significant, thus indicating that the experimental groups had overcome their initial relative inadequacy.

When the performance of the control groups is compared on a test-retest basis, the difference is very significant (p < .001). The same comparison for the experimental groups results in the same significant difference. In other words, both the combined experimental and combined control groups made significantly more correct responses in the post-test period.

TABLE 59

Means, Standard Deviations, t-Tests, and Probabilities of Chance Differences in Means for the Control and Experimental Groups on the Syracuse Visual Figure-Background Test: Number Correct

Group	N	X̄	σ	t
Combined Control Groups, Pre-test	20	5.40	2.69	
				2.71 †
Combined Experimental Groups, Pre-test	19	2.95	2.82	
Combined Control Groups, Post-test	20	7.50	2.85	
				1.49
Combined Experimental Groups, Post-test	19	6.05	3.07	
Comparison of Control Group, Pre-test, and Control Group, Post-test	20	2.10	1.54	5.92 #
Comparison of Experimental Group, Pre-test, and Experimental Group, Post-test	19	3.1	2.15	6.13 #

† p < .05
# p < .001

The above results show that both the control and experimental groups increased in ability to indentify pictures flashed on a screen for varying speeds of time. The children in the control classes were able to do this much better than the children in the experimental classes at the beginning of the academic year, but by the end of the year this difference had disappeared, i.e., there was no longer a significant difference between them.

Number Background. Table 60 shows the means, standard deviations, and *t*-tests of the significance of differences between means for the SVFB Test, Number Background. Neither of the control groups showed significant improvement between the pre-test and post-test phases. On the other hand, one of the experimental groups made significantly fewer background responses in the post-test phase (p < .05); and the other experimental class approached significance (p < .10). The total group of 39 children made significantly fewer (p < .02) background responses at the end of the academic year.

Table 61 shows a comparison of the combined control and combined experimental groups. At the beginning of the school year, the mean of the combined control groups (2.65) was slightly less than the mean of the combined experimental groups (2.89); but this difference was not statistically significant. By the end of the academic year, however, this situation was reversed: the mean of the combined control groups

TABLE 60

Means, Standard Deviations, t-Tests, and Probabilities of Chance Differences in Means for the Syracuse Visual Figure-Background Test: Number Background *Score*

Class	N	Pre-test		Post-test		t
		$\overline{X}$	σ	$\overline{X}$	σ	
C-1	10	3.10	2.47	2.00	1.55	1.48
C-2	10	2.20	1.99	2.10	1.58	.19
E-1	10	3.10	2.47	1.60	1.56	2.36 †
E-2	9	2.67	2.71	1.11	1.29	2.22 *
Total	39	2.77	2.44	1.72	1.55	2.60 ‡

* p < .10
† p < .05
‡ p < .02

TABLE 61

Means, Standard Deviations, t-Tests, and Probabilities of Chance Differences in Means for the Control and Experimental Groups on the Syracuse Visual Figure-Background Test: Number Background Responses

Group	N	$\overline{X}$	σ	t
Combined Control Groups, Pre-test	20	2.65	2.29	
				.30
Combined Experimental Groups, Pre-test	19	2.89	2.59	
Combined Control Groups, Post-test	20	2.05	1.56	
				1.37
Combined Experimental Groups, Post-test	19	1.37	1.46	
Comparison of Control Group, Pre-test, and Control Group, Post-test	20	.65	2.10	1.35
Comparison of Experimental Group, Pre-test, and Experimental Group, Post-test	19	1.53	2.14	3.14 §

§ p < .01

(2.05) was slightly higher than the mean of the combined experimental groups (1.37). But, again, this difference was not statistically significant. When the pre-test and post-test responses of the combined control groups are compared, no significant improvement is noted; the experimental groups, on the other hand, show a significant improvement (p < .01).

The above data show that the children in the experimental classes produced significantly fewer post-test background responses than the children in the control classes. These data suggest that nonstimulating experimental classroom environments and the specialized teaching method may have partially improved the experimental subjects' abilities in the discrimination of the figure-background relationship and their abilities to withstand the impact of extraneous background stimuli.

TABLE 62

Means, Standard Deviations, t-Tests, and Probabilities of Chance Differences in Means for the Syracuse Visual Figure-Background Test: Number of Perseverations *Score*

Class	N	Pre-test		Post-test		
		$\overline{X}$	σ	$\overline{X}$	σ	t
C-1	10	3.20	2.82	1.10	1.45	2.40 †
C-2	10	1.90	2.66	1.50	2.80	.59
E-1	10	4.90	3.75	2.90	1.92	2.23 *
E-2	9	2.40	2.79	1.30	1.25	1.31
Total	39	3.13	3.25	1.72	1.78	3.36 §

* p < .10
† p < .05
§ p < .01

Perseveration. Table 62 shows the means, standard deviations, and *t*-tests of the significance of differences between means for the SVFB Test, Perseveration. One of the control classes showed significantly fewer Perseverations in the post-test period (p < .05), and the results of one of the experimental classes approached significance (p < .10).

Table 63 shows a comparison of the total control group and the total experimental group, and it indicates that both groups made significant gains over the course of the year.

The above data show that there was no difference in the number of perseverative responses on the SVFB between the children in the stimulus-free classrooms and those in the control classrooms. When all of the children are considered as a group, however, the difference between the pre-test and post-test means was significantly different (p < .01), showing that all the children were less perseverative at the end of the academic year.

SUMMARY

When the means of the pre-test and post-test results are compared, the total group showed significantly increased ability to identify figures

TABLE 63
Means, Standard Deviations, t-Tests, and Probabilities of Chance Differences in Means for the Control and Experimental Groups on the Syracuse Visual Figure-Background Test:
Number of Perseverations

Group	N	$\overline{X}$	σ	t
Combined Control Groups, Pre-test	20	2.35	2.82	
				1.13
Combined Experimental Groups, Pre-test	19	3.74	3.55	
Combined Control Groups, Post-test	20	1.30	1.65	
				1.23
Combined Experimental Groups, Post-test	19	2.00	1.81	
Comparison of Control Group, Pre-test, and Control Group, Post-test	20	1.25	2.53	2.16 †
Comparison of Experimental Group, Pre-test, and Experimental Group, Post-test	19	1.58	2.72	2.46 †

† $p < .05$

correctly. Although the children in the control classes gave significantly more correct responses at the beginning of the school year, the children in the experimental classes had caught up with them by the end of the year. The total group was much less perseverative at the end of the year. The children in the experimental classes were less distracted by the background at the end of the year. In contrast, the children in the control classes were almost as distracted and confused by the background at the conclusion of the academic year as they had been at the beginning.

The SVFB Test results are especially significant when considered in light of the views of Strauss, Werner and their associates (55, 59, 60). These results show the ameliorative effects of a stimulus-free environment and specialized teaching methods on visual-perceptual performance, and especially on figure-background distractions.

Vineland Scale of Social Maturity

BACKGROUND

The Vineland Scale of Social Maturity, which has been widely used to evaluate the social competence of children, is made up of items of increasing average difficulty concerning areas of maturation in social independence, such as self-help, self-direction, locomotion, occupation, communication, and social relations. The interested reader is referred to review sources by Doll (25, 26, 27) which cover the research concerned with this instrument.

RESULTS

A summary of the Vineland Scale of Social Maturity social quotients is shown in Table 64. The statistically significant *t*-tests of the differ-

TABLE 64

Mean Social Quotients, Standard Deviations, t-Tests, and Probabilities of Chance Differences in Means for the Vineland Scale of Social Maturity: Social Quotients

Class	N	Pre-test		Post-test		
		$\overline{X}$	σ	$\overline{X}$	σ	*t*
C-1	10	89.20	11.80	97.40	14.11	2.16
C-2	10	81.50	16.54	96.50	10.49	2.62 †
E-1	10	85.60	11.83	99.00	8.79	4.87 §
E-2	9	89.67	10.54	98.22	10.87	3.02 ‡
Total	39	86.41	13.35	97.77	11.28	5.72 §

† $p < .05$
‡ $p < .02$
§ $p < .01$

ences between pre-test and post-test means indicates that three classes made a significant gain in the *rate* of social development over the course of the year. A further comparison of the combined control groups and combined experimental groups is shown in Table 65. A comparison of the combined control groups' pre-test scores with their post-test scores shows a significant increase in social quotients; the same comparison with the combined experimental groups' scores gives the same results.

The above results show that the total group made significant gains in the rate of development of social competence. The improvement of the children was independent of their placement in a control or experimental class.

Stanford Achievement Test

BACKGROUND

At the beginning of the academic period, an attempt was made to administer the Stanford Achievement Test, Form J, to all of the children. At that time, only 12 children were able to complete all or part of this test. Failure was caused in part by inability to follow directions,

TABLE 65

Mean Social Quotients, Standard Deviations, t-Tests, and Probabilities of Chance Differences in Means for the Combined Control and Experimental Groups on the Vineland Scale of Social Maturity: Social Quotients

Group	N	X̄	σ	t
Combined Control Groups, Pre-test	20	85.35	14.85	
				.48
Combined Experimental Groups, Pre-test	19	87.53	11.42	
Combined Control Groups, Post-test	20	96.95	12.44	
				.44
Combined Experimental Groups, Post-test	19	98.63	9.83	
Comparison of Control Group, Pre-test, and Control Group, Post-test	20	11.50	14.97	3.38 §
Comparison of Experimental Group, Pre-test, and Experimental Group, Post-test	19	11.11	8.48	5.55 §

§ p < .01

by distractibility, or by inability to read. In an attempt to obtain as good an estimate of academic achievement as possible, the pre-tests were administered individually by the staff psychologist in rooms provided by the school which were free of the distracting elements of the average classroom. The directions for administering these tests were carefully followed. In no instance was help given to the child other than that specifically allowed in the directions, and careful note was made of the time.

The Primary Battery, Form J, is for use at the end of Grade 1, in Grade 2, and in the first half of Grade 3. The Primary Battery consists of five tests: paragraph meaning, word meaning, spelling, arithmetic reasoning, and arithmetic computation. A brief description of each of the subtests follows:

1. *Paragraph Meaning.* This subtest consists of a series of paragraphs of increasing difficulty; a word is missing from each paragraph. The task of the child is to demonstrate his understanding of the paragraph by choosing the missing word from a list of four possible choices.

2. *Word Meaning.* This subtest consists of multiple-choice items; the child is required to select the proper answer for a given stimulus word from a series of four alternatives. The central importance of vocabulary knowledge in the development of reading skills and in the acquisition of all kinds of information needs no elaboration here.

3. *Spelling.* This subtest is made up of a dictation spelling test of 30 items. The examiner reads a word, then uses the word in an illustrative sentence, and then repeats the word again. The list of words is carefully chosen for level of difficulty.

4. *Arithmetic Reasoning.* Increasing attention is being paid to the desirability of laying a good, solid foundation of meanings and under-standings prior to the teaching of formal computational skills; this subtest attempts to assess this type of understanding. The first half consists of pictorial items designed to measure understanding of basic quantitative and numerical concepts. The last half attempts to meas-ure problem-solving ability.

5. *Arithmetic Computation.* This subtest consists of 46 exercises which primarily involve the skills of addition and subtraction of whole numbers, but which also has multiplication and division problems.

At the conclusion of the academic year, each teacher assumed the responsibility for administering the Stanford Achievement Test, Form J, to all the children in her class. The post-test was administered indi-vidually after the teacher became familiar with the directions. Careful note of time was kept, and the directions were followed to the letter. The teachers, rather than the staff psychologist, administered the post-tests because there was only a short period of time available for testing.

RESULTS

At the beginning of the academic year, only 12 children were able to finish all or part of the Stanford Achievement Test. The children were either unable to read or else they were so distractible that they could not follow directions. Table 66 gives the grade level means and

TABLE 66

*Mean Grade Levels, Standard Deviations, t-Tests, and Probabilities of
Chance Differences in Means for the Pre- and Post-test
Achievement Subtests on Which Ten or More
Children Were Able to Perform*

Subtest	N	Pre-test		Post-test		t
		$\overline{X}$	σ	$\overline{X}$	σ	
Paragraph Meaning	12	1.73	.52	2.54	.96	2.55 ‡
Average Reading	12	1.49	.94	2.64	.96	2.84 §
Spelling	11	2.11	.76	2.95	.59	2.74 ‡
Arithmetic Computation	10	2.20	.49	2.78	.49	.79

‡ $p < .02$
§ $p < .01$

standard deviations for the subtests that all 12 children were able to complete: Paragraph Meaning, Average Reading, Spelling, and Arithmetic Computation. The post-test means for the same 12 children are also given for comparative purposes, as well as the *t*-tests of the significance of differences between pre- and post-test means. The differences are significant for three of the four subtests: Paragraph Meaning, Average Reading, and Spelling. Although the post-test grade level mean for the Arithmetic Computation subtest is higher than the pre-test mean, the progress that had occurred was not statistically significant.

TABLE 67
Mean Grade Levels and Standard Deviations for Remainder of Subtests

Subtest	N	Pre-test		Post-test	
		$\overline{X}$	σ	$\overline{X}$	σ
Word Meaning	0	2.50	.98	3.35	1.14
Arithmetic Reasoning	3	2.73	.66	3.37	.37
Average Arithmetic	3	2.73	.39	3.33	.21
Battery Median	3	2.63	.48	3.17	.60

Table 67 shows the grade level means and standard deviations for the other subtests, as well as the number of children who completed each subtest. Although the number of children completing each subtest is too small for meaningful statistical comparison, it should be noted that the post-test mean for each subtest is larger than the pre-test mean, thus indicating substantial growth over the course of the academic year.

Table 68 gives a comparison of the number of control and experimental children who were able to do all or part of the achievement test at the beginning of the school year. The post-test grade levels are also given although, again, the number of children is so small that meaningful comparison cannot be made (N's vary from 7 to 1). It should be noted, however, that in every instance the post-test mean is larger than the pre-test mean, thus indicating improvement on each subtest.

Table 69 gives a comparison of the combined control and combined experimental groups for the post-test Stanford Achievement Test. There are no statistically significant differences between the control and experimental groups on the post-test grade scores. Tables 70 through 77 give the grade level and means, and standard deviations by class for each of the subtests.

Because of the very small number of students who were able to complete all or part of the Stanford Achievement Test at the beginning

TABLE 68

*Comparison of Pre-test and Post-test Achievement Test Grade
Levels for the Two Combined Experimental and Two
Combined Control Groups* [a]

| | Pre-test | | | | Post-test | | | |
| | Control | | Experimental | | Control | | Experimental | |
Subtest	N	$\overline{X}$	N	$\overline{X}$	N	$\overline{X}$	N	X
Paragraph Meaning	7	1.71	5	1.76	7	1.76	5	2.02
Word Meaning	3	3.13	3	1.87	3	4.2	3	2.50
Average Reading	7	1.56	5	1.40	7	2.97	5	2.18
Spelling	6	2.50	5	1.64	6	3.13	5	2.72
Arithmetic Reasoning	1	3.20	2	2.25	1	3.80	2	3.15
Arithmetic Computation	6	2.25	4	2.13	6	2.33	4	2.88
Average Arithmetic	1	3.10	2	2.55	1	3.6	2	3.20
Battery Median	1	3.30	2	2.30	1	4.0	2	2.75

[a] Only 12 children were able to finish all or part of the achievement test at the beginning of the academic year. The post-test scores for these same children are given above for comparative purposes.

TABLE 69

*Grade Levels Means, Standard Deviations, t-Tests, and Probabilities of
Chance Differences in Means for the Control and Experimental
Groups on the Stanford Achievement Test:*
Primary Battery, Form J

| | Combined Groups | | | | |
| | Control | | Experimental | | |
Subtest	$\overline{X}$	σ	$\overline{X}$	σ	t
Paragraph Meaning	2.29	3.07	2.07	.41	.69
Word Meaning	2.51	1.07	2.41	.50	.28
Average Reading	2.35	1.01	2.25	.45	.33
Spelling	2.21	.87	2.41	.68	.68
Arithmetic Reasoning	1.52	1.61	2.06	.85	1.26
Arithmetic Computation	2.21	.77	2.27	.68	.02
Average Arithmetic	2.02	.85	2.21	.71	.72
Battery Median	2.04	1.04	2.55	.36	1.53

TABLE 70

Grade Level Means and Standard Deviations for the Post-test
Achievement Scores: Paragraph Meaning

Class	N	$\overline{X}$	σ
C-1	7	2.23	.71
C-2	7	2.36	1.18
E-1	8	2.15	.38
E-2	4	1.93	.43
Total	26	2.19	.77

TABLE 71

Grade Level Means and Standard Deviations for the Post-test
Achievement Scores: Word Meaning

Class	N	$\overline{X}$	σ
C-1	7	2.51	1.16
C-2	6	2.50	.96
E-1	8	2.49	.51
E-2	4	2.25	.45
Total	25	2.46	.85

TABLE 72

Grade Level Means and Standard Deviations for the Post-test
Achievement Scores: Average Reading

Class	N	$\overline{X}$	σ
C-1	7	2.36	.92
C-2	7	2.36	1.10
E-1	8	2.31	.45
E-2	4	2.13	.43
Total	26	2.31	.81

TABLE 73
Grade Level Means and Standard Deviations for the Post-test Achievement Scores: Spelling

Class	N	X̄	σ
C-1	9	2.30	.82
C-2	8	2.11	.92
E-1	8	2.85	.37
E-2	7	1.90	.61
Total	32	2.30	.80

TABLE 74
Grade Level Means and Standard Deviations for Post-test Achievement Scores: Arithmetic Reasoning

Class	N	X̄	σ
C-1	10	2.05	.97
C-2	10	1.99	.84
E-1	10	2.18	.86
E-2	9	1.92	.83
Total	39	2.04	.88

TABLE 75
Grade Level Means and Standard Deviations for Post-test Achievement Scores: Arithmetic Computation

Class	N	X̄	σ
C-1	9	2.27	.91
C-2	10	2.15	.61
E-1	10	2.23	.61
E-2	8	2.33	.76
Total	37	2.24	.73

TABLE 76
Grade Level Means and Standard Deviations for Post-test Achievement Scores: Average Arithmetic

Class	N	X̄	σ
C-1	10	2.03	1.02
C-2	10	2.01	.64
E-1	10	2.18	.71
E-2	8	2.24	.72
Total	38	2.11	.79

TABLE 77

Grade Level Means and Standard Deviations for Post-test
Achievement Scores: Battery Median

Class	N	$\overline{X}$	σ
C-1	10	1.89	1.07
C-2	6	2.28	.93
E-1	7	2.60	.34
E-2	4	2.48	.36
Total	27	2.25	.87

of the year, a statistically meaningful comparison between the combined experimental and control groups was not possible. At the end of the year, however, enough children were able to perform on the test so that such a comparison could be made; it showed that there was not a statistically significant difference between the groups on their post-test performance. The post-test means were, in all cases, greater than the pre-test means for all the children, showing that definite progress in all classes had occurred.

Summary of Psychological Data

On the four intelligence tests given at the beginning of the project (Stanford-Binet, Goodenough Intelligence Test, Ammons Full-Range Picture Vocabulary, and Coding and Block Design from the WISC), no differences between classes, or between the combined control and combined experimental groups, were observed. Only two of the intelligence tests were administered on a pre-test and post-test basis (Stanford-Binet and Goodenough Intelligence Test), and no statistically significant differences were found between scores made at the beginning of the year and scores made at the end.

Careful matching of the groups was also reflected in the similar scores of the four groups on the perceptual tests (Bender-Gestalt, SVFB, Tactual-Motor Test, and Marble Board Test) at the beginning of the school year. Only two of these tests were administered on a pre-test and post-test basis (Bender-Gestalt and SVFB). On the Bender-Gestalt Test, the experimental group made significant improvement on six of the ten scoring categories (Incorrect Elements, Rotations, Distortion of the Configuration, Size, Inadequate Method, and Total Number of Errors).

At the beginning of the academic year, the combined control groups identified significantly more correct figures on the SVFB than did the experimental groups. By the end of the year, however, the experimental groups had caught up with the control groups. What is of even more importance from a theoretical point of view is that the children in the experimental groups had improved significantly in their ability to withstand distractibility from background stimuli; this may be seen in the significantly fewer background responses which were made on the SVFB in the post-testing phase.

Social growth and development, as measured by the Vineland Scale of Social Maturity social quotients, showed a significant increase in the *rate* of development for all of the children. Improvement in the development of social skills seemed to be independent of placement in a control or experimental group.

Adequate evaluation of academic achievement during the course of the year was not possible, as only 12 of the children were able to perform on all or part of the achievement test at the beginning of the school year. Failure to perform on the achievement test was due to inability to read, because of hyperactivity or attention difficulties or both. By the end of the year, however, all of the children were able to perform on at least part of the achievement test, and 25 were able to perform on all of it.

At the beginning of the project, it was generally agreed among the diagnostic staff that one academic year was not enough time to see the maximum growth and development which might be expected to occur as a result of the experimental procedures. For instance, it was felt by some in special education that the IQ's of these children would increase as a result of the special education experience. The present data lend no support for this belief, although isolated children did show major gains. (The pre-test mean Binet IQ was 80.39, and the post-test mean IQ was 80.23.)

In the light of what has been written about the relationship of perceptual difficulties to learning problems, it is interesting to note that the main influence of the experimental conditions was to increase visual-perceptual performance. All of the children in the project received perceptual training, but the children in nonstimulating environments made significantly more growth in this ability than did the children in control classrooms.

In order to adequately assess the long-term effects of the experimental conditions, as well as the value of the specialized methodology, it is, of course, necessary to evaluate these children again at some future time, preferably after an interval of one or two years.

TWELVE MONTH FOLLOW-UP

An additional grant by the Eugene and Agnes E. Meyer Foundation made possible the collection of further psychological and educational test data covering the academic year 1958–1959. The term, "pre-test," of the project refers to the testing done prior to or at the beginning of the project (1957); the term, "post-test," refers to the testing done at the end of the project year (1958). "Follow-up" (1959), refers to the test data made possible by the above-mentioned Meyer Foundation grant.

Follow-up I

The Follow-up I psychological and educational test battery consisted of:
Stanford-Binet, Form L,
Bender-Gestalt,
Syracuse Visual Figure-Background Test,
Goodenough Draw-a-Person,
Block Design and Coding from the WISC,
Vineland Scale of Social Maturity,
Stanford Achievement Test.

The Stanford Achievement Test was administered individually by a special education teacher [6] whose full-time services during the month of May and part of June were contributed by the Montgomery County Board of Education. The psychological tests were administered during the period from June 3 to July 6, 1959.

The 1959 results are noted on the tables as Grouping II. Each class in the second-year grouping (1959) contained a core of 4 or 5 children who were carried over from the preceding year; the remainder were children who had been shifted from the other project classes, or they were children who had been brought in from other special education classes. The statistics presented in this chapter are based only on the performance of those children who had been in the original project.

None of the second-year grouping classes had modified physical environments, and all of the teachers were free to vary teaching techniques as they saw fit. No attempt was made to insure close adherence to the highly structured teaching techniques of the project. One of the control teachers from the project year was not available during the second year, but she was replaced by a teacher who had had experience working with children of the type included in the project.

It was desirable to make a comparison of the control and experimental groups during the second year, even though the actual class placement had been changed, in order to assess the influence of the project year on subsequent psychological and achievement test per-

[6] Miss Mary Morningstar, Department of Special Education, Montgomery County Board of Education.

formance. A number of children had moved from the area or were for other reasons unavailable for testing. As reported in the following tables, the statistics for the pre-test and post-test phases were computed on the basis of the number of children from the original project who still remained in the four classes at the end of the second year.

Statistical analyses of the test results are presented in the following order:

1. comparison of the experimental and control classes,
2. test results of the classes during the second year.

Stanford Binet

Table 78 shows the means, standard deviations, *t*-tests, and probabilities of chance differences in means for the Stanford-Binet intelligence quotients. The figures for the pre-test and post-test results are based on

TABLE 78

Means, Standard Deviations, t-Tests, and Probabilities of Chance Differences in Means for the Stanford-Binet:
Intelligence Quotients

Class	N	Pre-test $\overline{X}$	σ	Post-test $\overline{X}$	σ	Follow-up I $\overline{X}$	σ	Follow-up I and Post-test t	Pre-test t
C-1	10	80.20	11.58	80.00	14.16	80.10	14.43	.04	.04
C-2	9	79.33	11.20	80.44	9.37	79.22	12.24	.42	.06
E-1	8	81.63	12.03	78.25	10.38	79.25	10.88	.85	1.45
E-2	8	82.00	15.67	83.25	15.04	82.25	19.77	.43	.08
Total	35	80.71	12.68	80.46	12.62	80.17	14.69	.25	.49

the number of children who remained in the project for the entire two-year period. The mean IQ is remarkably consistent: 80.71 in the pre-test phase, 80.46 in the post-test phase, and 80.17 in the Follow-up I phase.

Comparison of the combined control and combined experimental groups is shown in Table 79. No statistically significant differences in means occurred, again reflecting the very careful matching of these children. Table 80 shows the means, standard deviations, and *t*-tests for the children as they were grouped during the second year.

Table 81 shows the age-range on the Stanford-Binet for the three testing periods. At the end of the project, a statistically significant differ-

TABLE 79

Means, Standard Deviations, t-Tests, and Probabilities of Chance
Differences in Means for the Combined Control and
Experimental Groups for the Stanford-Binet:
Intelligence Quotients

Group	N	$\overline{X}$	σ	t [a]
Combined Control Groups, Follow-up I	19	79.68	13.44	
				.19
Combined Experimental Groups, Follow-up I	16	80.75	16.03	
Comparison of Control Group, Pre-test, and Control Group, Follow-up I	19	—.11	6.18	.07
Comparison of Control Group Post-test, and Control Group, Follow-up I	19	—.53	7.66	.29
Comparison of Experimental Group, Pre-test, and Experimental Group, Follow-up I	16	—1.06	6.64	.62
Comparison of Experimental Group, Post-test, and Experimental Group, Follow-up I	16	.19	5.53	00

[a] *t*-test computed on basis of paired observations. The mean and standard deviation reported on are based on the differences between pairs of observations.

TABLE 80

Means, Standard Deviations, and t-Tests, of the Significance of Differences
between Means for the Grouping II Stanford-Binet:
Intelligence Quotients

Group	N	Pre-test		Post-test		Follow-up I		Follow-up I and Post-test	Pre-test
		$\overline{X}$	σ	$\overline{X}$	σ	$\overline{X}$	σ	t	t
A	8	88.88	14.53	86.00	14.41	89.88	16.63	1.76	.37
B	10	72.90	8.81	74.10	9.52	70.90	8.63	3.49 §	
C	9	81.67	11.66	81.22	9.52	80.89	12.78	.11	.44
D	7	78.29	6.50	77.29	6.18	77.29	10.07	.00	.39

§ $p < .01$

ence had been found between the Form L administered at the beginning of the year, and the Form M administered at the end. The mean age-range in the pre-test period was 5.26; in the post-test period it was 4.57. At first it was assumed that this might reflect an improvement in the children's capacity to handle tasks at the low end of the scale; that

TABLE 81

*Means, Standard Deviations, and t-Tests, of the Significance of
Differences between Means for the Stanford-Binet:* Age-Range

Class	N	Pre-test X	σ	Post-test X	σ	Follow-up I X	σ	Follow-up I and Post-test t	Pre-test t
C-1	10	5.30	1.49	5.10	1.58	5.90	1.81	1.44	.90
C-2	9	5.22	1.31	3.89	1.29	5.11	1.10	3.77 §	.17
E-1	8	5.38	.86	4.50	.77	5.38	.99	2.49 †	.00
E-2	8	5.13	1.54	4.75	1.20	5.50	1.58	1.43	.81
Total	35	5.26	1.34	4.57	1.34	5.49	1.46	4.12 §	.79

† p < .05
§ p < .01

TABLE 82

*Means, Standard Deviations, t-Tests, and Probabilities of Chance
Differences in Means for the Combined Control and
Experimental Groups on the Stanford-Binet:*
Age-Range

Group	N	X	σ	t
Combined Control Groups, Follow-up I	19	5.53	1.57	
				.17
Combined Experimental Groups, Follow-up I	16	5.44	1.32	
Comparison of Control Group, Pre-test, and Control Group, Follow-up I	19	.21	2.01	.56
Comparison of Control Group, Post-test, and Control Group, Follow-up I	19	1.00	1.38	3.09 §
Comparison of Experimental Group, Pre-test, and Experimental Group, Follow-up I	16	.19	1.24	.59
Comparison of Experimental Group, Post-test, and Experimental Group, Follow-up I	16	.81	1.18	2.66 ‡

‡ p < .02
§ p < .01

is, it was assumed that the specialized teaching method might have
"filled in" the capacity to perform those which had caused failures in
the lower age levels. However, the results at the end of the second year
which are shown in Table 81, do not substantiate this interpretation,

because they show a significant *increase* in age-range when the post-test and the Follow-up I for the total group are compared, and when the age-range for two individual classes (C-2 and E-1) are compared. The mean age-range on the Follow-up I Stanford-Binet, Form L, for the total group was 5.49 as contrasted to 4.57 on the post-test Form M. In the two administrations of the Form L, the age-range means are extremely close, the pre-test being 5.26, the Follow-up I, 5.49. Thus, the mean age-range on the Form M seems to be at variance with the means on the Form L.

Table 82 shows comparison of the combined control and combined experimental groups.

Table 83 shows second-year grouping.

TABLE 83
Means, Standard Deviations, and t-Tests of the Significance of Differences between Means for the Grouping II Stanford-Binet: Age-Range

Group	N	Pre-test $\overline{X}$	σ	Post-test $\overline{X}$	σ	Follow-up I $\overline{X}$	σ	Follow-up I and Post-test t
A	8	6.00	1.06	4.50	.87	6.00	1.17	3.97 §
B	10	4.40	1.11	4.50	1.20	4.70	1.00	.61
C	9	5.44	1.34	4.56	1.26	6.00	1.63	3.51 §
D	7	5.00	.76	4.14	.99	5.00	1.19	1.23

§ P < .01

TABLE 84
Means and Standard Deviations for the Stanford-Binet: Mental Ages, *Original Grouping*

Class	N	Pre-test $\overline{X}$	σ	N	Post-test $\overline{X}$	σ	N	Follow-up I $\overline{X}$	σ
C-1	10	80.60	13.08	10	89.60	16.66	10	100.10	19.49
C-2	10	80.10	14.69	10	91.40	13.89	9	97.00	17.05
E-1	10	73.50	10.35	10	80.70	13.68	8	95.25	13.11
E-2	9	78.89	16.39	9	88.67	20.11	8	100.75	26.91
Total	39	78.26	14.03	39	87.56	16.71	35	98.34	19.82

The mean mental ages and standard deviations for the original grouping are shown in Table 84; those for the second-year grouping are shown in Table 85. These tables indicate that the variability of

TABLE 85
Means and Standard Deviations for the Stanford-Binet:
Mental Ages, Grouping II

Group	Pre-test N	X̄	σ	Post-test N	X̄	σ	Follow-up I N	X̄	σ
A	9	84.67	16.39	9	92.11	18.31	8	112.50	19.12
B	10	71.50	8.99	10	80.60	13.57	10	86.30	13.93
C	9	81.22	13.85	9	90.00	11.89	9	100.11	17.59
D	7	73.14	7.94	7	81.71	8.71	7	92.00	14.46

mental ages was much greater in the second-year grouping than it was at the beginning of the project.

The drawing of a diamond still proved to be an extremely difficult item at the end of the second year, even though perceptual training had been an integral part of the teaching approach during the two-year period. In the pre-test period, 7 of the 39 children passed this item on the Stanford-Binet, Form L, at the 7-year level. In the Follow-up I Stanford Binet, Form L, 7 children again passed this item. It should be noted, however, that only 3 children passed this item on both the pre-test and Follow-up I period. For comparison, the mean age for all the children was 10–0, and the mean IQ was 80.17. The mean age of the 7 children who passed the diamond-drawing item on the Follow-up I, Form L, was 8–6, and the mean IQ was 89.43. Five had normal EEG's.

SUMMARY

Is the significant difference in age-range between the pre-test and post-test phases, and between the post-test and Follow-up I phases, due to changes in the intellectual functioning of the children, or is this difference the result of using two forms of the same test? In the standardization of the Stanford-Binet, the Form L and Form M correlate very highly, and in clinical practice they are considered equivalent scales. Many clinicians have felt for some time, however, that a revision should be made because a few of the items are generally considered to be obsolete. Although the over-all intelligence quotients from these two scales are, for all practical purposes, identical, it should be noted that the two scales are not composed of exactly the same items. For example, at the 7-year level on the Form M there is no item that would correspond *exactly* to the diamond-drawing item on the Form L at the same year level. As was pointed out earlier, this item proved extremely difficult for the children. If a child passed all items at the year 7 level except the diamond-drawing item, his age-range would automatically be extended one year, the basal age then being at the year 6 level rather than at the year 7. Similarly, several items at the upper end of the scale may be somewhat too easy, thereby augmenting the age-range by raising the ceiling. Thus, the differences noted in Table 81 could be caused by the internal construction of the scales.

Although there was some variability of individual IQ's, the mean IQ for the total group was very consistent for each of the three tests.

Many teachers who work with retarded children distrust the conventional measurement scales of intelligence. Too frequently the child who performs at a very low level on such tests demonstrates considerable capacities in various areas not ordinarily associated with "book learning." A "retarded" child may exhibit competency of a relatively high order in tasks involving mechanical aptitude or may show quite a high esthetic sense. As a result the teacher tends to discard the intelligence measures as meaningless or not really being important.

It is not the purpose here to criticize intelligence tests. Others have done a highly competent job in this respect. It has been pointed out that the tests do not take into account enough of the known or suspected elements which have been isolated in factor analysis studies; furthermore, little or no attempt has been made to correlate the processes involved in test performance with non-test problem solving. Whether or not the tests measure "real intelligence" is a problem to be answered through other investigations. One cannot escape the conclusion, however, that the tests do correlate highly with one form of intellectual endeavor that our society imposes upon its members: the activities and processes that make success possible within the school situation.

Masland, Sarason, and Gladwin (45) pointed out that many children who have been diagnosed as having borderline intelligence are labelled and treated as mentally retarded only within the context of the public school system; after passing the compulsory school age, many of these children "pass" into the normal population and lose the stigma of the earlier retardation label. The academic milieu, then, may be the only intellectual hurdle which such an individual will face within his lifetime. A search for a way of helping such children get over this hurdle would be justification enough for the present project.

Goodenough Intelligence Test

The means, standard deviations, and *t*-tests for the Goodenough IQ's are presented in Table 86. No statistically significant differences be-

TABLE 86

Means, Standard Deviations, and t-Tests of Significance of Differences between Means for the Goodenough Intelligence Test IQ's

Class	N	Pre-test		Post-test		Follow-up I		Follow-up I and Post-test	Pre-test
		$\overline{X}$	σ	$\overline{X}$	σ	$\overline{X}$	σ	*t*	*t*
C-1	9	82.22	19.79	84.00	12.56	79.89	16.05	.97	.56
C-2	9	71.89	12.68	76.00	12.34	69.56	13.72	.95	.37
E-1	8	73.13	9.06	76.63	11.37	70.50	15.12	1.26	.36
E-2	8	85.13	10.69	74.38	11.60	76.13	16.87	.36	2.76
Total	34	78.03	15.45	77.88	12.58	74.06	16.03	1.56	1.49

tween pre-test, post-test, or Follow-up I phases occurred, either for individual classes or for the total group.

Table 87 shows a comparison of the combined control and combined experimental groups. Again, no statistically significant differences were noted.

TABLE 87

Means, Standard Deviations, t-Tests, and Probabilities of Chance Differences in Means for the Control and Experimental Groups on the Goodenough Intelligence Test IQ's

Group	N	$\overline{X}$	σ	*t*
Combined Control Groups, Follow-up I	18	74.72	15.80	
				.24
Combined Experimental Groups, Follow-up I	16	73.31	16.26	
Comparison of Control Group, Pre-test, and Control Group, Follow-up I	18	−2.33	17.41	.64
Comparison of Control Group, Post-test, and Control Group, Follow-up I	18	−5.28	13.08	1.52
Comparison of Experimental Group, Pre-test, and Experimental Group, Follow-up I	16	−5.81	12.81	1.47
Comparison of Experimental Group, Post-test, and Experimental Group, Follow-up I	16	−2.19	11.54	.63

Table 88 compares the means, standard deviations, and *t*-test for the post-test and Follow-up I phases for the second-year grouping. No significant differences were noted.

TABLE 88

Means, Standard Deviations, and t-Tests of the Significance of Differences between Means for the Grouping II Goodenough IQ's

Group	N	Pre-test		Post-test		Follow-up I		Follow-up I and Post-test
		$\overline{X}$	σ	$\overline{X}$	σ	$\overline{X}$	σ	t
A	8	71.50	13.80	78.88	8.71	79.25	13.75	.12
B	10	82.60	11.93	76.90	10.68	72.70	17.22	.09
C	9	76.22	17.13	78.11	10.71	75.78	17.33	.38
D	7	81.29	16.15	77.86	19.21	69.00	10.70	2.04

SUMMARY

Machover (44) has devoted considerable attention to the personality dynamics involved in drawing the human figure. Without becoming involved in a complete analysis of her point of view, it should be noted that at the end of the two-year period these children produced drawings that were in marked contrast to those produced in the pre-test period. True, some of the children continued to produce bizarre, distorted figures which indicated that their skill was considerably below that expected from this age level, but even these few drawings are considerably better than those produced at the beginning of the project. It might be posited that with increasing personality integration, as noted in the psychiatric reports, there is a corresponding integration in the body image projected in this test. The improvement in drawing, however, cannot be attributed to any one factor. In addition to the academic experiences of the children, maturational and developmental factors may be assumed to play a role. The ratio of mental age, scored according to the Goodenough criteria, to the chronological age is very consistent. The perceptual training given the children did not result in an increase in this ratio.

Block Design and Coding
from Wechsler Intelligence Scale for Children

BLOCK DESIGN

A comparison of the pre-test and Follow-up I results is presented in Table 89. The mean equivalent test age for each individual class,

TABLE 89

Means, Standard Deviations, and t-Tests of Significance of Differences between Means for the Wechsler Intelligence Scale for Children Subtest: Block Design

Class	N	Pre-test $\overline{X}$	σ	Follow-up I $\overline{X}$	σ	t
C-1	10	73.60	12.32	103.40	18.20	5.55 §
C-2	9	75.33	22.07	113.11	41.90	4.95 §
E-1	7	64.86	11.05	121.14	33.33	3.39 ‡
E-2	8	78.50	13.03	115.50	42.56	2.65 †
Total	34	73.41	16.15	112.47	35.48	7.43 §

† $p < .05$
‡ $p < .02$
§ $p < .01$

as well as the mean for the total group of children, was significantly higher at the end of the second year. Table 90 shows a comparison of

TABLE 90

Means, Standard Deviations, t-Tests, and Probabilities of Chance Differences in Means for the Combined Control and Experimental Groups on the Wechsler Intelligence Scale for Children Subtest: Block Design

Group	N	X	σ	t
Combined Control Groups, Follow-up I	19	108.00	32.09	
				.78
Combined Experimental Groups, Follow-up I	15	118.13	38.63	
Comparison of Control Group, Pre-test, and Control Group, Follow-up I	19	33.58	19.32	7.37 §
Comparison of Experimental Group, Pre-test, and Experimental Group, Follow-up I	15	43.07	39.31	4.38 §

§ $p < .01$

the combined control and combined experimental groups. Although there was not a statistically significant difference between the combined control and combined experimental groups, each combined group had a significantly higher mean equivalent test age at the end of the second year than it had had in the pre-test period. Table 91 shows the statistics for the second-year grouping.

TABLE 91

Means, Standard Deviations, t-Tests, and Probabilities of Chance
Differences in Means for the Wechsler Intelligence Scale for
Children, Grouping II. Subtest: Block Design
(Equivalent Test Age in Months)

Group	N	Pre-test X	σ	Follow-up I X	σ	t
A	8	72.50	15.22	110.75	29.12	4.30 §
B	10	70.80	12.37	110.80	42.73	2.68 †
C	8	77.00	18.08	114.25	31.63	3.97 §
D	7	73.43	19.53	113.43	36.00	5.56 §

† p < .05
§ p < .01

CODING

Table 92 shows a comparison of the pre-test and Follow-up I mean
equivalent test age for the Coding test for individual classes and for
the total group. The two experimental groups had significantly higher

TABLE 92

Means, Standard Deviations, t-Tests, and Probabilities of Chance
Differences in Means for the Wechsler Intelligence Scale for
Children. Subtest: Coding (Equivalent Test Age in Months)

Class	N	Pre-test X	σ	Follow-up I X	σ	t
C-1	8	79.00	22.85	94.75	32.95	1.44
C-2	9	69.56	12.85	78.90	12.90	1.32
E-1	7	66.00	8.28	84.85	7.32	3.35 ‡
E-2	8	81.50	15.93	91.75	15.21	2.97 †
Total	32	74.13	17.18	87.38	20.68	3.68 §

† p < .05
‡ p < .02
§ p < .01

mean equivalent test ages, than did the total group, but the control
groups did not. Table 93 shows a comparison of the combined control
and combined experimental groups. Although there was not a significant difference between the combined control and combined experi-

TABLE 93

Means, Standard Deviations, t-Tests, and Probabilities of Chance
Differences in Means for the Combined Control and Experimental
Groups on the Wechsler Intelligence Scale for Children:
Coding (*Equivalent Test Age in Months*)

Group	N	$\overline{X}$	σ	t
Combined Control Groups, Follow-up I	17	86.35	25.72	
				.30
Combined Experimental Groups, Follow-up I	15	88.53	12.66	
Comparison of Control Group, Pre-test, and Control Group, Follow-up I	17	10.59	25.69	1.92
Comparison of Experimental Group, Pre-test, and Experimental Group, Follow-up I	15	14.27	12.33	4.33 §

§ p < .01

mental groups, the combined experimental group had a significantly higher equivalent test age on the Follow-up I test, while the combined control group did not. Table 94 shows the scores for the second-year grouping.

TABLE 94

Means, Standard Deviations, t-Tests, and Probabilities of Chance
Differences in Means for the Wechsler Intelligence Scale for
Children, Grouping II. Subtest: Coding
(*Equivalent Test Age in Months*)

Group	N	Pre-test		Follow-up I		t
		$\overline{X}$	σ	$\overline{X}$	σ	
A	8	78.00	14.70	78.00	13.45	.00
B	8	78.00	15.59	88.00	19.10	3.37 ‡
C	8	80.00	22.43	93.00	26.06	1.79
D	7	66.57	9.90	83.71	6.71	3.73 §

‡ p < .02
§ p < .01

SUMMARY

The equivalent test age is the WISC equivalent of the mental age obtained on the Stanford-Binet Intelligence Test. It is interesting to note how similar the mean equivalent test age on the Block Design test (6.12 years) is to the pre-test mean Stanford-Binet mental age (6.52

years). At the end of the second year, however, the mean equivalent test age had risen a full year above the mean mental age, the equivalent test age being 9.57 years, and the mean mental age being 8.20 years. These results are quite consistent with the perceptual training given the children. Parquetry blocks and other instructional block designs were used; thus, the children had experienced intensive drill in the processes measured by the test.

As noted above, training may be assumed to have played a very important part in the improvement of the total group's performance on the Block Design; but this was not the case with the Coding test, because there were no materials used in the training program that were similar to the test items. In the pre-test phase, the Coding mean equivalent test age was 6.12 years and the mean Stanford-Binet mental age was 6.52 years. In the post-test phase the Coding mean equivalent test age was 7.28 years and the mean Stanford-Binet mental age was 8.20 years.

Where instructional materials were quite similar to the WISC items, test performance was a full year above the Stanford-Binet mental age. Where the children had not had intensive training with similar instructional materials, test performance was a full year below the Stanford-Binet mental age.

The significantly higher equivalent test age of the combined experimental group may be attributed in part to the relatively greater emphasis on perceptual training. In all four classes perceptual training was an important part of the program, but there was somewhat greater freedom to vary instruction in the control classes.

Bender-Gestalt

PERSEVERATION

Table 95 shows the means, standard deviations, and *t*-tests of the significance of differences between means, for the total group, as well as for each control and experimental class, for the Bender-Gestalt category, Perseveration. There were no statistically significant differences either between the means of the pre-test and Follow-up I phase, or between the post-test and Follow-up I phase. Table 96 shows the results of the statistical analysis of the combined control and combined experimental groups. No significant differences were noted. Table 97 shows the statistics for the second-year grouping, and, again, no significant differences were noted.

There were no differences between the experimental and control

TABLE 95

Means, Standard Deviations, t-Tests, and Probabilities of Chance
Differences in Means for the Number of Perseverations on the
Bender-Gestalt Test, for the Experimental and
Control Groups

Class	N	Pre-test $\overline{X}$	σ	Post-test $\overline{X}$	σ	Follow-up I $\overline{X}$	σ	Follow-up I and Post-test t	Pre-test t
C-1	10	1.50	1.08	1.80	.92	.90	1.29	1.49	1.26
C-2	9	1.89	2.17	1.44	1.13	1.56	2.12	.21	.71
E-1	6	1.83	1.33	1.50	1.05	1.67	.52	.58	.28
E-2	8	1.50	1.51	1.50	1.20	.88	.80	1.18	1.05
Total	33	1.67	1.19	1.58	1.03	1.21	1.14	1.32	1.79

TABLE 96

Means, Standard Deviations, t-Tests, and Probabilities of Chance
Differences in Means for the Control and Experimental Groups
on the Bender-Gestalt Test: Perseverations

Group	N	$\overline{X}$	σ	t
Combined Control Groups, Follow-up I	19	1.21	1.32	
				.01
Combined Experimental Groups, Follow-up I	14	1.21	.77	
Comparison of Control Group, Pre-test, and Control Group, Follow-up I	19	—.47	1.39	1.44
Comparison of Control Group, Post-test, and Control Group, Follow-up I	19	—.42	1.76	1.02
Comparison of Experimental Group, Pre-test, and Experimental Group, Follow-up I	14	—.43	1.50	1.03
Comparison of Experimental Group, Post-test, and Experimental Group, Follow-up I	14	—.29	1.22	.85

TABLE 97

Means, Standard Deviations, and t-Tests of the Significance of Differences between Means for the Grouping II Bender-Gestalt Test: Perseveration

Group	N	Pre-test X	σ	Post-test X	σ	Follow-up I X	σ	Follow-up I and Post-test t
A	8	1.88	1.36	2.00	2.18	1.13	1.05	1.08
B	10	1.40	1.28	1.80	1.08	1.20	1.17	.97
C	8	1.38	.99	1.50	1.00	1.38	1.41	.21
D	6	2.17	.69	1.83	.69	1.33	.47	1.46

groups on this scoring category. The children who were in the more structured teaching situation of the experimental groups did not improve in perseveration during the project, nor was there any evidence of differential progress when they were assigned to different classes the second year. These results are in disagreement with the teachers' feeling that the children, as a total group, showed a reduction in perseveration over the two-year period. It may well be, however, that perseveration seen on the Bender-Gestalt Test, which may be considered a simple motor perseveration, may not be the same type of perseveration (process perseveration) with which the teachers are most concerned.

FORM DISSOCIATION

Table 98 shows the means, standard deviations, and *t*-tests of the differences between means for the Bender-Gestalt category, Form Dissociation. At the conclusion of the project one experimental class (E-1) had shown significant improvement on this category (p < .05), but this gain was not maintained when the children were assigned to different classes during the second year. None of the classes made significant gains on this category during the second year, nor did the total group make gains during the second year. The improvement made by the entire group during the first year was maintained, however, as may be seen in comparing the differences between the pre-test and Follow-up I phases, where one class (C-2) made significant progress (p < .05) and where the total group showed an over-all gain.

Table 99 shows comparison of the combined control and combined experimental groups. At the conclusion of the project, both the combined control groups and combined experimental groups had made

TABLE 98

*Means, Standard Deviations, t-Tests, and Probabilities of Chance
Differences in Means for the Number of* Form Dissociations *on
the Bender-Gestalt Test for the Experimental
and Control Groups*

Class	N	Pre-test $\overline{X}$	σ	Post-test $\overline{X}$	σ	Follow-up I $\overline{X}$	σ	Follow-up I and Pre-test t	Post-test t
C-1	10	2.90	1.91	2.40	1.78	2.20	1.62	.42	1.04
C-2	9	2.89	1.36	1.89	1.45	1.67	.81	.48	2.63 †
E-1	6	3.00	1.67	2.17	1.47	1.83	1.60	.68	1.12
E-2	8	3.13	2.36	1.25	1.04	1.63	1.77	.67	1.62
Total	33	2.97	1.78	1.88	1.56	1.85	1.44	.01	3.06 §

† p < .05
§ p < .01

TABLE 99

*Means, Standard Deviations, t-Tests, and Probabilities of Chance
Differences in Means for the Control and Experimental Groups
on the Bender-Gestalt Test:* Form Dissociation

Group	N	$\overline{X}$	σ	t
Combined Control Groups, Follow-up I	19	1.95	1.28	
				.45
Combined Experimental Groups, Follow-up I	14	1.71	1.58	
Comparison of Control Group, Pre-test, and Control Group, Follow-up I	19	−.84	1.75	2.29 †
Comparison of Control Group, Post-test, and Control Group, Follow-up I	19	.00	1.40	.64
Comparison of Experimental Group, Pre-test, and Experimental Group, Follow-up I	14	−1.36	2.41	2.03
Comparison of Experimental Group, Post-test, and Experimental Group, Follow-up I	14	.07	1.39	.18

† p < .05

significantly fewer errors in form dissociations. However, consideration of the pre-test and Follow-up I results indicates that only the control groups maintained their gains (p < .05).

Table 100 shows the results of the second-year grouping. None of the new class groups made significant gains on this category.

TABLE 100

Means, Standard Deviations, and t-Tests of the Significance of Differences between Means for the Grouping II Bender-Gestalt Test: Form Dissociation

Group	N	Pre-test $\overline{X}$	σ	Post-test $\overline{X}$	σ	Follow-up I $\overline{X}$	σ	Follow-up I and Post-test t
A	8	2.75	1.78	2.38	.99	1.63	1.32	1.43
B	10	3.40	1.56	2.00	1.41	2.70	1.95	1.48
C	8	2.63	1.49	1.50	1.50	1.63	.48	.23
D	6	3.33	2.05	1.83	1.34	1.50	1.26	1.59

Failure of the children to make gains the second year is not surprising since the intensive perceptual training occurred during the first year. Also, the highly structured environment and teaching approach had been modified during the second year. The gains that had been made during the first year tended to be maintained, however, even though the teaching emphasis had changed.

INCORRECT ELEMENTS

At the conclusion of the project, the children from the control classrooms actually made more errors on the Bender-Gestalt than they had made at the beginning. This was true at the end of the second year, the control group producing more errors than they did at the beginning of the project; but this difference did not reach statistical significance. Neither the experimental nor the control groups, singly (Table 101) or combined (Table 102), showed significant improvement between the post-test and Follow-up I phases, or between pre-test and Follow-up I phases. Even when the difference between the means of the pre-test and Follow-up I scores and post-test and Follow-up I scores for the total group were compared, there were no statistically significant differences. Table 103 indicates that the second-year grouping did not show significant improvement in this category between the post-test and Follow-up I phases.

DISTORTED ANGLES

Table 104 shows the means, standard deviations, and *t*-tests between means for the Bender-Gestalt category, Distorted Angles. When the

TABLE 101

*Means, Standard Deviations, t-Tests, and Probabilities of Chance
Differences in Means for the Number of Incorrect Elements on
the Bender-Gestalt Test for the Experimental
and Control Groups*

Class	N	Pre-test X̄	Pre-test σ	Post-test X̄	Post-test σ	Follow-up I X̄	Follow-up I σ	Follow-up I and Post-test t	Follow-up I and Pre-test t
C-1	10	2.10	1.60	3.40	1.08	2.60	1.84	2.06	1.05
C-2	9	2.22	.80	2.33	1.23	2.11	1.36	.51	.18
E-1	6	2.17	1.17	2.17	1.33	1.33	1.37	2.08	1.39
E-2	8	1.63	1.51	1.63	1.06	2.13	1.64	.76	.84
Total	33	2.03	1.29	2.46	1.30	2.12	1.58	1.34	.03

TABLE 102

*Means, Standard Deviations, t-Tests, and Probabilities of Chance Differ-
ences in Means for the Control and Experimental Groups on the
Bender-Gestalt Test: Incorrect Elements*

Group	N	X̄	σ	t
Combined Control Groups, Follow-up I	19	2.37	2.44	
				1.05
Combined Experimental Groups, Follow-up I	14	1.79	2.17	
Comparison of Control Group, Pre-test, and Control Group, Follow-up I	19	.21	1.61	.55
Comparison of Control Group, Post-test, and Control Group, Follow-up I	19	−.53	1.23	1.82
Comparison of Experimental Group, Pre-test, and Experimental Group, Follow-up I	14	−.07	1.62	.16
Comparison of Experimental Group, Post-test, and Experimental Group, Follow-up I	14	.07	1.58	.16

TABLE 103

*Means, Standard Deviations, and t-Tests of the Significance of
Differences between Means for the Grouping II
Bender-Gestalt Test:* Incorrect Elements

Group	N	Pre-test $\overline{X}$	σ	Post-test $\overline{X}$	σ	Follow-up I $\overline{X}$	σ	Follow-up I and Post-test t
A	8	2.63	1.11	2.75	1.30	1.50	1.50	3.99 §
B	10	1.80	1.33	2.80	1.43	2.80	1.72	.50
C	8	1.38	.99	2.38	1.22	2.25	1.39	.19
D	6	2.83	.69	2.17	1.04	1.83	1.67	1.59

§ p < .01

TABLE 104

*Means, Standard Deviations, t-Tests, and Probabilities of Chance
Differences in Means for the Number of Distorted Angles on
the Bender-Gestalt Test for the Experimental and
Control Groups*

Class	N	Pre-test X	σ	Post-test $\overline{X}$	σ	Follow-up I $\overline{X}$	σ	Follow-up I and Post-test t	Pre-test t
C-1	10	2.80	.60	2.90	.74	2.20	.90	2.09	1.97
C-2	9	2.78	.44	2.56	.53	1.89	.60	2.31	4.45 §
E-1	6	3.00	.00	2.83	.75	2.33	.82	1.46	3.16 †
E-2	8	2.75	1.17	2.75	.89	1.75	1.17	3.06 ‡	3.06 ‡
Total	33	2.82	.68	2.76	.71	2.03	.88	4.61 §	5.51 §

† p < .05
‡ p < .02
§ p < .01

individual control and experimental classes are examined for evidences
of continued progress during the second year, only one experimental
class (E-2) shows significantly fewer errors (p < .02). However, a comparison of the post-test and Follow-up I phases indicates that the total
group of 33 children made significantly fewer errors at the end of the
year (p < .01). When a comparison is made between the pre-test scores
and Follow-up I scores, two classes, one control (C-2) and one experi-

mental (E-2), show significantly fewer errors as did the total group of 33 children.

Table 105 shows the results of the comparison of combined control and combined experimental groups. The difference between the means of the combined control and combined experimental groups was not significant, but the groups considered separately made significant gains between the pre-test and Follow-up I (p < .01) phases, and between the post-test and Follow-up I (p < .01) phases.

Table 106 shows the figures for the second-year grouping. Two classes

TABLE 105

Means, Standard Deviations, t-Tests, and Probabilities of Chance Differences in Means for the Control and Experimental Groups on the Bender-Gestalt Test: Distorted Angles

Group	N	$\overline{X}$	σ	t
Combined Control Groups, Follow-up I	19	2.05	.76	
				.17
Combined Experimental Groups, Follow-up I	14	2.00	1.00	
Comparison of Control Group, Pre-test and Control Group, Follow-up I	19	—.74	.78	3.98 §
Comparison of Control Group, Post-test, and Control Group, Follow-up I	19	—.68	.92	3.15 §
Comparison of Experimental Group, Pre-test, and Experimental Group, Follow-up I	14	—.86	.83	3.71 §
Comparison of Experimental Group, Post-test, and Experimental Group, Follow-up I	14	—.79	.86	3.29 §

§ p < .01

TABLE 106

Means, Standard Deviations, and t-Tests of the Significance of Differences Between Means for the Grouping II Bender-Gestalt Test: Distorted Angles

Group	N	Pre-test $\overline{X}$	σ	Post-test $\overline{X}$	σ	Follow-up I $\overline{X}$	σ	Follow-up I and Post-test t
A	8	2.75	.43	2.75	.43	1.75	.97	2.65 †
B	10	2.90	1.04	2.80	.87	2.10	1.14	2.09
C	8	2.75	.43	2.75	.43	2.25	.43	2.65 †
D	6	2.83	.37	2.67	.94	2.00	.58	1.58

† p < .05

made statistically significant fewer errors at the end of the second year than they made in their post-test phase.

At the end of the project when the post-test period was completed, none of the groups showed statistically significant fewer errors on the category of Distorted Angles. By the end of the second year, however, one of the experimental classes had improved significantly on this category, as may be seen in a comparison of the post-test and Follow-up I phases; also, all of the comparisons made of the combined control and combined experimental groups considered separately show improvement. There was not a significant difference between the control and experimental groups as such on the Follow-up I test results.

ROTATIONS

Table 107 shows the statistical analysis for each control and experimental group considered separately, as well as for the total group. No statistically significant reduction in rotations was noted.

TABLE 107

Means, Standard Deviations, t-Tests, and Probabilities of Chance Differences in Means for the Number of Rotations on the Bender-Gestalt Test, for the Experimental and Control Groups

Class	N	Pre-test $\overline{X}$	σ	Post-test $\overline{X}$	σ	Follow-up I $\overline{X}$	σ	Follow-up I and Post-test t	Pre-test t
C-1	10	1.20	1.75	.70	.68	.40	.70	.90	1.35
C-2	9	.89	1.17	.89	1.05	1.00	1.32	.19	.24
E-1	6	.67	.82	.50	.84	.83	.98	1.58	.47
E-2	8	1.13	1.25	.63	.52	.38	.74	.68	1.43
Total	33	1.00	1.30	.70	.77	.64	.96	.03	1.36

Table 108 shows a comparison of the combined control and combined experimental classes. Again, no significant reduction in errors was noted, either between the pre-test and Follow-up I periods, or between the post-test and Follow-up I periods.

The results from the analysis of the second-year grouping are shown in Table 109. One class made significantly fewer rotations at the end of the second year than they did at the end of the project.

The above analysis is based on only those rotations that varied 45 degrees or more from the standard. The Pascal and Suttell criteria,

TABLE 108

Means, Standard Deviations, t-Tests, and Probabilities of Chance Differences in Means for the Control and Experimental Groups on the Bender-Gestalt Test: Rotations

Group	N	$\overline{X}$	σ	t
Combined Control Groups, Follow-up I	19	.68	1.29	
				.33
Combined Experimental Groups, Follow-up I	14	.57	.82	
Comparison of Control Group, Pre-test, and Control Group, Follow-up I	19	−.37	1.63	.96
Comparison of Control Group, Post-test, and Control Group, Follow-up I	19	−.11	1.37	.33
Comparison of Experimental Group, Pre-test, and Experimental Group, Follow-up I	14	−.36	1.34	.96
Comparison of Experimental Group, Post-test, and Experimental Group, Follow-up I	14	.00	.84	.00

TABLE 109

Means, Standard Deviations, and t-Tests of the Significance of Differences between Means for the Grouping II Bender-Gestalt: Rotations

Group	N	Pre-test $\overline{X}$	σ	Post-test $\overline{X}$	σ	Follow-up I $\overline{X}$	σ	Follow-up I and Post-test t
A	8	1.13	1.36	.38	.48	1.13	1.27	1.53
B	10	1.10	1.51	.70	.64	.40	.80	.82
C	8	.88	1.27	1.00	1.00	.25	.43	2.54 †
D	6	.83	.69	.67	.74	.83	.99	.74

† p < .05

which includes weighted scores for drawing errors and for partial rotations, were also used; the statistical analyses are shown in Tables 110, 111, and 112. One experimental class (E-1) made significantly fewer errors (p < .02) at the end of the second year (comparing post-test and Follow-up I results), while the other classes made fewer errors; but the *t*-tests did not reach the confidence level set for this study. The total group of 33 children, however, produced significantly fewer errors (p < .05) at the end of the second year for this same comparison. Table 111 shows that a comparison of the combined control and combined

TABLE 110

Means, Standard Deviations, and t-Tests of the Significance of Differences between Means for the Bender-Gestalt Test: Rotations, Scored According to the Pascal and Suttell Criteria

Class	N	Pre-test $\overline{X}$	σ	Post-test $\overline{X}$	σ	Follow-up I $\overline{X}$	σ	Follow-up I and Post-test t	Pre-test t
C-1	10	13.40	9.77	13.30	11.41	5.80	4.27	1.74	2.26 †
C-2	9	15.11	14.08	13.00	9.89	9.30	8.57	.97	1.39
E-1	6	14.50	11.90	9.67	2.98	3.67	3.30	3.74 ‡	2.35
E-2	8	14.50	13.72	6.38	7.24	8.13	7.03	.74	1.14
Total	33	14.33	12.44	10.88	9.42	6.94	6.61	2.20 †	3.43 §

† $p < .05$
‡ $p < .02$
§ $p < .01$

TABLE 111

Means, Standard Deviations, t-Tests, and Probabilities of Chance Differences in Means for the Control and Experimental Groups on the Bender-Gestalt Test: Rotations, Scored According to Pascal and Suttell Criteria

Group	N	$\overline{X}$	σ	t
Combined Control Groups, Follow-up I	19	7.47	6.89	
Combined Experimental Groups, Follow-up I	14	6.21	6.14	.53
Comparison of Control Group, Pre-test, and Control Group, Follow-up I	19	6.74	12.03	2.61 ‡
Comparison of Control Group, Post-test, and Control Group, Follow-up I	19	5.68	10.72	2.06
Comparison of Experimental Group, Pre-test, and Experimental Group, Follow-up I	14	13.62	4.10	2.19 †
Comparison of Experimental Group, Post-test, and Experimental Group, Follow-up I	14	1.57	6.04	.85

† $p < .05$
‡ $p < .02$

TABLE 112

Means, Standard Deviations, t-Tests, and Probabilities of Chance
Differences in Means for the Grouping II Bender-Gestalt
Test: Rotations, Scored According to the
Pascal and Suttell Criteria

		Pre-test		Post-test		Follow-up I		Post-test *t*	Follow-up I and Pre-test *t*
Group	N	X̄	σ	X̄	σ	X̄	σ	*t*	*t*
A	8	13.50	15.31	5.88	5.21	4.75	7.73	.45	2.01
B	10	14.10	13.63	13.80	11.62	8.80	6.95	1.09	1.26
C	8	11.38	7.58	12.88	9.89	8.50	6.65	1.32	.99
D	6	18.50	13.12	10.00	6.51	4.50	4.61	1.43	2.17

experimental groups reveals that both made significantly fewer errors at the end of the second year than they did at the end of the project year. Thus, improvement on the number of rotations produced cannot be attributed to the conditions of the experimental classes alone.

Rotations, as was pointed out in the preceding section, are considered an extremely important diagnostic sign by many people who work with the Bender-Gestalt. Most published findings have used a criterion of 45 degrees for rotations. These findings cannot readily be compared to those reports using the Pascal and Suttell scoring system, where partial rotations are considered, i.e., the "handle" of Figure 5 slanting toward the left rather than toward the right. In the scoring system used in this report, partial rotations would more properly be considered in the category of distortion of the configuration. Therefore, these results must be interpreted with caution.

INADEQUATE METHOD

Table 113 shows the means, standard deviations, and *t*-tests of the significance of differences between pre-test and post-test means for the Bender-Gestalt category, Inadequate Method, for the control and experimental classes considered separately. It should be pointed out that this category is a sum of four other categories: Immature, Concrete, Perseveration, and Erratic Approach. None of the individual classes, or the total group, made significantly fewer errors on this category. In the post-test phase one class (E-2) had made significantly fewer errors, and this gain was maintained in the Follow-up I testing phase (p < .02).

TABLE 113

Means, Standard Deviations, t-Tests, and Probabilities of Chance Differences in Means for the Inadequate Method *Category on the Bender-Gestalt Test for the Experimental and Control Groups*

Class	N	Pre-test $\overline{X}$	σ	Post-test $\overline{X}$	σ	Follow-up I $\overline{X}$	σ	Post-test t	Follow-up I and Pre-test t
C-1	10	2.80	1.87	2.70	2.50	1.20	1.55	1.77	2.18
C-2	9	3.56	1.94	2.33	1.12	2.56	3.05	.20	1.25
E-1	6	4.33	3.62	3.00	1.07	2.33	1.51	.67	1.17
E-2	8	4.00	2.51	3.38	2.72	1.13	.84	2.05	3.21 ‡
Total	33	3.58	2.39	2.82	2.08	1.76	1.99	2.00	3.79 §

‡ p < .02
§ p < .01

A significant gain for the total group is indicated when the pre-test and Follow-up I phases (p < .01) are compared.

Table 114 shows a comparison of the combined control and com-

TABLE 114

Means, Standard Deviations, t-Tests, and Probabilities of Chance Differences in Means for the Control and Experimental Groups on the Bender-Gestalt Test: Inadequate Method

Group	N	$\overline{X}$	σ	t
Combined Control Groups, Follow-up I	19	1.84	2.35	
				.28
Combined Experimental Groups, Follow-up I	14	1.64	1.23	
Comparison of Control Group, Pre-test, and Control Group, Follow-up I	19	−1.32	2.25	2.48 †
Comparison of Control Group, Post-test, and Control Group, Follow-up I	19	− .68	3.11	.93
Comparison of Experimental Group, Pre-test, and Experimental Group, Follow-up I	14	−2.50	3.11	2.90 §
Comparison of Experimental Group, Post-test, and Experimental Group, Follow-up I	14	−1.57	2.74	2.06

† p < .05
§ p < .01

bined experimental groups. There was a significant gain for both the control (p < .05) and experimental (p < .01) groups between the pre-test and Follow-up I phases, but there was not a difference between them.

TABLE 115

Means, Standard Deviations, and t-Tests of the Significance of Differences between Means for the Grouping II Bender-Gestalt Test: Inadequate Method

Group	N	Pre-test X	σ	Post-test X	σ	Follow-up I X	σ	Follow-up I and Post-test t
A	8	4.38	2.55	2.38	1.41	2.63	3.12	.18
B	10	2.90	2.21	3.70	2.87	1.60	1.36	4.36 §
C	8	4.13	3.69	2.38	1.22	2.00	1.50	.51
D	6	4.50	2.29	2.83	1.01	1.50	.76	3.16 †

† P < .05
§ P < .01

Table 115 shows the second-year grouping data. Two classes made significantly fewer errors at the end of the second year than they did at the end of the project year.

DISTORTION OF CONFIGURATION

This category is a combination of six other categories: Dissociation, Closure, Incorrect Elements, Unrecognizable, Distorted Angles, and Rotations. Table 116 shows the statistical analysis of the experimental and control classes considered separately and considered as a total group. One experimental class (E-1) made significantly fewer errors (p < .01) at the end of the second year while the other classes did not. The total group shows significantly fewer errors (p < .01) when this comparison is made. Thus, the improvement of the total group which was noted at the end of the project year was continued during the second year in the new class placements.

As shown in Table 117, at the end of the project year the combined experimental group made significantly fewer distortion of configuration errors, but the combined control group did not show similar progress. At the end of the second year this had been reversed, the combined control group now making significantly fewer errors (p < .05),

TABLE 116

Means, Standard Deviations, t-Tests, and Probabilities of Chance Differences in Means for the Number of Distortions of Configuration on the Bender-Gestalt Test for the Experimental and Control Groups

		Pre-test		Post-test		Follow-up I		Follow-up I and Post-test	Pre-test
Class	N	$\overline{X}$	σ	$\overline{X}$	σ	$\overline{X}$	σ	t	t
C-1	10	10.00	4.11	9.70	3.65	7.80	4.54	2.03	1.58
C-2	9	9.89	3.06	7.89	3.55	6.78	1.64	1.35	4.60 §
E-1	6	10.83	4.54	8.67	1.21	6.33	2.07	4.20 §	2.03
E-2	8	10.00	5.98	7.25	2.61	6.12	4.32	.83	2.19
Total	33	10.12	4.27	8.42	3.09	6.85	3.42	3.25 §	4.53 §

§ p < .01

TABLE 117

Means, Standard Deviations, t-Tests, and Probabilities of Chance Differences in Means for the Control and Experimental Groups on the Bender-Gestalt Test: Distortion of Configuration

Group	N	$\overline{X}$	σ	t
Combined Control Groups, Follow-up I	19	7.32	3.34	
				1.05
Combined Experimental Groups, Follow-up I	14	6.21	3.30	
Comparison of Control Group, Pre-test, and Control Group, Follow-up I	19	−2.63	3.33	3.36 §
Comparison of Control Group, Post-test, and Control Group, Follow-up I	19	−1.53	2.62	2.47 †
Comparison of Experimental Group, Pre-test, and Experimental Group, Follow-up I	14	−4.14	4.81	3.11 §
Comparison of Experimental Group, Post-test, and Experimental Group, Follow-up I	14	−1.64	2.89	2.05

† p < .05
§ p < .01

while the combined experimental group did not. It should be noted, however, that on all three tests (pre-test, post-test, and Follow-up I) every class made progressively fewer errors, even though this did not reach the level of confidence accepted in this study. Table 118 shows the second-year grouping.

TABLE 118

Means, Standard Deviations, and t-Tests of the Significance of Differences between Means for the Grouping II Bender-Gestalt Test: Distortion of Configuration

Group	N	Pre-test X	Pre-test σ	Post-test X	Post-test σ	Follow-up I X	Follow-up I σ	Follow-up I and Post-test t	Follow-up I and Pre-test t
A	8	10.50	4.69	8.89	2.26	6.00	2.78	4.62 §	2.77 †
B	10	10.40	4.34	8.90	3.45	8.20	4.81	.56	1.25
C	8	8.62	3.04	7.75	3.46	6.50	1.58	1.30	2.77 †
D	6	11.50	4.27	8.33	2.49	6.50	2.29	4.57 §	4.33 §

† p < .05
§ p < .01

SIZE

Three categories were combined to make this category: Compression, Enlargement, and Disproportion. At the end of the project year no individual class shows significantly fewer errors on the post-test results. The combined experimental group, however, made significantly fewer errors, while the combined control groups did not.

Table 119 indicates that at the end of the second year the total group of children showed significantly fewer errors (p < .01) in the Follow-up I period than they did in the post-test period; this is the case for three classes: one control (C-1), and the two experimental classes.

Table 120 shows a comparison of the combined control and combined experimental groups, both of which made significantly fewer errors (p < .01).

Table 121 shows the second-year grouping. One class (Class B) made significantly fewer errors during the second year.

TOTAL

At the end of the project year the entire group showed significantly fewer total errors on the post-test as contrasted to the pre-test results,

TABLE 119

Means, Standard Deviations, t-Tests, and Probabilities of Chance
Differences in Means for the Size Category on the Bender-
Gestalt Test for the Experimental and Control Groups

Class	N	Pre-test $\overline{X}$	σ	Post-test $\overline{X}$	σ	Follow-up I $\overline{X}$	σ	Follow-up I and Post-test t	Pre-test t
C-1	10	2.70	1.34	3.50	2.72	.30	.48	3.75 §	5.04 §
C-2	9	3.11	2.03	2.78	2.78	1.11	1.62	1.49	2.91 ‡
E-1	6	2.67	2.16	2.17	1.33	.50	.80	2.71 †	2.29
E-2	8	2.50	1.69	1.38	1.06	.13	.00	3.99 §	3.64 §
Total	33	2.76	1.71	2.55	2.27	.52	1.00	4.75 §	7.08 §

† P < .05
‡ P < .02
§ P < .01

TABLE 120

Means, Standard Deviations, t-Tests, and Probabilities of Chance
Differences in Means for the Control and Experimental
Groups on the Bender-Gestalt Test: Size

Group	N	$\overline{X}$	σ	t
Combined Control Groups, Follow-up I	19	.68	1.17	
				1.13
Combined Experimental Groups, Follow-up I	14	.29	.59	
Comparison of Control Group, Pre-test, and Control Group, Follow-up I	19	−2.21	1.73	5.50 §
Comparison of Control Group, Post-test, and Control Group, Follow-up I	19	−2.47	2.96	3.54 §
Comparison of Experimental Group, Pre-test, and Experimental Group, Follow-up I	14	−2.29	1.91	4.31 §
Comparison of Experimental Group, Post-test, and Experimental Group, Follow-up I	14	−1.43	1.12	4.61 §

§ P < .01

TABLE 121

*Means, Standard Deviations, and t-Tests of the Significance of
Differences between Means for the Grouping II
Bender-Gestalt Test: Size*

Group	N	Pre-test X	σ	Post-test X	σ	Follow-up I X	σ	Follow-up I and Post-test t
A	8	2.88	2.03	1.63	1.49	.38	.48	2.24
B	10	2.40	1.85	2.20	2.40	.10	.30	2.64 †
C	8	3.88	1.51	3.38	2.39	1.13	1.62	1.91
D	6	2.17	.99	2.83	2.27	.67	.75	2.01

† p < .05

as did two individual classes: one control (C-2) and one experimental
(E-2). The combined experimental groups also made significantly fewer
errors in the post-test period, but the combined control groups did not.

At the end of the second year the entire group showed significantly
fewer errors (p < .01) than they had shown on the post-test results
(Table 122), as did three individual classes: one control (C-1) and the
two experimental classes. Table 123 shows that both the combined

TABLE 122

*Means, Standard Deviations, t-Tests, and Probabilities of Chance
Differences in Means for the Total Number of Errors on
the Bender-Gestalt Test for the Experimental and
Control Groups*

Class	N	Pre-test X	σ	Post-test X	σ	Follow-up I X	σ	Follow-up I and Post-test t	Pre-test t
C-1	10	15.50	4.84	15.90	7.26	9.30	5.74	3.48 §	4.29 §
C-2	9	16.56	4.67	13.00	5.57	10.44	3.01	1.19	4.68 §
E-1	6	14.50	6.60	13.83	2.99	9.17	3.19	4.08 §	2.25
E-2	8	16.50	8.54	12.00	4.69	6.13	4.55	3.49 ‡	5.02 §
Total	33	15.85	5.95	13.79	5.58	8.82	4.50	5.32 §	7.89 §

‡ p < .02
§ p < .01

control and combined experimental classes made significant gains (p < .01) at the end of the second year.

Table 124 shows the analysis of the second-year groupings. One class made significantly fewer errors at the end of the second year.

On the basis of these results we can say that the entire group made significantly fewer errors at the end of the project year as well as at the

TABLE 123

Means, Standard Deviations, t-Tests, and Probabilities of Chance Differences in Means for the Control and Experimental Groups on the Bender-Gestalt Test: Total

Group	N	$\overline{X}$	σ	t
Combined Control Groups, Follow-up I	19	9.84	4.33	
				1.56
Combined Experimental Groups, Follow-up I	14	7.43	4.30	
Comparison of Control Group, Pre-test, and Control Group, Follow-up I	19	6.16	4.04	6.46 §
Comparison of Control Group Post-test, and Control Group, Follow-up I	19	−4.68	6.14	3.24 §
Comparison of Experimental Group, Pre-test, and Experimental Group, Follow-up I	14	−8.21	5.94	4.99 §
Comparison of Experimental Group, Post-test and Experimental Group, Follow-up I	14	−5.36	3.81	5.07 §

§ P < .01

TABLE 124

Means, Standard Deviations, and t-Tests of the Significance of Differences between Means for the Grouping II Bender-Gestalt Test: Total Errors

Group	N	Pre-test $\overline{X}$	σ	Post-test $\overline{X}$	σ	Follow-up I $\overline{X}$	σ	Follow-up I and Post-test t
A	8	15.25	5.47	12.88	4.37	9.00	4.50	2.06
B	10	15.70	6.68	14.80	7.30	8.90	6.09	2.77 †
C	8	14.75	3.70	12.50	6.52	8.75	3.38	1.65
D	6	18.17	6.96	10.50	3.41	8.67	2.43	1.69

† P < .05

end of the second year. Control and experimental conditions seemed to make little real difference; whatever differences there might have been at the end of the project year were equalized by the end of the second year.

SUMMARY

At the end of the project year the children who had been placed in the experimental rooms made significantly fewer errors than the children in the control classes on six of the ten scoring categories on the Bender-Gestalt. The scoring categories on which improvement was noted were: Incorrect Elements, Rotations, Distortion of the Configuration, Size, Inadequate Method, and Total.

At the end of the second year the children who had had the experimental class experiences the preceding year no longer did significantly better than the control group on a single scoring category. The total group, however, did produce significantly fewer errors. The categories on which the total group showed improvement were Distorted Angles, Rotations (scored according to the Pascal and Suttell criteria), Distortion of the Configuration, Size, and Total number of errors.

If the more structured, stimulus-free room made any real difference during the project year, this did not carry over into the succeeding year. The total group showed over-all improvement on every one of the scoring categories, although the reduction in errors reached statistical significance on only five of the nine categories. (One category, Immature, was not included in the second-year analysis, because so few errors were categorized as such.)

It is not possible to ascribe the children's improved ability in drawing geometric figures to any one thing in the educational program that was worked out for them. It is well known that the Gestalt function follows a maturational course of development, furthermore, there is no way of differentiating the influence of maturation from the influence of learning on the present data. There is impressive evidence in the literature which indicates that the children would have improved on the Bender materials with no special training, but the teaching staff felt that this development was greatly enhanced and accelerated by the children's educational experience.

Syracuse Visual Figure-Background Test

NUMBER CORRECT

At the end of the project year each group had improved significantly in ability to see pictures flashed tachistoscopically on a screen. Table

125 shows the results for the SVFB at the end of the second year. Both of the control groups and one experimental group (E-1) correctly identified significantly more correct figures in the Follow-up I test than they had identified in the post-test phase; and one of the experimental

TABLE 125

Means, Standard Deviations, and t-Tests of the Significance of Differences Between Means for the Syracuse Visual Figure-Background Test:
Number Correct

		Pre-test		Post-test		Follow-up I		Follow-up I and Post-test	Pre-test
Class	N	X	σ	X	σ	X	σ	t	t
C-1	10	5.40	3.07	7.40	3.32	10.10	2.30	2.83 ‡	5.57 §
C-2	9	4.89	2.18	7.11	2.86	9.33	2.79	2.71 †	5.67 §
E-1	7	2.43	1.76	5.86	2.99	9.00	2.14	3.45 ‡	12.45 §
E-2	8	4.00	3.67	7.38	2.74	9.38	4.18	1.76	3.53 §
Total	34	4.32	2.99	7.09	2.95	9.50	2.97	5.30 §	10.54 §

† p < .05
‡ p < .02
§ p < .01

groups (E-2) made a higher mean number of correct responses, but this did not reach the level of confidence accepted in this study. The same comparison for the total group indicates that they had identified significantly more correct figures (p < .01).

At the beginning of the project year the combined control groups correctly identified significantly more figures than did the combined experimental groups, and at the end of the project year the combined experimental groups had improved in ability to the point where this difference was no longer significant. At the end of the second year (Table 126) the combined control groups had a mean number of correct responses of 9.74, the combined experimental group mean being 9.20; this difference was not significant. Comparison of the combined control and combined experimental groups on a post-test, Follow-up I basis shows a significantly higher mean number of correct responses at the end of the second year.

Table 127 shows the statistics for the second-year grouping. Two of the grouping II classes made significant gains during the second year between the post-test and Follow-up I phases. The means for all of

TABLE 126

Means, Standard Deviations, t-Tests, and Probabilities of Chance Differences in Means for the Combined Control and Experimental Groups on the Syracuse Visual Figure-Background Test: Number Correct

Group	N	X̄	σ	t
Combined Control Groups, Follow-up I	19	9.74	2.57	
				.49
Combined Experimental Groups, Follow-up I	15	9.20	3.39	
Comparison of Control Group, Pre-test, and Control Group, Follow-up I	19	4.58	2.39	8.12 §
Comparison of Control Group, Post-test, and Control Group, Follow-up I	19	2.32	2.51	3.91 §
Comparison of Experimental Group, Pre-test, and Experimental Group, Follow-up I	15	5.93	2.61	7.44 §
Comparison of Experimental Group, Post-test, and Experimental Group, Follow-up I	15	2.53	2.73	3.48 §

§ p < .01

TABLE 127

Means, Standard Deviations, and t-Tests of the Significance of Differences between Means for the Syracuse Visual Figure-Background Test, Grouping II: Number Correct

Group	N	Pre-test X̄	σ	Post-test X̄	σ	Follow-up I X̄	σ	Follow-up I and Post-test t	Pre-test t
A	8	4.38	3.35	7.50	2.83	9.50	3.81	1.01	3.43 ‡
B	10	3.60	2.76	6.20	2.93	9.40	3.47	3.21 ‡	5.36 §
C	8	5.75	2.86	8.00	2.83	8.63	3.28	.96	4.87 §
D	7	3.57	2.56	6.43	2.82	9.00	2.88	2.96 †	9.49 §

† p < .05
‡ p < .02
§ p < .01

the groups were significantly higher at the end of the second year as compared to the test results obtained at the end of the project year.

BACKGROUND RESPONSES

At the end of the project year the children in the experimental classes made significantly fewer background responses than they had at the beginning of the year. The total group of children also showed significantly fewer background responses on post-test results than were shown on pre-test results.

TABLE 128

Means, Standard Deviations, and t-Tests of the Significance of Differences between Means for the Syracuse Visual Figure-Background Test: Number of Background Responses

		Pre-test		Post-test		Follow-up I		Follow-up I and Post-test	Pre-test
Class	N	$\overline{X}$	σ	$\overline{X}$	σ	$\overline{X}$	σ	t	t
C-1	10	3.00	2.49	2.00	1.55	1.30	2.47	1.91	1.85
C-2	9	2.44	1.95	2.22	1.62	3.00	2.67	.72	.68
E-1	7	3.57	2.61	2.29	1.38	3.71	1.98	1.64	.19
E-2	8	2.88	2.80	1.00	1.32	.88	.93	.21	1.82
Total	34	2.94	2.50	1.88	1.57	2.15	2.88	.24	1.65

At the end of the second year (Table 128) there were no statistically significant differences for the individual control and experimental groups, or for the total group between the post-test results and the Follow-up I results.

Table 129 shows the comparison of the combined control and combined experimental groups. There were no statistically significant differences either between post-test and Follow-up I results, or between pre-test and Follow-up I results.

Results for the second-year grouping are shown in Table 130. The second-year grouping did not result in statistically significant fewer background responses in comparing the post-test with Follow-up I.

Whatever decrease occurred in background responses during the project year did not persist to the end of the second year.

TABLE 129

Means, Standard Deviations, t-Tests, and Probabilities of Chance Differences in Means for the Combined Control and Experimental Groups on the Syracuse Visual Figure-Background Test: Number of Background Responses

Group	N	$\overline{X}$	σ	t
Combined Control Groups, Follow-up I	19	2.11	2.10	
				.12
Combined Experimental Groups, Follow-up I	15	2.20	2.72	
Comparison of Control Group, Pre-test, and Control Group, Follow-up I	19	—.63	2.79	.96
Comparison of Control Group, Post-test, and Control Group, Follow-up I	19	—.74	2.24	.00
Comparison of Experimental Group, Pre-test, and Experimental Group, Follow-up I	15	—1.00	2.71	1.38
Comparison of Experimental Group, Post-test, and Experimental Group, Follow-up I	15	.60	2.27	1.11

TABLE 130

Means, Standard Deviations, and t-Tests of the Significance of Differences between Means for the Syracuse Visual Figure-Background Test, Grouping II: Number of Background Responses

		Pre-test		Post-test		Follow-up I		Follow-up I and Post-test	Pre-test
Group	N	$\overline{X}$	σ	$\overline{X}$	σ	$\overline{X}$	σ	t	t
A	8	3.63	3.12	2.88	1.76	3.75	2.44	.71	.09
B	10	3.40	2.62	1.80	1.83	1.10	1.44	1.77	2.73 †
C	8	2.63	1.87	1.50	1.12	2.00	2.40	.63	1.26
D	7	2.00	1.85	1.14	.83	2.57	1.59	2.09	.57

† P < .05

PERSEVERATION

At the end of the project year the total group showed significantly fewer perseverative responses than they had shown at the beginning of the year; this was also the case for one control class (C-1).

A comparison of the post-test and Follow-up I results (Table 131) indicates that neither the entire group nor a single individual class made significantly fewer perseverative responses during the second year. How-

TABLE 131

Means, Standard Deviations, and t-Tests of the Significance of Differences between Means for the Syracuse Visual Figure-Background Test: Perseverations

Class	N	Pre-test X	σ	Post-test X	σ	Follow-up I X	σ	Follow-up I and Post-test t	Pre-test t
C-1	10	3.50	2.62	1.10	1.45	.70	1.79	1.50	3.01 ‡
C-2	9	2.11	2.73	1.44	1.89	1.11	2.18	.55	2.27
E-1	7	4.57	3.58	2.57	2.13	1.14	1.73	1.34	2.52 †
E-2	8	1.88	2.42	1.38	1.32	1.5	1.85	.50	.14
Total	34	2.97	3.15	1.56	1.79	1.15	1.94	.124	3.70 §

† $p < .05$
‡ $p < .02$
§ $p < .01$

ever, a comparison of the pre-test and Follow-up I results indicates that the total group made significantly fewer perseverative responses ($p < .01$), as did two classes (C-1, E-1).

Table 132 shows that at the end of the project year both the com-

TABLE 132

Means, Standard Deviations, t-Tests, and Probabilities of Chance Differences in Means for the Combined Control and Experimental Groups on the Syracuse Visual Figure-Background Test: Perseverations

Group	N	X	σ	t
Combined Control Groups, Follow-up I	19	.90	1.99	
				.81
Combined Experimental Groups, Follow-up I	15	1.47	1.82	
Comparison of Control Group, Pre-test, and Control Group, Follow-up I	17	−2.18	2.41	3.62 §
Comparison of Control Group, Post-test, and Control Group, Follow-up I	17	−.41	1.37	1.20
Comparison of Experimental Group, Pre-test, and Experimental Group, Follow-up I	15	−1.67	3.32	1.88
Comparison of Experimental Group, Post-test, and Experimental Group, Follow-up I	15	−.47	2.47	.30

§ $p < .01$

bined control and combined experimental groups made significantly fewer perseverative responses. At the end of the second year, however, only the combined control group showed a significant difference between pre-test and Follow-up I results.

TABLE 133

Means, Standard Deviations, and t-Tests of the Significance of Differences between Means for the Syracuse Visual Figure-Background Test, Grouping II: Perseverations

Group	N	Pre-test X	σ	Post-test X	σ	Follow-up I X	σ	Follow-up I and Post-test t
A	8	94.38	8.25	99.50	6.82	92.63	5.29	4.43 §
B	10	82.80	9.16	91.80	11.25	82.60	13.09	3.58 §
C	8	82.00	16.23	97.13	14.47	92.25	12.89	1.95
D	7	91.00	8.28	98.71	6.65	95.00	5.40	1.60

§ P < .01

Statistics for the second-year grouping are shown in Table 133. One class showed significantly fewer perseverative responses at the end of the second year than were shown in the post-test results.

SUMMARY

During the project year each of the two experimental classes had projectors with tachistoscopic attachments available for classroom use. The two control classes did not have projectors regularly assigned to them. An intensive program for using the tachistoscopic attachment was not developed by the teachers of the experimental classes; but it was occasionally used, and the projector itself was used regularly. The use of a projector with or without a tachistoscopic attachment could influence the results of the SVFB, even if the only learning that occurred was the centering of attention on the screen. Therefore, the improvement in the two experimental classes during the project year must be interpreted with the knowledge that the children had training which the control children did not. It is interesting and important to note, however, that this differential training did not result in permanent improvement in the accuracy of identifying tachistoscopically presented figures, or decrease in background responses.

The total group continued to improve in perceptual accuracy on this test during the second year, even when the children were reassigned to other classes. The children without special training improved as much as the children who did receive such training. This may indicate that maturation or some other unidentified factor, rather than perceptual training *per se,* played a crucial role in this improvement.

Vineland Scale of Social Maturity

During the project year each class showed a significant increase in social quotient (Table 134), the mean social quotient being 87.15 at the

TABLE 134

Means, Standard Deviations, t-Tests, and Probabilities of Chance Differences in Means for the Vineland Scale of Social Maturity:
Social Quotients

Class	N	Pre test $\overline{X}$	σ	Post-test $\overline{X}$	σ	Follow-up I $\overline{X}$	σ	Follow-up I and Post-test t	Pre-test t
C-1	10	89.20	11.80	97.40	14.11	90.40	15.54	2.55 †	.45
C-2	9	83.89	15.71	95.22	10.29	88.89	8.82	4.15 §	1.15
E-1	7	87.71	7.59	97.71	5.72	94.57	9.72	2.40	1.87
E-2	8	87.75	9.59	97.63	11.39	91.63	9.90	2.46 †	1.13
Total	34	87.15	12.00	96.94	11.18	90.53	11.64	5.63 §	2.10 †

† p < .05
§ p < .01

beginning of the year and 96.94 at the end. At the end of the second year, however, three classes had significantly lower social quotients (C-1, C-2, E-2) when compared with the post-test phase; this was also true of the total group. It should be emphasized that this refers to an analysis of the social quotient, which is the ratio of social age to chronological age. When the social ages are examined, growth can be seen over the two-year period. The mean social age in the pre-test period was 88.18, in the post-test period it was 105.77, and in the Follow-up I period it was 111.56. Thus, while the mean chronological age increased 12 months between the post-test and Follow-up I periods, the mean social age increased approximately 6 months.

An analysis of the combined control and combined experimental group is given in Table 135. Comparison of the post-test and Follow-up I results shows that both the combined control and combined experimental groups had significantly lower social quotients at the end of the second year.

TABLE 135

Means, Standard Deviations, t-Tests, and Probabilities of Chance Differences in Means for the Combined Control and Experimental Groups on the Vineland Scale of Social Maturity:
Social Quotients

Group	N	$\overline{X}$	σ	t
Combined Control Groups, Follow-up I	20	85.35	14.85	
				.48
Combined Experimental Groups, Follow-up I	19	87.53	11.42	
Comparison of Control Group, Pre-test, and Control Group, Follow-up I	20	96.95	12.44	
				.44
Comparison of Control Group, Post-test, and Control Group, Follow-up I	19	98.63	9.83	
Comparison of Experimental Group, Pre-test, and Experimental Group, Follow-up I	20	11.50	14.97	3.38 §
Comparison of Experimental Group, Post-test, and Experimental Group, Follow-up I	19	11.11	8.48	5.55 §

§ $p < .01$

Means, standard deviations, and t-tests for the second year grouping are given in Table 136.

TABLE 136

Means, Standard Deviations, and t-Tests of the Significance of Differences Between Means for the Grouping II Vineland Scale of Social Maturity Social Quotients

Group	N	Pre-test $\overline{X}$	σ	Post-test $\overline{X}$	σ	Follow-up I $\overline{X}$	σ	Follow-up I and Post-test t	Pre-test t
A	8	1.00	1.00	1.25	1.19	.13	.33	2.83 †	2.97 †
B	10	3.40	2.65	.90	2.63	1.40	1.69	.81	1.66
C	8	2.50	2.87	1.38	1.87	1.75	2.77	.89	1.66
D	7	3.71	3.28	3.29	2.19	1.43	1.84	1.93	1.66

† $p < .05$

SUMMARY

In evaluating the Vineland Social Maturity Scale, it should be emphasized that this is based on an interview between the parent(s) and an examiner. Parental biases and prejudices may thus influence the results.

The more rapid development reported during the project year may reflect the optimism freely expressed by a number of the parents. Many of the children were experiencing success in school for the first time, after having spent an ego-shattering year in a regular class. This may have resulted in a more rapid development of social skills and abilities during the project year while, during the second year, it may have leveled off. Although the children continued to develop in terms of social age during the second year their rate was slower than it had been during the preceding year, as reflected in the lower social quotients.

The way in which the Vineland Scale is constructed may have been another factor that played a role in producing a lower estimate of the children's social maturity at the end of the second year. As the chronological age increases the child is expected to show growth in communication skills ("Does he write occasional short letters?" "Does he enjoy books, newspapers, magazines?") and in self-direction generally ("Does he go about the neighborhood unattended?" "Does he engage in activities calling for simple creativity?"). The project children are academically retarded in the areas required for success in these communication skills.

Furthermore, a number of the parents tended to be very solicitous and protective. For example, many of the children were not trusted with even small amounts of money, were assigned no regular chores or responsibilities, and were in other ways protected from growth experiences.

Stanford Achievement Test

Tables 137 through 152 show the means, standard deviations, and tests of significance for the various subtests of the Stanford Achievement Test arranged according to the original grouping of control and experimental groups. Only t-tests of the significance of differences between means for the post-test and Follow-up I results, and between pre-test and Follow-up I results, are presented in these tables. The reader interested in a comparison of the pre-test and post-test results is referred to the preceding section.

All t-test scores for the total group, either post-test and Follow-up I,

TABLE 137

Means, Standard Deviations, and t-Tests of the Significance of Differences between Means for the Stanford Achievement Test: Paragraph Meaning *for the Experimental and Control Groups*

Class	N	Pre-test		Post-test		Follow-up I		Follow-up I and Post-test t	Pre-test t
		$\overline{X}$	σ	$\overline{X}$	σ	$\overline{X}$	σ		
C-1	9	.62	.75	1.32	1.05	2.23	1.23	4.38 §	6.52 §
C-2	9	.14	.43	1.28	1.06	2.30	.55	4.75 §	10.57 §
E-1	8	.54	.74	2.15	.41	3.11	.51	6.17 §	6.91 §
E-2	8	.56	1.04	.96	1.08	2.64	1.73	5.08 §	4.54 §
Total	34	.46	.75	1.42	1.00	2.55	1.12	9.20 §	12.60 §

§ p < .01

TABLE 138

Means, Standard Deviations, and t-Tests of the Significance of Differences between Means for the Stanford Achievement Test: Word Meaning *for the Experimental and Control Groups*

Class	N	Pre-test		Post-test		Follow-up I		Follow-up I and Post-test t	Pre-test t
		$\overline{X}$	σ	$\overline{X}$	σ	$\overline{X}$	σ		
C-1	9	.00	.00	1.37	1.05	2.24	1.09	3.40 §	6.14 §
C-2	9	.24	.73	1.17	1.15	2.41	.50	3.91 §	11.97 §
E-1	8	.21	.60	2.49	.54	3.16	.86	2.81 †	10.77 §
E-2	8	.49	.90	1.12	1.25	2.51	1.46	5.21 §	5.33 §
Total	34	.23	.64	1.52	1.13	2.57	1.04	7.48 §	14.71 §

† p < .05
§ p < .01

TABLE 139
Means, Standard Deviations, and t-Tests of the Significance of Differences between Means for the Stanford Achievement Test: Average Reading *for the Experimental and Control Groups*

Class	N	Pre-test X̄	Pre-test σ	Post-test X̄	Post-test σ	Follow-up I X̄	Follow-up I σ	Follow-up I and Post-test t	Follow-up I and Pre-test t
C-1	9	.32	.39	1.38	1.24	2.28	1.18	4.48 §	6.56 §
C-2	9	.20	.60	1.23	1.09	2.38	.51	4.42 §	14.52 §
E-1	8	.34	.47	2.23	.48	3.34	1.72	5.97 §	12.00 §
E-2	8	.54	1.00	1.06	1.30	2.59	1.59	5.41 §	4.96 §
Total	34	.34	.63	1.48	1.07	2.63	1.08	9.70 §	14.82 §

§ p < .01

TABLE 140
Means, Standard Deviations, and t-Tests of the Significance of Differences between Means for the Stanford Achievement Test: Spelling *for the Experimental and Control Groups*

Class	N	Pre-test X̄	Pre-test σ	Post-test X̄	Post-test σ	Follow-up I X̄	Follow-up I σ	Follow-up I and Post-test t	Follow-up I and Pre-test t
C-1	9	.63	1.03	1.87	.94	2.17	1.57	1.08	4.43 §
C-2	9	.32	.97	1.41	.93	2.27	1.49	3.79 §	4.95 §
E-1	8	.52	.76	2.85	.39	3.39	.97	1.91	5.24 §
E-2	8	.50	.93	1.50	1.08	2.24	1.47	3.60 §	3.71 §
Total	34	.49	.89	1.89	1.01	2.50	1.43	4.85 §	8.86 §

§ p < .01

TABLE 141

Means, Standard Deviations, and t-Tests of the Significance of Differences between Means for the Stanford Achievement Test: Arithmetic Reasoning *for the Experimental and Control Groups*

		Pre-test		Post-test		Follow-up I		Follow-up I and Post-test	Pre-test
Class	N	$\overline{X}$	σ	$\overline{X}$	σ	$\overline{X}$	σ	t	t
C-1	9	.00	.00	1.86	.87	2.57	1.47	2.81 †	5.23 §
C-2	9	.00	.00	1.83	.78	2.58	.86	3.51 §	8.95 §
E-1	8	.00	.00	2.42	.84	3.04	.77	5.03 §	11.21 §
E-2	8	.62	1.22	2.01	.90	2.98	1.50	2.96 †	6.23 §
Total	34	.15	.62	2.02	.84	2.78	1.17	6.51 §	14.37 §

† $p < .05$
§ $p < .01$

TABLE 142

Means, Standard Deviations, and t-Tests of the Significance of Differences between Means for the Stanford Achievement Test: Arithmetic Computation *for the Experimental and Control Groups*

		Pre-test		Post-test		Follow-up I		Follow-up I and Post-test	Pre-test
Class	N	$\overline{X}$	σ	$\overline{X}$	σ	$\overline{X}$	σ	t	t
C-1	9	.67	1.04	1.90	1.14	2.32	1.23	3.61 §	4.11 §
C-2	9	.27	.80	1.83	.43	2.39	.64	3.29 ‡	14.24 §
E-1	8	.41	.77	2.32	.69	2.71	.51	3.40 ‡	7.62 §
E-2	8	.65	1.20	2.14	1.13	2.32	1.29	.65	4.43 §
Total	34	.50	.94	2.04	.88	2.43	.95	4.43 §	12.02 §

‡ $p < .02$
§ $p < .01$

TABLE 143
Means, Standard Deviations, and t-Tests of the Significance of Differences Between Means for the Stanford Achievement Test: Average Arithmetic *for the Experimental and Control Groups*

		Pre-test		Post-test		Follow-up I		Follow-up I and Post-test	Pre-test
Class	N	$\overline{X}$	σ	$\overline{X}$	σ	$\overline{X}$	σ	t	t
C-1	9	.24	.49	1.86	.98	2.47	1.36	3.62 §	5.60 §
C-2	9	.13	.40	1.97	.71	2.57	.72	4.65 §	11.48 §
E-1	8	.00	.00	2.36	.74	2.89	.58	4.74 §	13.13 §
E-2	8	.64	1.19	2.00	1.11	2.68	1.35	3.36 ‡	5.89 §
Total	34	.25	.68	2.04	.87	2.64	1.04	8.04 §	15.33 §

‡ p < .02
§ p < .01

TABLE 144
Means, Standard Deviations, and t-Tests of the Significance of Differences between Means for the Stanford Achievement Test: Battery Mean *for the Experimental and Control Groups*

		Pre-test		Post-test		Follow-up I		Follow-up I and Post-test	Pre-test
Class	N	$\overline{X}$	σ	$\overline{X}$	σ	$\overline{X}$	σ	t	t
C-1	9	.39	.52	1.66	.86	2.30	1.22	4.70 §	6.33 §
C-2	9	.19	.57	1.56	.82	2.40	.71	7.09 §	11.89 §
E-1	8	.36	.57	2.44	.37	3.08	.64	5.40 §	8.35 §
E-2	8	.58	1.07	1.55	.98	2.54	1.32	5.37 §	6.21 §
Total	34	.37	.69	1.79	.84	2.56	1.01	9.44 §	15.01 §

§ p < .01

TABLE 145

Means, Standard Deviations, t-Tests, and Probabilities of Chance Differences in Means for the Control and Experimental Groups on the Achievement Test: Paragraph Meaning

Group	N	$\overline{X}$	σ	t
Combined Control Groups, Follow-up I	18	2.27	.90	
				1.56
Combined Experimental Groups, Follow-up I	16	2.88	.39	
Comparison of Control Group Pre-test, and Control Group, Follow-up I	18	1.83	.68	11.49 §
Comparison of Control Group Post-test, and Control Group, Follow-up I	18	.97	.61	6.62 §
Comparison of Experimental Group, Pre-test, and Experimental Group, Follow-up I	16	2.32	.11	7.96 §
Comparison of Experimental Group, Post-test, and Experimental Group, Follow-up I	16	1.32	.77	6.63 §

§ p < .01

TABLE 146

Means, Standard Deviations, t-Tests, and Probabilities of Chance Differences in Means for the Control and Experimental Groups on the Achievement Test: Word Meaning

Group	N	$\overline{X}$	σ	t
Combined Control Groups, Follow-up I	18	2.33	.85	
				1.39
Combined Experimental Groups, Follow-up I	16	2.84	1.17	
Comparison of Control Group, Pre-test, and Control Group, Follow-up I	18	2.21	.80	11.14 §
Comparison of Control Group, Post-test, and Control Group, Follow-up I	18	1.06	.84	5.23 §
Comparison of Experimental Group, Pre-test, and Experimental Group, Follow-up I	16	2.49	.99	9.76 §
Comparison of Experimental Group, Post-test, and Experimental Group, Follow-up I	16	1.03	.76	5.27 §

§ p < .01

TABLE 147
Means, Standard Deviations, t-Tests, and Probabilities of Chance Differences in Means for the Control and Experimental Groups on the Achievement Test: Average Reading

Group	N	X̄	σ	t
Combined Control Groups, Follow-up II	18	2.33	.86	
				1.69
Combined Experimental Groups, Follow-up II	16	2.96	1.17	
Comparison of Control Group, Pre-test, and Control Group, Follow-up II	18	.21	.68	12.60 §
Comparison of Control Group, Post-test, and Control Group, Follow-up II	18	1.02	.67	6.31 §
Comparison of Experimental Group, Pre-test, and Experimental Group, Follow-up II	16	2.52	1.00	9.56 §
Comparison of Experimental Group, Follow-up I, and Experimental Group, Follow-up II	16	1.28	.67	7.45 §

§ p < .01

TABLE 148
Means, Standard Deviations, t-Tests, and Probabilities of Chance Differences in Means for the Control and Experimental Groups on the Achievement Test: Spelling

Group	N	X̄	σ	t
Combined Control Groups, Follow-up I	18	2.22	1.44	
				1.17
Combined Experimental Groups, Follow-up I	16	2.81	1.30	
Comparison of Control Group, Pre-test, and Control Group, Follow-up I	18	1.74	.11	6.71 §
Comparison of Control Group, Post-test, and Control Group, Follow-up I	18	.56	.76	3.12 §
Comparison of Experimental Group, Pre-test, and Experimental Group, Follow-up I	16	2.30	.15	6.10 §
Comparison of Experimental Group, Post-test, and Experimental Group, Follow-up I	16	.64	.66	3.75 §

§ p < .01

TABLE 149

Means, Standard Deviations, t-Tests, and Probabilities of Chance
Differences in Means for the Control and Experimental Groups
on the Achievement Test: Arithmetic Reasoning

Group	N	$\overline{X}$	σ	t
Combined Control Groups, Follow-up I	18	2.57	1.14	
				1.04
Combined Experimental Groups, Follow-up I	16	3.01	1.12	
Comparison of Control Group, Pre-test, and Control Group, Follow-up I	18	2.57	1.14	9.32 §
Comparison of Control Group, Post-test, and Control Group, Follow-up I	18	.73	.66	4.55 §
Comparison of Experimental Group, Pre-test, and Experimental Group, Follow-up I	16	2.69	.94	11.18 §
Comparison of Experimental Group, Post-test, and Experimental Group, Follow-up I	16	.79	.67	4.52 §

§ P < .01

TABLE 150

Means, Standard Deviations, t-Tests, and Probabilities of Chance
Differences in Means for the Control and Experimental Groups
on the Achievement Test: Arithmetic Computation

Group	N	$\overline{X}$	σ	t
Combined Control Groups, Follow-up I	18	2.36	.93	
				.47
Combined Experimental Groups, Follow-up I	16	2.52	.94	
Comparison of Control Group, Pre-test, and Control Group, Follow-up I	18	1.89	.89	8.75 §
Comparison of Control Group, Post-test, and Control Group, Follow-up I	18	.49	.42	4.84 §
Comparison of Experimental Group, Pre-test, and Experimental Group, Follow-up I	16	.20	.96	8.05 §
Comparison of Experimental Group, Post-test, and Experimental Group, Follow-up I	16	.29	.59	1.90 §

§ P < .01

TABLE 151

Means, Standard Deviations, t-Tests, and Probabilities of Chance
Differences in Means for the Control and Experimental Groups
on the Achievement Test: Average Arithmetic

Group	N	$\overline{X}$	σ	t
Combined Control Groups, Follow-up I	18	2.52	1.03	
				.71
Combined Experimental Groups, Follow-up I	16	2.78	.99	
Comparison of Control Group, Pre-test, and Control Group, Follow-up I	18	2.33	.97	10.58 §
Comparison of Control Group, Post-test, and Control Group, Follow-up I	18	.58	.43	5.88 §
Comparison of Experimental Group, Pre-test, and Experimental Group, Follow-up I	16	2.46	.88	10.89 §
Comparison of Experimental Group, Post-test, and Experimental Group, Follow-up I	16	.50	.43	5.86 §

§ p < .01

TABLE 152

Means, Standard Deviations, t-Tests, and Probabilities of Chance
Differences in Means for the Control and Experimental Groups
on the Achievement Test: Battery Mean

Group	N	$\overline{X}$	σ	t
Combined Control Groups, Follow-up I	18	2.35	.94	
				1.27
Combined Experimental Groups, Follow-up I	16	2.81	1.01	
Comparison of Control Group, Pre-test, and Control Group, Follow-up I	18	2.06	.73	11.71 §
Comparison of Control Group, Post-test, and Control Group, Follow-up I	16	.74	.38	2.57 ‡
Comparison of Experimental Group, Pre-test, and Experimental Group, Follow-up I	16	.23	.93	6.77 §
Comparison of Experimental Group, Post-test, and Experimental Group, Follow-up I	16	.81	.44	7.06 §

§ p < .01
‡ p < .02

or pre-test and Follow-up I, are significant at the .05 level or beyond, showing substantial growth in those academic skills measured by the achievement test. Two classes (Table 140, C-1 and E-1) did not show a significant difference between means on the post-test and Follow-up I scores for the spelling subtest, and one class (Table 142, E-2) did not show a difference in means on the arithmetic computation subtest. In each case the failure to show increased growth can probably be attributed to the teacher. One teacher, for example, stressed word recognition and comprehension more than spelling, while the other emphasized arithmetic reasoning and process more than the mechanics of computation.

When the combined control and combined experimental groups are examined, statistically significant progress is indicated by both groups on all subtests except one: the combined experimental group did not show a significant difference between the post-test and Follow-up I results on the arithmetic computation section. When the individual scores are examined, it can be seen that all of the children in Group E-1 made small gains over the course of the second academic year, while in the E-2 group three children made lower scores at the end of that year. These three children had been in the E-1 group during the preceding year and had made substantial gains then.

These results are difficult to interpret. Perhaps the change in group composition had some effect on the children, or some unreported and unobserved change in teacher approach during the second year may have been a factor.

At the end of the first year (academic year 1957–1958), the children were re-assigned to classes. Each class had a core of 4 or 5 children remaining from the previous year, the other 5 children being new to that particular class. Tables 153 through 160 show the statistics for the second-year grouping, which, for convenience, have been labeled "Grouping II." The statistics have been presented for each class *as though* it had been similarly constituted in the pre-test and post-test period; they have been included for comparative purposes.

All classes made significant academic gains by the end of the second year on all subtests except three: spelling, arithmetic computation, and average arithmetic. These results probably reflect differences in teaching emphasis in relation to the above subjects.

INTELLIGENCE GRADE PLACEMENT

The question arises as to the grade level one might legitimately expect the children to perform at on the basis of their intelligence test scores. An attempt has been made to answer this question by using

TABLE 153

Mean Grade Levels, Standard Deviations, and t-Tests of the Significance of Differences between Means for the Grouping II Stanford Achievement Test Data: Paragraph Meaning

Group	N	Pre-test X	σ	Post-test X	σ	Follow-up I X	σ	Follow-up I and Post-test t
A	8	1.29	.82	2.24	.36	3.54	.94	4.03 §
B	10	.00	.00	.72	.72	2.02	1.07	5.70 §
C	9	.30	.57	1.49	.95	2.51	.49	5.03 §
D	7	.39	.62	1.40	.89	2.24	1.16	3.59 §

§ p < .01

TABLE 154

Mean Grade Levels, Standard Deviations, and t-Tests of the Significance of Differences between Means for the Grouping II Stanford Achievement Test Data: Word Meaning

Group	N	Pre-test X	σ	Post-test X	σ	Follow-up I X	σ	Follow-up I and Post-test t
A	8	.98	.98	2.39	.36	3.43	.88	4.36 §
B	10	.00	.00	.84	1.06	2.04	.94	4.60 §
C	9	.00	.00	1.48	1.17	2.63	.55	3.43 §
D	7	.00	.00	1.56	1.01	2.26	1.11	2.54 †

§ p < .01
† p < .05

TABLE 155

Mean Grade Levels, Standard Deviations, and t-Tests of the Significance of Differences between Means for the Grouping II Stanford Achievement Test Data: Average Reading

Group	N	Pre-test X	σ	Post-test X	σ	Follow-up I X	σ	Follow-up I and Post-test t
A	8	1.11	.81	2.34	.35	3.50	.86	4.40 §
B	10	.00	.00	.78	.98	2.05	1.01	5.47 §
C	9	.16	.29	1.48	1.03	2.59	1.59	4.47 §
D	7	.20	.32	1.47	.94	2.27	1.12	3.28 ‡

§ p < .01
‡ p < .02

TABLE 156

Mean Grade Levels, Standard Deviations, and t-Tests of the Significance of Differences between Means for the Grouping II Stanford Achievement Test Data: Spelling

Group	N	Pre-test X	σ	Post-test X	σ	Follow-up I X	σ	Follow-up I and Post-test t
A	8	1.56	1.05	2.68	.35	3.53	.73	3.17 ‡
B	10	.00	.00	1.42	.95	1.87	1.46	1.71
C	9	.13	.38	1.78	.77	2.44	1.05	.70
D	7	.44	.71	1.81	1.26	2.29	1.67	1.60

‡ p < .02

TABLE 157

Mean Grade Levels, Standard Deviations, and t-Tests of the Significance of Differences between Means for the Grouping II Stanford Achievement Test Data: Arithmetic Reasoning

Group	N	Pre-test X	σ	Post-test X	σ	Follow-up I X	σ	Follow-up I and Post-test t
A	8	.63	1.14	2.76	.53	3.51	.88	3.52 §
B	10	.00	.00	1.70	.83	2.31	1.24	2.27 †
C	9	.00	.00	2.01	.85	2.93	1.09	5.66 §
D	7	.00	.00	1.64	.32	2.40	.83	2.90 ‡

† p < .05
‡ p < .02
§ p < .01

TABLE 158

Mean Grade Levels, Standard Deviations, and t-Tests of the Significance of Differences between Means for the Grouping II Stanford Achievement Test Data: Arithmetic Computation

Group	N	Pre-test X	σ	Post-test X	σ	Follow-up I X	σ	Follow-up I and Post-test t
A	8	1.35	1.11	2.58	.50	3.06	.68	2.87 †
B	10	.00	.00	1.84	.97	1.94	1.18	.49
C	9	.23	.66	2.27	.83	2.57	.78	3.53 §
D	7	.57	.94	1.64	.82	2.43	.59	5.07 §

† p < .05
§ p < .01

TABLE 159

Mean Grade Levels, Standard Deviations, and t-Tests of the Significance of Differences between Means for the Grouping II Stanford Achievement Test Data: Average Arithmetic

Group	N	Pre-test X	σ	Post-test X	σ	Follow-up I X	σ	Follow-up I and Post-test t
A	8	.79	1.10	2.74	.49	3.30	.71	4.32 §
B	10	.00	.00	1.76	.84	2.14	1.18	2.14
C	9	.11	.31	2.13	.81	2.78	.92	5.86 §
D	7	.17	.32	1.51	.73	2.43	.71	8.46 §

§ p < .01

TABLE 160

Mean Grade Levels, Standard Deviations, and t-Tests of the Significance of Differences between Means for the Grouping II Stanford Achievement Test Data: Battery Mean

Group	N	Pre-test X	σ	Post-test X	σ	Follow-up I X	σ	Follow-up I and Post-test t
A	8	1.44	.78	2.54	.28	3.40	.65	5.46 §
B	10	.00	.00	1.29	.81	2.03	1.03	4.84 §
C	9	.13	.99	1.81	.74	2.60	.65	6.92 §
D	7	.29	.46	1.61	.82	2.33	1.01	4.35 §

§ p < .01

data supplied in the manual which accompanies the California Short-form Test of Mental Maturity. This is called an Intelligence (MA) Grade Placement Scale, which is a type of mental-age scale, expressed in grade-placement units. For example, an Intelligence Grade Placement of 2.5 indicates the median mental age of those cases in the standardization group whose actual grade placement is 2.5.

Correlations between the California Test of Mental Maturity and the Stanford-Binet have been uniformly high (from .70 to .88+). While it is recognized that there is a certain amount of risk in using the Stanford-Binet Mental Ages to arrive at Intelligence Grade Placement which is based on mental ages obtained from a different intelligence test, it is nevertheless felt that such a procedure was justified by the necessity to provide a basis for comparison. Tables 161 through 163

TABLE 161
Intelligence Grade Placement during the Pre-test Period (October, 1957)

Group	N	X̄	σ
C-1	10	1.41	.91
C-2	10	1.37	1.12
E-1	10	1.26	.72
E-2	9	1.62	1.26
Total	39	1.41	1.03

TABLE 162
Intelligence Grade Placement during the Post-test Period (June, 1958)

Group	N	X̄	σ
C-1	10	1.96	.89
C-2	10	2.13	.76
E-1	10	1.82	.97
E-2	9	2.49	1.62
Total	39	2.10	1.12

TABLE 163
Intelligence Grade Placement during the Follow-up II Period (June, 1959)

Group	N	X̄	σ
C-1	10	2.81	1.31
C-2	10	2.90	1.38
E-1	10	2.72	1.06
E-2	9	3.19	2.15
Total	39	2.90	1.53

present the Intelligence Grade Placement of the control and experimental groups.

Tables 137 through 144 show the Stanford Achievement Test data for the three tests. There was an attrition in the sample, reducing the total from 39 to 34. The pre-test and post-test data are based on the 34 remaining subjects. It must be remembered that the children had been assigned to other groups at the end of the project year. The Follow-up I data are reported *as if* the children had been assigned to the same experimental and control groups in which they belonged at the beginning of the project year. It was felt desirable to do this in order to see if the original experimental and control conditions had a lasting effect on academic performance. The second-year grouping will be shown in subsequent tables under the heading of Grouping II.

The achievement-test means reported in Tables 137 through 144 indicate that in the pre-test period none of the control and experimental groups performed at a level commensurate with the Intelligence Grade Placement. In considering the total group of 39 children, one child (C-2-10) had an Achievement Test Battery mean higher than his Intelligence Grade Placement score (IGP = .3; Battery Mean = 1.7).

In the post-test (June, 1958) results, all achievement-test group means were lower than the mean Intelligence Grade Placement with the exception of Experimental Group I. In Group I the achievement scores were higher than the Intelligence Grade Placements. Nine out of the 10 children had achievement scores higher than what would have been predicted on the basis of their mental ages alone. In considering the total group of 39 children, 14 had achievement-test battery means higher than their Intelligence Grade Placement, in contrast to the one child noted in the preceding paragraph who scored thus at the beginning of the project.

In the Follow-up I (June, 1959) one experimental group (E-1) maintained the superiority noted in the preceding paragraph. All groups except E-1 had group-achievement score means lower than the corresponding mean Intelligence Grade Placement. E-1 had higher achievement test means on every subtest with the exception of Arithmetic Computation (Intelligence Grade Placement = 2.72; Arithmetic Computation = 2.71). Even on this one subtest the difference is so slight that we can say that the group was performing at expected levels.

For the total group of children in the pre-test period (1957), the mean Intelligence Grade Placement was 1.41, and the Battery Mean was .37, which indicates an over-all academic retardation of 1.04 grade level. By the end of the project (June, 1958), however, the Intelligence Grade Placement was 2.10, and the Battery Mean was 1.74, which indicates an academic retardation of only .36 grade level. One year later, in June, 1959, the Intelligence Grade Placement was 2.90, and the Battery Mean was 2.56, showing academic retardation of .34. Thus, in the period from September, 1957, to June, 1959, the mean Battery Mean for the entire group had increased by 2.19 grade levels, and the total academic retardation had been reduced from 1.04 to .34.

In summarizing the Intelligence Grade Placement data, it can be said that at the beginning of the project all four groups of children were performing academically below the level one would predict on the basis of their mental ages alone. By the end of the project year, however, one group (Experimental Group I) was performing at a mean grade level higher than the mean Intelligence Grade Placement; and in the second year, even when these children were assigned to other groups, this higher level of academic performance was maintained. The mean increase in Battery Mean for this same period of time was 2.19 grade levels, and the academic retardation had been reduced from 1.04 to .34 grade level.

INTELLIGENCE AND ACHIEVEMENT

Inasmuch as most current intelligence tests have been validated against academic achievement, it comes as no surprise that there is a high correlation between both IQ and academic achievement, and MA and academic achievement, as may be seen in Tables 164 and 165.

TABLE 164

Pearson Product Moment Correlation Coefficients between Stanford-Binet Intelligence Quotients and the Stanford Achievement Test [a]

Subtest	Pre-test (N = 38)	Post-test (N = 38)	Follow-up I (N = 34)
Average Reading	.54	.46	.60
Average Arithmetic	.50	.63	.76
Battery Mean	.55	.57	.65

[a] All *r*'s reported in the above table are significant at less than the .01 level.

TABLE 165

Pearson Product Moment Correlation Coefficients between Stanford-Binet Mental Ages and the Stanford Achievement Test [a]

Subtest	Pre-test (N = 38)	Post-test (N = 38)	Follow-up I (N = 34)
Average Reading	.54	.49	.61
Average Arithmetic	.51	.69	.76
Battery Mean	.54	.66	.69

[a] All *r*'s reported in the above table are significant at less than the .01 level.

One very interesting thing about these tables, however, is the clear evidence that the correlation between intelligence and achievement became greater over the two-year period of this study. This may mean that the children with higher initial intellectual ability profited more from their school experiences and that this became a more important factor as time passed. It may be presumed that this trend would continue until all of the children reached an academic level completely in agreement with their intellectual potential.

Another inference from these two tables is that mental age and intelligence quotient are quite comparable in predicting academic achievement. This comparability is greatly enhanced, of course, by the relatively narrow range of chronological ages of the children chosen for the study.

SUMMARY

The area of most dramatic improvement over the two-year period is in academic achievement. At the beginning of the project only 12 children were able to score on part or all of the achievement test. This did not represent a true level of academic functioning, however, as many personal and environmental variables were operating to cause lowered test performance. The children's hyperactivity, perseveration, distractibility, difficulty with figure-background relationships, and inability to follow directions made it impossible for them to respond adequately in a standardized testing situation. By the end of the second year, however, the children had sufficiently overcome the problems mentioned above so that all were able to perform on at least part of the test.

One clear-cut inference that can be made from these results is that there were no demonstrable differences in academic achievement between the combined experimental and combined control groups. With few exceptions, however, the total group of children made substantial gains over this period.

Achievement Test Scores and EEG Patterns

Four of the 39 children were not considered in the following EEG analysis because their EEG reports were either not available at the time of writing, or else had been given and interpreted by someone other than the neurological consultant. Of the remaining 35, 14 had normal and 21 had abnormal EEG patterns. Tables 166, 167, and 168 show a comparison of the mean Stanford Achievement Test scores for the pre-test, post-test, and Follow-up I results of children having normal and abnormal EEG's. The abnormal EEG group did not have achievement test scores which were signficantly lower than those of the normal EEG

TABLE 166

A Comparison of the Pre-Test (October, 1957) Stanford Achievement
Test Scores of Children Having Normal and Abnormal
Electroencephalograms

| | Electroencephalograms | | | | |
| | Normal (N = 14) | | Abnormal (N = 21) | | |
Subtest	$\overline{X}$	σ	$\overline{X}$	σ	t
Average Reading	.67	.89	.20	.45	1.91
Average Arithmetic	.51	.91	.18	.39	1.34
Battery Mean	.67	.92	.21	.46	1.83

TABLE 167

A Comparison of the Post-test (June, 1958) Stanford Achievement
Test Scores of Children Having Normal and Abnormal
Electroencephalograms

| | Electroencephalograms | | | | |
| | Normal (N = 14) | | Abnormal (N = 21) | | |
Subtest	$\overline{X}$	σ	$\overline{X}$	σ	t
Average Reading	1.90	1.37	1.25	.98	1.50
Average Arithmetic	2.41	.86	1.81	.78	2.00
Battery Mean	2.16	1.02	1.54	.79	1.89

TABLE 168

A Comparison of the Follow-up I (June, 1959) Stanford Achievement
Test Scores of Children Having Normal and Abnormal
Electroencephalograms

| | Electroencephalograms | | | | |
| | Normal (N = 13) | | Abnormal (N = 19) | | |
Subtest	$\overline{X}$	σ	$\overline{X}$	σ	t
Average Reading	2.94	1.12	2.30	.94	1.77
Average Arithmetic	2.85	1.16	2.45	.91	1.10
Battery Mean	2.79	1.08	2.36	.92	1.22

group. It should be noted, however, that every mean achievement test score for the children having normal EEG's was higher than the corresponding mean achievement test score of children with abnormal EEG's, although this did not reach the level of confidence accepted in the present study. This difference is readily understandable when one considers that the mean IQ of the children having normal EEG's was 87.36, standard deviation 14.47, while for the children having abnormal EEG's the mean IQ was 75.95, standard deviation 9.48. The difference in intelligence level could account for the trend which has been mentioned.

DISCUSSION

As pointed out by Masland, Sarason, and Gladwin (45), psychometric patterning suggestive of brain injury can neither be confirmed nor denied in the absence of positive neurological data. The inability of the medical diagnostic staff to arrive at a unanimous diagnostic impression in regard to brain injury made it impossible to conduct an analysis of the children's test data in this regard. The EEG results are being reported with the full realization that any one single diagnostic procedure is at best highly unreliable. Within the limits of the present pilot study, however, it may be concluded that when the gross classification of records into a dichotomy of "normal" and "abnormal" patterns was made, the EEG did not discriminate between those children who achieved academically and those who did not.

Summary and Discussion of Psychological Data

It should be emphasized that this was a demonstration-pilot study, without rigidly controlled conditions that would permit the formulation of definite statements about very specific and carefully defined variables. This project demonstrated the ways in which interdisciplinary diagnostic findings shaped a certain type of educational philosophy and teaching methodology, and it demonstrated the ways in which such a program operated within the public school system. It is a *descriptive* study of an educational approach to the learning and behavior problems of the hyperactive child.

When one attempts to work within an already organized and structured situation, certain procedures may have to be changed to meet the existing framework. In large measure this is what happened in the current project. Scientific research methods were modified to meet the exigencies of the public school system.

An attitude shared by many school administrators must be recognized from the outset. This is the feeling that if one has information that might be of value in working with a child, there is a moral responsibility to see that this information is used. In other words, collecting diagnostic information about a group of children, and then assigning part of them to one type of treatment which may meet their needs ("experimental") and assigning the remainder to another type of treatment which may not meet their needs ("control") is morally repugnant to many school administrators. Thus, the design carefully worked out from a methodological point of view may be subjected to rude violation when it is thrust into the practical school setting. The end result, of course, is that when a program has to be modified to the extent that the present program was changed, then *explanation* of the results becomes impossible. One can only *describe* what happened.

In the foregoing section an attempt has been made to present descriptive statistics to show what happened to the project children. They grew in very important ways, both educationally and psychologically. The extreme learning problems of many of the children at the beginning of the project were greatly modified by the end of the second year. When the data are examined, however, it is not possible to say with certainty that the specialized methodology caused the growth. Other factors operative concomitantly with the project must have had far-reaching effects on the children's development, but they are impossible to evaluate. Such factors would include maturation, later participation of a number of the children in physical education classes at the University of Maryland, the participation of a number of children in psychotherapy, special swimming instruction during the summer, private tutoring by either an interested parent or even on a professional basis, experiences of some of the children in Boy Scout groups, speech therapy, and other activities. The children in this project are very fortunate to be living within the metropolitan District of Columbia area where many educational and growth experiences are available to them which would not be available to children living in other parts of the country. A number of the children have parents who are professional people, and the educational and social climate of the home is considerably above the average for the nation.

With the foregoing reservations in mind, the two following generalizations can be made on the basis of the psychological and achievement test results.

1. At the end of the project year, the experimental classes had made *temporary* gains in comparison to the control group on several of the scoring categories of the perceptual tests (Bender-Gestalt, Syracuse

Visual Figure-Background Test) and on the Vineland Scale of Social Maturity. By the end of the second year (Follow-up I), after the classes had been regrouped and the teaching approach had been varied, the children who had originally been in the experimental classes had lost these gains. The experimental conditions (reduction in stimulation by physical alteration of the rooms, and relatively increased structure and control in the teaching method) did not have a permanent measurable effect on the instruments under discussion. This conclusion raises a number of questions which cannot be fully answered by the present data. During the second year the children were regrouped for instruction in terms of their needs and in terms of growth which had been achieved during the first year. The teachers made use of specialized teaching techniques during the second year insofar as they felt the children needed them. In general, the children progressed smoothly during the second year from an academic-achievement point of view.

What led to the findings which have been noted regarding loss at the end of the second year of gains made during the first year in several categories of the perceptual tests? The loss may be due to the fact that, as with many studies of growth, the greatest spurt takes place during the first year. However, it may also be due to the fact that the children, during the first year, learned to tolerate the psychopathology which characterized them in the pre-test period. Having learned to tolerate it or having mastered it, pathology was no longer a unique factor in inhibiting achievement. Although it was still present, it no longer constituted an uncontrolled factor in learning. Hence, it was not measurable at the end of the second year and it was also not a factor which produced instructional problems for the teachers as they worked with the children during the second year. These assumptions both need further investigation.

2. The total group of 39 children, disregarding their placement in experimental or control classes, made significant academic improvement and showed considerably fewer errors on the perceptual and visuo-motor tests (Bender-Gestalt and Syracuse Visual Figure-Background).

The psychological test battery originally chosen on the basis of the usefulness of the individual tests in assessing brain injury did in fact show patterns suggestive of brain injury in the records of 33 children. As the medical staff was unable to arrive at criteria for diagnosing brain injury, however, an analysis of the psychological test performance in this regard was not possible.

PSYCHIATRIC EVALUATIONS [7]

Psychiatric evaluations were made individually with all of the children in the pilot-study groups during and as a part of the diagnostic examination period. The same psychiatrist was retained during the demonstration period to observe the children and to co-operate in interpreting their behavior for the teaching staff. At the close of the demonstration year, psychiatric re-evaluations were made for each child by the same psychiatrist.

Table 169 summarizes the psychiatric observations made during the pre- and post-test periods. No attempt has been made to quantify these data, since each comment consists of a subjective clinical impression. A careful reading of the data, however, is rewarding in providing the reader with a unique understanding of the psychiatric nature of the subjects, the way they appeared at the beginning of the educational experience, their status at the close of the ten-month educational period, and the behavioral changes which a number of the subjects achieved.

At the outset, it is immediately apparent that the observations made in the non-group setting of the playroom differ markedly in certain behavioral categories from those made in the classroom-group situation. While it was generally true in the latter setting that behavior was hyperactive, unpredictable, and aggressive, these characteristics were generally not seen in the playroom. However, other categories, such as impulsivity, poor self-image, and visual-perceptual problems were indeed demonstrated in both settings. This observation strengthens the growing awareness on the part of psychiatrists that their diagnostic responsibilities when dealing with children must be broadened to include classroom observation or data on classroom behavior, or both.

There are differences which are not yet understood in the psychiatric evaluation of those children who were previously enrolled in special education classes as opposed to those who have not had such experience. On the basis of a rating scale of one-plus to three-plus, clinical judgment was applied to the data to decide how much personality integration had occurred in nine months to determine the extent of the psychopathology of each child. While this is a manifestly rough rat-

[7] The authors are indebted to Christine W. Kehne, M.D., psychiatric member of the Diagnostic Team, who completed all of the initial and follow-up psychiatric evaluations and who prepared the material which appears in the following pages of this chapter.

TABLE 169
Psychiatric Observations of Subjects: Pre- and Post-test Data

Variable	Subject E-1-1	
Intelligence, Clinical Impression	Borderline capacity.	
	Pre-test	Post-test
Appearance	Friendly, co-operative, tall and thin, somewhat carelessly dressed, excessive drooling.	Ivy League clothes, serious-minded, drooling almost absent.
Attitudes	Trying to please; fears his destructive power; asks to have hands washed.	Likes school now achieving on his own.
Behavioral Observations, Characteristics	Showed no frustration over repeated attempts to put two parts of a tank together; perseverative thinking, irrelevant answers, distractible.	Not distractible.
Play Activities	Accurate, intense hitting of Bobo; fierce cowboy Indian fighting; offered story for every activity; played Old Maid with enjoyment.	More cowboys and Indians, toy train, talking a lot.
Motor Patterns, Co-ordination	Normal gross marked difficulty with name on line.	No change.
Draw-a-Person		
Memory Orientation, Time, Space		
Despert Fables, Phantasies, Dreams, and Wishes		Dreamed mother lion in bed with him.
Speech and Language	On and off stumbling over phrases; saliva, obscured words; rapid.	Defect less noticeable.
Parent Conference (Post)	Mother attended: alert, interested, notices that he must always play the "bad guy"; encouraged to revive use of Bobo by the children; over-protective.	
Parent Evaluation of Child (Post)	Much more relaxed, more a family member; parents less protective; feels he is still the "fall guy" to his peers.	
Summary and Comments	Has greater self-confidence, but has definite areas of insecurity; perceptual difficulties present; speech improved, drooling stopped; a child who still fears his resentful feelings (over being different) will erupt.	

Variable	Subject E-1-8	
Intelligence, Clinical Impression	Somewhat diminished normal capacity.	
	Pre-test	Post-test
Appearance	Neat, good looking, young for age.	No difference.
Attitudes	Friendly enthusiastic, co-operative, polite.	Friendly, not always co-operative or polite.
Behavioral Observations, Characteristics	Much singing to cover anxiety; no hyperactivity, but considerable energy expended.	Able to disagree; refused to draw picture; very reluctant to stop.
Play Activities	Cowboys beat Indians wounded in gun play; dollhouse, played toilet.	Guns broken, hence more hitting of Bobo; burned a house, leaving people within and removing only furniture.
Motor Patterns, Co-ordination	Gross movements average.	
Draw-a-Person	House with chimney at right angle.	
Memory Orientation, Time, Space		Good memory for last interview.
Despert Fables, Phantasies, Dreams, and Wishes	Bike, large; two guns.	
Speech and Language	Sing-song, high-pitched stammering, organic, unclear.	Much clearer, little stammering.
Parent Conference (Post)	Both parents present, anxious to report the child's progress.	
Parent Evaluation of Child (Post)	Calmer, more self-confident "independent type, eating and sleeping better"; speech clearer.	
Summary and Comments	Previously in an effort to please and be accepted he struggled with his handicaps, developing increasing tension; now he is more relaxed, speech improved, ego-development has occurred but brings concomitant anxiety; there is also anxiety due to greater recognition of the deprivation caused by handicaps.	

Variable	Subject E-2-7	
Intelligence, Clinical Impression	Retarded.	
	Pre-test	Post-test
Appearance	Neat, well-developed, bubbly saliva, attractive.	No difference.
Attitudes	Stubborn; expects to be dressed; overestimates ability to complete puzzles; desires to learn.	Tense, still overconfident.
Behavioral Observations, Characteristics	Friendly, affectionate; easily distractible except from painting; responded to firmness by co-operating; finally tied own shoe when not helped.	
Play Activities	Perseverated on finger painting; identified many objects; hesitated to use gun on Bobo freely.	Repeated same activities, but less concerned to take painting home.
Motor Patterns, Co-ordination	Jumbled normal gross.	
Draw-a-Person	Immature stick figure, quite good name writing.	
Memory Orientation, Time, Space	Marked difficulty with Johns of puzzle; receptive aphasia.	Absent receptive aphasia.
Despert Fables, Phantasies, Dreams, and Wishes	None given.	
Speech and Language	Prefers sign language, indistinct words if pressed to talk.	Relatively more verbal.
Parent Conference (Post)	Mother attended: she is interested and objective, though matter of fact; has compromised with Father who is spontaneous; week days better for child; inconsistency a family pattern—wonder if she understands them.	
Parent Evaluation of Child (Post)	Easier speech; more relaxed but has times of "3-year-old behavior"; surprised she is so much better at school and about the same at home.	
Summary and Comments	Through speech therapy and group has gained in communication; may tend to control parents by pretending not to understand their demands, as was once true; handicaps serving secondary gain at home; not needed at school where environment is consistent.	

Variable	Subject E-1-10	
Intelligence, Clinical Impression	Average	
	Pre-test	**Post-test**
Appearance	Handsome, well-developed.	
Attitudes	Coy, silent, except when he forgot himself.	Somewhat friendlier.
Behavioral Observations, Characteristics	Communicated angry feelings nonverbally in play; took suggestions readily; sensitive to noises; not easily distracted, no hyperactivity.	Essentially no change, provocative; silence prevailed; question of perseveration.
Play Activities	Shot Indians off the roof; tomahawked cowboys; with encouragement, hit Bobo with abandon; took out doll furniture and replaced it disorganized; made a clay bullet and knocked down girl, mother, boy, and father in that order.	More active pushing away of the punching toys.
Motor Patterns, Co-ordination	Normal gross and fine movements.	
Draw-a-Person		Primitive, lacks self-concept; poor spatial concept i.e., windows arise out of house wall.
Memory Orientation, Time, Space	Disoriented.	Continues disoriented.
Despert Fables, Phantasies, Dreams, and Wishes		Wishes for a horse.
Speech and Language		
Parent Conference (Post)	Mother attended: petite, well-groomed.	
Parent Evaluation of Child (Post)	Sees no real difference; "anything he does wears off fast"; still has "terrible temper"; "won't obey"; moderately accepting of a residential treatment center.	
Summary and Comments	The use of silence and play activities express his hostility and fear of aggressive drives in a family which has real difficulty accepting an alert, outgoing male child in other than an inconsistent, somewhat seductive fashion; greater ease with peers; has profited from brief psychotherapy.	

Variable	Subject E-2-3	
Intelligence, Clinical Impression	Low average.	
	Pre-test	Post-test
Appearance	Handsome, well-developed, neat.	No change.
Attitudes	Friendly, eager, frustration not obvious.	
Behavioral Observations, Characteristics	Took pleasure in activities; perseveration; interest span limited, reflects dull normal intelligence; no hyperactivity.	
Play Activities	Concentrated on Bobo, hitting squarely and increasing intensity; only observed toys; played checkers well; struggled to replace a series of various sized blocks.	Even greater interest and emotion displayed with Bobo.
Motor Patterns, Co-ordination	Gross = good; fine = impaired; could not hook trucks together.	No significant change.
Draw-a-Person	Primitive; insect with eyes outside of head.	Eyes now inside head; otherwise the same.
Memory Orientation, Time, Space	Form concepts very poor.	Still much difficulty but improved; now knows month.
Despert Fables, Phantasies, Dreams, and Wishes	Daily nightmares, but happy endings.	Average wishes.
Speech and Language	"Baby talk" plus omissions and substitutions; history of stuttering.	Moderate improvement, but still immature.
Parent Conference (Post)	Mother attended; still overprotecting.	
Parent Evaluation of Child (Post)	No significant changes within family; child more independent; has always preferred physical things to talking.	
Summary and Comments	This appealing, aggressive boy has had such marked perceptual difficulties that he needs both group experience to help his self-concept and concomitant individual speech, eye, and form training to establish realistic communication with the environment.	

Variable	Subject E-1-4	
Intelligence, Clinical Impression	Capacity for low average.	
	Pre-test	**Post-test**
Appearance	Stocky, overly plump; socially comfortable.	No change.
Attitude	Expected to be waited upon; cheerful; unconcerned about damage to toys.	Cheerful, self-satisfied.
Behavioral Observations, Characteristics	General enthusiasm; almost active; short attention span.	Waited quietly for his appointment; more controlled and orderly.
Play Activities	Short attention span; painting cheerful but formless; played with trucks mostly; played with and then threw train into stack of toys; did not seem interested in rules; moderate pleasure from Bobo.	Still satisfied to identify trucks and push them around; less interest in Boxer than in Bobo.
Motor Patterns, Co-ordination	Difficulty joining parts of trucks.	No clear data.
Draw-a-Person	Birdlike; cheerful, large head.	Less birdlike; still cheerful with large head.
Memory Orientation, Time, Space	Marked spatial disorientation; could not give dates, months.	
Despert Fables, Phantasies, Dreams, and Wishes	Bird would go to mother; elephant turned brown; he would lose the toy.	Not tested.
Speech and Language	Constant talker, questioner.	No change; irrepressible flow.
Parent Conference (Post)	Mother attended: feels guilty and responsible, but also blames lack of kindergarten.	
Parent Evaluation of Child (Post)	"Wonderful progress"; increased attention span.	
Summary and Comments	This child uses cheerfulness and enthusiasm to hide feelings of inadequacy; verbalization as a defense against overprotection and as expression of aggression; he is now more controlled, can permit reading to occur (let something through the verbal barrier); still immature.	

Variable	Subject E-1-2	

| Intelligence, Clinical Impression | Facile tongue, but demonstrates no more than average intelligence. | |

	Pre-test	**Post-test**
Appearance	Pudgy; large mouth, constant drooling.	No longer drools.
Attitudes	Friendly, cooperative, shy.	
Behavioral Observations, Characteristics	Quick rapport but superficial; fair amount of hyperactivity; perseveration; occasional grasping of trouser crotch.	Asked many questions checking whether other boys had been here too; more obvious masturbatory activity.
Play Activities	"Loved to fight"—as he hit Bobo; used finger paints, washing hands between colors.	Mostly hit Bobo.
Motor Patterns, Co-ordination	Heavy gait, clumsy; constant drooling (seemed oblivious to it); jerky when drawing, free when coloring.	No longer inco-ordinated.
Draw-a-Person	Bald man with crayons, stick figure.	
Memory Orientation, Time, Space	Disoriented.	Continues disoriented.
Despert Fables, Phantasies, Dreams, and Wishes	Feels things up against his face; wishes to walk with father.	
Speech and Language	Impaired but had clear moments; quite verbal.	Improved.
Parent Conference (Post)	Mother attended: (known to examiner in other setting): demanding, intelligent, dependent; has only high expectation for son.	
Parent Evaluation of Child (Post)	Most pleased that he comes home; without complaints; feels he is more bothered now that he has learned enough to see how wide the gap which separates him from the neighborhood.	
Summary and Comments	While the speech defect has diminished, this boy is markedly immature and has primary emotional problems as a member of this family-complex; there is a kind of castration anxiety symbolized by the nonacceptance of his intellectual limitations.	

Variable	Subject E-1-3	
Intelligence, Clinical Impression	Greater potential.	
	Pre-test	Post-test
Appearance	Attractive; pigeon-toed.	
Attitudes	Friendly, independent.	
Behavioral Observations, Characteristics	Refused help with lids of paint jars, opening doors etc.; perseveration, no hyperactivity.	Essentially same.
Play Activities	Eager to spend time with Bobo and finger paints—became very aggressive saying to Bobo "I'll kill you"; washed hands between colors; emphasized painting.	Further attack on Bobo— never slowed down by the marked pigeon-toed gait; freer use of colors in painting house and sky; emphasized Bobo.
Motor Patterns, Co-ordination	Pigeon-toed; gross and fine movements normal.	
Draw-a-Person	Compatible with poor form concept.	
Memory Orientation, Time, Space	Disoriented.	
Despert Fables, Phantasies, Dreams, and Wishes		
Speech and Language	Unclear, consonants missing: could "catch on" to his meanings; organic origin; appeared unconcerned.	Improved; expresses ideas more clearly as well as the words themselves with speech training.
Parent Conference (Post)	Mother attended: does not feel parents push him; child not troubled by competition from a younger sibling.	
Parent Evaluation of Child (Post)	Easier to handle; a happier child—used to come home from school tense and irritable, "now he fits at school"; social adaptation hard at home; few playmates his age; speech better; still an eating problem.	
Summary and Comments	Much anxiety is reflected by his aggressive play and is dealt with reasonably well by compulsive defenses; of late, some of this energy seems free of fears and more normal "boy spirits," less internalizing.	

Variable	Subject E-2-9	
Intelligence, Clinical Impression	Retarded.	
	Pre-test	**Post-test**
Appearance	Very neatly dressed; thin obviously handicapped.	Greater air of self-confidence.
Attitudes	Willing; no separation problem (from father); cooperative, polite.	
Behavioral Observations, Characteristics	Played quietly alone, but expected toys to be brought to him by examiner; perseveration; not hyperactive.	Less fearful of falling on stairs; placed examiner in role of teacher to agree with his play.
Play Activities	Pushed trucks back and forth, no story; identified puppet family once more; no interest in Bobo or punching bag.	Could fit Lok-Blocks together now; felt safe enough to pat and then push punching bag.
Motor Patterns, Co-ordination	Under stress: a myoclonic and choreoathetoid repetitive complex (five or six times).	Improved co-ordination complex occurs (three times); learned limb movements.
Draw-a-Person	Co-operative; (a) grotesque figure of boy, (b) trailer, but vaguely depicted.	Stated it was a puppet.
Memory Orientation, Time, Space	Mounted stairs so that both feet were on step, as though uncertain of spatial arrangement, similar to 4-year-old.	
Despert Fables, Phantasies, Dreams, and Wishes	Mumbled words.	Replied "nothing" on wishes.
Speech and Language	Severe speech impairment; a rare sentence.	Speech is more distinct.
Parent Conference (Post)	Father attended: recognizes "We have spoiled him I guess"; he thought too, they have tried to be firm—do not see themselves manipulated although child tries this.	
Parent Evaluation of Child (Post)	Could not say enough about the improvement they see: more independent, less scared, has clear concept of playing as something more than going out and moving around; parents are too optimistic about his catching up.	
Summary and Comments	There is obvious CNS damage along with psychogenic myoclonus under stress (which he can stop at will); autistic-like behavior has lessened but with limited assets and little guidance; he tends to give up and isolate himself.	

Variable	Subject E-1-6	
Intelligence, Clinical Impression	Greater capacity.	
	Pre-test	Post-test
Appearance	Friendly, likeable, eager.	Friendly, likeable, subdued.
Attitudes	Willing, displayed prowess.	Willing; liked school; liked reading best.
Behavioral Observations, Characteristics	Independent; took initiative; distractible; perseverative; no insight for errors of spelling.	Less distractible; perseverative; masturbatory movement.
Play Activities	Liked to punch Bobo; liked to draw; fingered doll furniture but had no people or plot.	Didn't punch Bobo; cars, Schmoo family bumped against table.
Motor Patterns, Co-ordination	Difficulty joining trailer to truck cab.	No change.
Draw-a-Person	Gaunt, grotesque boy "PDDIE" (Eddie his brother).	Insect, boy, self, "Douglas."
Memory Orientation, Time, Space	Disoriented.	Disoriented, except after hearing data on that day.
Despert Fables, Phantasies, Dreams, and Wishes	Noncommittal, changed topic.	
Speech and Language	Immature, intelligible.	Normal.
Parent Conference (Post)	Mother attended: intelligent (mother), co-operative; over-identified with child.	
Parent Evaluation of Child (Post)	Settled down a good bit; some improvement expressing positive or negative feelings; eats better; not as enthusiastic.	
Summary and Comments	Less anxious, better integrated, but perseveration continues and there is anxiety manifested in masturbation movements; speech improved; perceptual difficulties less apparent; currently has much anxiety arising from newly discovered awareness of *how* handicapped he is.	

Variable	Subject E-1-9	
Intelligence, Clinical Impression	Moderate mentally retarded; capacity puzzling.	
	Pre-test	Post-test
Appearance	Friendly, handicapped, co-operative.	No change.
Attitudes	Strongly motivated to learn; carefree, friendly.	Loves school; too friendly.
Behavioral Observations, Characteristics	Sucking noises; humming; infrequent marked perseveration; quite relaxed.	Little perseveration; masturbation.
Play Activities	Appropriate relish punching Bobo and bag; most of time with small train or joining sections of fence.	Immature; bulk of time hit Bobo, also used same train again.
Motor Patterns, Co-ordination	Poor gross; right hand for drawing, left hand for punching.	Fine: poor.
Draw-a-Person	Markedly immature.	"Happy man."
Memory Orientation, Time, Space	Disoriented but named day and month of birthday.	Time sense presents good concept of Schmoo family.
Despert Fables, Phantasies, Dreams, and Wishes		
Speech and Language	Defect definite, moderate.	
Parent Conference (Post)	Father attended; says makes friends; knows meaning of "no"; discussed readiness for sex education; masturbation infrequent.	
Parent Evaluation of Child (Post)	Father has found much improvement; more accepting; fewer tantrums, whining.	
Summary and Comments	Emotional growth occurred; still a mentally retarded picture; masturbation role unclear; co-ordination still poor; over-all good improvement.	

Variable	Subject E-1-5	
Intelligence, Clinical Impression	Average.	
	Pre-test	**Post-test**
Appearance	Drooling.	No change.
Attitudes	Denied neuro-handicap; no respect for property or command; begged not to have interview.	Less lack of respect for property now.
Behavioral Observations, Characteristics	Annoying teasing; provocative; pretended not to hear questions; moderately restless, begged to continue play interview; unpredictable.	Less teasing, less "I'll show you"; accepts limits 25 per cent (before 0 per cent); unpredictable.
Play Activities	Moved doll house furniture; scant attention to Bobo.	Much fanciful talk "owns a subway in New York City"; made overture to finger paint.
Motor Patterns, Co-ordination	Residual of right hemiparesis.	
Draw-a-Person	With urging, "boy whale."	
Memory Orientation, Time, Space	Disoriented.	No change.
Despert Fables, Phantasies, Dreams, and Wishes		
Speech and Language		
Parent Conference (Post)	Mother attended: stressed the value of three years' parent counselling for family.	
Parent Evaluation of Child (Post)	More independent, more mature in most respects; can be trusted with key to apartment.	
Summary and Comments	Has made significant gains in inner control, less need to engage in power maneuvers; definite aggressive drive still present.	

Variable	Subject E-2-10	
Intelligence, Clinical Impression	Not significantly retarded; appeared depressed.	
	Pre-test	Post-test
Appearance	Younger and smaller for age; strangely elongated head leads to old looking face; wears glasses.	As before except no longer needs glasses.
Attitudes	Cheerful, pleasant, friendly, cooperative.	As before.
Behavioral Observations, Characteristics	Fun-loving, curious; accepted limits; moderate perseveration; no hyperactivity; adequate attention span.	More relaxed.
Play Activities	"Oh! I love to draw"; intrigued by wind-up, circling train; little interest in guns, Bobo (but he owns latter); belated interest in finger painting but picture of pleasing color.	Succeeded surprisingly well with difficult puzzle, by using trial and error method.
Motor Patterns, Co-ordination	Bizarre motor pattern tremors —twisting of limbs, pill-rolling, good co-ordination otherwise.	Bizarre pattern absent; residual remains in arms and fingers but only occasionally present; left-handed.
Draw-a-Person	Talented quick action of cartoonist; demanded to take a picture home; cheerful stick man with some filling and with shaded pants.	Captivating little man resembling Herbie in Smitty cartoon, well-proportioned; acceptable for age level
Memory Orientation, Time, Space	Asked the time frequently.	Remembered activities of last hour in playroom.
Despert Fables, Phantasies, Dreams, and Wishes		
Speech and Language	Obvious stutter; trying hard to apply lessons from speech therapy; four times spoke easily without stutter.	Stutter markedly diminished.
Parent Conference (Post)	Mother attended: tries to hide concern over relative lack of academic growth; pleased that he will talk about school activities; we discussed present and future problems relating to adjusting to a younger and precocious brother.	
Parent Evaluation of Child (Post)	Much impressed with emotional and social comparable academic growth; stuttering much less; no apprehension over meeting new people, especially doctors; difficulties in neighborhood play because of size and poor game concepts.	
Summary and Comments	There has been marked ego development, less stutter, and disappearance of bizarre motor tic; predominant difficulties are with language not form; emotional tensions are secondary to adjustment problems arising out of handicaps, and will continue to require guidance.	

Variable	Subject E-2-1	
Intelligence, Clinical Impression	Depressed; capacity far greater.	
	Pre-test	Post-test
Appearance	Good looking, solid, large for age.	"Dressed up" in summer clothes but still remained boyish.
Attitudes	Co-operative, wary, "this is baby stuff."	
Behavioral Observations, Characteristics	Polite attention; slow to engage, perseveration; relaxed in hour; "finger painting is too messy"; in a drawing mood, sang to self and clicked tongue softly, watched adult reaction.	Definitely interested; more relaxed; no perseveration.
Play Activities	Couldn't explain why Bobo didn't bounce back; rejected checkers; slightly interested in wind-up train; made Play-Doh female pressed face down; followed Old Maid rules.	Less compulsivity to finger painting but still used a spoon; decided to "mix them up"; drew a Jap battle.
Motor Patterns, Co-ordination	Normal gait co-ordination.	Now seemed "loose hipped."
Draw-a-Person	"Balloon pumpkin" figure with centipede legs; drew his family people, his is most immature, all figures had long hair.	Drew his pictures with vertical lines but with fun picture of "you"; improved spatial concept.
Memory Orientation, Time, Space	"I just let time go by"; disoriented.	Oriented to date.
Despert Fables, Phantasies, Dreams, and Wishes		
Speech and Language	Normal speech.	
Parent Conference (Post)	Mother attended: Father with him (and her); more—we were both young and needed to learn what to do—now we talk things out; Father said to be "very shy."	
Parent Evaluation of Child (Post)	Is much happier—can accept difficulties, can make a mistake in reading now and it is OK, but lacks confidence; when reading to Father, "comes out with his feelings."	
Summary and Comments	There has been growth and the neurotic picture is now absent, but moderate anxiety (hesitancy) is present; the feeling of acceptance and achievement has still a doubtful permanency; definite reading disability still.	

Variable	Subject E-2-2	
Intelligence, Clinical Impression	Average or better than average.	
	Pre-test	**Post-test**
Appearance	Friendly, smiling, wears Denis leg braces; looks older and studious because of glasses.	
Attitudes	Not overtly bothered by appearance; good sense of humor.	
Behavioral Observations, Characteristics	Preferred conversation; moderate perseveration; no hyperactivity; adequate attention.	More active, more aggressive; clutched at crotch of trousers occasionally.
Play Activities	Hit Bobo with gusto using both hands but no strength; cowboys and Indians plot "goodies or baddies" but placed people without actual fighting.	Threw Bobo upside down, at the window, against examiner.
Motor Patterns, Co-ordination	Right arm spasticity and choreo-athetold movements.	
Draw-a-Person	Little boy with prominent arms, round feet; "everybody has feet."	Two bearded men with backs drawn on reverse side of paper; immature figures but clever idea.
Memory Orientation, Time, Space		
Despert Fables, Phantasies, Dreams, and Wishes	Baby will hop to Mother or Father, probably Mother; elephant's trunk was blown off by a high wind; 1) horse 2) all the soldiers, 3) all the money.	Continues with active phantasy life; same reply to elephant fable; wishes for a horse.
Speech and Language	Marked abnormal, "cluttered."	Much improved.
Parent Conference (Post)	Both parents attended: asking for specifics; undercurrent of doubt; asked to discuss finding of "immaturity," believe they were satisfied.	
Parent Evaluation of Child (Post)	Accepts sleeping in his own room; expresses more complicated thoughts; stuttering more; recently greater manual dexterity, follows Father's effort to build more models with him; diminishing dependence on parent participation in play.	
Summary and Comments	This physically handicapped child with marked speech and reading difficulties has lost some of his immaturity, improved his speech, and increased his use of normal developmental pathways; is more self-reliant but not without anxiety—trouser clutching at the crotch, for example.	

Variable	Subject E-2-6	
Intelligence, Clinical Impression	Low average? greater capacity.	
	Pre-test	Post-test
Appearance	Small, especially face; a lot of hair; grimaces.	No difference.
Attitudes	Wanted constant physical contact; personal basis to all talking, teasing.	More interested in asking than answering.
Behavioral Observations, Characteristics	Markedly hyperactive; perseverative speech; ground her teeth; poked examiner with whatever was handy; tried biting once; kissing and asking to be kissed.	No teeth grinding; no further kissing.
Play Activities	No interest in Bobo; desultory train play; disorganized card games.	Same messy painting, primitive circles.
Motor Patterns, Co-ordination		
Draw-a-Person	Bizarre, called hands "wings"; brief interest.	Declined.
Memory Orientation, Time, Space		
Despert Fables, Phantasies, Dreams, and Wishes	"Not telling, you don't live with me."	
Speech and Language	Constant, rapid talk under pressure, echolalia, some unclear.	Slower, clear.
Parent Conference (Post)	Mother attended: concerned, interested but holding herself under control regarding subject's future.	
Parent Evaluation of Child (Post)	Definitely improved; less restless; "has a ways to go."	
Summary and Comments	A prepsychotic child with anxiety, ambivalence, who has integrated somewhat through help in structuring her relationships at school but is still unable to deal with her instinctual drives on a continuing basis away from the group; is no longer feared, not violent.	

Variable	Subject E-2-4	
Intelligence, Clinical Impression		
	Pre-test	Post-test
Appearance	Solemn, serious, neat, average height.	Unchanged.
Attitudes	Co-operative, conforming; thinks he's dumb.	Continues.
Behavioral Observations, Characteristics	Passive, relaxed during hour; left hand preferred.	
Play Activities	Elected checkers; not timid but didn't "see" moves; could become absorbed in game.	
Motor Patterns, Co-ordination	Average, gross; suggestive delay in fine.	
Draw-a-Person	Small head but otherwise well-proportioned detailed tall man.	Undecided whether man or boy; less mature but well-proportioned.
Memory Orientation, Time, Space	Disoriented to time.	
Despert Fables, Phantasies, Dreams, and Wishes	Baby bird would probably die; elephant has big feet, is heavier; nightmares; wants more friends.	"A million dollars"; college.
Speech and Language	No spontaneity; clear speech.	
Parent Conference (Post)	Mother attended: begrudged him success; denies being told he has problems (has just returned from series of ECT); anxious to know whether we found improvement; Father thinks he is "just stubborn and lazy."	
Parent Evaluation of Child (Post)	Seems a little happier on his good days; "doesn't meet our high standards."	
Summary and Comments	Chronologically anxious, passive child with a psychotic mother and busy father who has begun to express resentments; is slow, more self-confident; has strong desire for Father's approval; perfectionistic; generally improved.	

Variable	Subject C-1-7	
Intelligence, Clinical Impression	Greater capacity than evidenced.	
	Pre-test	Post-test
Appearance	"Round" face, eyes, body,	No change.
Attitudes	Impersonal, co-operative.	Eager, impulsive.
Behavioral Observations, Characteristics	Restless, hyperactive perseverative; rather than move the ranch house from oncoming train said, "can't play with train now, it is destroying my house"; distractible artistic movements.	Still concerned with whether air-conditioner (self) was protected by a screen; less hyperactive.
Play Activities	Poked feebly at Bobo; opened closets, investigated everything; preoccupied with piece of heat lamp equipment; put train away when he saw it would not go in straight line; Play-Doh into bar, placed it away.	Much more assurance when knocking Bobo, even caressing it.
Motor Patterns, Co-ordination	Within normal limits but when tense, a little awkward; right-handed.	More at ease spatially on high places.
Draw-a-Person	Co-operative; of the picture, said in low voice, "I don't know the difference between them."	
Memory Orientation, Time, Space	Stated it was not wintertime "or I would plug in the lamps, not just pretend."	
Despert Fables, Phantasies, Dreams, and Wishes	Stopped listening when asked what baby bird did, became dreamy, said "my parents have not put me wise"; avoided talk of dreams.	
Speech and Language	Used third person often; intervals of dreamy, incoherent language, often suspended.	Could engage in conversation.
Parent Conference (Post)	Mother attended: intelligent, perceptive, impulsive; helpful in analysis of child's symbolic language; writes voluminous reports to teachers and therapist, many detailed observations, helpful.	
Parent Evaluation of Child (Post)	Has settled down a lot, can be trusted to "stay put most of time"; assumes routine chores; decreased demand for parental attention at merest whim; now likes school, so not worried and upset each morning.	
Summary and Comments	Has maintained reality contacts for longer periods before regressing to symbolic verbalization or activity; organic etiology may be debated but whether weight is given to these components, his response to stress has been a schizophrenic one; times are decreasing when this defense necessary. (In therapy.)	

Variable	Subject E-2-8	
Intelligence, Clinical Impression	Average.	
	Pre-test	Post-test
Appearance	Pleasant, shy, handsome.	Less shy.
Attitudes	Curious.	Less unhappy with himself; more trusting.
Behavioral Observations, Characteristics	Moved purposely and deliberately; bothered by mixed colors in same paint jar; aggressive but not hyperactive; acted-out, destructive feelings.	Less aggressiveness.
Play Activities	Gave Bobo "bloody nose"; methodically turned doll house upside down; returned to operate on Bobo; painted "deshorahum" very primitive; interested in watching turning train wheels.	Participated in friendly fashion with patching of Bobo; no interest in doll house.
Motor Patterns, Co-ordination	All movements adequate.	
Draw-a-Person	Refused a person.	Stick figure with big fat arms, no ears, pupils.
Memory Orientation, Time, Space		
Despert Fables, Phantasies, Dreams, and Wishes	"Didn't know about bird's nest." "Trunk gone" off elephant.	Still noncommittal about bird's fate.
Speech and Language	Immature but improved when relaxed.	Still immature; no spontaneity except a question about the train.
Parent Conference (Post)	Mother attended: pleasant and appreciative, but kept conversation on superficial level.	
Parent Evaluation of Child (Post)	"A different boy"; not on fringe of group; gives and takes; more relaxed at home with siblings.	
Summary and Comments	Along with perceptual and speech problems, child had a well-defined neurosis (hysterical and compulsive); he found relief (from castration anxiety) through acceptance and achievement at school; this led to increased self-confidence, greater group participation; more immaturity now than neurosis.	

Variable	Subject C-2-4	
Intelligence, Clinical Impression	Low average; capacity for average.	
	Pre-test	Post-test
Appearance	Wiry, well-developed; shows Latin parentage.	
Attitudes	Willing, co-operative, loathe to go.	Less anxious; cheerful.
Behavioral Observations, Characteristics	Hit Bobo with gusto, unaware of which hand he preferred; bothered by poor puzzle performance, especially lack of success on first attempt; no hyperactivity; short attention span; no perseveration.	Excited but controlled; amenable to suggestions; eyes lit up when school mentioned.
Play Activities	Stuck to rules of card game but got lost in each step; opened Play-Doh tin, but soon lost interest; took several splotches of colors at one time for finger painting, instead of the usual one at a time.	"Let himself go" in hitting Boxer and shooting clay bullets.
Motor Patterns, Co-ordination	Normal gait; good muscular strength; some clumsy fine movements with playing cards; awkward, if hitting Bobo; graceful, if drawing.	Better over-all co-ordination.
Draw-a-Person	Enjoyed this; surrounded the two stick figures (boys) with grass, blue clouds and buzzards which father would kill; somber colors.	Drew his 14-year-old sister —all details, good pictures.
Memory Orientation, Time, Space	Didn't know birth date, nor care.	
Despert Fables, Phantasies, Dreams, and Wishes	Bird would fly away; elephant was different because exchanged for tiger.	
Speech and Language	Moderate stutter.	More spontaneous, even; quite talkative; some stutter but less.
Parent Conference (Post)	Father attended: has 7 children; seemed relaxed, sensible; rotates three sons on archery dates per weekend; feels his wife is hard on son, not always his fault, "who is she to criticize his speech—hers is not right—or about spelling."	
Parent Evaluation of Child (Post)	"Has come along"; greater self-confidence, but added "truthfully don't see him often enough to notice any real difference."	
Summary and Comments	Motor inco-ordination; immature speech; mental retardation, short attention span have been modified; greater self-confidence is related to decreased anxiety and school achievement; source of present anxiety is partly rejecting home situation; cannot establish (acceptable) identity.	

Variable	Subject C-2-3	
Intelligence, Clinical Impression	Seems bright and alert.	
	Pre-test	**Post-test**
Appearance	Small for age; dark eyes and long lashes; thin.	Filled out.
Attitudes	Co-operative, self-examining: "people say I'm tricky. I guess I am but don't mean to hurt anybody"; cocky.	Happy; no longer needs to brag about "socking another boy."
Behavioral Observations, Characteristics	Much more talk than play; calmed down after "making as much noise as I wish"; much self-awareness and concern for others; not hyperactive.	Entered quickly, happily; perseverated on shooting doll house family until examiner pointed to the Boxer.
Play Activities	Quickly took gun and shot all the people in doll house; turned furniture upside down; all family members hit each other except child hitting adult; modeled a corral fence and then pounded away with gun butt for ten minutes.	Shot people in house until turned toward Boxer.
Motor Patterns, Co-ordination	Excellent co-ordination but knocked toes against heel of other shoe.	Right side better co-ordinated.
Draw-a-Person		Three primitives—one with each hand and one with both (latter best); "I don't know the difference between women and boys."
Memory Orientation, Time, Space	Disoriented for time.	
Despert Fables, Phantasies, Dreams, and Wishes	Wishes: (1) horses (2) six guns (3) new family at times; occasional nightmare.	(1) horse (2) real guns (3) wants policeman to OK shooting BB gun anywhere.
Speech and Language	Not remarkable.	
Parent Conference (Post)	Mother attended: a concerned, interested intelligent parent who wanted to discuss the present and future problems developing between siblings where younger brother is precocious; concerned about need to give sex facts (Father wants her to).	
Parent Evaluation of Child (Post)	"Has matured tremendously since" a new drug (unknown) was discontinued; accepts responsibility of A.M. routine without "buckling under"; better liked by group because he has concept of the games and doesn't muddle up the playing.	
Summary and Comments	A child with a convulsive disorder who has begun to develop inner controls; still reflects much anxiety related to seizures, perceptual problems and his small size; realistic threats posed by precocious younger brother; may be well advised to have psychotherapy as adjunctive support.	

Variable	Subject C-2-7	
Intelligence, Clinical Impression	Alert, intelligent.	
	Pre-test	Post-test
Appearance	Ultra-serious; big blue eyes peer out of large-framed glasses; earnest manner; scar between eyebrow and nose.	Continues to be a loveable Mr. Funny Face.
Attitudes	Willing to draw; wistful.	Same.
Behavioral Observations, Characteristics	Stood with feet twisted about one another, leaning against examiner's chair or desk; talked with adult inflections, rolling back and forth on his heels; did not back away from examiner.	Now went back and forth in front of examiner occasionally, but stood still most of the time, hands in pocket.
Play Activities	Noticeably disinterested in doll house, clay, toys; stories told revealed intensity of violently aggressive feelings.	Spent much time knocking the Boxer about, but still showed no interest in other toys, guns.
Motor Patterns, Co-ordination	Seemed normal.	
Draw-a-Person	Willing to draw his friend; one large ear partly painted green.	Drew a very small stick figure (boy); made a cat three times larger; drew a little larger person not a stick person.
Memory Orientation, Time, Space	Oriented to day and birth date.	
Despert Fables, Phantasies, Dreams, and Wishes	Compulsive need to make up ego-building stories, 99 per cent concerned violence; elephant's tail grew trunk in back too; afraid of alligator.	No longer needs to tell tall tales to gain status, identity.
Speech and Language	Profuse, outpourings adult inflections; slight British accent remains.	More realistic conversation.
Parent Conference (Post)	Mother and stepfather attended: both English; stepfather quiet and able to look realistically at problems; Mother now agrees Special Education is right school; now complained about U.S. schools last fall.	
Parent Evaluation of Child (Post)	Is socially better, but friendships "peter out if he goes to a child's home—wonder what parents are telling their children"; believes eye operation, several house moves, plus absent father contribute to anxiety.	
Summary and Comments	A clearly disturbed child whose intense feelings and rich phantasy life suggested a psychosis, but who was still well integrated; has gained enough security and feeling of adequacy to drop much of his compensatory story-telling and phantasy life.	

Variable	Subject C-1-4	
Intelligence, Clinical Impression	Decreased functioning.	
	Pre-test	Post-test
Appearance	Long, narrow head; marked drooling which he brushed away.	Same.
Attitudes	Quiet; gentle, willing; needed permission.	Same.
Behavioral Observations, Characteristics	Neat, methodical; planned ahead on play activities; didn't believe rules about Play-Doh applied to him too; tended to ignore, avoid examiner's conversation, especially regarding home relationships; perseverated.	Essentially same.
Play Activities	Painted cheerful rainbows; turned to trucks and then to cowboys and Indians; made permanent balls of Play-Doh, fascinated with it, mouthing it; uncertain toward end; no interest in going.	Began again by drawing; tired of it and then also of Play-Doh; didn't grasp idea of forms of different sizes; "fixed up" doll house, placing mother and little girl within.
Motor Patterns, Co-ordination	Slightly awkward gait.	Still present.
Draw-a-Person	Rapidly drew boy and flower of equal size—only slightly immature.	Split-level house, colorful.
Memory Orientation, Time, Space	Disoriented.	
Despert Fables, Phantasies, Dreams, and Wishes	Dreams about flowers, cowboys, bad animals (crocodiles).	
Speech and Language	Immature; sentences often were fragmentary and hard to understand.	Still hard to understand.
Parent Conference (Post)	Mother and Father attended: both quiet; Mother took lead; mindful of son's limitations; co-operative but feared questions as though to hear prognosis was even poorer.	
Parent Evaluation of Child (Post)	Much more independent; plays away from home but sets own limits; no wandering; no longer cries when left alone with strangers; worry about speech preventing rapport; has made effort now to seek peers.	
Summary and Comments	He fell apart when not able to use compulsive routines to handle anxiety derived from mental retardation, poor speech, immaturity, autistic-like modes now replaced by desire to communicate; considerable social and emotional growth.	

Variable	Subject C-1-3	
Intelligence, Clinical. Impression	Potentially average or above average.	
	Pre-test	Post-test
Appearance Attitudes	Smiling; alert; friendly.	No change.
Behavioral Observations, Characteristics	Accepted suggestions; tendency to give up; could discuss rules of checkers, reach a compromise without sulking.	No longer gave up; more aggressive.
Play Activities	Immediately seized trucks, cowboys, Indians, but merely lined them up—no plot; expert hitting at Bobo; suggested "Go Fish," knew correct rules; played checkers; perseveration tendency.	Spent most of the time hitting Boxer, then knocked down wooden figures with gun and clay bullets.
Motor Patterns, Co-ordination	Grand right hand uppercut; quite good co-ordination.	
Draw-a-Person	Drew stick woman, but complex transparent house.	Could not be diverted to drawing.
Memory Orientation, Time, Space		
Despert Fables, Phantasies, Dreams, and Wishes	"Gee, I don't know" response to fables; apprehensive; finally said baby bird went to Mother's tree; elephant tusk broken off; denied dreams.	
Speech and Language	Noticeable defect but intelligible; child unconcerned.	No significant change.
Parent Conference (Post)	Mother attended; wishes he read like two younger sisters (Father doesn't read much) but does not push him; Mother is somewhat afraid of authority persons.	
Parent Evaluation of Child (Post)	More responsible—and no fussing about baby sitting; cleaned room; doesn't sulk when his baseball team loses; has always played well with peers.	
Summary and Comments	Marked speech difficulties; perceptual problems have created anxieties, especially in learning areas, but ego rather well preserved; has improved speech and social ease; awkward gait but good arm co-ordination.	

400

Variable	Subject C-1-10	
Intelligence, Clinical Impression	Retarded.	
	Pre-test	**Post-test**
Appearance	Stocky, bullethead, big.	Same.
Attitudes	Anxious; temper tantrum; interested in spite of himself.	Same.
Behavioral Observations, Characteristics	Mounting resistance, increased crying and wish to return to his mother; soon played weepily and unconcernedly with a train; tantrum controlled by fear of spanking by father that night.	Separation anxiety continued.
Play Activities	Sized up principle of the switch to a train, asked an appropriate question about why it always went in a circle; hit Bobo until he remembered his mother.	Same ambivalence about enjoying himself away from mother; quickly saw relationship of Schmoo family.
Motor Patterns, Co-ordination	Normal gross co-ordination.	
Draw-a-Person	"I'll draw something and then that's all"—weeping drew boy; started to throw pencil and then replaced it carefully.	Drew, standing in the doorway, grotesque, baldheaded man with wings for arms, and detailed belt and buckle.
Memory Orientation, Time, Space	Disoriented.	
Despert Fables, Phantasies, Dreams, and Wishes	Has nightmares, sometimes afraid.	
Speech and Language	Clear.	
Parent Conference (Post)	Mother and Father attended: Mother feels she has overprotected because she is lonely and fearful; misses hometown support which she had for two older girls; doesn't get out much; will spend summer with cousins again in country.	
Parent Evaluation of Child (Post)	Much improved; more independent; reminds them his teacher said he should do more himself; plays with other children now; "he doesn't cry half as much now"; cries when stress put on routine and departure from it.	
Summary and Comments	This markedly dependent, immature child has a minimum of perceptual problems; a certain amount of weaning has occurred but he remains anxiety-ridden at separation and in need of much reassurance.	

Variable	Subject C-1-2	
Intelligence, Clinical Impression	Alert, average to above average.	
	Pre-test	**Post-test**
Appearance	Asthenic, well-built, dark, neat, small.	Same.
Attitudes	Friendly, outgoing, says his teacher thinks he is poorest in class—he does not.	More relaxed; no more self deprecation.
Behavioral Observations, Characteristics	Not hyperactive; organized but not compulsive play.	Essentially same.
Play Activities	Cowboys and Indians—originality in placement of men; lack of realism as to danger to a lone Indian on roof.	Stuck with Lok-Blocks until he completed a house.
Motor Patterns, Co-ordination	Good.	
Draw-a-Person	Boy with catcher's mitt is reaching for a ball—plus tall orange tree.	"We've been practicing at school"; small, thin smiling boy.
Memory Orientation, Time, Space	Not interested; mother keeps a calendar.	
Despert Fables, Phantasies, Dreams, and Wishes	"If a baby bird, it goes to mother; if older, goes to own tree; goes to both mother and father when worried."	
Speech and Language	Muddled, immature, alternated with clarity.	Clear.
Parent Conference (Post)	Mother attended: wonders "now and then" whether being special is good for him but "everyone knows he needs to build up his self-confidence"; sandwiched in between two sisters who are avid readers and honor students.	
Parent Evaluation of Child (Post)	"No doubt his school experience has been profitable"; Mother has five children and seems to have some understanding of needs; impresses as hoping he will grow up without too much attention from family, conserving her energies.	
Summary and Comments	Along with an apparently specific reading disability, there is an immature emotional pattern which has been modified, especially in speech area; but child is held back by family attitudes, as though they asked to slow down what they admit is an inevitable "growing up" process.	

Variable	Subject C-1-6	
Intelligence, Clinical Impression	Even allowing for expressive aphasia, appeared retarded.	
	Pre-test	**Post-test**
Appearance	Stocky, pleasant, babyfaced, blond.	"Put on a serious face to act like a grown up and behave myself."
Attitudes	Friendly, willing.	Same.
Behavioral Observations, Characteristics	Somewhat short attention span; wanted to take home a small car; perseveration?	Perseveration evident; marked dependency needs.
Play Activities	Ten-minute story about cowboys, Indians, using puppets; destroyed the examiner both as witch, as Indian; limited plot; longest time spent with several guns; copied lunging and diving of prize fighters, but punches were wild at Bobo.	No interest in anything but guns; shot down a man first; and then whole families; "who shall I get rid of now"? Examiner asked why —"They are too busy."
Motor Patterns, Co-ordination	Fair as seen in hitting Bobo.	
Draw-a-Person	Liked to draw boy-hit-Bobo; resembled beetles.	
Memory Orientation, Time, Space	Disoriented.	
Deepest Fables, Phantasies, Dreams, and Wishes	Confused when asked three wishes; spoke gibberish out of anxiety.	
Speech and Language	Motor aphasia; has been in therapy and is improving; made real effort and only occasionally was unintelligible.	
Parent Conference (Post)	Mother attended (brought baby and 3-year-old); was relaxed, intelligent, concerned; does feel that he would like more of Father's time and attention.	
Parent Evaluation of Child (Post)	"More confidence"; no longer fears dogs; feels this is explained by better speech; also sees him as asking questions he can answer to satisfy dependent needs.	
Summary and Comments	While there has been a gain in independent behavior, dependency is still marked; aggressive drives secondary to expressive aphasia are intensified by advent of new baby; needs more feeling of belonging and sense of accomplishment; would also diminish rhetorical questioning.	

Variable	Subject C-2-2	
Intelligence, Clinical Impression	Average if not potentially superior.	
	Pre-test	**Post-test**
Appearance	Neat, pleasant, elfin quality.	
Attitudes	Friendly, irrepressible.	
Behavioral Observations, Characteristics	Mischievous, attempted to tell or play jokes, continually tested limits; genuine, spontaneous remarks; spontaneously put toys away; hyperactive.	Same boundless energy difficult to follow directions; would not take "no" for an answer until he saw it was really meant.
Play Activities	Joined the fence sections easily; telling phantasy, played card games; hit Bobo and punching bags but preferred the popgun.	Talked as he played mostly with Bobo; drew a fort with Nazi guns and told a story.
Motor Patterns, Co-ordination	Gross and fine movements good; shuffled cards like an expert.	Good right-hand punch.
Draw-a-Person	"I will draw you—" (large rabbit); second was "here's you in your underwear out in the wetting (cloudburst outside)."	Started same way, but diverted, drew a boy.
Memory Orientation, Time, Space	Knew his birth month. Guessed at year.	
Despert Fables, Phantasies, Dreams, and Wishes	Wants: (1) to fly like Superman, (2) all the magic in the world, (3) jet plane.	
Speech and Language	In speech Rx for noticeable defect, but always understood.	Talked rapidly with adequate vocabulary.
Parent Conference (Post)	Mother attended: finds it hard herself to get anything done she should do; cannot discipline son.	
Parent Evaluation of Child (Post)	Has not seen "too much change"—you have to sit on him still—but he gets along within a larger group now; is apt to be critical and unforgiving of the trouble caused by himself.	
Summary and Comments	While there continues to be difficulty with impulse control, there is a healthy reaching out; the behavior patterns are reinforced unfavorably.	

Variable	Subject C-2-9	
Intelligence, Clinical Impression	Definitely retarded.	
	Pre-test	**Post-test**
Appearance	Neat, pleasant.	
Attitudes	Friendly, co-operative, shy.	Same quiet.
Behavioral Observations, Characteristics	Needed guidance and permission to involve himself.	Same quiet, passive behavior, perhaps less at ease.
Play Activities	Tentative punches at Bobo became stronger; drew a star.	Punched Bobo but it was starting to leak air; wrote name in a pleased fashion, one undetected error.
Motor Patterns, Co-ordination	Straight-legged gait big and important organic sign? Tremor of right arm unrelated to activity, time of day, etc.	
Draw-a-Person		Quite a primitive boy (ears and arms missing); much tension.
Memory Orientation, Time, Space	Knew age, birthday is "just half past"; disoriented to time.	
Despert Fables, Phantasies, Dreams, and Wishes	The baby bird went to another tree; there was another baby with the elephant; many dreams of bears.	Wishes: toys, cars, trucks.
Speech and Language	No spontaneity.	Continues passive; has slight lisp.
Parent Conference (Post)	Mother attended: feels guilty about neglecting son for foster children, also little time with son alone; more concerned than she realizes with his academic progress.	
Parent Evaluation of Child (Post)	Gets along better with peers, more independent, "can dress himself, etc."; goes off by himself rather than try to get his turn with his Mother; "has the best memory of any child"; "sensitive and appreciative of nature."	
Summary and Comments	He appears to have made academic progress, but remains essentially passive and ill-equipped to compete for his emotional needs within a large family; mental retardation is a factor here too.	

Variable	Subject E-1-7	
Intelligence, Clinical Impression	Depressed.	
	Pre-test	**Post-test**
Appearance	Well-developed; thick glasses; neatly dressed.	No change.
Attitudes	Willing, quiet, relaxed, curious.	Friendly, reached up with his hand for the examiner on leaving his mother.
Behavioral Observations, Characteristics	Free arm movement when painting; seemed to be enjoying himself; preferred larger chair.	Zipped his trouser fly a moderate amount throughout the hour.
Play Activities	Most anxious to paint; utilized many colors; played cowboys and Indians, talk to self but unintelligible; no interest in Bobo, bag, or clay.	Cowboys, Indians; perseverated with attaching fence sections with encouragement.
Motor Patterns, Co-ordination	Normal gait and manner; co-ordination adequate.	
Draw-a-Person	Spidery person (same as 1955).	Refused to draw person but chose a purple train, windows appropriately placed.
Memory Orientation, Time, Space	Gave month only correctly.	
Despert Fables, Phantasies, Dreams, and Wishes	Tried to make clear his wishes but mumbled.	
Speech and Language	Severe speech defect articulatory and omissions; persisted in trying to talk; considered organic.	Marked improvement but no spontaneity yet.
Parent Conference (Post)	Mother attended: somewhat older; sees difficulties and active sibling competition with 7-year-old sister at verbal level; less flattering picture emerged at end of interview.	
Parent Evaluation of Child (Post)	"I can't tell you all the things"—greatest gains in speech—but "is more certain of himself"; fewer tears and temper tantrums (rare); accepts correction and suggestion—"no longer in a shell"—but also he is "still a little nervous."	
Summary and Comments	History of abnormal EEG along with speech problem—indicates organic problem with secondary anxiety and immaturity; doggedly works at speech, with positive results—while greater self-certainty is present; child is acutely aware of his "differentness."	

Variable	Subject C-2-5	
Intelligence, Clinical Impression	Definite retardation but felt to have a higher capacity.	
	Pre-test	**Post-test**
Appearance	Tow-haired, neat, younger than stated age, beatific smile.	Usual smiling self.
Attitudes	Friendly, quiet.	
Behavioral Observations, Characteristics	Constantly sought approval; good concept of how toys worked; neither overly neat or messy in painting; proud of drawing.	Tried to show he was in control of Bobo at least.
Play Activities	Immediately drawn to Bobo; awkward; put fence sections together; persisted in trying to have all pieces upright at once; laughed at failures; enjoyed wind-up train going in circle.	Spent most of time with Bobo, sitting on him; shot Bobo "in his bottom" with B-B gun; stopped circular train with gun butt.
Motor Patterns, Co-ordination	Left-handed; awkward; in pokes at Bobo used right hand only.	
Draw-a-Person	Drew small house "nicer that way"; person was grotesque because distorted in size and position.	Person immature, disproportionate but larger; hesitated before saying boy.
Memory Orientation, Time, Space		
Despert Fables, Phantasies, Dreams, and Wishes		After much thought and persuasion wished for a pony.
Speech and Language	Began to speak in sentences, no stuttering today.	Speech muddled often by too broad and constant smiling; no spontaneity.
Parent Conference (Post)	Foster Mother attended; recognizes the limitations of this child (and his twin); has good picture of their needs and is warm, accepting.	
Parent Evaluation of Child (Post)	"Much better in every respect"; listens, understands better; less fidgety; rarely stutters now; participates now in neighborhood games, no longer on fringe.	
Summary and Comments	This child, known two years ago had made marked social and language progress before this study; he has continued to gain skills and self-esteem (he is the more alert of the twins) much is due foster home; awkwardness and immature speech still evident.	

Variable	Subject C-2-1	
Intelligence, Clinical Impression	Bright	
	Pre-test	Post-test
Appearance	Thin, wiry, rabbity facial grimacing.	No tics.
Attitudes	Quiet, evasive at times.	
Behavioral Observations, Characteristics	Perseverated? or concentrated on Bobo; uninterested in clay, painting, etc.	Reunion atmosphere; hid in the cupboard briefly playful this time; more controlled approach to finger painting, shooting; accepted suggestions readily.
Play Activities	Liked the planes; drew planes with bombs and told war stories; declined all other ideas.	Much hitting of Bobo; also of punching bag (alternate blows); tried gun, painting.
Motor Patterns, Co-ordination	Adequate; right-handed.	Better co-ordination.
Draw-a-Person	Drew airplanes but refused to do a person, "I can't."	
Memory Orientation, Time, Space	Oriented to all modalities.	
Despert Fables, Phantasies, Dreams, and Wishes		
Speech and Language	Slight lisp.	More spontaneity.
Parent Conference (Post)	Mother attended: still worried and guilty about mistake she made; no longer in treatment but husband is resentful of "spoiling" child; is perfectionist, uninterested.	
Parent Evaluation of Child (Post)	More independent, more realistic, but still hyperactive and fussy eater.	
Summary and Comments	While psychotherapy was stopped because of several factors, especially father's resistance, there has been a lessening of overt anxiety; but denial is still used to cope with family realities and he will not develop his potential until his parents use help.	

Variable	Subject C-2-8	
Intelligence, Clinical Impression	Moderate retardation.	
	Pre-test	**Post-test**
Appearance	Large for age, neat.	
Attitudes	Is aware of intellectual limits but not overly concerned; friendly, warm.	
Behavioral Observations, Characteristics	Took every chance to "show off" his learning but thereby revealed much difficulty; short attention span; oblivious to consequences of his actions.	Squeally laughter; less distractible.
Play Activities	Started to draw but turned to the wind-up train and then quickly to guns, running trains head on; much satisfaction punching Bobo.	Much time with popgun; shifted to more organized play but still only with himself; was a train robber.
Motor Patterns, Co-ordination	Right-handed; adequate co-ordination.	
Draw-a-Person	Never did finish his drawing, distracted to toys.	Happy-go-lucky stick figure who is smoking called "Dad."
Memory Orientation, Time, Space	Knew birth date and today's date.	Continues.
Despert Fables, Phantasies, Dreams, and Wishes	Worried whether dreams would come true.	Wishes: 1) croquet set, 2) model stage coach, 3) policeman's suit.
Speech and Language	Irrelevant answers; stream of consciousness but not psychotic proportions or quality; has slight lisp.	Slight lisp present, especially if excited; continued flow of conversation.
Parent Conference (Post)	Mother attended: felt they and past school had reminded him of his bad habits rather than praising his good ones; praised the teacher's guidance; neurologist is tapering off anticonvulsant drugs.	
Parent Evaluation of Child (Post)	"Everywhere I look, he has improved"; has learned to respect people of all ages.	
Summary and Comments	This child has been seizure-free but is on medication; he has had to deal with anxiety rising from handicaps plus family inconsistencies; these appear to be decreasing, and with it, aggressivity; immaturity is prominent quality—were seizures primarily psychogenic?	

Variable	Subject C-2-10	
Intelligence, Clinical Impression	Depressed functioning.	
	Pre-test	**Post-test**
Appearance	Freckled faced, sandy-haired, wiry.	
Attitudes	Groaned at going to playroom, loathed to stop.	Usual friendly self; more co-operative.
Behavioral Observations, Characteristics	Truly hyperactive in waiting room with his mother; sat still for the entire hour going from clay to crayon; very little effective coloring.	Not distractible but active so as not to waste time; more spontaneous in movements.
Play Activities	Direct wish to use Play-Doh, was followed by action—enthusiastic swinging at Bobo—only after brought to his attention (i.e. after permission received); rolled cars at each other to have large crash.	Marked activity, good workout to Boxer and punch bag.
Motor Patterns, Co-ordination		
Draw-a-Person		Drew a house, all but one window (9) done with correct cross bars, other shows perceptual difficulty.
Memory Orientation, Time, Space		
Despert Fables, Phantasies, Dreams, and Wishes	Baby bird would stay in tree without the nest; described all but elephant's nose or trunk, but the elephant was torn up by another boy.	Wouldn't commit himself to fables.
Speech and Language	Fast and high-pitched, careless speech.	
Parent Conference (Post)	Mother attended: tall, overbearing; calls herself "high strung," stoic; over-expectation; a certain detachment present—atmosphere of home not given—wondered why moved if doing so well—explanation seemed OK.	
Parent Evaluation of Child (Post)	Didn't think there had been much improvement at home; think summer camp helped him.	
Summary and Comments	He appears to have gained self-confidence, but still lacks insight into learning difficulties (see Mother's lack); seizures only at home since 3; potential intellectual functioning may be higher, but he is very anxious about failing his family's standards; tension flows out through motor activity.	

Variable	Subject E-2-5	
Intelligence, Clinical Impression		
	Pre-test	Post-test
Appearance	Large size, smiling.	
Attitudes	Noncommittal co-operative; *not* showing resistance.	
Behavioral Observations, Characteristics	Superficial relationship because of poor speech; quickly grasped concept of train switch; low frustration tolerance; restless toward the end.	
Play Activities	Spent most of the time with truck and self-winding train; hit Bobo with fair interest.	
Motor Patterns, Co-ordination	Right-handed, normal fine co-ordination.	
Draw-a-Person	A primitive house, which revealed difficulties with form— "I can't draw a person."	
Memory Orientation, Time, Space	Birth date and present date unknown.	
Despert Fables, Phantasies, Dreams, and Wishes	Wishes: "My sister took them" (*not* confusing dishes and wishes); denied troubles; "didn't know" to fables.	
Speech and Language	Structure and concepts were poorly developed.	
Parent Conference (Post)		
Parent Evaluation of Child (Post)		
Summary and Comments	Mother's history of ten foster homes prior to 16 years of age sets the stage for the very unstable home environment in which this child and his handicaps must try to develop; he is confused, immature, unrelated to most people and using denial and aggression as defenses.	

Variable	Subject C-2-6	
Intelligence, Clinical Impression	Below average.	
	Pre-test	**Post-test**
Appearance	Sturdy, heavy, large-boned.	
Attitudes	Friendly, cheerful, co-operative.	
Behavioral Observations, Characteristics	Opened heavy doors; Compulsive about finger painting, wanted to keep painting, but compromised; issued order-like requests; curious; enjoyed herself; not hyperactive.	Couldn't get concept of Schmoo family; didn't want to try certain answers, relying on being cute and coy; transient stubbornness and sulking.
Play Activities	Attracted briefly to Bobo; clay, finger painting; straightened disorderly doll house with appropriate furniture, but she put a large sofa across the front entrance and placed objects in line without imagination.	Less fuss about parting with drawing, squeezed Play-Doh with childish patting.
Motor Patterns, Co-ordination	Hit with better than expected co-ordination.	Clumsy with toys.
Draw-a-Person	Preferred finger-paint designs.	Disproportioned horse.
Memory Orientation, Time, Space	Did not answer.	
Despert Fables, Phantasies, Dreams, and Wishes	Could grasp meaning of bird's nest fable, but not recognize problem facing the baby bird.	
Speech and Language	Extremely immature; few words, but could make herself understood.	Fuller replies but still no spontaneous speech—using nonverbal communications.
Parent Conference (Post)	Mother attended: thinks she may be "too close to the scene."	
Parent Evaluation of Child (Post)	Not as much progress this year as last year, but steady pace; has learned more about home duties—except can do own pigtails; with improved speech plays better with peers —not as hurt by friends' remarks; usual big sister ambivalence.	
Summary and Comments	An essentially nonverbal child whose immature speech has improved and with it her social relationships, but who relies heavily on cuteness and coyness to maintain her big sister family position; she uses compulsive defenses and some aggression (demanding) to handle her moderate anxieties.	

Variable	Subject C-1-9	
Intelligence, Clinical Impression	Borderline.	
	Pre-test	Post-test
Appearance	Blond, nice-looking, good build.	Same.
Attitudes	Willing, friendly.	Same.
Behavioral Observations, Characteristics	Accepted suggestions easily; some perseveration; timidity in hitting Bobo; very alert to adult approval.	Usual talkative self; engrossed in family play; hitched up trousers periodically in a way suggesting masturbatory equivalent.
Play Activities	Immediately changed the doll house "all around," had MD's office downstairs (like own MD's); stereotyped play; no humans and furniture fitted together as jigsaw; absorbed in joining fence.	"Straightened things up a bit"; no longer stereotyped; furniture arranged realistically; people present and house called "mine"; hit Bobo, pushing like most girls, from shoulder girdle; triggered.
Motor Patterns, Co-ordination	Right-handed.	
Draw-a-Person	Had a fine time but very distorted limbs; drew both boy and girl; girl's hair twice as long; boy had hat.	
Memory Orientation, Time, Space	Disoriented.	
Despert Fables, Phantasies, Dreams, and Wishes		
Speech and Language	Clear.	
Parent Conference (Post)	Mother attended: feels the teacher's trips invaluable; given him a perspective and helped with fear of new places and things; wonders whether he is just lazy; as a busy mother she has closed her eyes to the amount of play with sister; seems overwhelmed with five children.	
Parent Evaluation of Child (Post)	"Developed in lots of ways"; doesn't cry as often over new situations; prefers to play dolls with 3-year-old sister than go out with 7-year-old brother and play with other boys; sleeps better but is still a light sleeper; "trigger happy" sounded right to this mother.	
Summary and Comments	By history idiopathic epilepsy but not needing medication; while anxiety secondary to organic limitation is present, the emotional problems are intensified and have earmarkings of a developing character disorder; he withdraws from peer groups, regressively playing house, families, etc., with sister.	

ing, the clinical impressions appear to correlate with more objective data.

Improvement	Old	New
3+	8	3
2+	7	10
1+	4	7

Would the old students have made greater strides this year in any type of special school setting? Or was their personality more in readiness for this particular methodology? Does the appearance in the two-plus category of 10 (50 per cent) new, opposed to 7 (37 per cent) old, children suggest that a project of this type can bring about personality integration at a faster rate; or is this a reflection of one kind of growth curve which is characterized by a sharp initial rise and a gradual leveling off? While there is wide variation in growth rates, nevertheless it is noteworthy that in all children there was social growth just as there was a measure of academic growth. Such was not the case in the areas of physical and emotional development where change was much less evident and more difficult to assess.

There was also a relation between parent attitudes toward, expectations for, and the evaluation of the child and his rate of emotional growth. Parents (13 known) who evidenced adjustment difficulties or neuroses had children who made the least progress in ego-identification and integration (object relationships and impulse control). Again, closer study may confirm the impression that some parents must see improvement effected in their child away from home before they can modify their own attitudes and thereby accelerate their child's learning processes.

Another observation is that the clinical level of anxiety appears unrelated to the degree of achievement in learning (when the subjectively arrived at level of anxiety is compared with the educational achievement grade level gain). Such an observation is a worthy reminder that anxiety in itself is only a symptom and that its origin must be understood. As the origin(s) becomes clear, one will have to determine the role of anxiety in the learning experience.

On the basis of the data made available by the current study, one may say that there appears to be no obvious correlation between particular attitudes or personality structures in teacher, child, or parent which explains the academic progress; for the gain in achievement levels among the four classes was not significantly different, statistically.

It cannot be stated too strongly that further study of over-all medical and educational data and their inter-relation is indicated, both for their educational implications and for their value to the diagnostic and therapeutic efforts of the psychiatric discipline.

REFERENCES

1. AARONSON, B. S. "The Porteus Mazes and Bender-Gestalt Recall," *Journal of Clinical Psychology*, XIII (1957), 186–87.
2. AMMONS, R. B., ARNOLD, P. R., and HERRMANN, R. S. "The Full-Range Picture Vocabulary Test: IV. Results For a White School Population," *Journal of Clinical Psychology*, VI (1950), 164–69.
3. AMMONS, R. B., and HOLMES, J. C. "The Full-Range Picture Vocabulary Test: III. Results For a Preschool-Age Population," *Child Development*, XX (1949), 5–14.
4. AMMONS, R. B., and HUTH, R. W. "The Full-Range Picture Vocabulary Test: I. Preliminary Scale," *Journal of Psychology*, XXVIII (1949), 51–64.
5. AMMONS, R. B., and MANAHAN, N. "The Full-Range Picture Vocabulary Test: VI. Results For a Rural Population," *Journal of Educational Research*, XLIV (1950), 14–21.
6. AMMONS, R. B., and RACHIELE, L. D. "The Full-Range Picture Vocabulary Test: II. Selection of Items For Final Scales," *Educational and Psychological Measurement*, X (1950), 307–19.
7. BAKWIN, H. "Cerebral Damage and Behavior Disorders in Children," *Journal of Pediatrics*, XXXIV (1949), 371–83.
8. BAROFF, G. S. "Bender-Gestalt Visuo-Motor Function in Mental Deficiency," *American Journal of Mental Deficiency*, LXI (1957), 753–60.
9. BECK, H. S., and LAM, R. L. "Use of the WISC in Predicting Organicity," *Journal of Clinical Psychology*, XI (1955), 154–58.
10. BENDER, L. "Organic Brain Conditions Producing Behavior Disturbances," in *Modern Trends In Psychiatry*. Edited by LEWIS, N. D. C., and PACELLA, B. L. New York: International Universities Press, 1945.
11. BENDER, L. "Psychological Problems of Children With Organic Brain Disease," *American Journal of Orthopsychiatry*, XIX (1945), 404–15.
12. BENDER, L. *Psychopathology of Children With Organic Brain Disorders*. Springfield, Illinois: Charles C. Thomas, 1956.
13. BENDER, L. "The Goodenough Test in Chronic Encephalitis," *Journal of Nervous and Mental Disease*, XCI (1940), 277–86.
14. BENDER, L. *Visual Motor Gestalt Test and Its Clinical Use*. Research Monograph No. 3. New York: American Orthopsychiatric Association, 1952.
15. BENTON, A. L. "A Multiple Choice Type of the Visual Retention Test," *Archives of Neurology and Psychiatry*, LXIV (1950), 699–707.
16. BENTON, A. L. "A Visual Retention Test for Clinical Use," *Archives of Neurology and Psychiatry*, LIV (1945), 212–16.

17. BENTON, A. L., and COLLINS, N. T. "Visual Retention Test Performance in Children," *Archives of Neurology and Psychiatry,* LXII (1949), 610–17.
18. BIJOU, S. W., and WERNER, H. "Language Analysis in Brain Injured and Non-Brain Injured Children," *Journal of Genetic Psychology,* LXVI (1945), 239–54.
19. BLAU, A. "Mental Changes Following Head Trauma in Children," *Archives of Neurology and Psychiatry,* XXXV (1936), 723–69.
20. BYERS, R. K., and LORD, M. E. "Late Effects of Lead Poisoning on Mental Development," *American Journal of Diseases of Children,* LXVI (1943), 471–94.
21. CORNELL, M. L., and COXE, W. W. *The Cornell-Coxe Performance Ability Scale Examination Manual.* Yonkers-on-Hudson: World Book Co., 1934.
22. COTTON, C. B. "A Study of the Reactions of Spastic Children to Certain Test Situations," *Journal of Genetic Psychology,* LVIII (1941), 27–44.
23. CRUICKSHANK, W. M., and BICE, H. V. "Personality Characteristics," in *Cerebral Palsy.* Syracuse, New York: Syracuse University Press, 1955.
24. CRUICKSHANK, W. M., BICE, H. V., and WALLEN, N. E. *Perception and Cerebral Palsy.* Syracuse, New York: Syracuse University Press, 1957.
25. DOLL, E. A. "Annotated Bibliography on the Vineland Social Maturity Scale," *Journal of Consulting Psychology,* IV (1940), 123–32.
26. DOLL, E. A. *The Measurement of Social Competence: A Manual for the Vineland Social Maturity Scale.* Philadalphia: Educational Test Bureau, 1953.
27. DOLL, E. A. *Vineland Social Maturity Scale: Manual of Directions.* Philadelphia: Educational Test Bureau, 1947.
28. DOLPHIN, J. E. and CRUICKSHANK, W. M. "The Figure-Background Relationship in Children with Cerebral Palsy," *Journal of Clinical Psychology,* VII (1951), 228–31.
     DOLPHIN, J. E. and CRUICKSHANK, W. M. "Visuo-Motor Perception in Children with Cerebral Palsy," *Quarterly Journal of Child Behavior,* III (1951), 198–209.
     DOLPHIN, J. E. and CRUICKSHANK, W. M. "Pathology of Concept Formation in Children with Cerebral Palsy," *American Journal of Mental Deficiency,* LVI (1951), 386–92.
     DOLPHIN, J. E. and CRUICKSHANK, W. M. "Tactual Motor Perception of Children with Cerebral Palsy," *Journal of Personality,* XX (1952), 466–71.
29. FEIFEL, H. "Qualitative Differences in the Vocabulary Responses of Normals and Abnormals," *Genetic Psychology Monograph,* No. 39 (1949), 151–204.
30. FELDMAN, I. "Psychological Differences Among Moron and Borderline Mental Defectives as a Function of Etiology. I. Visual-Motor Functioning," *American Journal of Mental Deficiency,* LVII (1953), 484–94.
31. FRAZEUR, H. A. and HOAKLEY, Z. P. "Significance of Psychological Test

Results of Exogenous and Endogenous Children," *American Journal of Mental Deficiency,* LI (1947), 384–88.

32. GOLDBERG, F. H. "The Performance of Schizophrenic, Retarded, and Normal Children on the Bender-Gestalt Test," *American Journal of Mental Deficiency,* LXI (1957), 548–55.

33. GOLDENBERG, S. "Testing the Brain-Injured Child with Normal I.Q.," in *Brain-Injured Child:* Vol. II. *Progress in Theory and Clinic.* Edited by STRAUSS, A. A. and KEPHART, N. C. New York: Grune and Stratton, 1955, Chapter 7, pp. 144–64.

34. GOLDSTEIN, K., and SCHEERER, M. *Abstract and Concrete Behavior: An Experimental Study with Special Tests.* Psychological Monograph 239, 1941.

35. GOODENOUGH, F. L. and HARRIS, D. B. "Studies in the Psychology of Children's Drawings. II. 1928–1949," *Psychological Bulletin,* XLVII (1950), 369–433.

36. GRAHAM, F. M., and KENDALL, B. S. "Performance of Brain-Damaged Cases on a Memory-for-Designs Test," *Journal of Abnormal and Social Psychology,* XLI (1946), 303–14.

37. HANVIK, L. J. "A Note on Rotations in the Bender-Gestalt as Predictors of EEG Abnormalities in Children," *Journal of Clinical Psychology,* IX (1953), 399.

38. HEALY, W., BRONNER, A., LOWE, C. M., and SHIMBERG, N. E. *A Manual of Individual Tests and Testing.* Boston: Little, Brown, & Co., 1932.

39. HOAKLEY, Z. P., and FRAZEUR, H. A. "Significance of Psychological Test Results of Exogenous and Endogenous Children," *American Journal of Mental Deficiency,* L (1945), 263–71.

40. HOPKINS, T. W., BICE, H. V., and COLTON, K. C. *Evaluation and Education of the Cerebral Palsied Child.* Washington: International Council for Exceptional Children, 1954.

41. HUDSON, A. "A Comparative Study of the Test Responses of Two Groups of Cerebral Palsied Children: Athetoid and Spastic." Unpublished doctoral dissertation, University of Wisconsin.

42. KLAPPER, Z. S., and WERNER, H. "Developmental Deviations in Brain-Injured (Cerebral Palsied) Members of Pairs of Identical Twins," *Quarterly Journal of Child Behavior,* II (1950), 288–313.

43. LORD, E. E., and WOOD, L. "Diagnostic Values in a Visuo-motor Test," *American Journal of Orthopsychiatry,* XII (1942), 418–28.

44. MACHOVER, K. *Personality in the Drawing of the Human Figure.* Springfield, Illinois: Charles C. Thomas, 1949.

45. MASLAND, R. L., SARASON, S. B., GLADWIN, T. *Mental Subnormality.* New York: Basic Books, 1959.

46. MEYERS, E. and SIMMEL, N. "Psychological Appraisal of Children With Neurological Defects," *Journal of Abnormal and Social Psychology,* XLII (1947), 193–205.

47. MYKLEBUST, H., and BRUTTEN, M. A. "Study of the Visual Perception of Deaf Children," *Acta Oto-laryngologica*, Supplementum 105 (1953).

48. PASCAL, G. R. and SUTTELL, B. J. *The Bender-Gestalt Test*. New York: Grune and Stratton, 1951.

49. SARASON, S. B. *Psychological Problems in Mental Deficiency*. New York: Harper & Brothers, 1949.

50. SHAW, M. C. "A Study of Certain Aspects of Perception and Conceptual Thinking in Idiopathic Epileptic Children." Unpublished doctoral dissertation, Syracuse University, 1955.

51. SHAW, M. C., and CRUICKSHANK, W. M. "The Use of the Bender-Gestalt Test with Epileptic Children," *Journal of Clinical Psychology*, XII (1956), 192–99.

52. SHAW, M. C., and CRUICKSHANK, W. M. "The Use of the Marble Board Test to Measure Psychopathology in Epileptics," *American Journal of Mental Deficiency*, LX (1956), 813–17.

53. SLOAN, W., and BENSBERG, G. J. "An Exploratory Study of the Full-Range Picture Vocabulary Test With Mental Defectives," *American Journal of Mental Deficiency*, LVIII (1954), 481–85.

54. SMITH, L. M., and FILLMORE, A. R. "The Ammons FRPV Test and the WISC for Remedial Reading Cases," *Journal of Consulting Psychology*, XVIII (1954), 332.

55. STRAUSS, A. A. and KEPHART, N. C. *Psychopathology and Education of the Brain-Injured Child*. Vol. 2. New York and London: Grune and Stratton, 1955.

56. TERMAN, L. M., and MERRILL, M. A. *Measuring Intelligence*. New York: Houghton Mifflin, 1937.

57. VERNON, M. D. "Different Types of Perceptual Ability," *British Journal of Psychology*, XXXVIII (1947), 79–89.

58. WECHSLER, D. *Wechsler Intelligence Scale for Children. Manual*. New York: The Psychological Corporation, 1949.

59. WERNER, H., and STRAUSS, A. A. "Pathology of Figure-Background Relation in the Child," *Journal of Abnormal and Social Psychology*, XXXVI (1941), 236–48.

60. WERNER, H., and STRAUSS, A. A. "Types of Visuo-Motor Activity in Their Relation to Low and High Performance Ages," *Proceedings, American Association of Mental Deficiency*, XLIV (1939), 163–69.

61. WOOD, L., and SHULMAN, R. "The Ellis Visual Designs Test," *Journal of Educational Psychology*, XXXI (1940), 591–602.

62. YOUNG, F. M., and PITTS, V. A. "The Performance of Congenital Syphiletics on the Wechsler Intelligence Scale for Children," *Journal of Consulting Psychology*, XV (1951), 236–42.

CHAPTER VII

Implications of the Demonstration-Pilot Study

A COMPLEX amount of information has thus far been presented concerning the demonstration-pilot study which was devised to evaluate a method of educating hyperactive children with and without diagnosed brain injury. It may be well first to summarize the essential elements of the project. Forty children were carefully screened by means of extensive medical and psychological diagnostic procedures; these children were assigned to four groups of 10 children each. The diagnostic phase of the study was concerned with isolating children, with or without brain injury, who showed the common psychological traits often associated with central nervous system disorders, i.e., hyperactivity and distractibility, perseveration, figure-ground pathology, reversals, angulation problems, dissociation, and a myriad of other related characteristics. Under the direction of skilled teachers these four groups of children, two experimental groups and two control groups, were studied intensively for one school year and were then re-evaluated twelve months after the close of the experimental year. The plan of education involved Cruickshank's modification of the Strauss-Lehtinen concept of education for brain-injured children. The plan consisted of the recognition of four essential principles:

1. the reduction of environmental space,
2. the reduction of unessential visual and auditory environmental stimuli,
3. the establishment of a highly structured daily program,
4. the increase of the stimulus value of the instructional materials themselves.

As has been pointed out earlier, research concerned with human beings is characterized by a great number of variables. It is obvious to the authors, and should be to the reader, that many of the variables in this particular experiment were uncontrolled and, indeed, could never be controlled. Consequently, it is often impossible to identify all the factors which influenced the results. The most significant uncontrolled factors involved:

1. variations in interpretations of the educational philosophy and method by the teachers;

2. variations in the personalities of the teachers of the children, and the way teachers and children related to each other;

3. variations in teacher skills and co-operation;

4. variations in the degree to which parents were informed of the program and the degree to which they supplemented it with home attitudes or instruction;

5. variations in the degree of effectiveness and uniformity of the directions given to the teachers by the Project Director, the Resident Co-ordinator, the staff psychologist, and others;

6. variations in the extent to which teachers made use of psychological and psychiatric consultation;

7. variations in numerous other quite obvious and extremely important factors which normally occurred in spite of structure of the program. (For example, a factor which was not measured, but which is undoubtedly important, involves the length of the instructional period for each child; variation in school attendance occurred because of illness, religious holidays, and the time of the child's entry into the instructional program at the beginning of the school year);

8. variations in home backgrounds of the children.

The extent of these influences has not been measured, in most instances could they be adequately appraised. However, they must be kept in mind as one evaluates the report and as one considers future research through which more definitive knowledge may be obtained.

Two different types of educational settings were developed by the authors: first, the experimental classes in which an attempt was made to fully test the four principles mentioned at the beginning of this chapter; second, the control classes wherein the teacher could implement the instructional program as she deemed appropriate, and wherein no modifications of the environmental structure were made, except as the teacher might herself direct. Insofar as achievement in learning is concerned, it has been demonstrated that the majority of all of the children in both types of settings made significant progress. It will be recalled that frequently there were no differences between the gains made by the children of the experimental classes and the children of the control classes. However, wherever statistically significant differences were obtained, the difference in gain was in favor of the children in the experimental classes. While still further evidence needs to be obtained, it is the opinion of the authors that hyperactive children in a nonstimulating environment and structured program demonstrate sufficient progress to warrant continuation of this approach with such children.

What were the gains noted in these children? While all children made some gain in their ability to differentiate figure from background—a skill essential to practically any type of abstract learning—the children of the experimental classes made somewhat greater gains in this respect. Similarly, almost all of the children made some growth in social maturity; but those in the experimental classes demonstrated this growth in more pronounced ways. The results of the Bender-Gestalt test did not always indicate statistically significant differences between the two types of classrooms. However, in those instances where statistically significant differences did appear the differences were again in the favor of the experimental groups. Hence it would appear that the elements essential to the experimental classroom settings were statistically valuable in appraising the gains made by those 20 children.

Was the fact that all of the children made great gains in school achievement due (1) to the presence of a professionally prepared teacher, (2) to the instructional method, (3) to the nature of the highly stimulating teaching materials, (4) to the isolation of the child within the classroom, (5) to the reduction of environment stimuli which was effected to some degree in each of the four rooms, or (6) to a combination of any or all of these factors? These questions remain to be answered. Something positive happened to the majority of the 40 children both in terms of school learning and in terms of social and emotional adjustment. Since they had had a history of failure and regression in school achievement and social growth prior to the study, it must be assumed that one or more of the factors inherent in the experimental design constituted the crucial motivational ingredient. It is the opinion of these authors that the controlled elements in the experimental classes provided a situation wherein greater positive conditioning could occur —a situation wherein highly distractible children were more able to concentrate for a sufficient length of time to permit the conditioning which leads to a success experience. The repetition of positive conditioning and the repetition of success experiences was sufficient to motivate the child and to ultimately permit him to function in social situations which contained a greater number of stimuli. The most important element which the children learned was to attend successfully to a given stimulus in the presence of a multiplicity of extraneous stimuli. While it is primitive, this single learned skill is probably the most important element in social growth and development. As the children learned to attend, growth in numerous areas was noted, i.e., in number concepts, in reading, in social and emotional behavior, and in an understanding of a positive self-concept.

The remainder of this chapter is devoted to two major topics. The purpose of the first section is to discuss some of the major theoretical implications and significant by-products of the pilot study's diagnostic and clinical findings. The final section is concerned with: (1) the early identification of children with learning disabilities, (2) the educational use of psychological and achievement-test data in developing more adequate methods of grouping children, and (3) the importance of the need for educators to understand the educational significance of developmental differences in children.

IMPLICATIONS

Implications from Psychiatry

The authors are strongly predisposed in favor of the assumption that disorders of learning and behavior result from, or are associated with, individual differences or dysfunction in the neurophysiological processes of growth, development, and maturation—even in the absence of tissue damage. This assumption does not necessarily suggest a viewpoint which is in conflict with psychiatric theories of personality dynamics. Rather, psychiatric concepts are viewed as having a neurophysiological counterpart in the processes and dynamics of body growth and conditioning.

Gerard has stated that:

. . . we all agree today that brain and mind are related . . . but the implications of this are often overlooked. A vital force does not move a molecule and an emotion does not discharge a neurone. When experience leaves an enduring trace, it must be some sort of material imprint; and, so to speak, there can be no twisted thought without a twisted molecule. Perhaps the simplest generalization to keep in mind is that all behavior in the external world, as well as all awareness of it, depends explicitly on the discharges of neurones. Certain neurones are fired by a given sensory input, these activate others, and still others, and in time certain final neurones activate particular muscles to contract or glands to secrete. Clearly, the properties of neural units and of their relations are crucial to all normal and disturbed behavior . . . (1, p. 82).

Whether one agrees or disagrees with Gerard, one should not rule out the possibility that a "twisted thought" may involve a "twisted molecule"; the "twist" may occur in response to a disturbance in one or more of the sensory motor processes by which a given human organism selects, translates, and integrates life experience into a behavioral response pattern. Thus, the psychiatrist who views a symptomatic behavioral response pattern as the result of disturbed parent-child relations may appropriately interpret reading disability "as a specific symptomatic manifestation of a disorder in ego function—the inhibition of learning and intelligence" (2, p. 299). He may then assume that the resolution of the reading disability is dependent upon the resolution of

. . . a constellation of factors, conscious and unconscious, particularly conflicts around curiosity and aggression involving oral and anal ambivalence. . . . Occasionally other problems such as prematurity, speech defects, variations of visual acuity, and handedness problems may be further handicapping factors—other sources of frustration. These physical and developmental factors, then, while they do not appear crucial in the origin of the reading problem, may be contributory. There may be some possibility that the reading disability child may more frequently have an irregular constitution and physical background which might influence his subsequent psychic maturation and structure (2, p. 299).

This reference to the physical and developmental factors that might contribute to the origin of the learning problem indicates recognition of the possibility that there can be no "twisted thought" without a "twisted molecule." At this point one must find out whether or not it makes any difference to the educator as to which assumption is uppermost in the minds of individuals engaged in research projects conducted within the framework of the public school. The viewpoint does matter since the psychiatric frame of reference generally is not compatible with nor appropriate to public school policies, procedures, and group instructional programs. This statement is based on the discussion which follows.

The pediatric psychiatrist works with children in terms of the psychopathology of personality dynamics. The success of treatment is measured by the degree to which interpersonal problems are resolved within the therapeutic relationship. The goal is to free the child from the restrictions of anxiety and fear through understanding and mastery of feelings. Whether the treatment involves group therapy or individual therapy, the energies of the child and the therapist are directed to the resolution of the psychopathology.

In contrast, the teacher works with children in terms of enlisting the support of the ego in acquiring mastery of the learning skills. The existence and resolution of psychopathological aspects of the personality is secondary to the instructional goal, and the success of the teaching situation is gauged in relation to the degree to which the children achieve academic progress. The success of the child is evaluated in terms of his academic achievement as compared to that of his classmates.

Frequently one observes attempts to superimpose a treatment-centered psychiatric frame of reference upon a teaching-centered classroom situation in "classes" for the emotionally disturbed children. The results of this practice have been discussed in an earlier portion of this monograph; it is sufficient at this time to simply point out that the existence of gross behavioral disturbances is hardly sufficient justification for grouping children together within an instructional frame of reference. There may be even less justification in expecting good group teachers to utilize one-to-one psychiatric procedures in a public school system where the policies, procedures and instructional goals have been established for a group setting. These considerations must be uppermost also in the minds of administrators who are planning educational programs for hyperactive and brain-injured children.

Adherence of psychiatrists to a philosophy of the importance of the one-to-one relationship may partially account for one of the main communication problems with people in other disciplines. Gerard states:

> I am satisfied that the greatest barrier to rapid advance in psychiatric research today is the continuous and anecdotal character of the descriptive material on which psychiatric insights and generalizations are almost exclusively based. When more useful categories have been recognized and at least ordinal scales established; when it is possible to *group* (italics ours) the phenomena into classes and categories in a meaningful manner, rapid progress is certain to follow (1, pp. 85–86).

One of the important findings in this study was the similarity in the pattern of individual differences which the children demonstrated to each of the diagnosticians. There was no doubt from the staff point of view that had it been possible to reproduce the pre- and post-psychiatric evaluations in full, the material would have been presented in a more meaningful form. Psychiatric data does not lend itself to easy summarization or tabulation (see Table 169). However, it was possible only to chart the material from the psychiatric interviews in an orderly, uniform sequence of diagnostic impressions. At best, it was possible only to report the pre- and post-test observations of the research psychiatrist. This ruled out any possibility of comparing the emotional growth of any given child with any other child in any form other than the psychiatric impressions.

It is apparent, however, that when extreme care is exerted in the grouping of children on the basis of their subtle nuances of psychopathology, they make progress in a purely educational setting. The school must understand that with hyperactive and brain-injured children its role is education, not psychotherapy. If grouping is carefully arranged and if an educational program is properly conceived, not only educational achievements may result, but also social and emotional development of a therapeutic nature may concomitantly occur.

The assumption, then, which underlies the writing of this section is that some kinds of learning and emotional disorders in hyperactive and brain-injured children result from the impact of stress (within the context and meaning of Seyle (3)) upon the neurophysiological systems and processes of the human organism. While recognizing the value and importance of psychiatric concepts and treatment procedures for the discipline of education, this point of view regards these concepts and procedures as inappropriate when superimposed upon a group teaching situation. Of value in the field of education, however, has been the translation and reformulation of psychiatric insights and generalizations concerning personality dynamics into an instructional frame of reference.

In this project an effort was made to utilize both the one-to-one approach and the group educational approach. The small cubicles and semi-isolation of the children one from the other required the teacher to work on a one-to-one basis with each child. She attempted to create a secure learning environment in which the children would be able through successful conditioning to move from very small group activities within the limits of the self-contained classroom into the highly complex group experiences of a regular or special grade group. Initially, the one-to-one approach was used extensively by the experimental-group teachers. Success gradually occurred; appropriate self-concepts began to develop; tolerance of unessential environmental stimuli was gained; and each child took part in small group activity. Group participation and instruction was substituted as rapidly as possible, but always the size of the group and the length of the group participation was maintained within the child's tolerance level.

The staff psychiatrist's impressions provide considerable supportive data of a qualitative nature for the above viewpoint and related observations. One cannot help but comment on the uniformity of the clinical psychiatric impressions concerning the children who were referred. In all 40 cases, at the time of the first evaluation, there was evidence of visual-perceptual distortion and visual-motor problems, and deficits in ego-organization, ego-strength and self-concept. Body-image concepts were grossly immature and sometimes bizarre. Sexual identification was often undetermined. The children appeared universally, although in varying degrees, to be unable to orient themselves in relation to time, space or other objects. Their play activities strongly suggested a preoccupation with fears of bodily hurt. It should be noted that this fear was in part a reality-based one. Because of their many visual-motor problems, the children ran into things and fell down more frequently than children without such problems. Anxiety over lack of control in the expression of basic drives was consistently demonstrated, as were strong dependency needs. The latter were sometimes expressed in the form of evasiveness and a noncommittal attitude when the examiner asked questions concerning dreams or wishes.

The major defense patterns included (1) obsessive compulsive behavior, (2) denial, and (3) projection. The defense pattern most commonly observed was obsessive compulsive behavior alone or in combination with the other patterns.

Although the children had many valid and complicated emotional and learning problems and although they resorted on occasion to symbolic language (primary process thinking), their over-all attitude was one of willingness to belong to the human race, if someone taught them.

Keeping in mind the fact that a limited number of projective tests were included in the psychological test battery, and the fact that the pilot project did not provide for a psychiatric social worker to represent his field on the diagnostic staff, it was still possible for the staff psychiatrist to arrive at a number of clinical impressions concerning the results of the use of the specialized grouping procedures and instructional program with this group of children.

First, is the psychiatrist's impression that there was evidence of social growth in all of the children, just as there was an objectively measurable degree of academic progress. This statement is corroborated by the results of the achievement tests, Vineland Social Maturity Scale, and the Goodenough Draw-A-Man. In connection with the latter, Bender states, "It is to be recalled that the body image is the most complete gestalt

experience involving the integration of all sensory experience imping-
ing on the organism; it is genetically determined and passes through
maturational stages which in the child can be followed through the
human drawing." (4, p. 159.)

There was, of course, wide variation in the rate of social growth
and in the degree of personality integration experienced by the individual children. Although objective evidence does not, at this time, support the clinical impression, a study of the pre- and post-test psychiatric
evaluations seemed to indicate that a major proportion of those children who had had no previous Special Education classroom experience
reached about the same level of ego integration from the experiences
as did those who had had previous Special Education programming.
In the absence of objective evidence supporting this impression, one
can only speculate as to the possibility that the specialized instructional
programming and grouping methods may have brought about personality integration at a faster rate than with other techniques available
to public school personnel. A second speculation is that the observed
change is a reflection of the frequently observed growth curve characterized by a sharp initial rise followed by a plateau.

Second, one of the most thought-provoking results of the psychiatric
pre- and post-test evaluations was that there appeared to be a decrease
in the amount of parental tension and anxiety.

As an area for further inquiry one might explore the possibility that
some parents may need to see evidence of improvement (increased academic proficiency, for example) in their child outside the home before
they are able to modify their own attitudes toward, and expectations
for, their child and thereby contribute directly to the child's increased
social and emotional growth and to his potential ability to utilize a
classroom learning situation.

Third, those children whose parents evidenced the most severe adjustment difficulties or frank neuroses made the least progress in ego
identification and personality integration. There appeared to be no
obvious correlation between a particular attitude or personality structure in the parent, teacher, or child which limited or contributed to
academic achievement. This impression is substantiated by the fact that
the increase in academic achievement was not statistically significant
among the four groups, outside of more favorable response by the experimental groups to various subtest items involving figure-ground
responses.

To what might one look for an explanation of the emotional gains?
In the discipline of psychiatry, experience (5) has shown that these

children need (a) one or more adults on whom they can depend; (b) firm environmental control of their impulse activity; (c) a minimum of daily stress (change of activity *per se* constituting one kind of stress); (d) reinforcement of gaps in their personality development through the use of other personalities (teacher and peers, for example); and (e) reinforcement, if possible, of the obsessive compulsive behavior patterns. Although these needs do not differ—with the exception of e— in kind from the usual requirements for healthy development, they do seem to differ in degree.

It is the opinion of the staff psychiatrist that the rigorous grouping and matching of the children, the structured classroom and predictable scheduling of activities, and the specialized instructional techniques, all met, to a significant degree, the five essential needs mentioned above. Within this frame of reference, it would appear that to the extent the classroom structuring, teaching approach, and the use of specialized instructional program led to and resulted in the children experiencing mastery over even one function, such as the acquisition of visual perceptual or motor skills, anxiety was lessened and learning took place.

There appear to be several major implications from this study which are for the discipline of psychiatry:

1. In view of the widespread attitude that the severely disturbed child is too disturbed to learn unless he has had the benefit of psychotherapy, it can be said that at least some of the children in this project who needed (and need) psychotherapy have achieved academically without it and without observable personality insults. Thus, there is an additional reason for requiring more complete diagnostic studies with fuller interdisciplinary representation in order for the psychiatrist and educator to keep the school door open to the child who can profit from an instructional program even while his name remains on a clinic or private-treatment waiting list.

2. According to the results of this study, the clinical level of manifest anxiety appeared to be unrelated to the rate and degree of increased academic achievement and learning. Such an observation is a worthy reminder that anxiety *per se* is only a symptom whose origin must be defined and understood before its handicapping or contributing role in problem solving situations can be evaluated. Only then will one be able to determine, define, and predict the role of anxiety in the learning process of the hyperactive, or indeed, of any other child.

3. At the early conferences of the diagnostic staff which were devoted to reporting the results of the individual examinations, it became apparent that the data which the psychiatrist obtained in the nongroup

setting of the playroom differed in certain behavioral categories from the data obtained in the classroom group situation. It was, for example, generally true that in the latter setting behavior of the children was hyperactive, unpredictable, and aggressive, while it was generally untrue that these behavioral characteristics were seen in the one-to-one playroom setting. This observation may help to strengthen the growing awareness of psychiatrists that diagnostic responsibilities should be broadened to include observation of the children in a classroom situation, rather than confined to behavioral evaluations in the playroom setting and secondhand reports from family or teacher.

4. It is the impression of the staff psychiatrist that had psychiatric social work case studies of the families and more complete projective test material been provided, more adequate information regarding the nature of the learning disabilities might have been available. Information from these sources would have made possible the evaluation of the effect of relationship patterns established by the child with significant adults and peers away from the school setting which, in turn, could then be correlated with teacher-child and peer-child relationships observed in the classroom setting. Ideally, these evaluative comparisons would need to be made at regularly scheduled intervals during the academic year. These results would put the psychiatrist in a more favorable position to consider what portion of the social and emotional growth achieved was school-determined, what part maturational, and what part family-determined. It must be emphasized that further study and investigation of the medical, clinical and educational data and their interrelationships in the area of children's learning is clearly indicated. This is not only in order to determine their educational implications, but to clearly identify the diagnostic and therapeutic efforts of the discipline of psychiatry.

Implications from Clinical Psychology

The children were carefully evaluated by the staff clinical psychologist. They presented a very uniform picture on the psychological tests. As a matter of fact, after the first 10 children were tested there was such a similarity in responses to the tests that it seemed as if the same child was being examined over and over again. One should perhaps temper this statement somewhat by adding that 4 children who had previous classification of strephosymbolia—a specific reading disability described by Orton (6)—and who met all the behavioral and medical criteria of the research design deviated from the general pattern of psychological-test responses in that they showed very minor disturbances of the Gestalt function on the various perceptual tests. The remaining 36 children showed a characteristic psychological test pattern. For example, on the Stanford-Binet Intelligence Scale the children had difficulty with items requiring ability in visuo-motor functioning (copying a diamond, bead stringing, copying forms), verbal abstractions, and memory for sentences and digits. On the Bender-Gestalt Test they produced drawings showing rotations, distortion of the configuration, perseveration, and dissociation. On the Syracuse Visual Figure-Background Test they showed disturbances in figure-ground relationships, such as reduced perceptual accuracy, distractibility by the background, and perseveration. Perceptual difficulties were also seen on the Coding and Block Design subtests from the Wechsler Intelligence Scale for Children. The drawing of a man showed very immature and poorly integrated body image, and the level of achievement was uniformly below age-grade expectancy.

Quantitatively, growth occurred on numerous psychological and educational tests. The children's perceptual abilities improved; their social maturity increased, and academic achievement advanced at the rate of 2.19 grade levels over the two-year period.

The teachers were unanimous in voicing their feeling that the children had also made substantial progress in many ways that could not be evaluated by psychological instruments. Much of the improvement thus described could be considered under the heading of social development, or development of emotional maturity to which the staff psychiatrist has previously made reference. In contrast to the need for individual instruction at the beginning of the academic period, by the end of the first academic year the children were operating as an instructional group for varying periods of time. Qualitative growth of this type is a subtle and evasive thing when one attempts to describe it objectively, but it was very real to the teachers.

At the conclusion of the project there were no statistically significant differences between the four groups in terms of gross measurements of academic achievement and social growth. There were, however, a number of statistically significant differences in various subtest items involving figure-ground responses and in the items of the Vineland Social Maturity Scale. These differences, while significant in all four groups, were greater among the children of the experimental classes.

It is not possible to say what caused these differences. The authors feel that the greater structure and reduction of stimulation in the experimental classes and the more rigid adherence to the specialized teaching methodology might have effected these differences. On the other hand, one can hardly discount, nor indeed measure, the effect of also having a full-time speech therapist available in the school which housed the two experimental groups. The speech therapist was well versed in the specialized techniques required by children with language-formulation problems and organic speech defects. It cannot be denied that all of the children improved. Although it is well known that maturation and normal growth processes often result in improvement, one cannot say specifically what the effect of the maturation factor combined with the specialized method actually has been; nor can we say what impact the specialized grouping and method had on the normal growth processes associated with maturation. In isolation or in combination they served to habilitate the children to a marked extent.

The lack of projective test information was felt keenly by the staff. The initial tests were chosen to determine the presence of specific psychopathology regarding the learning problems usually associated with organicity.

Rorschach tests were administered during the diagnostic period, but the results have not been included in the present study because the response total per record was so small that the value of the Rorschach in providing a valid personality picture appeared extremely doubtful. The children tended to give one response for each of the ten cards, even with repeated urging, and most Rorschach authorities (7) consider this to be inadequate for a valid personality description. The lack of projective information resulted in the necessity of making inferences about the emotional and anxiety status of the children on the basis of limited observations by the psychologists and others, combined with the results of the psychiatric interviews and teacher reports.

There is a logical fallacy in assuming that tests which have been standardized on a normal population and which are based on the assumption of quantitative differences can be applied to children who have specific learning disabilities, and who thus differ qualitatively from the standardization population. For example, the basic assumption of the usual intelligence test is that children have either more or less intelligence, and that if all children were administered the test, and the results were plotted graphically, the resulting curve would closely approximate the normal distribution curve. Indeed, the use of normal distribution theory assumes a continuous variation in the variable being tested. However, children may differ not only in *quantity* but also in *quality* of intellectual functioning.

Strauss and his co-workers (8), and Cruickshank and his associates (9), have demonstrated very convincingly that brain-injured children have characteristic intellectual processes that are qualitatively different from those of normal children. For example, consider the child who has a language-formulation problem. The assumption underlying the memory-for-sentences, or memory-for-digits subtests on the Stanford-Binet Scale is that the child with "more" intelligence will pass the item, while the child with "less" intelligence will fail. However, the child with a language-formulation problem may completely fail the item because of an inability to organize auditory experiences in a meaningful manner, even though his intelligence may be relatively high. This fact can be inferred from his ability to handle quite complicated problems which do not involve auditory functions beyond his ability.

A second example of this type of problem is associated with test items involving vocabulary. It is generally assumed that when a word is given to a child, the child will respond in a way which may be scored as either known or unknown. No allowance is made for the child who may have problems in the receptive processes in the central nervous system. Here, again, is a qualitative difference rather than a quantitative one.

Most clinical and school psychologists recognize problems of this type which result from qualitative differences in individual intellectual processes. Frequently an attempt is made to resolve this difficulty by pointing out that the test results indicate a *minimum* level of functioning and that the actual level may be much higher than the results indicate.

Other writers (10) have pointed out that no intelligence test has yet been devised which takes into account all of the known intellectual factors that have been isolated in factor analysis studies. This fact alone should provoke extreme caution when one is interpreting the test results of hyperactive or brain-injured children. Granting these limitations, however, it should be recognized that intelligence tests are of value—as was borne out in the present study—in predicting a child's ability or lack of it in relation to academic achievement. To use test results in attempting to predict anything about these children outside of the academic situation, however, is a questionable practice.

Another word of caution should be offered concerning the general limitations of test instruments. In the 1937 revision of the Stanford-Binet Intelligence Scale, all items which had been identified in terms of test responses associated with sex differences were systematically discarded as being "relatively less fair to one sex than the other" (11, p. 216). A comment on this fact follows:

It is of course clear that the philosophy of test construction, tied as it is now to the criterion of school performance, reflects little sophistication in the realities of our culture as a whole, but even if one were willing to accept a limitation on the applicability of intelligence tests strictly to school use this would not justify the obliteration of sex differences . . . (11, p. 262).

. . . .

. . . If the items on tests which differentiate between the sexes were not so systematically discarded, patterns would emerge from the intelligence test performance of normal children which we would say were characteristic of their respective sex roles. We would then have some standard against which to compare the test profiles of retarded boys and girls and thus perhaps obtain some idea whether we should look first at intellectual, emotional, or cultural aspects of the problem in search of a cause and therefore correction and prevention. However, the existing tests will not permit this, nor can they provide a test of any hypotheses our speculations might generate (11, p. 264).

It may well be that the boys in the project have a quite different rate of development (including intellectual development) from that of the girls. This fact may not be reflected by the type of intelligence tests and subtest items currently in use.

While the psychologist is able to make many inferences about learning processes and problems, it should be remembered that these are inferences based on an instrument which was designed for a different purpose. Consider, for example, the problem of perseveration. The existence of perseveration constitutes an important teaching and learning problem, and it is therefore an important factor in grouping children for instructional purposes. Many times children who show a great amount of perseverative behavior in the classroom fail to demonstrate this same trait on psychological tests. If perseveration on a behavioral level is as important as it appeared to be in this study, then it may be that a test or tests need to be designed to identify the existence of perseveration on a behavioral level. The same may be said for hyperactivity, distractibility, and lack of impulse control.

The staff psychiatrist has previously commented on the psychiatric implications of the success experience for the child with impaired ego strength. The impressions of the research psychologist, based on reports of teachers, neighbors, and interviews with the parents, supports the psychiatric impression. This stems from the observation that the children's behavior changed dramatically after they were placed in a class situation where they experienced success from the very first day. For example, some children who were considered unacceptable as playmates and who had been candidates for permanent exclusion from school were accepted as citizens of the community and the school at the end of the study. The therapeutic effect of success in a controlled teaching situation, combined with specialized grouping procedures, has implications for all those who work with children who have learning and behavior problems. While they are not substitutes for psychiatric treatment, appropriate educational diagnosis, grouping, and programming can go far to meet the total life needs of these children.

The growing tendency of clinical and public school psychologists to recommend neurological examinations for children whose tests show a characteristic "organic" pattern of behavior should be questioned. It is the opinion of these authors that the "signs of organicity" should be interpreted, within the framework of the public schools, in terms of learning problems rather than as indications of organicity *per se*. This opinion is strengthened by the fact that most of the children in the present study demonstrated visuo-motor problems in varying degrees—many showed rotations, and other "signs" of organicity—yet there was little or no correlation between these so-called signs and evidence of organicity as defined by medical and neurological findings, including EEG interpretations.

From the strictly educational point of view, which was the orientation of the present pilot study, the neurological and electroencephalographic data were of least value of any information received. It is of little educational consequence to know that the several cranial nerves are or are not functioning properly. Such information is significant for research and is basic to treatment programs in disciplines other than education. Much more important to educators, however, is the knowledge that the child is dissociating, perseverating, or in other ways functioning psychopathologically; on the basis of that knowledge, curriculum modifications can be effected, class placement can be made, and teaching materials can be prepared which will permit educators to teach to the apparent disabilities and to help rectify the influence of these disabilities on the child's growth and adjustment. Traditional neurological reports have little bearing on such a program. Educators and psychologists concerned for children with central nervous system impairments have too often utilized referral for neurological evaluation as an escape from the frustration of not knowing how to plan adequately for the child. It is of significantly more importance that a careful psychological description of the child's behavior, his thought processes, and his intellectual characteristics be obtained. Neurological diagnosis in itself can rarely be translated into a dynamic educational program; psychological diagnosis can.

Implications from Audiology and Speech Pathology

Two patterns of language and speech behavior were apparent:

1. there was clear evidence of a lack of awareness of the alternating roles of speaker and listener in verbal interchange;

2. there was difficulty in the interpretation and comprehension of verbal stimuli, a characteristic frequently associated with the effects of organic damage upon learning and memory.

In addition to these two patterns, there were many cases where the onset of speech was markedly delayed, while in others the onset occurred at a reasonable time, but progress was delayed or retarded. A few of the children talked in a compulsive fashion, which was not so much evidence of an attempt at communication as it was of self-expression. A number of the children demonstrated evidence of cluttered speech; others demonstrated severe dyslalia with additional evidence of poor auditory discrimination and memory. In general, the children's speech was characteristic of that of much younger children and included evidence of infantile perseveration, substitutions, omissions, reversals, and a wide variety of articulation problems. These difficulties might easily pass unnoticed since many of the children functioned quite adequately in verbal interchange structured in a one-to-one situation, although it was quite apparent that they would be unable to handle the verbal demands of normal conversation.

Hearing examinations revealed evidence of end-organ damage in only one child. Learning difficulties associated with problems of auditory comprehension and recall, however, were noticeable in at least 30 cases.

Learning to listen, to understand, and to talk are among the most complex tasks for the developing hyperactive or brain-injured child. This development is so intimately related to all other aspects of growth that its status at any stage becomes an index of the level of intrasensory function and cerebral organization, particularly as they relate to memory and learning. Any serious interference with the emergence of the complex, intricate sensory neural and cortical mechanisms—whether it be caused by organic inadequacy, environmental stress, or sensory deprivation—is often reflected in the child's language, speech, and behavior pattern. It is not strange, therefore, that approximately 80 per cent of the hyperactive, underachieving children had language and speech problems.

Hearing is fundamental in learning and adjustment. The auditory mechanism is devoted to the absorption of incoming information, encoding and decoding the information in highly complex neuro-psycho-physical activities. What the child perceives through audition becomes a part of him and, in terms of symbolic patterns, becomes a memory and a model. These models control the shifting phonetic events of his speaking; a feedback mechanism is set up, and the child is able to hear his own speech and compare it with what others say. Thus he learns to monitor himself. Once the hyperactive or brain-injured child has learned to monitor himself, it becomes possible for him to refine the details of incoming and outgoing messages, to learn language, to react appropriately to different levels of reference, and to develop the verbal symbolic nuances characteristic of the highest degree of intellectual development.

Unfortunately, hearing, however defined, is a highly complex activity, employing a neurophysiological circuitry that has not yet been fully described or understood. Moreover, the relationship of what is heard to what is understood, and the relationship of both these activities to what is expressed, is even less clear. Although most children develop language and speech and learn how to use verbal tools in the learning situation, many do not. The prevalence of language and speech disorders is particularly high in a group such as the children in this study who demonstrated evidence of impairment or delay in the development of the auditory feedback mechanism.

Many causal factors may contribute to this delay. Some may be identified and analyzed in terms of difficulties in learning and memory. Dysfunction would profoundly affect auditory and linguistic processing; it is of significant influence to account for the appearance of delayed speech, retarded speech, cluttering, and severe dyslalia. In a sense, the interrelated functions of hearing, language, and speech develop into an intricately balanced system of reflexes. The processes of conditioning and inhibition which serve in keeping these reflexes balanced require several years for development and are not fully mature until a child is 6 or 7 years old. Many conditions—prenatal, paranatal, or postnatal— may delay, retard, or impede this development. Fundamental chemical processes are involved, and apparently even slight imbalances may seriously affect a learning and behavioral component such as the capacity to pay attention. When this capacity is disturbed, a child may express himself but be unable to communicate because he is as yet unaware of the verbal interchange necessary for normal behavior.

Although this discussion has had to do with normal or aberrant development of the neuro-sensory mechanisms and processes in hearing, speech systems, and language development, the authors recognize the fact that all other aspects of growth and development must maintain a reasonable balance also; for when any aspect of the developmental balance is impaired, the intellectual tools of language and speech are apt to be profoundly affected.

The high incidence of speech and language problems in the population of this pilot study impresses on the authors the significance of extensive initial diagnostic data regarding the nature of hearing and language development in hyperactive or brain-injured children who may be considered for educational placement. It is not sufficient to know that the child is or is not characterized by a hearing loss. It is important that the nature of the hearing loss be thoroughly understood in terms of perception, memory, reproduction of language, and related speech characteristics. It is essential that the audiologist, speech pathologist, and the psychologist communicate frequently with one another regarding each child; for the characteristics of hyperactivity and of organicity which are herein being considered are closely related to each of the three disciplines. Their interrelationship must be understood by the diagnosticians before adequate information regarding the nature of the child can be provided to the teacher and before considerations regarding curriculum modification, grouping, and development of teaching materials can be undertaken.

Implications from Visual Examinations

Although ophthalmological examinations and optometric evaluations were not involved in the routine diagnostic study, visual examinations of both types were provided on a referral basis at the request of the staff pediatrician, neurologist, speech pathologist, and audiologist. In addition, the optometrist worked closely with the four research teachers in co-ordinating the classroom program with the visual training program in those cases where the children were also his private patients.

The following summary combines the findings of the ophthalmologists on the incidence of eye defects and the optometrist's evaluation of visual functioning among those children referred for examination.

Visual problems determined by ophthalmological examination were at a minimum; 5 children with nystagmus or strabismus had had corrective surgery performed, and their postoperative adjustment was successful.

From an optometric point of view, visual-perceptual disorders existed (as has been pointed out by the research psychologist and psychiatrist) in varying degrees in the majority of children. These disorders revealed themselves in the lack of eye-hand co-ordination, problems of fusion, rotations, and reversals. Alternating strabismus occurred under stress situations, such as those requiring sustained visual attention to desk work. Frequently, these disorders were associated with limited eye movements which resulted in difficulty in reproducing diagonal lines. In general, the children's capacity for binocular vision was characteristic of a much earlier developmental level.

In general, hand dexterity and control of eye movements in these children were very poor. Gross movements were more easily executed than were the fine movements required in visually centered, near-point work such as in drawing a diamond, copying a spelling list, or tying shoelaces. The response to tasks requiring fine motor abilities indicated a lag in the skills necessary to succeed in executing pencil and crayon drawings and placed serious limitations on any task requiring hand dexterity.

One aspect of the examination results indicated a need for special consideration in the classroom. It has been established (12) that visual discrimination and interpretation of visual material are hindered by inadequate control of eye movements. It is difficult for a child to really see a thing if his eyes cannot be quickly and economically centered on a given object. In the case of this group, the eye movements and control of visual centering were often poor, resulting in the child's need to turn the head and then the entire body toward an object rather than simply moving the eyes in the correct direction.

Most of the children had not yet learned the basic visual motor skills necessary for adequate visual functioning. One could not expect the children to completely overcome their difficulties—even with the aid of the intensive visual training they received as part of the specialized teaching method—because of the time already lost. There was, however, a good possibility that vision, through perceptual and motor integration, could be developed to an average level of efficient functioning.

Implications from Achievement Test Data

Since achievement-test findings and their educational implications are presented in detail in another section of this chapter, it is sufficient at this point to simply indicate that 33 children were nonreaders, 37 failed to score on the arithmetic subtests, and 29 were unable to spell even the simplest words at the beginning of the teaching period. This is not surprising in view of the fact that perceptual deficiencies, defective visual recognition, inability to recall visual patterns, and short attention span, all create confusion and difficulties in learning to read, write, spell, and develop number concepts.

THE DIAGNOSTIC TEAM

The implications thus far discussed strongly indicate the importance of adequate pre-educational diagnostic study. From the point of view of an extensive research study, diagnosis is one thing; from the point of view of practical educational programs, it may be another. In the view of the authors, what constitutes adequate diagnosis of hyperactive and brain-injured children in terms of the function of the public schools? Experience in the demonstration-pilot study gives some basis for response to this question.

In considering the education of hyperactive or brain-injured children, educators are dealing with extremes in their professional field. The nature of the individual differences in these children is so great that an extensive interdisciplinary diagnostic study is a minimum requirement before the development of an adequate educational program for each child can be undertaken. In spite of the often excessive cost, it is still necessary that full diagnostic data be received from diagnosticians who are familiar with the needs of the school personnel. A large number of the children in this study would have been permanently excluded from the public school system on the basis of the severity of their learning and social adjustment problems. However, as a result of the project, all of those children still living in the school district are retained in the public schools, many of them in regular grade placements in their neighborhood schools. This child salvage is significant enough to warrant the expense which was involved in the diagnostic phase.

A minimal diagnostic program will certainly include the following disciplines: pediatrics, clinical psychology, audiology, speech pathology, ophthalmology and optometry. The experience of the authors in the present study indicated that the nature of the pediatric examination provided a significant amount of psychiatric and neurological information. It was certainly sufficient to provide the educators with the basic data they required, and it was sufficient to make recommendations for referral to neurology or psychiatry when they were considered desirable. A well-prepared pediatrician with an orientation to pediatric psychiatry is essential to the ultimate educational program. The necessity of utilizing professionally adequate personnel clinical psychology, audiology, and speech pathology has already been sufficiently indicated. In view of the fact that visuo-motor and audio-motor disabilities are so characteristic of hyperactive and brain-injured children, extensive information regarding the nature of the auditory and visual sensory modalities is requisite to an adequate understanding of the child. Data from hearing, vision, and speech specialists can undoubtedly be integrated by psychological personnel into meaningful concepts for the educators who must interpret the diagnostic findings into an instructional program. The personnel indicated thus far constitute minimum planning.

If it is at all possible, pediatric psychiatry should be represented on the diagnostic team. The psychiatrist associated with this study was able to provide unique insights. Furthermore, the availability of the psychiatrist as a consultant to teaching personnel resulted in continuous acceptance by the teachers of the children in spite of emotional disturbances within the classroom. The children's extremes in behavior often violate all educational concepts of personal and classroom deportment. It is essential that there be available professional personnel from other disciplines who can assist the teacher to see the behavior of hyperactive and brain-injured children in its appropriate educational perspective and in terms of the individual growth and development of the child. The discipline of pediatric psychiatry has demonstrated that it can serve a major role in this connection.

EDUCATIONAL IMPLICATIONS

No other aspects of instructional programming more clearly reflect the changing trends in educational philosophy than do the factors considered important in grouping children for instructional purposes.

During the last fifty years, for example, the pendulum has swung from the period of grouping children on the basis of chronological age, dependence on rote methods of group instruction, and an unchanging curriculum to that period when the concept of individual differences precipitated a welter of various types of progressive reforms dedicated to the importance of the individual child, individualized instruction, and the use of a bewildering array of motivational materials. In spite of the psychologists' warnings, wholesale acceptance of psychological test instruments as infallible guides in developing the emotional and social growth of the whole child reached its height during this period.

In the first case, it appears that the educational philosophy was based on the assumption that all children of a given age learned the same things the same way at the same time; those who did not were not required by law to continue frustrating themselves and their teachers. Thus, the limitations of rote teaching remained undetected for many years.

In the second case, the basic assumption had shifted from a belief in the fundamental sameness of children to a concept of fundamental differences. During the last decade, there has been increasing evidence that the pendulum is swinging to a midway point which is concerned with the development of grouping criteria, group teaching methods, and curriculums based on patterns of or similarities in individual differences in the learning processes themselves. The current study illustrates this trend.

It would appear from a review of the current literature that experimental methods for grouping according to specialized instructional needs or individual differences have been most thoroughly explored and have been most rewarding with the following types of children: the physically handicapped (8), the blind and partially seeing (13), the deaf (14), the exceptionally gifted (15), the mentally retarded (11), and the brain-injured (16).

More recently, one sees the same trend appearing in public school systems which are initiating various types of track programs and ability grouping.

Educational Significance of Intelligence Test Data

The following comments concerning the possible uses of psychological test data in instructional grouping and programming can be seen as further refinements of a philosophy which recognizes the importance of grouping criteria based on patterns of individual differences.

Data concerning one of the four groups of children participating in the present pilot study will be presented in various grouping combinations, including that which the authors propose in utilizing standardized test results. The same group of children will be used in each example.

In Example 1, the grouping of the 10 hyperactive or brain-injured

EXAMPLE 1

Grouping by Chronological Age

Chronological Age	Expected Grade Assignment
6–11	Second
7– 8	Second
7– 8	Second
7–11	Third
8– 0	Third
8– 0	Third
8– 4	Third
8– 5	Third
8–10	Third
9– 7	Fourth

children would have been made on the assumption that chronological age equates with specific grade levels and that children can be taught the same subjects the same way because they learn at the same rate of speed.

In reality, only 2 of the 10 children could read, spell, or do arithmetic at all: one on the first grade level; the other, on the second. Presumably the children would have been assigned the same books, the same arithmetic problems, and the same spelling list year after year until they dropped out of school.

The grouping noted in Example 2 was made on the assumption that

EXAMPLE 2

Grouping by Chronological Age, Intelligence Quotient,
Mental Age and Achievement Test Scores

			Stanford Achievement Test, Form J							
Chronological Age	Intelligence Quotient	Mental Age	Paragraph Meaning	Word Meaning	Average Reading	Spelling	Arithmetic Reasoning	Arithmetic Computation	Average Arithmetic	Battery Mean
6–11	78	5– 5	0	0	0	0	0	0	0	0
7– 8	82	6– 4	0	0	0	0	0	0	0	0
7– 8	107	8– 2	2.2	2.6	2.4	3.4	0	2.1	1.1	2.1
7–11	73	5– 9	0	0	0	0	0	0	0	0
8– 0	69	5– 6	0	0	0	0	0	0	0	0
8– 0	68	5– 5	1.3	2.2	1.8	2.9	0	2.4	1.2	1.7
8– 4	106	8–10	0	0	0	0	0	0	0	0
8– 5	83	7– 0	0	0	0	0	0	0	0	0
8–10	70	6– 2	0	0	0	0	0	0	0	0
9– 7	85	8– 2	0	0	0	0	0	0	0	0

teaching efficiency can be expected only if a classroom group represents no more than three *instructional* levels and that the mental age of a child is more important than the intelligence quotient. It is interesting to note that the child with the highest IQ (107) and the child with the lowest IQ (68) had achieved a small degree of academic proficiency, the child with the 68 IQ having a mental age of 5–5 and the one with 107 IQ having a mental age of 8–2. In terms of chronological age, there is a difference of four months.

In Example 2, one sees the fallacy of assuming that chronological age can be equated with grade-level expectancy, intelligence quotient, or mental age in terms of academic achievement.

The above grouping criteria, combined with the additional matching factors from the medical and clinical studies (see Chapter III), represents the grouping criteria which was utilized in the project classes. Nowhere in this combination of factors was there any clue to the tremendous variation and range in the individual differences of each child.

In attempting to work through this problem, the research staff tabulated the results of individual test responses on the Stanford-Binet Form L subtest items. The results of this tabulation are shown in Table 170, and reveal beyond any doubt why when using traditional principles, in spite of what was considered to be grouping for maximum teaching efficiency, the four classes constituted exceedingly difficult and time-consuming instructional groups.

TABLE 170

Subtest Summary of the Stanford-Binet Intelligence Scale Form L and Achievement

Variable	Test Summary of Subjects									
	C-2-3	C-2-8	C-2-4	C-2-2	C-2-10	C-2-9	C-2-7	C-2-1	C-2-5	C-2-6
Chronological age	9–7	8–10	8–5	8–4	8–0	8–0	7–11	7–8	7–8	6–11
Intelligence quotient	85	70	83	106	68	69	73	107	82	78
Mental age	8–2	6–2	7–0	8–10	5–5	5–6	5–9	8–2	6–4	5–5
Stanford Achievement Test, Form J — Paragraph meaning	0	0	0	0	1.3	0	0	2.2	0	0
Word meaning	0	0	0	0	2.2	0	0	2.6	0	0
Average reading	0	0	0	0	1.8	0	0	2.4	0	0
Spelling	0	0	0	0	2.9	0	0	3.0	0	0
Arithmetic reasoning	0	0	0	0	0.0	0	0	0.0	0	0
Arithmetic computation	0	0	0	0	2.4	0	0	2.1	0	0
Average arithmetic	0	0	0	0	1.2	0	0	1.1	0	0
Battery mean	0	0	0	0	1.7	0	0	2.1	0	0
IV.		B			B	B				B
1 Picture vocabulary		+			+	+				+
2 Naming objects from memory		+			+	+				+
3 Picture completion: man		+			+	+				+
4 Pictorial identification		+			+	+				+
5 Discrimination of forms		+			+	+				+
6 Comprehension		+			+	+				+

Variable	Test Summary of Subjects									
	C-2-3	C-2-8	C-2-4	C-2-2	C-2-10	C-2-9	C-2-7	C-2-1	C-2-5	C-2-6
Chronological age	9–7	8–10	8–5	8–4	8–0	8–0	7–11	7–8	7–8	6–11
Intelligence quotient	85	70	83	106	68	69	73	107	82	78
Mental age	8–2	6–2	7–0	8–10	5–5	5–6	5–9	8–2	6–4	5–5
IV.6								B		
1 Esthetic comparison	+				+	+	+			+
2 Repeating four digits	+				+	+	+			o
3 Pictorial likenesses and differences	+				+	+	+			+
4 Materials	o				o	o	+			+
5 Three commissions	+				+	o	+			+
6 Opposite analogies	+				+	+	+			o
V.										
1 Picture completion: man	+				+	+	+			+
2 Paper folding, triangle	+				+	o	+			+
3 Definitions	+				+	+	+			+
4 Copying a square	o				o	+	+			+
5 Memory for sentences	+				o	+	o			o
6 Counting four objects	+				+	+	+			+
VI.		B	B					B	B	
1 Vocabulary	+	+	+	o	o	+		+	+	+
2 Copying a bead chain	o	+	+	+	o	o		+	+	o
3 Mutilated pictures	+	+	+	o	+	+		+	+	+
4 Number concepts	+	+	+	+	+	+		+	+	o
5 Pictorial likenesses and differences	o	+	+	+	+	+		+	+	+
6 Maze tracing	+	+	+	+	+	+		+	+	+
VII.						C	C			C
1 Picture absurdities	+	+	+			o		+	o	
2 Similarities	o	o	+			o		+	+	
3 Copying a diamond	o	o	+			o		o	o	
4 Comprehension	o	+	o			o		+	+	
5 Opposite analogies	o	o	+			o		+	+	
6 Repeating five digits	o	o	+				+	+	o	

Variable	Test Summary of Subjects									
	C-2-3	C-2-8	C-2-4	C-2-2	C-2-10	C-2-9	C-2-7	C-2-1	C-2-5	C-2-6
Chronological age	9–7	8–10	8–5	8–4	8–0	8–0	7–11	7–8	7–8	6–11
Intelligence quotient	85	70	83	106	68	69	73	107	82	78
Mental age	8–2	6–2	7–0	8–10	5–5	5–6	5–9	8–2	6–4	5–5
VIII.	B				C				C	
1 Vocabulary	+	+	+	+				+		
2 Memory for stories	+	+	o	+				+		
3 Verbal absurdities	+	o	o	o				o		
4 Similarities	+	o	o	+				+		
5 Comprehension	+	o	o	o				+		
6 Memory for sentences	+	o	o	+				+		
IX.	C									
1 Paper cutting	o		+	+				+		
2 Verbal absurdities	o		o	o				o		
3 Memory for designs	o		+	+				o		
4 Rhymes	o		o	+				+		
5 Making change	o		o	+				o		
6 Repeating four digits reversed	o		o	o				o		
X.										
1 Vocabulary	+		o	+				o		
2 Picture absurdities II	o		+	+				o		
3 Reading and report	o		o	o				o		
4 Finding reasons	o		o	o				o		
5 Word naming	o		o	o				o		
6 Repeating six digits	o		o	o				+		
XI.	C		C					C		
1 Memory for designs				o						
2 Verbal absurdities				o						
3 Abstract words				o						
4 Memory for sentences				+						
5 Problem situation				o						
6 Similarities, three things				+						
XII.				C						

B = Basal age
C = Maximum passing level
+ = Pass item
o = Fail item

The chronological age-range is approximately 7 through 9. One might assume that matters would have been less complicated if only eight-year-olds had been assigned to this group. However, the intelligence quotients for the 5 eight-year-olds range from 68 through 106. The most important piece of information derived from the tabulation of the subtest items is the total range in ability levels which this group represents, i.e., from the year 4 to the year 12. Almost of equal importance from an instructional standpoint are the individual patterns of pass and failure on the subtest items. One example will suffice. Study the pattern of test responses of the child, age 9–7 with an IQ of 85 and mental age of 8–2. The basal age is at the year VIII level; the ceiling is at the year XI level. The *scatter,* however, is most unusual. No items at year IX were passed, but vocabulary was passed at the year X level. Vocabulary is thus almost 2 years above the mental age.

When tabulated in the above fashion, the individual and group patterns illustrate the uneven developmental picture so characteristic of the hyperactive children participating in the project.

The Binet summary in Table 171 was prepared from the test results of the same children given at the termination of the project. The table demonstrates the impact of both the diagnostic grouping and the spe-

TABLE 171
*Subtest Summary of the Stanford-Binet Intelligence Scale
Form L and Achievement*

Variable	Test Summary of Subjects									
	C-2-3	C-2-8	C-2-4	C-2-2	C-2-10	C-2-9	C-2-7	C-2-1	C-2-5	C-2-6
Chronological age	11–9	10–11	10–4	10–2	10–1	9–11	9–10	10–0	9–10	8–11
Intelligence quotient	82	64	87	107	78	65	78	114	81	71
Mental age	9–8	7–0	9–0	10–10	7–10	6–5	7–8	11–5	8–0	6–4
Paragraph meaning	2.5	2.5	2.5	2.4	3.2	1.6	2.4	5.0	2.3	1.3
Word meaning	2.3	2.9	2.4	2.4	3.3	1.7	2.6	5.0	2.3	1.8
Average reading	2.4	2.7	2.5	2.4	3.3	1.7	2.5	5.0	2.3	1.6
Spelling	3.0	3.1	2.6	2.2	4.7	0	2.7	5.0	2.1	0
Arithmetic reasoning	3.1	2.0	3.2	3.8	3.2	1.3	2.0	5.0	3.0	1.6
Arithmetic computation	2.7	1.7	2.8	3.4	3.8	1.9	2.3	5.0	2.0	2.2
Average arithmetic	2.9	1.9	3.0	3.6	3.5	1.6	2.2	5.0	2.5	1.9
Battery mean	2.7	2.4	2.7	2.8	3.6	1.3	2.4	5.0	2.3	1.4

Stanford Achievement Test, Form J

VI.		B			B	B	B		B	B
1	Vocabulary	+			+	+	+		+	+
2	Copying a bead chain	+			+	+	+		+	+

Variable	Test Summary of Subjects									
	C-2-3	C-2-8	C-2-4	C-2-2	C-2-10	C-2-9	C-2-7	C-2-1	C-2-5	C-2-6
Chronological age	11–9	10–11	10–4	10–2	10–1	9–11	9–10	10–0	9–10	8–11
Intelligence quotient	82	64	87	107	78	65	78	114	81	71
Mental age	9–8	7–0	9–0	10–10	7–10	6–5	7–8	11–5	8–0	6–4
3 Mutilated pictures		+			+	+	+		+	+
4 Number concepts		+			+	+	+		+	+
5 Pictorial likenesses and differences		+			+	+	+		+	+
6 Maze tracing		+			+	+	+		+	+
VII.										
1 Picture absurdities		+			o	+	+		+	+
2 Similarities		+			+	+	+		+	o
3 Copying a diamond		o			o	o	o		o	o
4 Comprehension		+			o	+	+		+	o
5 Opposite analogies						+	o				+	o
6 Repeating five digits		o			+	+	o		+	o
VIII.	B		B					B		
1 Vocabulary	+	+	+		o	o	+	+	o	o
2 Memory for stories	+			+		o	o	+	+	+	+
3 Verbal absurdities	+	o	+		+	+	+	+	+	o
4 Similarities	+	+	+		+	+	+	+	+	o
5 Comprehension	+	+	+		o	o	+	+	+	o
6 Memory for sentences	+	o	+		+	+	o	+	o	o
IX.		C		B		C			C	C
1 Paper cutting	o		+	+	o		+	+		
2 Verbal absurdities	+		+	+	o		o	+		
3 Memory for designs	o		o	+	o		o	o		
4 Rhymes	+		o	+	+		+	o		
5 Making change	+		+	+	+		o	+		
6 Repeating four digits reversed	o		o	+	+		o	+		
X.										
1 Vocabulary	+		+	+	o		+	+		
2 Picture absurdities II	+		+	+	+		+	o		
3 Reading and report	o		o	o	o		o	+		
4 Finding reasons	o		o	o	o		o	+		
5 Word naming	+		+	o	+		o	+		
6 Repeating six digits	+		o	o	o		o	o		

Variable	Test Summary of Subjects									
	C-2-3	C-2-8	C-2-4	C-2-2	C-2-10	C-2-9	C-2-7	C-2-1	C-2-5	C-2-6
Chronological age	11–9	10–11	10–4	10–2	10–1	9–11	9–10	10–0	9–10	8–11
Intelligence quotient	82	64	87	107	78	65	78	114	81	71
Mental age	9–8	7–0	9–0	10–10	7–10	6–5	7–8	11–5	8–0	6–4
XI.			C		C		C			
1 Memory for designs	o			+				o		
2 Verbal absurdities	+			o				o		
3 Abstract words	o			+				o		
4 Memory for sentences	+			+				o		
5 Problem situation	+			o				+		
6 Similarities, three things	o			+				o		
XII.		C								
1 Vocabulary				o				+		
2 Verbal absurdities II				+				o		
3 Response to Pictures II				o				o		
4 Repeating five digits reversed				o				o		
5 Abstract words II				+				o		
6 Minkus completion				o				+		
XIII.										
1 Plan of search				+				o		
2 Memory for words				o				o		
3 Paper cutting I				+				o		
4 Problems of fact				+				o		
5 Dissected sentences				o				o		
6 Copying a bead chain				+				+		
XIV.								C		
1 Vocabulary				o						
2 Induction				o						
3 Picture absurdities III				+						
4 Ingenuity				+						
5 Orientation: direction				o						
6 Abstract words II				o						
XV.				C						

B = Basal age
C = Maximum passing level
+ = Pass item
o = Fail item

cialized teaching approach upon the uneven developmental pattern, particularly because they brought up the group's basal age level to a maturational level commensurate with academic readiness. This observation is substantiated by the individual and group gains in achievement as measured by the Stanford Achievement Test Form J, the average gain being 2.1 years for this group with a range from 2 months through 2 years, 8 months.

Recognizing the fact that the children were, on the whole 2 years older, one is still impressed with the mental age gains demonstrated in Table 171. Certainly this would tend to add support to the idea frequently advanced (11) that for purposes of instructional grouping, it would appear that mental age is more reliable than either chronological age or intelligence quotient.

Although it was not possible to incorporate the subtest response pattern into the matching and grouping criteria, the research staff was so intrigued with the possibilities of its future use that the original 40 children were regrouped, using the additional information. One such hypothetical group is reproduced in Table 172.

TABLE 172
*Subtest Summary of the Stanford-Binet Intelligence Scale
Form L and Achievement*

	Variable	Test Summary of Subjects									
		E-1-1	C-1-1	E-2-4	C-2-4	C-2-1	C-1-3	E-2-2	E-2-1	C-2-2	E-1-2
	Chronological age	6–10	8–2	9–9	8–5	7–8	9–2	8–2	8–3	8–4	8–4
	Intelligence quotient	102	102	80	83	107	89	106	107	106	94
	Mental age	7–0	8–4	7–10	7–0	8–2	8–2	8–8	7–0	8–10	7–10
Stanford Achievement Test, Form J	Paragraph meaning	0	2.9	0	0	2.2	1.5	2.2	2.3	0	1.3
	Word meaning	0	4.6	0	0	2.6	0	1.9	2.0	0	1.7
	Average reading	0	3.8	0	0	2.4	.8	2.1	2.2	0	1.1
	Spelling	0	3.0	0	0	3.4	0	1.8	2.2	0	1.7
	Arithmetic reasoning	0	3.2	0	0	0	0	3.2	1.8	0	0
	Arithmetic computation	0	3.0	0	0	2.1	0	2.7	2.5	0	1.8
	Average arithmetic	0	3.1	0	0	1.1	0	2.9	2.2	0	0
	Battery mean	0	3.3	0	0	2.1	.3	2.4	2.2	0	1.5

V.		B	B								
1	Picture completion: man	+	+								
2	Paper folding, triangle	+	+								

Variable	E-1-1	C-1-1	E-2-4	C-2-4	C-2-1	C-1-3	E-2-2	E-2-1	C-2-2	E-1-2
				Test Summary of Subjects						
Chronological age	6–10	8–2	9–9	8–5	7–8	9–2	8–2	8–3	8–4	8–4
Intelligence quotient	102	102	80	83	107	89	106	107	106	94
Mental age	7–0	8–4	7–10	7–0	8–2	8–2	8–8	7–0	8–10	7–10
3 Definitions	+	+								
4 Copying a square	+	+								
5 Memory for sentences	+	+								
6 Counting four objects	+	+								
VI.			B	B	B	B	B	B	B	B
1 Vocabulary	+	+	+	+	+	+	+	+	+	+
2 Copying a bead chain	o	o	+	+	+	+	+	+	+	+
3 Mutilated pictures	+	+	+	+	+	+	+	+	+	+
4 Number concepts	+	+	+	+	+	+	+	+	+	+
5 Pictorial likenesses and differences	+	+	+	+	+	+	+	+	+	+
6 Maze tracing	+	+	+	+	+	+	+	+	+	+
VII.										
1 Picture absurdities	+	+	+	+	+	+	+	+	+	+
2 Similarities	o	o	+	o	+	+	+	+	+	+
3 Copying a diamond	+	o	+	o	o	+	+	o	+	o
4 Comprehension	+	+	+	+	+	+	+	+	o	+
5 Opposite analogies	+	+	+	o	+	o	o	+	+	o
6 Repeating five digits	+	+	o	o	+	+	+	o	+	o
VIII.										
1 Vocabulary	+	+	+	+	+	o	+	+	+	+
2 Memory for stories	+	+	o	o	+	+	+	o	+	+
3 Verbal absurdities	o	o	+	o	o	+	+	+	o	o
4 Similarities	o	+	o	o	+	+	+	+	+	o
5 Comprehension	o	+	+	o	+	o	o	+	o	+
6 Memory for sentences	o	+	o	o	+	o	+	+	+	o
IX.										
1 Paper cutting	o	o	o	+	+	o	+	+	+	+
2 Verbal absurdities	o	o	o	o	o	o	o	+	o	o
3 Memory for designs	o	o	o	+	o	o	o	+	+	o
4 Rhymes	+	+	o	o	+	+	+	+	+	+
5 Making change	o	+	+	o	o	+	+	o	+	o

TABLE 172, *continued*

Variable	Test Summary of Subjects									
	E-1-1	C-1-1	E-2-4	C-2-4	C-2-1	C-1-3	E-2-2	E-2-1	C-2-2	E-1-2
Chronological age	6–10	8–2	9–9	8–5	7–8	9–2	8–2	8–3	8–4	8–4
Intelligence quotient	102	102	80	83	107	89	106	107	106	94
Mental age	7–0	8–4	7–10	7–0	8–2	8–2	8–8	7–0	8–10	7–10
6 Repeating four digits reversed	+	o	o	o	o	+	o	o	o	o
X.										
1 Vocabulary	o	o	+	o	o	o	o	+	+	+
2 Picture absurdities II	+	+	+	+	o	+	+	+	+	+
3 Reading and report	o	o	o	o	o	o	o	o	o	o
4 Finding reasons	o	+	o	o	o	o	o	o	o	o
5 Word naming	o	o	o	o	o	o	o	o	o	o
6 Repeating six digits	o	+	o	o	+	o	+	o	o	o
XI.	C		C	C	C					
1 Memory for designs		o				o	o	+	o	o
2 Verbal absurdities		o				o	o	o	o	o
3 Abstract words		o				o	o	o	o	o
4 Memory for sentences		+				o	+	o	+	o
5 Problem situation		o				o	o	+	o	o
6 Similarities, three things		o				+	o	o	+	+
XII.		C				C	C	C	C	C

B = Basal age
C = Maximum passing level
+ = Pass item
o = Fail item

The reader will note that the chronological age range is from 6–10 through 9–9, the mental age range is from 7–0 through 8–10, and the IQ range is from 80 through 107, representing a tightening up in the use of traditional criteria. The range in achievement levels is from 0 to 3.3, with 4 of the children unable to score at all. This range at first suggests an impossible instructional situation. However, a glance at the group's subtest response pattern shows that, with the exception of 2 children who failed one item at the VIII year level, their difficulties with test items began at the year VII. One might speculate, in such a case, as to whether the teacher would not be able to cut down on the amount of individual instruction and concentrate the major proportion of her time on group teaching. Since it was not possible to test the usefulness of the patterns of individual subtest responses to the Stanford-Binet Intelligence Scale in grouping the children for purposes of specialized instruction, one can only hope that others will find it a thought-provoking idea.

In the preceding section the discussion was mainly concerned with the general problem of grouping criteria and with speculation concerning the possible educational significance of standardized intelligence test data. With hyperactive and brain-injured children one of the most significant problems to the educator is grouping. These children present so many diverse problems and characteristics that time spent in grouping to achieve as much homogeneity as possible will be profitable in terms of effective teaching and child achievement.

In the following section the authors will consider some of the educational problems pointed up by the results of the achievement test data.

Educational Significance of the Achievement Test Data

The results and value of educational research—particularly when it occurs in public school classrooms and involves the use of experimental teaching methods with underachieving, disturbed children—quite sensibly will be measured in terms of whether or not the children increased their achievement level. That is, did the children participating in the project learn better and advance faster than they had previously?

This section of the monograph reports the evidence of increased academic proficiency in the total group and considers some of the problems of using standardized achievement tests with these children. It will also highlight the extreme need for cautious re-evaluation of some of the basic assumptions concerning the use of traditionally accepted indexes of the learning potential of children who do not achieve at grade-level expectancy.

Academic Achievement Results, Stanford Achievement Test, Form J, October, 1957–June, 1959

Thirty-nine of the 40 children remained in the research classes during the academic phase of the pilot study, September, 1957–June, 1958. One child was excluded.[1] The Stanford Achievement Test was administered

---

[1] One child was dropped from the study because his behavior disorders became so severe it was necessary to refer him for residential treatment. Follow-up contacts revealed that his parents had been so eager to have their child in the study that the mother gave a false history of severe birth injury and traumatic pregnancy.

at the beginning and at the end of the school year. Two children made enough academic, social, and emotional improvement during this period to be transferred out of the project and assigned to a regular class at their appropriate age grade expectancy level.[2] The diagnostic grouping and instructional aspects of the pilot study terminated at this point. Thirty-three of the original 40 children were still available at the time of the follow-up testing in June, 1959 when once again, the Stanford Achievement Test was included in the test battery. The results are reproduced in Table 173 in alphabetical order.

During the pre-test period only 10 children were able to participate in the test, and 4 of them made only partial scores. The IQ range of the 10 children is from 68 to 107. Of the 4 children who made partial scores, 1 had an IQ of 73, 2 had an IQ of 89, and 1 had an IQ of 91.

By the end of the instructional phase of the project, all 39 children, including the 33 identified in the above chart, demonstrated increased academic achievement in varying degrees.

Two children, one in each of the two control groups, made sufficient progress to warrant regular grade placement; they were the 2 children whose level of achievement at the beginning of the project was the most advanced. One child was 7 years and 8 months of age, had an IQ of 107, and achieved a battery mean of 2.1 on the achievement test. The other child was 8 years, and 2 months old, had an IQ of 102, and achieved a battery mean of 3.3. During the academic year following this test, the first child increased his academic proficiency to the point where he tested 4.0, a gain of 1.9 years. The second child made substantially

---

[2] The formula for age grade placement shown below is taken from Alice M. Horn, *Uneven Distribution of the Effects of Specific Factors*, Southern California Education Monograph, No. 12, Los Angeles: University of Southern California Press.

$$AGP = \text{Achievement grade placement}$$
$$MAGP = \text{Mental age grade placement}$$
$$CAGP = \text{Chronological age grade placement}$$

Ages: 12–0 and above

$$AGP = \frac{3\,(MAGP) + CAGP}{4}$$

Ages: 10–0 to 11–11

$$AGP = \frac{2\,(MAGP) + CAGP}{3}$$

Ages: 8–6 to 9–11

$$AGP = \frac{3\,(MAGP) + CAGP}{5}$$

TABLE 173
Stanford Achievement Test Results

Sub-ject	Pre-test October, 1957								Post-test June, 1958			
	Paragraph meaning	Word meaning	Average reading	Spelling	Arithmetic reasoning	Arithmetic computation	Average arithmetic	Battery mean	Paragraph meaning	Word meaning	Average reading	Spelling
C-2-7	0.0	0.0	0.0	0.0	0.0	0.0	0.0	0.0	1.5	2.1	1.8	1.5
E-1-4	0.0	0.0	0.0	0.0	0.0	0.0	0.0	0.0	3.0	3.6	3.3	2.5
E-1-3	1.5	0.0	.8	1.4	0.0	1.5	0.0	.9	1.9	2.3	2.1	2.6
C-1-5	1.2	0.0	.6	1.7	0.0	2.5	1.2	1.1	1.9	2.1	2.0	2.9
E-1-1	0.0	0.0	0.0	0.0	0.0	0.0	0.0	0.0	2.3	2.5	2.4	2.8
E-2-3	0.0	0.0	0.0	0.0	0.0	0.0	0.0	0.0	0.0	0.0	0.0	0.0
E-2-9	0.0	0.0	0.0	0.0	0.0	0.0	0.0	0.0	1.9	2.5	2.2	2.3
C-2-10	1.3	2.2	1.8	2.9	0.0	2.4	1.2	1.7	2.9	2.8	2.9	2.7
E-1-9	0.0	0.0	0.0	0.0	0.0	0.0	0.0	0.0	2.3	2.5	2.4	3.3
E-2-4	0.0	0.0	0.0	0.0	0.0	0.0	0.0	0.0	1.3	1.6	1.5	2.1
C-2-5	0.0	0.0	0.0	0.0	0.0	0.0	0.0	0.0	0.0	0.0	0.0	1.1
C-2-6	0.0	0.0	0.0	0.0	0.0	0.0	0.0	0.0	0.0	0.0	0.0	0.0
C-2-2	0.0	0.0	0.0	0.0	0.0	0.0	0.0	0.0	1.8	1.7	1.8	2.1
C-1-4	0.0	0.0	0.0	0.0	0.0	0.0	0.0	0.0	0.0	0.0	0.0	1.4
C-1-3	1.5	0.0	.8	0.0	0.0	0.0	0.0	.3	2.5	2.1	2.3	2.6
E-2-2	2.2	1.9	2.1	1.8	3.2	2.7	2.9	2.4	2.5	2.8	2.7	2.5
E-2-1	2.3	2.0	2.2	2.2	1.8	2.5	2.2	2.2	2.0	2.1	2.1	2.7
E-1-7	0.0	0.0	0.0	0.0	0.0	0.0	0.0	0.0	1.8	2.1	1.9	2.6
C-2-9	0.0	0.0	0.0	0.0	0.0	0.0	0.0	0.0	0.0	0.0	0.0	0.0
C-1-8	0.0	0.0	0.0	0.0	0.0	0.0	0.0	0.0	1.7	1.8	1.7	1.6
E-1-5	0.0	0.0	0.0	0.0	0.0	0.0	0.0	0.0	2.2	2.6	2.4	3.2
E-1-8	1.5	0.0	.8	1.1	0.0	0.0	0.0	.5	1.7	1.7	1.7	2.4
E-2-6	0.0	0.0	0.0	0.0	0.0	0.0	0.0	0.0	0.0	0.0	0.0	1.1
C-2-4	0.0	0.0	0.0	0.0	0.0	0.0	0.0	0.0	2.0	1.8	1.9	1.4
E-1-10	0.0	0.0	0.0	0.0	0.0	0.0	0.0	0.0	0.0	0.0	0.0	0.0
C-1-6	1.7	0.0	.9	2.8	0.0	1.4	0.0	1.2	2.5	2.5	2.5	2.8
E-2-8	0.0	0.0	0.0	0.0	0.0	0.0	0.0	0.0	0.0	0.0	0.0	0.0
C-1-7	0.0	0.0	0.0	0.0	0.0	0.0	0.0	0.0	0.0	0.0	0.0	1.1
E-2-10	0.0	0.0	0.0	0.0	0.0	0.0	0.0	0.0	0.0	0.0	0.0	1.3
C-2-3	0.0	0.0	0.0	0.0	0.0	0.0	0.0	0.0	2.0	2.1	2.1	2.1
C-2-8	0.0	0.0	0.0	0.0	0.0	0.0	0.0	0.0	1.3	0.0	.6	1.8
C-1-10	0.0	0.0	0.0	0.0	0.0	0.0	0.0	0.0	0.0	0.0	0.0	0.0
E-1-2	1.3	1.7	1.1	1.7	0.0	1.8	0.0	1.5	2.0	2.6	2.3	3.4
C-1-9	0.0	0.0	0.0	0.0	0.0	0.0	0.0	0.0	1.4	2.1	1.7	2.1
C-1-2	1.2	0.0	.6	1.2	0.0	2.1	1.0	.9	1.9	1.7	1.8	2.3

Post-test June, 1958				Follow-up June, 1959								Grade-level gain (1957–1959)
Arithmetic reasoning	Arithmetic computation	Average arithmetic	Battery mean	Paragraph meaning	Word meaning	Average reading	Spelling	Arithmetic reasoning	Arithmetic computation	Average arithmetic	Battery mean	
1.6	2.0	1.8	1.7	2.4	2.6	2.5	2.7	2.0	2.3	2.2	2.4	2.4
2.1	1.5	1.8	2.5	3.3	3.6	3.5	4.1	3.1	2.3	2.7	3.3	3.3
1.6	2.3	1.9	2.1	2.4	2.0	2.2	2.0	2.2	2.4	2.3	2.2	1.3
2.5	2.6	2.5	2.4	3.8	3.4	3.6	4.1	3.6	3.5	3.6	3.7	2.6
3.2	2.8	3.0	2.7	3.6	4.0	3.8	3.6	3.6	3.1	3.4	3.6	3.6
1.2	2.0	1.6	.6	1.3	1.5	1.4	—	2.8	1.9	2.4	1.5	1.5
1.5	1.3	1.4	1.9	3.4	3.0	3.2	3.1	1.6	—	.8	2.2	2.2
2.7	2.2	2.8	2.7	3.2	3.3	3.3	4.7	3.2	3.8	3.5	3.6	1.9
3.7	3.4	3.5	3.0	3.6	3.3	3.5	4.4	4.2	3.6	3.9	3.8	3.8
2.9	3.1	3.0	2.2	3.3	3.3	3.3	3.4	4.2	3.6	3.9	3.6	3.6
1.2	2.0	1.6	.9	2.3	2.3	2.3	2.1	3.0	2.0	2.5	2.3	2.3
1.0	1.2	1.1	.4	1.3	1.8	1.6	—	1.6	2.2	1.9	1.4	1.4
3.1	3.1	3.1	2.4	2.4	2.4	2.4	2.2	3.8	3.4	3.6	2.8	2.8
1.5	1.5	1.5	.9	1.5	1.9	1.7	—	2.4	2.1	2.2	1.6	1.6
3.4	3.8	3.6	2.9	3.3	2.9	3.1	3.1	4.8	4.1	4.5	3.6	3.3
3.4	3.1	3.3	2.9	5.8	4.8	5.3	3.8	4.8	3.7	4.3	4.6	2.2
2.9	3.2	3.1	2.6	3.3	3.5	3.4	3.0	4.8	3.6	4.2	3.6	1.4
1.8	1.5	1.6	2.0	2.5	2.6	2.6	2.7	2.4	2.4	2.4	2.5	2.5
1.5	1.9	1.7	.7	1.6	1.7	1.7	—	1.3	1.9	1.6	1.3	1.3
1.2	1.5	1.3	1.5	1.8	1.7	1.8	1.7	2.0	2.5	2.3	1.9	1.9
1.6	1.8	1.7	2.3	3.2	3.6	3.4	4.6	2.8	2.3	2.6	3.3	3.3
2.1	2.4	2.3	2.1	2.7	2.0	2.4	2.3	2.2	2.4	2.3	2.3	1.8
1.2	2.8	2.0	1.0	1.9	2.0	2.0	2.5	3.0	2.3	2.7	2.3	2.3
1.5	2.1	1.8	1.8	2.5	2.4	2.5	2.6	3.2	2.8	3.0	2.7	2.7
1.2	1.8	1.5	.6									
1.8	1.6	1.7	2.2	3.6	3.3	3.5	4.4	2.6	2.0	2.3	3.2	2.0
1.5	0.0	0.0	.3	0.0	0.0	0.0	0.0	1.0	1.4	1.2	.5	.5
1.3	1.2	1.2	.7	1.3	1.7	1.5	1.5	1.3	1.3	1.3	1.4	1.4
1.5	1.6	1.6	.9	2.1	2.0	2.1	2.1	1.6	2.1	1.9	2.0	2.0
2.7	2.4	2.6	2.3	2.5	2.3	2.4	3.0	3.1	2.7	2.9	2.7	2.7
1.2	1.2	1.2	1.1	2.5	2.9	2.7	3.1	2.0	1.7	1.9	2.4	2.4
1.0	0.0	.5	.2	0.0	0.0	0.0	0.0	0.0	0.0	0.0	0.0	0.0
3.3	2.9	3.1	2.8	3.6	4.2	3.9	3.4	3.8	3.2	3.5	3.6	2.1
1.1	1.7	1.4	1.7	2.3	2.1	2.2	2.3	2.2	2.1	2.2	2.2	2.2
2.9	3.2	3.0	2.4	2.5	3.2	2.9	2.4	4.2	3.3	3.8	3.1	2.2

less gain, a total of 7 months. This gain was, however, all he needed in order to meet his age grade expectancy level. The functioning IQ in the case of the first child increased 7 points (107–14), an increase which is within normal variation. The gain in the second case was 12 points (102 to 114), a substantial indication of the increased ability.

In evaluating the impact of the use of diagnostic grouping and the specialized teaching method upon specific learning disabilities in relation to specific subject areas, it is worth reporting that 23 of the 39 original children made greater progress in arithmetic during the first year, while 15 made greater progress in reading. Only one child increased his achievement level in both subjects equally (from 0 to 1.8).

It is the opinion of the authors that the discrepancy in the scores on reading and arithmetic subtests reflected the general pattern of uneven development in the children. This observation would tend to be supported by the results of the follow-up testing in the spring of 1959.

It is apparent in this case that the children not only continued to gain in achievement but, as indicated above, that the gains were consolidated in terms of subject matter. That is, where the previous testing results demonstrated a substantial gain in terms of battery mean, all except one child were substantially more proficient in one subject than in another. This fact alone perpetuated the teachers' instructional problems referred to earlier in this chapter. The teacher, for example, when preparing her instructional materials and lesson plans, was required to prepare in all but one case material at two or more grade levels for each child. In the majority of cases, by the time the follow-up testing took place, this was no longer necessary; the children had consolidated their gains.

Table 174 summarizes the gains of the children in terms of their age-grade levels as determined by their Stanford Achievement Test scores for the three testing periods.

The following discussion is concerned with some questions concerning the validity of using IQ scores and mental age in predicting the achievement potential of hyperactive and brain-injured children.

Table 175 presents the scores of the children who participated in all three test situations. The reader will note that the information includes the mental age and intelligence quotients for all three periods, the 1959 Stanford Achievement Test individual battery mean achieved by each child, and a comparison between those means and the achievement status in relation to their mental-age expectancies. Those cases where the actual achievement score equates with mental-age-grade expectancy are marked "average," those whose achievement scores are above their

TABLE 174
Stanford Achievement Test, Form J

Pre-test, October, 1957
Total Number of Children Tested = 40

Achievement Levels: Grade Placement

Reading: First grade . . . . 3 children
            Second grade . . . . 2 children
            Third grade . . . . 1 child
     Total Number of Children Scoring on Test 6
     Total Number of Children Who Failed to Score 34

Spelling: First grade . . . . 7 children
            Second grade . . . . 2 children
            Third grade . . . . 2 children
     Total Number of Children Scoring on Test 11
     Total Number of Children Who Failed to Score 29

Arithmetic: First grade . . . . , , , , . 0 children
            Second grade . . . . 2 children
            Third grade . . . . 1 child
     Total Number of Children Scoring on Test 3
     Total Number of Children Who Failed to Score 37

Follow-up I, June, 1958
Total Number of Children Tested = 39

Achievement Levels:

Reading: Readiness level . . . . 8 children
            First grade . . . . 9 children
            Second grade . . . . . . 12 children
            Third grade . . . . 1 child
            Fourth grade . . . . 2 children
     Total Number of Children Scoring on Test 32
     Total Number of Children Making No Measurable Gain . . . 7

Spelling: First grade . . . . 10 children
            Second grade . . . . . . 17 children
            Third grade . . . . 4 children
            Fourth grade . . . . 1 child
     Total Number of Children Scoring on Test 32
     Total Number of Children Making No Measurable Gain . . . 7

TABLE 174, *continued*

Arithmetic: First grade   .   .   .   . 24 children
            Second grade .   .   .   . 5 children
            Third grade .   .   .   . 10 children
    Total Number of Children Scoring on Test 39
    Total Number of Children Making No Measurable Gain 0

Follow-up II, June, 1959
Total Number of Children Tested = 34

Achievement Levels: Grade Placement
    Reading: First grade   .   .   .   . 6 children
            Second grade .   .   .   . 13 children
            Third grade .   .   .   . 12 children
            Fourth grade .   .   .   . 0 children
            Fifth grade   .   .   .   . 1 child
    Total Number of Children Scoring on Test 32
    Total Number of Children Making No Measurable Gain 2

    Spelling: First grade   .   .   .   . 2 children
            Second grade .   .   .   . 11 children
            Third grade .   .   .   . 9 children
            Fourth grade .   .   .   . 6 children
            Fifth grade   .   .   .   . 0 children
    Total Number of Children Scoring on Test 28
    Total Number of Children Making No Measurable Gain 6

    Arithmetic: Readiness level   .   .   .   . 1 child
            First grade   .   .   .   . 6 children
            Second grade .   .   .   . 14 children
            Third grade .   .   .   . 9 children
            Fourth grade .   .   .   . 3 children
            Fifth grade   .   .   .   . 0 children
    Total Number of Children Scoring on Test 33
    Total Number of Children Making No Measurable Gain 1

---

mental-age-grade expectancy are marked "high," and those whose score
was below mental-age expectancy are marked "low." The final figure
demonstrates the total grade level gains from 1957 through 1959.
Table 175 indicates that 6 children made a grade level gain of 3 or
more years; 16 made a grade level gain of 2 or more years; 10 made a
gain of 1 or more years; 1 made a gain of less than a year; and 1 child,
who demonstrated a gain of .2 by the end of the first year, lost this gain
after the termination of the project.

These gains should be examined in terms of some generally accepted assumptions. The comparison in Table 175 between the achievement test battery mean and the mental age is based on the assumption that age-grade expectancy levels are derived from valid norms of mental-age-grade expectancy levels. Examination of the tabulated data reveals

TABLE 175

Stanford-Binet Intelligence Tests: Forms L and M

Subject	Pre-test Form L		Follow-up I Form M		Follow-up II Form L		Battery	Grade Level Gain
	MA	IQ	MA	IQ	MA	IQ	Mean [a]	1957–59
C-2-7	5– 9	73	7– 4	83	7– 8	78	2.4 LA	2.4
E-1-4	5–10	84	5–10	74	6–10	76	3.3 H	3.3
E-1-3	6– 6	89	7– 0	82	8– 0	83	2.2 L	1.3
C-1-5	7– 0	82	7– 8	83	9– 8	94	3.7 L	2.6
E-1-1	7– 0	102	7– 0	88	8– 8	95	3.6 H	3.6
E-2-3	5–11	86	6– 6	83	7– 0	79	1.5 LA	1.5
E-2-9	5– 8	67	6– 6	69	6–10	65	2.2 H	2.2
C-2-10	5– 5	68	7– 0	78	7–10	78	3.6 H	1.9
E-1-9	5– 5	64	6– 4	68	7– 2	68	3.8 H	3.8
E-2-4	7–10	80	10– 0	95	10– 6	90	3.6 L	3.6
C-2-5	6– 4	82	8– 0	91	8– 0	81	2.3 L	2.3
C-2-6	5– 5	78	6– 0	77	6– 4	71	1.4 A	1.4
C-2-2	8–10	106	8–10	96	10–10	107	2.8 L	2.8
C-1-4	5–11	87	6– 6	82	6–10	77	1.6 LA	1.6
C-1-3	8– 2	89	9– 0	90	9– 6	86	3.6 L	3.3
E-2-2	8– 8	106	9–10	108	12– 0	118	4.6 L	2.2
E-2-1	8–10	107	9– 4	101	11– 2	108	3.6 L	1.4
E-1-7	5– 6	71	6– 6	74	6–10	69	2.5 H	2.5
C-2-9	5– 6	69	7– 0	79	6– 5	65	1.3 A	1.3
C-1-8	6– 8	71	6–10	66	7– 3	63	1.9 LA	1.9
E-1-5	6– 4	76	6– 6	71	7– 6	73	3.3 H	3.3
E-1-8	6– 8	73	7– 2	69	8– 2	72	2.3 L	1.8
E-2-6	6– 0	77	6– 4	73	6– 2	64	2.3 H	2.3
C-2-4	7– 0	83	8– 0	86	9– 0	87	2.7 L	2.7
E-1-10	4– 8	51	4– 9	48	—	—		
C-1-6	6– 3	76	7– 0	74	7– 2	68	3.2 H	2.0
E-2-8	5– 5	69	6– 0	68	6– 4	64	.5 L	.5
C-1-7	5– 6	72	6– 2	75	6–10	73	1.4 LA	1.4
E-2-10	5– 8	64	6– 4	69	7– 2	70	2.0 A	2.0

TABLE 175, *continued*

Sub-ject	Pre-test Form L		Follow-up I Form M		Follow-up II Form L		Battery	Grade Level Gain
	MA	IQ	MA	IQ	MA	IQ	Mean [a]	1957–59
C-2-3	8– 2	85	7– 6	70	9– 8	82	2.7 L	2.7
C-2-8	6– 2	70	6– 4	64	7– 0	64	2.4 A	2.4
C-1-10	5– 0	61	5– 8	61	6– 2	60	0.0 L	0.0
E-1-2	7–10	94	9– 6	100	10– 4	98	3.6 L	2.1
C-1-9	6– 4	71	7– 4	73	8– 8	78	2.2 L	2.2
C-1-2	8– 0	91	7–10	81	10– 2	95	3.1 L	2.2

[a] Battery Mean, June, 1959. Comparison: Battery Mean—Mental Age.

H = High   Pre-test—October, 1957
A = Average   Follow-up I—June, 1958
LA = Low Average   Follow-up II—June, 1959
L = Low

that 6 of the children would be considered overachieving, 6 would appear to be achieving at grade-level expectancy, and 23 would appear to be somewhat below mental-age-grade expectancy. Of special interest, however, is the fact that the 6 children, all of whom failed to score on the initial achievement test, made the greatest over-all gains in achievement and at approximately the same rate of speed over the two-year period and had an IQ range of 27 points (68–95).

The 1959 achievement test scores, mental ages and IQ's of these six children are listed below.

Total Grade Level Gain	Achievement Score	MA	IQ
3.3	3.3	6–10	76
3.6	3.6	8– 8	95
3.8	3.8	7– 2	68
3.6	3.6	10– 6	90
3.3	3.6	9– 6	86
3.3	3.3	7– 6	73

One may question the validity of the assumption that IQ and mental age in relation to a given chronological age are necessarily predictive of an individual child's learning potential. For example, in the above group the child with the lowest IQ made the greatest academic gain (IQ 68; total gain, 3 years and 8 months).

The most thought-provoking problem concerns the predictive value of the results of standardized intelligence and achievement tests when they are used to classify *children* in terms of mental retardation. These traditional classifications, based on the IQ score, purport to define degrees of mental retardation. For example, of the 22 children whose academic gain was 2 or more years over the two-year period, only 3 would have qualified as being of normal intelligence (IQ 96–118).

The intelligence quotients of the remaining 19 were as follows:

IQ	Number of Children
64–75	9
76–85	4
86–95	6
Total	19

Curiously enough, it appears that the greatest number of potentially able learners had the lowest IQ's. It is also worth pointing out that the IQ range in this group of 22 was 54 points (64–118).

One additional example will suffice to point out the extreme need for caution in assuming that deviations from population or IQ norms is an index of learning potential and a valid guide for classifying children for purposes of educational programming. The 6 children referred to earlier, in spite of three previous years of total and complete academic failure, severe emotional problems and myriad of specific learning disabilities, increased their academic standing 3 academic years over a two-year period, and would have been classified as follows:

Number of Children	IQ	Classification
2	68–73	Mentally retarded
2	76–86	Slow learner
2	90–95	Borderline normal

In the following statement, one sees reflected not only the dilemma of the many hundreds of thousands of counterparts to the above 6 children who are assumed to be mentally retarded, but also a recognition of the limitations of the test instruments by which the authors themselves appear to asume a child is retarded.

In sum then, if we accept the fact that we cannot at present materially change the culturally determined standards of adequate performance, and that most intelligence tests will do little more for the retarded child than to confirm existing suspicions of inadequacy, we must turn our attention to determining which test or tests best differentiate among retarded children, between those who have more promise and those who have less, and in what directions the assets or liabilities of all of them lie (11, p. 262).

The comments made in the preceding paragraphs may appear at variance with those derived from Tables 164 and 165. Such is not the case, for the latter are based upon the total group data whereas the statements in the immediate section are based upon only those 6 children who received the highest scores on achievement tests.

The Educational Implications of the Use of Achievement Test Data

The following discussion is concerned with educational programs which classify children on the basis of individual and group achievement test scores. Two examples come to mind: first, the growing practice in public school systems of classifying children in track programs or ability levels; and, second, the so-called "firming up" of retainment policies in contrast to the practice of automatic promotion.

The authors do not favor automatic promotion over retainment policies; rather they believe that track programs, retainment, and automatic promotion all share the same limitations as devices for educational programming because they do not make provision for recognizing the myriad causes of underachievement among children. For example, one fourth-grade child who obtains a second grade achievement score in reading may be underachieving because he has difficulty learning words. A second fourth-grade child of the same age and intelligence, with the same second grade reading score, may be able to remember word forms easily but may lack the ability to associate words with their appropriate concepts. Under track programs the two children would presumably be assigned to the same ability group and receive the same instruction, despite the fact that if they are to learn to read, they need to be taught by entirely different instructional methods.

Under a retainment policy, the two children would be retained in the fourth grade and would repeat not only the same subject matter taught the same way, but they would also probably repeat the same failure on the achievement test.

Under the policy of automatic promotion, the children's learning disabilities would be considered secondary to the emotional and social gains anticipated by grouping them with their peer groups.

One suspects that in some cases the adherence to a policy of automatic promotion grows out of the assumption that children who are underachieving at one grade level may, and sometimes do, catch up or outgrow their academic difficulties. One also occasionally hears the suggestion that automatic promotion fosters a generally accepted practice of passing on failing students and behavior problems to the next grade in order to get rid of the child. It is, of course, only reasonable to assume that this practice does exist and, in some cases, is resorted to by some individuals because they are more interested in expediency than education. Experience with the teaching profession, however, would suggest that in most cases teachers pass on such children when they honestly believe they have exhausted their resources and consequently, in promoting the child, are acting in the child's best interest.

Public schools once exercised considerable caution in subscribing wholeheartedly to a belief in the over-all instructional value of track retainment, or automatic-promotion programs. The authors do not reject the value of ability grouping, retainment and automatic promotion; nor do they question the importance of achievement and intelligence scores in grouping children for instructional purposes. However, the authors do suggest that provisions should be made for identifying the causes of underachievement in order to avoid grouping together children who have the same level of ability but who have different instructional needs, such as the two fourth-graders referred to earlier.

The Use of Achievement Test Data as an Aid in Detecting Learning Problems

The research staff found that achievement-test results can be useful guides to a child's specific learning disabilities. Wide discrepancies, for example, between language and non-language scores, failure to discriminate between similarities and differences, and evidence of right-left confusion are, as most teachers are aware, general guides in identifying the strengths and weaknesses of a given child in terms of his potential for achievement when compared with the strengths, weaknesses and achievement level of classmates of the same chronological age. The subtest score profile of underachieving children, if properly understood, acts as a clue to developmental differences and deviations. The profile reflects the maturational levels of far more complex combinations and kinds of abilities than the ability to achieve.

Imagine a third-grade child in a group achievement test situation. The test booklet is on the child's desk. The teacher reads the directions: "Look at the bottom of the booklet. It says, 'To Boys and Girls.' This booklet has some games you will like. In taking the first part, you will show how many words you know and how well you can read. Do as many of them as you can. Do not turn this page until told to do so. No one is expected to finish all of the parts nor to do everything correctly. You may do very well, even if you do not finish on time. If you do not know the answer, go on to the next question. You may come back to it later if you have time. Now open the booklet to the next page which has a big 1 near the top and fold it back so that the 1 shows."

The teacher will demonstrate the proper page, and then she will read the directions for the first subtest: "Read the directions for this game silently while I read them aloud. They are: Below are some pictures of familiar objects. They are arranged in four rows. There are four pictures in each row. Look now at the first row and put an X on the object which begins with a T sound." At this point the teacher asks her pupils if they understand the directions; she answers any questions and demonstrates an X on the blackboard.

The third-grade child in the example has been given a set of simple directions and has been asked to identify the line drawing of a table. Now consider a few of the various associative and integrative processes involved in a satisfactory completion of the test, and some of the basic assumptions made about the child if he is to follow the directions. These comments are meant to illustrate some of the sensory motor processes involved in accomplishing certain tasks.

TASK 1: FOLLOWING DIRECTIONS

Since the teacher gave the directions verbally during a time span of at least three minutes, the following assumptions have been made.

1. There is no evidence of impaired hearing; or if there is, it has been identified and the results will be evaluated accordingly.

2. It has also been assumed that the developmental processes involved in auditory functioning have matured to the point where the child recognizes the T sound as a separate auditory unity and is able to identify it as the initial sound (not consonant) of the name (not object) of a representational drawing of a table.

3. Maturation in the above-mentioned developmental processes is anticipated in normal children somewhere around 8 years of age. One would hope that the child is at least 8 and that all the developmental processes have matured evenly. He would be helpless if he heard and understood the directions but was unable to remember them.

4. It has been assumed that the child has no speech handicaps, nor difficulties in language formulation; or, if he has, it is assumed that they have been identified and evaluated in terms of their effect upon the test results. That is, that the language formulation processes have developed sufficiently so that the child is able to associate the words used in the teacher's language with their correct concepts in a meaningful, orderly sequence.

5. Finally, to have heard and understood the directions, it has been

assumed that the child has an attention span of three minutes or more, and that during that three minutes he has not been distracted from the listening task.

TASKS 2 AND 3: IDENTIFYING THE TABLE AND MARKING IT WITH AN X

The following basic assumptions have been made concerning the child's eyes and his level of visual functioning.

1. There is no evidence of eye damage or impaired vision, or if there is, provision has been made for it in evaluating the test results.

2. The developmental processes involved in visual functioning have all matured sufficiently for the child to perceive the following things correctly: the four rows of four objects and the vertical legs of the table, the oblique lines of the X drawn on the blackboard, and the square shape of the table top. In short, one would be requiring a 9-year-old to demonstrate a type of development which is not fully mature in some children until they are approximately 12 years of age (12).

3. There is no evidence of damage or impairment to the brain or central nervous system; or if there is, it has been taken into consideration. In the absence of such damage, it has also been assumed that the integrative processes and associative systems of the body have matured sufficiently for the child to integrate the above auditory and perceptual experiences and relate them immediately to the motor skills appropriate to completing the task at hand.

If the child *has heard, understood,* and *remembered the directions,* if he has *perceived the object* correctly, *integrated* complicated sensory motor stimuli into the action of making an X on the table—then he has followed the test directions and given the correct answer.

But what if he fails? Is it not reasonable to suggest that children who do not score at grade level expectancy be accorded at least the same professional attention that an expensive piece of delicately balanced machinery receives when it fails to perform efficiently?

The Educational Implications of Teacher Selection and Training for Hyperactive Children

In the previous section, the discussion was conducted with little reference to the project children. This appeared appropriate because the educational implications of the use of test instruments goes far beyond this particular group of children. The discussion concerning teacher selection and assignment which follows is confined to teachers for hyperactive children.

One would like nothing better than to be able to define the specific criteria on which teachers for classes of hyperactive children, comparable to the project groups, can be selected, professionally prepared and assigned to their classes with satisfaction guaranteed to both the teacher and children. This certainly is not possible. What can be offered are some very general guides which the project staff found helpful in selecting the four research teachers, all of whom demonstrated such a high degree of professional competence in their respective classrooms that one will never know just how much they contributed to the growth of the children.

Prior to discussion of these selection guides, a philosophical concept shared by the project staff responsible for the selection of the teachers should be stated. This concept should be thoroughly understood in all its many implications if one is to comprehend the importance which the staff attributes with the following statement.

. . . Classroom conditions that challenge and satisfy one teacher can threaten and disorganize another. Recognition of a teacher's personal characteristics can . . . be utilized constructively through timely and skillful professional supervision that can support and help correct areas of insecurity as well as encourage and fortify strengths. Thus, the taking of teachers' personal make-up into account can significantly reduce job-connected anxieties. . . . This in turn can improve the classroom experience for both teachers and pupils . . . (17, p. 190).

The staff would tend to avoid the use of teachers whose total professional experience has been confined to small groups; they are not the best teachers for this particular kind of group because they tend to do their best work on a one-to-one basis. The teacher of hyperactive and brain-injured children must be able to perceive various types of grouping within a classroom and must be able to adjust to different approaches as the child progresses both academically and socially. Initially, much, if not all, of the teacher's work will be on a one-to-one basis. Here she must be able to give the child as much individual attention as he needs without causing the child to panic. As the child grows more secure and is able to tolerate greater space and more stimulating situations, the teacher must be able to move with the child into small group instruction processes. A teacher of brain-injured and hyperactive children must be able to carefully, continuously, and successfully assess the progress of the child and modify the instructional climate to meet the child's newly achieved levels of behavior. It is essential that teachers not be used who identify with the pathology of the children or who utilize the instructional situation, consciously or unconsciously, to act out their own unresolved authority problems in power struggles with the children or with their parents.

It would be the authors' impression that the teacher most comfortable and competent with this particular type of group is one who loves teaching and enjoys the children. The teacher should be professionally competent; she should have several years experience and possess the skills which are essential in the management of an elementary school class of around 30 children. The teacher should have demonstrated exceptional ability in meeting the individual and group instructional needs of children in kindergarten, first, second, or third grades. The teacher should also have a thorough knowledge and understanding of the social, emotional, and educational abilities associated with the maturational processes at each developmental level.

Such teachers are usually professionally challenged, curious, and intrigued by the unresolved instructional problems of the times and, consequently, their attitude toward new and unfamiliar teaching concepts, instructional methods and techniques is characterized by elasticity, creativity, and professional objectivity. They are more of an eclectic than a devotee of curriculum guides and methods, and are able to determine quickly the particular techniques and procedures to use at a specific time with a given youngster with a particular problem. Since the group they teach is easily distracted, has a short attention span, and lacks impulse control, it is important that their sense of timing and skill in utilizing transition devices be developed to such a degree that the instructional day is experienced by the children as a smooth, flowing, many-faceted continuum of learning.

Teachers of this caliber can be predicted to be good group teachers. That is, they use the individual or group structure as an instructional technique by which they communicate the skills which, in the end, make it possible for the children to learn how to proceed in completing assignments, independent of the group situation. Herein the teacher of hyperactive and brain-injured children will be expected to be able to mobilize her talent, experience, drive, and professional understanding in an effort to provide previously unsuccessful, disorganized, underachieving children with those skills which lead to successful learning experiences and to help promote a sense of healthy well-being while participating in well-organized classroom activities.

Once such a teacher is selected and assigned to her class, she should be expected, and expect, to teach and nothing else. The experience of children with a teacher of this caliber is described by Biber in the following words.

She, the teacher, can lead him to become skilled, knowing, perceptive and effective in his world; to master confusions; to reorder experience through his own invention; to communicate in the modes of his culture and sustain the idiom of himself; to extend his "interest" world to far places and times; to act, to organize, to accomplish, to reason, to reflect. For this exciting and challenging task, there are special techniques and skill in using them that determines the extent to which the child's learning, achievement, and mastery become the framework for positive ego-growth, and contribute to the child's growing feeling as a knowing, doing, confident self in relation to a knowable, manageable world (18, p. 173).

It is the feeling of the authors that these ingredients of positive growth take on an added dimension of significance when they are the very ones which represent the greatest developmental deficits of the hyperactive child.

Educational Significance of the Diagnostic and Clinical Data for Over-all School Programming

In this chapter as well as those which precede it, a great deal of attention and time has been given to a discussion of the social, emotional, and educational needs of hyperactive and brain-injured children. The results of medical and clinical study, combined with specialized grouping and teaching of a very small number of these children have been reported, tabulated, analyzed, compared, and the results subjected to intensive speculation. Attempts have been made, perhaps unwisely and with too much complacency, to explain the increased learning and emotional adjustment of the children in terms of meeting the instructional and emotional needs of all children.

Many significant by-products of the project have been ignored; others, perhaps less significant in terms of the pilot study, have been reported in detail because of what appeared to be their unique significance to educators and public school administrators.

In this concluding section, the discussion is concerned with what the research staff learned from each other and from the children, knowing full well that what is actually being offered may not be evidence of learning as much as evidence of a new set of professional biases. One can only hope that, in either case, professional support will be proffered where it is justified just as readily as criticism will be accepted by the research staff when it is justified.

The project brought to the staff's attention what appears to be an educational system which recognizes the importance of individual differences but which makes little or no provision for identifying the differences or classifying them into meaningful patterns or developmental scales for instructional purposes. This dichotomy between philosophy and implementation is reflected in a number of ways.

First, one of the most serious results is the lack of procedures, personnel, and facilities for identifying the causes of developmental deviations and individual differences.

Second, instructional programs, curriculum guides, and the results of psychological and achievement testing programs are evaluated in terms of normative data derived from statistical rather than from developmental studies. Furthermore, our educational system makes no provision for the developmental difference between boys and girls. This lack of differentiation becomes even less tenable when one recalls that:

. . . Sex is an important factor in determining birth size and the course of postnatal development. Newborn boys weigh about four per cent more than girls, and throughout later months of growth of bone and flesh, as well as oxygen consumption per unit of body surface, males are ahead of females. The difference becomes even more striking when we recall that, biologically, girls are older than boys of the same chronological age. At birth, this developmental difference is slight, girls being biologically only one month older than boys, but they are six months older at two, twelve months older at five, and eighteen months older at nine. Girls reach puberty at thirteen, fully two years ahead of boys (19, p. 172).

Keeping in mind the above statement of the biological age difference between boys and girls, and the diagnostic pattern of neurophysiological immaturity of the project children (37 of whom were boys), is it not time for educators to consider the very real possibility that current educational procedures may be *creating* learning disabilities and emotional disorders among boys through the use of traditional grouping procedures and instructional programs which are not appropriate to sex-linked differences and developmental variations in the learning rate between boys and girls? One only has to think of the approximate two-to-one ratio of boys to girls in reading disabilities, speech and hearing problems, deafness, blindness, and various types of emotional disorders to sharpen this suspicion into real concern. Further exploration of this possibility is urgently needed, if for no other purpose than to dispel it.

A third result of the dichotomy between an educational philosophy which recognizes the importance of the individual and the lack of procedural implementation of that philosophy, appears to be a direct result of the absence of concrete factual information defining the normality of individual differences in learning.

The failure to dissociate learning from behavior problems has given rise to the common practice of classifying children with emotional and learning disorders as problem children, or at best, atypical children;

the underlying assumption is that the difficulty is in the child or his parents.

In order to illustrate the point being made, one only needs to contrast this method or approach to the educational and emotional problems of children, with those developed in other disciplines with an established body of knowledge concerning the relationship between cause and effect. Contrast, for example, the difference between the medical term "childhood diseases" and the utter inappropriateness of such a term as "diseased children."

Would it not appear reasonable to make an all-out attempt to determine the clinical basis of underachievement and emotional disorders? The results of such inquiries would provide educators with the kind of information which would make it possible to classify various kinds of learning problems of children, rather than the children themselves.

The effectiveness of this approach is illustrated by the experience of the research staff of the pilot project. It will be recalled that a major proportion of the children in the research classes, prior to their selection as project participants, were classified as "problem children"; their failure to achieve academic mastery was explained away by still another semantic substitute for clinical data: they were "emotionally disturbed, underachieving problem children."

It was a refreshing and thought-provoking experience to see how quickly the use of these labels disappeared as the clinical basis for the children's underachievement and behavioral response pattern was established.

Thus it was that the earlier description of a composite profile of an underachieving, emotionally disturbed, problem child in Chapter III emerged from the diagnostic study as a hyperactive child with specific learning disorders, and was taught as such by his teacher.

THE ROLE OF INTERDISCIPLINARY RESEARCH AND PILOT STUDIES IN PUBLIC SCHOOL SYSTEMS

Much has been written on the theoretical value of interdisciplinary research and its contributions to knowledge of human behavior. From a practical standpoint, multidisciplinary research and pilot studies of public school problems are the quickest, most efficient, most orderly and, in the long run, least expensive methods of attacking and resolving the problem areas of education. At no time in the history of this country's educational history and philosophy has the need for pooling up-to-date information on the causes of children's learning and emotional disorders been so great or so urgent. Neither have the results of not having such information available, including the educational implications, been so disastrous to professional morale and instructional efficiency.

One contributing factor to this situation is, of course, a lack of communication among those disciplines concerned with investigating the processes and deviations in human growth, development and maturation, and an even greater gap between those disciplines and education. When some method has been established for communicating and integrating new concepts among all disciplines, including methods of making such concepts available to educators who are working on an operational level, a major step will have been taken in providing the kind of information which will eventually make it possible to meet the educational needs of all children.

A second communication problem exists within the field of education itself. Outside of the educational journals there is no nationwide clearing house for educational problems.

A third factor contributing to the lack of interdisciplinary communication is the resistance in all disciplines to social change. This resistance becomes particularly intensified whenever a new discipline threatens to erupt within the ranks of older, more established disciplines.

The resolution of these very large, complex, interdisciplinary communication problems will take many, many years. Interdisciplinary research projects, however, provide a means of cutting directly through these difficulties, provided the personnel comprising the staff are carefully selected. This statement in no way implies that there were no interdisciplinary communication problems in the project staff, but rather that it was possible to work through these difficulties for two reasons.

First, the various reports of each discipline were on the same children and were evaluated and interpreted in the immediate presence of the total group. This meant that the "basic data" was identical for all members of the staff and on-the-spot provision was made for working through communication problems; and second, although the research problem meant different things to different disciplines, the solution to the problem and the educational aims and goals were of equal importance to all.

Another very practical aspect of utilizing this type of research project in public schools is that the pooling of information on the educational implications of current research on growth and maturation processes takes place as the staff works together on a problem with clearly defined goals. Furthermore, since monographs or formal reports of some kind are required by almost every fund-dispensing agency, it is essential that the participating staff formulate and integrate the results of the project experience in such a way that it becomes available to others.

If one accepts the importance of the urgent need for intensive study of the role of individual differences in the learning process, it becomes very clear that such studies are not, and cannot become the responsibility of any one discipline, but are the proper province of interdisciplinary research projects and pilot studies.

Adler, while not referring directly to the problem as it is presented here, in making the following statements defines his own concern wisely and well.

We need [he says] to reorganize and reorient our whole school system; to educate our teachers as few are now educated; to invent materials and techniques of teaching which do not now exist; and to devise graded courses of study which are designed to do for every level and kind of ability exactly what the traditional liberal curriculum once did effectively in Colonial times for the few and most gifted children (20).

Adler has stated what needs to be done if the United States is to cease being a country which "fails to honor knowledge." It is the authors' hope that this monograph may suggest some methods for meeting that need.

REFERENCES

1. GERARD, R. W. "The Biological Roots of Psychiatry," *American Journal of Psychiatry*, CXII, No. 2 (August, 1955), 225–29.
2. SILVERMAN, J. S., FITE, M. W., and MOSHER, M. M. "Clinical Findings in Reading Disability Children: Special Cases of Intellectual Inhibition," *American Journal of Orthopsychiatry*, XXIX, No. 2 (April, 1959), 298–314.
3. SELYE, H. *The Stress of Life*. New York: McGraw-Hill Book Co., 1956.
4. HOCH, P. H., and ZUBIN, J. (eds.). *The Psychopathology of Communication*. New York: Grune and Stratton, 1958.
5. LOURIE, R. S. "Basic Science and the Future of Orthopsychiatry," *American Journal of Orthopsychiatry*, XXVIII, No. 3 (July, 1958), 445–52.
6. ORTON, S. *Reading, Writing and Speech Problems in Children*. New York: W. W. Norton & Co., 1937.
7. HALPERN, F. *A Clinical Approach to Children's Rorschachs*. New York: Grune and Stratton, 1953.
8. STRAUSS, A. A., and LEHTINEN, L. E. *Psychopathology and Education of Brain Injured Children*. Vol. 1. New York: Grune and Stratton, 1947.

9. CRUICKSHANK, W. M., BICE, H. V., and WALLEN, N. E. *Perception and Cerebral Palsy*. Syracuse, New York: Syracuse University Press, 1957.

10. SARASON, S. B. *The Clinical Interaction*. New York: Harper & Brothers, 1954.

11. MASLAND, R. L., SARASON, S. B., and GLADWIN, T. *Mental Subnormality*, New York: Basic Books, 1958.

12. HEBB, D. O. *Organization of Behavior*. New York: John Wiley & Sons, 1955, p. 34.

13. ALLAN, L. G. "Life Planning for the Partially Seeing," *Journal for Exceptional Children*, XXIII, No. 5 (February, 1957), 202–6.

14. FRISINI, R. "Children with Deafness," *Journal for Exceptional Children*, XXVII, No. 2 (October, 1959), 94–97.

15. STALNAKER, J. N. "National Program for Discovering Students of Exceptional Ability," *Journal for Exceptional Children*, XXIII, No. 6 (March, 1957), 234–37, 266.

16. BURKS, H. "The Effect of Learning on Brain Pathology," *Journal for Exceptional Children*, XXIV, No. 4 (December, 1957) 169–72, 174.

17. BERNARD, V. W. "Teacher Education in Mental Health from the Point of View of the Psychiatrist," *Orthopsychiatry and the School*. New York: American Orthopsychiatric Association, Inc., 1958.

18. BIBER, B. "Teacher Education in Mental Health from the Point of View of the Educator," *Orthopsychiatry and the School*. New York: American Orthopsychiatric Association, Inc., 1958.

19. HEILBRUNN, L. V. *An Outline of General Physiology*. Third edition. Philadelphia: W. B. Saunders, 1952.

20. ADLER, M. J. Special Report. *Washington Post and Times-Herald*, April 6, 1959.

Appendix

DIAGNOSTIC EXAMINATION REPORTS FOR CHILDREN IN GROUP C-1

Note: Group C-1 was chosen solely because its members are typical of the children in the remaining three groups and because space limitations prevented including studies of all 40 children. The studies are the unedited reports of the several co-operating diagnosticians.

PEDIATRIC HISTORY C-2-1

The pediatric history was obtained by interviewing the mother while C-2-1 waited outside playing with blocks in the presence of his younger brother and the Resident Co-ordinator.

The mother is an attractive petite woman who seemed to be a little depressed and not anxious to talk about C-2-1's problems, although she did volunteer information without too much difficulty. The general attitude may have been due to the fact that she had gone through similar interviews innumerable times in the past.

Problem

"He can't be quiet; he balks—gets too emotionally upset, especially with other people and mostly with strangers. When he is by himself he's fine, although he doesn't prefer to be by himself; he will seek out other people."

"It is difficult to complain now. He's better than he was last year." "Can't get to him or reason with him. You don't feel like you're getting to him."

The mother became aware of her son's difficulties at the age of 2 years when he began playing with other children. It was at this time that she noted that he would scream during the middle of the night as if he were having nightmares. She had no way of knowing whether this was normal or abnormal since she had no other children and no basis of comparison. At approximately 1½ years of age he started getting up at night only once. She would pat him and put him back into his crib. At first this would suffice. Then it became necessary to repeat this two or three times during the night. Although she would try picking him up, it appears that this is not what he wanted. When holding him did not seem to do any good, she would take him into bed with her, but that did not seem to work either. At such times he would be found to be standing up in his crib and would scream for long periods at a time. At first he would be spanked and this did no good. Then finally, in desperation, she would shut the door and let him cry it out, sometimes letting him cry for an hour and a half before he would fall off to sleep. He had a room to himself since the age of 5 months. After consulting her pediatrician about this condition, he was given phenobarbital a half hour before bedtime. This worked for as long as he was taking the phenobarbital. However, whenever it was discontinued, the same pattern was seen again. At about the same time it was noted that he did not have much interest in or with other children. In their presence he would make noise and throw sand and other things. The mother qualified this as "attention getting." She stated that he still does not get along too well with children, although he is beginning to have friends. He prefers larger boys or boys of his own size rather than smaller children.

His activity consists in building forts or playing with blocks. He seems to be constantly running around. When he is by himself he will sit and play with blocks. However, when he is with others, he always has to be doing something. His mother stated that he seems to have antagonized just about everyone, regardless of their age, although she notes improvement. When questioned about how his behavior was handled at first, the mother said that at first she tried reassuring him. When this failed, she tried spanking. However, nothing seemed to do any good. It appeared to her as if the child knew what was expected of him, or wanted of him, but paid no attention to this. Punishment was ineffectual because there seemed to be little he cared for, and so nothing seemed to matter that much to him. He did not seem to accept extra attention. He did not want to be held or loved.

Although the father was away a good part of the time, he did know what was going on and was well aware of the situation. It was his opinion that they were not strict enough with the boy. He undertook disciplinary measures, both on a positive and on a negative side. The mother said that fathers are not as easy on children as mothers are. The father looked on some of this behavior as negativism.

When C-2-1 was 3 years of age he underwent a T & A. It was following this operation that the nightmares stopped. He began sleeping better and eating better. It would appear that he was a poor eater as well, always having to be bribed or coerced into eating. However, the mother states that following the T & A, C-2-1's eating habits became better.

When asked what the reason for the T & A was, the mother said that C-2-1 had had repeated colds and sore throats. There was not any evidence of mouth-breathing or snoring. He did have nose bleeds and was unable to blow his nose.

Family History

1. His mother's mother living and well? Answer: Yes
2. His mother's father living and well? Answer: Yes
3. His father's mother living and well? Answer: Yes
4. His father's father living and well? Answer: Yes

5. Are all of mother's brothers and sisters living and well? Answer: Mother has one sister and four brothers all of whom are living and well.

6. Are all of father's brothers and sisters living and well? Answer: Father is an only child.

There is no family history of epilepsy, nervous breakdown, hospitalizations for mental illness, convulsions, heart disease, syphilis, tuberculosis, diabetes, or cancer. There is no history of co-sanguinity.

Family Background

Father. (Age 42.) He is a nice person, not too social and prefers his family to other people. He is a complainer about things in general. He is not too easy-going and fusses a great deal. He shows concern about the children's welfare, although he does not seem to get down to their level in play or in fantasy. His wife remarked that his parents were very strict with him, although he does respect his parents, adding, "A lot more than other people do." He is a salesman. He completed high school and business school. When asked how he feels presently about his son's situation, the mother said that her husband feels that C-2-1 should be in his own school, instead of having to come to special classes at Rockville. He feels that he will pick up bad habits.

Mother. (Age 39.) She says she used to be even-tempered. However, she is now mean because of the tension about C-2-1 and feels that perhaps the fact that she is approaching 40 years of age might have something to do with it. She completed high school and business college, and was employed as a secretary. She feels that C-2-1 is so much better than he was a year ago, and she states that she is willing to go along with whatever is necessary for his well-being. She expressed the desire that she would prefer that the boy behave himself, whereas his father prefers for him to be able to learn. This is her second marriage, having been married for six years before without any children.

Siblings. A sister, 5½ years of age, presently in kindergarten and in good health. Brother, 2 years of age, in good health. It would appear that C-2-1 behaves the same way toward his brother and sister as with others. He shows no resentment of them and did not seem upset when they arrived on the scene. He shared his room with his sister until she reached the age of 2, and now shares his room with his brother.

Mother's Medical History during Pregnancy with Child

The pregnancy with C-2-1 was desired, although it came somewhat as a surprise after being married for two years and trying to have a child. She was

30 years of age at the time and received prenatal care during first months of the pregnancy. Just prior to conceiving, the mother had undergone surgery for the removal of an ovarian cyst. The delivery itself was not remarkable. There were no accidents during her pregnancy and she said she felt wonderful, having worked during the entire pregnancy up until the last month. Her diet was adequate, there was no physical or emotional strain, and she received no medication.

Labor and Delivery Factors

Baby was born at a local hospital. Length of labor was 24 hours in the hospital. Baby was born with forceps scars on each side of the head. The bag of waters was ruptured artificially. C-2-1 was seen by his mother within the first six hours following his birth. He weighed 6 pounds, 3 ounces at birth, although he apparently lost so much weight that he could not be circumcised at the time he left the hospital. Even in the hospital it was noted that he kept crying. He did not seem to eat well at all; he did not seem to be interested in food. The mother volunteered the information that perhaps he should have had special care and attention. He was placed on an evaporated milk formula and apparently settled down after the first month.

Past Medical History of Patient

Immunization: DPT, no sequela, and he has had his Salk vaccinations. He had chickenpox at the age of 6 years. Apparently it was very severe. He had a fever for about a week and was confined to bed. He could not even swallow water, his mother says. Except for circumcision and the T & A, he has had no other operations.

Developmental History

C-2-1 has always been a feeding problem. This became more apparent at the time that regular food was introduced at the age of one year. He had been given vitamin supplements adequately. He voluntarily gave up his bottle at the age of 5 months, and started drinking from a cup. He has difficulty tying his shoes, although he is not clumsy; he is sure-footed and walks with a steady gait. He can build things and follows instructions very well. He achieved bladder control and bowel control at 2 years of age. When he is by himself his attention span is O.K. He is able to button his own buttons, zip a zipper, and although he can not tie his shoes too well, he is able to. When he is being watched, however, he will not even try. At the end of our physical examination, when we asked him about tying his shoes, at first he ignored the remark and then said that this was something his mother would do.

Interests. He likes to look at books, although he is not given any comic books. He likes tools or anything connected with building things. He can sit through cartoons at a movie and will watch certain programs on TV.

Personality. In answer to the question as to how C-2-1 handles punishment, the mother said that at first he used not to react at all. Now he behaves as if an injustice were being done. He is belligerent or resentful and he talks back but does not sulk. He does not seem interested in fighting and will not fight at all, and he is not mean to young children. When he is frustrated he will talk back and bluster. He seems to like school now, although he did not use to. He used to feel the teachers were mean to him.

Physical Examination

Blood pressure 90/60.

General appearance. C-2-1 is an alert, pleasant-looking, hyperactive, and asthenic child. He did not seem particularly withdrawn or afraid of the doctor or the various procedures entailed in this examination. He recognized the various instruments and seemed to know what their function was. It seemed difficult for him to remain quiet and still, but as his confidence was won he became more co-operative. He is tall and slender—his rib cage being prominently visible. He was not particularly pale and his state of hydration was good. There were no gross speech defects or impediments, and he only occasionally blinked his eyes more frequently than is ordinarily seen. His posture was good and his gait normal.

Skin and mucous membranes. There were no skin eruptions, nor discolorations or other evidence of trauma. *Lymph nodes.* There was no significant lymphadenopathy. *Head.* The head is of normal shape and position, being freely movable on the neck in all directions. The hair was cut closely and of normal consistency with no evidence of seborrhea or parasites. *Face.* There was voluntary facial control with no asymmetry. The expression was that of an alert youngster. *Ears.* The otological exam was not significant. Gross hearing was apparently normal. *Mouth and throat.* C-2-1 did not breathe with his mouth open. His lips were of normal color with no evidence of any fissures or eruptions. His teeth were poorly aligned but in satisfactory condition, numbering 11 on the top and 10 on the bottom. The arch of the palate was normal. The tongue was normal-looking and neither trembled nor deviated when protruded. The tonsils were absent. *Neck.* The neck was perfectly supple with no apparent masses or thyroid enlargement. The trachea appeared to be in the mid-line and there was no evidence of venous enlargement. *Vertebral.* There were no abnormal curvatures of the spine, nor was motion limited or painful. No spasm or tenderness could be elicited. *Chest.* Rib cage was prominent but no abnormal masses were palpable. The chest was symmetrical as were the respiratory excursions. The lungs were clear to percussion, palpation. The heart did not appear to be enlarged. The PMI was in the midclavicular line of the fifth interspace on the left and was quite forceful. There were no murmurs or trills. The radial pulses were not easily palpable but were present, as were the femoral pulses. *Abdomen.* The abdomen was scaphoid in contour. There were no masses palpable, nor were the liver, spleen, or kidneys palpable. There was no spasm or tenderness. *Genitalia.* The scrotum was well developed and both testicles were palpable therein. The penis was circumcised and there was no evidence of inguinal hernia. *Anal region.* Not remarkable. *Extremities.* There were no gross deformities; mild pes planus; good muscle tone and normal range of motion in all extremities. *Neurological.* The deep tendon reflexes were not easily elicitable, but the pateller reflex was hyperactive bilaterally. There was no clonus. The Babinski reflex was not elicitable. The cremasteric reflex was hyperactive. The cranial nerves were intact. Abnormal cerebellar signs were absent.

Neurological Examination

C-2-1 went along willingly with the Examiner. He was co-operative, very alert, and followed things very closely. He was curious about things, but it took a little time for him to catch on. *Cranial nerves.* The first cranial nerve was not tested. Second cranial nerve: the boy is able to see without any difficulty. Visual fields on gross confrontation were normal. The fundi showed discs that were well outlined and without any palor. There were no hemorrhages or exudates present. The vessels seemed normal. Third, fourth, and sixth cranial nerves: the extra-ocular movements were intact. No mystagmus could be seen on bilateral gaze. Pupils reacted to light and to accommodation. Fifth cranial nerve: corneal reflexes were present bilaterally. He was able to feel touch and pinprick on his face equally on both sides. The muscles of mastication were all intact. Seventh cranial nerve: there is no evidence of facial paresis. Eighth cranial nerve: tuning fork was heard without difficulty bilaterally. Gross hearing tests were completely normal. Ninth and tenth cranial nerves: child was able to swallow without difficulty. The uvula was in the midline. Gag reflex was not tested. Phonation seemed to be intact. There is no evidence for difficulty with his speech. Eleventh cranial nerve: he was able to shrug his shoulders without difficulty and he was able to hold his head to one or the other side with great strength. Twelfth cranial nerve: the tongue protruded in the mid-line, showed no signs of atrophy or phthisications. *Sensory.* The boy is able to feel pinprick, vibratory, and touch on all parts of his body without difficulty. In addition he is able to make two-point discrimination and pinprick localization. He is able to localize his body parts when asked to do so. *Reflexes.* The reflexes in the arms are equal and active bilaterally. Reflexes in the legs are equal and active bilaterally. The ankle jerks are somewhat more brisk than the knee reflexes. Pathological reflexes are absent. Abdominal and cremasteric reflexes were not done. *Motor.* He shows good muscle strength throughout. His hand grips are normal. He has no deviation of the arms or legs when held out in space. *Cerebellar.* Boy shows good co-ordination throughout. He is able to do such things as spin a jack to make it act like a top with his right hand and somewhat with his left hand. In addition to that, hand-patting tests are normal bilaterally as are the finger-to-nose and heel-to-shin tests. He is able to get up from a sitting position without any difficulty. There are no signs of ataxia, either trunkal or in the extremities. *Station and gait.* The boy stands in an erect position. The Romberg is negative. He is able to stand on one foot without too much difficulty. He is able to walk on his heels and on his toes without any great difficulty. He walks in a normal fashion, swinging his arms as he walks. *Movements.* No extra-pyramidal movements could be seen. He seemed to be somewhat more active than would be usually found at this age. However, he was able to calm himself down when requested and acted in a fairly normal fashion. *Comment.* The boy seemed to be able to do such simple things as add 1 and 1. When asked what 3 from 100 was, he said 89, then changed himself to 98 and then changed himself to 97. He seemed to be able to reason things fairly well, although sometimes it took him a little bit longer. He often jumped to conclusions which were wrong without thinking, and then went back and corrected himself without being asked to correct himself.

Electroencephalogram

Attitude and condition of patient: alert, unusually restless. Fundamental frequency: is ill-defined at around 8 and 9 waves per second. Slow waves: throughout the baseline is choppy, and short sequences of bioccipital 6 per second waves are observed (these are not prominent). Fast waves: except of muscle origin, are not prominent. Amplitude characteristics: average voltage; poorly modulated. Additional feature: no paroxysmal activity is recognized. Hyperventilation: not accomplished. Impression: within the range of normal variation.

Speech and Hearing Evaluation

General appearance. C-2-1 came eagerly into the room and freely engaged in conversation. He was interested in what we were going to do, and did not appear the least bit disturbed by the "hospital" appearance of the examining room. He is a thin, wiry lad whose over-all co-ordination was good. He was clutching the remains of a bottle of Coke which he offered to share with the Examiner. He had a golf ball, from which the cover had been removed, that he was unwinding. During most of the examination he clutched this ball of thin rubber and his major interest was to string it from object to object around the room to make a telephone line. He discussed his project very freely. When asked to come over to the Examiner for various parts of the examination, he co-operated willingly, but as soon as the immediate task at hand was over he immediately went back to stringing his telephone line. At the end of the examination he apparently sensed that I was in a hurry to get upstairs. When he was urged to wind it up so we could go, he became even slower in his movements. He was very pleasant about it, showed no negative behavior, but he could not be budged until he had completed his task. He explored everything in the room during the course of the examination. This could not be described so much as hyperactivity as an intentness to do what he wanted to do. No tic was observed today.

Speech and language development. The child's mother was not present today so no details of speech and language development could be obtained. It would be my impression from reading over the pediatric history that there has been no significant delay.

Oral examination. There is a marked overbite. The lips are held in an open position because of the oral structure. However, this child has no difficulty in closing his lips in order to produce the labial sounds. The velum is of adequate length, and there is equal lift. There is good nasopharyngeal closure. The tongue has good motility. It is used with precision and accuracy in the production of all speech sounds. He can move his tongue into any required position.

Articulation. Speech is intelligible. There are no defective sounds. Sibilant affricatives are sharply articulated. All the blends are good. He has a good ear for speech imitation and reproduced any polysyllabic words with great ease.

Voice. Voice is of good quality. There was no unusual hoarseness or breathiness. Voice is not nasal.

Propositional speech. C-2-1 converses easily on a variety of topics. He talks at rather a slow rate, but this is felt to be his way of monitoring his own speech. His language comprehension is good, as is his use of language. His sentences tend to be 6 and 7 words in length. He has a good vocabulary range for his age. Thought content is good. He is using complex sentences. He has no difficulty in naming objects or selecting the appropriate object when it is described to him. He demonstrated a good memory for complex sentences and repeated them accurately.

Hearing. No audiometer was available today. When he was stood 15 feet away, in as soft a voice as could be articulated, he quickly and readily repeated some 25 phonetically balanced words. This, along with his ready understanding during the whole examination, precludes any marked hearing difficulty.

Initial impression. Speech and language comprehension are up to his age level.

Psychiatric Evaluation

C-2-1 (with whom the Examiner had had previous contacts), on entering the examination room, immediately asked whether we still had that "train." He was obviously excited to be back.

He began by saying that school was too hard and that he and some friends were going to run away to an island, taking his father's gun and some B-B shot. This story was accompanied by facial grimacing and a serious expression. As he told the plan, he attempted to crawl into the bottom shelf of a cupboard (an activity he enjoyed in past interviews) but gave the idea up, saying as he did so, "I'm too big now."

C-2-1 continued to express his dissatisfaction with school, but when pressed for specific comments, his reply was "I do not like to work; I like to play." And with this comment squirmed his way into the cupboard and closed the door making noises like a train to keep the Examiner informed of his presence.

In previous interviews, C-2-1 played with planes, bombs, and racing cars. He declined to draw or play with puppets. He appeared to be a serious-minded youngster, smiling only occasionally. During this interview, the subject appeared more anxious and the facial tic was more prominent than in the past hours, although his drawings were less confused than in the past and he appears from classroom observations to have made definite progress in group participation.

Psychiatric Re-evaluation

C-2-1 put himself in the cupboard, as he had in a previous interview, but after a short period came out. He seemed to enjoy hitting the punching bag. He showed better co-ordination than in the past. No facial tics were present today.

He talked spontaneously about school saying that he liked the people all right but that he did not like the work. As this discussion continued he said "You mean life is hard for everybody?" This matter of school being hard has been a recurrent theme.

In general, the child's approach to finger painting and to the gun shooting was much more controlled. He could stop and start activities, as well as accept suggestions readily. In an earlier interview, the subject pleaded to continue the hour and asked when there would be a second visit. Today he accepted the reality of the situation and left in a cheerful frame of mind.

C-2-1's mother finds him to be much more independent. She can rely on him now to go to the store, or to be safe on his bicycle, or leave her when they go shopping. She feels that he continues to be hyperactive.

The child appears to have developed considerable emotional maturity over the course of the past year and evidently to have profited from the classroom experiences.

Psychological Examination

Stanford-Binet, Form L (Pre-test) (2–25–57).
CA: 7–8; MA: 8–2; IQ: 107.

C-2-1's mental age is 8–2, with an IQ of 107. In previous testing (10–6–55), using the Form M of the Stanford-Binet, the mental age was 6–10, with an IQ of 109. Thus, the rate of intellectual development is quite constant. The only item missed at Year VII was the copying of a diamond. At Year VIII, C-2-1 could not handle the verbal absurdities. He was inclined to give up too easily. "That's too hard," and "I don't know," were ways of handling the problem. No amount of questioning or prompting could elicit further effort.

At Year IX, C-2-1 was unable, again, to see verbal absurdities, copy designs from memory, make change, or repeat four digits reversed. He was able, however, to make rhymes and repeat six digits forwards. Vocabulary was passed at an eight-year level. He is a very verbal little boy who seems to find pleasure in using words, and uses them quite accurately. Some of his responses on the vocabulary test indicate a fairly high level for his age.

Stanford-Binet, Form M (Post-test) (5–15–58).
CA: 8–11; MA: 10–2; IQ: 114.

There is a 7 point difference between the pre- and post-test Stanford-Binet

IQ's, both being within the Average range. The eight-year performance range extends from a Basal Age at Year VIII to a Ceiling at the Average Adult level.

Two items were failed at Year IX. C-2-1 was unable to see the absurdity in verbally presented situations. Neither could he see the similarities and differences between quite common things. He could see the similarities, but not the differences.

Two items were failed at Year X. Auditory organization, as involved in memory of stories, was quite poor, as was repetition of six digits. Number concepts are relatively well developed as was the definition of abstract words and word naming.

At Year XI, one item was passed, seeing the similarity of three things. C-2-1 gave qualitatively very good similarities. He was unable to solve verbally presented problem situations, copy a bead chain from memory, or repeat sentences from memory.

At Year XII, two items were passed, memory for designs, and repeating five digits reversed. Memory for sentences was passed at Year XIII, on the second attempt. This was an unexpected success in view of the fact that memory for sentences was not passed at Year XI.

At Year XIV, one item was passed, the reconciliation of opposites. C-2-1's responses were quick and qualitatively quite good on this item. For example, when asked how *winter* and *summer* are alike, he said: "Both are a month." For *happy* and *sad,* he said: "Ways you feel about something." For *much* and *little,* he said: "Both amounts of something."

Ammons Full-Range Picture Vocabulary Test (11–27–57).

CA: 8–6; MA: 9–6.

The mental age obtained on this test is about 6 months greater than the Stanford-Binet IQ. The following words, expected at a higher chronological age, were passed by C-2-1: mercury, perspiration, sympathy, and mishap.

Goodenough Intelligence Test.

Pre-test (2–26–57)	Post-test (5–12–58)
CA: 7–8; MA: 7–9	CA: 8–10; MA: 6–3

There is little change in the pre- and post-test drawings. In fact, the post-test figure is somewhat less detailed, lacking the eyebrows and ears of the pre-test figure. Both drawings have a square trunk on which the arms and legs seem to be hung, with arms outstretched, and hat perching precariously on top of the head.

Block Design and Coding from WISC (2–26–57).

	Raw Score	Scaled Score	Equivalent Test Age
Block Design	13	12	9–6
Coding	46	14	10–2

Designs A and B were constructed very rapidly and accurately on the first attempt, while Design C was completed just short of the time limit on the second attempt. Designs 1 and 2 were constructed without difficulty, but from that point on C-2-1 could not make the correct designs, and became quite anxious. On the Coding, Form A, C-2-1 substituted all of the symbols with fifteen seconds to spare. Both subtests from the WISC score considerably above the mental age obtained on the pre-test Stanford-Binet.

Bender-Gestalt Test. On the pre-test (2–26–57), there were 13 errors, with 1 concrete, 1 perseveration, 2 dissociations, 2 incorrect elements, 1 unrecognizable, 3 distorted angles, 1 rotation, and 1 disproportion. On the post-test (5–12–58) there were eight errors, with 2 dissociations, 1 incorrect element, 2 distorted angles, 1 compression, and 1 disproportion.

Syracuse Visual Figure-Background Test. On the pre-test (11–18–57), there were 7 correct responses to the figure, with no instances of perseveration or background reactions. Post-test (5–12–58), however, there were 9 correct responses to the figure, 1 background response, and 2 perseverations. Thus, at the end of the year, there was greater accuracy, but also evidences of disturbance in figure-background relationships that were initially lacking.

Tactual-Motor Test (2–26–57). After feeling the triangle, C-2-1 said: "I can't draw exactly what it was. It felt *something* like a valentine." He then proceeded to draw a circle with a slight indentation near the top. Bender Designs 4 and 6, with plain background, were incorrectly drawn. When a thumbtack background was added, C-2-1 was quite confused, and tried to draw in the background as well as his misinterpretations of the stimulus figures.

Marble Board Test (2–26–57). Marble Board 1 was correctly reproduced rapidly and accurately. The drawing C-2-1 made of it shows a good grasp of the basic pattern. Marble Board 2, despite the efforts of C-2-1 to count, was not entirely accurate, having three misplaced marbles. In his drawing the basic pattern was recognizable, but was greatly elaborated.

Vineland Social Maturity Scale.

Pre-test (*11–18–57*)		Post-test (*5–15–58*)	
Total Score:	56.5	Total Score:	76
Age Equivalent:	5–1	Age Equivalent:	9–8
Social Quotient:	60	Social Quotient:	108

The mother served as informant in both interviews. C-2-1 has developed many new social skills and abilities over the course of the year, which is reflected in the difference of 48 points between pre- and post-test social quotients. Some of the things that he could do at the end of the year that he could not at the beginning include playing simple table games, going to school unattended, using a pencil for writing, telling time to a quarter hour, using a table knife for cutting, participating in pre-adolescent play, combing and brushing his own hair, making minor purchases, writing occasional short letters, making telephone calls, and being left to care for himself and younger children.

The mother feels that, at home, C-2-1 is as noisy and active as he has been in the past, but that he is now more reliable and will do what is asked of him.

Summary. Intelligence is within the average range. Ability to see similarities, which involves a relatively high abstract ability, was especially note-worthy. C-2-1 was able to see similarities and reconcile opposites at the Year XIV level.

There was improvement on four out of the five psychological tests on which there is a pre- and post-test available for comparison. The post-test Binet was 7 points greater, there were fewer errors on the Bender-Gestalt Test, greater accuracy on the Syracuse Visual Figure-Background Test, and a 48 point greater social quotient on the Vineland Social Maturity Scale. The only test which showed no improvement, and in fact was slightly poorer, was the Goodenough Intelligence Test.

The most striking improvement over the course of the past year has been in the development of social skills and abilities. This was especially noticeable in observations of classroom behavior.

PEDIATRIC HISTORY C-2-2

The information was obtained from both parents who were not particularly sure that they wanted C-2-2 included in this Study. They had just spoken to the Resident Co-ordinator and had not quite made up their minds. Some of the questions they had indicated that the father, especially, wanted as-surance that this would be the best placement and he apparently was not willing to do it unless these assurances were met. Initially, he did most of the talking, not looking directly at the Interviewer, and later on the mother entered into the discussion and information giving.

Problem

The difficulties of C-2-2 apparently started off with speech. He received speech therapy and was making progress. Then he had some difficulty reading (which father said he had supposed would be the case). Last year there was a question of discipline in school as well. Because of the discipline problem and the speech and reading difficulties, he was placed in Special Education (at the end of his first year in school).

He seems to get excited when something new occurs and this difficulty became more apparent when he entered the second grade. At home apparently he is not much of a discipline problem, although he is said to be quite strong-willed. His reading difficulty seems to center around a reversal problem with his *b*'s and *p*'s, his *s*'s, *w*'s, and *m*'s. This was noticed by the parents. He has had a neurological examination, including an EEG which apparently was normal. At the Clinic where this was done, no reason could be found for some of his difficulties and at that time the suggestion was made that a psychological test should be done and Special Education might be helpful. Last year, when in Special Education, he seemed to do well. He presently is receiving remedial reading instruction from a neighbor who apparently does this work quite well. There was no apparent retardation in appearance of speech; it is just that it was always unclear and immature. His speech has markedly im-proved, although there are one or two sounds which he still does not get right.

His dislike for school might have stemmed from the difficulty with some of his playmates who were making his life rather miserable because of his inability to function on their level. He tends to get excited easily in groups and is certainly easier to handle in a smaller group setting, or when alone. He is said to open up more with other people than he will at home with his parents.

Family History

1. Maternal grandmother living and well.
2. Maternal grandfather living and well. The grandparents are separated.
3. Paternal grandmother died when he was only 2 years of age in the epidemic of influenza.
4. Paternal grandfather died of cancer.
5. Mother has one brother who is living and well.
6. Father has one brother and one sister, both of whom are living and well. The sister has two girls who apparently are also having reading difficulty.

Family Background

Father. (Age 41.) He is in good health, wears glasses for myopia, and has retenitis pigmentosa. He is a research assistant at a physics lab, has a master's degree in electrical engineering. Interests: reading, community discussion groups. Problems: he was raised by an aunt but traveled about quite a bit, from one relative to another, until he was 7 years of age, at which time his aunt and himself went to live with his father. He was always small for his age and therefore had difficulty defending himself. Personality: quiet, retiring individual who is said not to be an extrovert. Attitude toward patient's difficulties: he tried to be very understanding and patient and he said that he might be a litt'e more strict than other parents in the neighborhood.

Mother. (Age 38.) She is in good health. Used to do clerical work and finished high school. Interests: handiwork and photography. Personality: quiet, calm and cheerful. Attitude: not nearly as concerned as other people seem to be with some of the difficulties of C-2-2.

Marriage. The parents have been married fourteen years. It is the first marriage for both. The marriage is said to be compatible. Although they are not of the same religion, this is not a problem.

Siblings. None. C-2-2 has a cat and more recently has acquired a rabbit.

Mother's Medical History during Pregnancy with Child

The mother has had three miscarriages, one at six weeks, one at four weeks, then C-2-2 was born, and the third one since his birth, at four weeks. Apparently no explanation for these miscarriages has been given. During her pregnancy with C-2-2 she received hormonal therapy. Apparently there was an indication of her losing C-2-2, due to bleeding, and so she was put to bed where she remained for about six months of the pregnancy and received Stilbesterol. She was 30 years of age at the time of his birth. C-2-2 was born in a local hospital. The bag of water was ruptured six or eight hours prior to delivery. The delivery itself was uneventful except that C-2-2 apparently was born a month earlier than the due date. His birth weight was 5 pounds, 7 ounces. He was seen within the first twelve hours. He was placed on formula feeding and was slow in eating and sucking. Apparently he tired easily, although there was no difficulty in the actual nursing or in swallowing.

Past Medical History of Patient

DPT and smallpox vaccination during first year of life. He has had his polio immunizations. He had chickenpox at the age of 5, measles at the age of 7, mumps at the age of 6. At 3 years of age, on the way back from a trip, he was hospitalized. Apparently he had a type of breathing difficulty which was described as asthma, and at that time, during his hospitalization, an anemia was discovered and he was transfused. Since then he has been on medication for the anemia and apparently at present is back to normal. He has never had any convulsions and concurrently is on no medication.

Developmental History

C-2-2 was always a slow feeder, he was slow in sitting up, standing, walking and teething, as well as speech. He seemed to be a happy baby though. His bottle was propped. There was no sleeping difficulty. He started counting when he went to kindergarten and was able to understand and perform instructions and commands. There was apparently no visual or auditory difficulty. He likes to be outside playing a great deal and will sit and watch TV only if he is really interested. Does not like to sit through Sunday School. His toilet-training was uneventful being accomplished by 3 years of age with no history of enuresis. He is said to be right-handed and at one time there was a question of whether he might not have been ambidextrous. He is said to be able to dress himself and does better with one other playmate, rather than a large group. He is said to be able to ride a two-wheeler bicycle and to roller-skate, and is said to be active in general. At the table he used to fidget quite a bit, but is much better now. He does not suck his thumb, bang his head, or rock. Personality: logical, loves to argue. He is not particularly friendly. Punishment: he is either spanked or put in his room. He will argue at first and then sort of respond. Fighting: he is able to fight and will fight. Frustration: he gets and throws things but does not have actual temper tantrums.

Physical Examination

Blood pressure 100/90.

General appearance. C-2-2 was a pleasant boy who came along without difficulty and who was noted to talk in a rather babyish, immature way. When we walked into the examining room he recognized the pipe on the table and immediately put it into his mouth, saying that he smokes and asked me to light the pipe for him. He wanted to know what I was going to do, adding, "You are not going to put me to sleep and cut me open—I'm tough—I could knock your brains out." He kept jabbering away about this and was somewhat hyperactive.

His three wishes included (1) jet bomber, (2) helicopter, (3) horse. He said he didn't know about a good mommy or a bad mommy. To the ambulance story he said, "A man who was driving it was killed with a twelve gauge shotgun." He recognized a penny, nickel, dime, and quarter, and knew their value. In counting, he said "thorty" for thirty and "thorteen" for thirteen. Of note is the fact also that he kept saying, "I don't know," rather than risking an answer which he was unsure of. However, when reassured, he frequently did give a proper answer. C-2-2 was able to hop equally well on both feet and could skip. He was able to walk on both heels and toes.

The remainder of the physical examination, including the neurological exam, was negative. When approached for an examination of his genitalia, he made a movement to protect them. He was able to dress himself rather well, including the tying of his shoelaces.

Neurological Examination

Cranial nerves. First cranial nerve was not tested. Second cranial nerve: visual fields were normal; fundi normal. Third, fourth, and sixth cranial nerves: pupils were equal and round and reacted to light and accommodation. Extra-ocular movements are intact. No nystagmus is seen. Fifth cranial nerve: normal for motor and sensory function. Seventh cranial nerve: normal for motor function. Taste was not tested. Eighth cranial nerve: the boy was able to hear the tuning fork on both sides without difficulty. Air conduction is greater than bone conduction. There is no lateralization. Ninth and tenth cranial nerves: gag reflexes normal. The boy was able to swallow without difficulty. The uvula went up in the mid-line. Eleventh cranial nerve: the boy was able to shrug his shoulders without difficulty. Twelfth cranial nerve: the tongue protrudes in the mid-line. *Sensory.* Normal for pinprick, touch, vibratory, position and stereognosis. Two-point discrimination and other modalities involving the cortex are also normal. No extinction is seen in this boy. *Reflexes.* Reflexes are equal and active throughout. No pathological reflexes were present. *Motor.* Motor system is normal. There is good strength throughout. *Cerebellar.* Finger-to-nose and heel-to-shin tests were well performed. He was able to spin the jack well with his right hand, but not so well with his left hand. *Station and gait.* The boy was able to walk on his heels and on his toes without difficulty. His gait is normal. *Comment.* There is some slurring of speech when he talks. The boy is right-eyed and right-handed.

Electroencephalogram

Attitude and condition of patient: alert and co-operative. Fundamental frequency: ranges between 8.5 and 9 waves per second. Slow waves: occasional short volleys of approximately 5 per second waves are observed in the frontal derivations (bilateral). With the onset of sleep this activity became more prominent. With sleep the normal frontal and parietal slow activity became dominant. Fast waves: are not prominent, but short runs of bifrontal 18 per second activity is observed. Amplitude characteristics: average to high voltage (100 microvolts); irregular modulation. Hyperventilation: accentuates the prominence of the bioccipital slow output. Impression: moderate generalized abnormal EEG.

Speech and Hearing Evaluation

General appearance. His early difficulties centered around his speech and he has been having difficulties with reading. The general developmental picture suggests considerable retardation. C-2-2 sat up at 10 months and walked at 30 months, with no following difficulties in locomotion reported. Mother reported that he babbled a lot as a young infant, but there was evidently a long period of pre-speech jargon. Around the age of 3 he began to talk in phrases, rather than in words. Speech was then very unclear. The summer before he entered kindergarten the child was taken to the Speech Clinic where they worked with him for about two years. In first grade he received his speech therapy in school. His speech has been described as follows: ". . . shows a marked dyslalia, with many details of infantile articulation carried over. There is a fairly severe lateral lisp and distortion of all the alveolar sounds as they occur in the sound blends. The blends are generally poor, as is his connected discourse." Mother reports that he has not been having speech therapy for the past year. Improvement has been gradually occurring. Mother feels that he still has some occasional errors.

Behavioral observations. C-2-2 came willingly with the Examiner. He is a well-dressed, clean-looking youngster. At first his manner was very tentative and all his gestures were in "slow motion." This is in line with his speech which is quite prolonged. He would engage in some of the test procedures, but would immediately return to those objects in the room that had attracted his attention. He was not unco-operative, but determinedly willful.

Oral examination. There is a marked overbite. Teeth are widely spaced and there is a high palatal arch. Tongue and palatal mobility are good, as is pharyngeal stricture. He has good control of his tongue and lips.

Articulation. This child's speech has improved. The *s* and *s* blends are still unstable. *J* is pronounced as *ch* and there is still distortion of the alveolar sounds as they occur in sound blends. There are many vowel distortions, particularly on the diphthong, but these are not consistent.

Voice. Voice is unprojected and prolonged.

Propositional speech. The content of this child's connected discourse is good. We started talking about airplanes and he indicated that he was going to be a pilot. He then got into a discussion on the differences between a propeller and a jet plane. When he is talking freely about a topic in which he is interested, he is using complex sentences and a good vocabulary. His vocal utterance stands out because of the prolongation rather than the articulation errors. He knew all the animals and gave a sentence about each one. He was quite scornful about the idea of telling the story about the picture. He started to tell about the picture of shopping at the A & P: "They went shopping too," and then he broke in with a loud, "No." He then grabbed the picture about the family and muttered scornfully, "They kissing and all that crazy junk—peuh!" The ejaculation was said with real feeling. He looked over the one about fishing and commented, "They already caught some fish—they are just beside some boats." He was finally induced to tell the story of the Three Bears, which he did in quite some detail, but interspersed with giggles and playing with cigarette tobacco which he took from a pack lying on the desk.

Hearing. This child's hearing is well within normal range. He gave the following pure-tone audiogram:

Right	15	20	10	0	−10	5
	125	250	500	1000	2000	4000
Left	10	15	10	0	−10	0

He repeated the spondee words quickly and accurately. He missed three of the PBK words. It was felt that this was more the lack of attention than inability to hear.

Initial impression. While this child's speech has improved, it is still conspicuous in its prolongation and vowel and alveolar distortion.

Psychiatric Evaluation

C-2-2 is a friendly youngster whose speech defect was quite noticeable today, but everything he wished to say was understood without difficulty. He was quite mischievous during the hour and attempted to tell jokes and play jokes on the Examiner. In testing a bullet from the cork gun, he lined up a good target and fired, but discovered that the bullet went a few inches and dropped down without having any projectile force. At this point he said, "Oh, that's not much of a gun."

He joined the fence sections quite easily, building up a little phantasy around the fence and the ranch house, having one side of the house on the edge of a 200-foot cliff. He arranged it so that when the button was pressed, the house would swing 180 degrees and three airplanes which had been hidden in there, would be brought into the yard, and after 40 seconds, would move into its former position, "And the airplane that didn't get off in time would just have to know what was coming to it." He offered some technical knowledge about the anti-aircraft truck he was playing with. He would not divulge his source, but facts, as well as a good phantasy life, were demonstrated.

When asked what the baby bird would do when its nest was blown away, he replied, "The bird would build his own nest." When asked about the elephant, said it would be "bigger and heavier."

There was good gross and fine motor co-ordination. He shuffled playing cards quite well. He asked to play Old Maid and this was done with lots of spirit and gusto. It was established that he could not read the names on the cards, e.g., one out of four tries was correct.

This was the only boy seen for the Project who ventured to give a month for his birthday. He was unwilling to state what month we were in, though he did talk of the summer season. He guessed the year when asked, saying 108. His three wishes were: (1) to fly himself like Superman, he illustrated with flowing gestures and said, "Fly"; (2) "All the magic in the world," and he smiled in an impish manner; (3) a jet plane.

At the end of the hour he was asked to draw a person, and said, "I will draw you," at which he drew a big head and ears of a rabbit. Another head appearing below on the paper was egg-shaped with the egg laying on its side. The facial features were added, finally, in pencil. He drew a very immature, odd body which was not a stick figure and had a pair of shorts only for clothing. His remark was, "Here's you in your underwear out in the wetting." It should be said that a few moments before the drawing was begun, there was a cloudburst.

Psychiatric Re-evaluation

C-2-2's behavior was essentially the same as the initial contact, i.e., the same boundless energy, difficulty in following directions, and much aggressive drive. In the absence of the popgun, he spent the majority of the hour hitting Bobo's replacement around the room. He showed good strength and his coordination was above average. As he punched he talked rapidly and with an adequate vocabulary. He did not mention his mother nor his father. Much of what he had to say was superficial, and he continued to speak with a kind of babyishness, but his words were understood at all times.

The child was asked to make a drawing of anything he wanted, plus a drawing of a person. He drew an action picture in which a Nazi plane fired at an enemy fort. When asked who this fort belonged to, he said, "The Germans." He gave the same reply as last year to Draw-a-Person, saying, "I'll draw you"; but this time he was asked to try something else. He drew a man with ears and a face resembling a rodent. The bizarre distorted hands and fingers, which were larger than the hand, were placed upon a trunk which dwindled away into tapering feet.

Conversation with mother. The child's mother stated that she had not seen too much change in her son. She said it was still hard to get him to do things. Also, she found it hard to do the things that she was supposed to do in her relationship with the child. She does feel, however, that he has been able to get along with a larger group than his usual number of two or three youngsters. But he may have trouble with certain friends because he is apt to be a little critical and not too forgiving.

Psychological Examination

Stanford-Binet, Form L (Pre-test) (7–19–57).
CA: 8–4; MA: 8–10; IQ: 106.
Present intellectual functioning falls within the Average range with an IQ of 106 and mental age of 8–10. This is consistent with testing done 7–30–56, when an IQ of 100 was obtained, mental age 7–4. Thus the rate of intellectual

development seems to be quite consistent. The seven-year range of perform-ance was from Year VI through Year XII. The Basal Age was at Year VI, while the ceiling was at Year XII.

All items were passed at Year VII with the exception of comprehension. In this item a situation is verbally described in which the child is expected to grasp the essential factors involved. For example, when asked what he should do if he accidentally broke something which belonged to someone else, he said, "Nothing." When asked what he should do if he were on his way to school and saw that he was in danger of being late, he said, "I wouldn't go at all then." Abstract ability, as in seeing the similarity between two things, was good, and he was able to make three good diamonds.

At Year VIII two items were missed, verbal absurdities, and, again, compre-hension. Auditory organization, as in repeating sentences, was good, as was ability to see similarities and differences.

At Year IX two items were failed, verbal absurdities and repeating four digits reversed. In the absurdities, for example, when asked what was absurd about the statement that only recently a small skull had been discovered in Spain which was believed to be that of Christopher Columbus when he was about 10 years old, C-2-2 said, "He wouldn't die when he was ten, because he wasn't old enough to die." Attention span, as measured by repetition of digits, was inadequate at this age level.

At Year X two items were passed. Eleven words must be defined to pass the vocabulary test at this level, which C 2-2 did. He was also able to analyze a situation presented pictorially. He was unable to read even the simplest words at this level. For example, he read "I" for "a." He could not find reasons for various problem situations. He did not pass the word naming test. In this test the child is instructed to say as many words as he can in one minute. At least 28 words are expected at this level, and he was able to produce only 18. He started out very well and named the objects in the testing room, but then he "blocked" and could not continue. He also could not repeat six digits.

At Year XI two items were passed, the memory for sentences and similari-ties of three things. This indicates that auditory organization, at least as far as meaning is concerned, is relatively good, as is abstract ability.

Stanford-Binet, Form M (Post-test) (5–23–58).

CA: 952; M: 8–10; IQ: 96.

Intelligence is Average, with a performance range of seven years from a Basal Age at Year VI to a ceiling at Year XII.

At Year VII one item was failed, memory for sentences. C-2-2 transposed phrases and left out words.

Comprehension was failed at Year VIII. This item involves a problem situa-tion presented verbally. In answer to an inquiry as to what a man should do if he came home and found that his house had been robbed, he said, "Go out and try to find the burglar."

At Year IX he was unable to draw designs from memory, rearrange a series of disarranged words so that they made a sentence, or make rhymes. He knew what rhymes are, as may be seen in the first series of responses, but was unable to produce enough rhyming words. He saw the absurdity in verbal absurdities, gave good similarities and differences, and repeated four digits reversed.

At Year X he was able to name more than 12 animals in one minute, and count the number of blocks presented on a card. He could not repeat six digits, define abstract words, or remember the details of a story that was read to him.

At Year XI two items were passed, verbal absurdities and abstract words. He was unable to find reasons for problem situations, copy a bead chain from memory, see similarities between three things, or repeat a sentence from memory.

All items were failed at Year XII.

Ammons Full-Range Picture Vocabulary Test (7–19–57).

CA: 8–4; MA: 9–0.

The mental age obtained on this test was only two months greater than that obtained on either of the Stanford-Binets. C-2-2 passed a number of words that the average child of this chronological age is not expected to pass, including purchase, panels, sudden, sympathy, and gravitation.

Goodenough Intelligence Test.

Pre-test (7–19–57)	Post-test (5–12–58)
CA: 8–4; MA: 6–3	CA: 9–1; MA: 6–3

Both the pre- and post-test drawings are very crude for this chronological age level. The first drawing is a tightly compressed figure near the extreme upper edge of the paper, with huge, wing-shaped ears, and one single hair coming from the top of the head. The second figure lacks the facial detail of the first, but has the correct number of fingers represented. In general, the post-test figure was more poorly executed than the pre-test.

Block Design and Coding from WISC.

	Raw Score	Scaled Score	Equivalent Test Age
Block Design	14	11	9–6
Coding	20	7	6–10

All of the block designs up to Design 2 were done quickly and accurately on the first attempt. He could not form the diagonals in Design 3, attempting to rotate the complete design instead. On the Coding test, form B, 21 symbol substitutions were attempted, with one error.

Bender-Gestalt Test. On the pre-test (7–19–57) 14 errors were made with 1 immature, 1 perseveration, 2 dissociations, 1 incorrect elements, 2 distorted angles, 1 rotation, 3 enlargements, and 3 disproportions. Only 10 errors were made on the post-test (5–12–58), with 1 immature, 2 perseverations, 2 distorted angles, 2 rotations, and 3 enlargements. The main improvement may be seen in fewer errors categorized as dissociation and disproportion.

Syracuse Visual Figure-Background Test. In the pre-test (10–24–57) there were 8 correct responses to figure, 2 perseverations, and 1 background response.

On the post-test (5–12–58), there were 10 correct responses to figure, 1 background reaction, and no perseverations. Thus improvement may be seen in accuracy and lessened perseveration, but no change was shown in distractibility by background stimuli.

Tactual-Motor Test (10–24–57). He correctly drew the diamond, both with plain and with structured backgrounds. The other drawings have no resemblance to the stimulus figures.

Marble Board Test (11–18–57). Marble Board 1 was reproduced quickly and accurately. The drawing shows a good grasp of the basic configuration, i.e., overlapping squares. Marble Board 2, however, proved to be too difficult. He counted the correct number of marbles for the horizontals, but could not construct the diagonals, despite many shifts and changes. His drawing shows two dissociated pentagons.

Vineland Social Maturity Scale.

Pre-test (11–19–57)		Post-test (5–15–58)	
Total Score:	65	Total Score:	17
Age Equivalent:	7–0	Age Equivalent:	10–0
Social Quotient:	81	Social Quotient:	109

The mother served as informant at both interviews. The post-test, social quotient is 28 points higher than the pre-test, reflecting the observed progress made in classroom behavior over the course of the year.

C-2-2 can do several things at the present time that he could not do formerly, such as using a pencil for writing, going to bed unassisted, doing routine household tasks, bathing himself unaided, caring for himself at the table, going about home town freely, making telephone calls, doing small remunerative work, and being left to care for himself and other smaller children.

At the beginning of the year his mother commented than in *doing things* he was like a 9-year old, but in a group his behavior was more like that of a 7-year old. Although he does not contribute much information about his school activities, his mother feels that he is widening his circle of friends and is much more competent in dealing with other children now.

Summary. Intelligence is within the Average range. Difficulty was noted on the Stanford-Binet with tasks requiring auditory organization, such as repetition of sentences from memory, problem situations, and memory for a story that was read to him. Vocabulary and abstract thinking, as involved in seeing similarities, were passed at a level higher than his chronological age would indicate. Visuo-motor tasks were also difficult for him, such as the stringing of beads according to an example presented by the Examiner.

C-2-2 showed improvement on three of the five tests on which both a pre- and post-test is available for comparative purposes. He made fewer errors on the Bender-Gestalt, showing fewer dissociations, and disproportions. On the Syracuse Visual Figure-Background Test accuracy was greater and perseveration less, but there was no change in reactions to background stimuli. There was a great change in the rate of development of social skills and abilities, C-2-2 now being able to do many things that were either absent or just emerging at the beginning of the year.

PEDIATRIC HISTORY C-2-3

Problem

When asked about C-2-3's problems, the mother seemed quite suspicious and guarded. She thought a good deal before answering and presenting his problems. In her own words she felt that basically it is the fact that the child has a brain injury, supposedly occurring at birth. She went into further detail, stating that he had motor seizures which were actually the first symptoms for which she sought help. At approximately 11 months of age she noticed for the first time that he would blink his eyes and tense his upper extremities. It seemed at first as if he were playing. When she called this fact to the attention of the pediatrician he felt there was not very much to be concerned about and tried to reassure her. At 2 years of age these same symptoms were apparently becoming more frequent. It was at this time that a neurologist began seeing the boy and he diagnosed the difficulty as minor convulsions due to brain injury, probably due to hemorrhage at birth. The mother said there was no loss of consciousness, no rolling of the eyes and no gross convulsive movements, just the fine movement of both hands and the blinking of the eyes. She hastened to add that he slept well and did all the things he was supposed to do, turning his head, gaining weight, and teething. He was put on medication by the neurologist and only had occasional seizures, the last one having occurred about six years ago and none since. He has been having repeated EEG's which are said to be showing some improvement.

It was not until I specifically asked whether C-2-3 was having any school problems that the mother talked about them. It seems he started nursery school at 3 years of age. He was thought to be "brilliant," but displayed a short attention span. He was quite verbal with an excellent vocabulary. He did, however, have a tendency to ramble. At the end of the school year when he was 5, the school suggested private school, because—according to the mother—of his small physical size, and because it was suggested that he would benefit from a smaller group in such a setting. Apparently he was having difficulty with eye-to-hand co-ordination. It was at about this time that a physician tested the boy and found that he had a distorted pattern of function. The physician is said not to have interpreted the test results in terms of brain injury. It was at this point that the mother mentioned that C-2-3 could count abstractly but not specific objects. At the private school he attended the teacher thought that he might be having some visual difficulty (actually he was not recognizing written words). However, upon testing, his vision was found to be normal. At age 5½ it was suggested (based on psychological testing) that he remain in kindergarten for another year instead of going on to the first grade.

Apparently it was not until after psychological testing at a local clinic that the term "retardation" was used and it was then suggested that the mother see the Supervisor of Special Education. The mother apparently is pleased with the progress that her son is making at school presently.

Description of Parent

She is a rather pleasant-looking woman who spoke quite freely and had excellent control and knowledge of medical terminology. I have the distinct impression that she was perhaps not being very honest, not only with me but with herself. She played with the matchbox and kept swinging her foot up and down while seated in the chair. She explained perhaps some of the difficulties in school upon the fact that she never told anyone, even the neighbors, nor the teachers, about the motor difficulties or the minor convulsions that C-2-3 had had. She, of course, said that the neurologist had suggested that there was no need to tell anyone as it was not very serious. However, after the various psychological testings, and when it became necessary for C-2-3 to be placed in a Special Class, she could no longer hide it. Actually, after she told others, she seemed to be quite relieved.

Family History

1. Mother's mother is living and well. Has hypertension.
2. Mother's father died of a brain tumor.
3. Father's mother is living and well and also has hypertension.
4. Father's father died of a coronary occlusion.
5. Mother has one brother who is living and well.
6. Father has one sister who is living and well.

The mother further stated that a cousin of hers had some trauma of the head which resulted in convulsive-like seizures. An uncle of hers has diabetes and it would appear that the mother's grandmother and grandfather were cousins.

Family Background

Father. (Age 40.) In good health, physicist—has a Ph.D. His interests include gardening, photography, tennis, and bicycling with the boys. He too is said to have been small physically as a child and his parents were concerned about this. He had a duodenal ulcer which was treated medically and has had no recent recurrences. When confronted with C-2-3's problem, at first he was confused, but apparently has accepted it with "faith in nature doing right." In describing his personality, the mother said he is a scholar, has lots of wisdom and a great deal of faith; he is an introvert, does not need social contacts or lots of people around him. He is self-sufficient and well-controlled (rarely loses temper).

Mother. (Age 39.) Good health, has a master's degree and has taught school. Interests: at first she said she had none; then she said she likes to sleep. Talking about her personality, she said she loves people, she is explosive, she is much more temperamental than her husband and she has been accused of being "the managerial type." Her initial reaction to C-2-3's problems was described as feeling "sunk." She felt that he would melt away. She cried a good deal. She would look at the baby and just cry. She said her husband came to the rescue in terms of expounding about faith and realism. She said she recovered rapidly. She said she was greatly disturbed at first by the burden placed upon her in concealing his difficulty, that is, in having to tell little white lies. She feels much more comfortable now that she can talk about it and she keeps thinking about what he might have been like.

Marriage. The mother was 26 years of age and the father was 27 years of age at the time of the marriage and they have been married for thirteen years. It is described as a compatible, happy marriage. They have the same religion now, one having converted from another faith. Both are said to share in the marital responsibilities. She was teaching for a while, two nights a week, and then the father would stay home and take care of C-2-3.

Siblings. Brother, 6 years of age; he was described as being a "little mathmetician." The boys get along well together and the younger brother is said to be a model child. C-2-3 will tease him, but he apparently shows a great deal of restraint and understanding. He recognizes the undesirable actions of C-2-3, but doesn't verbalize to C-2-3 or to his parents. (The mother says she has heard him use the expression to his friends "You're just like my brother," whenever they do something which displeases him.) She did not further elaborate, but stated that sometimes C-2-3 resents his brother's normalcy. C-2-3 has the following pets: a dog, a bird, and a turtle. The mother spoke of the dog with disdain. She said it is dirty and smells, and actually she doesn't want him around the house; however, the father felt that C-2-3 should have a dog, and so she actually bought the dog for the boy.

Mother's Medical History during Pregnancy with Child

The mother was 30 years of age at the time of C-2-3's birth. The delivery was attended by an obstetrician. Prenatal care was begun four weeks following conception. The mother said she had back trouble and received physical therapy throughout most of the pregnancy. This therapy consisted of infrared lamp treatments and massage. There was no hyperemesis, no medication, and no X-ray during the pregnancy. The delivery occurred two weeks past the expected date of confinement. There apparently was a fast labor, and C-2-3 was rotated by high forceps from a posteria position. His birth weight was 7 pounds, 8 ounces, and he was seen by his mother within the first twenty-four hours following the delivery. He was breast-fed for four weeks but apparently had diarrhea and was not gaining too well. He always seemed hungry. As a result he was placed on an evaporated milk formula.

Past Medical History

C-2-3 received his DPT immunizations during the first year of life. He received his smallpox vaccination at 18 months of age. The reason for the delay was that they had moved from their former place of residence in the meantime. He has had his Salk vaccine immunizations. He had chickenpox and measles, both of which were rather mild. He still has his tonsils and an occasional sore throat. He is said to have had an enlarged thymus at birth and received one X-ray treatment in addition to the original X-ray taken of his chest. The latter was done routinely at the hospital in which he was born. Two years ago he had a dental extraction for which he was given ether. He is said to have been exposed to chickenpox at three months of age although he never came down with the disease at that time.

Developmental History

As previously stated, C-2-3 was breast-fed for four weeks but he did not seem very interested. He sucked well and mother finally gave it up. (It was too time consuming and made the mother nervous.) He had no difficulty on the evaporated milk formula. He is said to have had diarrhea at one month of age and later again at 3 months of age. The bottle was never propped. He started drinking from a cup at 9 months of age and was weaned from the bottle at 13 to 14 months of age. He gave up his night bottle at 15 months of age, then he threw it away. He was started on solids at 3 months—had no difficulty swallowing and ate well. There is no history of pica. There was never any difficulty with speech. He has always been manifestly right-handed. Bladder control was achieved at 2 years of age and bowel control at about the same age. Toilet-training usually terminated every meal and so there was no difficulty. He is said to prefer to play with older boys. He seems solicitous of younger children and wants to take care of them. He is said to be an extrovert, likes to watch TV, and can sit through movies. He likes to play all sorts of games. At the moment he is fond of guns; it used to be cars. He likes to be read to and is able to ride a two-wheel bicycle. He can feed himself, zip zippers mother says she avoids anything with buttons to make it easier for him. He can tie his own shoelaces. He is able to bathe himself. He will avoid fighting as much as possible, and, although he does not have overt temper tantrums, he cries when frustrated.

Additional Information

When C-2-3 was in a private school, the mother requested a study and evaluation of her son "because of lack of speech."

At home, C-2-3 was said to be a behavior problem caused by indulgence after a diagnosis of brain damage was made. The mother described her disciplinary methods as "wishy-washy" and without strength. He is small for his age, is a feeding problem, but is able to care for other needs. The parents seem to be struggling with and are having difficulty in accepting the patient's limitations.

The mother said that she was a spoiled child, one of two children, the other a brother eight years younger who was a "tyrant." She has difficulties in the area of interpersonal relationships, which seem to stem from underlying hostility. She formerly taught school, and she recently undertook private tutor-

ing and became active in civic work to compensate for her husband's absence
from the home. She indicated that there has been some friction in the marital
relationship from the time of her first pregnancy. She had not wanted children—"was talked into it"—and was left to care for the children herself.
There was one pregnancy between the two children. The second child was
planned for after the father agreed to spend more time at home.

Medical Summary of Another Physician

C-2-3 has been under private neurological care since his second year of life.
The presenting signs of brain damage were "staring spells" and EEG studies
confirmed the diagnosis of organic difficulty.

Physically, C-2-3 is a small, 8½-year old boy with slightly prominent ears.
X-ray of the wrists reveals slight retardation in bone age. Neurological exam
within normal limits. Psychological evaluation mentioned on this same fa-
vored organic brain damage.

Physical Examination

Blood pressure 90/60.

There was no difficulty in getting C-2-3 to come along with the Examiner.
Throughout the entire examination he was very active and seemed all wound
up. He verbalized quite easily. He knew his age, said he liked school, and he
was quite curious about the various objects in the room, and was able to
identify most of the more common ones. His three wishes were: (1) horse;
(2) sun; (3) a pear tree, because he could pick off the pears and eat them.
The child was noted to have a liquid "*i*" in his speech. A good mommie is
somebody who takes care of you. A good daddy is fairly nice. A bad daddy
doesn't like you very much. When somebody doesn't like someone he socks
them in the jaw. To be liked means not to be mean. Not to be liked means he
threw a rock. His spontaneous conversation and rambling seemed to consist
a great deal about firemen and policemen, about fires, sleeping and closets
for twenty-four hours a day. In response to the ambulance question he said
somebody would get hurt, maybe a neighbor, maybe the home was on fire.
It is interesting to note that V-2-3 was dressed in a fancy T-shirt and that his
trousers had neither belt nor buttons, but elastic at the waist and clips in
front. However, he was able to tie his shoes. He expressed concern about his
T-shirt not being put on correctly after the examination. When asked why,
he said it would look silly.

General appearance. C-2-3 is a pleasant, short, slight-of-build, boy. A very
fine but prominent hirsutism was noted on the extremities and thorax. *Skin
and mucous membranes.* Not remarkable. *Lymph nodes.* Occasional cervical
lymph nodes. *Head.* The head was of normal shape and size and freely movable. *Face.* The expression on the child's face was rather alert. He seemed to
breath with his mouth open and spoke with a stuffy nose, as if he had a cold.
He had good facial control and no tic was apparent. *Ears.* There were no
discharges or mastoid tendernesses. His bearing was grossly normal, and

otoscopic examination was negative. *Eyes.* The extra-ocular movements were normal, there was no strabismus, the pupils were equal and round, reacted to light and accommodation. Gross vision was normal. Fundiscopic examination was normal. *Nose and sinuses.* The nares were not entirely patent. The mucous membrane seemed rather boggy and pale. *Mouth and throat.* The teeth were in good condition and numbered 12 on top and 12 on bottom. The tongue did not tremble nor deviate when protruded. There appeared to be a prognathism. The palate and uvula were normal. The tonsils were of normal size. *Neck.* The neck was freely movable, no masses palpable; the thyroid was not enlarged; the trachea was in the mid-line. *Chest.* The rib cage was rather prominent, the chest was symmetrical, the lungs were clear to palpation, percussion and auscultation. The heart size was normal clinically. PMI was in the fifth interspace in the mid-clavicular line on the left. No murmurs were audible. Radial and femoral pulses were easily palpable. *Abdomen.* Contour was scaphoid. No tenderness, no spasm, liver, spleen, and kidneys were not enlarged, bladder was not distended, and no masses were palpable. *Genitalia.* Testicles were in the scrotum; remainder of genital examination was negative. *Extremities.* There were no deformities, muscle power and range of motion was good. There was no cyanosis or clubbing of the digits. *Neurological examination.* Not remarkable.

Neurological Examination

Cranial nerves. The first cranial nerve was not tested. Second cranial nerve: visual fields were grossly intact. The fundi were normal. Third, fourth, and sixth cranial nerves: extra-ocular movements were intact. No nystagmus was present. Fifth cranial nerve: motor and sensory parts were normal. Seventh cranial nerve: muscles of facial expression were all in excellent shape. Eighth cranial nerve: boy was able to hear the tuning fork bilaterally. Air conduction was greater than bone conduction. Ninth and tenth cranial nerves: swallowing was well performed. The uvula was in the mid-line. Gag reflexes were not attempted. Twelfth cranial nerve: the tongue protruded in the mid-line. No sign of atrophy or fasciculation. *Sensory.* Pinprick, vibratory, position, two-point discrimination, pinprick localization were all well performed once the patient understood what was expected of him. Stereognosis was normal bilaterally. *Motor.* The boy shows good strength throughout. The muscle tone is normal. Reflexes were equal and active bilaterally. There were no Babinski present. *Cerebellar.* Finger-to-nose, finger-to-nose-to-finger, heel-to-shin tests were well performed. Diadochokinesis was normal. Co-ordination seemed to be fairly good, although he had some difficulty with rapid alternating movements of the hands, tending to have large gross movements rather than fine movements. He was unable to spin the jack with the left hand; however, he could do a moderately fair job with the right hand. Hand-patting tests were normal. *Station and gait.* The gait was normal. He was able to walk on the heels and on the toes without any difficulty. Romberg was negative.

Electroencephalogram

Attitude and condition of patient: alert, co-operative. Fundamental frequency: 9 per second waves are scattered in short sequences throughout the record. Slow waves: 4 to 6 per second activity dominates the record, sometimes this slow activity is more prominent over the left occiput. Fast waves: around 20 to 22 per second waves are increased in amount over each frontal region. Amplitude characteristics: high voltage (120 microvolts); irregular modulation. Additional characteristics: *no paroxysmal* activity is observed in the record. Hyperventilation: generates high voltage 2.5 per second activity in all leads, persists long after the cessation of deep breathing. Impression: generalized abnormal EEG.

Speech and Hearing Evaluation

Speech and language development. There is no family history of hearing or speech problems. The child's mother has read Gesell and had constantly checked his development by a baby book she kept. According to the mother's recounting and documented by the baby book, the child had precocious language and speech development. She claims that he was saying "Hi, Daddy," and "All gone," by 6 to 8 months of age. At 22 months she had tabulated his vocabulary of some 400 words and a few sentences. She comments that both she and the nursery teacher were aware that he had a short attention span. It was felt that he now has vocabulary that is up to his age level and can express his ideas quite well. He had to have some help in organizing his ideas around a topic.

General behavior. Although this child charged down to the examining rooms as though he was not going to be led any place, he was pleasant and co-operated quite well. He was easily distracted and tended to wander around the room, but could be brought back to the task at hand. Occasionally he tended to perseverate on something that had been done in the past.

Oral examination. Oral examination is unimpressive. There is a good deal of pharyngeal closure. There is an overbite. This child has good control of his tongue and uses it well in articulation.

Voice. He tends to talk rapidly and with somewhat of a monotone.

Articulation. This child can articulate all sounds accurately and with precision in imitation. There are no outstanding articulation errors.

Propositional speech. This youngster talks volubly. His speech becomes slurred in conversation because of his rapid articulation. However, this speech is quite typical of many boys his age. He is using complex sentences and has good vocabulary range. He could not be persuaded to tell a story about a picture.

Hearing. This child has normal hearing. He gave quick, accurate responses to the pure-tone test. He gave sharp, quick responses to spondee words and the PBK words.

Diagnostic impression. Speech is rapid and slurred but is not unusual.

Psychiatric Evaluation

C-2-3's muscular co-ordination was excellent, although he had a bad habit of knocking the toes of one foot against the heel of the other as he walked. On entering the playroom he immediately picked up a gun, shot down all the people figures in the house and turned over all the furniture. He had the husband and wife hitting each other, the children hitting one another, but no children hitting the family. In connection with this activity he gave Bobo the Clown a hard punch, but left him alone after that. When asked what he did when people didn't like him, the child responded "I sock them, that's what." He went on to say "I don't hit my brother though, he's too big for me." (His brother is much younger.) When asked about other brothers and sisters, the reply was, "we have two children, that's all we intend to have."

As he was modeling a corral fence he named a classmate and asked whether the Examiner knew him. "I have a score to settle with him, he calls me Mr. Monkey and I call him Mr. Stupid." The Examiner replied that we only tease people we like and that she bet he and the classmate he named were good friends. He continued to deny this fact in the interview, but the record states that he and this boy are good friends.

As he worked the Plasticene onto the existing metal fence he pounded extremely hard with the butt end of a gun deriving real satisfaction from the activity. "Yes, it's very nice—I can make as much noise as I wish." After about ten minutes of this, which rounded out the first half hour, he had calmed down considerably as far as hyperactive movements were concerned.

The discussion showed that the child had social maturity: "I did something not so good the other day, I laughed at a midget. Mother and I talked it over and I saw where I had hurt his feelings" . . . "People say I'm tricky, I guess I am, but I don't mean to hurt anybody really." He had three wishes: horse; two six-guns; and lastly, "A new father, mother, brother and sister—at times." The phrase "at times" was first spoken by the Interviewer.

General information was fairly average. On the other hand there are some basic facts which he was unable to give me today, such as the days of the weeks, or the months which appear in the spring season. He glowed with pleasure when praised for a correct answer.

Psychiatric Re-evaluation

C-2-3 entered the playroom quickly and happily. He was anxious to point out articles that had been here before, and immediately took the gun and began shooting people as well as furniture in the doll house. In order to direct his attention away from this activity, the Examiner nodded towards Bobo's replacement, the Boxer, saying, "How about this for a change?" The child immediately went at the rubber balloon and hit it with both arms, though with better co-ordination in his right-hand punch. Although his initial activity on both interviews was to shoot down the people, during the present session there was less hostility shown. He omitted having the husband and wife, as well as the children, hit each other.

His first two wishes remained the same, i.e., to have a horse and to own some real guns. He refrained this time from wanting, "A new father, mother and sister—at times," and wished instead that he could be allowed by the policeman to shoot his B-B gun anywhere and not just at the Boys' Club.

When the child was asked to draw a picture, he wanted to use both of his hands, the left hand for the left-hand side of his body and the right hand for his counterpart. Also he wished to use the right hand to guide the left. He completed one drawing with his left hand, followed this with a drawing with his right hand, and then did a drawing with both hands. He then wrote his name feeling very pleased with himself that he did not have to print this year. The other picture on the paper is that of a dog. The drawing made with the use of both hands is the best integrated, though they were all disproportionate. In every case there were five fingers and five toes, ears, hair and all the facial features. As he was making the drawings, he commented "I'll never in the world know what the difference is between woman and boys, I don't believe I'll ever know . . . girls look different than boys when they have all their clothes off."

Conversation with mother. C-2-3's mother felt that when a new drug was added to the regular medication he was "worse off than they had ever seen him." She said, when the new medicine was discontinued, he began to settle down and has ". . . matured tremendously. . . ." He has been able to accept responsibility for morning routine in terms of getting off to school and has not "buckled" under the addition of bed-making and picking up his clothes in recent weeks.

There appears to be a difficult relationship between this child and his brother, who is three years younger and seems to be gifted. His brother is anxious to give the answers to questions addressed to C-2-3. Also, his brother cannot understand why C-2-3 is slow in arithmetic which is "so easy." This parent is a very concerned and interested mother who has considerable intellectual ability.

The child's mother feels that he is better accepted by the group now because he has developed a better concept of the games and hence has not tended to muddle them up in his effort to be friendly.

The value of Bobo the Clown was stressed, and if Bobo was ordered, it was recommended that his activity with the bag should be structured so as not to wear the child out, but while he was at it let there be no "holds barred."

The possible implication of the child's remark concerning the difference between boys and women were discussed. It was learned that he is quite aware of the relationships. He said to his mother, "I know that you love me Mommy, but my Daddy doesn't love me the way he loves you, I'm not so sure about him."

Stanford-Binet, Form L (Pre-test) (4–3–57).

CA: 9–7; MA: 8–2; IQ: 85.

Present intellectual functioning falls within the Slow Learning range. The mental age is 8–2, and IQ is 85. Previous tests have ranged from IQ's of 95 to 78. It is important to note that the highest IQ, that of 95, was obtained in 1952 when C-2-3 was 5 years old. As he has grown older the obtained IQ's have been quite consistent. If only the test results obtained in 1955, 1956, and 1957 are compared, the IQ range is only 7 points. It is the earliest test results, obtained at an age when the IQ is typically least stable, that appears to be most out of line.

The Basal Age, at which all items were passed, was at Year VIII, while the Ceiling, at which all items were failed, was at Year XI.

The scattering in this test is rather peculiar. No items at Year IX were passed, but vocabulary was passed at Year X. Vocabulary is thus almost two years above the Mental Age.

Stanford-Binet, Form M (Post-test) (6–9–58).

CA: 10–9; MA: 7–6; IQ: 70.

The IQ obtained on this test was 15 points lower than the pre-test IQ, which places the intelligence within the Retarded range. The range of performance is from a Basal Age at Year VII to a Ceiling at Year IX.

Three items were passed at the Year VIII. Comprehension of problem situations was quite good, as was seeing opposite analogies. He was also able to name the days of the week by rote, as well as telling the days that come before certain specified days. More involved abstract tasks, such as verbal absurdities and similarities of two things, proved too difficult.

All items were failed at Year IX. Memory for designs was very poor, and he could not tell the similarities of two things, although he was able to see differences. He could not repeat four digits reversed, but could reverse three digits. In giving rhymes he gave a series of words beginning with the same sound, *d*. The directions were carefully repeated, and he then gave a series of words beginning with *h*.

Ammons Full-Range Picture Vocabulary Test (7–19–57).

CA: 9–10; MA: 10–0.

The mental age on this test is considerably higher than that obtained on the Stanford-Binet. The following words, which the average child of this chronological age can pass, were failed by C-2-3: vegetable, sale, garment, perspiration, protection, and cleanliness.

Goodenough Intelligence Test.

Pre-test (4–3–57)	Post-test (5–12–58)
CA: 9–7; MA: 8–0	CA: 10–8; MA: 7–9

The mental ages obtained on these tests were both quite close to the Stanford-Binet mental ages, the post-test being lower than the pre-test in both cases. The first drawing is a robot-like figure, with box-body, square arms outstretched, and square head. The post-test figure has considerably more detail, but is more crudely drawn. The figure is wearing eye-glasses, has outstretched arms with fingers carefully arranged around the circumference at the end, and club-like feet with the correct number of toes arranged around them almost up to the knees.

Block Design and Coding from WISC.

	Raw Score	Scaled Score	Equivalent Test Age
Block Design	5	6	6–6
Coding	24	8	7–10

Design A was completed on the first attempt, Design B on the second, and Design C on the first. On Design 1, he chose the correct blocks, but could not arrange them correctly. On the Coding test, Form B, 24 symbol substitutions were attempted, with no errors.

Bender-Gestalt Test. On the pre-test (4–3–57) there were 22 errors, with 3 immature, 3 perseverations, 3 dissociations, 3 incorrect elements, 1 unrecognizable, 3 distorted angles, 3 compressions, and 3 enlargements. There were only 10 errors on the post-test (5–15–58) with 1 concrete, 1 perseveration, 3 dissociations, 3 incorrect elements, 2 distorted angles. Improvement is mainly seen in fewer immature drawings, less perseveration, and fewer compressions and enlargements.

Syracuse Visual Figure-Background Test. Pre-test (10–24–57) there were 3 correct figure responses, 1 background response, and 2 perseverations. Post-test there were 7 correct figure responses, no background responses, and 3 perseverations. Thus improvement is seen in increased accuracy and reduction of background reactions.

Tactual-Motor Test (10–24–57). C-2-3 did not draw the correct figure for any of the designs presented. For the triangle, with plain background, he drew a square. When a thumbtack background was added, he drew incorrect figures enclosed in a square.

Marble Board Test (10–1–57). C-2-3 was unable to construct the design for Marble Board 1, even though he took much time and made many changes of the marbles. His drawing shows the basic pattern, but there is a marked disproportion in the sizes of the overlapping squares. After many shifts he managed to construction the design for Marble Board 2. His drawing, again, shows disproportion and dissociation of the design, but is readily recognizable.

Vineland Social Maturity Scale.

Pre-test (11–9–57)		Post-test (5–16–58)	
Total Score:	76	Total Score:	73
Age Equivalent:	9–7	Age Equivalent:	8–10
Social Quotient:	94	Social Quotient:	83

The mother, who served as informant for both interviews, expressed concern with the increased medications C-2-3 is getting, and feels that it is slowing him down very much. The main skill which he is not displaying now, and which he was at the beginning of the project, is in making telephone calls. His teacher last year made this activity part of the regular school program, but he has not continued calling classmates this year.

Summary. Periodic intelligence tests over the past five years have shown a steadily decreasing IQ, with a high of 95 in 1952 to the present low obtained in 1958 of 70. The main intellectual strength of this child is vocabulary, but when faced with abstract tasks such as similarities and problem situations, his performance is very poor. Visuo-motor performance is also well below age level.

He showed improvement on two of the five tests on which there are pre- and post-test results for comparative purposes. On the Bender-Gestalt Test he produced fewer errors, as seen in fewer immature drawings, less perseveration, and less compression and enlargement. Improvement is seen in accuracy and reduction of background disturbances on the Syracuse Visual Figure-Background Test. The Stanford-Binet, Goodenough Intelligence Test, and Vineland Scale of Social Maturity all show a reduced level of performance. The mother had indicated the very strong possibility that an extremely heavy medication for the control of seizures may be retarding over-all development and efficiency.

PEDIATRIC HISTORY C-2-4

The information was obtained from the mother, a pleasant looking, modestly dressed woman who spoke with a foreign accent, having been born and raised outside of the U.S. She seemed to be under a great deal of tension in discussing C-2-4's problems and, with understanding coaxing, did give most of the information desired.

Problem

C-2-4 is said to be nervous. This nervousness manifests itself in wringing his hands when put under any pressure. The mother was unable to elucidate any further and I did not want to press the point at that time. This nervousness might be attributed to a prenatal factor, or so the mother said. She explained that about two or three weeks before C-2-4 was born she fell from a table and following this she was very upset, unsteady, and unsure of her gait; and on one or two occasions was afraid of slipping and falling again. C-2-4 was born with his eyes crossed, which remained so for a long period of time. The mother felt perhaps the fall might have had something to do with it. There were no particular ill-effects following her fall. She was confined to bed, but more for nervousness than for any physical reason. There was no spotting or premature rupture of the bag of water. The fall apparently did not bring on labor. If anything, C-2-4 was said to have been born a little later than had been anticipated. With prompting, the mother added that the teachers tell her that C-2-4 has a mind of his own because he does not obey too easily and therefore creates a problem in school. He is said to get along fairly well with the children unless there are too many of them, or they try to boss him or tell him what to do. Presently, he is in regular school and is to be placed in the second grade next year. Actually, he had been scheduled for Special Education classes, but apparently a place could not be found for him until now.

Sometimes, when he is asked to do something, he ignores the question or the request almost as if he might have some trouble hearing. This apparently seems to be getting worse. The mother did add, however, that maybe this just is his way of ignoring the question, or perhaps he is so preoccupied with other things that he isn't paying enough attention.

Again when asked directly about any speech difficulty, the mother said that he did have some speech difficulty; however, this is getting better. When asked specifically what the speech difficulty consisted of, she said that C-2-4 used to stutter and would leave off prefixes or suffixes from words.

In summary, she said that, except for the speech problem, prior to his going to school, she didn't think there was anything remarkable about his behavior. As a matter of fact, his two older brothers were pretty much the same in general, and they too had stuttering problems with speech. They apparently have gotten over these difficulties and are doing fairly well in school.

Family History

1. Mother's mother died at the age of 35 of tuberculosis.
2. Mother's father died at the age of 48 of a kidney ailment.
3. Father's mother is 56 years of age and well.
4. Father's father is living and well, although he is not living with his wife. They apparently separated when C-2-4's father was a youngster.
5. Mother has three brothers and two sisters all of whom are living and well.
6. Father has two sisters who are living and well.

The mother's mother, grandmother and aunt all had nervous breakdowns. The difficulty seemed to have stemmed from marital difficulties and other difficulties with children and home. All three were institutionalized, and the grandmother and aunt actually died in the institutions.

Family Background

Father. (Age 36.) In good health. His occupation is that of a printer. He finished school through the ninth grade. Although he was born in another state, he has lived in the area most of his life. Interests: archery, hunting, fishing and sports in general. Problems: had difficulty in school as a child and so he quit at the ninth grade. He apparently didn't like school. His mother and father separated when he was about four or five. His mother remarried when he was five or six and apparently he got along fairly well with his stepfather. Personality: he is said to be well liked and friendly. This was all the mother had to say on that score. Attitude toward patient's difficulties: apparently he feels that the mother should leave C-2-4 alone and not punish him as much and not keep after him as much.

Mother. (Age 33.) (She actually looks quite a bit older than this.) In good health. She was born outside of the U.S. and has been in this country for the last thirteen years. She too finished school through the ninth grade. Interests: homemaking and volunteer work. Problems: she was a very shy girl. When asked specifically, she said she didn't remember too much about her mother's breakdown, as well as her grandmother's and aunt's, except that she remembered an unpleasant experience of visiting them in an institution. Her mother remained home under care of a private physician and a nurse. This, plus the fact that her father apparently did a good deal of drinking, made her "nervous." Personality: she said she likes everybody and couldn't say anything more about her own personality. Attitude: at this point she broke out into tears and it took a little bit of time before she could compose herself to continue. Afterward, all she could say is that she felt he could be helped and is very much concerned about him. When asked what it was she was concerned about, she said that his behavior, like throwing stones at people or cars or misbehaving in general, is what is causing her some concern.

Marriage. The parents have been married for fourteen years. They met and were married in the wife's homeland while the husband was in the Navy. He was 22 years of age and she was 18. It was the first marriage for both. They are of different religions. Apparently this does not cause any outward difficulties and the children are being raised in the mother's faith. The marriage was described as average and it was further stated that the father is not in the home too much, as he works long and irregular hours. As a result of this the mother said that she has the job of taking care of the house and raising the children. She has never been back to homeland and did not express a desire to do so.

Because of the peculiar and long hours that the father worked, he is home very little of the time and so cannot be with the boys as much as the mother would like. Apparently, more recently, his hours are much better and he does spend quite a bit of time with the boys, taking them fishing and hunting, and taking them out to the archery range for bow and arrow practice.

Siblings. (1) Sister, age 13½, doing average work in school. Seems to get along fine with other children and with C-2-4. (2) Brother, 10½ years of age. He is said to be a little slow in school. He too had a speech problem which is O.K. now. He and C-2-4 will tease and fight "like brothers." They always play together. (3) Brother, 9½ years of age. He too is said to be a slow reader, otherwise doing O.K. He also had a speech problem for awhile. C-2-4 will play equally well with both of these brothers and seems to show no preference for either. The boys sleep in the same room, either in a bed together or in separate beds, depending on what is happening at the time. (4) Sister, 22 months old "a ball of dynamite," very active. (5) Brother, three months old and doing well.

In addition the children have a dog who is not anyone's in particular, but belongs to and is enjoyed by everybody.

Mother's Medical History during Pregnancy with Child

There is no history of miscarriages or still-births. The mother was 25 years of age at the time she delivered C-2-4. She was being cared for by a Health Department Clinic and she gave birth at a local hospital. The pregnancy was a desired one and apparently was uneventful up until the time when she fell from the table, two or three weeks before term. Following this, as previously stated, she became nervous and jittery and would have to go to bed on and off. She received no medication during the pregnancy and had no X-rays.

The labor and delivery itself was not remarkable. The mother said she doesn't remember very much of either, except that it did not take very long. C-2-4 weighed 6 pounds, 4 ounces at birth, was seen within the first twenty-four hours and both mother and infant left the hospital together. He was nursed for the first two weeks. However, because he didn't seem to be getting along enough, and because he was seen to be hungry all the time, he was placed on bottle feedings. All the other children were nursed also for about three weeks, apparently the mother always having some difficulty with her milk.

Past Medical History of Patient

DPT and smallpox vaccination during the first year of life. C-2-4 has had two Salk vaccine immunizations. German measles at the age of 3 or 4, chickenpox at the age of 4 or 5. He had a history of repeated attacks of sore throat and ear infections so that, at the age of 6, he had a T & A at the County General Hospital. C-2-4 himself has never had any convulsions, although his youngest sister had convulsions last year and currently is on Phenobarbital. C-2-4 is on no medication at the present time. The crossed eyes which the mother described as being present from birth, apparently has straightened out and at the present time he is not wearing any glasses nor has he ever.

Developmental History

C-2-4 had no trouble feeding or swallowing, although he did a great deal of crying for the first six months of his life. There were no sleeping problems. Solids were started at the age of 3 or 4 months. He was weaned at about 2 years of age by himself when he gave up the bottle. The bottles were always propped up until that time. He would also pick up sand and dirt and put it into his mouth. Toilet-training was accomplished by about 2 years of age without any difficulty by himself and occasionally there is an episode of enuresis. The mother explained that this is when he drinks a lot before going to bed. He is said to be right-handed, and there are no left-handed individuals in the family. His motor development was said to have been not remarkable. There is no thumbsucking, head-banging, or rocking. Speech did not appear until about 18 months of age and then there was the difficulty already mentioned. There is a question of visual difficulty as well as some hearing impairment.

Present Status

C-2-4 prefers to play with other children rather than be by himself. Usually the children are older. He seems to get into fights with the younger children. He likes to play with little toys, cars, and can't do puzzles too well. He likes to play with blocks, but as yet hasn't been exposed to an Erector set. He likes to color and colors well. He is said to be able to print. He is a slow reader, is able to ride a two-wheeler bicycle, sits and watches his favorite programs on television. He had been going to Sunday School, but was unable to make Communion this year. He used to have nightmares in which he would cry out and would be found awake in bed crying. There are times when he likes to go to school and other times when apparently he says he doesn't want to go back. He has been making progress in school, especially this last year. He is said to be unable to button the buttons on his cuffs, but is able to tie his shoes and button other buttons. He is said not to be able to use a knife too well, and he behaves fairly well at the table. There is no difficulty in getting him to sleep. Personality: he is said to be very likeable, wants attention all the time. When punished, like being sent to his room or withholding things like TV or occasionally being hit, he "throws a fit," stamps his feet and gives back-talk. There apparently is some disagreement between the parents on the question of punishment. C-2-4 knows how to fight and will fight to protect himself. When frustrated, he has an actual temper tantrum, although not on the floor, but in his bed.

Physical Examination

General appearance. C-2-4 is a rather slight youngster who came with the Examiner without hesitation. He is pleasant looking and has a winning smile. At the onset there was no obvious speech difficulty, nor any hesitation in talking. He knew his age. Said he goes to school and is in the first grade. He was unable to identify a quarter, although he knew a penny and a nickel, but he didn't know how many pennies there are in a nickel and was unable to give the days of the week in sequence. He seemed a little fidgety, moving his legs and hands a bit.

When asked would he like to write or draw, he picked the pencil up in his right hand and drew a picture of a mouse and a deer. Although he held the pencil fairly well, it was noteworthy that his left hand remained in his lap, immobile, not even holding the paper (almost as though he was trying to suppress its use).

Following the drawing of a deer, he spoke about hunting, said that his brother shot a rabbit, but they couldn't eat it because it was "all dirty and bloody." When asked about dreams, he spoke about throwing the rabbit, that had previously been referred to, into a tree and it was at this point that the first stutter response appeared. As he continued talking about the dreams the stuttering became more pronounced and obvious. Bad dreams were about his brother shooting things. At this point, the speech became even more immature and indistinct, and ended with a sort of half-laugh. Although he was unable to say what a good mommy or a bad mommy was, or a good father, he said a bad father "is someone going around and being mad." To the ambulance story he said, "My little sister had a convulsion and that was why the ambulance was there."

In getting undressed, it was noted that he took his left shoe off first, then he took his right sock off, and took the left trouser leg off first. In getting dressed, he used the same sequence, in terms of right and left, for the various things mentioned. Though he was able to hop on either foot, he was unable to skip, but he walked pretty well on both heels and toes. The gait was normal, he did not deviate to any side, even when standing on one foot. His eyelashes were very long, his teeth were in good condition but poorly aligned and numbered 12 on top and 12 on bottom. His hearing seemed to be grossly normal. Reflexes were physiologic bilaterally and there was a very mild right convergent strabismus. In getting dressed, he was able to tie his shoes, but in putting his shirt on he put his right sleeve on first and left both cuffs unbuttoned. When told about this he was able to button the right one, using the left hand; however, the left one which required the use of his right hand, he was unable to do and the Examiner had to do this for him. The remainder of the physical examination was not too remarkable.

Neurological Examination

Cranial nerves. First cranial nerve was not tested. Second cranial nerve: fundi are normal. Visual fields seem to be intact. Third, fourth and sixth cranial nerves: the extra-ocular movement are intact. The pupils reacted to light and accommodation. No signs of strabismus or nystagmus. Fifth cranial nerve: corneal reflexes are equal and active. Motor and sensory powers of this particular nerve are normal. Seventh cranial nerve: muscles of facial expression are both normal. Eighth cranial nerve: air conduction is greater than bone conduction. The boy was able to hear the tuning fork without difficulty. Ninth and tenth cranial nerves: the uvula went up in the mid-line. The boy was able to swallow without difficulty. Eleventh cranial nerve: the boy was able to shrug his shoulders and turn his head from side to side against pressure without difficulty. Twelfth cranial nerve: the tongue protrudes in the mid-line. *Sensory.* Pinprick, vibratory, touch, position, and stereognosis are all well performed. Two-point discrimination, pinprick localization, double simultaneous stimulation on both arms, left arm and left face, right arm and right face, both legs, are normal. *Reflexes.* Reflexes are equal and active throughout. No pathological reflexes are present. *Motor.* Motor strength is good throughout. Muscle tone is normal. *Cerebellar.* Finger-to-nose and heel-to-shin tests were well performed. Diadochokinesis is normal. The boy was able to spin the jack better with the left hand than with the right. *Station and gait.* The boy was able to walk on his heels and on his toes without difficulty. Romberg is negative.

Electroencephalogram

Attitude and condition of patient: alert, co-operative. Fundamental frequency: ranges between 8 and 9 waves per second. Slow waves: 4 and 5 per second activity is fairly prominent in the homologous post-rolandic derivations. Fast waves: are not prominent. Amplitude characteristics: average to high voltage (100 microvolts); iregular modulation. Additional feature: no paroxysmal activity is recognized. Hyperventilation: moderately accentuates the generalized slow wave output. Impression: moderate generalized abnormal EEG.

Speech and Hearing Evaluation

Language and speech development. The mother speaks with an accent, as she was born and raised outside the U.S. She states that the only time her mother tongue is spoken in the home is when her sister comes to visit. This is very rare. None of her children have learned to speak any language other than English.

Mother is greatly concerned about C-2-4's hearing. She thinks his greatest difficulty is in following instruction. She finds it necessary to tell him two or three times if she wants him to do something. This is true even if it is something in which he is interested. She expresses this as giving her a feeling as though he shuts her out. This youngster had frequent earaches until a T & A which was done two years ago.

C-2-4 is reported to have babbled normally as a young infant. He was the slowest of the children in starting to talk. She does not remember when he said his first word. However, she is sure he was beginning to use two word phrases by 24 months of age. His speech, as it developed, was not different from the others. She reports that his vocabulary and language have been expanding since he has gone to school. She estimates that his vocabulary is about a year behind his age level. He apparently has a number of words which he mispronounces and which are very difficult to correct. She gives as an example: he says "afore" for before. He has always liked to be read to and has enjoyed thumbing through magazines and books since he was a little boy.

She does not think he is more of a behavior problem than the other children. When he gets angry he hits out. She is aware of this fact when he is watching the 2-year-old baby and is very quick to "discipline." "He smacks her." This was particularly interesting in light of the fact that the only real stutter block that was observed here today was when we talked about the baby sister.

Behavioral observations. C-2-4 is a slender child with a very sensitive face. He came along willingly with the Examiner and talked almost constantly. He was most co-operative and apparently enjoyed the experience.

Oral examination. There is rather a high palate with a velum of adequate length and lift. There is slight overbite and front teeth are widely spaced. There is adequate control of the tongue and lips.

Articulation. Articulation on isolated words is good, except for *th – f* substitution.

Voice. Voice is very tentative and has a breathy quality because it is unsupported.

Propositional speech. C-2-4 talked on and on without any prodding from the Examiner. As a matter of fact he initiated the conversation with a discussion about a Halloween party which he had attended. He wanted advice as to how he should dress up this year—whether he should be a Hobo or an Indian.

While talking he exhibited many nervous mannerisms. His phrases were punctuated by audible intakes of air and frequently he talked on the ingoing breath stream. His speech is filled with many circumlocutions and fillers. He will repeat words and phrases interspersed with "you know" and "uh, uh." His vocabulary and language usage was better than had been anticipated from the discussion with his mother. The only grammatical errors that were observed were concerned with verbs, as he used "shotted" for shot, and "I seen." More cluttering was heard than stuttering. As a matter of fact, the only evidence of a stutterer was when he talked about his baby sister.

When presented with a page of animals he made an adequate comment about each one and named the entire series. Rather than telling a story about each picture, he described what he saw. This was limited to one or two sentences about each of the three pictures. He was somewhat reluctant to tell the story of the Three Bears. He started out in a very tentative, insecure fashion. He finally got wound up and told the story amidst constant giggles. When asked to repeat a fairly long sentence, he appeared to have real trouble, indicating some difficulty in auditory perceptual organization.

Hearing. This child has a normal end organ of hearing. He had no difficulty in giving quick, accurate responses to the test by pure-tone audiometry. The following audiogram was obtained:

Right	10	15	5	−5	−5	−5
	125	250	500	1000	2000	4000
Left	10	10	0	−5	5	−5

He repeated the spondee words quickly and accurately at very soft levels. He missed one word on the PBK list, for a score of 96 per cent. Any difficulties with hearing are a matter of inattention or difficulties in organizing complex material.

In summary, this Examiner felt that C-2-4 was a nervous, insecure child whose speech reveals more of a clutter than a stutter. He is verbose but poorly organized in his output.

Psychiatric Evaluation

This wiry, well-developed youngster gave his age correctly as 8. He came willingly to the playroom, showing normal gait and good muscular strength.

He looked around the playroom with obvious pleasure, but his first activity reflected the need to establish a foothold. He lined up all the trucks he could find (in the course of which he was discovering what toys were there to be played with). He made a point of saying he had no trucks at home now, but that he once had. He asked the Examiner what she did and when she replied that she played with boys and girls so as to learn and help them with some of their worries, he replied "Oh." He denied worries—"especially my father, he doesn't have worries." At this, his eyes gleamed. Further evidence for a good identification with father is evidenced by his desire to have the same job as the father when he grows up.

We played a card game called War. He abided pretty faithfully to the rules he had already laid down, but seemed to lose himself in each particular step and was not able to stick to the original objective of the game. Handling of the cards revealed clumsiness of fine movement, but not overly significant in his age group. When introduced to Bobo the Clown and the punching bag, it was clear, however, that he was somewhat awkward in gross co-ordination also. He tended to push out from his chest to the object rather than developing a good swing of the arm. However, he hit with obvious pleasure and satisfaction. He did not use his left hand until specifically asked to do so.

On the occasion, the Examiner particularly asked him whether he was holding back his left hand. His reply was a look of genuine surprise and puzzlement at the question. He was apparently not aware when he used a particular hand.

To the Despert Fables, he responded that "The baby bird would fly away," even after the questions, "He didn't go to the mother bird, or the father bird? Or to his own nest?" which were offered to make certain he understood the meaning of the story.

He noticed the Play-Doh and reached for it, attempting to open it, even as the Examiner had opened one of the cans. This looked like healthy initiative, but he soon saw that the lid would not work and so handed everything over to her. There seemed to be no perseveration. He observed that the material smelled like dough, wondered what he should make, but shortly turned his attention back to Bobo the Clown, which he correctly named by reading the letters on the side.

When asked to draw, he very quickly drew some artistic blue clouds, several buzzards circling over a green field where two young boys stood, each with an orange hat. They were stick figures and looked more like upright grasshoppers. Nevertheless, C-2-4 seemed quite proud of this picture. He stated his father would kill the buzzards, and that buzzards did not eat anything that wasn't already dead or "suffering." He denied any fear of buzzards.

Shortly before the end of the hour C-2-4 asked, "Say, do you finger paint?" He was given the equipment and for a few minutes did finger painting, during which he showed exceptionally easy, graceful motions; his whole body became relaxed and expressive. The colors were largely somber. His approach to this activity was different from other children so far seen. He took up several splotches of color out of each jar and placed them close together and then began to finger paint. Other children have taken one color, moved their fingers through and around with it for a while before turning to another color.

He seemed reluctant to go, and worked in a puzzle which is rather good at catching difficulties with form. He missed some of the more obvious shapes which were very simple because of a solid color distinction. It seemed to bother him that he could not place each piece on the first attempt.

C-2-4 appeared to have good general information about the countryside, and animal life, compatible with most 8-year olds. However, he did not know his birthday, and seemingly did not care. He was disoriented to time in general.

He gave the names and ages of his siblings accurately, putting an extra note of pleasure into his voice when describing his big brother.

The over-all emotional picture of C-2-4 reveals a child who operates well on a one-to-one relationship, accepting limits, showing initiative, trying hard to please, even to the extent of answering when he is not altogether sure of the question. There was no observable perseveration and no hyperactivity. However, there was definitely a short attention span and a measure of distractibility. C-2-4 can deal more effectively with concrete and specific activities than with ideas. There is considerable anxiety which is handled by obsessive-compulsive means.

Psychiatric Re-evaluation

There have been some striking gains in C-2-4's attitude as compared with the last interview. While he had come willingly to the playroom previously, today he was much less anxious and much more willing to engage in spontaneous conversation. In fact, he was quite talkative, stating, "Did you hear about the robbery?" and then giving details about it; or, "Did you hear the jet and the plane crash the other day?" He had heard about the news event, it seems, from his older sister.

He was most cheerful and seemed to be having a great deal of fun. His excitement never led him to lose control of himself. He was at all times amenable to suggestions.

Most of the time he spent hitting the replacement of Bobo the Clown and shooting play bullets at various objects on the play table and in the play cupboard. He was thought to have much better co-ordination and also was able to "let himself go" in the two latter activities to a greater degree than previously.

When asked to draw a person, he drew his 14-year old sister. He filled in all the details, such as hair, lipstick, fancy dress, and high heels. C-2-4 wrote his name clearly and with little difficulty.

There was still some of the stutter which had been noted before—perhaps this should be called stammer—but he was easily understood. When asked about school his eyes lit up and he said "It was very fine." The father accompanied C-2-4 and seemed a very relaxed, sensible, level-headed individual. He mentioned how he takes his three sons in rotation along with him on the two Sundays a month when he shoots archery and he tried to find time to play with them on the weekends. He feels that C-2-4 has come along and has somewhat greater self-confidence. However, he added that he did not see very much of C-2-4 and could not truthfully say just how much difference there really was.

In the Examiner's mind C-2-4 has gained a degree of self-confidence with a concomitant decrease in anxiety. It would seem that the source of the anxiety is now not primarily academic frustration secondary to perceptual difficulties, as it was in the previous interview.

Stanford-Binet, Form L (Pre-test) (7–11–57).

CA: 8–5; MA: 7–0; IQ: 83.

Intelligence is within the Slow Learning range, with an IQ of 83 and mental age of 7–0. The Basal Age, at which all items were passed, is at Year VI, while the Ceiling, at which all items were failed, is at Year XI.

At Year VII C-2-4 was unable to repeat five digits forwards. He became quite upset at this failure and despite what seemed to be maximum effort only became hopelessly confused. He appeared to hear what was said, but could not organize the stimulus in a manner that would help him retain it. Abstract thinking, as in seeing similarities, was too difficult for him. For example, when asked how wood and coal are alike, he said: "They're dirty." For apple and peach, he said: "Apple has a stem, but a peach has a round thing." For ship and automobile he said: "A car can't go across the ocean." He was unsuccessful in making a good diamond, producing figures with additional angles. He was successful in the differentiations required in seeing the absurdity of situations presented pictorially, and was quick to comprehend the situations described verbally that involve "common sense."

At Year VIII C-2-4 was unable to repeat from memory a story that was read to him. Again, this would indicate difficulty in perceptual discriminations of auditory stimuli. He seemed to get the over all sense of the story, but fabricated the details. He could not bring together the intellectually irreconcilable elements of situations described to him. For example, when asked what is foolish about the statement that they found a young man locked in his room with his hands tied behind him and his feet bound together, he said: "He locked himself in. He thinks someone robbed his place." He could not see the similarities and differences between various common items. For example, when asked how a *baseball* and *orange* are alike and how they are different, he said: "Batting a ball." For *airplane* and *kite*, he said: "Kite is more hard to do." Further questioning elicited no further information. In attempting to repeat sentences it was again obvious that he had difficulty with organization of the auditory stimulus. For example, in repeating the sentence "Fred asked his father to take him to see the clowns in the circus," he said, "Fred asked his father to bring the circus to the clowns." The only item passed at this age level was vocabulary. Eight words are needed to pass, and C-2-4 correctly defined 10.

At Year IX two items were passed, paper cutting and memory for designs. He could not repeat four digits reversed or see the absurdity of situations described verbally. He could not give rhymes, which is usually the easiest task at this level. For example, when asked to give a number that rhymes with tree, he said: "Two." When asked to give the name of an animal that rhymes with fair, he said: "Tiger." He gave the correct answer, however, to the first question giving the name of a color that rhymes with head.

At Year X only one item was passed, picture absurdities. This was the easiest item at this age level for most children in the present project.

Stanford-Binet, Form M (Post-test) (5–22–58).

CA: 9–3; MA: 8–0; IQ: 86.

The IQ is three points greater than that obtained at the beginning of the year. The mental age is 8–0, IQ 86, and performance range is from Year VIII to Year IX. Intelligence is within the Slow Learning range.

The extremely narrow performance range of two years indicates lack of outstanding strengths or weaknesses. It should be noted, however, that several items were minimal failures, i.e., three verbal absurdities must be correct for success on this item, while C-2-4 passed two. In attempting to rhyme words he said: "Cap, cat, kitten, cap, taxi driver." He was able to give similarities, but not differences, could not reassemble a dissected sentence, or repeat four digits reversed.

Ammons Full-Range Picture Vocabulary Test (11–27–57).

CA: 8–7; MA: 7–0.

The mental age obtained on this test is exactly the same as that obtained on the pre-test Stanford-Binet. The following words, expected successes at this age level, were failed by C-2-4: vegetable, dessert, transport, customer, sale, cheerful, collision, listening, safe, and intersection.

Goodencugh Intelligence Test.

Pre-test (6–27–57)	*Post-test (5–13–58)*
CA: 8–5; MA: 8–6	CA: 9–2; MA: 9–6

The ratio of mental age to chronological age is practically the same for both drawings. The most outstanding difference between the drawings is the addition of hands to the post-test drawing. Both are fairly well detailed, with hats, belt, shoes with heels, and cuffs.

Block Design and Coding from WISC.

	Raw Score	*Scaled Score*	*Equivalent Test Age*
Block Design	15	12	9–6
Coding	15	5	6–6

Designs A, B, and C of the Block Design test were completed accurately and rapidly on the first attempt. Design 3 was completed well within the time limitations. On the Coding test, Form B, 17 symbol substitutions were attempted with two errors. He seemed to have much difficulty in keeping his place, and performance was extremely slow on this task.

Bender-Gestalt Test. On the pre-test (7–11–57) 8 errors were made, including 1 perseveration, 1 dissociation, 2 incorrect elements, 3 distorted angles, and 1 compression. Post-test (5–13–58) 8 errors were again made, including 3 perseverations, 1 dissociation, 2 incorrect elements, and 2 distorted angles.

Syracuse Visual Figure-Background Test. On the pre-test (10–24–57) there were 8 correct responses to the figure, 1 background response, and no perseverations. Post-test (5–14–58) there were 11 correct responses, and no perseverations. The main change on this test is in improvement in accuracy.

Tactual-Motor Test (10–24–57). C-2-4 was able to draw the triangle, both with plain and with thumbtack backgrounds. Drawings of the other figures, however, were completely unrecognizable.

Marble Board Test (10–1–57). The first design was accurately reproduced, the method of approach was continuous, and organization was aggregate. His drawing was one of the best in the present series, showing a good grasp of the basic configuration.

Marble Board 2 was quite inaccurate, which C-2-4 recognized, but despite many shifts and changes, he was unable to correct it. The method of approach on this design was incoherent, and organization was aggregate. The drawing shows an hour-glass figure, but is easily recognizable.

Vineland Social Maturity Scale.

Pre-test (11–18–57)		Post-test (5–16–58)	
Total Score:	71.1	Total Score:	73.5
Age Equivalent:	8–3	Age Equivalent:	8–11
Social Quotient:	95	Social Quotient:	96

The mother served as informant at both interviews. Very little change in the rate of social development has occurred over the course of the year, as may be seen in the similar social quotients. C-2-4 has mastered several skills since the beginning, such as making telephone calls to his friends, dialing the numbers himself, and looking them up. He cares for himself at the table, choosing foods and spreading his own bread and butter. He is also trusted to make minor purchases, which he does satisfactorily.

Summary. Little change is noted in this child's rate of development, which seems to be very consistent in all areas on which psychological test data is available. Intelligence is within the Slow Learning range as shown on the Stanford-Binet and Ammons Full-Range Picture Vocabulary Test. The main intellectual weaknesses are in organizing auditory perceptions, abstract ability, and number concepts. Relative strengths are in vocabulary and visual-perceptual discrimination. The Goodenough Intelligence Test gives almost identical results for pre- and post-tests when the ratio of mental age to chronological age is considered. No improvement was noted on the Bender-Gestalt Test, the same number of errors being obtained on both tests. There was a slight change toward greater accuracy on the SVFB test, but the Vineland Social Maturity Scale gives almost identical social quotients. The over-all impression is of slow development with few outstanding strengths or weaknesses.

PEDIATRIC HISTORY C-2-5

C-2-5 is one of twins, both of whom are living in a foster home. The foster mother brought him and supplied whatever information is available in this report. More information is needed and perhaps could be obtained from the agency responsible for him.

Problem

The problem as stated by the foster mother is that C-2-5 stutters and has ever since he came to her. This has improved a great deal since he started school in Special Education. He apparently has done pretty well this past year.

His attention span and memory are not too good. Teachers indicate that he would need some drilling on this. At home he never forgets, and it only took three evenings to teach him the alphabet, and he was then able to recognize letters afterward. Otherwise he seems very bright. He is obedient and apparently knows right from wrong. He writes with his left hand and there was some difficulty getting him to hold a pencil correctly. As previously stated, he is one of twins, the older one. The boys have been living with the foster mother for the past three years. When they arrived she said she couldn't understand anything C-2-5 said. He apparently witnessed his mother's burning to death and for a while afterward he would talk about this. He has never wanted to go back to his father. His father will come around when he is drunk and make things miserable in general for both the foster parents and the children. Whenever C-2-5 gets upset he stutters. This happened yesterday when he was told about coming in for an examination. The foster mother spoke of the children's needs and feels very strongly about the possibility of her losing them to the father. The children were 5 years of age when they came to the foster home. C-2-5 is said to be able to dress himself completely. He wasn't toilet-trained at that time; however, he is now. He is not messy at the table and is able to use a fork and a spoon although he is not permitted to use a knife. He sleeps O.K. He is able to ride a tricycle and he is said to speak well, except when upset. He can become upset when he is scolded, or when he is speaking to strangers. He plays well with other children. The others seem to like him. He is able to watch funnies and cowboy stories on TV. He is said to color and write fairly well. He is able to count up to one hundred when encouraged and is able to read. As far as the foster mother knows, he has had the measles at the age of 7 and a T & A at the age of 5. As previously stated, he is left-handed. He doesn't fight, as the foster mother doesn't approve of this. When punished by being spanked or placed on a chair, he takes it without any display outwardly. He never really has a temper tantrum. He gets peeved when he is frustrated. He has always been a good eater. There is no difficulty getting him to bed at night, or getting him up in the morning to go to school. He sleeps in a bed by himself in the room with his brother. In addition to the twins there is an older brother, a younger brother, and one older sister. The children are all in foster homes and have visited C-2-5 on different occasions.

This was all the information that the foster mother was able to give.

Physical Examination

Blood pressure 100/60.

C-2-5 came to the examining room willingly. He said he likes school and likes to play there. He is a very polite little boy, answering "Yes, sir," and "No, sir." He was able to recognize a penny, nickel, and dime, but was unable to give their values. There were no dreams, he said. He was able to count up to 10 and was able to recite the alphabet fairly well. The child was not very verbal.

He was left-handed, was unable to hop on his left foot, but could do so on his right. He was unable to skip. C-2-5 knew the parts of his body and his speech was noted to be grossly normal. The child undressed and dressed himself fairly well and could tie his shoelaces. There was no other evidence of any visual-motor inco-ordination.

He had a high-arched palate. Teeth were carious, but numbered 10 on top and 10 on bottom. Harrison grooves were present but minimally so.

Neurological examination was grossly negative.

Neurological Examination

Cranial nerves. First cranial nerve was not tested. Second cranial nerve: fundi are normal. Visual fields are grossly normal. Third, fourth, and sixth cranial nerves: the extra-ocular movements are intact. No nystagmus is present. There is no sign of strabismus. Pupils reacted to light and accommodation. Fifth cranial nerve: corneal reflexes are normal. This nerve is normal as far as motor and sensory is concerned. Seventh cranial nerve: normal for motor function. Taste was not tested. Eighth cranial nerve: air conduction is greater than bone conduction. The boy was able to hear the spoken voice and the tuning fork without difficulty. Ninth and tenth cranial nerves: the uvula went up in the mid-line and the boy was able to swallow without difficulty. Eleventh cranial nerve: the boy is able to shrug his shoulders without difficulty. The sternocleidomastoid muscle is normal. Twelfth cranial nerve: the tongue protrudes in the mid-line and there is no sign of atrophy or fasciculation. *Sensory.* Pinprick, touch, vibratory, position and stereognosis are all normal. Pinprick localization, double simultaneous stimulation, using both arms, the left arm and left face, right arm and right face and both legs, is normal. *Reflexes.* Reflexes are equal and active throughout. No pathological reflexes are present. There is good motor strength throughout. *Cerebellar.* Finger-to-nose and heel-to-shin tests were well performed. Diadochokinesis is very poorly performed. The boy is not able to spin the jack but he was able to do patting movements without difficulty. *Station and gait.* The boy was able to walk without difficulty on his heels and toes. Romberg is negative.

Electroencephalogram

Attitude and condition of patient: alert, co-operative. Fundamental frequency: ranged between 8 and 9½ waves per second, isolated and short sequences of 150 to 200 millisecond waves are scattered throughout the record. Fast waves: were not prominent. Amplitude characteristics: average voltage; transient irregular modulation. Additional feature: no paroxysmal activity was observed. Hyperventilation: generated approximately 4 per second activity, primarily in the homologous frontal and temporal derivations. Impression: within the range of normal variation.

Speech and Hearing Evaluation

Speech and language development. The details of this child's development are not known. His stuttering is almost completely under control; he only stutters when he gets excited. The parent feels that stuttering in the child is no longer a problem.

General behavior observations. C-2-5 came willingly into the examining room. He stuttered a bit in the waiting room and during the initial part of the testing situation, and then there was no stutter block or hesitation in his speech. He talked freely, if not volubly, during the entire examining session.

Oral examination. The oral musculature is normal. The velum is of adequate length and there is good bilateral lift. He has good control of his tongue and lips. Teeth are in fair occlusion, as there is a slight overbite.

Articulation. Articulation is good. He substitutes an *f* for a *th* in most words. He can correct this readily if asked to do so, but it is not maintained.

Voice. Voice is of good quality. While he tends to talk slowly and carefully, the rate is within normal limits and is not conspicuous.

Propositional speech. The child seemed to have taken undue care with his articulation during this interview. As a consequence, it was slow in rate. He enjoyed talking and expressed his ideas well. His story of the Three Bears was well organized, told with a great many details, and with many dramatic flourishes. A number of errors were observed with verbs in the telling of this story: "She seen, she taste of it," and the like. It was also noted that he told the story directly to the listener and many times looked in the Examiner's eyes. In the past, there was a great deal of avoidance of eye contact. A fair number of complex sentences were used. When presented with the three pictures about which to tell a story, he had the beginning of a story formed, albeit it was without elaboration. The one about fishing consisted of two sentences: "These men went fishing. This man caught a fish." The story about the A & P was much more disconnected. In the third picture, consisting of a family bidding good night, he said that it was Christmas morning and the children were very happy and came running down with their pajamas on.

Hearing. This child gave very quick, accurate responses to the test by pure-tone audiometry. There was good localization from ear to ear. The following audiogram was obtained:

Right	15	0	5	0	0	10
	250	500	1000	2000	4000	8000
Left	20	10	5	5	5	5

He readily repeated the spondee words as well as the PBK list with no errors. Hearing is well within normal range.

Psychiatric Evaluation

C-2-5 was a towheaded, friendly but quiet 7-year old who looked at least a year younger. He was neatly dressed in long dark trousers and a very white shirt with matching bow-tie and cuff-links out of cloth. While he was slow to open up in conversation, he was immediately fascinated with Bobo and, after saying "Clown" and being shown what he could do with Bobo, he spent the next ten minutes hitting him down, picking him up, and smiling his beautific smile. He was somewhat awkward in his pokes, despite the history of left-handedness, as well as a statement by C-2-5 to the same effect, he did all his hitting with the right hand, until specifically asked to try it once with his left. His right-hand motions were awkward but less so than the left-hand. In much the same fashion, he turned to the punching bag, accepting the suggestion to move baseboard farther out into the room so that he could take a wider swing. However, he had been ready to oblige with a swing, even in close quarters. This lad constantly seeks approval.

He turned from Bobo to some toys, picking the sections of fence. He had a good concept of what was right-side-up and how to join the sections. Several fit poorly into one another and C-2-5 would no sooner get two sections joined when two others would separate. He laughed about this and would have kept it up until the sun set, trying to have everything stay together at one time, if the Examiner had not suggested we do this together. He next turned to the favorite wind-up train and was much surprised and puzzled that it went around in a circle all by itself. He decided it would be nice to build a fence around it, saying, "There, let it rest awhile." When he had the fence all built, again with help at points *but not* where it concerned the concept of the joint in this particular fence, he ran the train around within the fence.

In the finger painting, he wanted to help pin up the paper, although initially he hung back. He had a fine time applying one color after the other, and his movements became far less awkward as he relaxed. He decided first to draw the inside of the house. This led him to smear one-quarter of the page with green. This was followed by the living room, which was made black, and then he forgot about this idea altogether, it would seem, and continued with colors as part of a design. He was not overly neat nor overly messy in his paint play; when through, he washed his hands and looked around for towels, climbing up to get one for himself and then, seeing the Examiner, going back and getting one for her. Lastly, he drew a house and a person on request. As he drew the house, he said "It's a small house, isn't it? . . . It's nicer that way." Then he put a window in for each room starting again with the bathroom, followed by the living room, and then kitchen, then bedroom. He drew the door and pointed it out to the Examiner, naming handle, and then adding windows in the door. His Draw-a-Person was somewhat grotesque looking. On the other hand, there were no stick arms and legs. All the essential elements were there, but distorted in size and position. Particularly distorted was the relationship of the trunk to the legs. The blue crayoning represented trousers and the legs were indicated by the white areas, off which were placed the toes. He was quite proud of this drawing. When he was asked for his name, he spelled it out first, looking very pleased but having omitted one letter. With some encouragement, he wrote his name.

We are continuing to see a child whose intellectual capacity may be still greater, as must be determined by the extent to which he widens his social and cultural experiences in the growing-up process. While there was no stuttering today, language was immature. The Examiner was most impressed with the improvement which has occurred in the past two years, in a very warm, accepting foster home. It is felt that C-2-5 will be able to develop to his highest potential within this particular family setting, and that what is seen of shyness and passivity will continue to be ameliorated as he gains further social acceptance and academic recognition.

Psychiatric Re-evaluation

C-2-5 was his usual smiling self. There was no spontaneity to his conversation. Also, there was no stuttering.

He spent a great deal of time hitting Bobo's replacement about. He took the B-B gun and shot the boxer with great glee "in the bottom." His play with the train consisted of stopping it with the butt of the gun and letting it continue again. His only wish was for a pony. His drawing of a person was very immature; tiny, stick-like extremities, square body, huge round head, eyes placed in a very lateral position with nose, mouth and moustache in dead center.

Conversation with foster mother. She sees child "as much better in every respect." He listens better, seems to understand what is spoken, and is not as fidgety as he was. She notices that the child hardly stutters now. He is also more willing to go out and play with other youngsters and participates in neighborhood games, whereas before he had tended to hang back on the fringe of the group.

Stanford-Binet, Form L (Pre-test) (5–15–57).

CA: 7–8; MA: 6–4; IQ: 82.

This child's learning ability is at a Slow Learning level. The mental age is 6–4, and IQ 82. The Basal Age is at Year VI, while the Ceiling is at Year VIII. The present test is consistent with testing done 11–5–55 when a Stanford-Binet, Form L, was administered, with resulting IQ of 77.

The range of only three years suggests an over-all dullness, with neither extreme relative weaknesses nor strengths.

At Year VII C-2-5 was unable to see the absurdity of situations presented pictorially. Seeing absurdities in pictures involves some of the same elements that are involved in pointing out the incongruities of situations presented verbally, although there is a concrete stimulus to which the child can react when pictures are used. When shown a picture of a man and woman sitting in rocking chairs in front of their house, with the rain pouring down on them, and asked what is foolish about the picture, C-2-5 said, pointing to some shrubbery in the distance: "Because a tree is growing in the house." This same lack of ability to differentiate and discriminate the important aspects of a situation may be seen in his response to the picture showing a man carrying an umbrella in such a position that it offers no protection: "The man is wearing an umbrella." When questioned about this he said: "He's not supposed to." Further questioning resulted in: "Because he's wearing a hat." Another weakness is in comprehension of problem situations. When asked what he should do if on his way to school he saw that he was going to be late, he said: "Run back home." When asked what to do if another boy hit him without meaning to do so, he said: "Hit back." He was unable to copy a diamond or repeat five digits. It should be noted that he repeated the correct digits, but repeated them in improper sequence.

At year VII two items were passed. He passed the similarities item, although his responses were so immature and the concepts so poorly developed that they were minimal passes. For example, when asked how an apple and peach are alike, he said: "Got seeds in them," seizing upon an inconsequential similarity. When asked how a ship and automobile are alike he said: "Cause they run."

At Year VIII all items were failed. C-2-5 was unable to keep the details of a story in mind. When asked what he should do if he were in a strange town and someone asked him how to find a certain address, he said: "Tell them to go up a block and turn." He was unable to repeat a sentence, again showing a weakness in immediate memory. When presented with similarities and differences at this level, he was able to give similarities *or* differences, but without prompting was unable to maintain the directing notion of giving *both*.

Vocabulary was passed at Year VI. There was a tendency to respond to the terms of their sounds rather than meanings. When asked to define *lecture* he said *lectric* and for *haste*, he said *hate*. When asked to define *eyelash* he at first said that he did not know, but after the vocabulary words were completed he was asked if he had an eyelash, and pointed to his eyebrow.

Stanford-Binet, Form M (Post-test) (6–22–58).

CA: 8–9; MA: 8–0; IQ: 91.

The present IQ of 91 is 9 points higher than the pre-test. The four-year range of performance is from a Basal Age at Year VII to a Ceiling at Year X. It is important to note that over the three-year period from 1955 to the present the IQ has steadily increased, from a low of 77 in 1955 to its present level.

At Year VIII S was unable to pass the similarities item, the only item failed at this level. When asked how a *mosquito* and *sparrow* are alike, he said: "They look alike." For *bread* and *meat,* he said: "They are square, that's how they are alike." This was evidently a perseveration from the question asked immediately preceding, in regard to the similarity between *window* and *door.*

Only one item was passed at Year IX, repeating four digits reversed. When asked for words that rhyme, C-2-5 resorted to alliteration instead, saying: "Dale, day, did." Similarities and differences was a minimal failure, with 3 being correct when 4 are needed at this age level. He could not see the absurdities in described situations, reassemble a dissected sentence or draw designs from memory.

All items were failed at Year X.

Ammons Full-Range Picture Vocabulary Test (11–27–57).

CA: 8–3; MA: 7–6.

The mental age on this test is somewhat higher than that obtained on the pre-test Stanford-Binet. The following words, expected successes at this age level, were failed: vegetable, customer, fuel, skyscraper, razor, cheerful, broadcast, and protection.

Goodenough Intelligence Test.

Pre-test (5–15–57)	Post-test (5–15–58)
CA: 7–8; MA: 4–9	CA: 8–9; MA: 7–9

There is a very marked improvement on the post-test drawing. In the pre-test drawing the figure was extremely primitive, consisting of a circular head with eyes but no nose or mouth, with legs attached directly to the head, and no trunk. Arms were attached directly to the legs. The post-test drawing was much more detailed, with hat, nose and mouth, arms that bent with fingers attached, belt, pockets and a gun. He called his drawing "A cowboy," and it was quite recognizable as such. The mental age on the post-test was much more nearly in line with the Stanford-Binet test results.

Block Design and Coding from WISC (5–15–57).

	Raw Score	Scaled Score	Test Age Equivalent
Block Design	5	5	6–6
Coding	15	4	5–2

Designs A and B of the Block Design were drawn correctly on the first attempt, and Design C was correct on the second. C-2-5 could not progress beyond that point, being unable to grasp the principle of using diagonal blocks. On the Coding 15 substitutions were attempted, with no errors. He was extremely slow and careful on this test, which reduced his score considerably. The Block Design equivalent test age is quite close to the Stanford-Binet mental age, but the Coding is quite a bit lower.

Bender-Gestalt Test. On the pre-test (5–15–57) there were 17 errors, including 2 immature, 3 perseverations, 1 dissociation, 1 closure, 2 incorrect elements, 3 distorted angles, 3 enlargements, and 2 disproportions. On the post-test (5–15–58) marked improvement is seen in that only 4 errors were made, including 1 incorrect element, 2 distorted angles, and 1 compression.

Syracuse Visual Figure-Background Test. Pre-test (11–18–57) there were 6 correct figure responses, 5 background, and 1 perseveration. Post-test (5–15–58) there were 7 correct responses to the figure, 3 background responses, and no perseveration noted. Thus improvement is seen in accuracy of perception, decreased distractibility by background stimuli, and lessened perseverative tendencies.

Tactual-Motor Test (11–18–57). C-2-5 drew the triangle, both with plain and with thumbtack backgrounds, but the other drawings were completely unrecognizable. He called Bender Figure 4 a "circle," and promptly drew one.

Marble Board Test (11–18–57). Marble Board 1 was correctly reproduced, the method of approach being continuous, and organization articulate. His drawing of the design shows good comprehension of the basic configuration. Marble Board 2 was incorrect with three misplaced marbles, the method of approach segmental, and organization was global. While the drawing is rather distorted, it nevertheless is recognizable.

Vineland Social Maturity Scale.

Pre-test *(12–13–57)*		Post-test *(5–23–58)*	
Total Score:	63.5	Total Score:	75
Age Equivalent:	6–6	Age Equivalent:	9–3
Social Quotient:	79	Social Quotient:	105

The foster mother served as informant at both interviews. The social quotient was 26 points higher in the post-test period, showing a greatly increased rate of social development. C-2-5 has developed a number of skills, absent at the beginning of the academic year, such as participating in pre-adolescent play. This includes such games as tag, ball, and cowboys and Indians. He does small remunerative work, mostly chores around the house, for which he is paid spending money. He also does simple creative work, such as building objects like sleds, airplanes, etc. The foster mother feels that much progress has been made, and that this is not something she alone can see, for various neighbors have commented on it.

Summary. C-2-5 shows improvement on all five of the psychological tests on which there is pre- and post-tests for comparison. Intelligence is now within the Average range, although at the beginning of the year it was in the Slow Learning range. The IQ has shown a steady increase over the past three years, from a low of 77 in 1955 to the present high of 91. The main intellectual weakness was in abstract ability, as involved in seeing similarities or solving problem situations. The post-test Goodenough Intelligence Test mental age was almost identical with that on the Stanford-Binet, while the pre-test indicated much lower ability. Marked improvement occurred on the Bender-Gestalt Test, where 17 errors were obtained on the pre-test, and only 4 on the post-test. There were fewer immature drawings, i.e., drawings at least two years below the mental age, and considerably less perseveration. On the Syracuse Visual Figure-Background Test there was increased accuracy, less distractibility by background stimuli, and less perseveration. A marked increase in the rate of social development was seen on the Vineland Social Maturity Scale, where a 26 point higher social quotient was obtained on the post-test.

Neighbors and other interested adults made frequent comments concerning his growth and development this past year. He is a much more comfortable child in the classroom, and has earned himself a place with the other children.

PEDIATRIC HISTORY C-2-6

The pediatric history was obtained from both parents. They seemed quite young, relaxed and easy-going. Both of them participated in supplying the information. The mother was seen to be constantly picking on her fingers, playing with a rubber band or with her wallet. She also spoke quite loudly.

Problem

One of the most outstanding difficulties which C-2-6 is said to be experiencing is the difficulty with her speech. She is said to be unable to talk properly. She makes herself understood to some degree; however, adults do not try to understand her and seem to lose patience because of this language difficulty.

She is in a Special Education class. She is slow in picking up certain things at school (it was the father who mentioned this bit of information). For example in things like numbers and arithmetic, she is apparently able to recognize words much better than numbers. Parents have tried working with her around this difficulty she seems to be having with numbers. Although she is able to recognize a number and point to similar figures, she has difficulty in remembering or recognizing the word for the number.

She is said to have a good memory for places. For example it was stated that she recognized a road that they had traveled on only once ten months previously. She was able to pick out one store from many on a street in a shopping area because the mother had taken her there once. Apparently she has always had this ability for fine details.

C-2-6 is said to have a terrific fear of fire engines. As a possible explanation it was noted that at about the age of 2 the family lived behind a fire-house and frequently she would be awakened at night by the noise of the siren. At these times it appeared that she was quite terrified. There was also an experience when mother was pregnant with the baby sister (C-2-6 was about 5½ years old) that the bag of waters broke and apparently C-2-6 has always remembered this because there was a great deal of excitement associated with it. Once when noticing men who were on a construction job nearby filling up their buckets with water, she said something about that they were silly to do this as the water would break.

It was further stated that C-2-6 was always an easily frightened child. She, for example, likes to watch TV as long as there is not too much action or peculiar characters (things like Howdy Doody or other puppets). She is also afraid of rain and thunder. Presently she will only go out in the rain if she is properly protected so that her head especially does not get wet. It was further stated that as an infant she was rather inactive, slept a good deal of the time, and was a very quiet baby.

Family History

1. Maternal grandmother is living and well.
2. Maternal grandfather living and well.

3. Paternal grandmother living and well.

4. Paternal grandfather is dead; died of a coronary thrombosis at the age of 56.

5. Mother has three brothers and three sisters all of whom are living and well. One sister had rheumatic fever at the age of 12.

6. Father has three sisters all of whom are living and well. There were one brother and one sister who died as infants, one following a fall during which she struck her head and the brother having died from some congenital malformation of the gut.

There is a maternal grandmother who had diabetes. The remainder of the family history is not remarkable. No history of co-sanguinity.

Family Background

Father. (Age 32.) In good health. He is an aircraft mechanic in the Navy, has been in the Navy for the past fourteen years. He finished high school and had various specialized courses in mechanical training. Interests: outdoor sports, gardening; likes to make things and repair things around the house. Problems: none in particular. Personality: mother said "lovable." She said he has little temper. His attitude toward the child's problem: he said he felt that he was realistic enough and would see what could be done for her and try to do the best they could.

Mother. (Age 25.) In good health. Used to be employed as a seamstress in a factory for about one year. She finished three years of high school. Interests: sewing, bowling, "hen-parties." Problems: none. Personality: quick tempered, but really other than that everything is O.K. Attitude: she felt badly; however, the main thing is to do as much for her as can possibly be done. She would like for her never to feel that she was unwanted. She feels that C-2-6 should be permitted to make use of what she has. She does not want anyone to push the child around, or take advantage of her, and this is especially true as she is said to be easy going and very susceptible to suggestion of others.

Mother's Medical History during Pregnancy with Child

The mother had two miscarriages at approximately six weeks of gestation; one was between C-2-6 and her brother and the other was right after the brother. There was apparently no reason given for these miscarriages. She was 18 years of age when C-2-6 was born and was under constant attention of doctors. Of note is the fact that at approximately three months she began spotting and was put to bed for approximately two weeks. She never went back to work after that. At the time there was a serious question as to whether she would be able to continue to carry the baby to term. At five months gestation the physician who took over was the one who delivered C-2-6 after ten months gestation—she was definitely a late baby. The delivery took place at a hospital. At nine months gestation the mother fell and broke her ankle but made an uneventful recovery. Six days after the date of confinement, her pelvis was X-rayed and she was told that the baby's head was in an abnormal position and this is why she was late in being born. Finally 19 days after the X-rays, she was taken to the hospital and a caesarean section was performed because of signs of impending toxemia. Immediately following the birth, both the mother and the baby were said to be jaundiced and each stayed in the hospital for two weeks, then left. Birthweight was 8 pounds and 5 ounces, and, except for the jaundice, the neo-natal period was said to be unremarkable.

Marriage. The parents have been married for eight years and this is said to be a compatible marriage. First marriage for both. They are of the same religion; both share the responsibility equally in the home and in raising the children. The father is not away for any length of time except perhaps for a two-week period during the summer when he is out on a training cruise.

Siblings. (1) A brother, 5 years of age. He too has a speech problem—articulation; otherwise he is fine. He gets along well with C-2-6. (2) A sister, 18 months of age, who is not yet talking, but is beginning to say words. She had a congenital dislocation of the left hip which was castered at about 6 weeks of age and is perfectly well now.

Past History

C-2-6 did not have her DPT and smallpox vaccination until she was 3 years of age because she had so many colds, upper respiratory infections, etc. She has had many injections of penicillin during the first year in order to "break the colds." Since then she has had her Salk vaccine.

Measles at the age of 5. She has never had any convulsive seizures and presently is on no medication. She apparently is said not to react violently when given injections of penicillin or when undergoing any type of pain. An example of this was that when she was scalded with hot water, she did not even cry, mentioning it to her parents: "Look, I didn't even cry."

Developmental History

C-2-6 was bottle fed, sucked well, had no difficulty swallowing. Solid food was started at approximately 2 months of age. She was weaned from the bottle at approximately 12 months of age without any difficulty whatsoever. There is no history of pica. Her sleeping habits were always very good and she still naps in the afternoon. She sucks her thumb and the satin edge of her blanket when in her bed. There is no rocking or head-banging. Toilet-training was accomplished by 15 or 18 months of age without any difficulty. Now there is only an occasional episode of enuresis. She is right-handed and apparently always seemed to be. Mother and brother are left-handed. It was stated that for awhile C-2-6 did not seem to know whether she would be right- or left-handed, but then apparently made the choice of being right-handed by herself. She did not roll over until the age of 8 months. She sat up at about 8 months, never crawled; she stood alone at 12 or 13 months of age. She did not begin walking until about 15 months of age. Her teething was normal, her speech was definitely and markedly delayed and abnormal in its quality. Her bottles were propped, and she was never able to hold them by herself. When she was weaned, she did hold the cup alone. She was always able to follow instructions, always had short attention span, and there was no evidence of any visual, auditory difficulties. She is said not to be particularly hyperactive; on the contrary she, if anything, is rather on the lethargic side.

Present Situation

C-2-6 is said to be able to dress herself completely including tying bows on her dresses, laces on her shoes; she can button buttons, zip zippers and even work safety pins. She eats with a fork and spoon because she is not permitted to use a knife. Her attention span is rather short. She will sit now and allow herself to be read to. She watches TV and has been in drive-in movies. She goes to Church, Sunday School. Games: she likes to play with dolls, puzzles. She prefers to play with younger children and especially babies and to sort of take care of them. She is able to roller skate and ride a tricycle. She is said to be able to count up to 12. Personality: when punishment is meted out, which is very seldom as it is not really necessary too often, she is so sensitive that she will respond to a simple scolding. She cries and says she is sorry. Fighting: makes no attempt to fight or protect herself. Frustration: she will either sulk or cry.

Physical Examination

Blood pressure 90/60.

General appearance. C-2-6 is a very pretty, well built, stocky, 7-year-old girl with blond hair and blue eyes. When walking, she started with her head down and walked somewhat clumsily about, slapping the soles of her shoes on the floor. It was felt, however, that this was an intentional type of gait rather than one over which she had no control. Upon giving her name and her age, a speech impediment was quite noticeable. Her fingers are very short, stubby and approximately the same length. She had epicanthic folds in both eyes as in mongoloid children. There are, however, no other features of mongolism. She has a pale flame nevus on her forehead above the bridge of her nose. It was almost impossible to do any type of subjective or projective tests on a verbal level, due to the speech and language formulation problems. When asked to undress, she became quite frightened and refused to remove anything other than her shoes and socks. After taking off her socks, it was noticed that her toes were short and stubby, the fourth and fifth toes being of equal length. She was able to count up to 12. She was unable to recognize and did not know the value of coins.

She was unable to hop on her right foot nor to skip. The remainder of the examination was not remarkable. In getting dressed, it was noted that she put her left sock on first and tried to put her right shoe on her left foot, then realizing the error she changed it. She was able to tie her shoelaces quite well.

Neurological Examination

Cranial nerves. First cranial nerve: not tested. Second cranial nerve: determination of the visual field on this little girl was not possible. She *appeared* to see everything within the usual range of vision. Fundi were normal on a very brief examination. Third, fourth and sixth cranial nerves: pupils reacted to light and also to accommodation. Extra-ocular movements were intact. No nystagmus was present. Fifth cranial nerve: normal for motor and touch. Seventh cranial nerve: taste was not tested. Muscles of facial expression were normal. Eighth cranial nerve: hearing seemed to be normal for tuning fork. She heard what was said to her. Ninth and tenth cranial nerves: could not be adequately tested. Eleventh cranial nerve: was intact. Twelfth cranial nerve: the tongue protruded in the mid-line and showed no furrowing or atrophy. *Sensory.* The child is able to feel touch, pinprick and vibration. Position sense, two point discrimination, and pinprick localization could not be carried out. Stereognosis was normal. *Reflexes.* Reflexes were equal and active throughout. No pathological reflexes were present. *Motor.* Motor appeared to be normal. *Cerebellar.* Finger-to-nose and heel-to-shin tests were all performed. She was unable to spin the jack with either hand, not so much from lack of co-ordination but from inability to understand directions for completing task. *Station and gait.* Station and gait were normal. Romberg was negative. She was able to walk on heels and on toes without any difficulty. *Movements.* No extrapyramidal movements were seen. *Mental status.* This child seems to be rather immature in writing, the letters lacking proportion and her copy ran off the end of the page. She leaves out letters, and was unable to draw a diamond. Her drawing of a house was primitive. The child is right-eyed, right-handed and right-footed. There is no apparent dominance problem.

Electroencephalogram

Attitude and condition of patient: alert, co-operative. Fundamental frequency: ranges between 6 and 7 waves per second. Slow wave: isolated 200 to 250 millisecond waves are seen in each occipital derivation. Fast waves: are not prominent. Amplitude characteristics: average to high voltage (90 microvolts peak); irregular modulations. Additional feature: no paroxysmal activity is observed. Hyperventilation: accentuates the prominence of the bioccipital slow wave output. Impression: minimal generalized abnormal EEG.

Speech and Hearing Evaluation

The parents report that C-2-6 was a very quiet baby and "slept all the time." At first they congratulated themselves on having such a "good" child. As an infant she demonstrated very little vocal play and limited babble. Parents commented that they began to be concerned when she was quiet in Church and did not make sounds like other children. At age 3½ it was estimated that she had no more than 6 words and even these were not very clear. At this point they requested advice on what to do about the delayed speech. She did not start to group words into two-word phrases until about 5 years of age. She used no more than two-word groupings for the next six months.

After this period there was a tremendous spurt in vocabulary and language. Hearing or language comprehension has never been questioned by the parents. She couldn't or wouldn't imitate words until after 4 years of age.

In July 1956 she was seen at a Diagnostic Speech Clinic. At that time her speech was diagnosed as a severe dyslalia in an immature, distractible child with very short attention span. Arrangements were made for speech therapy. As a result C-2-6 became more speech conscious and was able to make some corrections with guidance.

It is the parents' impression that their daughter is now using a great many new words. They feel she is trying hard to talk correctly, and when she is not understood, will make repeated attempts to correct herself.

Behavioral observations. Her over-all reactions to the test situation were those of a much younger child. Her general behavior could not be described as hyperactive. Her speech and language reflect over-all immaturity. She related well when her attention could be held and on some occasions giggled easily. Under pressure, she played with her shoes and generally fingered things on the desk.

Oral examination. The oral examination is unimpressive. Teeth are in good occlusion and the velum is of good length. She has a good nasopharyngeal closure and good control of her tongue and lips.

Articulation. Articulation shows marked infantile perseveration, including omissions, elisions, distortions, substitutions and defective sounds. C-2-6 can imitate all sounds readily in isolation. There is little or no carry over in propositional speech. *S, sh, ch,* and *j* are usually pronounced as *d*. Most final *th* sounds are omitted. She substitutes *w* for *l* and *r*, though these substitutions are inconsistently used in an initial position. Most blends are defective.

Voice. Voice is of good quality with no nasality or breathy emission. There are great changes in pitch, rate, and inflection.

Propositional speech. General conversation shows immature grammatical structure. C-2-6 now uses a fair number of simple sentences, but frequently omits words, and there is evidence of a great deal of disorganization and clutter. There was a great deal of dramatic inflection and change of voice as she took the voice of the various characters in the story of the Three Bears. Typical of her manner of conversing was this kind of sentence: "Baby Bear too hot."

When presented with picture and asked to tell a story she did much better than anticipated. For example, she talked in some 6 or 7 incomplete sentences about a picture of the two children getting ready for bed, before launching into random discussion and forgetting her idea about this particular picture. It is felt that her poor attention span and short memory contribute to her inability to express herself clearly, as well as her inability to imitate polysyllabic words which are unfamiliar to her.

Hearing. C-2-6's short attention span made the hearing test a real struggle. However, she repeated enough of the spondee words to indicate that there is no hearing difficulty *per se.* Her articulation was so poor that the PBK words were of little value. Test by pure-tone audiometry was done with the following results:

Right	10	5	5	15	10	20
	250	500	1000	2000	4000	8000
Left	15	10	5	10	15	15

C-2-6 had to be tested skillfully and quickly, due to her short attention span. As a result she may have had some difficulty in localizing in which ear the test tone was heard. Localization appeared better when the tones were loud. My impression is that hearing is within normal range.

Impression. An immature, distractible child with a very short attention and memory span whose delayed language, speech development, and infantile perseveration reflect her immaturity. There is some self-monitoring of speech output, but C-2-6 still has a long way to go.

Psychiatric Evaluation

C-2-6 gave her stated age correctly as 6 and during the interview, was at all times a friendly, cheerful, co-operative, young lady. Despite simple sentences and a small vocabulary, she made herself understood to the Examiner with the help of only occasional repetitions.

C-2-6 came willingly to the office, opening the stairway doors herself. Once inside the playroom, she was attracted briefly to Bobo the Clown then, in rapid sequence, to the clay, finger painting and doll house. She settled for the doll house (which was in total disarray) and fixed an orderly house with the furniture appropriately placed with only one exception. The sideboard piece was placed directly across the entrance to the house. She saw nothing incongruous about this arrangement and readily accepted the suggestion that it might be a good idea to look for another place to put it, which she did.

C-2-6 appeared interested in finger painting, and between us we pinned the paper on the easel and opened the jars. She began her painting with yellow, followed by red. She insisted upon sitting down on the floor and stretching up to the easel in order to paint. She informed the Examiner that purple was made by mixing red and yellow, but she listened carefully when she was corrected, and after several attempts to say, "Red and blue make purple," was able to repeat the words correctly. After completing two pictures, she said "That's enough—now I want to do something with Bobo and then use Play-Doh." "Put tops on please."

C-2-6 was curious about the punching bag, and hit it with fairly good co-ordination. This activity did not interest her more than a few minutes, after which she moved on to Mr. Bobo saying, "What's new with you."

She appeared to wish to "do for herself," and struggled to complete an activity. For example, she was very loathe to give up in her efforts to pry the lid off the Play-Doh; however, there was no overt sign of impatience or anxiety evidenced during her struggle.

While she understood the story of the father, mother, and baby bird in the Despert Fables she apparently failed to grasp the problem facing the baby bird.

Psychiatric Re-evaluation

While the Examiner's over-all impression remained approximately the same, C-2-6 has made definite progress in certain areas. For example, while she still wanted to keep the drawings she made, she did not protest to the same degree as in the previous interview. Also, her replies to some questions were more detailed.

C-2-6 played with the Play-Doh much as she had before, mixing the colors by squeezing and patting them together in the fashion of a much younger child. She was clumsy with toys. There was obvious difficulty in grasping the mechanics of the Schmoo family (a series of white penguin forms in graduated sizes one within the other).

Her continued perceptual problems were clearly illustrated in her drawing which showed little understanding of forms. On occasions she became stubborn and sulky when questions necessitated answers she was unprepared to give, but the moods passed quickly.

Parent evaluation. C-2-6's mother does not feel the improvement in her daughter's problems is as noticeable this year as it was the previous year. Rather that there has been continued improvement at a very steady pace. Specifically, she feels her daughter has learned more about home duties (picking up her clothes for example) and helping with her appearance—such as keeping her hair neat and attractive.

She plays better with her peers, her mother feels, perhaps because she has improved in speech and they can understand what she wants. However, she does not get hurt so easily by what other children do or say to her and does not come running home crying, except at infrequent intervals.

Stanford-Binet, Form L (Pre-test) (6–7–57).

CA: 6–11; MA: 5–5; IQ: 78.

Learning ability is within the Slow Learning range. The mental age is 5–5, and IQ 78. The Basal Age is at Year IV, while the Ceiling is at Year VII. Previous intelligence testing, 4–19–56, with the Stanford-Binet Form M, resulted in an IQ of 68.

At Year IV-6 all items were passed except opposite analogies and repeating four digits. C-2-6 did not seem to grasp the concept involved in the opposite analogies test. Immediate memory span was very poor, and even three digits were too difficult for her.

At Year V the only item failed was, again, concerned with immediate memory span, but this time it involved meaningful material in the form of sentences. When asked to repeat the sentence: "Tom has lots of fun playing ball with his sister." C-2-6 said: "Tom likes playing with his sister." In the directions before administering this item the child is asked to say "big girl," and then "I am a big girl." She could only say: "I big girl."

At Year VI two items were failed, number concepts, and copying a bead chain from memory. She seemed to have a good concept through fourness, but could not handle number concepts above four. In copying a bead chain from memory she seemed to get the concept of alternating forms, but her bead chain was quite unrelated to the stimulus.

All items were failed at Year VII. Items involving abstract ability, such as seeing the similarity between two things, was quite beyond her. Comprehension of concrete, practical situations was also poor. For example, when asked what she should do if she should accidentally break something which belonged to someone else, she said: "Call the police." When asked what she should do if she were on her way to school and saw that she was in danger of being late, she said: "Go back home." Her diamonds were very poor, having but slight resemblance to the stimulus figure.

Stanford-Binet, Form M (Post-test) (5–22–58).

CA: 7–10; MA: 6–0; IQ: 77.

There is only one point difference between the IQ obtained on pre- and post-test Stanford-Binets. The intelligence is within the range of the Slow Learning group, and the four-year performance range extends from a Basal Age at Year V to a Ceiling at Year VIII.

At Year VI the only item failed was differences. In this item the child is asked the difference between quite common objects. For instance, when asked how a slipper and boot are different, she replied: "A little girl has a boot and the little boy has a slipper."

The only item passed at Year VII was giving the number of fingers. She gave the correct number on one hand, on the other, and then the total number. In repeating sentences from memory, she left out the most important qualifying words, and in repeating three digits reversed, said any number that occurred to her. Picture absurdities, sentence building, and counting taps were too difficult for her.

All items were failed at the Year VIII.

Ammons Full-Range Picture Vocabulary Test (11–27–57).

CA: 7–5; MA: 6–0.

The mental age obtained on this test is only slightly higher than that obtained on the pre-test Stanford-Binet. The following words, expected successes at or below this child's chronological age level, were failed: vegetable, human, customer, island, manufacturing, cheerful, collision, listening, uniform, safe, and protection.

Goodenough Intelligence Test.

Pre-test (6–7–57)	*Post-test (5–12–58)*
CA: 6–11; MA: 6–0	CA: 7–10; MA: 5–3

The post-test drawing is somewhat more crudely drawn than the pre-test. The first drawing shows a trunk, hair, but no mouth or arms. Post-test there is no trunk, the arms and legs being attached directly to the head.

Block Design and Coding from WISC (6–7–57).

	Raw Score	Scaled Score	Equivalent Test Age
Block Design	2	6	4–10
Coding	13	5	4–10

C-2-6 was able to do the first Block Design on the first attempt, but could do no other designs. She got colors confused, and showed no grasp of the basic form necessary for this task. The equivalent test age of 4–10 represents the lowest score possible on this subtest. The same score was earned on the Coding, Form B, where only 13 substitutions were attempted.

Bender-Gestalt Test. Pre-test (6–7–57) there were 22 errors, including 3 immature, 3 perseverations, 4 dissociations, 1 closure, 3 incorrect elements, 1 unrecognizable, 3 distorted angles, 2 rotations, 1 enlargement, and 1 disproportion. Post-test (5–12–58) there were 18 errors, including 1 immature, 1 perseveration, 2 dissociations, 1 closure, 3 incorrect elements, 3 distorted angles, 1 rotation, 4 compressions, and 2 disproportions. Thus slight improvement is seen in the fewer number of drawings categorized as immature, fewer dissociations, and less tendency to perseverate.

Syracuse Visual Figure-Background Test. Pre-test (10–24–57) there were 4 correct responses to figure, no background responses, and 4 perseverations. Post-test (5–12–58) there were 6 correct responses to figure, 2 background responses, and 5 perseverations. Thus there was a slight increase in accuracy, but this was offset by more distractibility by background responses and more perseveration.

Tactual-Motor Test (10–24–57). C-2-6 seemed to be completely unable to appreciate a figure felt through a screen. Even when the Examiner drew the child's fingers over the raised figure, she seemed unable to grasp the fact that there was "something there" that could be drawn.

Marble Board Test (10–24–57). On Marble Board 1 C-2-6 started at the upper left-hand corner, and proceeded to fill in every available space with marbles. When she attempted to draw the design made by the Examiner, she made many horizontal *x* lines across the paper. In reproducing Marble Board 2 she made one long diagonal line from corner to corner, and then started to fill in all available spaces. Her drawing consisted of a very large *X*.

Vineland Social Maturity Scale.

Pre-test (11–20–57)		Post-test (5–13–58)	
Total Score:	67	Total Score:	71
Age Equivalent:	7–4	Age Equivalent:	8–4
Social Quotient:	100	Social Quotient:	106

The mother, who served as informant at both interviews, expressed satisfaction with C-2-6's progress. She feels that the improvement in speech has helped with her relationship to other children. There is but a slight difference between social quotients, showing a rate of development of social skills that has remained quite consistent over the course of the year. There are only a few skills that have been developed that C-2-6 was unable to do at the beginning of the project, including using a table knife for spreading, participating in pre-adolescent play, with such games as tag, ball, etc., and making minor purchases.

Summary. All of the psychological tests show reduced functioning. The intelligence quotient falls within the Slow Learning range, with relative weaknesses in attention span, number concepts, and visuo-motor performance. Relative strengths are in vocabulary and simple discriminatory tasks. On three of the tests—Binet, Goodenough, and Vineland—no improvement was noted, but slight improvement was noted on the Bender-Gestalt Test and Syracuse Visual Figure-Background Test. On the Bender-Gestalt Test there were fewer immature drawings, less tendency to dissociate, and a reduced number of perseverations. On the Syracuse Visual Figure-Background Test there was greater accuracy, but somewhat more distractibility by background stimuli. The rate of social development was about the same in the pre- and post-test periods.

PEDIATRIC HISTORY C-2-7

The pediatric history was obtained from the mother, a rather attractive young woman wearing sun glasses. She explained that she had left her regular glasses in the car and couldn't see a thing without her glasses.

Problem

The pupil personnel worker had told her that C-2-7 wasn't doing too well in school and it was upon her recommendation that a work-up was done at a local hospital for placement in Special Education. It was upon the further advice of the pupil personnel worker that C-2-7 is being worked-up currently for possible inclusion in a research project. The mother and son were recent arrivals in the United States. When her son started school abroad, he was said to be hostile and aggressive with the other children. Mother always felt that he was slow, but teacher never really indicated any abnormality. Apparently he progressed fairly well and was promoted at that time. After coming to this country, the mother started working and the woman who took care of C-2-7 did not treat him too well.

When he started school here he was hostile and aggressive, especially with other children. He was hyperactive ("raising hell"). He upset the class routine consistently. His mother felt that discipline in school here was not what it should be or what it had been abroad, and perhaps this was in some way responsible for his behavior. The school personnel felt that he was unable to do the work. The mother mentioned that when she worked at home with him he seemed to do well. He still goes to regular school and is in the first grade (actually he had done this same work elsewhere, but the mother felt it would be better to place him in the first grade rather than try to have him go ahead). He was tested at a local hospital and said to have been found of normal intelligence and that his problems were emotional in origin. Mother didn't follow the recommendations of the hospital. She said that she had some reservations about the program under discussion inasmuch as she didn't know what type of children would be included and she had fears that the children would either be physically deformed or of retarded intelligence.

At this point again, she complained about the living conditions that her apartment house offered and again complained about the woman who originally cared for the boy. She said that she hadn't moved before because she did not want him to change schools. However, she was told that if he is accepted for this program, it wouldn't matter where he lives, as he would be picked up by bus. At this point, the mother further mentioned that her son was slow in talking and in walking. He had been placed in the day nursery at one year of age when she had returned to work. Immediately following the marriage and after C-2-7 was born the mother lived with her mother and father. She worked, and her mother took care of the child for the most part. Both grandparents died within a three month period when C-2-7 was approximately five years of age, and he was unhappy about this as he was quite close to them. He was quite upset and for awhile following this, whenever anyone left the room he thought that they would not come back.

Family History

1. Mother's father died at the age of 66 following an operation for strangulated hernia.
2. Mother's mother died at the age of 76 of cancer of the kidney.
3. Father's mother died of cancer.
4. Father's father is living and well.
5. Mother has two brothers and three sisters living and well.
6. Father has two brothers living and well.

Family Background

Father. Deceased.

Mother. (Age 26.) In good health. Employed as a secretary. Finished high school, came to the United States one year ago. Throughout most of the interview, although she spoke rather freely, she avoided the direct gaze of the examiner. Her interests are swimming, reading, and sailing. All she could say about her personality was that she was irritable. She had problems as a child from the age of 8 to 11 when she was evacuated from her home. She is quite worried about C-2-7. The mother stated she would like to remarry at some point so she could stay home and wouldn't have to work, in addition to which C-2-7 would have all the advantages of having a father.

Marriage. The father and mother had been married eight years. There was considerable difficulty. Her mother had been against the husband, and things were quite strained when, prior to his death, they were obliged to live with her parents after the marriage.

Mother's Medical History during Pregnancy with Child

The mother was 18 years of age when she delivered C-2-7. The pregnancy itself was rather uneventful except for hyperemesis. The delivery was un-eventful, C-2-7 weighing 5½ pounds. He was described as looking squashed, and the mother heard someone say that he looked peculiar but normal. She remained in the hospital for three weeks, apparently because of difficulty in finding a place to live. The baby was breast-fed for nine months. There was some difficulty in weaning him which was started at 6 months of age. The mother went back to work when he was 12 months of age.

Past History

DPT and smallpox vaccination during first year of life. Salk vaccine given. He wears glasses for myopia and for strabismus and has been wearing them since the age of 2. He had measles and mumps at the age of 4 and chickenpox at 6 years of age. He was given tranquilizers on two occasions, but has been off all medication for several months now.

Developmental History

C-2-7 gained well and thrived on breast feeding. Solids were not started un-til after he was weaned. Although he had no particular sleeping problem, his habit was to lie awake in bed and jabber away, which he still does. Apparently he dreams quite a bit, mostly about cowboys and other similar-natured activ-ity. He is said to have been slow in development, generally speaking. As to handedness, he is said to be ambidextrous, that is, equally poor with either hand. Toilet-training was accomplished by 2½ years of age, except for enuresis on and off, even to the present day. He has always been reluctant to use other people's toilets and would prefer to stand rather than to sit. His attention span is said to be very poor unless he is particularly interested in something.

Present Situation

He plays with children older or of the same age, does not like to play with younger children or by himself. He is subject to terrific fantasy. He likes to play cowboys; he isn't interested in puzzles or coloring. He can ride a two-wheel bicycle, can't catch ball too well, has poor co-ordination, is able to count and is said to be able to tie his shoes if he wants to. He can use a knife, if permitted to, and will sit through movies and TV. Punishment consists of withholding TV, being sent to his room or being slapped. He usually doesn't cry and the mother says she has the impression that he is almost asking to be disciplined. He will fight back, although he isn't too good at fighting, and when he is frustrated he grumbles and does not have outright temper tan-trums.

Physical Examination

General appearance. C-2-7 is a short boy who wears glasses. He started talking immediately after coming in contact with the Examiner and didn't stop until he left the room. His speech was normal. He began by saying, "My friend talks crazy; his brain is funny." It is possible that C-2-7 was unable to differentiate reality from his fantasy world. He spoke of being naughty and robbing a bank, and said, "My friend is crazy. When he was asleep, he was afraid he might roll off onto the floor." He spoke with feeling and expression, and kept his fists clenched throughout the entire interview. He said his dreams of giants, gorillas, and little dogs did not frighten him.

In answer to the ambulance story, he said, "Somebody's been badly hurt—one of my friends—it was a girl. One of her bones broke." The elephant story was different in that it would be "painted by Mr. Tooth Decay." He then said that "He caught Mr. Tooth Decay and should have shot him but I squeezed him in my hand," and he clenched his fists even tighter. "So I punched him and he fell out of the window and broke his head to bits," he concluded. To the bird story, he replied, "Little baby bird would die."

He was unable to undo the collar button and undid the other buttons with his left hand in a rather clumsy way. His shoelace became knotted and he was unable to undo it, asking the Examiner to do it for him. When it was time to put his shoes back on, he was unable to tie them. He was able to hop better on his right foot than on his left. He skipped fairly well spontaneously. He was able to identify the various parts of his body. The right eye showed a convergent strabismus, was irritated, and had a slight corneal abrasion. He seemed to past point and not to do it as smoothly with his right. His teeth were carious. The neurological examination was not remarkable except for hyperactive reflexes bilaterally. He was able to distinguish the right from the left shoe and put them on properly. There were indications that he has confused but definite knowledge about both men and women's bodies.

Neurological Examination

Cranial nerves. First cranial nerve: not tested. Second cranial nerve: fundi are normal. Visual fields appear to be intact. He does have very thick glasses which seem to be necessary for any good visual acuity. Third, fourth, and sixth cranial nerves: he had nystagmus on lateral gaze to either side and some on upward gaze. The extra-ocular movements appear to be intact. The pupils are round and equal and react to light and accommodation. Fifth cranial nerve: corneal reflexes are present bilaterally. The motor and sensory functions of this particular nerve are normal. Seventh cranial nerve: muscles of facial expression are all normal. Taste was not tested. Eighth cranial nerve: he is able to hear the tuning fork and the spoken voice without difficulty. Air conduction is greater than bone conduction. Ninth and tenth cranial nerves: the uvula went up in the mid-line. He is able to swallow without difficulty.

Gag reflex was not tested. Eleventh cranial nerve: he is able to shrug his shoulders without difficulty. Twelfth cranial nerve: the tongue protrudes in the mid-line. There is no sign of atrophy or fasciculation. *Sensory*. Normal for pinprick, touch, vibratory, position, pinprick localization, two-point discrimination and double simultaneous stimulation on both arms, both legs, left arm and left face, as well as right arm and right face. *Motor*. The reflexes are equal and active throughout. No pathological reflexes were found. Motor power seems to be good in all of the muscles. Muscle tone seems normal. *Cerebellar*. The boy showed good finger-to-nose tests bilaterally as well as heel-to-shin tests. Diadochokinesis was not too well performed on either side. He was able to spin the jack fairly well with his right hand but not at all with his left hand. The boy is right-handed. *Station and gait*. The Romberg is negative. He can walk on his heels and on his toes without any difficulty. The gait is normal.

Electroencephalogram

Attitude and condition of patient: alert, co-operative. Fundamental frequency: ranges between 7 and 8 waves per second. Slow waves: a 2 per second spike-dome variant pattern transiently dominated the left occipital output. Fast waves: are not prominent. Amplitude characteristics: high voltage (250 microvolts); irregular modulation. Hyperventilation: does not markedly alter the basic EEG pattern. Impression: maximum electric abnormality of paroxysmal quality over the left occipital region.

Speech and Hearing Evaluation

Language and speech development. C-2-7's language and speech development have been more precocious than his other aspects of development. He sat at eight months and walked independently around 22 months of age. He used his first words at about 9 to 10 months of age and consistently added vocabulary. He began to use phrases around 24 months of age. It is mother's impression that he did not fluently express his ideas until around the age of 4. She has never questioned his hearing or his ability to comprehend language. She is aware that his conversation is a mixture of fact and fancy.

General behavioral observations. C-2-7 has an intent, studious expression, which is emphasized by the big shell-rimmed glasses. He came willingly to the examining room. He talked incessantly, demonstrating the same vivid imagination and mixture of fact and fantasy that was observed while he was playing with the toys in the waiting room. He has many nervous mannerisms and is constantly in motion. This took the form of twisting around on one foot or the other to wild frantic flailing with his hands and arms. Occasionally he would clench his fists. In telling stories, he grew more and more excited until he almost became hysterical in his verbal output. When he became "wound-up," definite stutter symptoms were observed.

Oral examination. Teeth are in fair occlusion. There is an overbite. The velum is of adequate length and there is good nasopharyngeal closure. He can move his tongue in all directions with control.

Articulation. He can imitate all sounds with accuracy and precision. In isolated words he had no articulation errors except a *th* substitution; for *th* he usually uses an *f* or a *v*. However, in propositional speech, he does not maintain this accuracy and there is a color of infantile perseveration.

Voice. The voice reflects a strong emotional component. Many times he was breathless and gasping; he rapidly changes pitch and inflection. Sometimes he speaks with extreme rapidity and at other times with prolongation and repetition.

Propositional speech. When presented with three pictures in which to tell a story, there was marked variation in his performance. The first picture was that of shopping at the A & P; for this he gave a very elaborate story about a robbery. He could not volunteer any information about a family picture until direct questions were asked. His comments were very limited and centered about the fact that it was a mother, a father, a boy, and a girl. He did not know what the little girl was doing even though it was obvious that she was kissing the father. The third picture (people fishing) once again provoked a series of tall tales. All the stories were told with frantic gestures. As he got engrossed, his speech became louder and louder. It was punctuated with many giggles and almost hysterical laughter. In the middle of "The Three Bears" tale, he lost track of the story and began telling a story about "my friend." This child has an excellent vocabulary and uses English well. He uses many complex sentences and has the ability to express nuances.

Hearing. This boy has normal hearing. He could repeat spondee words with precision and accuracy. This was also true of a list of PBK words. The following pure-tone audiogram was obtained.

Right:	10	5	0	10	15	15
	250	500	1000	2000	4000	8000
Left:	15	5	5	10	15	10

He listened intently while giving the audiometric responses and his responses were consistent and sharp.

Impression. This boy has excellent language comprehension and expression. He is almost a compulsive speaker, weaving fact and fancy. When he gets wound-up, his speech is almost compulsive and hysterical. There are many evidences of a stutter pattern in his repetitions and perseveration. He has many nervous mannerisms and is constantly in motion.

Psychiatric Evaluation

C-2-7 had a compulsive need to "make-up" many ego-building stories-tales of prowess against Indians—"one of these cars belong to my policeman who is about to take some money to one of my banks; I've forgotten how many," etc. Most of his stories were about violence he has inflicted on others or what others have perpetrated on him. He was not interested in the doll house, clay, toys, etc. In response to Despert Fables (I), he replied, "Mother bird is brighter than Father; if I don't get Father bird away, he will kill all the little ones. I didn't know this at first, but then I got a wolf to kill the Father and lost it." To Despert Fables (VI) he replied, "The (elephant's) tail grew. He calls his mother and says he has a trunk in the back too, but you know it's really a tail."

The child willingly drew a person for the Examiner. He gave a running comment: "His hair is really messy; this is a friend of mine." ". . . he has one big ear . . . he had some paint so he painted part of this ear green . . . didn't know what to do with the paint."

He had no wishes that he could think of but stated, "My wishes go with wild." He circumvented questions regarding his family with irrelevant remarks. As the Examiner and the child came down the corridor, the child stayed behind and pushed at the air saying, "Stop that." In response to the Examiner's questioning look, he explained that his "horses were acting rough and were kicking a bit."

Psychiatric Re-evaluation

The conspicuous difference between the interview last year and the present one is that C-2-7 no longer had the need to tell such "tall tales." There was less anxiety manifested through the use of his limbs. Also, during this interview, the child went after Bobo the Clown and spent quite some time knocking it about. It will be remembered that he had no desire to play with toys during the last interview. During this session, his conversations were much more realistic. He agreed that he told "tall tales" last year, but was unable to remember a story he related regarding four-year olds in the Foreign Legion.

His first attempt in drawing a person consisted of a circle for the head and a stick figure for the body. He drew an animal that was three times the size of the person. He was asked to draw another person; this figure had ears, eyes and mouth and was no longer made as a stick figure. He was disappointed in his signature which was started off well but ended up rather cramped.

The mother is still concerned that C-2-7 has not progressed academically, but she says that he is socially better and that they do not hear him telling so many fancy stories now. She agrees that Special Education is the proper type of experience for her child at the present time.

Stanford-Binet, Form L (Pre-test) (6–6–57).

CA: 7–11; MA: 5–9; IQ: 73.

Intelligence falls within the Retarded range, with a mental age of 5–9 and IQ of 73. The Basal Age is at Year IV–6, while the Ceiling is at Year VII. These results are in accord with previous psychological testing done 9–27–56, which resulted in an IQ of 69.

At Year V all items were passed with the exception of repeating sentences from memory, thus showing a short attention span for immediate meaningful material. He left out major words in attempting to repeat the sentence, and it was obvious that he was relying on rote memory rather than meaning.

At Year VI all items were passed with the exception of copying a bead chain from memory.

At Year VII all items were failed. Visual-perceptual analysis of situations presented pictorially were beyond him. He could not distinguish essential from nonessential elements in the pictures. He could not see similarities between objects. When asked how wood and coal are alike he said: "Looks like wood and like coal." For apple and peach he said: "An apple is orange." Comprehension of problem situations was poor. When asked what he should do if he were on his way to school and saw that he was in danger of being late, he said: "Get my mummy." When asked what he should do if another boy hit him without meaning to do so, he said: "I'd do it straight back. Hit him back hard." His attempts at reproducing diamonds resulted in figures bearing scant resemblance to the stimulus figures.

Stanford-Binet, Form M (Post-test) (5–15–58).

CA: 8–10; MA: 7–4; IQ: 83.

The present IQ of 83 is 10 points higher than the pre-test results, and places the functioning level of intelligence within the Slow Learning range. The four-year performance range is from a Basal Age at Year VI to a Ceiling at Year IX.

Two items were failed at Year VII. C-2-7 was unable to repeat sentences from memory, making many mistakes. In fact, for the first sentence he remembered only the first word. He also failed the sentence building item. When given three words, *horse, bigger, dog,* he made up the following sentence: "The horse ran after the little dog and chased him until the dog tripped, and the horse tripped over the dog." He passed the number of finger item, saw the absurdities in pictorially presented material, repeated three digits, and counted the number of times a block was tapped on the table (up to 8 taps).

Two items were failed at Year VIII. He was unable to see the absurdities in situations described verbally. He was also unable to see opposite analogies.

All items were failed at Year IX.

Ammons Full-Range Picture Vocabulary Test (11–17–57).

CA: 8–4; MA: 6–6.

The mental age obtained on this test is quite close to that obtained on the Stanford-Binet. He failed a number of words ordinarily expected from a child at this chronological age, including vegetable, human, phonograph, transport, customer, sale, manufacturing, skyscraper, cheerful, collision, broadcast, protection.

Goodenough Intelligence Test.

Pre-test *(6–6–57)*	Post-test *(5–12–58)*
CA: 7–11; MA: 7–6	CA: 8–9; MA: 6–6

The first picture shows a boy standing with arms outstretched. A fair amount of detail is presented, including hands and fingers (incorrect number of fingers), shoes with heels, good facial features with eyebrows, teeth, and a large letter "S" on the chest, standing for Superman. The second drawing, however, is much more primitive. The body is made like a figure eight, with large club-like appendages for arms and legs, no hands or feet, and mouth in one dimension.

Block Design and Coding from WISC.

	Raw Score	Scaled Score	Test Age Equivalent
Block Design	3	6	4–10
Coding	12	3	4–10

Block Design A was completed successfully on the first attempt, and Design B was completed on the second. Design C was completed accurately, but in excess of the time limit. The equivalent test age of 4–10 is the lowest possible on this test. The same equivalent test was obtained on the Coding subtest, Form A, where 12 symbol substitutions were attempted with no errors. He was extremely slow on this subtest, frequently losing his place.

Bender-Gestalt Test. Pre-test (6–5–57) there were 17 errors, with 2 perseverations, 4 dissociations, 2 incorrect elements, 1 unrecognizable, 3 distorted angles, 3 rotations, 1 compression, and 1 enlargement. Post-test (5–13–58) there were 18 errors, with 3 concrete, 1 dissociation, 2 incorrect elements, 3 distorted angles, 1 rotation, 6 compressions, and 2 disproportions. Thus only slight improvement is seen in Bender-Gestalt performance, mostly in perseveration, dissociation and rotation. There were more errors post-test categorized as concrete and compression.

Syracuse Visual Figure-Background Test. Pre-test (10–24–57) there were 2 correct responses to the figure, 2 background responses, and 1 perseveration. Post-test (5–12–58) there were 4 correct responses to figure, 3 responses to background and no perseveration. As can be seen, only slight improvement is noted on this test.

Tactual-Motor Test (10–24–57). C-2-7 was able to draw correctly the triangle, both with plain and with thumbtack background. He failed all other designs. There was a marked tendency to concretize the designs. For Bender Figure 6 he said: "It's a spider!" For Bender Figure 4 he said: "It's an airflyer," and proceeded to draw an airplane.

Marble Board Test (11–18–57). Marble Board 1 was incorrectly reproduced. The first square was correct, but he could not overlap the second. The method of approach was incoherent, while the organization was linear. The drawing shows a square with a rotated "1" protruding from the top. Marble Board 2 was started with a diagonal that extended from the extreme upper left-hand corner to the lower right-hand corner. It was quite apparent that he was reacting to the design as a whole, rather than seeing it as being made up of parts. His drawing was incomplete, being drawn with one diagonal missing.

Vineland Social Maturity Scale.

Pre-test (11–18–57)		Post-test (5–21–58)	
Total Score:	62.0	Total Score:	70
Age Equivalent:	6–3	Age Equivalent:	7–0
Social Quotient:	76	Social Quotient:	80

The mother served as informant at both interviews. There is only a 4-point difference between pre- and post-interviews, showing a very consistent rate of social development. C-2-7 can do a number of things at this time that he could not do at the beginning of the school year. He is given much greater freedom now, and goes about the immediate neighborhood unattended. He plays competitive exercise games, such as Blind Man's Bluff, Tag, Cowboys and Indians, etc. He does small remunerative work, such as washing the car, returning bottles to the store, etc. He is occasionally left to care for himself, prepares his own food on these occasions, and is quite responsible. He also disavows a literal Santa Claus.

Summary. C-2-7 shows a reduced level of functioning on all psychological tests administered. Perceptual ability, as shown on the Bender-Gestalt, Syracuse Visual-Background Test, Tactual-Motor Test, and Marble Board Test was uniformly poor. On the two items from the Wechsler Intelligence Scale for Children (Block Design and Coding) he received the lowest possible equivalent test age. Post-test improvement was noted on only one test, the Stanford-Binet, Form M, on which an IQ 10 points higher than the pre-test was obtained. It should be noted that in the three intelligence tests given since 1956, all using forms of the Stanford-Binet, the IQ has steadily increased, from 69 in 1956, to 73 in 1957, to its present level of 83 in 1958. No comparable improvement was noted on the Bender-Gestalt Test (more errors post-test then pre-test), Syracuse Visual Figure-Background Test, or Vineland Social Maturity Scale.

While there was marked improvement in this child's general behavior over the course of the year, his behavior was still impulsive, at times uncontrollable, and he was a generally disruptive influence in the classroom. He continued to "tell stories" and make wild exaggerations of his experiences—both actual and vicarious experiences from television performances—that bordered on the delusional. The general impression is that the primary growth of this child over the academic period was in social growth, especially in ability to get along with peers, and there seemed to be but little change in the types of performances measured by the psychological tests.

PEDIATRIC HISTORY C-2-8

The history was obtained from both parents.

Problem

At two-and-a-half years of age C-2-8 started having convulsions. The doctors decided that it was both grand mal and petit mal epilepsy. Most of the seizures occurred early in the morning, while he was still asleep. The petit mal consisted of dropping his head forward. For the past three-and-a-half years he he has had no seizures and has been on Mysoline, Dilantal and Phenobarbital. Actually he is doing very well except for outbursts of temper, belligerency and hyperactivity. There is some difficulty in keeping him relaxed. Both parents seem to think that the Phenobarbital might actually be excitatory. There is a plan to reduce or to discontinue the various medications. An EEG, which was taken at one point, was normal. Up until 6 months of age he is said to have been a perfect baby. From 6 months of age on he began to whine almost constantly and seemed rather unhappy. He has always been rather active but not abnormally so. He has always been a determined child, doing what he sets out to do unless he was spanked or stood over, in order to be sure that something was done or was not done. As a matter of fact it was stated that the main problem really, is that he needs and demands constant individual attention. He started kindergarten at 5 years of age, went for about a month and then was told that he wasn't ready. He sought and needed too much individual attention. He would do things other than what he was supposed to and so he stayed out for the remainder of that school year. The following year he started in special classes and has been making steady progress since. Of late, he has been asking his parents for help with his work. Before, he claimed that he knew something or could do it without help. His attention can be obtained and held more readily now.

The history was obtained from both parents. The father was rather tall, good-looking, and straight-forward. Actually, he did not do most of the talking. The mother was rather obese; it was she who signed the medical release forms and actually did most of the talking.

Family History

1. Maternal grandmother living and well.
2. Maternal grandfather living and well.
3. Paternal grandmother deceased. Died when the father was 9 years of age of tuberculosis.
4. Paternal grandfather died also of tuberculosis.
5. Mother has one brother who is living and well.
6. Father has one brother who is living and well.

There is no co-sanguinity in the family.

Family Background

Father. (Age 40.) In good health, bus operator. Did not finish high school. He was born and raised in the area. Interests: sports. Problems: following mother's death, he kicked about from one relative to another. Personality: (wife answered) very well liked, no enemies. He spent two-and-a-half years in the service before the children were born. Presently, he is at home a good deal of the time. However, he used to go out quite a bit in the evenings to lodge meetings in which he was an officer and quite involved. At different times C-2-8 asked why Daddy couldn't stay home more with him (or at least so the mother said). More recently a closer relationship has been established. Attitude: at first the father didn't want to accept it. However, once the diagnosis of epilepsy was made, he felt a little better, since he had heard of other people having this illness and who were successfully treated. He accepts it more readily now but occasionally still wonders "why."

Mother. (Age 36.) Short, obese and in good health. Prior to marriage, worked as a beautician. She too is from the area and has completed high school. Interests: she likes to do beautician work, she finds it very relaxing and is quite accomplished in this field. Right now her interests are mainly in the children. Personality: she is able to find good in just about everybody. Attitude: at first she was upset, especially before she found out what it was. Now she says that she has resigned herself and is more accepting, feeling that eventually he will be cured. She feels that his education is the greatest concern to her.

Marriage. The parents have been married for fourteen years. It is the second marriage for Mr. and the first for Mrs. They are compatible and are of the same religion.

Siblings. (1) A brother, 10 years of age, doing well in school and a good boy. He is very tall and looks older than his 10 years. The two boys do a lot of scrapping; however, the brother takes a great interest in C-2-8 and they share things. They do not sleep in the same room, as C-2-8 sleeps in his parents' room because they want to keep an eye on him should he have his seizures. There are times when the brother is upset and hurt by C-2-8's difficulties.

Mother's Medical History during Pregnancy with Child

It was the mother's second pregnancy. She was 27 years of age when she was delivered by an obstetrician at a local hospital. The medical history during the pregnancy was not remarkable at all. The labor itself was quite short. C-2-8 was born of a normal, spontaneous delivery. They both left the hospital within three days (mother had had a phlebitis following her first delivery and so she was discharged earlier). Birth weight 9 pounds, 6 ounces; 23 inches long. C-2-8 was seen within the first twenty-four hours and was placed on bottle feedings.

Past History

DPT and smallpox vaccination during first year of life. Has had two polio shots. Measles at $4\frac{1}{2}$ years of age, mumps at 5, chickenpox at 5. There were no seizures for the first three-and-a-half years. He fell in school once and injured his left kidney which subsequently healed. This fall was not as the result of a seizure. The first convulsion did not occur accompanying a fever.

Developmental History

There was no difficulty feeding although there was some difficulty breathing through the nose. He ate well, swallowed O.K. There was no trouble weaning him. He threw the bottle away by himself at 9 months of age. He walked at 9 months of age and always liked to climb. No history of pica. Was never able to count well, even today. He is right-handed. There was a little difficulty toilet-training him, inasmuch as the Dilantin was inserted rectally. However, he was toilet-trained by the age of 4. No enuresis. His attention span has always been short, although for puzzles and putting things together, his attention span is much better. His school progress has been good.

Present Condition

He can button his buttons except for cuffs and collar, is able to use a spoon and a fork, can bathe himself. Interests: he likes puzzles and games, likes to play with plastic cowboys and animals; he likes to look at books, and cut out, and paste and color. He does better by himself or with one person rather than with a group. He is said to be able to ride a bicycle in his yard. He watches TV and goes to Sunday school. He is unable to tie his shoes. Personality: (Punishment consists of spanking, rewards or threatening to withhold things from him.) he says he is very sorry when he is punished but seems to forget easily and will do the same thing again. He is whining less now than he used to. However, he still does, especially when he is tired. He has no difficulty getting up in the morning to go to school, but there is a great deal of difficulty at night getting him quiet enough to go to sleep. He handles fighting quite well and father sounded rather proud when he stated that he is somewhat of a bully, attacking children regardless of their size. He does not have temper tantrums when frustrated.

Physical Examination

Blood pressure 100/70.

General appearance. C-2-8 went willingly with the Examiner. He knew his name and his age. He has a definite speech impediment.

His three wishes consisted of (1) horse, (2) cat, (3) dog. A good mommy "cooks for you and does nice things for you." A bad mommy "is real mean to you, screams at you." A good father "loves his boy," and a bad father "screams with his wife." On a desert island he would "take his sister." On a few occasions he would laugh or hum after giving an answer. He was able to name the coins that were shown to him but he did not know their value. Also he was able to count up to 10 without difficulty. *Skin and mucous membranes.* Not remarkable. *Lymph nodes.* Not remarkable. *Head.* Not remarkable. *Face.* Not remarkable. *Ears.* Not remarkable. *Eyes.* Not remarkable. *Nose and sinuses.* Not remarkable. *Mouth and throat.* Teeth—12 over 12; carious with wide spaces in between. *Neck.* Not remarkable. *Vertebra.* Not remarkable. *Chest.* Not remarkable. *Abdomen.* Not remarkable. *Genitalia.* Not remarkable. *Extremities.* Not remarkable. *Neurological examination.* He was able to hop on each foot and reflexes were normal.

C-2-8 was unable to dress himself well. He was unable to tie his shoes.

Neurological Examination

Cranial nerves. First cranial nerve: not tested. Second cranial nerve: the fundi are normal. Visual fields are normal on confrontation. Third, fourth and sixth cranial nerves: the extra-ocular movements are intact. Pupils react to light and accommodation. Fifth cranial nerve: good motor and sensory power is present. Seventh cranial nerve: no evidence for facial paralysis. Taste was not tested. Eighth cranial nerve: air conduction is greater than bone conduction. The tuning fork is heard with equal ease on both sides. The child was able to hear spoken voice. Ninth and tenth cranial nerves: the child has some defect in speaking. However, it is difficult to place this on the basis of vocal chord difficulty. He is able to swallow without difficulty. In addition the uvula goes up in the mid-line. Eleventh cranial nerve: normal. Twelfth cranial nerve: the tongue protrudes in the mid-line. There is no sign of atrophy or fasciculation. *Sensory.* Pinprick, vibratory, positions were all normal. Stereognosis was normal. Two-point discrimination and pinprick localization was normal. *Reflexes* were equal and active throughout. No pathological reflexes were present. *Motor.* Motor power was good. Muscle tone was normal. *Cerebellar.* Finger-to-nose and heel-to-shin tests were fairly well performed. Diadochokinesis was not too well performed, being better performed on the left than on the right. He had some difficulty in spinning the jack, spinning it better with the right hand than with the left. Fine movements were not well performed. *Station and gait.* He was able to stand on either leg without difficulty. He could walk on his heels and on his toes. Romberg was negative. The gait was normal. *Movements.* No extrapyramidal movements were present.

Electroencephalogram

Attitude and condition of patient: alert, co-operative. Fundamental frequency: ranges between 7 and 10 waves per second. Slow waves: occasional short sequences of approximately 4 per second output are observed in all leads. Fast waves: short run of 20 to 22 per second waves are seen in the homologous frontal derivations. Amplitude characteristics: high voltage (150 microvolts); irregular modulation. Additional feature: no definite paroxysmal activity is recognized. Hyperventilation: minimally accentuates the prominence of the generalized slow activity. Impression: moderate generalized abnormal EEG.

Speech and Hearing Evaluation

Language and speech development. According to his mother, C-2-8's general development was more advanced in all areas than her other children. He had the usual baby babble. His first word "dada" appeared at nine-ten months of age. He steadily added vocabulary and was using two-word phrases before the age of 2. It was the mother's impression that he was talking in short sentences at 30 months of age. It was at this time that his first seizure occurred. His speech declined thereafter, but after drug therapy it began to improve. The mother feels that her son can express his ideas adequately and that he has a good vocabulary. She also felt that he continued to improve in school work and in his ability to figure things out for himself. He recently has become curious and asks the meaning of words he hears or reads. The child has never had any speech therapy.

General behavior. C-2-8 is a friendly, outgoing child, who related well to the Examiner. He eagerly walked down the hall inquiring what they were to do. He co-operated well in all the various tasks set before him. He laughs and giggles easily and many things amused him.

Oral examination. Upper jaw is somewhat narrow and the hard palate has a high, narrow vault. The soft palate is of adequate length and lifts evenly. There is good nasopharyngeal closure. Tongue is controlled well and can be protruded in the mid-line without a tremor. He can move it from side to side and in various places with fair precision. He can imitate rapid, successive tongue placement, with or without vocalization. Teeth are rather short and there is a wide space between the upper incisors. Occlusion is adequate.

Articulation. Single words are well articulated. He says them with more emphasis and precision than is manifested in connected discourse. However, speech is intelligible. The only defective sound is the *s* and *z*. Apparently he once had a lisp and has not learned to jet an air stream for the *s*. Blends, with the exception of the *s* blend, are good.

Voice. Voice is clear and resonant when he projects. He tends to talk in a monotone without much inflection.

Propositional speech. C-2-8 verbalizes easily. However his utterance is not consistent. At times it is quite clear and quite precisely articulated. He tends to draw out his speech, prolonging vowels and changing stress and phrasing. As a result, it is difficult to follow him. A defective sibilant and the prolongation tend to make his speech sound different. He talks in fairly long sentences, if it is appropriate, and is using compound as well as complex sentences. He employs a variety of verb tenses.

He eagerly told a story about the pictures. He enjoyed it and went into some detail. He told the story of the Three Bears with quite good organization and with a variety of dramatic touches. He showed more animation in his speech while telling these stories than was observed in most conversation.

The child's hearing is essentially normal. He repeated the spondee words with great surety. He also gave back the PBK words with accuracy. This was further confirmed by the pure-tone test. The following audiogram was obtained.

Right:	0	15	5	15	20	20
	250	500	1000	2000	4000	8000
Left:	5	15	10	20	20	15

Impression. This child has relatively good language comprehension and expression. Speech is made somewhat deviant by the drawl and prolongation of vowels, as well as by the somewhat deviant stress pattern. It is further colored by a defective *s*.

Psychiatric Evaluation

This pleasant looking youngster's manner was quiet and he willingly came to the playroom. He gave his birthday correctly adding, "I'll be 9 on my birthday." He took every chance to show his knowledge, but he had difficulties. For instance, he gave the difference between an apple and a ball after ten minutes thought and then with prompting he was unable to suggest a way in which they are similar. He showed awareness of his limitations by saying very matter of factly "That's the way it always is at school"; and added with apparent genuine enthusiasm "You know, I'm lucky, I'm going to summer school."

There was little other verbal communication of feeling. C-2-8 did remark, when asked about his worries, that he worried over whether his dreams would come true. There was a very short attention span. Although he readily accepted the idea of drawing a boy, girl, and himself, he drew a house, and then turned to a wind-up train, and then quickly to the guns. He returned to the drawing, only to talk about wanting a sister and to mentioning a girl friend; "But she won't marry me," he added.

His answers to questions were often irrelevant and many of his remarks were made in the form of a stream of consciousness.

Psychiatric Re-evaluation

C-2-8 willing joinedly the Examiner in the playroom. His slight lisp becomes more prominent when he is excited. He has an almost continual flow of conversation with a fair amount of it running together. For example, he said "If my mother and I lived in two hundred houses we would need two hundred pounds of food and two hundred dollars." This was said with a cheerful beaming countenance and laughter characteristic of a much younger child. His play with the toys became more organized during the last half hour of the interview, but he continued to play by himself.

He quickly drew a stick-figure for the Examiner. Although the man is smoking, there is no cigarette or pipe present. He named this picture "Dad." When asked to draw a diamond, he drew a diamond bracelet. When an example was placed before him, his second of three attempts was what was asked for. The first and third attempts were done by drawing each line separately.

Conversation with parent. His mother stated that, "Everywhere I look he has improved." She feels that the positive aspects of the child's behavior had not been praised enough in the past and that the child had been "living up" to his bad reputation. There was much praise for C-2-8's teacher and the school conference that she attended. The mother also feels that her child has learned to respect people of all ages; this attitude seems to have been missing in the past.

Stanford-Binet, Form L (Pre-test) (4–7–57).

CA: 8–10; MA: 6–2; IQ: 70.

This child is functioning at a retarded level. The Mental Age is 6–2 and IQ 70. The Basal Age is at Year VI. The present test results are in agreement with psychological testing done 10–15–53, when a Stanford-Binet IQ of 70 was obtained. Thus it can be seen that the rate of intellectual development is quite constant.

At year IV–6 all items except that dealing with materials were passed. In this item the child is asked the material certain things are made from. When asked what a dress is made of, C-2-8 thought for a long interval, and then said: "A blouse." Repeating the question did not improve the answer. When asked: "What are shoes made of?" he responded with "Wood." When asked if the shoes he was wearing were made of wood, he answered in the affirmative. This latter is probably a perseveration from the first question which he answered correctly, namely, "What is a chair made of?"

At Year V all items were passed with the single exception of copying a square. Each attempt made by C-2-8 resulted in a figure more nearly resembling a rectangle than a square.

At Year VI he was unable to copy a bead chain from memory. He grasped the idea that different beads were to be used, but did not differentiate the very simple pattern used at this age level.

At Year VII only one item was passed, picture absurdities. This was one of the easiest tests at this age level for the children in this project. Attention span and memory for immediate material (repeating five digits) was not up to age level. Abstract ability also represented a weakness, as shown in an ability to see opposite analogies, comprehend problem situations, or see similarities. For instance, when asked in what way wood and coal are similar, he replied: "Coal is black." No further elaboration was obtained. When asked what he should do if another boy hit him without meaning to do it, he replied: "Tell my mother." He was unable to reproduce a diamond.

At Year VIII C-2-8 was able to remember the main aspects of a story that was read to him and vocabulary was at chronological age. Several times during the test he responded with a word and then spelled it. For instance when asked what an orange is, he replied: "What you eat. E-A-T, Eat." He seemed very pleased with himself when he could spell a word.

Stanford-Binet, Form M (Post-test) (5–23–58).

CA: 9–10; MA: 6–4; IQ: 64.

There is only a 6-point difference between this examination and the pre-test, the present IQ being 64, which, again, places C-2-8 in the range of the Retarded. The performance range is three years, from a Basal Age at Year VI to a Ceiling at Year VIII.

At the Year VII two items were passed, giving the number of fingers, and sentence building. C-2-8 was unable to repeat sentences from memory, see picture absurdities, repeat three digits reversed, or count the number of times a block was tapped.

All items were failed at Year VIII.

Ammons Full-Range Picture Vocabulary Test (11–27–57). The mental age was ten months greater on this test than on the pre-test Stanford-Binet, Form L. The following words, expected successes at this age level, were failed: vegetable, human, transport, customer, sale, manufacturing, skyscraper, cheerful, collision, broadcast, uniform, protection, and cleanliness.

Goodenough Intelligence Test.

Pre-test (4–7–57)	Post-test (5–12–58)
CA: 8–10; MA: 5–9	CA: 9–10; MA: 6–5

The first drawing was very poor, showing a huge balloon-shaped head with arms and leg attached, huge fan-like ears, and a minimum amount of detail. The post-test was little better, showing, in addition to the pre-test, an attempt to reproduce teeth, nostrils, and a hat flying through the air above the figure. When the ratio of mental age to chronological age is taken into consideration the post-test drawing is even poorer than the pre-test.

Block Design and Coding from WISC.

	Raw Score	Scaled Score	Equivalent Test Age
Block Design	1	3	4–10
Coding	7	3	4–10

Design A of the Block Design was completed on the second attempt, just short of the time limit. C-2-8 was unable to construct any other designs, becoming confused by the colors. Nine substitutions were attempted on the Coding, Form B, with 2 errors. Both subtests received the lowest possible equivalent test age on this test.

Bender-Gestalt Test. Pre-test (5–7–57) there were 21 errors, including 3 immature, 2 perseverations, 5 dissociations, 1 closure, 1 incorrect element, 3 unrecognizable, 3 distorted angles, 1 compression, 1 enlargement, and 1 disproportion. Post-test (5–12–58) there were 21 errors, including 1 concrete, 3 perseverations, 3 dissociations, 1 closure, 4 incorrect elements, 3 distorted angles, 3 rotations, 2 enlargements, and 1 disproportion. Fewer errors were made post-test which were categorized as immature, dissociations, unrecognizable, or compression. More errors were made post-test which were categorized as concrete, perseveration, incorrect elements, rotations, and enlargements.

Syracuse Visual Figure Background Test. Pre-test (10–24–57) there were 2 correct responses to figure, 2 background responses, and 9 perseverations. Post-test (5–12–58) there were 4 correct responses to figure, 2 background responses, and 4 perseverations.

Tactual-Motor Test (10–24–57). C-2-8 was completely unable to grasp the notion of this test. He felt the design behind the curtain for the minimum amount of time, and then, when asked to draw what he felt, proceeded to draw men. This test was attempted again a week later, with essentially the same results.

Marble Board Test (11–18–57). C-2-8 constructed Marble Board 1 by filling in every available space with marbles. His drawing showed no grasp of the basic pattern, being composed of disconnected lines. Design 2 was reproduced in a similar manner, and the drawing shows a background with scattered dashes supposedly representing marbles.

Vineland Social Maturity Scale.

Pre-test (11–18–57)		Post-test (5–13–58)	
Total Score:	60.5	Total Score:	71.5
Age Equivalent:	5–9	Age Equivalent:	8–5
Social Quotient:	63	Social Quotient:	86

The mother served as informant at both interviews, and indicated that she feels much progress has been made. She said: "I think he is improving, especially since we cut down on Phenobarbital." At the first interview she said that she felt that, in many cases, C-2-8's lack of ability might be due to her over protection or failure to provide opportunity, while in the second interview she indicated that she has been trying to give him considerably more freedom.

C-2-8 can do several things now that he could not do at the beginning of the year. He goes about the neighborhood unattended, at least so far as visiting friends' homes and local store. He goes to school unattended, while formerly his mother accompanied him. Going to bed was a problem for everyone concerned at the beginning of the year, he resisting sleep, but now he goes to bed unassisted. He also uses table knife for cutting, bathes himself unassisted, cares for himself at the table and is allowed to make minor purchases.

Summary. Both tests of intelligence on which there is a pre-test and post-test available for comparison (Stanford-Binet, Goodenough) show a retarded level of functioning. Both tests also show a slightly lower level of ability post-test. Little change was noted on the Bender Gestalt Test, 21 errors being made both pre- and post-test. Slight improvement was noted on the Syracuse Visual Figure-Background Test, where there was somewhat greater accuracy of perception and less perseveration. The most improvement as shown by the psychological testing was on the Vineland Social Maturity Scale, where the post-test social quotient was twenty-three points higher than the pre-test, showing an accelerated rate of social development. Social change was also observed in the classroom. At the beginning of the school year C-2-8 was considered a behavior problem, defying the teacher and making many aggressive remarks to her. By the end of the year he was very co-operative, and little aggressiveness remained.

PEDIATRIC HISTORY C-2-9

The information was obtained from the mother who is a rather large, elderly woman with white hair, who wears glasses. She seemed rather pleasant throughout the interview. She spoke quite freely and of significance was the fact that she spoke with very homey expressions.

Problem

The problem as stated by the mother is that C-2-9 is unable to learn to read and write. As a result of this he has a tendency to stand off from the rest of the children in school and elsewhere. He is very unsure of himself, never takes the lead, has to be told what to do, apparently has no confidence in himself. The latter points are true, specially in reference to other children. However, he does not seem to show the same manifestations, at least not to the same extent, with his mother.

If he is out playing (or as in the waiting-room while playing with blocks) and he notices his mother or father, he will stop and sort of look to them to see what their reaction will be. He apparently is freer with his mother than he is with his father. He likes to play "pretend machinery." For example, he pretends he is an airplane, or a tractor, or some other moving appliance. Sometimes this kind of play gets him so excited that he has difficulty falling asleep at night, and he will continue to talk about it even the following day. Other times he seems to get carried away with pretty flowers, or trees, or a mountain, or a sunset. His facial expressions are also said to be so different from other children; the fact that he takes notice of his surroundings and is so much aware of them makes his mother more appreciative of his having some positive qualities. "If only they can be brought out!" He is said to refuse to or be unable to, concentrate, and therefore is a problem at school. He loses interest quite readily, has an extremely short attention span, and again this is either because he won't or can't concentrate. If any type of pressure is brought to bear on him he gets nervous and upset, and at this time his hands begin to quiver; otherwise he does not have this quivering motion of his hands.

In discussing some of these problems, the mother said that she really never noticed (I wonder if it wasn't more a refusing to notice) many of the aforementioned difficulties prior to starting school. It was at this point that the mother stated that she had had a son, 15 months younger than C-2-9, who had leukemia, and while she was so occupied with this son, she wondered if perhaps C-2-9 hadn't been neglected to some extent by his parents. This lasted for six months at the end of which time the boy with leukemia died. C-2-9 was about 3 years of age at the time. In addition to the illness of his brother, he was sort of left out of things because his baby brother had to be cared for too. This preoccupation with both the baby and the son with leukemia was also given as a possible explanation for why the mother had not perhaps noticed anything unusual about C-2-9.

C-2-9 was said to be always a "quiet one" and never gave them any trouble by "getting into anything." His younger brother has always been the leader between the two of them and always tells C-2-9 what to do. It was he who actually taught C-2-9 to dress himself (mother says she was unable to do this as he either refused to do something or, if he had difficulty, she would automatically do it for him). He seems to be quite dependent on his brother who is the leader in getting both of them into mischief. C-2-9 is said to be very happy to follow his brother and doesn't seem to resent the arrangement whereby his brother is the leader and he follows. He is said to give up quite easily.

Family History

1. Maternal grandmother died at the age of 69 of a heart attack following surgery for an ovarian cyst.
2. Maternal grandfather died at the age of 72; he was burned to death in a fire.
3. Paternal grandmother died at the age of 60 of "dropsy."
4. Paternal grandfather died at the age of 73 of a stroke.
5. Mother had three brothers. One died following a heart attack, the other two are living and well.
6. Father has four brothers and five sisters. One brother died of tuberculosis

which he apparently contacted during the First World War. The other brothers and sisters are living and well. No other significant information of diseases.

Family Background

Father. (Age 48.) In good health. He is a dairyman. Finished school through the seventh grade. Currently the family lives on a farm. Interests: father loves to tinker with machinery or electrical devices. Mother says she doesn't see why he sticks to dairying when he could be a very good mechanic. Problems: there were none in particular except perhaps that of being part of a large family often who was very poor but happy. Personality: father is said to be very hard to get to know. He is very quiet, does not have anything to say for himself. Attitude toward boy's problem: he would do anything to get him started and straightened out. At first, however, he refused to accept that anything was wrong with C-2-9. He would get very angry, didn't want to admit to himself the possibility. Now he is able to admit this (at least for the past year) and is willing to permit diagnostic tests and placement in special classes. Father takes an active interest in the children. Apparently he lives for his children and his home.

Mother. (Age 50.) In good health. She taught school before her marriage; has done nothing since except raise a large family. Completed school through the seventh grade and then Teacher's College for a certificate to teach. Interests: mother says that she does not have too much time to do anything but take care of the home and the children. She still however teaches Bible school. Personality: she just accepts whatever comes along. (She laughed and wanted to know what I thought about her personality.) Problems: mother says that she comes from a divorced family and the six children were scattered about pretty much. She said she had a good home but it was a rather lonely childhood. She was further quite upset when one of her children died of leukemia. And then she just added that she has the usual problems one has in raising a large family and educating them, seeing that they are brought up properly, etc. Attitude: at first she worried a great deal. She wondered if he did not have the ability to make a good citizen and get along. However, now she sort of seems quite sure that he is capable of making a good citizen. She added rather philosophically that "somebody has to do the more menial difficult and unpleasant work." It would appear that the mother never had any help with the home or the children. (When asked about this, she did not give the information with any rancor.) She further stated that all her children come to her with their problems and ask her advice—things like doing homework and what they should do, etc. She feels that she is more sympathetic, or rather she said that perhaps the children came to her rather than her husband because they found her to be more sympathetic than he. She added that even the father tends to lean on her and comes to her with most of his problems. One of the children once asked: "What would become of the family if anything should happen to you?"

Marriage. They have been married twenty years. It is the second marriage for both. They have the same religion and apparently the marriage is quite compatible. As previously stated the mother has to handle all of the family troubles and make the decisions for the family.

Siblings. The mother had thirteen children in all, ten of whom are living at the present time. Sister, 30 years of age, happily married and in good health. Has not been in the home for the past eleven years. Brother, 28 years of age, married, in good health and out of the home for the past nine years. Brother, 26 years of age, married and in good health. He has been out of the home for the past two years, although prior to that he was in and out of the home, having been in the service. The mother mentioned that she is having somewhat of a problem with him because he is alcoholic. She loves him and said that he loves C-2-9 and vice versa and they get along very well. Brother, 24 years of age, in the Air Force and out of the home for the past three years. He is just wonderful. The children all love him and he loves them as a real brother. (The above named children are actually the children from the father's first marriage.) Brother, 18 years of age, living at home and in good health. He gets along well with the children. Sister, 16 years of age, living at home, still in school and doing quite well. Both this sister and the 18-year old brother don't seem to worry C-2-9 and seem to protect him. Brother, 14 years of age, living at home and doing well; he is said to be very critical of C-2-9. It was he who first pointed out why or how C-2-9 was different from other kids. He tries to make him stop some of his foolishness, tries to teach him. A brother who died at age 7 of leukemia. C-2-9 does not seem to remember him and does not say very much about him. He used to talk about him and ask about him whenever the parents said they were going to the hospital to visit anyone, since the brother went to the hospital and never returned. A brother, 10 years of age, doing well, gets along fine with C-2-9. Subject, age 8. A brother, 6 years of age, extra good in school and learning, and he is said to be "sharpest of the young ones." C-2-9 depends on him a great deal and is very concerned about him and tries to protect him when other older children might pick on him. The mother says C-2-9 seems to love his brother more than he does his mother or father. This is not true on the part of the brother, however.

The family lives on a farm and only recently the parents took a welfare baby, a little boy one week old (father is said to be home this afternoon baby sitting). It is interesting to note that previously, earlier in the interview, the mother mentioned that her husband couldn't come out with her because he had to work—perhaps both of these are factors as there are many things to be done on a farm which could not necessarily be put off.

There is a dog who is everybody's. C-2-9 has cats which he likes better and especially the kitten, and is said to love anything that is small and little such as a kitten.

Mother's Past History Including Pregnancy with Child

The mother had one miscarriage at three months. Does not know what the cause of it was, or where it occurred along the line. She had one infant who died at 6 months of age of whooping cough; both of the above were from her first marriage. Of her present marriage, one baby died during the first day, apparently from birth trauma. She was 42 years of age at the time she delivered C-2-9 and is said to have been quite upset during the pregnancy. She felt at this time that there were just too many children closely together; her mother died at this time as well. The son who later died of leukemia seriously burned himself and required hospitalization. As a result, she was very tense and nervous throughout the pregnancy. In addition she sort of hoped that C-2-9 would be a girl. She said that she was very difficult to live with at this time and came quite close to "cracking up." (She questioned whether this might not perhaps have had an effect on C-2-9 being so nervous.)

Past Medical History

DPT and smallpox vaccination during first year of life; has had two polio immunizations.

Had whooping cough at 4 months of age; apparently he was very sick with it; although he was not hospitalized he was ill for about six weeks. He had chickenpox at 1 year of age which was very serious and seemed to be more like smallpox rather than chickenpox. He had "asthma" at about approximately 1½ years of age. This was described as difficulty in breathing and turning blue. Everytime he would become upset up unto the age of 3 or 4, he would apparently have one of these attacks. It was at this time, after the first attack, that he became quite nervous and he began jerking and couldn't control his hands. The mother describes what she thinks was a convulsion; he seemed to have jerked all over; his teeth clicked. This too, was at a time during one of his "asthmatic" attacks. He was given paragoric on one or two occasions for these attacks and apparently this seemed to make him more nervous. He has not had one of these attacks for the past three years. Currently he is on no medication and never had any medicine before these attacks. The father is said to have gotten quite upset and excited every time C-2-9 had one of these attacks because of what happened to the son who had leukemia.

Developmental History

C-2-9 is said to have cried a lot for the first three months. He was always tense and nervous and not being able to relax even when asleep. Because of this he was picked up a bit. His bottles were propped about half of the time because of the needs of the rest of the family. He had no difficulty swallowing, solids were started at the usual time. Apparently there was normal growth and development in terms of sitting up, standing, walking, etc. There never seemed to be any difficulty with speech, any delay. He was able to follow instructions O.K. He is right-handed and always was, although one brother is said to be left-handed. The mother feels C-2-9 has some visual difficulty; she was unable to say how or why. He has a very short attention span. Toilet-training was prolonged and only was accomplished when his younger brother was completely toilet-trained. This happened at about 3½ years of age for the patient. There was never any history of thumbsucking, head-banging or rocking. He is a sound sleeper, has never had any difficulty sleeping.

Present Condition

He always seems to be quite happy, eats well, sleeps well. Prefers to play with smaller children and prefers to run around and engage in physical activity like making believe he is a machine, than do more sedentary type activity. He is said to be able to color O.K. for a short while; likes to be read to, but again only for awhile. Up until one year ago, he would not watch TV. He is a little better on that score now. He is said to be able to sit through Sunday School, loves music and has learned the words to songs quite easily. He can repeat the Lord's Prayer and is able to recite the Pledge of Allegiance. He has an uncanny ability for recognizing infrequently traveled roads and has quite a memory for fine small details. He is able to button his buttons and tie his shoes. He is sort of messy at the table and is unable to use a knife. Mother feels perhaps a lot of this is due to the fact that this is done for him. Although he bathes himself, he is unable to get his ears and neck clean. He has never been punished too much, and when he is, he cries and is very unhappy and wants to make up immediately. He has to get real mad before he will fight. He just cries and shouts. Usually he will avoid it as much as possible. When frustrated he does not have a temper; he says that he will have a spell. He nags quite a lot and whines.

Physical Examination

C-2-9 came with the Examiner without any hesitation or difficulty. He had a whistling *s* which was quite noticeable when he said 66, referring to his weight. He speaks haltingly and screws up his face quite a bit and makes other grimaces when he is thinking or responding. He was able to name his friends at school. He said he likes to play with toys and build and is able to color. He thought a great deal about his three wishes and said he couldn't think of any. Good mummy treats you good, a bady mummy hurts you. A good daddy doesn't hurt you, a bad daddy, "He hurts you, slaps you." On a desert island he would take one of his school friends. In response to the ambulance story he said, "Someone got hurt, a man was in a car wreck—he hurt his back real bad." To the bird story he said the baby bird would die and wants his mummy and daddy. Bad dreams make you get scared because real bad things happen. However, he was unable to say what some of these bad things were. He wants to be a farmer when he grows up and was able to mention some of the various things that a farmer does. He recognized a penny but called a nickel a dime, gave no response when shown a dime and said a quarter was a dime. He can count up to 13, skip 14, then he can count well up to 30. He knew the days of the week. He did not undress with too much dexterity. Teeth are normal for his age. There were wide spaces in between. They were quit carious and he had a high-arched palate. Neurological examination was not remarkable. The child was able to hop on either foot equally well and he was able to skip. He had quite a bit of difficulty in buttoning his trousers and in zipping the zipper. There were no gross or fine tremors seen with his arms outstretched. There was some perseveration in his finger-to-nose test which was not performed too well. He did some things with his right hand and foot and others with his left. He was unable to pick out his right shoe and it was only after trial and error that he did. He wore moccasins so that he did not even have to attempt to tie his shoe laces. The remainder of the examination was not remarkable.

Neurological Examination

Cranial nerves. First cranial nerve: not tested. Second cranial nerve: visual fields appeared to be normal on confrontation. The fundi were also normal. Third, fourth and sixth cranial nerves: the boy had a slight nystagmus on lateral gaze to either side. No strabismus was noted. Extra-ocular movements were all intact. Fifth cranial nerve was normal, as was the seventh, ninth, tenth, eleventh and twelfth. *Sensory.* Pinprick, vibratory, touch, position, and stereognosis were all well performed. Two-point discrimination, pinprick localization, and extinction phenomena were all normal. *Reflexes* were equal and active throughout. No pathological reflexes were present. *Motor.* Muscle tone was good. The motor system appeared normal except for co-ordination. Diadochokinesis was not well performed. *Station and gait.* Station and gait were normal. *Movements.* There was a fine tremor, particularly in movements of the right hand. *Comment.* This boy had difficulty in performing other than very simple tasks. He was unable to draw a diamond and he could not draw a house very well. In addition to that, the printing of his name is not very well done. He has a great deal of difficulty in differentiating right from left, continually calling the right the left, and the left the right. He is right-handed, but left-eyed.

Electroencephalogram

Attitude and condition of patient: alert, co-operative. Fundamental frequency: ranges around 10.5 waves per second. Slow waves: none of brain origin. Fast waves: are not prominent. Amplitude characteristics: average to high voltage (100 microvolts peak); regular modulation. Hyperventilation: generates no slow waves. Impression: Within the range of normal variation.

Psychiatric Evaluation

C-2-9 gave his age correctly and was friendly, co-operative but quite shy throughout our time together. He left his mother easily and walked upstairs with the Examiner demonstrating a rather straight-legged gait. At all times during the interview he was in need of guidance, as well as permission to involve himself in the play activities. For example, he took a few tentative punches at Bobo until encouraged to hit out, at which point he did so, catching on to the explanation as to why Bobo remained upright. He showed this by tossing Bobo into the air and tipping him so that we both could hear the sand move from one side to the other. After a while, in quite a normal fashion, he said "I'm getting a bit tired of this now," but added "May I do" such-and-such "now?"

He drew a very poor star and said as much. While drawing, the tremor mentioned earlier was in evidence. It did not seem a true intentioned tremor because it was present before, during and after the activity. C-2-9 told me, on questioning, that it comes and goes. It appeared before he ever started school but has, at no time, affected more than his two hands, nor has the trembling become worse. The tremor is unrelated to the time of day. In answer to other questions of information, he stated that his birthday "is just half past." Knowing that his birthday was about two weeks ago, perhaps what was meant was, "it was just passed." There was a definite degree of mental retardation and he was disoriented for time.

When asked two of the fables, he stated that the baby bird "went to another tree," and when asked what was different about the elephant, he replied that there was "another baby with the elephant."

When asked about his family, he named four brothers and where they were.

The child dreams some, but he did not elaborate except to say that there were many bears in his dreams, and sometimes he saw shadows on the wall that scared him.

After the Examiner defined what wishes meant, he answered by suggesting items which were around him in the playroom, despite the Examiner's encouragement to think of other things, perhaps at home. He gave (1) toys, (2) cars, (3) trucks.

Psychiatric Re-evaluation

C-2-9 was less at ease and more passive in the playroom during this interview than previously. He limited his play activities to hitting Bobo's replacement, but this activity was performed with some uncertainty. There was no spontaneity in his conversation. When asked about school his face lit up and he said, "I can write my name, and I can do arithmetic, too. I like arithmetic." There was a slight lisping quality to his speech, but it was not remarkable. When asked if anything was different at home, he said "No."

His three wishes included a horse, a cow, and a cat. When asked to draw a picture of a person, the child drew a boy. The boy he drew had a head, body, and legs, but the ears and arms were missing, and the drawing was quite primitive. It was made with considerable muscular tension, as though he found it hard to control the direction of his lines. In a very pleased fashion he printed his name.

Conversation with mother. The child's mother was her usual calm, friendly self. She stated that the child has improved a lot in getting along with people, that he is more independent and can dress himself, etc., without requiring as much or any help. She noticed that he soon had better drawings at home and stated that "he must have been a little excited today." His drawings at home contain arms, but in most respects are not too different. She was pleased to see that he was spelling, stating that this was something he could not do before this year.

She resented the fact that she could not spend time with her children. There seemed to be some difficulty in trying to work up a schedule whereby more attention could be given to the child. His mother stated that "he has the best memory of any child I know and is much more observant than his brother." She described how sensitive and appreciative he is of nature. He can describe all the flowers, the sunset, etc. "He sees the beauty in everything," she concluded.

Stanford-Binet, Form L (Pre-test) (6–25–57).

CA: 8–0; MA: 5–6; IQ: 69.

Intelligence is within the Retarded range. The mental age is 5–6, and IQ 69. The Basal Age is at Year IV, while the Ceiling is at Year VIII. Thus the performance range is over a six-year period. The mental age is retarded two and one-half years below the chronological age. The present results are in agreement with testing done 11–10–55, when an IQ of 66 was obtained.

At Year IV–6 C-2-9 was unable to give the materials of which several very common articles are made. For example, when asked what a dress is made of, he said: "Wood." When asked what shoes are made of, he said: "Wood." This latter was perseverated from a previous item. Giving the materials of which familiar objects are made is a test of language comprehension and of information. He was also unable to follow directions in carrying out three commissions, leaving out one of the tasks assigned to him. It should be noted that giving the materials of common articles and the ability to carry out three commissions are the two most difficult items at this age level for cerebral palsy children known to have central nervous system dysfunctioning.

At Year V C-2-9 was unable to copy a square. This test requires an appreciation of spatial relationships and the ability to make use of visual perception to guide a rather complex set of motor co-ordinations. The figures produced by C-2-9 became progressively worse the further removed they were from the stimulus. He was unable to fold a paper triangle, producing instead a paper folded in a very haphazard manner. The motor co-ordinations involved are not so complex as those required in the drawing of a square, but the paper folding involves the imitation of remembered movement. These are the two items at this age level usually found most difficult by cerebral palsy children known to have central nervous system dysfunctioning.

At Year VI vocabulary was failed. Five words are required to pass at this level, and he successfully defined only four. Verbal concepts were poorly developed. For example, when asked to define *eyelash* he said: "When your eye gets bad you have to wear it." For *gown* he said: "Some kind of machine." For *muzzle* he said: "Some kind of round thing." At this age level he was unable to copy a bead chain from memory. He grasped the notion of alternating forms, but could not differentiate shapes.

At Year VII C-2-9 was successful with only one item, repetition of five digits. This is the item which was found easiest by the children in this project. Comprehension of problem situations was poor. When asked, for example, what he should do if he accidentally broke something which belonged to someone else, he said: "Pick it up." When asked what he should do if he were on his way to school and saw that he was in danger of being late, he said: "Get out of it." C-2-9 could not see the absurdities of situations presented visually, nor could he perform at the abstract level required in seeing the similarity between two things. The diamonds produced were very poor, having little relationship to the stimulus figure. He was aware of the need for angles, and carefully drew rather peculiar looking "ears" to satisfy this need.

Stanford-Binet, Form M (Post-test) (5–23–58).

CA: 8–11; MA: 7–0; IQ: 79.

The IQ obtained on this test is 10 points higher than that on the pre-test, which places the functioning level of intelligence in the Slow Learning range. The four-year range of performance was from a Basal Age at Year VI to a Ceiling at Year IX.

At Year VII C-2-9 was able to see the absurdity of situations presented pictorially, build sentences from three words that were given, and count the number of times a block was tapped on the table. He did not know how many fingers he had, could not repeat sentences from memory, and could not reverse three digits.

At Year VIII he could see the similarities between two things, the absurdities in situations described verbally, and could not only name the days of the week by rote but could also give the day coming before certain specified days. Comprehension of problem situations was poor, however, as was opposite analogies.

At Year IX all items were failed.

Ammons Full-Range Picture Vocabulary Test (11–27–57). The mental age obtained on this test was quite consistent with that obtained on the Stanford-Binet. The following words, expected successes from a child of this chronological age, were failed: vegetable, customer, fuel, sale, island, laundry, razor, cheerful, broadcast, uniform, and safe.

Goodenough Intelligence Test.

Pre-test (6–25–57)	Post-test (5–12–58)
CA: 8–0; MA: 5–9	CA: 8–10; MA: 5–9

Both drawings were quite similar, the main difference being in the slightly greater detail in the post-test drawing, which showed hair and ears, details left out in the pre-test drawing. Both were very crudely drawn, with a box-like trunk, buttons down the midline, no arms, and very long pipe-stem legs.

Block Design and Coding from WISC (6–25–57).

	Raw Score	Sealed Score	Equivalent Test Age
Block Design	0	0	4–10
Coding	0	0	4–10

In attempting to reproduce the block design C-2-9 used the wrong colors, choosing whatever was closest. Even when the colors were pointed out to him, he could not construct the designs. He attempted 4 substitutions on the Coding, with 4 errors. He skipped several squares in the process, and kept losing his place. The equivalent test ages obtained are the lowest possible.

Bender-Gestalt Test. Pre-test (6–25–57) there were 15 errors, with 3 immature, 3 dissociations, 3 incorrect elements one unrecognizable, 3 distorted angles, 1 compressions, and 1 disproportion. Post-test (5–12–58) there were 16 errors, with 2 perseverations, 4 dissociations, three incorrect elements, 3 distorted angles, 1 rotation, 2 enlargements, and 1 disproportion. Little improvement was noted on the post-test.

Syracuse Visual Figure-Background Test. Pre-test (11–18–57) there were 5 correct responses to the figure, 6 background responses, and no perseverations. Post-test (5–12–58) there were 9 correct responses to figure, 2 background responses, and 1 perseveration. Thus improvement is noted in accuracy and lessened distractibility by background stimuli in the post-test results.

Tactual-Motor Test (11–18–57). C-2-9 was unable to reproduce correctly a single design from the series of six shown him. He recognized the triangle, but in drawing it produced a long, blunted canoe-shaped figure, open at one end.

Marble Board Test (11–18–57). Marble Board Designs 1 and 2 were reproduced in much the same manner, by filling in all adjacent holes. The drawings showed no understanding of the basic forms, being disconnected lines ranging over the entire page.

Vineland Social Maturity Scale.

Pre-test (11–18–57)		Post-test (5–23–58)	
Total Score:	55.5	Total Score:	65
Age Equivalent:	4–9	Age Equivalent:	7–0
Social Quotient:	58	Social Quotient:	79

The mother served as informant at both interviews. She is a large, "motherly" type of person, who seemed to have a very good understanding of C-2-9 and his problems. He can do many things now that were quite beyond him at the beginning of the school year. He can now print quite well, although spelling is poor and must be constantly corrected. The table knife is used for cutting, and spreading. Baseball, Follow-the-leader, Cowboys and Indians, etc., are some of the pre-adolescent play activities in which he engages.

The mother feels that much progress was made by C-2-9 this past year. Observation in the classroom during the Christmas party (11–23–58) corroborates this. He is very much a part of the group, and participates in classroom activities very well. Much of his shyness and awkwardness are no longer apparent.

Summary. Improvement was noted on three of the five psychological tests on which there was pre- and post-tests for comparison. The post-test Stanford-Binet was 10 points higher than the pre-test, which placed the intelligence level within the Slow Learning range. On the Syracuse Visual Figure-Background Test there was greater accuracy of form perception, and lessened distractibility by background stimuli. The post-test Vineland Social Maturity

Scale resulted in a social quotient 21 points higher than the pre-test, showing that C-2-9's rate of social development had increased. Behavioral observations in the classroom situation corroborated this finding.

Performance on all other tests was uniformly poor. The Goodenough Intelligence Test mental age was exactly the same post-test, and there was one more error on the Bender-Gestalt Test. The equivalent test ages on the Block Design and Coding subtests from the Wechsler Intelligence Scale for Children were the lowest possible. C-2-9 was unable to perform on either Tactual-Motor Test or Marble Board Test.

PEDIATRIC HISTORY C-2-10

The history was given by the boy's mother.

Problem

C-2-10's biggest problem is said to be that of nervousness and tenseness, and being high-strung. When he does try to work he doesn't seem to have the patience to follow through—feels the pressure of doing arithmetic problems and then is unable to complete a task. His reading is said to be good, but when it comes to figuring, as in arithmetic, something seems to be wrong. However, he is said to have made quite a bit of improvement and it is felt that this is due, in large part, to his teacher who is said to handle him beautifully (he is repeating first grade). He is made to bring home second-grade work and mother works with him at home. She feels that he is making progress along these lines. Apparently there were no problems or outstanding trouble until he started school, except for convulsions which he has been having since the age of 3 years. These convulsions are one-sided seizures which affect the arm, leg and face; he foams at the mouth, loses consciousness and is incontinent of urine. He is on Phenobarbital and unless he continues to take the Phenobarbital he has convulsions, the last convulsion having taken place as late as January 1957 when he was taken off the medication to see what would happen. The mother stated that she thought that C-2-10 might be on a tranquilizer; however, this will have to be checked with the physician. The mother stated that neither she nor the teachers are able to see any difference since he has been placed on what she feels is a tranquilizer. It is apparently the difficulty at school, apart from the convulsions, which seem to be of greatest concern to the parents. The father and grandparents find it difficult to believe that C-2-10 is abnormal since they seem to think at home that they are unable to see any gross abnormal behavior. The mother is a rather tall, thin, blonde woman. We had the impression almost immediately that she had an accent and it turns out that she is of foreign extraction, having come to the United States about ten years ago. However, she does have excellent control of the language. She spoke freely but seemed rather nervous and tense, tapping her feet and clasping and unclasping her hands.

Family History

1. Maternal grandmother is living and well.
2. Maternal grandfather is living and well.
3. Paternal grandmother is living and well.
4. Paternal grandfather is living and well.
5. Mother has two sisters and one brother living and well.
6. Father is an only child.

Family Background

Father. (Age 29.) In good health, manager of a hardware store (which is owned by parents). He finished high school. He was born and raised in this area. Interests: golf, (little time for this actually, since he works from 9:00 A.M. to 9:00 P.M.). He is very handy around the house and likes to putter around. Personality: he is said to be tense and nervous and quite different from his father; has to be on the move all the time. Problems: he had difficulty in school as a child, in that he did not want to go and played hooky quite a bit, and it was not until he was discharged from the service, after serving two years, that he completed his high school education. Attitude toward patient and his difficulty: he was very disappointed at first. He wanted him to be like the other children and at first would not hear of special education. He was upset when C-2-10 was put back to repeat the first year. However, now he realizes more of what is involved and seems to be more accepting of the idea of special education for the child. Since the father is quite busy he does not have too much time to spend with C-2-10. However, he has more time on Sunday, but does not do too much with him. They are becoming closer now because they are able to play sports together.

Mother. Age (32.) In good health. Born and raised outside the U.S. where she was educated and completed the equivalent of high school. After she left her homeland, she came to this area. Interests: sewing and sports. Presently she works part time as a receptionist while C-2-10 is in school. (She felt that she did not have enough to do at home.) Personality: the mother described herself as nervous and has to be doing something most of the time. She said that she wishes she could relax and that she gets upset quite easily with C-2-10. Attitude: at first, she was scared and upset by the convulsions. She was then unhappy with the knowledge that he would need special education. However, she prefers the latter to his being kept back and having to repeat a year, feeling that this way he is not keeping up with his peers. She feels that perhaps with special education he will catch up.

Marriage. The parents have been married for nine years. A fairly compatible marriage. There is a difference of religion, the child taking the same religion as the father. However there does not seem to be any real difference or difficulty on that score. The parents have always lived with their in-laws and this has been somewhat of a problem (the mother added that this is as would be expected in any family), even though the in-laws do not apparently meddle too much in the raising of C-2-10.

Grandmother. (Age 53.) Is a hard-working woman who still works in the hardware store.

Grandfather. (Age 54.) He is very close to C-2-10 and loves him very much. The mother stated that her in-laws feel that she is spoiling C-2-10; however, there is no real friction between them. The mother did say that there was some interference with the raising of the child.

Siblings. C-2-10 has no brothers or sisters. The mother expressed the wish that he had. There is a dog who, at first, did not get along too well with C-2-10 and vice versa, however, they are doing better now.

Mother's Medical History during Pregnancy with Child

The mother was 24 years of age at the time she delivered C-2-10. He was a desired pregnancy. He was born in the mother's homeland. After becoming pregnant, the mother had a desire to see her parents, feeling that afterward it would be practically impossible for her to return. The father felt the same way and it was agreed that she would return there while she was pregnant. She made the trip when five months pregnant and remained separated from her husband for about eight or nine months. The in-laws apparently did not object to this either. The pregnancy itself was completely uneventful, no illnesses, no X-rays, no medicines were taken. She entered the hospital one week prior to the expected date of delivery for a blood transfusion. However, she never did receive the blood transfusion and labor was induced artificially, was apparently prolonged and anesthesia was given, so that the mother described the delivery as "pretty rough." C-2-10 was seen within the first twenty-four hours. His birth weight was 6 pounds, 4 ounces, and he was 19 inches long. He was breast-fed for about the first three months with supplemental bottle feedings. However, the mother developed a breast abscess, and so he was weaned from the breast at about that time. He remained in the hospital for two weeks after the mother left. The reason for this was that he had developed an infection of his navel (without jaundice). Mother and child returned to the States when C-2-10 was $4\frac{1}{2}$ months old.

Past History

DPT and smallpox vaccination during first year of life. B.C.G. Polio immunizations. Infection of navel at about two weeks of age. Measles at about $3\frac{1}{2}$ years of age. T & A at $5\frac{1}{2}$ years. His first convulsions seemed to have been associated with fever. Convulsions are said to occur just before he actually goes to sleep and while he is in bed. When he was 4, teeth extracted under anaesthesia. He apparently had a rough time of this because he awakened screaming, and was frightened and upset.

Developmental History

C-2-10 nursed well, had no trouble swallowing and is said to have shown temper at 3 months of age because, when he was hungry, he would bite his mother (apparently teethed quite early). He was weaned from the breast at 3 months of age and from the bottle at one year of age. He was a thumb-sucker, but did not rock. Solids were started at 2 months of age. He never had any difficulty with his sleeping habits, no history of pica (swallowed pennies and marbles, though). He started to walk at 12 months of age and was walking alone at 14 months of age. He teethed early. He was a late talker, but once he started he apparently spoke well. He held a spoon and a glass quite early. His toilet-training was begun at 6 or 7 months of age and completed by 2 years of age. He was enuretic up until $5\frac{1}{2}$ or 6, when an apparatus consisting of a bell was used and apparently was successful in breaking him of this habit. He was unable to count up until the time he started kindergarten. He is right-handed (father is left-handed and maternal grandmother is ambidextrous). There was never any difficulty with vision or hearing. His attention span is poor and he has a lack of patience.

Present Condition

C-2-10 is on Phenobarbital, takes his medicine satisfactorily and by himself, wants to be like everyone else. He has asked about his being put back in school and is said to have expressed a desire not to leave the regular school because he wants to be with his friends (I wonder if this isn't the way the parents themselves feel about the problem). He is said to be able to dress himself; he can tie his shoes, combs his hair and bathes himself. He uses a spoon and fork O.K. but is not too handy with a knife.

Interests

He draws and colors very well and likes to do this. He likes to play with children, but is content when he is by himself. He has friends, some of whom are his own age and some are older. He gets upset easily when others criticize his work. He is able to ride a two-wheeler bicycle and doesn't do too well with building-type of games or activities, unless someone else is around to help. He can drive nails into wood, but is unable to make anything useful by this type of procedure. He likes to play ball and apparently can (is said to have good co-ordination). He goes to Sunday School; he sits through television and movies. Punishment consists of spanking, threatening and rewards. His response to any and all of them is to get mad and sulk. At first he was unable to fight. He used to come home crying and was overprotected by mother. However, now he will hit back when attacked. When frustrated he cries and gets upset, but no real temper tantrums.

Physical Examination

Blood pressure 90/50.
General appearance. C-2-10 is a pleasant-looking child who was neatly

dressed and came along with the Examiner willingly. He was able to state his age and that he likes reading most at school. It was noted that he spoke with a hoarse voice. His speech was adequate but he did not seem too alert. A good mommy "is a good cook and baker." A bad mommy "doesn't give any food— she doesn't like the boy who is bad but my mommy is playing too much." His three wishes included games like croquet, baseball and football. He says he never dreams. He gave an inadequate response to the elephant story and the baby bird "would die or get hurt—when people die they go to Heaven." The child wore a wristwatch and was able to tell time. He recognized a penny and a nickel but did not know how many of the former were in the latter. He was very fidgety and although not particularly hyperactive, seemed rather uncomfortable. He undressed rather sloppily, leaving his clothes where they fell. He didn't unbutton the buttons too well and was unable to undo the cufflinks.

C-2-10 is rather skinny, with his thorax prominent. He has a hemangioma on the inner aspect of his right arm. He is able to hop on each foot, but cannot skip. His teeth numbered 10 on top and 10 on bottom. Reflexes were easily elicited and equal in all four extremities. In getting dressed he had some difficulty with his shirt buttons. *Skin and mucous membranes.* Not remarkable. *Lymph nodes.* Not remarkable. *Head.* Not remarkable. *Face.* Not remarkable. *Ears.* Not remarkable. *Eyes.* Not remarkable. *Nose and sinuses.* Not remarkable. *Mouth and throat.* Not remarkable. *Neck.* Not remarkable. *Vertebra.* Not remarkable. *Chest.* Not remarkable. *Abdomen.* Not remarkable. *Genitalia.* Not remarkable. *Extremities.* Not remarkable. *Neurological examination.* Not remarkable.

Neurological Examination

Cranial nerves. First cranial nerve: not tested. Second cranial nerve: visual fields are grossly intact by confrontation. Fundi are normal. Third, fourth and sixth cranial nerves: pupils are round and equal, and react to light and accommodation. Extra-ocular movements are intact. No nystagmus is present. Fifth cranial nerve: motor and sensory powers are normal. Seventh cranial nerve: taste was not tested. Muscles of facial expression are normal. Eighth cranial nerve: the tuning fork and spoken voice were heard without difficulty. Air conduction is greater than bone conduction. Ninth and tenth cranial nerves: the uvula goes up in the mid-line. Phonation seems to be normal. Eleventh cranial nerve: normal. Twelfth cranial nerve: the tongue protrudes in the mid-line. There is no sign of atrophy or fasciculations. *Sensory.* Pinprick, touch, position, vibratory senses are all normal. Two-point discrimination and pinprick localization were well performed. Stereognosis is normal. Reflexes are equal and active throughout. No pathological reflexes are present. *Motor.* Boy shows good strength throughout. Muscle tone is normal. *Cerebellar.* Finger-to-nose and heel-to-shin tests were fairly well performed. There is some difficulty with diadochokinesis on both sides. He had a great deal of difficulty in spinning the jack. Fine movements seemed to be rather awkward for this boy. *Station and gait.* Romberg is negative. He is able to walk on his heels with some difficulty. He can walk on his toes without any difficulty. Normal gait. *Movements.* No extrapyramidal movements were seen.

Electroencephalogram

Attitude and condition of patient: alert, co-operative. Fundamental frequency: ranges around 8 waves per second. Slow waves: isolated and short sequences of 200 to 300 millisecond waves dominates the record; at times 100 millisecond biphasic spike-like discharges are prominent, particularly over the left brain. Fast waves: are not prominent. Amplitude characteristics: high voltage (100 to 150 microvolts); irregular modulation. Hyperventilation: accents the prominence of the spike-like output. During a prolonged series of spike-activity the patient was seen to engage in an automatic type of pulsion movement of the extremities. Impression: generalized abnormal EEG. Right-left orientation disturbed. Double simultaneous testing. Unable to resolve any pairs of stimuli.

Psychiatric Evaluation

C-2-10 is truly hyperactive, both in the playroom and with his mother, though somewhat more so in the latter situation. He groaned about going to the playroom for an hour, "That's sixty minutes, isn't it?" but once there was loathe to stop at the end of this time. He singled out the Play-Doh immediately and said, "I want to work with clay." He asked the Examiner to do something "hard, like a horse," but backed away from the joking reply that he try something hard also. The Examiner's, he said, was not going to turn out too well because clay work was not as easy for her as other things. He was asked the Despert baby bird fable and he replied that "the baby would stay on the tree without the nest . . . even though the mother and father bird flew somewhere else." As to the elephant story, C-2-10 first described the elephant as having big eyes, big tail, big tummy, big nose, etc., but was unable to say that the nose or trunk was bigger than any other part of his body. In reply to the question "What is different about the elephant?" he smiled stating, "It was all torn up—by another little boy—no, he was not a friend."

C-2-10 sat still for the entire hour, turning from the clay to crayon drawing. He drew first a house with brown color, followed by another house on a separate sheet of paper, then a rabbit, a tree, and his signature. He was very proud of this last drawing. He drew their dog, and on the Draw-a-Man test, at the very bottom of the page, he drew a small, bizarre head and body resembling that of a dog which he described as a "baby." For several of these drawings it was important that the Examiner not look at his drawing. He would ask certain questions about the drawing, "Do you think the house door is five or six inches high? But don't look now, remember." It was evident that this hour was a test situation for him because he asked more than once "Is this the last time I have to come for tests?"

He denied bad or good dreams.

He had the ability to count to 12 but could not use these figures in any meaningful way. Likewise, he was disoriented for time, although he did remember his birthdate.

His speech was not remarkable except to describe it as fast and rather high-pitched. The speech difficulties, such as they were, appeared to indicate careless speech rather than gross immaturity.

After the Examiner called Bobo and the punching bag to the boy's attention, he was more than enthusiastic to hit them. He gave good right blows to both Bobo and the bag which continued in a furious vigorous fashion for about five minutes. He returned abruptly to his crayon drawing without registering verbally how he liked it or why he had stopped. His co-ordination was within normal limits and he evidenced good muscular strength throughout.

We wound up the hour vigorously rolling toy cars and trucks headlong into one another, the harder and faster the better. However, he was able to control his enthusiasm and after one sentence to prepare him that the end of the hour was approaching, he was able to leave once he had made small "quick drawing."

Psychiatric Re-evaluation

C-2-10 was his usual very active, friendly self. He had been spending the summer at camp and has had many opportunities in which to achieve, and has allegedly done so. His mother stated, "This has been better than anything else for him . . . it has been wonderful."

In the playroom he first gave the training boxer a good work-out and then turned to the punching bag. He seemed eager to use every moment and did not wish to waste any of the minutes available for spontaneous behavior.

Once again he was unwilling to commit himself to any of the Despert Fables and he remained silent. However, he was much more spontaneous in his movements and in his responses to the Examiner's questions; in fact it was hard to stop his verbalizations about what fun it was to be at camp.

He was most co-operative when asked to do some drawing. He started by creating partial diagonals and squares, each of which he colored in various fashions. He was less interested in drawing a person and chose to picture a house in which he put ten windows. Nine windows had crossbars and one had diagonal window sections.

C-2-10 appears to have gained tremendously in the realm of social interaction. He gave no indication of any problems in getting along with his peers and/or his academic work. He was not interested in his academic performance and talked very little about this except to say that he had not liked his "bossy" teacher. The striking features about this interview were his apparent self-confidence and his willingness to talk in detail about his family and his school life.

Conversation with mother. The mother exhibited a certain detachment. She did not in any way communicate the atmosphere of their home. She felt that her child profited a great deal from summer camp. There was some concern on her part about the child's change of classrooms. She wondered why he was being moved. Following a discussion informing her that much was gained through such a placement, she was satisfied that her son was in a good position this year because of what was learned about him during the past year.

Stanford-Binet, Form L (Pre-test) (5–24–57).

CA: 8–0; MA: 5–5; IQ: 68.

Intelligence is within the Retarded range with the mental age being two-and-one-half years below the chronological age. The Basal Age is at Year IV, while the Ceiling is at Year VII. The results of this psychological examination are in close agreement with the psychological testing done 11–15–55, when a WISC was administered and a Full Scale IQ of 64 was obtained. On the same instrument a Verbal IQ of 72 and Performance IQ of 61 were obtained.

At Year IV–6 all items were passed with the exception of materials. To pass this item a child must be able to identify correctly the materials of which several common objects are made, such as a chair, dress, and shoe. Giving the materials of which familiar objects are made involves language comprehension and information. C-2-10 correctly identified the material of which a chair is made, but could not tell the materials involved in a dress or shoe. At the conclusion of the test direct questions were asked. When asked what his shirt was made of he said: "Paper." When asked what his shoes were made of he said: "Wood."

At Year V two items were failed. C-2-10 was unable to copy a square. This test requires an appreciation of spatial relationships and the ability to make use of visual perception to guide a complex set of motor co-ordinations. He was also unable to remember a sentence at this age level. Thus two areas of weakness can be seen: perceptual activities requiring visual-motor co-ordination, and immediate memory span.

At Year VI two items were failed. Vocabulary was not passed at this level, only four words being correctly defined when five are required. The vocabulary responses indicated a paucity of well-developed verbal concepts. His definitions were very concrete. Comprehension was very poor. For example, when asked to define eyelash, he said: "It lights." After the conclusion of testing he was asked if he had an eyelash. He said: "Yes, in our basement." Further questioning did not elicit further elaboration. When asked to define roar he said: "Chocolate pudding." He could not elaborate on this. He was also unable to pass the mutilated pictures item. In this test item the child must choose from the given parts of a whole the missing parts. This also involves choosing the essential from the nonessential of a meaningful, structured situation.

At Year VII all items were failed. He was unable to see the absurdity of situations presented pictorially. Again, this involves seeking the essential meaningful elements. When he was shown a picture of a man sawing wood with the saw turned upside down, he said: "He's sawing wood." When asked what was foolish about it he said: "Because he has to." When shown a picture of a dog chasing a rabbit but running in the wrong direction, he said: "The rabbit's running away from the dog." Comprehension of practical situations was also difficult for him. When asked what he should do if another boy hit him without meaning to do so, he replied: "Hit him back." Abstract ability, as involved in opposite analogies and similarities between two things, were also failed, as was repeating five digits. He was unable to draw a diamond.

Stanford-Binet, Form M (Post-test) (5–22–58).

CA: 950; MA: 7–0; IQ: 78.

The IQ on the post-test is 10 points higher than that obtained on the pre-test, which places the level of intelligence within the Slow Learning range. The four-year performance range is from a Basal Age at Year VI to a Ceiling at Year IX.

At Year VIII C-2-10 could see opposite analogies, comprehend problem situations, and tell what day preceded certain given days in the week. He was unable to see the similarity between two things or absurdities in verbally described situations.

All items were failed at Year IX.

Ammons Full-Range Picture Vocabulary Test (11–27–57). The mental age obtained on this test is very close to that obtained on the Stanford-Binet. A number of words, expected successes at this chronological age level, were failed: vegetable, phonograph, customer, sale, island, laundry, manufacturing, cheerful, collision, listening, broadcast, uniform, cleanliness, and intersection.

Goodenough Intelligence Test.

Pre-test (5–24–57)	Post-test (5–12–58)
CA: 8–0; MA: 4–6	CA: 8–11; MA: 7–0

The pre-test drawing is extremely crude, being constructed of spidery lines, barely recognizable as an attempt to draw the human form. Post-test is much better, although still very poor. The latter is two dimensional, with hair, and eyes with pupils.

Block Design and Coding from WISC.

	Raw Score	Scaled Score	Equivalent Test Age
Block Design	4	6	5–2
Coding	15	5	6–6

The first design was reproduced accurately on the first attempt, Design B and C on the second, and S was unable to progress beyond this point. His first attempt to reproduce Design B was a perseveration of the preceding design. Seventeen substitutions were attempted on the Coding Test, Form B, with 2 errors.

Bender-Gestalt Test. The pre-test drawings (5–24–57) were rather firm and definite, but a fair number of deviations occurred which were categorized as errors. There were 2 perseverations, 3 dissociations, 3 incorrect elements, 2 distorted angles, 2 rotations, and 1 disproportion, which totals 13 errors. Post-test (5–12–58) 12 errors were made, 1 concrete, 1 perseverations, 3 dissociations,

3 incorrect elements, 3 distorted angles, and 1 compression. Thus, in terms of over-all performance, there was practically no change between the tests given at the beginning and those at the end.

Syracuse Visual Figure-Background Test. Pre-test (11–18–57) there were 6 correct responses to the figure, four background responses, and no perseverations. Post-test (5–12–58) there were 9 correct responses to the figures, 6 background responses, and, again, no perseverations, thus, while there was a slight increase in accuracy, there was also evidenced a somewhat greater distractibility by background stimuli.

Tactual-Motor Test (11–18–57). C-2-10 was unable to reproduce correctly a single design from this test. After feeling the diamond, which is the easier figure in the series, he proceeded to draw a square. With the addition of a thumb-tack background he became even more confused, and proceeded to draw only the background.

Marble Board Test. Design 1 was started in the extreme upper left hand corner of the board, and the first side of the figure contained the correct number of marbles. The next side had additions, however, and C-2-10 was unable to resolve this error. He was aware of the inaccuracy of his reproduction, as may be inferred from his comments: "I'm getting all mixed up . . . how many do I have right?" He attempted to count the marbles, but this did not resolve the problem. His drawing of the design shows two squares, one directly on top of the other.

Design 2 was started correctly, but he was unable to make the diagonal lines required. After many errors, he said: "That don't look like it," but was unable to improve his reproduction. When he attempted to draw the figure, he produced two dissociated rectangles.

Vineland Social Maturity Scale.

Pre-test (11–22–57)		Post-test (5–13–58)	
Total Score:	74	Total Score:	74
Age Equivalent:	9–0	Age Equivalent:	8–11
Social Quotient:	106	Social Quotient:	100

There is very little change in the rate of development of this boy's skills and abilities as shown on this instrument. The major skills that seem to be emerging at the present time are an increased desire and ability to participate in pre-adolescent play activities, and a beginning use of tools and utensils. His father is encouraging him in this latter activity.

Summary. The level of functioning intelligence was in the retarded range at the end of the academic year. On three of the five tests on which there was a pre-test and post-test for comparative purposes improvement was noted (on the Stanford-Binet, Goodenough Intelligence Test, and Syracuse Visual Figure-Background Test) . . . On this latter test, while improvement was noted in accuracy, a slight tendency toward greater distractibility by background stimuli was also noted. Practically no change was noted on the Bender-Gestalt Test or the Vineland Scale of Social Maturity.